Values and Norms in the Age of Globalization

Dia-Logos

Schriften zu Philosophie und Sozialwissenschaften
Studies in Philosophy and Social Sciences

Herausgegeben von/Edited by
Tadeusz Buksiński und Piotr W. Juchacz

Bd./vol. 9

PETER LANG

Frankfurt am Main · Berlin · Bern · Bruxelles · NewYork · Oxford · Wien

Ewa Czerwińska-Schupp (ed.)

Values
and Norms
in the Age of
Globalization

PETER LANG

Europäischer Verlag der Wissenschaften

Bibliographic Information published by the Deutsche Nationalbibliothek
The Deutsche Nationalbibliothek lists this publication in the Deutsche Nationalbibliografie; detailed bibliographic data is available in the internet at <http://www.d-nb.de>.

Published with kind support of the Federal Ministry for Education, Science and Culture in Vienna,

bm:bwk

of the Österreichisches Kulturforum in Warschau

austriackie forum kultury[waw]

Reviewer Bogusław Bukowski, Ph.D.

ISSN 1619-005X
ISBN-10: 3-631-55171-1
ISBN-13: 978-3-631-55171-4
US-ISBN 0-8204-9892-0

© Peter Lang GmbH
Europäischer Verlag der Wissenschaften
Frankfurt am Main 2007
All rights reserved.

Printed in Germany 1 2   4 5 6 7

www.peterlang.de

Contents

Part IV. Science and Globalization Processes

Part V. Law and Politics in the Context of the Challenges of Globalization

Part VI. Democracy and Globalization

Introduction

In autumn 2005 representatives of various scientific disciplines met in Poznań to jointly deliberate about the direction of transformations in ideas, outlooks and morality as well as in social and political life (including political systems) in the contemporary world. These representatives included philosophers, ethicists, sociologists, lawyers and political scientists, who spoke for research institutions from different countries ranging from Germany, Austria, through the United States, Spain, Kirghizia, to Poland. It was not by accident that they focused on globalization, a project that is problematic in the present day and, at the same time, controversial in the light of reviving fundamentalisms in outlooks and religions, the movements that guard the preservation of the national and cultural identity, and growing euroscepticism.

Opinions on the unification process taking place before our very eyes are definitely varied: they range from optimistic, through moderately optimistic and critical, to sceptical or even unfavourable to globalization. The disputes over globalization are by no means just a scientific or theoretical or political debate, but they are transposed into real activities and diverse forms of protest. Perhaps, in the age of expansion of democracy, the attitudes and the opinions that are most important are those shared by "common people" who are disappointed with the practical implementation of the "globalization project" and lip-service paid to it. This book, which is an outcome of the Poznań Conference, shows how deeply men of science and politics are involved in the changes taking place in the contemporary world and respective responses to them. The authors of the articles in the book address an exceptionally wide range of issues linked with globalization. These include: 1) the question of globalization itself, its present forms, range, dimensions or aspects, 2) the question of values, standards, principles and mechanisms supporting or hindering the unifying processes, 3) assessments of benefits and risks that unification entails in mental, cultural, social and political terms. These briefly mentioned issues are supplemented by works by authors who address the complex problems of the globalization epoch, as well as the issues and questions representative for the period that preceded it.

Despite the diversity and multiplicity of the questions being raised, the book has, in our opinion, retained clarity. It focuses mainly on the challenges that are posed to philosophy and related sciences by the epoch of unification of nations and states. The challenges apply to the problems that are important to globalization, such as the establishment of rights and rules and institutions governing the existence of supra- and international communities, the development of a common system of ethical values, moral standards and norms (or even the creation of a system of entirely new values, standards and norms) supporting the unification process. They also apply to the legitimacy and validity of transferring the values and standards and the models of economy and politics characteristic of European culture to other cultures and civilisations (the countries of the Middle East, Latin America or Asia), which, as signified by national and religious movements growing in strength in different parts of the globe, are much sceptical about the projects in question and cannot see any possibility or even need for the reification of the values present in their cultures and social and political practices.

Conclusions that are particularly significant to the present-day political practice in its global dimensions are provided by those works whose authors i.e. philosophers, ethicists and political scientists raise questions of the place, role and dimension, as well as the relevance of or transformations undergone in the post-modern world order of such moral values, standards and norms present in politics as human rights, freedom, justice, responsibility, solidarity, tolerance, forgiveness, peace, security, education, modernization or democracy. The debate concerning the place of traditional and post-modern values and norms in the contemporary world has also encompassed the law and it has been directly linked with the need to change the role and function of the law in the new global reality. One challenge that the law and lawyers are facing is the development of a new informational and communicative legal theory at the level of the global community that would be addressed to and implemented by global actors: states and communities. It is also necessary to develop new branches of jurisprudence that would meet, to a greater extent than now, the ethical and normative challenges of technological civilisations and, furthermore, to integrate legal thought with legal practice in the area of protection of human life and natural environment.

The subject matter of the book is enriched by articles on European integration. They can be regarded as making a valid point in a discussion that is aimed at recognizing whether this integration is a symptom of post-modernity and thus results from and supports globalization changes or rather a defensive reaction to modernity, a peculiar relic of the pre-globalization world. As shown by the texts of many authors, the dilemmas (including legal and political) of the European Union and the difficulties it experiences, also in the sphere of values (e.g. the inability to create a common cultural European identity in the light of the expansion of mass culture and the domination of homogenized and marketised liberal and democratic values), reflect the complexity of contemporary globalization processes. The question whether and how the project of the Common Europe can be revitalized is today a question about the need for or legitimacy and usefulness of the community idea, as well as about its real and apparent beneficiaries.

The topic of globalization is indisputably open and it brings more questions than final answers. A number of such questions are raised in the context of this book. The principle questions include: Do post-modern (integration, community and cosmopolitan) values gain precedence over traditional (national, local, religious) values in the course of transition from the fragmentized world to geoculture? Does the success of the unification processes depend on the creation of new, post-modern values or is it just sufficient to resort to old, recognized and proven values and standards in political practice and ensure their greater, international range? Is the present shift from the domination of liberal democracy based on a national state and its political system and an institution of a welfare state to a neoliberal economic and social order with its consequences – free market economy, destabilised position of national states, marketised and mass culture – a natural progress of modernity transformations or rather a straying from the path chosen, due to the interests of the strongest economies and countries? Finally, there is a question that recurs in the whole book by implication, though it is not raised directly: What will be the shape of the future civic society, what norms and standards will it apply and what forms of regulation of the public life will it employ? This question can only be answered when the community of nations, states and societies becomes a reality. However, to achieve this, we must first talk, so that with our knowledge of our cultural roots, we could determine who we are today and where we are heading.

* * *

The texts presented in the book were initially delivered at an international interdisciplinary conference entitled *Values and Norms in the Age of Globalization*, which was held in Poznań between 13th and 15th October 2005. The idea of the conference originated at the Institute of Philosophy of the Adam Mickiewicz University, Poznań and it was taken up by the Polish and foreign research institutions: The Poznań Society for the Friends of the Sciences, the University of Vienna, the Karl Renner Institute in Vienna, the Austrian Forum of Culture in Warsaw and the Hans Jonas Center in Berlin. It was an honor for the conference to have Prof. Karl-Otto Apel as a guest, who is an eminent figure in world philosophy and the most outstanding contemporary ethicist.

As the organizer of this conference and the editor of this volume, I would like to express my heartfelt thanks to those people and institutions that contributed to the success of both projects.

I am also sincerely grateful for the financial and organizational support of the conference granted by the Vice Chancellor and Dean's Offices of the Adam Mickiewicz University, Poznań, the Poznań Society for the Friends of the Sciences, Poznań City Hall, the Ministry of National Education of Warsaw, Foundation for Polish-German Cooperation in Warsaw, the Austrian Forum of Culture in Warsaw, and the Karl Renner Institute in Vienna. I would like to thank the Mayor of the Poznań City Mr. Ryszard Grobelny for the honorary patronage of the conference and the warm reception of its participants at Poznań City Hall.

I would like to express my deep gratitude to Austrian scientific and cultural institutions with which I have been honored to cooperate fruitfully over the years: the Ministry of Federal Education, Science and Culture in Vienna and the Austrian Forum of Culture in Warsaw. Both institutions funded the release of this book. I especially appreciate the kindness shown and assistance provided by the representatives of these institutions: Ministerial Counselor Dr Alois Söhn, Ministerial Officer Gottfried Prinz MA and the Director of the Austrian Forum of Culture in Warsaw, Doctor Walter Maria Stojan.

In the course of work on the book, its reviewer, Doctor Bogusław Bukowski, a sociologist and implementer of EU programs, offered advice and invaluable help. His precious suggestions had a strong influence on the shape of the book as a whole. While thanking him for many months of continuous friendly cooperation, I would like to underline the fact that it was this cooperation that greatly expedited publication of this book.

Poznań, June 2006 *Ewa Czerwińska-Schupp*

Part I
Rights and Values in Philosophy

Karl-Otto Apel
Frankfurt am Main

Jus gentium or „Cosmopolitan law"?
The Topicality of a Kantian Aporia Today

Kant suggests, on the one hand, that perpetual peace between sovereign states can only be established, if the single states give up the pertinent part of their sovereignty (e.g. the *ius ad bellum)* in favour of the cosmopolitan state. (This holds by analogy to the constitution of the internal law of single states). But, on the other hand, Kant thinks that this sacrifice cannot be demanded because it destroys the very idea of *jus gentium* and moreover, may result in a "soulless despotism" and "cemetery of freedom".

In face of this dilemma Kant proposes a "negative surrogate" for the cosmopolitan state, namely a league of nations which would hold in check the inclination to war, although with a constant risk of its outbreak.

I will try to show in my lecture that this Kantian exposition may be used as a key to understanding the present situation of international politics, especially the relationships between the UN as representation of an international law and the most powerful national states.

1. Introduction:
The Ambiguity of the Conceptualisation
of "International Law"

My lecture wants to deal with a problem of law and politics the conceptualization of which was ambiguous from the beginning and throughout its discussion in modern times and has reached a disturbing stage of unclearness in our day. How should we at least address what I have in mind by an adequate term? Should we use the German term *Völkerrecht*, which is a translation of the traditional Latin term *jus gentium*, or should we prefer the term "international law", which is rather used in English, or should we speak of "cosmopolitan law", as Kant did for the first time using the German word *weltbürgerliches Recht*?

In order at least to intimate a relevant difference between these terms, one could point to some aspects of European history, in which the concept of *jus gentium* has developed. At the beginning – let us say, from the work of J. Bodin (Bodinus) through the time that was determined by the peace treaties after the 30 years war – the classical period of *jus gentium* was determined by the concept of the "sovereignty" of the single states or, respectively, their rulers. The classical *jus gentium* recognized e.g. an unrestricted *jus ad bellum* of the sovereign states, since their rulers had no legislative and executive authority above themselves except God. (This was different in the middle ages and still with the Spanish founders of *jus gentium* in the 16th century. For these jurists and theologians still presupposed a certain paramount authority of the pope and / or the emperor (i.e. Charles V), and they discussed intensively the problem of *just* and *unjust wars*, even of the wars of Christian rulers against the American Indians. Thereby they practically discussed also the question of *human rights* within the context of "natural law".

By contrast, the classical *jus gentium* of the sovereign states excluded any intervention into their politics by external powers in the name of international law, including the external protection of "human rights." This connotation of the meaning of classical *jus gentium* was still influential in the 20th century, although by the Brian-Kellog pact (1928) the *jus ad bellum* was abolished and 1948 the declaration and protection of human rights was connected with the Charta of the United Nations. An example of the persistent unclearness of the situation of international law was provided by the Kosovo conflict, when initially China and Russia blocked the intervention of UNO by appeal to the sovereignty of Serbia.

From this short sketch of the history of the concept of *jus gentium* it becomes already understandable, why Kant in his attempt of a novel foundation of international law and its political institution in his essays of 1784 and 1795 had problems with the terms *jus gentium* (*Völkerrecht*) and *jus cosmopoliticum* (*Weltbürger-recht*). For Kant indeed considered a completely new conception with regard to the philosophy of history and the philosophy of law, and his vision included a conception of cosmopolitan rights (*Weltbürgerrechte*) of single persons as well as a conception of *jus gentium* (*Völkerrecht*) that for the first time strictly excluded the *jus ad bellum*.

In what follows, I shall first try to give a pertinent account of Kant's innovative conceptions in his essay "Idea of a general history in cosmopolitan intention" of 1784 and especially in his so called "philosophical project: toward perpetual peace" of 1795.[1] I will try to show that Kant in the second essay for the first time introduced the relevant terminological distinctions with regard to our problem and that he, precisely for this reason, arrived only at an aporetical solution of his "philosophical project": to propose a political institution of a *cosmopolitan order of law* that could guarantee the protection of cosmopolitan rights of human beings and the preservation of perpetual peace. Kant, on the one hand, saw the need for a restriction of the sovereignty of the single states by a *cosmopolitan state* (*Weltstaat* or *Völkerstaat*), but on the other hand he considered its realization to be impossible for conceptual and empirical reasons and therefore pleaded for a "negative surrogate" of the "cosmopolitan state", that is, for a *federation of peoples* (*Völkerbund*) that should approximately fulfil the task of a cosmopolitan order of law.

Now, with a certain simplification, one could say that this Kantian proposal has been followed two times in the 20th century: first, after the first world war, by the Geneva League of Nations, and again, after the second world war, by the UNO. But I will show in the second part of my lecture that the aporetic aspect of the Kantian proposal was still effective in both cases and that a new response to our problem has been challenged especially by the recent developments of global politics.

---

[1] See Immanuel Kant, *Akademie-Textausgabe*, Bd. 8, 2. ed., Berlin: De Gruyter, 1968.

2. The Aporia of Kant's Attempt at a Novel Foundation of a Political Institution of International Law as Cosmopolitan Law. His Proposal of a Federation of Peoples (*Völkerbund*)

The widest horizon for a novel foundation of the problem of international law was opened by Kant in his essay on the *philosophy of history* of 1784 where he tried to illustrate the hypothesis that there is an "intention of nature" or of "providence" which throughout the human history uses the short-sighted intentions of the human beings, in order, even by way of conflicts and wars, in the long run to reach a state of cosmopolitan law and peace. But I shall not deal with Kant's philosophy of history in this place, but only with the sentence 7 of his essay. In this sentence Kant opens a new horizon for the conception of *jus gentium*, in which he – and that remained almost unnoted till today – gives priority to *international law* over the law of a single republic.

He states:

> The problem of instituting a perfect civil constitution is dependent on the problem of a legal (lawful) external relationship between states and cannot be solved without the solution of the latter problem.

In my opinion, the topical significance of this sentence still today lies in the insight that the philosophically relevant solution of the problem of political justice in general and hence of a universally valid law of a constitutional state cannot be reached by thematizing only the legal constitution of a particular state, even of a democracy, under abstraction from the problems of so called foreign policy. In our time especially the problems of "human rights" and in that context e.g. the problem of immigration and asylum points to the fact that the study of just one state and its hierarchical or democratic structure cannot suffice for dealing with constitutional law even of one state.

But for Kant in his first essay on the need for "cosmopolitan law" the topic is not primarily that of "human rights" but rather that of the relationship between the different states which was thematized by the classical *jus gentium*. And, obviously alluding critically to Thomas Hobbes, Kant suggests that human beings had not only to leave the pre-legal "state of nature" by joining a constitutional state, but moreover had to join a *federation of states* (a *Völkerbund*), because this latter could end not only the conflicts between human individuals but also the wars between the states "according to laws of a united will" (p. 24).

At this point already the ambiguity of the problem and concept of "international law" which we mentioned in the preceding, becomes obvious, but Kant´s talk of the need of a "cosmopolitan law" or "state" as well as of the *external relationship between states* shows that he has not yet become aware of the ambiguity.

This is quite different ten years later, in the famous essay "Toward perpetual peace" of 1795. Here Kant makes a distinction between three possible dimensions or aspects of a lawful relationship, in which human persons can stand. And he emphasizes that his threefold distinction is *a priori* necessary and hence is a basic presupposition of reason for politically relevant law.

The three dimensions are: First, "that according to the law of citizens in one state or people (the *jus civitatis*)", second "that of the law of peoples as law between states" (i.e. *jus gentium*), third, "that according to 'cosmopolitan law' (*Weltbürgerrecht*) in so far as human persons and states ... can be considered as citizens of one general state of human beings" (i.e. *jus cosmopoliticum*). (p. 349)

The new problem dimension that Kant here has introduced obviously is that of "cosmopolitan law". He no longer equates this law with the traditional *jus gentium* but relates it to the single human persons as citizens of the world (i.e. cosmopolitans). But now one could ask: Which of the two last dimensions of Kant´s novel partition provides a sufficient basis for his philosophical project: toward perpetual peace? Could it be the traditional *jus gentium* that deals with the relationship between peoples and thus indeed deals also with war and peace? But at this point the following argument in the spirit of Hobbes comes into play:

In order to secure perpetual peace between individuals occasional peace agreements between them are not enough, but it is necessary for them to surrender once for all their personal autonomy of using violence to the higher authority of a *constitutional* state. Now, by way of analogy, Kant argues:

according to reason, there is no other way for states to escape from the
prelegal state (of nature), which contains a constant risk of war, than that
they, in the same way as single human beings, surrender their wild anarchic freedom by submitting to public laws of coercion (compulsion) and
thus shape one (always growing) "state of peoples" (*Völkerstaat*) which
finally would comprise all "nations of earth". (p. 357)

Thus Kant's solution of the problem of *perpetual peace* seems to be
presented by the institution of a *unitary cosmopolitan* state. But this
opinion is immediately disclaimed by Kant. He makes the objection,
that the different peoples, according to their idea of *jus gentium* (*Völkerrecht*), would by no means accept that conception of a *cosmopolitan
state* of all nations. (p. 357)

(In the preceding Kant had indeed declared that a cosmopolitan
state of nations would contradict the very idea of *jus gentium*, since
the single peoples in one unitary state would melt together to one
people and thereby would abolish the subject of *jus gentium*.) (p. 354)
Thus Kant arrives at the result that a cosmopolitan state, i.e. a unitary
"state of peoples" (*Völkerstaat*) for conceptual reasons is impossible as
a solution of his problem of securing perpetual peace by international
law.

One should add here that Kant also mentions empirical reasons
for his definite rejection of *one state of nations*. Thus he remarks that a
melting together of all peoples in one homogenous cosmopolitan state
could lead to a "soulless despotism" that would bring about a
"cemetery of freedom" (p. 367). And at an other place he even points
to a concrete fact of history, in order to suggest that and how the *third*
dimension of the human law of reason, namely that of cosmopolitan
rights of human persons in relation to foreign states, must be restricted in favour of the rights of the single sovereign states. Kant here
thinks of the fact of *European colonialism*. He explains this fact first
from the point of view of a cosmopolitan right of all human beings,
namely their common property of the surface of the earth, which
allows them to visit all foreign countries, e.g. in the interest of trade.
But, Kant complains that the Europeans confused the right of *visiting*
foreign countries with the right of *conquering* them and include them
into their empire. Thereby, he states, they considered the foreign
peoples to be nothing.

In order to prevent this danger, Kant demands to restrict the cosmopolitan right of all persons with regard to other countries to a right of "hospitality" (*Besuchsrecht*). This restricted cosmopolitan right, Kant suggests, would even promote peace by founding trade relations between the different countries. (p. 358 f.)

But these remarks only illustrate but do not dissolve the aporetic main result of Kant´s argumentation quoted so far. For Kant does not forget or disregard the argument he derived by analogy to Hobbes: In order to secure *perpetual peace*, there had to be some surrender of the sovereignty of the single states in favour of a higher authority of power, although the possibility of a homogenous state of all peoples, Kant thinks, was not possible or even desirable. In this aporetic situation Kant presents his main proposal: "If not everything should be lost", he claims, "the positive idea of a cosmopolitan republic" (*Weltrepublik*) can only be replaced by the "negative surrogate" of an existing and always expanding federation, which could repel (fend off) the war and resist the stream of hostile and unlawful inclination, but together with a "constant risk of its new outbreak" (p. 357).

Now, I think, this is a key for understanding the situation of *international law* and its political institutionalization that came about in the 20th century and still prevails in our time. For, the Kantian project of a federation of peoples (*Völkerbund*) was indeed realized first after 1918 by the "Geneva league of nations", which came about by an initiative of the American president Wilson, and again after 1945 by the UNO.

3. The Problem of a Political Institution of International Law as Cosmopolitan Law in the Present Era: the Rise of a New Alternative: Continuation of Kant's Project of a *Völkerbund* by the UNO or Substitution of a Cosmopolitan State by a World Empire?

Looking back on the whole history of the project of the "Geneva league of nations" and its continuation by the UNO, one could *first* say that it was an implementation of the Kantian aporia with regard to the problem of securing perpetual peace. For in this respect it was a *verification* of Kant´s own characterization of his "negative surrogate" of a cosmopolitan state by judging that it might provide a means against hostilities, but together with the constant risk of their new outbreak.

This began already with the retreat of the United States of America from the Geneva league which they themselves had initiated, at the occasion of the treaty of Versailles which they did not accept; and the growing conflicts, which led to the second world war, seemed to be continued after 1945 in the era of the cold war between the two world powers, USA and the Soviet Union, which dominated the UNO as well.

Even later, after the dissolution of the Soviet Union and the end of cold war, we were witnesses of many international conflicts that could not immediately be pacified by the UNO, since the five potent members of the "security council" were not interested in an engagement or could not arrive at a common line of reaction. Thus the UNO, which was in charge of the administration and execution of *international law*, more and more lost its authority and was exposed to the complaint of inactivity or helplessness (I think in particular of the lasting civil wars in Africa as e.g. in Angola and in Rwanda.)

However "in the course of these failures of the UNO, and partly because of them, a novel constellation of international pacification politics has developed in the last years.

Thus in the Balkan wars after the dissolution of Yugoslavia and in the wars in the Middle East, the initiative of intervention and pacification with and without a mandate of the UNO was taken over by the USA or, respectively, the Atlantic alliance of the NATO under the leadership of the USA. And it was precisely in these wars that it turned out that the USA now is the *only superpower* among the world powers of today. It was demonstrated that the USA by its technological equipment is capable to win each classical war only from the air with minimal losses of its own troops. (But I am not speaking as yet of a war against terrorism)

Now, with regard to the relationship between the USA and the UNO, it is revealing, I suggest, to compare the short war of the NATO against Serbia in Kosovo and the war of the USA and Great Britain in Iraq (against Saddam Hussein).

Already the intervention of the NATO in Kosovo[2] began without a mandate of the UNO. This was essentially caused by the fact that two of the members of the Security Council of the UNO, Russia and China, refused any interference in the sovereignty of Serbia thereby appealing to the *classical jus gentium*. But the high-handed intervention of the NATO was justified in the spirit of *International law* as it was re-established after 1945 by the Convention of Human Rights that were included in the Charta of the UN; in this vein the intervention in Kosovo was claimed as *emergency help* in face off an imminent ethnocide of the Albanians and indeed legitimized belatedly by the UNO.

Thus far the intervention of the NATO in Kosovo did not yet call into question the validity of *international law* and the authority of the UN as political representation of international law. There was no open rivalry as yet between the UNO and the USA.

This was different, I think, in the second Iraq war.[3] In this case the USA from the beginning argued publicly and in the forum of the UNO for the need of their planned intervention in Iraq by appeal to the principle of self-defence and they declared several times that they would not tolerate any obstruction or hindrance in that strategy by arguments from outside.

Now it is true indeed that the right of *self-defence* is acknowledged by *international law*, and it must be realized that the appeal to this right by the USA was supported afresh by the terroristic attack of 11th September in NY. But in the mean time it has become clear and was

---

[2] Cf. Karl-Otto Apel, „Das Spannungsfeld zwischen Ethik, Völkerrecht und politisch-militärischer Strategie in der Gegenwart. Philosophische Retrospektive auf den Kosovo-Konflikt", in: *Diskursethik, Grundlegung und Anwendungen*, ed. by Marcel Niquet et al., Würzburg: Königshausen & Neumann, 2001, pp. 205–218. English Version: "On the Relationship between Ethics, International Law and Politico-military Strategy in Our Time: a Philosophical Retrospective on the Kosovo-Conflict", *EJST* 4/1, 2001, pp. 29–40.

[3] Cf. Karl-Otto Apel, "Internationale Beziehungen. Was ist wünschenswert: das Imperium als Weltstaat oder die Völkergemeinschaft", in: *Neue Kolonialismen in den Nord-Süd-Beziehungen*, ed. by Raul Fornet-Betancourt, Frankfurt am Main: IKO-Verlag für Interkulturelle Kommunikation, 2005, pp. 29–44.

even admitted by the former American foreign minister, that the arguments of the USA that supported their claim of self-defence were based on false suppositions. Thus it turned out more and more for the global public that the USA had simply ignored the UNO as representation of international law as they started a *preemptive* war against Iraq which before was refused by veto of two members of Security Council.

Thereby a new global situation came about which by some reviewers was interpreted as a tendential replacement of the global authority of the UNO by that of a *hegemonial* power or even by an *empire*. Adherence to this new tendency then was called *unilateralism* whereas the resistance to this tendency was called *plurilaterism*.

Now, from the point of view of our philosophical problem of providing a juridical and political foundation and institution of international law as cosmopolitical law, the question arises, how we could or should interpret the present crisis situation in light of the primordial, as I said, aporetical analysis by Kant and his proposed solution of a *Völkerbund* which still is represented by the UNO.

I think, in a first approach, that the present situation in many respects confirms and even displays and illustrates Kant's aporetic analysis. Thus, to begin with the external political circumstances and their assessment by the reasoning public, there are indeed strong arguments on the side of both the *plurilateralists* and the *unilateralists*.

The strongest argument of the *multilateralists* against the *unilateralists* refers of course to the danger of an imminent *despotism* in the Kantian sense. In a modern explication this would mean that the one hegemonic power – even if in its formal domestic structure it is and remains a democracy – would become the center of a political and economical neo-colonialism and imperialism, at the cost of the UNO. For those functions by which the UN have integrated the many new nations of the third world, which became independent by the dissolution of the classical colonialism, – these functions would first be tendentially replaced by the economical and political functions of the multinational companies and the international organizations (like WTO, the World Bank, the International Monetary Fund etc), and then these functions would loose their original connections with the

UNO and would practically become strategical annexes of the hegemonical power. And the improvements of international law, which by the UNO without doubt have been reached through an integration of many agreements and conventions – especially about human rights, and the protection and preservation of the natural environment and the cultural heritage of humankind – these achievements would loose their practical bearing on the level of globalization.

This much against the rise of a *global empire* at the cost of the UNO. But, on the other side, there are the arguments of the *unilateralists* against the *plurilateralists* whom they consider to be real enemies of a cosmopolitan order of law and peace.

These arguments are primarily directed against the obstruction of the effectivity of the UNO by the diverging interests of the second strong global powers. I think, it is indeed possible to show that most of the failures by inactivity of which the UNO was reproached, were in reality consequences of the fact that there was no *unitary political power* or *united will* that could or wanted to get through international law in the name of the UNO. (Thus it was one of the stronger arguments of the USA in the debate of the Security Council *before* the Iraq war that most of the conditions imposed on Iraq by the UNO could not be put through before the threat of an intervention by the USA.)

Now this argument of the *ineffectivity* of the *UNO* corresponds of course to the Hobbesian insight, that the binding force of positive Law must be based on the coercive force of a constitutional state, – the argument from which Kant first by analogy draw the conclusion of the rational necessity of a *world state*. Hence we stand again at the aporetical point, at which Kant suggested his compromise proposal of a *federation of peoples*. And it has to be added at this point that today there are also novel crises problems which deepen the risk of our situation between the Skylla of the loss of freedom and the Charybdis of the loss of peace.

Thus there is the danger of a further proliferation of weapons of mass destruction, a problem that transcends the horizon of classical warfare by the fact that a few of these weapons in the hands morally unscrupulous leaders suffice for an extortion of the strongest powers of constitutional states.

Somehow related to this danger is the whole scene of *terrorism*, especially the planned use of *suicide attacks* based on religious or quasi religious fanatism – a strategy the results of which seem to lie out of range for immediate military repulse.

The background of this scene seems to be the new global danger of a *clash of cultures* which has an economical but also a religious side. Also this background phenomenon seems to lie out of range for a global empire that is only based on a military and technological superiority.[4]

It almost goes without mentioning that the problems of the *ecological crisis* which were also recognized only in the last century, remain topical also in our day, although some people seem to have immunicized themselves against this outlook by habituation. But the energy shortage in our day reminds us of the fact that this and many other problems of our natural resources have by no means been settled by pertinent rules of international law.

But let us again focus on the main problem of international law and its political institution which has led us to the optional alternative of either continuing the often ineffective institution of the UNO or replacing it by the acceptance of a *global empire*. After what we have said about the unpleasant aspects of both of these options, we should ask the question, whether it might be possible to find a *third* answer to our problem which avoids the negative aspects of the dilemma.

We should remember that also Kant´s proposal of a *federation of peoples* was already a compromise with regard to an original alternative: namely, either to a *jus gentium*, which included a *ius ad bellum* and gave priority to the sovereignty of the single states over the human rights of single persons, or, on the other hand, a *cosmopolitan law* (*Weltbürgerrecht*). This latter conception was Kant´s ultimate aim in his philosophy of history; and the "negative surrogate" of a "federation of peoples" was not to preclude the historical progress toward the *cosmopolitan state of law* as a *regulative idea*, I suggest. It was only considered to be an up-to-date solution that could be acceptable

---

[4] Cf. Samuel P. Huntington, *The Clash of Civilization*, 3. ed., New York: Simon & Schuster, 1996.

for the citizens of the single states who already were protected by a state of law and wanted to preserve (save) their political freedom.

Hence, we could ask, whether there is not the possibility of developing the present order of the UNO in the direction of *cosmopolitan law* through conventions of international law. This would mean: the UNO would not be totally replaced by a homogenous world state or the function of an empire, but only be supplemented by a *minimal state*. This *minimal world state* would be in charge of fulfilling only a few crucial functions of a cosmopolitan law according to the principle of subsidiarity, thus e.g. the maintenance of peace and the protection of human rights and some functions of an international order of economy.[5]

Of course, there would again be the problem of balancing these subsidiary functions against those many functions that would remain in charge of the primary states: the subsidiary functions of a *world police*, so to speak, had to be bound in and controlled by the same federation which it is to protect against war and terrorism by its powers and thus far by its monopoly on force.

This sounds again paradoxical, but one has to consider that the task of establishing such an order of *subsidiarity* has not to be shaped (created) at one blow but developed gradually by a series of different steps within a network of institutions of international law. These institutions are already developing today on a global scale through a networking of political and economical organizations in a post-national constellation. And not only governmental but also non-governmental groups and initiatives are in the play.[6]

An important requirement would be, I think, that the three functions of legislation, political execution and jurisdiction would remain separately working even on a post-national scale. Thus e.g. an *international court* had to be available for an appeal at law by all individuals

---

[5] Cf. Otfried Höffe, "Völkerbund oder Weltrepublik?", in: Immanuel Kant, *Zum ewigen Frieden*, ed. by Otfried Höffe, Berlin: Akademie Verlag, 1995, pp. 109–132, and idem, *Demokratie im Zeitalter der Globalisierung*, München: Beck, 1999.

[6] Cf. Hauke Brunkhorst, „Demokratie in der globalen Rechtsgenossenschaft. Einige Überlegungen zur poststaatlichen Verfassung der Weltgesellschaft", *Zeitschrift für Soziologie. Sonderheft Weltgesellschaft*, 2004.

as cosmopolitan citizens, and even the subsidiary state that is in charge of the function of a *world police* had to subject its soldiers to the jurisdiction of the international court. (As is well known, this is not accepted today by the USA with regard to the International Court Justice of the UNO at The Hague).

Since I myself have worked on a conception of *discourse ethics* in the last 30 years[7], I should mention at the conclusion of my lecture one point of view that was already emphasized by Kant but in our time has displayed a novel dimension of institutional power. What I mean is the development of a *quasi-institution of the reasoning public* that could be characterized as "the thousand dialogues and conferences" about global questions of humankind that take place almost every day in many countries. These dialogues and conferences have very different forms, topics and degrees of significance, reaching from intellectual explorations and discussions to international conferences the results of which are agreements and treaties with far reaching political and economical consequences.

Of course, they are also vehicles of different political and economical interests. But I think, as dialogues that are constantly accompanied and communicated by the mass media, they have so great a share in reaching *social consensus through arguments* that they today must become a *fourth* power, so to speak, in supplementing the three classical power functions of a republic. Thus far, I would hope, they will help to make possible a *cosmopolitan government of law without a cosmopolitan empire.*

---

[7] Cf. for a summary: Karl-Otto Apel, *The Response of Discurse Ethics*, Leuven/Belgium: Peeters, 2001.

Dietrich Böhler
Berlin

Sich-Verantworten in der globalisierten high-tech-Zivilisation. Ein Diskurs zwischen Hans Jonas, Karl-Otto Apel und der sokratischen Dialogpragmatik

Als im Jahre 1972 die Industriegesellschaften vom *Club of Rome* die erste drastische Warnung vor den *ökologischen Langzeitgefahren* des quantitativen ökonomischen Wachstums und den *kumulativen Folgeschäden* der (damals teils kapitalistischen, teils staatssozialistischen) technologischen Zivilisation erhielten, fanden sich die Philosophen auf die neuen Verantwortungsprobleme sehr schlecht vorbereitet. An der New School for Social Research in New York und an der Universität des Saarlandes waren jedoch zwei, durchaus komplementäre, Denker bereits dabei, eine Ethik der solidarischen Menschheitsverantwortung zu entwerfen: Karl-Otto Apel und Hans Jonas, ein rationaler Postkantianer und ein metaphysischer Postaristoteliker (mit biblisch jüdischer, z.T. kantischer Moralmotivation).

Nach einer sowohl von Jonas als auch von Apel inspirierten Skizze der hochtechnologischen Problemsituation erörtert dieser Essay folgende, noch zu differenzierende zukunftsethische Fragen:

– Wie läßt sich moralische Verantwortung in der technologischen Gefahrenzivilisation begreifen – als neuartige *Für*-Sorge für echtes menschliches Leben und dessen Umwelt oder als Sich-Verantworten *vor* der regulativen Instanz einer idealen Kommunikationsgemeinschaft?

– Läßt sich *überhaupt* eine solche moralische Verantwortung als einsehbar verbindlich erweisen?

– Können wir Embryonen den Anspruch der Menschenwürde verweigern?

Die Beobachtung, daß „die ganz unbeabsichtigten, aber unausweichlichen Nebenwirkungen" der technologischen industriellen Zivilisation, etwa „die Verschmutzung der Atmosphäre, der Gewässer, des Bodens, die Ausraubung der Biosphäre, der ganzen Lebenswelt durch Überbeanspruchung, durch Ausrottung von Arten"[1] unermeßlich sind, führte Jonas zu der Erkenntnis, daß die Wirkungsmacht des Menschen „nach Maßstäben unserer irdischen Umwelt ... enorm gestiegen ... und ein Zustand erreicht worden ist, in dem beinahe alles möglich scheint".[2] Daraus erwachse die Einsicht, daß proportional zu dieser Wirkungsmacht auch die Verantwortung des Menschen größer werde, daß es nunmehr eine Verantwortung für die Umwelt, für die Zukunft und für die Menschenwürde gebe. Aus dieser Einsicht entstand Jonas' bescheiden betitelter, aber groß angelegter „Versuch einer Ethik für die technologische Zivilisation", das 1978 erschienene *Prinzip Verantwortung*.[3]

Hans Jonas' Denkweg und Karl-Otto Apels kommunikationsbezogene *Transformation der Philosophie*, 1973 in zwei Bänden vorgelegt, zumal seine transzendentalpragmatische Rekonstruktion der normativ ethischen Präsuppositionen des Denkens und ihr Resultat, nämlich die Einheit von theoretischer und praktischer Vernunft in der Metapraxis des Argumentierens, sind in je eigener Weise von einer faszinierenden Geistesgegenwart. Infolgedessen hat die Arbeit an meinem Lehrstuhl und am Berliner Hans Jonas-Zentrum zum Teil der Auseinandersetzung mit dem intuitionsbezogenen, meta-

---

[1] So Jonas in dem Gespräch „Erkenntnis und Verantwortung", in: *Orientierung und Verantwortung. Begegnungen und Auseinandersetzungen mit Hans Jonas*, hrsg. von Dietrich Böhler u. Jens P. Brune, Würzburg: Königshausen & Neumann, 2004, S. 451: „Diese Zeitbombe tickt, während wir einfach so leben, wie wir es tun als Mitglieder der westlichen technischen Zivilisation, und woran jeder von uns mitwirkt" (S. 450).

[2] Ibidem, S. 452 f.

[3] Erschienen in Frankfurt a. Main, Insel Verlag.

physischen Denken von Jonas einerseits und der kommunikations-bezogenen Transzendentalphilosophie Apels andererseits gegolten. Die sokratische Diskurspragmatik und dialogbezogene Verantwortungsethik kann Grundgedanken jener beiden komplementären Ansätze präzisieren und weiterentwickeln. – Soviel zum Hintergrund, vor dem ich hier die Prinzipienfrage erörtere: „Was heißt und wohin orientiert Verantwortung als Moralprinzip?" So fragend, diskutieren wir auf der Begründungsebene, die Apel den Teil A der Diskursethik nennt.

Für die Situationsanalyse der technologischen Zivilisation ist es an der Zeit, sich klarzumachen, daß charakteristische Begriffe, mit denen Öffentlichkeit, Wissenschaft und Philosophie auf die planetare Selbstgefährdung der Menschheit reagieren, beschönigend und verfälschend sind. So suggeriert die deutsche Diskussion, daß wir in einer bloßen „ökologischen *Krise*" und eben in einer *„Risiko"*-*Gesellschaft* leben. Freilich kann die hochtechnologische Zivilisation gerade durch ihre Innovationen mehr zerstören, als sich im Einzelnen prognostizieren und gegenüber künftigen Generationen verantworten läßt. In diesem Betracht ist sie eher eine *Gefahrenzivilisation* und *Zukunftsgefährdungsgesellschaft*. Scheint es doch ihr Gesetz zu sein, daß sie permanent kumulative Langzeitwirkungen hervorbringt, welche die Anerkennung des Prinzips Menschenwürde und die Fortdauer „echten menschlichen Lebens auf Erden" in Frage stellen. Denn sie bringt nicht allein kumulative Langzeitwirkungen hervor, die zusammen mit ökologischen und soziokulturellen Lebensgrundlagen auch Freiheits- und Verantwortungsbedingungen künftiger Generationen fortwährend verschlechtern oder gar zerstören; sie trägt darüber hinaus zur Aushöhlung der moralischen Prinzipienorientierung bei. Macht sie doch Forschungs- und Medizin-Versprechungen, die individuellen Interessen dienen, während hinderliche moralische Orientierungen als fortschrittsfeindlich, illiberal, ja als inhuman hintangestellt werden.

Was die Analysebegriffe angeht, so ist etwa der Begriff „ökologische Krise" sinnlos, weil euphemistisch. Daher wurde er in dem von der Forschungsgruppe „Ethik und Wirtschaft im Dialog" des Hans Jonas-Zentrums edierten Buch *Zukunftsverantwortung in der Marktwirtschaft*

einer entsprechenden Sinnkritik unterzogen.[4] Schon 1978 hatte Hans
Jonas seine Leser für „das metaphysische Ausmaß" und für die Permanenz der technologisch-kapitalistischen Gefahrensituation sensibilisiert:
sie werde der Menschheit nunmehr wie ein Schatten anhaften.[5] In den
politisch-ethischen Überlegungen und Diskussionen müssen wir m.E. in
der Tat davon ausgehen, daß wir weder in einer „ökologischen Krise"
leben, die wie jede Krise zeitlich begrenzt wäre, noch in einer bloßen
„Risikogesellschaft", sondern in der kapitalistisch-dynamischen technologischen Gefahrenzivilisation, deren weitreichende Zerstörungen und
Zerstörungspotentiale neue, stets zu erneuernde Verantwortungs-
Engagements und Verantwortungs-Institutionen erfordern.

Die anstehenden Probleme werde ich in den folgenden sechs Ab-
schnitten erörtern:

1. Zum Problem einer globalen Verantwortungsethik – nach Max
   Weber.
2. Hans Jonas, Karl-Otto Apel und die Berliner Diskursethik –
   prinzipienethische Antworten auf die neuartigen Herausforderungen der praktischen Vernunft durch die technologische Zivilisation.

---

[4] *Zukunftsverantwortung in der Marktwirtschaft. In memoriam Hans Jonas*, hrsg. von
Thomas Bausch, Dietrich Böhler, Michael Stitzel u.a., EWD, Bd. 3, Münster: LIT, 2000,
bes. S. 58 f., 37 ff., 168 f., 199 f.

[5] Hans Jonas, *Das Prinzip Verantwortung, Versuch einer Ethik für die technologische Zivilisation*, Frankfurt a. Main: Insel, 1979, bes. 1. und 2. Kap. Idem, „Technik, Freiheit und
Pflicht", in: idem, *Wissenschaft als persönliches Erlebnis*, Göttingen: Vandenhoeck und Ruprecht, 1987, S. 45 f.: „Über eines müssen wir uns [...] im klaren sein: eine Patentlösung für
unser Problem, ein Allheilmittel für unsere Krankheit gibt es nicht. Dafür ist das technologische System viel zu komplex, und von einem Aussteigen daraus kann nicht die Rede
sein. Selbst mit der einen großen 'Umkehr' und Reform unserer Sitten würde das Grund-
problem nicht verschwinden. Denn das technologische Abenteuer selber muß weitergehen;
schon die rettenden Berichtigungen erfordern immer neuen Einsatz des technischen und
wissenschaftlichen Ingeniums, das seine eigenen neuen Risiken erzeugt. So ist die Aufgabe
der Abwendung permanent, und ihre Erfüllung muß immer Stückwerk bleiben und oft
nur Flickwerk. Das bedeutet, daß wir wohl in alle Zukunft im Schatten drohender Kala-
mität leben müssen. Sich des Schattens bewußt sein aber, wie wir es jetzt eben werden,
wird zum paradoxen Lichtblick der Hoffnung: er läßt die Stimme der Verantwortung nicht
verstummen. Dieses Licht leuchtet nicht wie das der Utopie, aber seine Warnung erhellt
unseren Weg – zusammen mit dem Glauben an Freiheit und Vernunft".

3. Metaphysische oder reflexiv dialogische Begründung des Prinzips Mitverantwortung?
4. Gedankenexperimente zum Prinzip Verantwortung.
5. Was heißt ‚Verantwortung'? Keine Fürsorge ohne Rechtfertigung, kein praktischer Diskurs ohne Verständigungsgegenseitigkeit und Öffentlichkeit.
6. Verantwortungspflicht gegenüber Embryonen? In dubio pro Menschenwürde.

1. Zum Problem einer globalen Verantwortungsethik – nach Max Weber

Hans Jonas' metaphysisch wertethisches Verantwortungsdenken und die transzendentalpragmatisch oder diskurspragmatisch begründete Verantwortungsethik teilen die Auffassung, daß infolge der (hoch-)technologischen Lebensbedingungen, die seit Mitte des 20. Jahrhunderts herrschen, der Ethik eine ganz neue Stunde geschlagen hat: Alle Menschen seien selbst irgendwie *verantwortlich* dafür, daß auch künftig menschenwürdiges Dasein möglich ist.

Die Diskurs-Verantwortungsethiker schlagen hier die Präzisierung „Mitverantwortlichkeit" vor. Sie beziehen diesen Begriff vor allem darauf, daß eine direkte Verantwortungszuschreibung für die einzelnen oft weder angemessen noch konkret durchführbar sei, daß aber in der modernen Kommunikationswelt und zumal im Falle rechtsstaatlicher Bedingungen allen diskursfähigen Menschen – unabhängig von ihren institutionalisierten Verantwortlichkeiten – eine *Mit*verantwortung *als* Diskurspartner für die Bewußtmachung und mögliche Bewältigung der Zukunftsprobleme zukomme. Warum? Wer von moralischen Problemen wissen kann und irgendwie zu ihrer Verringerung beitragen kann, der weiß *als* Diskurspartner, daß er eine Mitverantwortung für das Problembewußtsein ebensowenig zurückweisen kann wie für die Verringerung und letztlich für die Bewältigung der Probleme.[6]

---

[6] Vgl. *Prinzip Mitverantwortung. Grundlage für Ethik und Pädagogik*, hrsg. von Karl-Otto Apel u. Holger Burckhart, Würzburg: Königshausen & Neumann, 2001.

Jonas und die Diskursethiker sehen die Philosophie vor der Aufgabe, diese – verglichen mit aller traditionellen Ethik – ungeheure Mitverantwortung zu *denken*, also das neue Problem aus dem ihm anhaftenden Ungefähr, jenem „Irgendwie", zu befreien. Die Philosophie sei einmal zu der Begründungsaufgabe herausgefordert, die *Verbindlichkeit* einer noch nie dagewesenen und kollektiven Verantwortung zu erweisen; zum anderen stehe sie vor zweierlei Anwendungsaufgaben, nämlich sowohl die idealisierende *Konkretion* des Moralprinzips zu moralischen Situationsmaximen bzw. Normen, die eigentlich gelten sollten, neu zu denken als auch *Strategien* bzw. Konterstrategien für deren Realisierung und Durchsetzung in der Gesellschaft, etwa gegen amoralische Interessen und Funktionssysteme, zu entwickeln und auf ihre Moralverträglichkeit hin zu prüfen.

Kant hatte jene Konkretionsaufgabe nochmals vorkommunikativ, nämlich in Beschränkung auf eine vom einsamen Subjekt zu leistende *gedankenexperimentelle* Anwendung des Kategorischen Imperativs zu lösen versucht. Ohne an Kants methodischem Solipsismus Anstoß zu nehmen, hat Max Weber generell eine bloß innermoralische Orientierung als unzureichend kritisiert: als Leistung einer Gesinnungsethik, die blind sei für die unverantwortlichen Folgen, die ein unmittelbar moralgetreues Verhalten *inmitten* der „ethischen Irrationalität der Welt" haben könne.[7] In der Tat sieht sich der realistische Ethiker und der ernsthaft Verantwortliche Gesinnungskonflikten ausgesetzt, da die reale Welt Dilemmata bereithält, die in der Perspektive einer reinen Gesinnung unlösbar erscheinen mögen. Sind „schmutzige Hände" (Sartre) und „Schuldübernahme" (Bonhoeffer) unausweichlich?

Karl-Otto Apel hat Webers Anstoß als eigenständiges, konkret geschichtsbezogenes Begründungsproblem 'B' der Ethik pointiert. Im Jonas-Zentrum wird es sowohl kontrovers diskutiert[8] als auch wirt-

---

[7] Max Weber, „Politik als Beruf", in: *Gesammelte Politische Schriften*, hrsg. von Johannes Winckelmann, Tübingen: Mohr/Siebeck, ³1971, S. 553, vgl. S. 550 ff.

[8] Vgl. einerseits Dietrich Böhler, „Idee und Verbindlichkeit der Zukunftsverantwortung", in: *Zukunftsverantwortung in der Marktwirtschaft. In memoriam Hans Jonas*, hrsg. von Thomas Bausch u.a., op. cit., bes. S. 63 ff., 199 ff. und Karl-Otto Apel, „Diskursethik als Ethik der Mitverantwortung vor den Sachzwängen", in: *Prinzip Mitverantwortung. Grundlage für Ethik und Pädagogik*, hrsg. von Karl-Otto Apel u. Holger

schaftsethisch präzisiert.[9] Meines Erachtens geht es um zwei Arten von geschichts- und situationsbezogenen Realisierungsfragen. Einmal um die moral*strategische* Durchsetzungsfrage, welche Widerständigkeiten gegen eine moralische (das Moralprinzip konkretisierende) Situationsnorm durch welche Strategien überwunden werden sollten, und andererseits um die moral*konservative*, gleichsam wertkonservative Frage, welche ethischen Traditionen und Institutionen dem Moralprinzip entsprechen, so daß sie bewahrt bzw. entwickelt werden sollen.

Die intrinsisch moralische Konkretionsaufgabe besteht darin, vom abstrakt Prinzipiellen zu Maximen, gewissermaßen zu regulativen Sollensperspektiven für das Handeln zu kommen. Dabei geht es zuallererst um einen begrifflichen und methodischen Rahmen für die moralische Konkretion der neuen Zukunfts-Verantwortlichkeit, welcher alsdann interdisziplinär auszufüllen wäre. Noch auf der Begründungsebene A können wir die reflexive Letztbegründung des Moralprinzips als ersten Zug der Diskursethik (*A 1*) von einem zweiten Zug (*A 2*), nämlich der diskursvermittelten Anwendung des Moralprinzips zur Normenrechtfertigung, unterscheiden.[10] Und wenn *Habermas* von '*praktischen Diskursen*' sprach, hatte er, bei kritischem bzw. realistischem Lichte besehen, an nichts anderes gedacht; denn er hat dabei stets die kontrafaktische Unterstellung gemacht, *alle* würden sich *als* Teilnehmer eines moralischen Diskurses verhalten – auf

---

Burckhart, op. cit., bes. S. 74 ff. Andererseits Micha H. Werner, *Diskursethik als Maximenethik*, Würzburg: Königshausen & Neumann, 2003, bes. S. 199 ff., 237 ff.

[9] So von Thomas Bausch, „Unternehmerische Verantwortung im Lichte universalistischer Prinzipienethik", in: *Zwischen Universalismus und Relativismus. Philosophische Grundlagenprobleme des interkulturellen Managements*, hrsg. von Horst Steinmann u. Andreas G. Scherer, Frankfurt a. Main: Suhrkamp, 1998, S. 322–347. Ferner Thomas Rusche, *Aspekte einer dialogbezogenen Unternehmensethik*, EWD, Bd. 4, Münster: LIT, 2002, S. 58 ff. und Teil III.

[10] Vgl. Dietrich Böhler, „Diskursethik und Menschenwürdegrundsatz zwischen Idealisierung und Erfolgsverantwortung", in: *Zur Anwendung der Diskursethik in Politik, Recht und Wissenschaft*, hrsg. von Karl-Otto Apel, Matthias Kettner, Frankfurt a. Main: Suhrkamp, ²1993, S. 201–231; idem, „Ethik der Zukunfts- und Lebensverantwortung. Teil I", in: *Orientierung und Verantwortung. Begegnungen und Auseinandersetzungen mit Hans Jonas*, hrsg. von idem u. Jens P. Brune, op. cit., S. 135 ff.

argumentativen Konsens gerichtet *und* mit dem guten Willen, die diskursiv gerechtfertigten Situationsnormen stets zu beachten. Daher konnte er durchgängig auf *„allgemeine* (sic!) *Normenbefolgung"*[11] und *reine* Verständigungsorientierung abstellen, *ohne* daß er diese normativen Gehalte des Diskursgrundsatzes 'D' für die *reale* Handlungsorientierung verantwortungsethisch, nämlich moralstrategisch differenziert hätte.

Hingegen hat Apel eine solche situationsrealistische Differenzierung mit seinem, allerdings unglücklich so genannten, „Ergänzungsprinzip" der moralischen Grundnorm gemäß eines moralstrategischen „Teils B der Diskursethik" ins Auge gefaßt.[12] Denn als universalistisches Moralprinzip verlangt 'D', daß man auch diejenigen Situationen berücksichtigt *und* jene Sachzwänge prüft, die einer ausnahmslosen, allgemeinen Befolgung moralischer Normen entgegenstehen. Kritisch an Apel und Böhler anknüpfend hat Horst Gronke diesen Übergang vom idealisierten praktischen Diskurs zur erfolgsverantwortungsethischen Fragestellung diskursarchitektonisch geklärt.[13]

Im Sinne einer „Verantwortung für den Erfolg des Moralischen" (Böhler) geht es um die konterstrategische Durchsetzung der moralischen Gehalte gegen die Widerstände einer teilweise amoralischen Systemwelt und einer teilweise „ethisch irrationalen" Handlungswelt. Denn in der realen Lebenswelt müssen wir damit rechnen, daß moralische und bereits rechtliche Normen gerade nicht allgemein befolgt, sondern egoistisch bzw. partikular interessiert unterlaufen oder auch

---

[11] Jürgen Habermas, *Moralbewußtsein und kommunikatives Handeln*, Frankfurt a. Main: Suhrkamp, 1983, S. 53–126, bes. S. 103.

[12] Karl-Otto Apel, *Diskurs und Verantwortung*, Frankfurt a. Main: Suhrkamp, 1988, S. 256 ff., 270 ff. u.ö.; idem, *Auseinandersetzungen in Erprobung des transzendentalpragmatischen Ansatzes*, Frankfurt a. Main: Suhrkamp, 1998, Sachregister: „Diskursethik – Begründungsteil A und B"; idem, „Diskursethik und die systemischen Sachzwänge der Politik, des Rechts und der Marktwirtschaft", in: *Diskursethik. Grundlegungen und Anwendungen*, hrsg. von Marcel Niquet, Franciso J. Herrero, Michael Hanke, Würzburg: Königshausen & Neumann, 2001, S. 181–204.

[13] Horst Gronke, „Apel versus Habermas: Zur Architektonik des Diskursethik", in: *Transzendentalpragmatik*, hrsg. von Andreas Dorschel, Matthias Kettner u.a., Frankfurt a. Main: Suhrkamp, 1999, S. 273 ff., bes. S. 232 ff.

aus Verantwortungs- bzw. Fürsorgegründen (z.B. angesichts einer Notlage) dispensiert oder uminterpretiert werden. In der gesellschaftlichen Systemwelt kommt hinzu, daß sie neutralisiert oder gar konterkariert werden können durch die Eigensinnigkeit, den Selbstbehauptungscharakter und die 'Sachzwang-Macht' der gesellschaftlichen Systeme (wie Recht, Politik, Wirtschaft). Zudem kanalisieren und modifizieren Institutionen die normativen Gehalte durch ihre Routinen und Mechanismen.

Daraus ergeben sich zumindest *zwei* moralphilosophische Realisierungsaufgaben, die bei Jonas zwar anklingen, aber weder eingeführt und differenziert noch aus dem Moralprinzip abgeleitet werden. Es ist dies einmal die Prüfung, welche *ethischen Institutionen und Traditionen* dem Moralprinzip gerecht werden, so daß sie *bewahrt* und entfaltet werden sollten. Das wäre ein Diskursschritt *B 1*. Außerdem stellt sich nun die heikle Aufgabe, in theoretischen Diskursen, und zwar mit zweckrational strategischer Einstellung – die Tradition spricht hier verunklarend von „Klugheit" –, *Durchsetzungsstrategien* zu suchen, die zunächst einmal erfolgsfähig sein müssen. Das wäre eine zweckrational strategische Diskursstufe *B 2*. Dann steht die moralische Legitimationsaufgabe an, in praktischen Diskursen zu prüfen, ob die entwickelten Strategien ihrerseits mit dem *Moralprinzip* vereinbar sind. Das wäre die moralstrategische Diskursstufe *B 3*, eine spezifisch verantwortungsethische Erörterung.

Erforderlich ist dazu ein Moralprinzip mit Kriterien für die rationale Abwägung jener Folgelasten, welche eine moralische Konterstrategie für die durchaus verschiedenartigen „Betroffenheitslagen", die „komplexen Entwicklungspfade" der Gesellschaften (M. Werner)[14] *und* für die schutzwürdigen Moral-, Freiheits- und Kulturgüter einer Gesellschaft nach sich ziehen kann. Daher wäre eine bloß vermeidungsethische Fassung des Moralprinzips, welche geböte, die Vernichtung der Menschheit zu vermeiden, unzureichend. Es bedarf,

---

[14] Micha Werner, „Erfaßt das 'Prinzip Verantwortung' die Probleme moderner Technologie?", in: *Hans Jonas. Von der Gnosisforschung zur Verantwortungsethik*, hrsg. von Wolfgang E. Müller, Stuttgart: Kohlhammer, 2003, S. 227 ff., hier S. 233 f. Micha Werner, „Hans Jonas' Prinzip Verantwortung", in: *Bioethik. Eine Einführung*, hrsg. von Marcus Düwell u. Klaus Steigleder, Frankfurt a. Main: Suhrkamp, S. 41 ff., hier S. 43 f.

wie Apel und Werner gegen Jonas ins Feld geführt haben, mehr als eines puren Bewahrungsprinzips und mehr als einer bloßen Ergänzungsethik.

Doch bietet Jonas dazu nicht Ansätze? Leistet er nicht für die Herausarbeitung der normativen Gehalte des Moralprinzips einen wichtigen Beitrag durch seinen phänomenologischen Umgang mit ethischen Intuitionen? Können und müßten hier nicht beide 'Seiten' voneinander lernen? Freilich betrifft Jonas' Beitrag eher die Konkretionsaufgabe (in Apelscher Architektonik die Ebene *A 2*) als die Entwicklung und Prüfung moralischer Strategien (nach Apel die Ebene B).

2. Hans Jonas, Karl-Otto Apel und die Berliner Diskursethik – prinzipienethische Antworten auf die neuartigen Herausforderungen der praktischen Vernunft durch die technologische Zivilisation

Das, worauf Jonas' „Prinzip Verantwortung" reagiert, sind zumal die *äußeren* Herausforderungen der praktischen Vernunft, die mit den, von der technologisch-kapitalistischen Zivilisation verursachten Gefährdungen von Menschheit und Natur gegeben sind. Die transzendentalpragmatischen bzw. diskurspragmatischen Diskursethiker teilen seine Gefahrenanalyse im wesentlichen, wenngleich sie das Erfordernis einer – möglichst durch öffentliche *Verständigung* mit den Beteiligten und Betroffenen zu ermittelnden – sichernden Interpretation der Bedürfnisse und Betroffenheitslagen betonen. Außerdem sehen sie mit den äußeren Herausforderungen eine *innere* verbunden: eine „Selbstparalyse der Vernunft" (Apel) infolge der vorherrschenden Gleichsetzung von Vernunft mit theoretisch analytischer und zweckrational kalkulierender Rationalität. Daraus ergeben sich bei Jonas und den Transzendentalpragmatikern unterschiedliche Ansätze.

Jonas' Analyse der äußeren Herausforderung der praktischen Vernunft führt ihn zunächst zu drei Erweiterungen des Problemhorizonts der Ethik, die sich gut mit den Begriffen der drei Auswirkungsdimensionen menschlichen Verhaltens in der technologischen Zivilisation erläutern lassen, die Karl-Otto Apel 1973 eingeführt hatte.[15]

Die *Dimension* der ethischen Probleme sei in der Tradition räumlich und zeitlich eingeschränkt gewesen, nämlich auf das Verhalten zwischen Personen, also auf eine *soziale Mikro*-Dimension, und dann, politisch-ethisch, auf das Verhältnis zwischen Staaten und Völkern, in der *politischen Meso*-Dimension. Nun führe aber die technische Praxis neuartige Faktoren in die „moralische Gleichung" ein, nämlich einmal die hochtechnologische „Unumkehrbarkeit im Verein mit ihrer zusammengefaßten Größenordnung". Die ganz neue, zumal *ökologische Makro*-Dimension ergibt sich (was bereits Apel als neue, externe Herausforderung der praktischen Vernunft analysiert hatte) daraus, daß die Wirkungen des hochtechnologisch vermittelten Kollektiv- und Systemverhaltens zunehmend weder räumlich noch zeitlich eingrenzbar sind. Hinzu komme „ihr kumulativer Charakter: gewisse Wirkungen addieren sich, so daß die Lage für späteres Handeln und Sein nicht mehr dieselbe ist wie für den anfänglich Handelnden, sondern zunehmend davon verschieden und immer mehr ein Ergebnis dessen, was schon getan ward." Demgegenüber rechnete „alle herkömmliche Ethik [...] nur mit nicht-kumulativem Verhalten".[16]

Naiv erscheint Jonas auch der Erkenntnisbezug des traditionellen ethischen *Urteils*. Sowohl die aristotelisch-thomasische Tradition der Wertethik des guten Lebens als auch die normative Ethik seit Kant gingen ganz selbstverständlich von der Voraussetzung aus: da die sittlichen Probleme aus dem ‚mir' jeweils vertrauten „Nahkreis des Handelns" entspringen, kann ‚ich' auch jeweils aufgrund ‚meines' alltagsweltlichen Erfahrungswissens und ‚meines' *common sense* erkennen, was moralisch richtig oder praktisch gut ist.[17] Demgegenüber

---

[15] Karl-Otto Apel, *Transformation der Philosophie II*, Frankfurt a. Main: Suhrkamp, 1973, S. 359–361. Idem, „Die Situation des Menschen als Herausforderung an die praktische Vernunft", in: *Funkkolleg Praktische Philosophie/Ethik: Dialoge*, hrsg. von idem u. Dietrich Böhler, Gerd Kadelbach, Bd. 1, Frankfurt a. Main: Fischer-TB, 1984, hier: S. 49 ff.

[16] Hans Jonas, *Das Prinzip Verantwortung, Versuch einer Ethik für die technologische Zivilisation*, op. cit., S. 27.

[17] Ibidem, S. 23 ff.

pointiert Jonas, daß die kumulative technologische Veränderung der Welt „lauter präzedenzlose Situationen" schaffe, für die „die Lehren der Erfahrung ohnmächtig" seien, woraus er die Konsequenz zieht: „Unter solchen Umständen wird Wissen zu einer vordringlichen Pflicht [...], und das Wissen muß dem kausalen Ausmaß unseres Handelns größengleich sein."[18]

Wir sehen uns also dem neuen moralischen Erfordernis gegenüber, uns bestmögliches Folgenwissen zu beschaffen. Nicht zuletzt diese Einsicht ist es auch, welche einen wichtigen Aspekt der Diskursethik hervorgebracht hat, nämlich das Postulat, eine Ethik müsse heute mit theoretisch-empirischen Diskursen verbunden werden, um das zur Urteilsbildung erforderliche weitreichende, beispielsweise ökologische, Wissen zu erhalten. Freilich blieben die konkreten praktischen Diskurse über die Frage, was wir in einer bestimmten Situation tun sollen, gerade wegen ihrer Abhängigkeit von empirisch theoretischer Wissensbildung grundsätzlich fallibel, so daß ihre Irrtumsfähigkeit zu berücksichtigen, mithin die *Revisionsfähigkeit* der praktischen Urteile und Maßnahmen zu gewährleisten sei. Eine ähnliche Statusüberlegung findet sich bei Jonas.

Jonas stellt eine höchst ernüchternde Reflexion jener Einsicht an, deren wissenschaftstheoretischer Gehalt – von beiden unbemerkt – mit einer Grenzerkenntnis Karl R. Poppers übereinkommt[19]: das Folgenwissen in nicht-geschlossenen Systemen, für die geschichtliche Welt und für die Biosphäre der Erde könne nie das der bedingten Prognose sein. Folglich bleibe es stets unzulänglich.

Jonas pointiert nun, daß sich aus der Nichtprognostizierbarkeit der ökosozialen Technologiefolgen ein scheinbar paradoxes Ausgangsproblem der Verantwortungsethik als einer *Wissens-Ethik* ergibt:

Daß das vorhersagende Wissen hinter dem technischen Wissen, das unserem Handeln die Macht gibt, zurückbleibt, nimmt selbst ethische Bedeutung an. Die Kluft zwischen Kraft des Vorherwissens und Macht des

---

[18] Ibidem, S. 28.

[19] Vgl. Karl R. Popper, „Naturgesetz und theoretische Systeme", in: *Theorie und Realität*, hrsg. von Hans Albert, Tübingen: Siebeck/Mohr, 1964. Auch in *Logik der Sozialwissenschaften*, hrsg. von Ernst Topitsch, Köln: Kiepenheuer, [4]1967.

Tuns erzeugt ein neues ethisches Problem. Anerkennung der Unwissenheit wird dann die Kehrseite der Pflicht des Wissens und damit ein Teil der Ethik[20].

Was Apel und die anderen Transzendentalpragmatiker darüber hinaus ins Spiel bringen, ist eine diskurs- und wissenschaftspragmatische Einsicht: bereits das Kernstück der naturwissenschaftlich-technologischen Rationalität, das theoretisch-empirische Wissen, als *wahrheitsfähiges* Wissen lasse sich allein in der dialogischen und daher moralisch geladenen Form eines Diskurses unter gleichberechtigten Argumentationspartnern geltend machen. Insofern setze auch der Naturwissenschaftler beispielsweise voraus, daß er andere Wissenschaftler – logisch gesehen aber alle möglichen kompetenten Diskursteilnehmer – als gleichberechtigte Diskurspartner *anerkennen* soll und *will*. Schon diese Gerechtigkeitspräsupposition zeigt, daß die Herausarbeitung der *Diskussionsform* des Wissens moralisch von Belang ist.[21]

Bereits hier kommt die Diskursethik, als genitivus subiectivus verstanden, ins Spiel. Erschließt sie doch aus der diskurspragmatischen Dimension der wissenschaftlichen Forschung – das Forschen ist ja zugleich ein *Geltendmachen* von Hypothesen und Theorien bzw. ein Kritisieren solcher, mithin ein argumentativer Diskurs – eine implizite Wissenschaftsethik als Ethik der Diskurspartner. So lieferten Apels Programm einer transzendentalpragmatischen Aufdeckung des Kommunikationsaprioris[22] und das einer *Rekonstruktiven Pragmatik*[23]

---

[20] Hans Jonas, *Das Prinzip Verantwortung, Versuch einer Ethik für die technologische Zivilisation*, op. cit., S. 28.

[21] Karl-Otto Apel, *Transformation der Philosophie II*, op. cit., S. 324 ff., 395 ff. Dietrich Böhler, „In dubio contra projectum", in: *Ethik für die Zukunft*, hrsg. von idem, München: C.H. Beck, 1994, bes. S. 255 ff., 268 ff.

[22] Karl-Otto Apel, „Sprache als Thema und Medium der transzendentalen Reflexion", in: idem, *Transformation der Philosophie II*, op. cit., S. 311 ff., bes. 327 ff. Idem, „Das Apriori der Kommunikationsgemeinschaft. Grundlagen der Ethik", ibidem, S. 358 ff.

[23] Dietrich Böhler, *Rekonstruktive Pragmatik. Von der Bewußtseinsphilosophie zur Kommunikationsreflexion: Neubegründung der praktischen Wissenschaften und Philosophie*, Frankfurt a. Main: Suhrkamp, 1985, Kap. II. und VI.

den Grundriß einer *Ethik für Diskurse* und schlossen gleichsam sokratisch-kantisch an Popper an. Dessen kritisches Wissenschaftsethos, von ihm selbst als eine bloße *Entscheidungsangelegenheit* des Vernunftgläubigen angesehen, wurde (hinsichtlich *dieser* Deutung) als ein dezisionistisches Mißverständnis zurückgewiesen; doch konnte sein normativer Gehalt, das *Ethos des selbstkritischen Forschers in einer offenen Gemeinschaft,* als angemessene Entsprechung zur intersubjektiv-dialogischen Form des Habens, Beanspruchens und Geltendmachens einer Erkenntnis aufgewiesen werden. Denn das Erheben von Geltungsansprüchen schließt Moralität ein – zunächst in Form der Anerkennung substantieller moralischer Verpflichtungen gegenüber allen möglichen Diskurspartnern.

Wenn aber in den Präsuppositionen der wissenschaftlichen Rationalität und in den Präsuppositionen des Argumentierens moralische Verbindlichkeiten aufweisbar sind, dann ist *Vernunft,* nun rekonstruiert als dialogische Praxis des Argumentierens, nicht bloß theoretischer, technischer, ökonomischer Natur, nicht ein bloßes Vermögen des Analysierens und Rechnens, sondern zugleich moralisch orientierend und verpflichtend. Dann ist eine moralisch bedeutsame Selbsterkenntnis der Vernunft möglich, welche die moderne Selbstinfragestellung der praktischen Vernunft als gegenstandslos erweist – als Selbstverfehlung der Praxis des Geltung-Beanspruchens und Etwas-Geltendmachens.

Jene *innere Herausforderung* der Idee einer moralisch-praktischen Vernunft durch das vorherrschende moderne Vernunftverständnis hat Karl-Otto Apel als Komplementarität analysiert: Einerseits werde die wissenschaftlich-theoretische Ratio und das formale Kalkül der Zweckrationalität als die Vernunft schlechthin monopolisiert; andererseits würden Wert- und Normfragen zu einem 'act of faith' (Popper), einem existenziellen und irrationalen Entscheidungsakt subjektiviert. Diese auch von Jonas berührte *Komplementarität*[24], welche Apel als „Komplementaritätssystem" des modernen westlichen Geistes entfaltet, führt dazu, daß die Idee einer praktischen Vernunft als obsolet

---

[24] Hans Jonas, *Das Prinzip Verantwortung, Versuch einer Ethik für die technologische Zivilisation,* op. cit., S. 57.

Auf der einen Seite ...

steht die (von Max Weber an Hand des großen neuzeitlichen Säkularisierungs- / Rationalisierungsprozesses beschriebene) Entwicklung von

zweckrationalen Standards

im weitesten Sinne mit ihren (z.B. von Jürgen Habermas untersuchten) Sub- und Nebenformen

– der *wissenschaftlich-technischen Rationalität* einer am Erfolg kontrollierten Naturbeherrschung,

– der *ökonomischen Rationalität* des effizienten Mitteleinsatzes bei vorgegebenen Zwecken,

– der *strategischen Rationalität* wechselseitiger Instrumentalisierung zu je eigenen Zwecken,

– der *pragmatischen Verfahrensrationalität* der öffentlichen Willensfeststellung per Mehrheitsbeschluß usw.

Auf der anderen Seite ...

steht eine Verdrängung aller moralischen Wert- und Normgesichtspunkte in den Bereich des rational nicht Fassbaren, des Irrationalen, eine Entwicklung, die sich gesellschaftspolitisch in der

Privatisierung der moralischen Urteilsbildung

und philosophisch in der Strömung des *Existentialismus* niedergeschlagen hat.

Komplementär sind diese Seiten insofern, als (a) alles, was in den Bereich des Irrationalen fällt, im Bereich des Rationalen nicht vorkommt und umgekehrt, andererseits aber (b) die Annahme eines Bereichs des Irrationalen Voraussetzung für den Bereich des Rationalen ist und umgekehrt: der Wissenschaftler, der im Labor seine erfolgskontrollierten Experimente durchführt, muß, indem er experimentiert, moralische Wert- und Normfragen aus dem Blickfeld nehmen (methodologische Werturteilsenthaltung); der Existentialist, der sich in der außergewöhnlichen Situation einer „Ur-Entscheidung für/gegen Vernunft" wähnt, setzt selbstverständlich voraus, daß die Welt um ihn herum weiterhin „funktioniert" und dieses „Funktionieren" anhand von Rationalitätsstandards zu erklären ist.

Abb. 1. Analyse der technologischen und liberalen Zivilisation
als 'Komplementaritätssystem' im Anschluß an Apel

und illusorisch gilt[25]. Unter diesen Voraussetzungen erscheint es sinnlos, moralische Ansprüche auf der objektiven oder intersubjekti-

---

[25] „Die Komplementarität zwischen wertfreiem Objektivismus der Wissenschaft einerseits, existentiellem Subjektivismus der religiösen Glaubensakte und ethischen

ven Ebene der Vernunft, also des Erweisbaren, prüfen und rein argumentativ darüber befinden zu wollen. Praktische Fragen wie die Frage nach dem „Vorrang eines Ziels gegenüber anderen unter dem Aspekt der Vernunft zu diskutieren..."[26] gilt als unmöglich. Vernunft wird auf formale Logik plus theoretisch-empirische und Zweckrationalität verkürzt, sie schrumpft zur „subjektiven" und „instrumentellen Vernunft" (Max Horkheimer).

Dann verfällt freilich das Sich-Verantworten gegenüber den (moralischen) Ansprüchen Anderer einem Wertsubjektivismus, einem Rückzug auf 'meine' Wertwahl, die allenfalls noch plausibel gemacht werden kann. Von jener Subjektivierungsgefahr, letztlich Beliebigkeitsgefahr der Ethik ist Jonas durchdrungen. Das motiviert ihn dazu, die traditionelle *substanzielle*, nämlich *objektive Vernunft*, die den Wert des Seins aus diesem selbst vernehmen will, zu erneuern. Es ist dies ein metaphysisch teleologischer, auf die aristotelisch-thomasische Tradition zurückgreifender Ansatz, der das „Prinzip der Ethik" aus der „Natur des Ganzen", nämlich aus dem im Menschen gipfelnden Leben begründen will, – und insofern aus dem, „was die Theologie als *ordo creationis* zu bezeichnen pflegte".[27] So formulierte Jonas programmatisch im Epilog zu seiner evolutionären Ontologie des Lebendigen: „*Organismus und Freiheit*".

Zuvor hatte er jedoch unmißverständlich klargemacht, daß er *nach* Nietzsches Proklamation des Todes Gottes und *nach* Heideggers „Sein und Zeit" denkt. Denn er vertritt nicht etwa objektivistisch eine

---

Entscheidungen andererseits erweist sich als der moderne philosophisch-ideologische Ausdruck der liberalen Trennung zwischen öffentlichem und privatem Lebensbereich, der sich im Zusammenhang mit der Trennung von Staat und Kirche herausgebildet hat." In: Karl-Otto Apel, *Transformation der Philosophie II*, op. cit., S. 370, vgl. S. 361–378. Weiterentwickelt in: idem, „Die Selbstinfragestellung der praktischen Vernunft in der Gegenwart", in: *Funkkolleg/Studientexte*, hrsg. von idem u. Dietrich Böhler, Karlheinz Rebel, Bd. 1, S. 130–137. Vgl. Karl-Otto Apel, *Diskurs und Verantwortung*, op. cit., S. 26–36, 58 ff.

[26] Max Horkheimer, *Zur Kritik der instrumentellen Vernunft*, hrsg. von Alfred Schmidt, Frankfurt a. Main: Fischer, 1967, S. 17.

[27] Hans Jonas, „Epilog – Gnostizismus, Existentialismus und Nihilismus", in: idem, *Gnosis. Die Botschaft des unbekannten Gottes*, Frankfurt a. Main: Insel, 1999 (zuerst als „Gnosis und Nihilismus" in: *Kerygma und Dogma*, 1960, S. 155–171).

Ontotheologie, derzufolge Gott das Sein selbst bzw. der Grund des Seins sei *und* auch als dieses principium des Seins erkennbar sei, sondern er nimmt die *Immanenz* der Welt, die *Endlichkeit* des Lebens und die *Zeitlichkeit* des menschlichen Daseins ernst. Darin ist er so konsequent, daß er in seinem spekulativen Mythos eines möglichen Schöpfergottes die Idee dieses Gottes selbst jenen Bestimmungen und insofern das Transzendente der Immanenz unterwirft.[28] Insofern entsubstantialisiert Jonas seinen metaphysischen Ansatz und verbindet ihn mit dem methodischen Atheismus, der den modernen Wissenschaften zugrundeliegt und der vom nachkierkegaardschen Existentialismus aufgenommen wird.[29]

Dazu paßt es, daß Jonas schon 1964 Heideggers mystisch-ontotheologische „Kehre" als Flucht vor der Rechtfertigungsaufgabe des Denkens verwirft. Er unterzieht sie einer schneidenden Sinnkritik: diese neue Ontotheologie verbinde den demütigen Gestus des Vernehmens des Seins mit dem hybriden Anspruch, daß durch den Seinsdenker, also durch Heidegger, „das Wesen der Dinge selbst spricht" und daß dadurch die (in Wahrheit doch von jeder Theorie erneut zu überbrückende) „Subjekt-Objekt-Spaltung erlassen, vermieden, überwunden werden könne". So aber mache sie sich durch Erschleichung unangreifbar. Diese selbstimmunisierte Ontotheologie sei „die enormste Hybris in aller Geschichte des Denkens".[30]

Gegen den ontotheologischen, den „anfänglichen" und „wesentlichen" Denker Heidegger, den er geradezu als „Bauchredner des Seins" apostrophieren kann, macht Jonas geltend, daß das Denken verantwortlich sei und daß es „entscheidend von der Auffassung seiner Verantwortlichkeit" abhänge.[31] In diesem Sinne legt er großen

---

[28] Idem, *Philosophische Untersuchungen und metaphysische Vermutungen*, Frankfurt a. Main: Insel, 1992, bes. S. 190–197, 243–247.

[29] Idem, *Erinnerungen*, Frankfurt a. Main: Insel, 2003, S. 93. Idem, Gespräch mit H. Koelbl, in: *Jüdische Portraits*, hrsg. von Herlinde Koelbl, Frankfurt a. Main: Fischer TB, 1998, S. 170, Sp. 2.

[30] Hans Jonas, „Heidegger und die Theologie", Vortrag von 1964, deutsch in: *Heidegger und die Theologie, Beginn und Fortgang der Diskussion*, hrsg. von Gerhard Noller, München: Christian-Kaiser-Verlag, 1967, S. 316–340, hier S. 335 f.

[31] Ibidem, S. 336.

Wert darauf, den geltungsmäßigen Stellenwert sowohl seiner metaphysischen Ontologie als auch seiner spekulativen Theologie distanziert und kritisch zu erörtern. Mit selbstkritischer Redlichkeit wahrt
er die ontologischen Differenzen zwischen Denker und Gedachtem,
zwischen Endlichkeit und möglicher Nicht-Endlichkeit. So spricht er
von Gott nur in doppelter Einklammerung: als möglichem Gott, über
den er wiederum nur „Vermutungen" ohne Wahrheitsanspruch vor-
zubringen habe.[32]

Die Subjekt-Objekt-Differenzen ernstnehmend und in Einklammerung des Wahrheitsanspruchs über das Sein-Können eines möglichen Schöpfergeistes nachdenkend, zeigt sich Jonas als ein nachkanti-
scher und nachhusserlscher Metaphysiker. Das trennt ihn sowohl von
der klassischen und thomistischen Ontotheologie als auch von der
des späten Heidegger. Diesem kritischen Zug wird weder Vittorio
Hösle gerecht, wenn er Jonas schlicht eine „ontotheologische Begründung der Ethik" zuspricht[33], noch Micha Werner, der bei Jonas eine
„objektivistische Moralbegründung" erblickt.[34] Ohne objektivistische
seinstheologische Prämissen will Jonas den naturalistisch monisti-
schen Zug und die Teleologie der klassischen bzw. thomistischen
Ontologie neu denken. Ohne Rückgriff auf göttliche Autorität oder
auf Allmachtsannahmen will er schöpfungstheologisches Erbe, so die
„Heiligkeit des Lebens" und die „Hütung des Ebenbildes", in Besitz
nehmen.[35] „Philosophierend habe ich von Möglichkeiten gesprochen,
nicht von Wirklichkeiten".[36]

In der Tat ist ein hypothetisches Denken der *Möglichkeit* eines
Schöpfergottes, der sich gänzlich dem Weltabenteuer der Immanenz

---

[32] Hans Jonas, *Philosophische Untersuchungen und metaphysische Vermutungen*, op. cit.,
3. Teil, S. 171–255.

[33] Vittorio Hösle, „Ontologie und Ethik bei Hans Jonas", in: *Ethik für die Zukunft*,
hrsg. von Dietrich Böhler, op. cit., S. 120 f. Zur Sache: Walther Ch. Zimmerli, „Philosophie in einer Gott-verlassenen Welt", ibidem, S. 151 ff., bes. S. 159 ff.

[34] Micha Werner, „Hans Jonas' Prinzip Verantwortung", op. cit., S. 48.

[35] Hans Jonas, *Das Prinzip Verantwortung, Versuch einer Ethik für die technologische
Zivilisation*, op. cit., S. 57 f., 63, 392 f.

[36] Idem, „Im Kampf um die Möglichkeit des Glaubens. Erinnerungen an Rudolf
Bultmann und Betrachtungen zum philosophischen Aspekt seines Werkes", in: idem,
Wissenschaft als persönliches Erlebnis, op. cit., S. 75.

überantwortet habe, etwas grundsätzlich anderes als das (gegenstandsbezogene, Wahrheit beanspruchende) Schauen bzw. Vernehmen von Gott als tatsächlichem Grund bzw. Prinzip des Seins. Jonas' ontologisch-teleologischer Ansatz – er nennt ihn mit Vorliebe „metaphysisch" und „ontologisch" –, bringt ihn von Anbeginn in die *Prinzipiendimension* und läßt ihn auch das Ethische aus dieser denken. Außerdem gewinnt er durch den Rückgriff auf die biblisch priesterschriftliche Lehre von der Gottesebenbildlichkeit des Menschen (1. Buch Mose, 1,26 f.) den normativen Gehalt des Grundsatzes der (zu achtenden) *Menschenwürde*. Dadurch erweitert er die Perspektive einer bloßen Bewahrung der Gattung, in deren Sinne sich die erste Formel seines kategorischen Imperativs der Zukunftsverantwortung unter Umständen verstehen läßt: „Handle so, daß die Wirkungen deiner Handlungen verträglich sind mit der Permanenz echten menschlichen Lebens auf Erden".[37] Karl-Otto Apels Kritik hat Jonas darauf festlegen wollen.[38] Unangemessenerweise; denn sie überspringt den Kontext und den Rekurs auf Menschenwürde, mit dem das Werk auch schließt: „Um die Hütung des 'Ebenbildes'".[39]

Allerdings ist zu fragen, was Jonas zum Begründungsproblem, d.h. zu einem Verbindlichkeitserweis des Prinzips der Ethik beiträgt, ob bzw. inwiefern ein Verantwortungsprinzip der aussichtsreiche Kandidat für die Bestimmung des grundlegenden Moralprinzips sein kann und wo ein solches Prinzip gleichsam zu lokalisieren ist: primär im Sein oder primär im Dialog, in welchem auch ein Seinsdenker, dadurch, daß er denkend etwas geltend macht, sich je schon befindet?

Schließlich stellt sich die Frage, welche differenzierenden Kriterien bzw. normativen Bedeutungsgehalte (etwa Gerechtigkeit, Öffentlichkeit und Kommunikationsfreiheit) intern mit dem Verantwortungsprinzip verbunden werden müßten – besser: *als* mit ihm

---

[37] Hans Jonas, *Das Prinzip Verantwortung, Versuch einer Ethik für die technologische Zivilisation*, op. cit., S. 36.

[38] Karl-Otto Apel, „Verantwortung heute...", in: idem, *Diskurs und Verantwortung*, op. cit., S. 179 ff., vgl. auch das Gespräch mit Apel in: *Prinzip Mitverantwortung. Grundlage für Ethik und Pädagogik*, hrsg. von idem u. Holger Burckhart, op. cit., S. 97 ff.

[39] Hans Jonas, *Das Prinzip Verantwortung, Versuch einer Ethik für die technologische Zivilisation*, op. cit., S. 392 f.

verwoben aufzuweisen sind. Müßte Jonas, wenn er diese Frage ernstnimmt, nicht die „doppelte Vereinfachung" zurücknehmen, die in den Kollektivierungen der *vielerlei* Beteiligten zu der jetzt lebenden Menschheit und den *sehr unterschiedlichen* Betroffenen zu der künftigen Menschheit steckt? Micha Werner hat darauf mit Recht hingewiesen.[40] Die hier nötigen Differenzierungen sind *Diskursdifferenzierungen*. Sie ergeben sich als solche mit innerer Logik, wenn man das Verantwortungsprinzip aus dem Dialogprinzip entwickelt: durch Rückgang auf das Sich-im-Diskurs-Verantworten. Eben das ist der komplementäre, nicht-metaphysische Prinzipienansatz der Berliner Diskurspragmatik und Dialogpragmatik: eine sokratische Ethikbegründung durch rationale Beweisführung und sinnkritische Prüfung im Dialog mit dem Skeptiker, deren Wahrheit jeder aus stichhaltigen Gründen zustimmen würde – auch der ex professo Ungläubige, der *skeptische* Diskursteilnehmer, dem wir mit keiner bloßen Glaubensannahme kommen können.

3. Metaphysische oder reflexiv dialogische Begründung des Prinzips Mitverantwortung?

Seinen metaphysisch ontologischen Begründungsweg fortsetzend, entwarf Jonas 1985, überarbeitet 1992, den „Versuch einer 'metaphysischen Deduktion' der Verantwortungsethik".[41] Bemerkenswerterweise geht er hier in einer sokratisch kantischen Manier zurück auf das, was Menschen als ethische *Fähigkeit* mitbringen und was sie als normative *Verpflichtung* nicht bezweifeln können:

> Der Mensch ist das einzige uns bekannte Wesen, das Verantwortung haben kann. Indem er sie haben *kann*, *hat* er sie. Die Fähigkeit zur Verantwortung bedeutet schon das Unterstelltsein unter ihr Gebot: das Können

---

[40] Micha Werner, „Erfaßt das 'Prinzip Verantwortung' die Probleme moderner Technologie?", op. cit., S. 227 ff., hier S. 234 und 240.

[41] Hans Jonas, Brief an H.-G. Gadamer, 9. Nov. 1985, in: *Orientierung und Verantwortung. Begegnungen und Auseinandersetzungen mit Hans Jonas*, hrsg. von Dietrich Böhler u. Jens P. Brune, op. cit., S. 480.

selbst führt mit sich das Sollen. Die Fähigkeit aber zur Verantwortung – eine *ethische* Fähigkeit – beruht in der *ontologischen* Befähigung des Menschen, zwischen Alternativen des Handelns mit Wissen und Wollen zu wählen. Verantwortung ist also komplementär zu *Freiheit*.[42]

Das Manuskript hatte Jonas Hans-Georg Gadamer mit der Bitte um dessen Urteil zugesandt. Dieser hebt in seiner Antwort hervor[43], daß Jonas seine Deduktion einer Pflicht zur (Mit-)Verantwortung für „die Permanenz echten menschlichen Lebens auf Erden" eigentlich durch Rückgang auf ein moralisches Grundfaktum der Vernunft gewinne. „Im Grunde folgen ja auch Sie Kant, wenn Sie von der Gegebenheit der Verantwortung reden: das *ist* das Vernunftfaktum der Freiheit."[44]

Gadamer übergeht allerdings, daß der Rückgang auf die Verantwortungsfähigkeit *als* „ursprüngliches Erfahrungsdatum" in einen naturalistischen Fehlschluß[45] führt oder gar in einen, wie Jonas selbst erörtert, „logischen Zirkeltrug" nach Art des ontologischen Gottesbeweises. Letzterem will Jonas" dadurch entgehen, daß er aus der begrifflichen ‚Essenz' eines ursprünglichen Erfahrungsdatums (nämlich aus dem Begriff der Menschheit) allein die Pflicht zur Fortsetzung von deren Existenz ableitet. Das sei dann:

zwar ein Schluß von Essenz zu *geforderter* Existenz, doch kein Zirkelschluß von Essenz zu *gegebener* Existenz. Also ist unser Argument kein

---

[42] Hans Jonas, *Philosophische Untersuchungen und metaphysische Vermutungen*, op. cit., S. 130 f.

[43] Hans-Georg Gadamer, Brief an H. Jonas, 21. April 1986 in Antwort auf das Schreiben von Jonas vom 9. November 1985, in: *Orientierung und Verantwortung. Begegnungen und Auseinandersetzungen mit Hans Jonas*, hrsg. von Dietrich Böhler u. Jens P. Brune, op. cit., S. 471–482, hier: S. 481 f.

[44] Hans-Georg Gadamer, Brief an H. Jonas, vom 21. April 1986, ibidem, S. 481. Gadamer pointiert also die Analogie zu Kants These einer Verwobenheit der moralischen Autonomie mit der Einsicht in das Sittengesetz als dem „Faktum der reinen Vernunft", nach: *Kritik der praktischen Vernunft*, 1787, S. 55 ff.

[45] So Karl-Heinz Ilting, „Der naturalistische Fehlschluß bei Kant", in: *Rehabilitierung der praktischen Philosophie*, hrsg. von Manfred Riedel, Freiburg i.Br.: Rombach, 1972, Bd. 1, S. 113–130. Wiederum in: Karl-Heinz Ilting, *Grundfragen der praktischen Philosophie*, Frankfurt a. Main: Suhrkamp, 1994, S. 277–295.

leeres. Aber es ist auch kein *Beweis*. Es ist an gewisse unbewiesene, axiomatische Voraussetzungen gebunden: nämlich, daß Verantwortungsfähigkeit an sich ein *Gut* ist, also etwas, dessen Anwesenheit seiner Abwesenheit überlegen ist; und daß es überhaupt ‚*Werte an sich*' gibt, die im Sein verankert sind – daß letzteres also *objektiv* werthaltig ist.[46]

Als Philosoph, dem die, von Kant als Selbstverpflichtung der Vernunft geltend gemachte, Tugend der Wahrhaftigkeit eingeschrieben ist, zieht Jonas daraus die Konsequenz: „Letztlich kann mein Argument nicht mehr tun, als vernünftig eine *Option* begründen [...]. Besseres habe ich leider nicht zu bieten".[47]

In seinem Brief an Gadamer schließt er damit, daß er glaube, über dieses „Wagestück" nicht mehr „hinauszukommen (was zwar nötig wäre)".[48] Einerseits räumt Jonas damit ein, die Komplementarität des modernen westlichen Geistes nicht überwunden zu haben – eine bloße Option gehört auf die subjektiv existenzielle Seite der Komplementarität. Sein Begründungsziel, die Subjektivität in Wert- und Normenfragen aufzuheben, hat er demnach verfehlt. Andererseits transzendiert – darauf weist Gadamer hin – seine sokratisch kantische Denkweise hier sein metaphysisches Selbstverständnis. Was bedeutet das für uns *als* Skeptiker?

Ohne Gefahr der petitio und ohne naturalistischen Fehlschluß können wir Jonas' Intuition aufnehmen und – in zwei Schritten – zwingend neu denken: zuerst durch eine *Rekonstruktion* von Voraussetzungen des argumentativen Dialogs, sodann durch eine *sokratische Dialogreflexion*; nämlich durch einen dialogreflexiven, aktuell im Diskurs mit Skeptikern geführten Erweis einer ursprünglichen, unhintergehbaren Anerkennung von Verantwortung. Ursprünglich ist diese Anerkennung, weil sie zugleich mit dem Ins-Spiel-Bringen der eigenen Freiheit entspringt; argumentativ unhintergehbar ist sie, weil sie bereits dem Etwas-Denken und Etwas-Geltendmachen zugrunde

---

[46] Hans Jonas, *Philosophische Untersuchungen und metaphysische Vermutungen*, op. cit., S. 139.

[47] Ibidem, S. 140.

[48] Idem in: *Orientierung und Verantwortung. Begegnungen und Auseinandersetzungen mit Hans Jonas*, hrsg. von Dietrich Böhler u. Jens P. Brune, op. cit., S. 480.

liegt – eine Sinnbedingung des Denkens als Selbstgespräch und als Gespräch aufgrund von Argumenten.

Werfen wir zunächst einen Blick auf die diskurspragmatische Rekonstruktion: *kommunikative Freiheit*, die wir in Anspruch nehmen, indem wir etwas Eigenes, das wir geltend machen wollen, vorbringen (etwa 'meinen' Gedanken über Freiheit jetzt), und *Verantwortung im Dialog*, die wir anerkennen, indem wir Anderen gegenüber etwas zur Geltung bringen, sind von vornherein an dem ebensowohl logischen wie ontologischen Ort verwoben, an dem wir beide voraussetzen und ins Spiel bringen. Dieser Ort ist der Dialog. Denn im Dialog machen wir von unserer Freiheit Gebrauch, indem wir Ansprüche auf Geltung für das, was wir vorbringen, erheben. Diese kommunikative Freiheit können wir jedoch nur in dem Maße verwirklichen, als wir auch zur Verantwortung bereit sind gegenüber den Anderen, die am Dialog teilnehmen, und gegenüber denen, über die wir reden bzw. um deren Ansprüche es geht. Gleichursprünglich mit 'meiner' Freiheit ist im Dialog 'meine' Anerkennung dessen, daß 'ich' anderen Rede und Antwort stehen können muß. In der Dialogsituation ist meine Freiheit gleichursprünglich mit meiner Bereitschaft, mich zu verantworten für das, was 'ich' frei äußere. – Der erste Begründungsschritt, die rekonstruktive Pragmatik des Diskurses, bestünde also darin, die Verantwortungsfähigkeit in ihrer Verwobenheit mit der kommunikativen Freiheit als diejenige Seinseigenschaft *und* soziale Erwartung aufzudecken, die jeder implizit schon anerkannt hat, wenn er überhaupt – sich bzw. anderen – etwas zu verstehen gibt und etwas geltend macht.

In einem *zweiten* Begründungsschritt würde dann die rekonstruierte Argumentations- und Kommunikationsvoraussetzung hinsichtlich ihrer Allgemeingültigkeit bezweifelt, damit nun – im reflexiven Dialog mit dem Zweifler – die Möglichkeit *dieses* Bezweifelns sokratisch sinnkritisch getestet werden kann. Wenn sich in dieser Prüfung herausstellt, daß der angemeldete Geltungszweifel für die konkreten Dialogpartner des Skeptikers *nicht* als prüfbarer *Dialogbeitrag verstehbar* ist, dann *kann* er nicht triftig sein, dann trifft der Zweifel nicht das *Sein* des Zweifelgegenstandes. D.h.: dann gehört dieses Sein zum Sein des *Dialogs*, es ist also ein Stück des Geltungsbodens und des Seins-bodens, auf dem der Zweifelnde *als* Etwas-Denkender und Kommunizierender selber steht. So zeigt sich in einem reflexiv sokratischen Dialog mit dem Skeptiker: Eine Bezweiflung der These, daß Freiheit und Verantwortung gleichursprünglich sind, so daß 'ich' prinzipiell zur Verantwortungsbereitschaft für den Dialog verpflichtet bin, wäre sinnlos, wäre ein performativer Widerspruch. Einen solchen Zweifel kann 'ich' meinen Dialogpartnern gegenüber nicht ernsthaft vertreten.

Warum kann ich das nicht? Weil 'meine' Diskurspartner nur einen solchen Zweifler *verstehen* und hinsichtlich seiner Dialogbeiträge *ernstnehmen* können, der zugleich seine kommunikative *Freiheit* (z.B. die Freiheit, jetzt eine Zweifelsthese zu vertreten) und seine Bereitschaft zur *Verantwortung* in das dialogische Verhältnis einbringt *und* der beide darin auch aufrechterhält. Im Dialog muß er verantwortlich dafür sein, daß er den Anderen sinnvolle, diskutierbare Diskursbeiträge vorlegt: Beiträge, für die er glaubwürdig, ohne Selbstwiderspruch, Rede und Antwort stehen kann. Eben das tut er *nicht*, wenn er dasjenige in Zweifel zieht, was er (im Verhältnis zum Anderen und zu sich selbst) notwendigerweise als gemeinsame Sinnbasis beansprucht und vorausgesetzt hat – im Sinne eines apriorischen Perfekts, welches mit einer Diskurspartnerrolle gegeben ist.

Ich kann nur hoffen, daß Hans Jonas diese zugleich dialogische (mithin geltungslogische) und ontologische (auf das Sein des Zweiflers und seiner Gemeinschaft zurückgehende) Argumentation überzeugt hätte. Leider war ich selbst zu seinen Lebzeiten im sokratisch reflexiven Denken noch nicht weit genug gekommen, um sie ihm klar genug vorzutragen. Jedenfalls läßt sich die Kantische, Hans Jonas durch Gadamer offerierte, Lehre vom Faktum der Vernunft auf diese Weise dialogpragmatisch dechiffrieren. So ließe sie sich überführen in eine Lehre des *einsehbaren* Anerkannthabens von Verantwortlichkeit *und* Gewährthabens von Freiheit auf dem gemeinschaftlichen Seinsboden und Geltungsboden des Dialogs. Problemgeschichtlich gesehen, wäre das eine dialogreflexive Aufhebung Kants, nämlich seines mißlungenen Aufhebungsversuchs der metaphysischen Vernunftlehre, durch Rekonstruktion eines moralisch gehaltvollen „Faktums" der dialogischen Vernunft. Den Anstoß dazu hatte Apel 1967/1973 gegeben, als er Kants Rede vom „Faktum der Vernunft" als „Ergebnis transzendentaler Selbstbesinnung" interpretierte und vorschlug, sie transzendentalpragmatisch zu „dechiffrieren".[49] 1990 präzisierte er gegenüber Karl-Heinz Ilting und dem Dezisionismus, daß der Rückgang auf die diskurs- und damit vernunfttragenden Verpflichtungen nicht etwa ein kontingentes Faktum zutage fördere, sondern es handele sich um „ein *einsehbares in Freiheit Anerkannthaben*, das für die Selbstreflexion der Vernunft immer schon ein 'Faktum der Vernunft' (apriorisches Perfekt!) ist".[50] Der reflexive Rückgang darauf sei weder ein naturalistischer Fehlschluß noch eine *petitio principii*, denn er besage:

> Wer mit dem Willen zur Selbstkonsistenz argumentiert – und dies kann man als nichthintergehbar unterstellen –, der hat insofern nicht mehr die Wahlfreiheit, sich auch gegen das Sittengesetz zu entscheiden; denn dieses hat er ineins mit dem Willen zur selbstkonsistenten Argumentation – d.h. ineins mit dem Adressieren einer idealen Argumentationsgemeinschaft – schon *notwendigerweise* anerkannt.[51]

Die Unhintergehbarkeit von Freiheit und Verantwortlichkeit, von Jonas metaphysisch und von Apel transzendentalpragmatisch angenommen, läßt sich demonstrieren: in einem realen Dialog mit einem Zweifler als leibhaftem Dialogpartner, kann 'ich' diesem 'meinem' Partner demonstrieren, daß er aus dem Dialogverhältnis ausbrechen müßte und von 'mir' (und anderen möglichen Partnern) nicht mehr als glaubwürdiger Diskurspartner anerkannt werden kann, wenn er das Verwobensein seiner Freiheit mit seinem Verantwortlichseinwollen und damit die Verbindlichkeit des Moralprinzips bzw. des Sittengesetzes in Zweifel zu ziehen versucht. Geht nämlich ein solcher Dialogtest für den Zweifler negativ aus, dann ist dialogevident, daß die bezweifelte Annahme eines Prinzips in der Tat eine Sinnbedingung argumentativer Diskurse ist – also ein wahrhaft verbindliches Prinzip.

Die reflexiv sokratische Dialog- und Diskurspragmatik kann also auf der Ebene allgemeingültiger Kriterien zweierlei nachkantische

---

[49] Karl-Otto Apel, *Transformation der Philosophie II*, op. cit., S. 418.

[50] Idem, *Auseinandersetzungen in Erprobung des transzendentalpragmatischen Ansatzes*, op. cit., S. 231.

[51] Ibidem.

Errungenschaften in das Gespräch mit Jonas einbringen. Erstens bietet sie einen Gültigkeitstest der ethischen *Intuitionen*, die wir aus der Lebenswelt mitbringen. Mit Recht legt Jonas auf die Erschließung lebensweltlicher Intuitionen großen Wert. Und es ist der bedeutsame Rückgang auf allgemein einsichtsfähige Moralintuitionen, der seinem normen- und wertphänomenologischen Ansatz – im Unterschied etwa zu dem transzendentalphilosophischen Diskursansatz Apels und zu Habermas' verfahrensförmigem Diskursansatz – eine attraktive Konkretheit und starke Motivationskraft verleiht. Beides kann eine Vernunftethik wie die Diskursethik m.E. nur gewinnen, wenn sie – im Anschluß an Jonas – transformiert wird zu einer sokratischen Ethik des Sich-im-Dialog-Verantwortens. Sie würde dann einen sinnkritischen Verbindlichkeitstest auf den prinzipiellen Begründungsstufen A1 und A2 etablieren: „Welche lebensweltlichen moralischen Intuitionen mußt du – der du ein glaubwürdiger Diskurspartner sein willst – als ein solcher anerkennen, um dich nicht in einen performativen Selbstwiderspruch zu verwickeln und dadurch die beanspruchte Glaubwürdigkeit des Diskurspartners zu verlieren?"

Zweitens kann die sokratisch reflektierende Diskurspragmatik Jonas' Begründungsdefizit beheben. Denn sie kann erweisen, daß Jonas' kategorischer Imperativ unhintergehbar ist und infolgedessen als *verbindliches* Prinzip zu gelten hat[52] – unbeschadet möglicher Konkretionen auf der Orientierungsebene idealer praktischer Diskurse (für die Jonas Gedankenexperimente wie das von der Wette in allem Handeln einsetzt) *und* unbeschadet nötiger erfolgsverantwortungsethischer Strategien auf der Handlungsebene. Damit ist, wie ich hoffe, die *innere* Herausforderung der praktischen Vernunft durch die wissenschaftlich-technische Zivilisation angenommen und die Komplementaritätsstruktur des modernen westlichen Geistes wirklich aufgehoben.

---

[52] Dietrich Böhler, „Idee und Verbindlichkeit der Zukunftsverantwortung", in: *Zukunftsverantwortung in der Marktwirtschaft. In memoriam Hans Jonas*, hrsg. von Thomas Bausch, u.a., op. cit., S. 34 ff. Dietrich Böhler, „Warum moralisch sein?" in: *Prinzip Mitverantwortung. Grundlage für Ethik und Pädagogik*, hrsg. von Karl-Otto Apel u. Holger Burckhart, op. cit., S. 15 ff. Dietrich Böhler, „Glaubwürdigkeit des Diskurspartners", Abschn. 1.4.1 – 1.4.2, in: *Wirtschaft und Ethik. Strategien contra Moral?*, EWD, Bd. 12, Müster: LIT, 2004.

Mit dem *reflexiv philosophischen Begründungsdiskurs*, der einen solchen Prinzipienerweis erlaubt, haben wir den *zweiten Namensgeber der strikten Diskursethik* vor uns: im Sinne des *genitivus obiectivus*. Die dialogpragmatische Form der Diskursethik – nicht zu verwechseln mit Habermas' „formalpragmatischer" bzw. „diskurstheoretischer" Schwundstufe von Diskursethik – ist eine allgemeine Prinzipienethik. Ihre nicht metaphysische, sondern dialogreflexive Begründung des Moralprinzips und der moralischen Grundnormen vollzieht sich *durch* Diskurs und *im* Diskurs. An einem solchen Begründungsdiskurs kann *jeder* teilhaben; seine Resultate sind allgemeingültig, insofern sie jederzeit intersubjektiv nachprüfbar sind. Gemäß des Berliner Dialogdenkens bedeutet „Diskursethik" in diesem zweiten Sinn so viel wie: Prinzipienethik aufgrund von reflexiven Dialogen im Gespräch mit dem Skeptiker, insofern er einen Zweifel an der Gültigkeit und Verbindlichkeit eines Prinzips vorbringt.

Allerdings ist das, was nach der Prinzipienbegründung – also nach geleistetem Verbindlichkeitserweis des Prinzips der Mitverantwortung für den Fortbestand der Menschengattung und für Fortschritte in Sachen Menschenwürde und Gerechtigkeit – noch zu denken und immer wieder zu tun bleibt, mehr als genug: die Bewältigung der *äußeren* bzw. materialen Herausforderungen der praktischen Vernunft durch die technologische Zivilisation, also die Eindämmung der Menschheits- und Naturgefährdungen – zugunsten nicht allein einer „Weiterwohnlichkeit der Welt", sondern auch zugunsten der „künftigen Integrität des 'Ebenbildes'"[53], wie wir in biblischer Sprache mit Jonas sagen können.

4. Gedankenexperimente zum Prinzip Verantwortung

In „Das Prinzip Verantwortung" schlägt Jonas, um angesichts der Menschheits- und Naturgefährdungen zu moralischen Handlungsorientierungen zu gelangen, zwei Wege ein: die phänomenologische

---

[53] Hans Jonas, „Technik, Freiheit und Pflicht", in: idem, *Wissenschaft als persönliches Erlebnis*, op. cit., S. 46 und idem, *Das Prinzip Verantwortung, Versuch einer Ethik für die technologische Zivilisation*, op. cit., S. 393.

Herausarbeitung ethischer Intuitionen *und* die Durchführung von Gedankenexperimenten zu deren Prüfung. Diese „Denkexperimente" sollen die praktische Diskurs-Frage „Was sollen wir tun?" beantworten, und zwar vor dem Hintergrund der unvermeidlichen Risikobeladenheit menschlichen Handelns im allgemeinen und des technologievermittelten bzw. technologischen Handelns im besonderen. Es wird also – moralintrinsisch – nach richtigen, moralisch legitimierbaren Maximen gesucht.

In dem Gedankenexperiment der „Heuristik der Furcht" nimmt Jonas zwei ethische Intuitionen auf: die zukunftsethische Grundintuition, daß die Bewahrung des Menschen, so wie er ist, ein lohnendes Ziel ist[54], und die diskursethische Intuition, man solle die Rechts- und Lebensansprüche der möglichen Betroffenen zur Geltung bringen, indem man deren Standpunkt einnimmt. Jene Grundintuition, die die Zukunftsethik zunächst zu einer Ethik der Menschheitsbewahrung macht, gibt den normativen Rahmen ab: mit der Permanenz moralfähigen Lebens auf Erden muß jedes Risiko vereinbar sein. Im Hintergrund steht die „moralische Furcht", die „Furcht um den Menschen" in der hochtechnologischen Zivilisation[55]. Wachsen die kumulativen Folgen der industriegesellschaftlich normalen Konsumpraxis und ihres Fortschritts- und „Wachstums"-Gangs den sittlichen Fähigkeiten des Menschen über den Kopf?

Zu jener, vor allem ökologisch ethischen Furcht tritt eine andere, eine *intern* moralische Sorge. Denn nicht allein die ökologische Ausdehnungsdimension der hochtechnologisch vermittelten Lebenspraxis ist so gut wie grenzenlos geworden, auch die Tiefendimension der

---

[54] Jonas grenzt sich damit von dem metaphysischen bzw. anthropologischen Utopismus ab, wie er radikal von Ernst Bloch, die Hoffnung auf ein „Sein wie Utopie" zum Prinzip des Daseins erklärend, vertreten worden ist. Vgl. Hans Jonas, *Das Prinzip Verantwortung, Versuch einer Ethik für die technologische Zivilisation*, op. cit., S. 340 f., 371–373, 380–387. Idem, *Technik, Medizin und Ethik*, Frankfurt a. Main: Insel, 1985, S. 298 ff. Idem, *Fatalismus wäre Todsünde. Gespräche über Ethik und Mitverantwortung im dritten Jahrtausend*, Münster: LIT, 2005, S. 110 f, 76–80 und 95. Dazu: Dietrich Böhler, „Verstehen und Verantworten", Einl. zu: ibidem, S. 15–18.

[55] Hans Jonas, ibidem, S. 137. Idem, *Das Prinzip Verantwortung, Versuch einer Ethik für die technologische Zivilisation*, op. cit., S. 63–65.

hochtechnologischen Forschung überschreitet längst jedes gewohnte ethische Maß: Die molekularbiologischen Manipulationsmöglichkeiten und Konstruktionsmöglichkeiten menschlichen Lebens überrennen alle Grenzen, welche unsere ethischen Intuitionen und judäochristlichen Traditionen vom Menschen als dem unantastbaren Ebenbild Gottes gesetzt hatten.

Für die konkrete Risikobeurteilung bringt die „Heuristik der Furcht" zunächst eine Art diskursethischen Rollentausches ins Spiel. Jonas nimmt hier den Standpunkt der Betroffenen ein, indem er den Lesern einen negativen Wert-Test vor Augen führt, der Gefühl und Dialog, jedenfalls einen impliziten Dialog mit möglichen Betroffenen, verbindet; etwa so: 'Überlege zunächst, welche Folgen deiner Handlung dir, dessen Wollen in die Richtung des Guten geht, aus dem Blickwinkel der Betroffenen Furcht einflößen würden.'

Das Denkexperiment provoziert die „moralische Phantasie" (Günther Anders),[56] indem es uns auf die Suche nach dem moralisch (nicht etwa privat und lebensplanerisch) zu Fürchtenden schickt. Zur Begründung führt er eine bekannte logische Asymmetrie in der ethischen Urteilsbildung an: Dasjenige, „was wir *nicht* wollen, wissen wir viel eher als was wir wollen. Darum muß die Moralphilosophie unser Fürchten vor unserm Wünschen konsultieren, um zu ermitteln, was wir wirklich schätzen".[57] Vorsichtig hebt Jonas hervor, das wertethische Gedankenexperiment der vorgestellten schlechten Fernwirkungen, gleichsam das worst-case-Szenario, sei kein hinlänglicher Kompaß, sondern bloß eine *erste* Klärung. Ihm komme nur der Stellenwert einer Findekunst bzw. eines brain storming zu, eben einer „*Heuristik der Furcht*".[58]

Jonas' zweites Gedankenexperiment geht von der realistischen Einsicht aus, die Hannah Arendt im Sinne einer lebensweltlichen

---

[56] Günther Anders, *Die Antiquiertheit des Menschen. Über die Seele im Zeitalter der zweiten industriellen Revolution*, München: C.H. Beck, 1956, bes. S. 15 ff. und 267 ff.; dazu Micha Werner, „Kann Phantasie moralisch werden?", in: *Anthropologie und Ethik*, hrsg. von Jean-Pierre Wils, Tübingen: A. Francke, 1997, S. 41–63.

[57] Hans Jonas, *Das Prinzip Verantwortung, Versuch einer Ethik für die technologische Zivilisation*, op. cit., S. 64.

[58] Ibidem, S. 63 ff.

Anthropologie entwickelt hat[59], der Einsicht, daß alles Handeln des Menschen riskant und nach seinem Risiko schwer einschätzbar ist. Er pointiert dieses intuitive Lebenswissen durch den Vergleich des Handelns mit einem Glücksspiel: „Das Prinzip" auch der neuartigen, der technologischen Handlungs- bzw. Auswirkungsdimensionen könnten wir erfahren, „wenn wir auf das Element des *Glücksspiels* oder der *Wette* reflektieren, das in allem menschlichen Handeln hinsichtlich des Ausgangs wie der Nebenwirkungen enthalten ist, und uns fragen, um welchen *Einsatz* man, ethisch gesprochen, wetten darf".[60] Das Gedankenexperiment der Wette ist ein zur Abhandlung stilisiertes moralisches Selbstgespräch: Es ähnelt einem praktischen Diskurs, den ein moralisch orientierter und hinsichtlich der technologischen Folgendimension aufgeklärter Projektbefürworter – ein Vernunft- und Moralfreund, der seinen Kant gelesen haben mag – mit sich selbst führt. Er führt seinen Diskurs faktisch zwar allein mit sich – aber logisch geurteilt vor der *Geltungsinstanz* einer *unbegrenzten Argumentationsgemeinschaft*. Auf diese Instanz beruft sich Jonas implizit, indem er stillschweigend das Universalisierungsprinzip Kants zum Leitfaden nimmt und seinen Vernunftfreund vermittels Selbsteinwänden nach dem *besten Argument* suchen läßt.

Komplementär zum vorausgegangenen Denkexperiment setzt dieses mit der Perspektive eines Handelnden in der technologischen Zivilisation ein, welcher bereits weiß, daß seine Handlungen eine kaum begrenzbare Auswirkungsdimension haben können, und auch, daß eine Prognose ihrer Auswirkungen prinzipiell unsicher bleibt.[61] In die, von Jonas angespielte, Form des moralischen Selbstgesprächs gebracht, können wir sein Diskurs-Gedankenexperiment folgendermaßen beginnen lassen:

> Du, der du Interesse an einer technischen Innovation hast, überlege dir, welchen Einsatz deine technologische Wette haben darf und stelle dir die Frage: „Darf ich die Interessen Anderer in meiner Wette einsetzen?" Die

---

[59] Hannah Arendt, *Vita activa oder Vom tätigen Leben*, München: Piper, [7]1994, §§ 26–34.

[60] Hans Jonas, *Das Prinzip Verantwortung, Versuch einer Ethik für die technologische Zivilisation*, op. cit., S. 77.

[61] Ibidem, S. 76.

erste Antwort ergibt sich aus der moralischen Intuition, daß „man, streng genommen, um nichts wetten darf, was einem nicht gehört".[62]

Doch damit kann es nicht sein Bewenden haben. Denn wenn 'du' weiter argumentierst, erkennst 'du' alsbald, daß sich jene Antwort nicht absolut nehmen läßt, weil all dein Handeln „das Schicksal Anderer in Mitleidenschaft zieht", so daß du, wenn du daraus ein direktes Handlungsprinzip machtest, gar nicht mehr handeln dürftest. Ein gewisses Risiko gehört zu den Anfangsbedingungen menschlichen Handelns in der vielfach verflochtenen und nicht (mit Sicherheit) prognostizierbaren Welt. Hierin trifft sich Jonas ebenso mit Hannah Arendt wie mit Popper, Skirbekk[63] und der Diskurspragmatik.

Daß die erste Antwort gleichwohl eine gewisse Berechtigung hat, zeigt sich erst, wenn eine Qualifizierung des Wettverbots vorgenommen wird. „Der Einsatz darf nie das *Ganze* der Interessen der betroffenen Anderen sein, vor allem nicht ihr Leben".[64] Nun kann man hiergegen wiederum einwenden, es gebe doch Krisensituationen, in denen sich das drohende größte Übel nur durch den höchsten Einsatz, hier des Lebens Vieler, abwenden lasse. Demnach ist also auch das neue Prinzip, das die Unverfügbarkeit des Gesamtinteresses der Betroffenen geltend macht, nicht unbedingt gültig, nämlich nicht in der Alternative Sein oder Nichtsein, welche zur Notwehr und zum höchsten Noteinsatz berechtigt, sondern gleichsam nur in mittleren Problemlagen.

Nun fragt es sich ohnehin, ob das eingewandte Extrembeispiel überhaupt auf denjenigen zutrifft, der das Interesse eines technologischen Fortschritts geltend macht. Die heutigen „großen Wagnisse der Technologie" werden doch nicht, so setzt Jonas das diskursive Gedankenexperiment fort,

> zur Rettung des Bestehenden oder Behebung des Unerträglichen unternommen, sondern zur stetigen Verbesserung des je Erreichten, das heißt

---

[62] Ibidem, S. 77.

[63] Gunnar Skirbekk, *Une Praxéologie de la Modernité*, Paris: Harmattan, 1999, chap. III, V, VIII. Idem, *Praxeologie der Moderne*, Weilerswist: Velbrück, 2002.

[64] Hans Jonas, *Das Prinzip Verantwortung, Versuch einer Ethik für die technologische Zivilisation*, op. cit., S. 78.

für den *Fortschritt*. [...] Also gewinnt hier, wohin der Schutz des Proviso nicht reicht, der Satz, daß mein Handeln nicht „das *ganze*" Interesse der mitbetroffenen Anderen (die hier die Zukünftigen sind) aufs Spiel setzten darf, wieder Kraft.[65]

Bemerkenswerterweise geht Jonas mit diesem Gedankenexperiment über seine kontemplative phänomenologische und ontologische Perspektive hinaus, indem er in der Dialogform eines argumentativen Selbstgesprächs denkt. Wenngleich er nicht *aus* dem Dialog denkt und sich selbst keineswegs diskursethisch versteht, arbeitet er hier (wie auch anderwärts) im Sinne einer Grundforderung des diskursethischen Prinzips 'D'. Denn sein Moralfreund ist de facto sorgsam darauf bedacht, die Diskursnorm der gleichberechtigten *Berücksichtigung der Interessen aller Anderen* zu befolgen, insoweit gute Gründe für sie geltend gemacht werden können. Damit entspricht er 'D'. Denn diesem regulativen Geltungs- und Orientierungsprinzip zufolge soll man sich um eine Handlungsweise bemühen, die *universal zustimmungswürdig* ist, so daß sie unter *reinen* Argumentations- und Dialogbedingungen den Konsens der Argumente erzielen würde.

Allerdings leistet das diskursbezogene Gedankenexperiment der Wette dreierlei nicht: einmal gibt es nichts für die Begründung her, *daß* jeder und jede *überhaupt* unabweisbare moralische Verpflichtungen habe; zudem fehlt eine moralstrategische Fortsetzung zur Lösung von Max Webers Problem einer Verantwortung für den Erfolg des Moralischen in der realen, nicht moralischen Welt. Ähnlich wie Kants Gedankenexperiment des Kategorischen Imperativs oder Habermas' Verfahren des praktischen Diskurses bleibt auch Jonas' Diskursexperiment der Wette gleichsam auf einer idealisierenden Begründungsstufe A 2 stehen. Drittens gibt es kein Kriterium für die Zuerkennung moralischer Ansprüche her. Es bleibt stumm, wenn es um die „Inklusionsfrage" geht, welche Wesen wir als moralisch Anspruchsberechtigte anerkennen sollen. Eben das ist etwa bei der Diskussion über die In-vitro-Fertilisation und die Forschung an embryonalen menschlichen Stammzellen umstritten.

---

[65] Ibidem, S. 79.

Auch ein Rückgriff auf das Menschenwürdeprinzip fruchtet hier nicht, weil ja gerade strittig ist, von welchem Entwicklungsstadium an Embryonen der Menschenwürdestatus und der volle Menschenwürdeschutz zukomme.

Angesichts der weltgeschichtlich neuen Situation *unbegrenzter,* die Gattung gefährdender Handlungsfolgen klärt und rekonstruiert das Gedankenexperiment jedoch den *Gehalt* einer schon mitgebrachten Verpflichtungsintuition. Indem Jonas solche allgemeinen lebensweltlichen Moralintuitionen rekonstruiert *und* diese direkt auf die neuartige technologische Problem- bzw. Handlungssituation bezieht, gewinnt seine Verantwortungsethik eine zugleich motivierende und orientierende Kraft. Daran hat es der Diskursethik bislang gefehlt.[66] Kommt es aber nicht darauf an, bereits in der *Logik* der verantwortungsethischen Beratungen und Erörterungen die sozialanthropologisch tiefliegenden Fürsorgeintuitionen zu berücksichtigen, die an den lebensweltlichen Verantwortungsinstitutionen der Elternschaft und der Regierung haften? Muß hier nicht die Diskursethik der verantwortungsethischen Bewahrungsaufgabe besonderen Nachdruck verleihen?

Aus Raumgründen präzisiere ich hier nur das erste der erfolgsverantwortlichen Kriterien (B 1): „Prüft, welche Institutionen, Traditionen und ethischen Intuitionen dem Moralprinzip (D) gerecht werden, schützt und entfaltet sie sorgsam!"[67]

Wenn wir nunmehr zurückblicken, um Jonas' und Apels Ansätze als Antworten auf die technologische westliche Moderne zu interpre-

---

[66] Vgl. Wolfgang Kuhlmann, „'Prinzip Verantwortung' versus Diskursethik" in: *Ethik für die Zukunft,* hrsg. von Dietrich Böhler, op. cit., S. 277–302. Erstaunlicherweise hat K.-O. Apel, wiewohl er stets den teleologischen Verpflichtungssinn des Moralprinzips auf der moralstrategischen Ebene B betont und dabei nicht nur die Herstellung fehlender Bedingungen für moralisches Handeln, sondern auch die *Bewahrung* der bereits geschichtlich gegebenen ins Auge fassen konnte, an dieser Stelle kein Kooperationsverhältnis zu Jonas erkannt. Das mag auch daher rühren, daß Apel auf der Ebene B keine eigenständige *Fragestellung,* was denn das zu Bewahrende sei, und also keinen eigenen *Diskurs*schritt B 1 vorgesehen hat.

[67] Dazu die Entfaltung der verantwortungsethischen Diskurse auf der moralstrategischen „Ebene B" in: Dietrich Böhler, „Ethik der Zukunfts- und Lebensverantwortung. Erster Teil", in: *Orientierung und Verantwortung. Begegnungen und Auseinandersetzungen mit Hans Jonas,* hrsg. von idem u. Jens P. Brune, op. cit., hier S. 137 ff., 147 f.

tieren, wenn wir außerdem Apels Ansatz transformieren in ein so-
kratisches und intuitionssensibles *Denken aus dem Dialog,* dann mag
sich folgendes Schema ergeben.

Jonas	Von Apel zum Dialog-Denken
Verantwortungsprobleme durch Hand-lungs- und Wirkungsdivergenzen: (1) technologische Wirkmacht – Ohnmacht des Folgen-Wissens, (2) Macht der Naturwissenschaften – Verunsicherung (u. Bezweiflung) religiös-ethischen Normwissens.	**Paralyse des Verantwortungsdenkens durch das „Komplementaritätssystem" der westlichen Moderne:** (a) zweck-rationalistisch verengt auf das moralfrei Analysierbare/Kalkulierbare, (b) Moral privatisiert und irrationalisiert als Sache existentieller bzw. religiöser Entscheidungen.
Behebungsversuch:	*Aufhebungsversuch:*
(Moral.) *Motivation* durch Sensibilisierung für moralische Ansprüche zukünftiger Generationen: – „Heuristik der Furcht" – Um was darfst du (nicht) wet-ten? – „Prinzip Verantwortung!" Unklar: Unter welchen Voraussetzungen können moralische Ansprüche Künftiger mißachtet werden? Offen: Verbindlichkeitserweis der Pflicht, sie zu berücksichtigen	Sokratisch-sinnkritischer Rückgang auf das, was du als Dialogpartner nicht sinnvoll bezweifeln kannst, wenn du (a) und (b) im Dialog vertrittst, z.B. die Pflicht, *alle* sinnvoll im Dialog vertret-baren Ansprüche zu berücksichtigen **Dialogreflexive Begründung von und Motivation zu universaler und Zu-kunfts-Verantwortung** → Einsicht in meine Ansprüche/Pflichten als Dialog-partner: Prinzip D

Abb. 2. Technologische und geistige Herausforderungen der technologischen, liberalen Zivilisation

5. Was heißt 'Verantwortung'?
Keine Fürsorge ohne Rechtfertigung, kein praktischer Diskurs ohne Verständigungsgegenseitigkeit und Öffentlichkeit

Auch wenn Jonas eine Begründungsarchitektonik fehlt, die für die
moralstrategische Urteilsbildung eine differenzierte Orientierung für
moral*restriktive* Verhältnisse vorsieht – wie Apels „Teil B der Ethik",

so sieht er sich doch einem moralstrategischen Dilemma gegenüber. Vereinfacht lautet es: ökologische Verantwortung oder demokratische Interessenwahrnehmung. Im Hintergrund steht sein Gedanke: Verantwortungsfreiheit setze ein *Sein* voraus, das der Verantwortung *Sinn* gibt. Insofern bestehe die unbedingte Pflicht, dieses Sein, nämlich die Existenz der Gattung als Teil der Natur *und* die moralische Idee der Menschheit samt ihrem Kernbegriff „Menschenwürde", zu bewahren.

Um diesen Bewahrungspflichten gerecht zu werden, hat Hans Jonas unter bestimmten Umständen einen zeitweiligen Dispens der Demokratie und die Errichtung einer Diktatur für sinnvoll gehalten. Wenn sich, wie zumal heute, das Dilemma zwischen Zukunftsverantwortung und demokratischer Politik, die zum Interessenopportunismus neige, dramatisch zuspitze, müsse der Philosoph „durchaus den Mut haben, zu sagen, Demokratie ist höchst wünschbar, aber kann nicht selber die unabdingbare Bedingung dafür sein, daß ein menschliches Leben auf Erden sich lohnt".[68]

Läßt sich dieser Not-Vorbehalt als erfolgsverantwortungsethische Konter-*Strategie* rechtfertigen? Jonas hat dafür heftige Kritik hinnehmen müssen, besonders massiv von Karl R. Popper.[69] Unberechtigt ist die Kritik jedenfalls dann, wenn sie nicht genügend zwischen faktischer öffentlicher Meinung bzw. Mehrheitsentscheidung *und* normativer Rechtfertigung differenziert. Denn eine Ethik, der es um normative Legitimität und eine unbedingte Verpflichtung geht, steht und fällt damit, daß sie keinerlei *faktische* Übereinkunft, weder einen empirischen Konsens von Beteiligten noch gar einen Mehrheitsentscheid, als *Geltungsgrund* für die gesuchte Verantwortlichkeit oder Richtigkeit akzeptieren darf. Das liefe auf einen naturalistischen bzw. faktizistischen Fehlschluß hinaus, der allein aus dem Faktum einer Übereinkunft auf deren Sollensgeltung schlösse. Erforderlich ist ein *nichtrelativierbarer Maßstab*, damit sich ein irgendwie zustandegekommener Konsens und erst recht eine Mehrheitsentscheidung jeweils auf die

---

[68] Gespräch mit E. Gebhardt, in: *Ethik für die Zukunft*, hrsg. von Dietrich Böhler, op. cit., S. 210, 211. Vgl. Hans Jonas, *Das Prinzip Verantwortung, Versuch einer Ethik für die technologische Zivilisation*, op. cit., S. 254 f., 259–270, 302–305.

[69] Vgl. das Interview mit Karl R. Popper in: *Die Welt*, 8. Juli 1987.

moralische Zustimmungs*würdigkeit* hin überprüfen läßt. Es ist die Suche nach einem Verbindlichkeitskriterium jenseits von Subjektivismus und Relativismus, die Jonas' ontologische und intuitionistische Wertethik mit der dialogreflexiv verfahrenden, normativen Diskursethik vereint. Beide Ansätze kommen darin überein, daß der gesuchte Maßstab in dem Umkreis zu finden sein müßte, der sich mit den normativ geladenen Begriffen „Idee der Menschenwürde und des moralfähigen Menschen" und „Verantwortung dafür, daß künftige Generationen diesen Ideen noch gerecht werden können, indem sie sich ihrerseits verantwortlich und moralisch verhalten" beschreiben läßt.

Diese Konzepte enthalten eine in ihrer Verbindlichkeit unbedingte, doch gleichsam regulative Pflicht, die die Richtung des Verhaltens angibt, der immer nachzustreben sei. Wenn aber die Durchsetzung *kurzfristiger Nahinteressen mittels Demokratie* jener Richtungspflicht gefährlich zuwiderläuft, dann gehört – genau insoweit – auch eine Demokratie auf den Prüfstand; entweder müßte sie verändert werden, oder es stünde, falls die Veränderung scheitert, als ultima ratio ein zeitweiliger Dispens der Demokratie an.

> Was ich [aber] mit der potentiellen Möglichkeit einer Tyrannei als äußerste Rettungsmaßnahme gemeint habe, ist einzig dem vergleichbar, was sein wird, wenn ein Haus brennt oder ein Schiff untergeht. Dann nämlich kann man keine Abstimmung mehr machen, und dann kann man nicht die normalen Gesetzesverfahren laufen lassen, sondern es müssen gewisse Notmaßnahmen ergriffen werden ...

Freilich würde Jonas die Demokratie „mit großem Kummer verschwinden sehen und würde ausschließlich akzeptieren, daß sie *zeitweilig*, sagen wir mal, *suspendiert* würde".[70] Um für dieses Problem klare Kriterien zu erarbeiten, ergänzen die Diskursethiker Jonas' Ansatz durch die moralstrategische Perspektive der Ebene B und fragen nach einer *moralischen Erfolgsverantwortung* in der Gefahrenzivilisation.[71]

---

[70] *Ethik für die Zukunft*, hrsg. von Dietrich Böhler, op. cit., S. 210, 211.
[71] Dazu Dietrich Böhler, „Idee und Verbindlichkeit der Zukunftsverantwortung", in: *Zukunftsverantwortung in der Marktwirtschaft. In memoriam Hans Jonas*, hrsg. von Thomas Bausch, u.a., op. cit., hier bes. S. 63 ff.

Die Kritik an Jonas' Relativierung der demokratischen Staats- und Regierungsform ist aus mehreren Gründen nicht abwegig. Ein Grund liegt darin, daß Jonas die begründungslogisch zuerst anstehende verantwortungsethische Frage dessen, der eine moralische Maxime gegen Widerständigkeiten durchsetzen will, hier überhaupt nicht stellt: die Frage, welche Institutionen und Traditionen im jeweiligen Veränderungsfeld dem Moralprinzip gerecht werden und daher bewahrt und möglichst weiterentwickelt werden sollten. Dieser erste Prüfauftrag der verantwortungsethischen Diskurse, als Stufe B 1, fehlt bei Jonas. Er bezieht sein Verantwortungsprinzip *unmittelbar* auf mögliche Widerstände, die aus der Demokratie entstehen können. Hier fehlt eine Diskursdifferenzierung, die nötig ist, damit die Anwendung des Verantwortungsprinzips nicht rigoristisch wird, sondern damit sie sich ihrerseits verantworten läßt; so nämlich, daß nach Maßgabe verantwortungsethischer Kriterien Rechenschaft über die möglichen Folgen abgelegt wird.

Ein zweiter Grund ergibt sich direkt daraus: Weil die Frage nach der moralischen Bewahrungswürdigkeit geschichtlicher Institutionen von ihm nicht als eigenständige verantwortungsethische Stufe berücksichtigt wird, nimmt Jonas unmittelbar die Demokratie als Mehrheitsherrschaft ins Visier, ohne den (moralisch hoch relevanten) *rechtsstaatlichen Rahmen* der Demokratie, den modernen Verfassungsstaat mit den *menschenrechtlichen Ideen* der französischen und der amerikanischen Revolution, eigens zu berücksichtigen. Beziehen wir die moralische Bewahrungsfrage hingegen auf den modernen Verfassungsstaat, so leuchtet ein, daß eine Demokratiekritik weithin als *immanente* Kritik zu üben ist: geleitet von *Grundsätzen* des demokratischen Rechtsstaats selbst. Dazu gehören solche, deren normativer Kerngehalt reflexiv letztbegründbar ist, so daß sie als Momente bzw. Konkretionen des Diskurs-Moralprinzips erwiesen werden können. Wenn das der Fall ist, dann ist hier bei der Entwicklung einer moralischen Konter-*Strategie* äußerste Vorsicht geboten. Deren Grenze ist dann sofort in Sicht: die Strategie darf nicht pauschal 'Dispens der Demokratie' heißen.

Läßt sich aber ein Moralitätserweis tragender normativer und prozeduraler Elemente der rechtsstaatlichen Demokratie antreten? In gewisser Weise ja: durch den sokratischen Rückgang der *Diskurspragmatik* auf die dialogförmige Argumentationssituation[72], in der man sich auch befindet, wenn man die begründete Verbindlichkeit eines Prinzips bezweifelt. Dieser Rückgang führt über eine dialogische Sinnlosigkeits- bzw. Sinnprüfung des Zweifels – als eines Beitrags im argumentativen Dialog – zum Erweis der Verbindlichkeit des bezweifelten normativen Gehalts. Denn dasjenige, was sich in einer aktuellen Argumentation unter Diskurspartnern *nicht* sinnvoll bezweifeln läßt, das ist prinzipiell gültig, so daß sein normativer Gehalt als *verbindlich*, als einsichtige Pflicht, zu gelten hat und daher *befolgungswürdig* ist. Auf diese Weise kann m.E. die Dialog- bzw. Diskurspragmatik zeigen, daß *alle*, welche überhaupt die Rolle eines Denkenden als Argumentationspartner einnehmen können – einzig auf die Potentialität kommt es in Geltungsfragen an –, daß also *wir alle* bereits gewisse demokratisch-rechtsstaatliche Grundwerte von vornherein *dadurch* als befolgungswürdig vorausgesetzt haben, daß wir ernsthafte Diskurspartner sein wollen. Denn *als* solche haben wir gewisse rechtsstaatliche Prinzipien (notwendigerweise) *für uns* selbst in Anspruch genommen – also impliziert.

Welche Prinzipien sind das? Einmal ist es das rechtsethische Prinzip, *die Würde, nämlich die Unverletzlichkeit und Freiheit allen menschlichen Lebens zu achten*.[73] Sodann ist es das Prinzip, keine Beschlüsse

---

[72] Der aktuelle Forschungsstand der Diskurspragmatik spiegelt sich zumal in den Büchern *Prinzip Mitverantwortung*, 2001 (s.o. Anm. 6); sowie *Philosophieren aus dem Diskurs. Beiträge zur Diskurspragmatik*, hrsg. von Holger Burckhart u. Horst Gronke, Würzburg: Königshausen & Neumann, 2002; in den Studien Böhlers, Brunes, Gronkes, Rähmes und Werners in: *Reflexion und Verantwortung. Auseinandersetzungen mit Karl-Otto Apel*, hrsg. von Dietrich Böhler, Matthias Kettner, Gunnar Skirbekk, Frankfurt a. Main: Suhrkamp, 2003; ferner in: *Orientierung und Verantwortung. Begegnungen und Auseinandersetzungen mit Hans Jonas*, hrsg. von Dietrich Böhler u. Jens P. Brune, op. cit. In Vorbereitung: Dietrich Böhler, *Verbindlichkeit aus dem Diskurs*, Freiburg i.Br.: Alber, 2006/7.

[73] Dietrich Böhler, „Diskursethik und Menschenwürdegrundsatz zwischen Idealisierung und Erfolgsverantwortung", in: *Zur Anwendung der Diskursethik in Politik, Recht, Wissenschaft*, hrsg. von Karl-Otto Apel und Matthias Kettner, Frankfurt a. Main: Suhrkamp, 1992, S. 201–231. Dietrich Böhler, „Menschenwürde und Diskursethik", Nachwort zu: Thomas Rusche, *Aspekte einer dialogbezogenen Unternehmensethik*, op. cit., hier S. 247 ff.

und Maßnahmen in Kraft zu setzen oder anzuerkennen, die im Geheimen zustande kommen, sondern allein solche, die der öffentlichen Kritik ausgesetzt und der öffentlichen Zustimmungsfähigkeit unterworfen worden sind; also das *Prinzip der Öffentlichkeit.*[74] Verbunden mit dem Grundrecht der Kommunikationsfreiheit, enthält das Prinzip der Öffentlichkeit den dritten Grund einer unabweisbaren Kritik an Jonas' Geltungseinklammerung der Demokratie. Warum? Dieses Prinzip bezeichnet eine Bedingung der Möglichkeit moralischer Rechtfertigung, weil eine zureichende *Beurteilung* der Handlungen Anderer ebenso wie eine wahrheitsfähige *Einschätzung* der Bedürfnisse bzw. Interessen Anderer nur in dem Maße möglich ist, als man sich dabei auf die *freie Artikulation* ihrer Interessen stützen kann. Wahrheitsfähig, nämlich situationserkennend, und (darauf aufbauend) legitim, also durch gute Gründe gerechtfertigt und in diesem Sinne ›gerecht‹, können moralische Urteile, Maximen oder Normen einzig dann sein, wenn sie nicht bloß auf der subjektiven Vermutung eines einsamen Gedankenexperimentators oder einer Experten-Elite beruhen, sondern wenn sie die *wirkliche Situation* der Betroffenen berücksichtigen – ausgehend von deren Selbstverständnis.

Aus dieser (hermeneutischen) Überlegung hatte ich in der Entstehungszeit der Diskursethik, und zwar während einer kontroversen Diskussion des „Funkkollegs Praktische Philosophie/Ethik" im Jahre 1980, die geltungslogische Folgerung abgeleitet:[75] Keine Gültigkeit

---

[74] Vgl. Dietrich Böhler, „Kritische Moral oder pragmatische Sittlichkeit", in: *Funkkolleg: Studientexte*, hrsg. von Karl-Otto Apel, Dietrich Böhler, Karlheinz Rebel, Bd. 3, Weinheim und Basel: Beltz, 1984, S. 845–886.

[75] Ich beziehe mich auf die aufschlußreiche Kontroverse zwischen dem Personalismus Manfred *Riedels* mitsamt dem Quasi-Kantianismus Otfried *Höffes* auf der einen Seite und dem transzendentalpragmatischen Ansatz bei der realen Kommunikationsgemeinschaft und deren kontrafaktischen Normen auf der anderen Seite: *Funkkolleg: Studientexte*, hrsg. von Karl-Otto Apel, Dietrich Böhler, Karlheinz Rebel, Bd. 1, Weinheim und Basel: Beltz, 1984, S. 269–277. Hier konnte das Hintergrundproblem der traditionellen Philosophie, der *methodische* Solipsismus, kontrovers herausgearbeitet werden.

Vor diesem Hintergrund ließ sich dann eine kommunikativ hermeneutische Vorstufe für praktische Diskurse als unabweisbar begründen: Dietrich Böhler, „Transzendentalpragmatik und kritische Moral", in: *Kommunikation und Reflexion. Zur Diskussion*

ohne argumentative Geltungsgegenseitigkeit, keine Geltungsgegenseitigkeit ohne Verständigungsgegenseitigkeit. Anders pointiert: Ohne „Verständigungs-Gegenseitigkeit" (über die Bedeutung der Situation
und der situationskonstitutiven Interessen) keine Wahrheit und Gerechtigkeit, also keine „Geltungs-Gegenseitigkeit" für moralische
Urteile und für moralische Normen bzw. Handlungsorientierungen.

Das ist es, was Jonas selbstwidersprüchlich – nämlich in Widerspruch zu seiner moralischen Absicht einer Einbeziehung der Interessen der mitbetroffenen Anderen[76] – als traditioneller Phänomenologe und als methodisch einsamer Gedankenexperimentator
überspringt. Das ist es, was in der Weiterentwicklung der Transzendentalpragmatik zur Begründung und diskursethischen Anwendung einer „phänomenologisch-hermeneutischen Maxime" geführt hatte.[77] Ist aber eine Verständigungsgegenseitigkeit unabdingbar, so
folgt eine tiefgreifende Kritik des, von Jonas noch ein gutes Stück
geteilten, Selbstverständnisses der traditionellen Philosophie als
theoria.[78] Die theoria-Tradition dachte zugleich objektivistisch und
methodisch solipsistisch; und sie konnte das Eine tun, weil sie das

---

der Transzendentalpragmatik, hrsg. von Wolfgang Kuhlmann und Dietrich Böhler,
Frankfurt a. Main: Suhrkamp, 1982, hier S. 108 ff., S. 206 und 243 f. Dazu: Jon Helles-
nes, „Ethischer Konkretismus und Kommunikationsethik", in: Die pragmatische Wende,
hrsg. von Dietrich Böhler, Tore Nordenstam und Gunnar Skirbekk, Frankfurt a. Main:
Suhrkamp, 1986, bes. S. 183 f.

[76] Hans Jonas, Das Prinzip Verantwortung, Versuch einer Ethik für die technologische
Zivilisation, op. cit., S. 78 f. Dazu hier: Kap. 4.

[77] Dietrich Böhler, Rekonstruktive Pragmatik. Von der Bewußtseinsphilosophie zur
Kommunikationsreflexion: Neubegründung der praktischen Wissenschaften und Philosophie,
op. cit., S. 123 ff.

[78] Jonas überschreitet dieses klassische theoretische Selbstverständnis der Philosophie jedoch mit Argumenten, die auf ein „Leib-Apriori" (M. Merleau-Ponty) der Erkenntnis und auf eine Sinnkritik hinzielen, indem sie – gegenüber Descartes und
Husserl – das Sinnkriterium einer, wie Gronke formuliert, leibpragmatischen Wider-
spruchsfreiheit geltend machen. Vgl. Hans Jonas, Organismus und Freiheit, Göttingen:
Vandenhoeck & Ruprecht, 1973, S. 32 ff. – Das Prinzip Leben, Frankfurt a. Main: Suhrkamp, 1994, S. 38 f. Dazu Horst Gronke, Das Denken des Anderen, Würzburg: Königshausen & Neumann, 1999, S. 161 f. Vgl. in diesem Zusammenhang die differenzierte
diskursethische Kritik an Jonas von Micha Werner: „Dimensionen der Verantwortung", in: Ethik für die Zukunft, hrsg. von Dietrich Böhler, op. cit., S. 303–340, bes. S. 324 ff.

Andere tat. Sie setzte nämlich voraus, daß die Seinsstrukturen (Platons Ideen) und die Kriterien richtigen Handelns (Platons Paradigmen) eigentlich durch eine geistige Schau (theoria) erkennbar seien, zu der es einer Kommunikation mit Anderen nicht bedürfe – Erkenntnis des Seins unabhängig von Verständigung und Sprache, jenseits einer Kommunikationsgemeinschaft. Eine grundsätzliche Kritik an dem seither wirksamen methodischen bzw. transzendentalen Solipsismus der Philosophie, ja des abendländischen Geistes, hat als erster Apel sprachphilosophisch und problemgeschichtlich vorgetragen.[79] Habermas hat sie in seinem Ansatz einer *„Theorie des kommunikativen Handelns"* fruchtbar gemacht.[80] Ich selbst hatte in den 68er Jahren aus der theoria-Kritik die Konsequenz einer radikalen Metakritik des Historischen Materialismus und der marxistischen Ideologiekritik gezogen.[81]

Jene kommunikativ hermeneutische Einsicht und die daraus folgende Traditionskritik der theoria-Tradition (von Platon über Marx bis zum modernen Szientismus, zur analytischen Philosophie und zur Phänomenologie) gab einen wichtigen Anstoß für die Entwicklung einer neuen, einer *kommunikativen Ethikform* – eben der Diskursethik. Diese erkennt erstmals an, daß die Gültigkeit moralischer Sätze von der Kommunikation mit den betroffenen Interessensubjekten abhängt; infolgedessen verpflichtet sie die moralisch Urteilenden dazu, sich um eine solche Kommunikation zu bemühen. In diesem Sinne haben Habermas und Apel, Kuhlmann und ich seinerzeit die Diskursethik pointiert als *Ethik der Kommunikation* eingeführt – etwa gegenüber Kants und Rawls' Moralfindung durch pure Gedankenexperi-

---

[79] Karl-Otto Apel, *Transformation der Philosophie II*, op. cit., daraus die Studien „Sprache als Thema und Medium der transzendentalen Reflexion", ibidem, S. 311–329; sowie „Der transzendentalhermeneutische Begriff der Sprache", ibidem, S. 330–357.

[80] Jürgen Habermas, *Theorie des Kommunikativen Handelns*, 2 Bde, Frankfurt a. Main: Suhrkamp, 1981; idem, *Legitimationsprobleme im Spätkapitalismus*, Frankfurt a. Main: Suhrkamp, 1973, bes. S. 96 ff.

[81] Dietrich Böhler, *Metakritik der Marxschen Ideologiekritik. Prolegomenon zu einer reflektierten Ideologiekritik und 'Theorie-Praxis-Vermittlung'*, Frankfurt a. Main: Suhrkamp, 1971; idem, „Kritische Theorie – kritisch reflektiert", *Archiv für Rechts- und Sozialphilosophie*, Vol. LVI/4, 1970, S. 511–525.

mente, die vermeintlich ein einsames Subjekt anstellen könne; dem-gemäß auch in Opposition zu Kohlbergs universalistischer Moralstufe 6,[82] in Opposition zum ethischen Kantianismus und Personalismus, schließlich in Opposition zum Naturrecht und zur objektiven Wert-ethik. Praktisch *politisch* führt dieser kommunikative Ansatz, wie schon erwähnt, zur Opposition gegen jede Expertokratie: von Platons Philosophenherrschaft bis zur modernen Technokratie. Glücklicher-weise hat sich die zugrundeliegende kommunikativ hermeneutische Einsicht in Politik und Recht der Bundesrepublik Deutschland soweit durchgesetzt, daß – bis hin zur Ermöglichung von Verbandsklagen der Umweltverbände – *Anhörungs*prozeduren und andere Verfahren der Verständigung mit Betroffenen institutionalisiert worden sind. Leider Gottes hat es nach der deutschen Vereinigung zum Zwecke einer beschleunigten Modernisierung im Rahmen des „Aufbaus Ost" zahlreiche Rücknahmen und Einschränkungen dieser Partizipations-rechte gegeben, die sogenannten „Beschleunigungsgesetze".[83]

Was die Ethikbegründung anbelangt, haben wir hier einen *dritten* Bedeutungsaspekt von ‚Diskursethik': Ethik, die zur Kommunikation verpflichtet – und das bereits, um die *Erkenntnis* der Situation zu ge-währleisten. Keine Situationserkenntnis ohne Sinnverständigung mit den Menschen. Für den diskursethischen Begründungsweg habe ich daraus eine architektonische Konsequenz gezogen, die auch die Diffe-renz zu Jonas augenfällig macht: Direkt nach der dialogreflexiven Letztbegründung des Moralprinzips, der transzendentalpragmati-schen Begründungsstufe (A 1), müsse als erster Konkretionsschritt die *öffentliche Verständigung* (oder ersatzweise ein hermeneutisches Ver-fahren zum Zweck einer möglichen Verständigung) über den kon-kreten Sinn der Interessen und Bedürfnisse möglichst aller Betroffe-nen vorgesehen werden: Sinnverständigung mit den möglichen

---

[82] Vgl. Jürgen Habermas, „Moralentwicklung und Ich-Identität", in: idem, *Zur Re-konstruktion des historischen Materialismus*, Frankfurt a. Main: Suhrkamp, 1976, S. 63–91, bes. S. 84 f.

[83] Dazu: Wilfried Erbguth u. Bodo Wiegand-Hoffmeister, „Umweltrecht im Ge-genwind? Ein ethisch orientiertes Umweltrecht ist nötig", in: *Zukunftsverantwortung in der Marktwirtschaft. In memoriam Hans Jonas*, hrsg. von Thomas Bausch, u.a., op. cit., S. 411 ff., bes. 422 ff.

Betroffenen als Diskursstufe eigenen Rechts (A 2).[84] Erst nach einer solchen Verständigungsbemühung fänden – als dritte Begründungsstufe – die konkreten situationsbezogenen Diskurse ihren logischen Ort. Zunächst wären in theoretischen Diskursen die Fragen 'Wie ist die Situation beschaffen?' und: 'Ist die vorgeschlagene Situationsinterpretation zutreffend?' zu beantworten (A 3). Darauf baue dann der praktische oder moralische Diskurs auf, der die Frage stellt, was wir in der so beschaffenen Situation eigentlich tun *sollen* (A 4); hier sei zu prüfen, ob eine vorgeschlagene Situationsnorm legitim ist, ob ihr argumentative „Geltungs-Gegenseitigkeit" zukommt (A 4).

Insofern die Demokratie das Prinzip der Öffentlichkeit etabliert und praktiziert, ist sie eine Realisierungsbedingung für moralische Diskurse. Stellt sie doch den institutionellen Rahmen für eine freie Sinnverständigung mit den Adressaten moralischer Normen und den Gegenständen moralischer Urteile bereit. Aus diesem Grunde und in dieser Hinsicht läßt sich ein Dispens der Demokratie nicht rechtfertigen. Wohl aber kann – auf der verantwortungsethischen Ebene B – in Form einer moralischen Konter-Strategie Widerstand gegen *einzelne* Mehrheitsbeschlüsse und Regierungsmaßnahmen in einer Demokratie legitimiert werden.

Jonas' kontemplativ eingestellte, an die antike *theoria* angelehnte Phänomenologie kann dem Prinzip der Öffentlichkeit eine solche grundlegende Rolle nicht einräumen. Sein Selbstverständnis und seine Methode stehen dem entgegen, weil er „die universale Verantwortung gegenüber allem lebendigen Sein 'monologisch' aus dessen werthafter Struktur selbst" gleichsam abliest bzw. intuitiv abschaut.[85] „Sieh hin und Du weißt"[86], wofür Du verantwortlich bist, nämlich für das schutzbedürftige, werthafte, organische Leben um Dich herum – sagt Jonas intuitionistisch: Du weißt es, so wie Eltern, die ihren

---

[84] Dietrich Böhler, „Kritische Moral oder pragmatische Sittlichkeit?", in: *Funkkolleg Studientexte,* hrsg. von Karl-Otto Apel, Dietrich Böhler, Karlheinz Rebel, op. cit., Bd. 3, bes. S. 855–870.

[85] Vgl. Micha Werner, „Dimensionen der Verantwortung", in: *Ethik für die Zukunft,* hrsg. von Dietrich Böhler, op. cit., S. 332, vgl. S. 314–318.

[86] Hans Jonas, *Das Prinzip Verantwortung, Versuch einer Ethik für die technologische Zivilisation,* op. cit., S. 235.

schutzbedürftigen Kindern gegenüberstehen, 'normalerweise' (!) wissen, daß sie ihnen Fürsorge und Vorsorge zu gewähren haben. Handlungs- und gefühlsphänomenologisch ansetzend, nimmt Jonas allein das *asymmetrische* Verhältnis der Ausgangs- und Handlungsbedingungen eines Verantwortlichen in den Blick. Einzig diese praktische und intuitive Asymmetrie sei es, die den Verantwortungsbegriff konstituiere.

Trifft das zu? Recht hat Jonas als Phänomenologe, insoweit er zeigt, worin die *Ausgangslage* und die direkte praktische Aufgabe der Verantwortung besteht – nämlich *stellvertretend*, mithin fürsorgend für ein wertvolles, um seiner selbst willen schutzbedürftiges Wesen zu handeln. Diesen Verantwortungsaspekt stellt die Abb. 3 auf der rechten Seite dar, während ihre linke Hälfte den dialogförmigen, mithin symmetrischen Rechtfertigungsaspekt veranschaulicht:

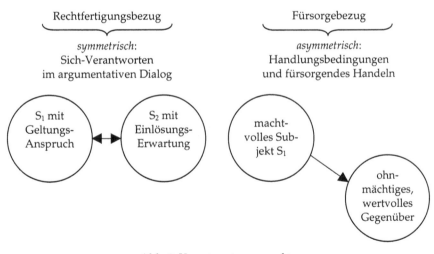

Abb. 3. Verantwortungsaspekte

Logisch und diskurspragmatisch gesehen, ist Jonas im Unrecht. Denn logisch hat sowohl die Situation der *Prinzipienbegründung*, in der einer dem anderen im argumentativen Dialog demonstriert, daß man prinzipiell zur Mitverantwortung für schutzbedürftige Wesen verpflichtet sei, eine symmetrische Form, als auch die *konkrete Rechtfertigungssituation* einer oder eines Verantwortlichen, die bzw. der über seine Praxis befragt wird oder sich selbst Fragen stellt. So befragt, muß sie bzw. er in einem *symmetrischen Dialog* mit Argumenten begründen können, daß die im Sinne der Fürsorge praktizierten Handlungsweisen den legitimen Ansprüchen gerecht werden bzw. gerecht geworden sind, die man im Namen seines Betreuten geltend machen kann oder die jener – später einmal – selbst gegenüber den Verantwortlichen vorbringen kann, etwa das herangewachsene Kind gegenüber den Eltern. Dann sind die Verantwortlichen gefordert, die Asymmetrie des fürsorgenden Handelns zu verlassen und sich auf die Symmetrie des argumentativen Dialogs einzulassen.

Es ergeben sich dann zweierlei Diskurs-Symmetrien: sowohl die im engen Sinne *logische* oder semantisch syntaktische Symmetrie zwischen Rede und Gegenrede, als Aussagen betrachtet, wie auch die *dialogpragmatische* bzw. kommunikationsethische zwischen Frage und Antwort, Gründefordern und Gründegeben, Anerkennungserwartung und Anerkenntnis, wie sie sich in der Interaktion gleichberechtigter Diskurspartner einstellen. Das ist die Form der Verantwortung als Rechtfertigung: das Sich-im-Dialog-Verantworten. Keine Verantwortung ohne mögliche Rechenschaft.

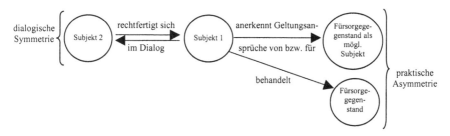

Abb. 4. Verantwortung: Verwobenheit von Fürsorge und Rechtfertigung

Beide Aspekte, das Rede-und-Antwort-Stehen und das stellvertretende Handeln des Fürsorglichen sind miteinander *verwoben*. Das eine verlöre ohne Bezug auf das andere seinen Sinn. Das Verwobensein der Fürsorgebeziehung mit der Rechtfertigungsbeziehung zeigt sich schon daran, daß 'ich', der Fürsorgende, bei Fragen nach dem Warum meiner Handlungsweise sowohl zum 'Gegenstand' meiner Fürsorge als auch zu dem Fragenden die symmetrische Stellung eines Diskurspartners werde einnehmen müssen. 'Ich' komme dabei nämlich nicht umhin, sowohl dem Frager Geltungsansprüche für seine Frage (als ernstgemeint, verständlich und wahrheitsdienlich) zuzubilligen und ernsthaft, verständlich, wahrheitsbemüht darauf einzugehen, als auch analog meinen Fürsorgegegenstand anzuerkennen und mich seinen möglichen Geltungsansprüchen zu stellen. 'Ich' muß zur Rechtfertigung, zum Geltungsdiskurs über meine Fürsorge bereit sein.

Warum? Ich bin einerseits Handelnder, ein faktisches Subjekt, aber 'ich' bin zugleich virtueller Diskurspartner, der zu seinen Handlungen Stellung nehmen kann. Daher kann 'ich' als Diskurspartner meinem Fürsorgegegenstand nicht einerseits (in der Fürsorgerelation) *Wert* beimessen resp. unterstellt haben *und* andererseits (in der Rechtfertigungsbeziehung) in Zweifel ziehen oder gar bestreiten, daß ich ihn *als* mögliches Subjekt von *Geltungsansprüchen* anerkennen soll. Wer das behauptete, verstrickte sich in einen performativen Widerspruch. Hinsichtlich dieser These verlöre er seine Glaubwürdigkeit als Diskurspartner. 'Ich' müßte vielmehr über ihn sagen können, daß man für ihn mit Recht Wert und Schutzwürdigkeit beanspruchen könne bzw. daß ihm dieser Anspruch zukomme, so daß 'ich' ihn aus guten Gründen ernstnehmen solle.

Der von Jonas verabsolutierte Fürsorgeaspekt bezieht sich auf die appellative wertethische Ausgangssituation eines Handlungsmächtigen im Verhältnis zu einem wertvollen, vergleichsweise ohnmächtigen Gegenüber, während sich der Geltungsaspekt aus der, damit von vornherein verbundenen, dialogethischen Rechtfertigungssituation ergibt. Erst beide Aspekte, miteinander und ineinander, machen den vollen Sinn von 'Verantwortung' aus.

Zur Verantwortung gehört das Sich-Verantworten, die Rechtfertigung ggf. des *Warum* und des *Wie*, der Mittel und Wege: der Fürsorgende muß sich vor allem konkret *verantworten* können gegenüber Anderen bzw. gegenüber den Ansprüchen des Adressaten seiner

Fürsorge. Das gilt auch dann, wenn der 'Fürsorgegegenstand' faktisch selbst keine Ansprüche erheben aber ein „moralisches Mandat" beanspruchen kann[87] – auch im Falle von Embryonen?

6. Verantwortungspflicht gegenüber Embryonen? In dubio pro Menschenwürde

Wenn wir Jonas' Gedankenexperiment der Wette und damit seinen neuen Imperativ der Zukunftsverantwortung auf den Streit über die Legitimität der In-vitro-Fertilisation und der Präimplantationsdiagnostik (PID) sowie der 'verbrauchenden' Forschung an embryonalen menschlichen Stammzellen anwenden, so zeigt sich zunächst dieses: *Wenn* gilt, daß die genannten Technologien bzw. Forschungstätigkeiten das Ganze der möglichen künftigen Interessen der von ihnen betroffenen Embryonen aufs Spiel setzen, *ohne* daß sie zur Rettung der Menschheit beitragen, dann sind sie moralisch nicht zu rechtfertigen. Es drängt sich gleich der Einwand auf, daß die umstandslose Anwendung des Gedankenexperiments zum Zweck der Überprüfung von PID und 'verbrauchender Embryonenforschung' das eigentliche Problem überspringe: ob nämlich das Ganze der künftigen Interessen von Embryonen, auch von Embryonen „in vitro", moralisch zu berücksichtigen ist, ob also Embryonen ein *moralischer Status* mit Anspruch auf Menschenwürde etc. zukomme, das sei doch gerade eine *offene* Frage – jedenfalls umstritten. Und das umso mehr, als bereits über die Frage nach dem Anfang menschlichen Lebens im öffentlichen Diskurs faktisch Dissens herrsche.

Wenn aus guten Gründen Uneinigkeit über den Gegenstandsbereich der Verantwortung besteht, dann hilft Jonas' Verantwortungsbegriff, der sich auf den Gegenstand der Verantwortung beschränkt *und* sich mit der schwachen Argumentationskraft eines metaphysi-

---

[87] Jens Peter Brune, „Menschenwürde und Potentialität: Eine diskursethische Skizze", in: *Philosophieren aus dem Diskurs. Beiträge zur Diskurspragmatik*, hrsg. von Holger Burckhart u. Horst Gronke, Würzburg: Königshausen & Neumann, 2002, hier S. 443.

schen Glaubens auf dessen motivationsfähigen Seinswert verläßt,
nicht weiter. Eine metaphysische Theorie, die dem Leben, zuhöchst
dem menschlichen Leben, Seinswürde und Schutzanspruch zu-
schreibt, also an eine „Ehrfurcht vor dem Leben" appelliert, *begründet*
hier letztlich nichts. Sie artikuliert nur den eigenen Wert- und Nor-
men-Standpunkt, eine schon mitgebrachte Motivation. Selbst eine
Differenzierung der Motivation durch Entfaltung von ethischen Intuitionen führt kaum weiter, da der Skeptiker deren universale Verbindlichkeit (für diesen Fall) in Zweifel ziehen dürfte.

Was wir an diesem Dissenspunkt benötigen, ist ein Verbindlichkeitserweis, der auch den argumentationsbereiten Skeptiker oder den
Andersmeinenden einbezieht bzw. das skeptische Argument ent-
kräftet. Für die Begründungsarbeit würde das bedeuten: erforderlich
ist ein nicht-metaphysischer *und* nicht-intuitionistischer Weg; schließlich kann jede metaphysische und intuitionistische Theorie vom
Skeptiker mit Recht als fallibel gekennzeichnet und bezweifelt werden, weil sie, wie Jonas zuletzt selbst einräumte, bloß „eine Option
[...] zur Wahl stellt".[88] Zudem darf der Argumentationsweg nicht de-
duktiv sein, weil sich alle Ableitungen einer moralischen, also ver-
bindlichen, Sollensvorschrift in der Ausweglosigkeit eines Begrün-
dungstrilemmas verlieren, wie Karl R. Popper bzw. Hans Albert
nachdrücklich in Erinnerung gebracht haben.[89] Was bleibt, ist die
sokratische Besinnung darauf, daß man auch als Skeptiker mit seinem
Etwas-Bezweifeln jeweils schon *in* einem argumentativen Dialog mit
Anderen ist *und* daß man *in* diesem Dialog die eigene Zweifelsthese
müßte verantworten können. Hier kommt der in der Umgangsspra-
che verwurzelte Tätigkeitsbegriff der Verantwortung ins Spiel: Verantwortung als ein *Sich* für die eigene These bzw. Zweifelsbehaup-

---

[88] Hans Jonas, „Zur ontologischen Grundlegung einer Zukunftsethik", in: idem,
Philosophische Untersuchungen und metaphysische Vermutungen, op. cit., S. 140. Vgl.
Jonas' selbstkritische Äußerung in: *Ethik für die Zukunft*, hrsg. von Dietrich Böhler,
op. cit., S. 39.

[89] Vgl. Hans Albert, *Traktat über kritische Vernunft*, Tübingen: Mohr/Siebeck, 1968.
S. 11–15; Wolfgang Kuhlmann, „Ist eine philosophische Letztbegründung moralischer
Normen möglich?", in: *Funkkolleg Studientexte*, hrsg. von Karl-Otto Apel, Dietrich
Böhler, Karlheinz Rebel, Bd. 2, Weinheim und Basel: Beltz, 1984, S. 572–605.

tung *Verantworten*. Dieser responsorische Verantwortungsbegriff deutet sich an bei Sokrates, er findet sich mehr oder weniger bei W. v. Humboldt und dem frühen Löwith. Jonas zehrt zwar an wichtigen Stellen von ihm[90], holt ihn jedoch nicht in seinem primär gegenstandsorientierten phänomenologischen Denkansatz ein.

Die sokratisch-postkantianische Dialogpragmatik rekonstruiert zunächst das Beziehungsgeflecht des Sich-Verantwortens als sechsstelliges Verhältnis des Rede-und-Antwort-Stehens: Eine Person (1) legt durch Dialogbeiträge (2) Rechenschaft ab über eine Handlung (3) und deren Wirkung (4); nämlich gegenüber (realen oder möglichen) Anderen (5) und kraft ihrer Geltungsansprüche vor der Instanz einer unbegrenzten Argumentationsgemeinschaft (6). Dieses sechsstellige dialogbezogene Verhältnis ermöglicht 'meine' Selbsteinholung als eines Dialogpartners. Das ist der Witz der sokratisch-dialogreflexiven Begründung: Bei sich selbst als *jetzt* Denkendem, als Diskursteilnehmer ansetzend, besinnt man sich darauf, daß man selbst mit seinem Zweifel einen *Dialogbeitrag* gegenüber Anderen *als* Partner *im* argumentativen Dialog *geltend* macht bzw. gemacht hat. Man geht reflexiv auf das zurück, was beide Seiten, die ja als Diskurspartner ernst genommen sein wollen, in Anspruch nehmen müssen – nämlich, daß sie sich als *irrtumsfähige* Menschen *für* ihr Projekt *im* Dialog der Argumente verantworten können. Durch eine solche Besinnung auf den Diskurs sowie auf 'mich' resp. 'dich' als Skeptiker und Partner in einem Diskurs kann die Diskurspragmatik dem Metaphysiker Jonas beispringen.

Wie? Die Diskurspragmatik macht mit der von ihm eingeklagten „Anerkennung der Unwissenheit" *im* Diskurs ernst. Sie bezieht nämlich diese Anerkennung so auf die offene Frage nach dem moralischen Status von Embryonen, daß die Antwort mit ihrer (nun anerkannten) Fallibilität von Situationseinschätzungen und konkreten

---

[90] Z.B. Hans Jonas, *Technik, Medizin und Ethik*, op. cit., S. 200. Ferner: idem, *Macht oder Ohnmacht der Subjektivität? Das Leib-Seele-Problem im Vorfeld des Prinzips Verantwortung*, Frankfurt a. Main: Insel, 1981, Einleitung, S. 13–18. Dazu Dietrich Böhler, „Ethik der Zukunfts- und Lebensverantwortung", in: *Orientierung und Verantwortung. Begegnungen und Auseinandersetzungen mit Hans Jonas*, hrsg. von idem u. Jens P. Brune, op. cit., S. 97–160.

Diskursen moralisch vereinbar ist: Wer etwas behauptet und sich damit Anderen gegenüber rechtfertigen will, ist einsehbar und unbestreitbar dazu verpflichtet, die Möglichkeit der Rechtfertigung zu bewahren: die Möglichkeit, sich dialogförmig für ein Projekt oder eine These zu verantworten. Das aber heißt, er ist zunächst gehalten, „das Ganze der Interessen" von (möglichen) Anspruchssubjekten nicht aufs Spiel zu setzen, sondern deren Rechte im Diskurs zu berücksichtigen. Und letztlich ist er verpflichtet, die zugleich normative und ontologische Idee des Menschen, welche nicht allein die Bewahrung der Gattungsexistenz sondern auch die Hütung von Menschenwürde und Moralfähigkeit einschließt, in seinen Entscheidungen zur Geltung zu bringen.

Solange nicht mit Sicherheit ausgeschlossen werden kann, daß gravierende Einwände gegen eine Handlungsweise möglich sind – etwa aus der Perspektive von Embryonen, deren moralischer Status jetzt faktisch noch offen sein mag –, solange besteht die grundsätzliche Verpflichtung, den Rechtfertigungsdialog und das Irrenkönnen in concreto ernst zu nehmen, statt in eine folgenirreversible Handlungsweise, die nicht irren dürfte, überzugehen. Mithin gilt: Im Zweifel für die Verantwortung (als Sich-im-Dialog-Verantworten-Können) und also für das Leben und die Menschenwürde.

Diese Pflicht zur Vorsicht beim Sich-im-Dialog-Verantworten erstreckt sich auch auf den faktisch noch umstrittenen moralischen Status menschlicher Embryonen. Mit Blick auf Jonas' Gedankenexperiment über die Wette im technologischen Handeln ergibt sich dieser Verbindlichkeitserweis:

– Eine Technologie, deren Einsatz mit dem Risiko verbunden ist, das Ganze der möglichen Interessen moralisch anspruchsberechtigter Wesen aufs Spiel zu setzen, ohne dadurch zur Rettung der Menschheit beizutragen, ist moralisch nicht zu verantworten.

– PID und 'verbrauchende Embryonenforschung' setzen das Leben von Menschen-Embryonen aufs Spiel, ohne zur Rettung der Menschheit beizutragen.

– Ob Embryonen moralisch anspruchsberechtigte Wesen sind, ist noch nicht eindeutig geklärt und faktisch umstritten (faktischer Dissens, faktisches Unwissen).

– Solange nicht mit Sicherheit ausgeschlossen werden kann, daß gravierende Einwände gegen eine Handlungsweise möglich sind, bleibt die grundsätzliche Pflicht bestehen, die Instanz des argumentativen Dialogs *und* die Irrtumsfähigkeit in konkreten Fragen ernst zu nehmen, statt eine folgenirreversible, nicht irren dürfende Handlungsweise zu wählen.

Ergo: im Zweifel für das Leben und für die Nichtverfügbarkeit von Embryonen. Indem 'wir' zwar die Streitsache selbst offen lassen, aber uns auf unsere Rollenpflichten *im* Diskurs besinnen, erkennen 'wir' Diskurspartner *das*, was 'wir' absolut nicht dürfen – absolut nicht, solange ein Sachstreit besteht, in dem das menschliche Ganze auf dem Spiele steht bzw. stehen kann. Denn die Achtung der Menschenwürde ist ein unbedingtes Prinzip. Es gebietet, menschliches Leben als „Zweck an sich selbst" (Kant) zu achten, mithin jegliche Instrumentalisierung dessen zu unterlassen. Eine solche hat man freilich schon begonnen, wenn man hier bloß, wie es zeitgeist- und politiküblich geworden ist, im landläufigen Sinne 'pragmatisch' verfährt: statt streng zu argumentieren, vermischt man die argumentationstragende Besinnung auf die Verantwortungsbedingungen von Argumentationspartnern sofort mit einer Kalkulation von Nutzen und Nachteil hinsichtlich besonderer Interessen. Für Klarheit und Strenge einzustehen, ist jedoch des Denkens Pflicht. Ohne eine Wachsamkeit über jene Prinzipien, die auch das Denken tragen, verkäme es selbst – und damit die Menschenwürde, welche die Denkenden je schon selbst in Anspruch genommen haben. Es gilt heute mehr denn je, sie als Prinzip zu hüten und sie in ihrer Unbedingtheit zu achten.

Christoph Menke
Potsdam

From the Dignity of Man to Human Dignity: the Subject of Rights

1.

Human rights are a specific category of "subjective rights". Ever since the 19th century, the term "subjective right" or "right in the subjective sense" denotes what had earlier – towards the end of the Middle Ages – been understood as quality (*qualitas*), ability (*facultas*), freedom (*libertas*), or power (*potestas*), of an individual. This distinguishes "right" in the subjective sense from "right" in the objective sense. Right in the objective sense is simply the right thing (*das Richtige*) according to the virtue of justice – Aquinas approvingly quotes Isidor in this way: "Something is called 'right' because it is just".[1] Or to quote Suarez: "'Right' denotes ... the law that is the norm for morally good action, and it determines certain equality among things".[2] Justice (the morally good with respect to equality) determines certain relations amongst men in regard to what someone has done; this is called "right" in the objective sense. For example, if a victim's property is returned to him or her according to the laws of commutative justice, it is a right (in the objective sense). In distinction to this, if someone "has a claim on an object", we speak (as Suarez does) of a right in the subjective sense. Furthermore, we then speak of a capacity

---

[1] St. Thomas Aquinas, *Summa theologica*, Qu. 57, Art. 1 [the translations of all quotes are the translators' own].

[2] Federico Suarez, *De legibus*, bk. 2, chap. 17.

or freedom of the one entitled to this claim to treat the object in question as he or she chooses. When speaking of subjective rights as capacity or ability, two things are implied: a subject's "(moral) capacities for putting others under obligations", as Kant says[3]; i.e. under the obligation to respect and not to intervene with the subject's exertion of this ability in respect to an object. Subjective rights enable, in this they are subjective: They enable someone (a subject) to something *vis-à-vis* others.

Human rights are a specific category of "subjective rights". They are a category of subjective rights, because they are a subject's "capacities for putting others under obligations". What kind of capacity of obligation we speak of here is disputed; it is a dispute that concerns the question of the relation between morality and legality. No matter for which of the two one may opt, a further question remains: how can we delimit *which* subjective rights are in fact human rights? Obviously, this delimitation has far reaching consequences. It consists in attributing a role or a power to these specific subjective rights in relation to all other rights, a power that Ronald Dworkin has compared to that of trumps in a card game. They outdo all other claims; they overtrump all other interests, obligations, or needs one might have. If someone's human right is at stake, other interests such as economic welfare or political stability have to stand back.

Without a doubt, human rights can only have this particular power, because as subjective rights they are about something very specific. To be more precise: in the case of human rights, the capacity to put others under obligations can only function as a trump in respect to all adversary rights and interests, because the subject's capacity or ability, which the others are obliged to respect, is of special significance. This special significance is often expressed as the very capacity of being a human being, or – if one wants to stress the normative character of the predicate of human beings – it is expressed as the capacity called the dignity of man. Human rights are about human dignity; this is why they overtrump all other claims. The con-

---

[3] Immanuel Kant, *The Metaphysics of Morals*, Introduction to the Doctrine of Rights.

junction of the notion of "human rights" with that of "human dignity" does not have to, or in fact should not, be understood as if human dignity was an independently given derivative ground (*Ableitungsgrund*) for human rights; as if there existed a normative act of grasping the dignity of (every) human being, from which one could then deduce that he or she has overtrumping rights, and what these rights might be. Rather, we need the concept of human dignity in order to be able to say what this category of rights essentially is about.

The concept of human dignity contained in and presupposed by the idea of human rights has to be such that it can designate the status of each individual as being the bearer of certain claims that trump all other claims. Human dignity, thus, refers to the individual human being *as* a bearer of rights or *as* a subject of rights. Two thoughts converge in this notion of human dignity: that of the subjective right on the one hand and that of the dignity of man (which I would like to distinguish – so far only terminologically – from human dignity) on the other hand. On their own, none of these two thoughts amounts to the concept of human dignity such as it is presupposed in the concept of human rights. While human rights are a specific category of subjective rights and refer to an individual as the bearer of such rights, this concept of a subject of rights does not suffice to denote the special status of being the bearer of human rights which the concept of human dignity aims at. The idea of human rights is not yet contained in the form of subjective rights; to be the "subject" of human rights does not merely *mean* to be the bearer of subjective rights. The reverse, however, is also true: human dignity does not coincide with the traditional definition of the dignity of man, since man, to whom dignity in this traditional definition had been attributed, is not yet understood as a subject (of human rights). Thus, we have to differentiate between the idea of the dignity of man and that of human dignity, whereby I historically refer to the difference between the traditional idea of a dignity of man – such as it can be found e.g. (examples which are relevant to us) in the traditions of monotheistic religions and Stoic philosophy – and the specifically modern idea of human dignity, which from the start was connected to the idea of human rights. While the modern idea of human dignity only developed through the appropriation and reinterpretation of the traditional idea of the dignity of man, the latter, be it the Christian or Stoic type, *is* not yet the idea of human dignity.

2.

Fundamental to the traditional concept of the dignity of man is a delimitation that was terminologically phrased as that between honour and dignity. According to Cicero, dignity belongs to the "role" (*persona*) "common to all men"; honour, on the contrary, belongs to that other role "that is personally (*proprie*) assigned to each individual (*singulis*)".[4] All men are endowed with dignity; this is the fundamental determination with which already the traditional conception begins and which it develops in three steps.

The *first* and fundamental step of the traditional concept of the dignity of man is the ontological distinction of man from all other beings, a distinction primarily explicated by the delimitation of the human from the animal. More precisely, then, what is at stake is the special ontological position of humans as a *species*, their elevation or sublimity in respect to all other living beings: "how far human beings in their essence are superior to cattle and all other animals".[5] The Jewish Bible characterizes this elevated position by the godlikeness of man (*imago dei*)[6]; Stoic philosophy, on the contrary, by human reason. The role of which Cicero said, as quoted above, that it is common to all men, "rests on the fact that we all partake in reason and in the privileged status whereby we are superior to animals; on this depends all moral good, honesty and decorum (*honestum decorumque*), and the analysis of all dutiful action is based upon it".[7] This anthropologico-ontological determination of the specifically human mode of being is followed, in a *second* step, by the assertion of a corresponding ethos. The fact that I as a human being am endowed with "dignity" in

---

4 Cicero, *De officiis*, I 107.
5 Ibidem, I 105.
6 *Genesis* 1, 26–27.
7 Cicero, *De officiis*, I 107.

the sense explained above – that is, for Cicero, the fact that reason privileges me over animals – obliges me to act in a specific (namely: in an "adequate") manner. Cicero concludes "that bodily pleasure is not adequate to the dignity of man, and that it shall be despised and rejected".[8] I owe it to my dignity as a human being, endowed with reason, to be prudent, moderate, self-controlled, i.e. to be virtuous. Here, the anthropologico-ontological determination of the dignity of man becomes an ethical task or an ethical measure.

Finally, the *third* step in this traditional concept of the dignity of man stresses that the (anthropologico-ontological) dignity of man does not only imply an (ethical) obligation of each individual towards him- or herself to a particular, rationally controlled way of life, but it also always implies an obligation towards others. According to the second step, these virtues are grounded in the fact that I am interested in acting in accordance with my dignity, with my status as a human being. In their normative content, however, these virtues at the same time also refer to others: "Nature has endowed us with the role (*persona*) ["due to which we outshine all other living beings by far"] of steadfastness, modesty, self-control, and restraint, and it teaches us not to disregard the question of how we behave towards our fellow human beings (*nos adversos homines*)".[9] Cicero calls this concession of virtues to others – the "consideration for other human beings" – "justice and restraint" (and he distinguishes between the two). And as much as the ground of virtue is the dignity of man, so does the dignity of man determine the justice and restraint in regard to others. Each human being has to consider the other (i.e., any other) as a human being; this was already part of traditional Christian and Stoic philosophy: "Thus, one has to pay (a certain) respect (*reverentia*) to human beings, as much to the noble ones as to all others".[10]

Whatever this might mean or imply, this "respect" that we, according to Christian and Stoic philosophy, owe (to) the other due to the dignity of man, does *not* (yet) mean one thing: it does not attribute

---

[8] Ibidem, I 106.
[9] Ibidem, I 98.
[10] Ibidem, I 99.

human dignity, i.e. the status of bearer of fundamental or human rights, to the other. This becomes evident in the behaviours and institutions which are, according to the traditional concept – be it Christian or Stoic –, compatible with the idea of the dignity of man, but definitely not with the idea of fundamental or human rights (however one may interpret them). In a moment we will ask, *why* they are compatible in one case and incompatible in another, and what the reason for such difference might be. The most extreme example for this difference is perhaps that neither the Jewish nor the Christian idea of the godlikeness of man (*imago dei*) necessarily rules out slavery, as little as this is the case in the Roman thought of the dignity of man based on reason. We find this e.g. in Paul's letter to Philemon, to whom he sends his slave Onesimus with the request to "welcome him as you would welcome me", "so that you might have him back forever, no longer as a slave but *more* than a slave, a beloved brother".[11] Paul does precisely not mean for Philemon to free Onesimus from slavery. In Paul's view, one can have someone as a beloved brother and *simultaneously* as a servant or slave. The universally understood "society of mankind" (*humani generis societas*) for which Paul stands and of which Cicero speaks[12] is all-comprising only in that sense that it comprises all men; at the same time, however, it is limited and restricted because it strictly categorizes human beings into different "roles" (Cicero: *personae*), and sees their being respected in one "role" (that of man) as compatible with their being subjugated and oppressed in another. The dignity of man in its traditional understanding – as pertaining to all men in distinction to the animal – cannot found an egalitarian order of human rights.

3.

One could probably show that this is already entirely different in the case of Samuel Pufendorf, the thinker who was mostly responsible for introducing the Stoic concept of the dignity of man into the mod-

---

[11] *Philemon*, 15–17.
[12] Cicero, *De officiis*, III 21, see 28.

ern discourse on (human) rights. Unable to pursue this here in detail, I just want to refer to the terminological turn that occurred in the German translation (of 1711) of his *De iure naturae et gentium* (1672). It happened without him knowing – Pufendorf had died already in 1694 –, but what it brings to the fore is the difference between his usage of (the concept of) dignity and the traditional one. In Pufendorf we read "that by nature all men are to be held equally dignified".[13] He explains this equality, which all men are worthy of due to their godlikeness (*imago dei*) and their endowment with reason, immediately afterwards as one of "rights".[14] While it is, of course, permissible if not inevitable – as is the case for any concept of equal justice – that inequalities of all kinds arise in political, social, economic, or other interaction, the relation of such equal dignity to these inequalities is here no longer understood according to a model of spatially separated realms or roles. Rather, it is understood as a normative relation of conditions: social inequalities can now only be justified for as long as they do not contradict equal dignity in this very same social realm. This is precisely what the concept of fundamental rights aims at: they shall provide the minimal conditions that need to be fulfilled in every conduct or institution in order to bring about equal respect for the dignity of each human being in the face of all the inequalities by which this conduct or these institutions are characterized. It is, thus, precisely the point of the concept of fundamental rights to guarantee the equal dignity of each human being in each social realm, and thus in each role (*persona*). The traditional concept of the dignity of man only becomes the modern concept of human dignity when linked to this decisive claim – decisive in the sense that it does away with the traditional differentiation between general and particular *persona*, between this world and a beyond – and precisely (and only) this claim *is* one to fundamental or human rights.

So far, we have only *described* the difference (in its functioning) between the traditional and the modern concept of dignity; we have, however, not yet explained it. But for as long as we are unable to ex-

---

[13] Samuel Pufendorf, *De iure naturae et gentium*, Lund 1672, p. 567 ff.
[14] Ibidem, pp. 572, 575.

plain it, it seems reasonable to suppose that the step from one concept to the other was merely a simple learning process: merely the resolution of the paradox (or the inconsistency) into which Paul and Cicero manoeuvred themselves when they did *not* understand the godlikeness (*imago dei*) or the dignity of man the way the modern concept of equal rights does. In reverse, this would mean to understand the modern concept of equal rights merely as the (logical) consequence of the traditional idea of the dignity of man; as basically already contained in this idea. If we want to avoid such an odd understanding of human history – and with it avoid the difficulty to explain why European civilization should have needed seventeen centuries to carry out nothing but a logically correct deduction – we have to look for a different explanation. We have to note that we cannot hold a lack of coherence responsible for the fact that the traditional concept of the dignity of man cannot be related to the concept of fundamental rights. It is rather a different kind of lack (if we want to phrase things in these terms at all): it is the lack of the concept of subjectivity. Such a concept of subjectivity has to be presupposed in order to link dignity and rights – in order to see the dignity of man in a conceptual relationship with the equal rights of each human being, and in order, thus, to understand the dignity of man as human dignity. Or putting it the other way around: the surplus (of the modern idea) of human dignity in respect to (the traditional idea of) the dignity of man consists in an internal relation between dignity and rights, because this modern idea of human dignity understands the human being as a subject.

I cannot adequately elaborate this specifically modern concept of subjectivity here; a concept that, as the normative core of the idea of human dignity, underlies the concept of human rights. But let me just briefly sketch how such an elaboration could proceed. Its starting point would be the relation of "mineness" in the sense of authorship that defines, according to Kant, the concept of personality or subjectivity in a moral sense. It aims at the normative (and not just epistemic) sense of the fact that something – e.g. avolition or an action – is "mine". Something is "mine" insofar as I understand myself as its "author", and insofar as I am responsible for it. Furthermore, this idea of authorship that defines subjectivity would further need to be elaborated in three steps. On a first level, I am the author of certain occurrences whenever it is correct to describe them as my performances in the sense that they realize an ability or capacity that I possess. The "freedom [or authorship] of a *rational* being", by means of which Kant defines the concept of personality, does, however, not only consist in realizing one's abilities, but it also consists in a self-conscious relationship to the normative content that defines the ability as a rational one – a relationship of applying, and thus accepting this content. On this second level then, being a subject means being the (applying and realizing) authority, the medium of a law, a value, or a norm. The third and decisive step in elaborating the idea of subjectivity refers to how this norm does indeed exist (i.e. has validity) for the subject: the norm only exists for the subject when it exists through the subject. The concept of subjective authorship articulates the idea that I can call an action "mine" in this complex sense if I not only realize my ability in it – that was the first meaning of authorship –; also if I not only apply a norm (and thus conform to it) – that was the second meaning of authorship –; but if I (and here I would like to use an ab-used, but indispensable term) "realize myself" in it: The norm has to be my own. The capacity to make normative orientations my own (or: to have them as my own) in such a way that they can be understood as the expression of myself is fundamental to subjectivity or personality in this complex sense. To be a "subject" means to realize a double, mutual relation of expression: It means to express my norms in my actions, indeed in my life, because my norms are but an expression of my life. A subject is someone for whom only those norms are valid that can be expressed by and in his or her life; someone who is able to make his or her life an expression of those norms.

Human rights, as I have said already in the beginning, are a specific category of "subjective rights". Now we can say that human rights are those specific subjective rights that can be understood as the capacity to oblige others to respect just that ability or that capacity which Kant has called "humanity", and which I have called "subjectivity". This is why (according to Kant, in his *Metaphysics of Morals*) there is but *one* human right: "*Freedom* (independence from being constrained by another's choice), insofar as it can coexist with the freedom of every other in accordance with a universal law, is the only original right belonging to every man by virtue of his humanity." The formal structure of this one human right corresponds to that of subjective rights. Having this right consists in the capacity or in the quality to oblige others to respect my capacity to do or to refrain from doing something. However, in the case of this one human right the capacity, which to respect I have the capacity to oblige others, is a peculiar one: there is only one human right because it is the subjective right to subjectivity; the ability of each individual to oblige all others to respect his or her ability to be a subject. We need to spell out more clearly what this means, and this happens in an in principle open and contestable list of subjective rights that comprises what we usually call human rights (in the plural). Kant's (hypo)thesis of only one single human right does not mean to say that these other human or fundamental rights do not exist. It rather asserts the meaning of the many other rights. It asserts that their meaning is a single and unified one: the unfolding of the one human right to a humanity or subjectivity. Human rights are those subjective rights that have their meaning in their bearer's subjectivity.

This fundamental definition of human rights, which results from the concept of human dignity as dignity of the subject, entails the two dimensions of the *egalitarian* and *fundamental* character of human rights, which, as I said above, cannot be found in the traditional conceptualizations of dignity, respectively cannot be founded upon them. (1) The first, the egalitarian point is obvious: the (sole) human right to subjectivity, and all that follows from it, *can* only be the same for everyone because the subjectivity to which it refers is always the same (it either exists – or it does not; there are neither different degrees nor modes of subjectivity). (2) If human rights are those subjective rights whose significance lies in the subjectivity of the bearer of these rights, then they have to be not only *egalitarian* but also *fundamental*. In as much as human rights cannot be distributed unequally amongst human beings, they cannot be restricted to certain areas of life. Herein lies the difference of human rights to both the traditional idea of diverse privileges and the traditional concept of the dignity of man. What I have described (in view of Paul and Cicero) as role-theoretical distribution – as the categorization in(to) different *personae* – was characteristic of such a concept: dignity pertains to human beings only in their "general" role, from which other social roles are to be distinguished, and onto which dignity has no effect. Such a distribution is unthinkable for a notion of human dignity whose content is subjectivity as self-realization: either one is a subject or one is not. Any restriction to practice my capacity of subjectivity in a specific area of my acting and life, "damages me" (*lädiert mich*), as Kant says, as a subject on the whole. Subjectivity is indivisible, or: subjectivity is not a role, it is not a *persona*. Human rights are meant to guarantee that I can sustain my practice as a subject in every respect, in every area of my life; they serve the self-preservation of subjectivity. Or, to be more precise: since the self-preservation of subjectivity is not (wholly) within our powers (we can lose it through accidents and strokes of fate), human rights provide us with the moral capacity to oblige others to respect the preservation of our subjectivity.

4.

Therefore, the thesis that I would like to suggest in this essay is that only the modern understanding of human dignity as "subjectivity" (and correspondingly as "free" in a certain sense) leads to a concept of fundamental or human rights. I have attempted to expound this thesis in three steps: I began by understanding human rights via their function in social practices, and by defining this function with the Dworkinian analogy of trumps in a card game. What remains unexplained in this concept, however, is the presupposition that these overtrumping claims can be made by human individuals *only*, not by groups, and not by communities and organizations. If, by this presupposition, we do understand that the special status of each individual is expressed in his or her "dignity" as a human being, the question that still remains is what we mean by this. To answer this question I have distinguished between two concepts of dignity: a traditional one which I called "dignity of man" and which I took primarily from Cicero, and a modern one which I terminologically distinguished from the former as "human dignity" and which I took mostly from Kant. A second step, then, demonstrated that Cicero already had an idea of "respect" that should not only be paid to the "nobles" but also to "all others". This, however, does not prevent Cicero from distinguishing between the role of a human being and his different social roles in such a way that respect for the former is compatible with inequality and oppression in the latter. On the very contrary now, the idea of fundamental or human rights has to be understood as doing away with this distribution: fundamental or human rights articulate the minimal conditions for each social realm and for each social role. In order to be able to do so – and this was my third step – they have to understand "human being" in a manner different from the traditional concept of the dignity of man: They have to understand "human being" as personality or as subject. To be a subject or to have subjectivity in this sense means to follow only those normative orientations that are "my own" in the complex sense of the term. This capacity is indivisible; it concerns everything I do. The concept of fundamental or human rights relates to this in such a way that they are to guarantee the conditions under which each human being, in each social realm of action, can be a "subject" or have a "personality". In this sense, as "personality" or as "subjective" freedom, the modern idea of human dignity is the precondition of the concept of fundamental or human rights. While in fact a society can have rules that *materially* resemble those of fundamental or human rights even without this idea of a subject – one does not need the concept of human rights in order to condemn homicide, cruelty, and oppression –, there is a *formal* difference between such rules and fundamental or human rights. This difference cannot be found (i.e. not always at least or not necessarily) in their content but only in their form, and therefore it can only be found in their meaning and functioning. Fundamental or human rights are (with Kant) those "capacities" of a subject, which are guaranteed by "external" legislation, and which are needed for the sake of the capacity of a subject – the capacity of the (moral) "personality"; the capacity to be a subject.

Translated by Birgit M. Kaiser and Kathrin Thiele

Manfried Welan
Wien

Drei Weise aus dem alten Österreich: Friedrich August von Hayek, Karl Raimund Popper, Hans Kelsen

Unwissenheit als Grund von Freiheit und Toleranz

1. Der Mensch weiß wenig und Sicherheit ist nirgends

Der Mensch weiß wenig. Er ist auch in der Google-Gesellschaft informationsarm. Deshalb neigt er zum Irrtum und zu Fehlern, vor allem in Beziehung auf die Zukunft. Die Unwissenheit in Bezug auf die Zukunft ist unser aller Problem, macht aber vielleicht unser Leben erst schön.

„Ich weiß, dass ich nichts weiß". Das angebliche Wort des Sokrates blieb im Gedächtnis der Welt. Als ich diesen Satz im Gymnasium hörte, merkte ich ihn mir sofort und bis heute. Als Alter weiß ich, dass die Erkenntnis unserer Unwissenheit ein Anfang der Weisheit sein kann. Für unser Verständnis der Gesellschaft hat dieser Satz große Bedeutung.[1] Die erste Voraussetzung für dieses Verständnis ist, dass wir uns der notwendigen Unkenntnis des Menschen von vielem, das ihm seine Ziele zu erreichen hilft, bewusst werden. So sagt Friedrich August von Hayek, dass die Zivilisation beginnt, „wenn der Einzelne in seiner Verfolgung seiner Ziele mehr Wissen verwerten kann,

---

[1] Friedrich August von Hayek, *Die Verfassung der Freiheit*, Tübingen: Mohr und Siebeck, 1971, S. 30.

als er selbst erworben hat und wenn er die Grenzen seines Wissens überschreiten kann, indem er aus Wissen Nutzen zieht, das er nicht selbst besitzt."[2]

Die Erfahrung hat uns gelehrt, dass es die Sicherheit nicht gibt, die wir gerne hätten. Der Dichter Arthur Schnitzler lässt seinen Paracelsus sagen: „Sicherheit ist nirgends." Seit dem 11. September 2001 ist das evident. Trotzdem oder gerade deswegen hat sich die Wissenschaft der Unsicherheit systematisch angenommen. Aber „Garantien für eine überraschungsfreie und gesicherte Zukunft gibt es letztlich keine."[3] Erziehung und Selbsterziehung zu Ungewissheit und Unsicherheit sind daher für unser Leben wichtig geworden.

Unser Verstand ist ein Ergebnis der Kultur, in der wir aufgewachsen sind. Von der Erfahrung, die ihn geformt hat, weiß er zum großen Teil nichts. Diese Erfahrung ist in Gewohnheiten, Gebräuchen, Spielregeln verschiedener Art und in der Sprache verkörpert. Das Wissen, das wir bewusst verwenden, ist nur ein kleiner Teil dessen, was zum Erfolg unserer Handlungen beiträgt. Hayek erkannte, dass das Wissen anderer immer mehr eine wesentliche Vorbedingung für die Verfolgung unserer eigenen individuellen Ziele wird. Das Ausmaß unseres Unwissens und unserer Unkenntnis der Umstände, von denen die Ergebnisse unseres Handelns abhängen, ist überwältigend.

Wissen nach Hayek umfasst alle Anpassungen des Menschen an die Umgebung, die auf vergangener Erfahrung beruhen. Wissen und Wissenschaft hängen zusammen, aber auch wenn die Wissenschaften und die Wissenschaftler insgesamt mehr denn je sind, so erschöpft sich darin keineswegs das Wissen, von dem wir Gebrauch machen. Kulturwissenschaften als Sammlung dieser Erfahrungen sind umso wichtiger geworden, je mehr wir Geschichte vergessen und „geschichtslos" werden, eine Entwicklung, die wir seit einigen Jahrzehnten erleben. Man erkennt immer mehr, wie viel mehr unser aller Wissen ist als das bewusste Wissen oder gar die Wissenschaft. Der Bereich der zugestandenen Unkenntnis wird mit dem Fortschritt der Wissenschaft nicht kleiner, sondern größer. Dieser Prozess erhöht

---

[2] Ibidem.
[3] Adalbert Evers, Helga Nowotny, *Über den Umgang mit Unsicherheit*, Frankfurt am Main: Suhrkamp, 1987, S. 324.

notwendigerweise die Unkenntnis des Einzelnen vom größten Teil dieses Wissens. Je größer das Wissen insgesamt, desto geringer wird der Anteil des Einzelnen daran. Deshalb ist Tradition und Kommunikation so wichtig. Deshalb nennt Sir Karl Raimund Popper die Tradition die wichtigste Quelle unseres Wissens. Sie muss freilich immer wieder kritisch untersucht werden, ob sie noch hält, was sie einmal als Problemlösung versprochen hat. Aber ohne Tradition ist Erkenntnis kaum möglich.

Leben ist Problemlösen und Leben ist Lernen. Das müssen alle. Popper hat alle Menschen als Philosophen verstanden. Ebenso hat Hayek alle Menschen und nicht nur Wissenschaftler als „Wissende" angesehen. Er hat der Wissenschaft nur einen bescheidenen Anteil an Gesamtwissen zugestanden.

Beide erkannten, dass jede Lösung eines Problems neue ungelöste Probleme schafft. Diese neuen Probleme sind umso interessanter, je schwieriger das ursprüngliche Problem war.

Unser Wissen kann nur begrenzt sein. Unsere Unwissenheit dagegen ist grenzenlos. Popper hat diese Unermesslichkeit mit der Unermesslichkeit des Sternenhimmels anschaulich umschrieben. Je mehr wir über die Welt erfahren, desto klarer wird unser Wissen über das, was wir nicht wissen. Ich wiederhole: Wir wissen wenig. Niemand weiß genau, was anderen oder vielen oder gar allen im Einzelnen gut tut. Kein Mensch, keine Institution, und (noch) kein Instrument kann die Information über die Lebenssituationen aller Individuen besitzen und verarbeiten. Hayeks Argument für die Freiheit beruht auf dieser Erkenntnis unserer Unkenntnis. Aufgrund der allgemeinen und besonderen Unwissenheit ist niemand legitimiert, fremde Lebensräume und andere Lebensführungen inhaltlich zu gestalten. Weil wir wenig wissen und auch nicht wissen, wer etwas am Besten weiß, brauchen wir politische Freiheit. Wir brauchen Freiheitsrechte und wir brauchen politische Rechte. Hayek definiert Freiheit vor allem aus dem Fehlen von Zwang und Willkür, also formal und negativ, als „Freiheit vom", insbesondere als „Freiheit vom Staat". Aber auch die Freiheit zum Staat und im Staat, das Wahlrecht und andere Rechte der Mitwirkung an der politischen Willensbildung ergeben sich als Folge der Unwissenheit.

2. Grundlagen der Freiheit

Welches Argument gäbe es für die Freiheit, wenn wir nicht nur alles wissen könnten, wovon die Erfüllung unserer gegenwärtigen Wünsche abhängt, sondern auch wüssten, was unsere zukünftigen Wünsche sind und wie sie erfüllt werden?

Artikel 1 der allgemeinen Erklärung der Menschenrechte 1948 bestimmt: „Alle Menschen sind frei und gleich an Würde und Rechten geboren. Sie sind mit Vernunft und Gewissen begabt und sollen einander im Geiste der Brüderlichkeit begegnen." Aus großen Evidenzen wird hier die politische Freiheit der Menschen abgeleitet. Die Menschenwürde gilt als Grundlage der Freiheit. Sie liegt in der Einzigartigkeit und Einmaligkeit jedes Menschen. Daraus folgt sein Recht, Mensch zu sein. Sein aufrechter Gang, seine Sprachbegabung und seine verantwortliche Freiheit, seine Geschichts- und seine Zukunftsbezogenheit unterscheiden ihn von der übrigen Natur. Aus dieser anthropologischen Sicht wird der Menschheit als Ganzes und jedem Einzelnen das Recht zugestanden, Mensch zu sein und Recht zu haben.

Humanistisch wird die Menschenwürde im vernünftigen, sittlich autonomen und deshalb freien Subjekt begründet. Nach der reinen Vernunft haben alle Menschen gleiche angeborene Rechte und eine gleiche rechtliche Freiheit, neue Rechte zu erwerben. Dementsprechend bestimmt § 16 des österreichischen Allgemeinen Bürgerlichen Gesetzbuches 1811:

> Jeder Mensch hat angeborene, schon durch die Vernunft einleuchtende Rechte und ist daher als eine Person zu betrachten. Sklaverei oder Leibeigenschaft und die Ausübung einer sich darauf beziehenden Macht werden in diesen Ländern nicht gestattet.

Die christliche Lehre vertritt die Freiheit und Gleichheit aller Menschen, weil alle Menschen Kinder Gottes und seine Ebenbilder sind.

Hayek ist bescheidener. Für ihn ist die Unwissenheit die wichtigste Grundlage der individuellen politischen Freiheit. Unsere notwendige Unkenntnis von vielen Dingen bedeutet, dass wir es weitgehend mit Wahrscheinlichkeiten und Möglichkeiten und nicht mit Wahrheiten und Wirklichkeiten zu tun haben.

Freiheit ist wesentlich, um Raum für das Unvorhergesehene und Unvoraussagbare zu lassen. Es geht bei der Ordnung der Gesellschaft um die größtmögliche Gelegenheit für den Eintritt von Zufälligkeiten.

So demütigend es für unseren Stolz sein mag, wir müssen anerkennen, dass der Fortschritt und selbst die Erhaltung unserer Zivilisation von der größtmöglichen Gelegenheit für den Eintritt von Zufälligkeiten abhängt. Es ist natürlich richtig, dass im gesellschaftlichen ebenso wie im persönlichen Leben Zufälle gewöhnlich nicht einfach geschehen. Wir müssen sie vorbereiten. Aber sie bleiben immer noch Möglichkeiten und werden keine Gewissheiten. Sie bedeuten bewusst eingegangene Risken, mögliches Missgeschick von einzelnen Gruppen, die ebenso verdienstvoll sind wie andere, die Erfolg haben, sie bedeuten die Möglichkeit ernsten Fehlschlages oder eines Rückschlages sogar für die Mehrheit, und nur eine hohe Wahrscheinlichkeit eines Nettogewinns im Ganzen. Alles, was wir tun können, ist, die Wahrscheinlichkeit zu vergrößern, dass ein besonderes Zusammentreffen von persönlicher Begabung und Umständen zur Schaffung eines neuen Werkzeuges oder zur Verbesserung eines alten führen wird, und die Aussichten zu verbessern, das solche Neuerungen schnell allen jenen bekannt werden, die Verwendung dafür haben.[4]

Dazu dient vor allem der Wettbewerb als Entdeckungsverfahren.

3. Einrichtungen der Freiheit sind Anpassungen an Ungewissheit und Unwissen

Hayek wiederholt immer wieder, dass alle Einrichtungen der Freiheit, auch wenn wir uns dessen nicht bewusst sind, Anpassungen an die grundlegende Tatsache unseres Unwissens sind. Sie sind Anpassungen daran, dass wir es in menschlichen Angelegenheiten nicht mit Gewissheiten zu tun haben.

Gewissheit können wir in menschlichen Angelegenheiten nicht erreichen und das ist der Grund, dass wir, um von unserem geringen Wissen den besten Gebrauch zu machen, uns an Regeln halten müssen, die sich in der Erfahrung am zweckdienlichsten erwiesen haben, auch wenn wir

---

[4] Friedrich August von Hayek, *Die Verfassung der Freiheit*, op. cit., S. 39.

nicht wissen, was die Folgen ihrer Einhaltung im einzelnen Fall sein werden.[5]

Das gilt für die Grund- und Freiheitsrechte, für die Gewaltenteilung, für das Wahlrecht und den Parlamentarismus, für die Bindung an Verfassung und Gesetz, für Kontrollen, kurz für den demokratischen Rechtsstaat.

Wir wissen auch nicht, wie die Freiheit gebraucht werden wird. Wenn wir das wüssten, „würde sie in weitem Maße ihre Rechtfertigung verlieren."[6] Wenn der Freiheit durch Gesetze Schranken gezogen werden, weil sie missbraucht wird, dann wird sie in der Folge immer mehr beschränkt und schließlich kommt es dazu, dass auch Schranken gegen die Schranken der Freiheit gezogen werden müssen. Jedenfalls sollte es erlaubt bleiben, auf eigene Kosten Dummheiten zu machen.

> Freiheit bedeutet notwendig, dass vieles getan werden wird, das uns nicht gefällt. Unser Vertrauen auf die Freiheit beruht nicht auf den voraussehbaren Ergebnissen in bestimmten Umständen, sondern auf dem Glauben, dass sie im Ganzen mehr Kräfte zum Guten als zum Schlechten auslösen wird.[7]

Wir wissen wenig und das nur bis auf weiteres. Wir können aber lernen. Wir lernen vor allem durch die Enttäuschung von Erwartungen. Aber wir sollen auf eine direkte Lenkung der individuellen Lebensführung verzichten. Eine solche Gesellschaft freier Menschen kann von viel mehr Kenntnissen Gebrauch machen als wir es verstehen. Die Gesellschaft ist für uns weder durchschaubar noch vorhersehbar. Keine menschliche Entscheidung und auch nicht politische Entscheidungen lassen sich in ihren Konsequenzen voll angeben. Die Gesellschaft lässt sich nicht planen. Nur die Planer wissen das nicht. Denn die Gesellschaft ist das Ergebnis von Verhaltensweisen und nicht das Resultat eines human design. Unsere Verhaltensweisen und die von ihnen gestalteten Institutionen sind nicht Konstrukte des Intellekts, sondern das Ergebnis von Geschichte und Erfahrung, a work of art and time.

---

[5] Ibidem, S. 40.
[6] Ibidem, S. 40.
[7] Ibidem, S. 40.

4. Ordnung der Freiheit
– Hayek und Popper

Man hat Hayek vorgeworfen, dass er zu einem veralteten Laissez-faire-Standpunkt zurückgekehrt sei. In der Hoffnung, dass alles gut gehen werde, wolle er den Dingen ihren Lauf lassen. Sicher ist nach Hayek der Wettbewerb nicht zuletzt dadurch gerechtfertigt, dass man nicht weiß, was dabei herauskommt. Jeder Wettbewerb ist ein Entdeckungsverfahren und eines der wichtigsten Werkzeuge zur Verbreitung von Wissen. Er führt gewöhnlich den Wert des Wissens jenen, die es nicht besitzen, vor Augen. Dabei kann die Verbreitung und Verwertung des Wissens durch bewusste Bemühungen gesteigert werden. Deshalb soll Gelegenheiten und Zufällen zu ihrem Recht verholfen werden. Hayek will die Dinge nicht einfach laufen lassen. Es geht ihm um eine Ordnung für die Freiheit, um die Verfassung der Freiheit. Sie ist Grund, Weg und Mittel. Es geht um ein dezentrales, ungeplantes Entstehen von Regeln, nicht um zentrale Pläne und Befehle einer Autorität. Es geht um freie Gesellschaftsentwicklung, nicht um einen Sozialplan. Es geht um gesellschaftliche Regeln, die in einem großen unpersönlichen Prozess wirken. Dieser Weg ist das Ziel der Verfassung der Freiheit.

Nicht was der Einzelne in seinem Freiheitsraum tut, ist wichtig, sondern die Abgrenzung der vielen individuellen Bereiche der Freiheit durch allgemeine und abstrakte Regeln. Freiheit kann nur als Freiheit unter dem Gesetz und als Gleichheit vor dem Gesetz bestehen. „Es ist eines der Merkmale einer freien Gesellschaft, dass die Ziele der Menschen offen sind, d.h. dass neue Ziele für die bewussten Bemühungen auftauchen können, zunächst bei ein paar Einzelnen, um mit der Zeit Ziel der meisten zu werden."[8]

Hier trifft sich Friedrich August von Hayek mit Popper:

> Aber wenn wir Menschen bleiben wollen, dann gibt es nur einen Weg, den Weg in die offene Gesellschaft. Wir müssen ins Unbekannte, ins Ungewisse, ins Unsichere weiter schreiten und die Vernunft, die uns gegeben ist, verwenden, um, so gut wir es eben können, für beides zu planen: nicht nur für Sicherheit, sondern zugleich auch für Freiheit.[9]

---

[8] Ibidem, S. 45.

[9] Karl R. Popper, *Die offene Gesellschaft und ihre Feinde*, 1. Bd.: *Der Zauber Platons*, Frankfurt am Main: Suhrkamp, 1964, S. 268.

5. Popper: Ich weiß, dass ich nichts weiß, und kaum das

Sokrates folgend sagte Popper gern: „Ich weiß, dass ich nichts weiß, und kaum das."[10] Er war aber nicht ein Sophist, sondern ständig auf der Suche nach der Wahrheit. Die Idee der Wahrheit war für ihn das grundlegende regulative Prinzip. Dabei hat er die Welt der Freiheit, die Welt des demokratischen Rechtsstaates, zwar nicht als die beste aller denkbaren oder logisch möglichen politischen Welten bezeichnet, aber doch als die beste aller politischen Welten, von deren historischer Existenz wir Kenntnis haben. „In dieser Hinsicht bin ich also ein wilder Optimist".[11]

Der Weg zur Wahrheit war für ihn vor allem durch Diskussion gegeben. Wir wissen nichts endgültig, Wissen ist revidierbar und wir können und sollen voneinander lernen. Der Wahrheitsbezug war für ihn auch eine Frage der Sprache und der Verständlichkeit, der Überprüfbarkeit durch andere und der Nachvollziehbarkeit durch andere. Wissen durch Diskussion war für ihn wesentlich.

Drei Prinzipien gab er an, die erkenntnistheoretische und gleichzeitig ethische Prinzipien sind:

1. das Prinzip der Fehlbarkeit, das bedeutet: Vielleicht habe ich Unrecht, und vielleicht hast Du Recht. Aber wir können auch beide Unrecht haben.

2. das Prinzip der vernünftigen Diskussion: Wir wollen versuchen, möglichst unpersönlich unsere Gründe für und wider eine bestimmte kritisierbare Theorie abzuwägen.

3. das Prinzip der Annäherung an die Wahrheit. Durch eine sachliche Diskussion kommen wir fast immer der Wahrheit näher und wir kommen zu einem besseren Verständnis; auch dann, wenn wir nicht zu einer Einigung kommen.[12]

Ethische Prinzipien sind diese drei deshalb, weil sie Toleranz implizieren. Hier trifft sich Popper wieder mit Hayek. Denn die klassi-

---

[10] Die Verantwortung der Intellektuellen, in: Karl R. Popper, *Alle Menschen sind Philosophen*, München – Zürich: Piper Verlag, 2002, S. 202.

[11] Karl R. Popper, *Freiheit als Aufgabe*, ibidem, S. 241.

[12] Ibidem, S. 202.

sche Begründung der Toleranz, wie sie von Erasmus, Montaigne, John Milton, John Locke, Voltaire und von Lessing formuliert und von John Stewart Mill und Walter Bagehot neu formuliert wurde, beruht auf der Erkenntnis unserer Unwissenheit.[13]

Wenn man voneinander lernen kann und will, dann muss man in Augenhöhe miteinander reden und sich gegenseitig gleichberechtigt anerkennen. „Die potentielle Einheit und Gleichberechtigung aller Menschen sind eine Voraussetzung unserer Bereitschaft, rational zu diskutieren."[14]

Popper hat die alte Frage „Wer soll regieren?" durch eine neue ersetzt: „Wie kann man eine Regierung einigermaßen unter Druck halten, dass sie nicht allzu schlimme Dinge tut?" Seine Antwort dazu: „Indem man sie absetzen kann!" Es geht ihm vor allem um politische Einrichtungen, in und unter denen schlechte und böse Menschen möglichst wenig Schaden stiften können. Dafür ist die rechtsstaatliche Demokratie, der demokratische Rechtsstaat, die bisher zweckmäßigste Lösung. Ein Staat ist nach Popper politisch frei, wenn seine politischen Institutionen es seinen Bürgern praktisch möglich machen, ohne Blutvergießen, einen Regierungswechsel herbeizuführen, falls die Mehrheit einen solchen Regierungswechsel wünscht. „Wir sind frei, wenn wir unsere Herrscher ohne Blutvergießen loswerden können."[15]

Wie Hayek klärt uns Popper darüber auf, dass wir über die Zukunft wenig, ja nichts wissen. Der Lauf der Welt ist weder vorherbestimmt, noch zielgerichtet. Es ist auch nicht alles schon da gewesen. Die politische Weltgeschichte hat keinen verborgenen und auffindbaren Sinn und es gibt in ihr auch keine verborgenen und auffindbaren Entwicklungstendenzen.[16] Damit steht Popper nicht nur zu den Fortschrittstheorien des 19. Jhdts. – z.B. zu den Theorien von Comte, Hegel und Marx – im Gegensatz, sondern auch zur Untergangstheorie von Oswald Sprengler und zu den zyklischen Theorien von Plato, Vico und anderen. Popper warnt uns. Wir sollten uns davor hüten, unsere höchst pluralistische Geschichte als eine Schwarz-Weiß-

---

[13] Friedrich August von Hayek, *Die Verfassung der Freiheit*, op. cit., S. 39.
[14] Karl R. Popper, *Alle Menschen sind Philosophen*, op. cit., S. 203.
[15] Ibidem.
[16] Karl R. Popper, *Vom Sinn der Geschichte*, ibidem, S. 248.

Zeichnung oder als ein in nur wenigen Kontrastfarben koloriertes Gemälde anzusehen. „Und wir müssen uns noch mehr davor hüten, in sie Entwicklungsgesetze hineinzulesen, die zu Fortschrittsprognosen, zyklischen Prognosen, Untergangsprognosen oder zu irgend welchen ähnlichen historischen Voraussagen verwendet werden können."[17]

Was die Zukunft bringen wird, wissen wir nicht.

Aber wissen wir viel oder gar alles von der Geschichte? Der Kantianer Theodor Lessing hat die Geschichte als die „Sinngebung des Sinnlosen" bezeichnet. Das versteht Popper folgendermaßen:

> Wir können es versuchen, einen Sinn in die an sich unsinnige Geschichte hineinzulesen, z.B., indem wir an das Studium der Geschichte mit der Frage herantreten, wie es denn unseren Ideen und besonders unseren ethischen Ideen – wie der Idee der Freiheit und der Idee der Selbstbefreiung durch Wissen – im Laufe der Geschichte ergangen ist.[18]

So können wir der Geschichte einen Sinn geben, ohne *den* Sinn zu finden.

Als Aufklärungsphilosoph hat Popper die Grundüberzeugung, dass es so etwas wie eine absolute Wahrheit gibt. Durch Versuch und Irrtum können wir uns dem Wahrheitsbezug nähern, indem wir unsere Vorstellungen immer wieder kritisch überprüfen und der Diskussion und Widerlegung freigeben. Nicht Antworten und Lösungen, sondern Fragen und immer wieder Fragen sind das Wichtigste, auch in der Politik. Wie Hayek erinnert er uns, dass wir aus unseren Enttäuschungen und vor allem aus unseren Irrtümern lernen können. Um zu lernen, Fehler möglichst zu vermeiden, müssen wir aus unseren Fehlern lernen. Der Politologe Karl Deutsch sagte einmal: Wer Macht hat, braucht nicht zu lernen. Aber wie lange besteht diese Macht?

Eine Autorität, die keinen Irrtum begehen kann, und nicht mehr zu lernen braucht, gibt es nicht. Wir werden aber nur dann aus unseren Enttäuschungen, Irrtümern und Fehlern lernen, wenn wir solches auch bei anderen als Schritte zur Wahrheit sehen. Wir sollen uns von

---

[17] Ibidem, S. 252.
[18] Ibidem, S. 254.

unseren eigenen Ideen distanzieren können, statt uns mit unseren Ideen zu identifizieren. Dieses Lernen ist vielleicht der wichtigste Sinn der Verfassung der Freiheit.

6. Kelsen:
Absolute Gerechtigkeit ist eine Illusion

Für viele liegt der Sinn der individuellen Freiheit in der Steigerung der sozialen Gerechtigkeit. Hayek warnte uns vor allen, die das Wort soziale Gerechtigkeit in den Mund nehmen, ohne genau zu sagen, was sie darunter verstehen. Die Frage der Gerechtigkeit führt mich zu Hans Kelsen, dem dritten der drei Weisen. Er erlebte das Habsburger Imperium noch länger als Hayek und Popper. Sein ganzes Leben setzte er sich mit der Frage auseinander: Was ist Gerechtigkeit?

Er durchwanderte die geistige Erfahrung der Vergangenheit und stellte fest: Wenn wir daraus etwas lernen können, so das: Auf rationalem Wege kann eine absolut gültige Norm gerechten Verhaltens nicht gefunden werden. Absolute Gerechtigkeit ist ein irrationales Ideal, eine Illusion.[19]

Vom Standpunkt rationaler Erkenntnis gibt es nur menschliche Interessen und daher Interessenkonflikte. Für deren Lösung stehen nur zwei Wege zur Verfügung: Entweder das eine Interesse auf Kosten des anderen zu befriedigen, oder einen Kompromiss zwischen beiden herbeizuführen. Es ist nicht möglich, zu beweisen, dass nur die eine, nicht aber die andere Lösung gerecht ist. Wenn sozialer Friede als höchster Wert vorausgesetzt wird, mag die Kompromisslösung als gerecht erscheinen. Aber auch die Gerechtigkeit des Friedens ist nur eine relative, keine absolute Gerechtigkeit.

Kelsen meint aber, dass wir doch etwas aus dem geistigen Erfahrungsschatz der Vergangenheit lernen können. Nämlich, dass menschliche Vernunft beschränkt ist und daher nur relative Werte begreifen kann. Er vertritt eine relativistische Gerechtigkeitsphiloso-

---

[19] Hans Kelsen, *Was ist Gerechtigkeit?* Stuttgart: Reclam, 2000, S. 50.

phie. Sie sei weder amoralisch oder noch unmoralisch. Das moralische Prinzip, das einer relativistischen Wertlehre zugrunde liegt oder aus ihr gefolgert werden kann, ist das Prinzip der Toleranz. Das ist die Forderung, „die religiöse oder politische Anschauung anderer wohlwollend zu verstehen, auch wenn man sie nicht teilt, ja gerade weil man sie nicht teilt, und daher ihre friedlichen Äußerungen nicht zu verhindern."[20]

Wie Hayek und Popper kommt also auch Kelsen aufgrund unserer Unwissenheit zur Toleranz. Unsere Unwissenheit ist auch sein Argument für die politische Freiheit und die Demokratie. Demokratie ist ihrer innersten Natur nach Freiheit. Freiheit aber bedeutet Toleranz. Das moralische Prinzip seiner Lehre ist das Prinzip der Toleranz.

Aus Kelsens relativistischer Weltanschauung kann sich kein Recht auf absolute Toleranz ergeben. So ist es das Recht jeder Demokratie, Versuche, sie mit Gewalt zu beseitigen, mit Gewalt zu unterdrücken und durch geeignete Mittel zu verhindern. Grenzziehungen schließen Gefahren in sich. „Aber es ist das Wesen und die Ehre der Demokratie, diese Gefahr auf sich zu nehmen; und wenn Demokratie die Gefahr nicht bestehen kann, dann ist sie nicht wert, verteidigt zu werden."[21]

Das Buch des Agnostikers Hans Kelsen „Vom Wesen und Wert der Demokratie" endet mit dem Prozess Jesu, der in diese Welt gekommen ist, „um Zeugnis zu geben für die Wahrheit", worauf Pilatus fragt: „Was ist Wahrheit?" und „das Volk" entscheiden lässt. Das Ergebnis ist bekannt.

Die über drei Jahrzehnte später erschienene Schrift „Was ist Gerechtigkeit" beginnt mit dem Prozess Jesu: Er war wie Kelsen formuliert – geboren „Zeugnis zu geben für die Gerechtigkeit, jene Gerechtigkeit, die er im Königreich Gottes verwirklichen wollte. Und für diese Gerechtigkeit ist er auf dem Kreuze gestorben."[22]

So erhebe sich, hinter der Frage des Pilatus: Was ist Wahrheit?, aus dem Blute des Gekreuzigten eine andere, eine noch viel gewaltigere Frage, die ewige Frage der Menschheit: Was ist Gerechtigkeit?

---

[20] Ibidem, S. 50.
[21] Ibidem, S. 51.
[22] Ibidem, S. 9.

Und Kelsen, seinen Streifzug durch die geistige Erfahrung der Vergangenheit vorwegnehmend, stellt fest:

> Und doch ist diese Frage heute so unbeantwortet wie je. Vielleicht, weil es eine jener Fragen ist, für die die resignierte Weisheit gilt, dass der Mensch nie eine endgültige Antwort finden, sondern nur suchen kann, besser zu fragen.[23]

---

[23] Ibidem, S. 9.

Mercedes Torrevejano
Valencia

Über das Menschliche
als Struktur von Möglichkeiten

1. Einleitung

Diese Arbeitstage machen sich ausgehend von unserer Situation
als Europäer mutig das große Problem der Werte in einer Ära der
Globalisation zu eigen. Unsere Denktradition, das, was wir abendländische Philosophie nennen, ist zweifellos „mehr als Europa", und
mehr als das territorial oder geographisch verstandene „Abendland".
Es ist für uns ein Gemeinplatz zu denken, dass die ungeheure Dichte
dieser Worte – „Europa" oder unserer „abendländische Kultur" –
Hinweise enthält, die auf Griechenland oder Athen, auf Rom, Jerusa-
lem und die christianisierte römische Welt abzielen. Je mehr das
abendländische Denken von sich aus die wissenschaftliche Entwicklung und die demokratischen politischen Systeme gepriesen hat, um
so mehr wird dadurch die territoriale Dimension Europa irrelevant
oder relativiert. Denn solche Dynamik scheint „jeglicher Territoriali-
tät" gegenüber, gleichgültig zu werden.
  Wenn wir uns, ausgehend von den durch das Projekt der Europäischen Union eröffneten Perspektiven, auf unsere aktuelle europäische Lage beziehen, finden wir vor uns

- Ein Projekt, das in einem unmittelbar soziopolitischen Szenari-
  um entworfen wird.
- Einige Begriffe und Kategorien, die sich auf bestimmte Subjekte
  beziehen, die dies alles gliedern: es handelt sich um Programme,
  Vorträge, usw. zwischen *Staaten* oder *Nationen* oder *Ländern*, die

von der Plattform ihrer *politischen Strukturen* ausgehen, und die durch die demokratischen Regierungen dieser Länder aktiviert und verwaltet werden. Im Grenz- und Grundlagenbereich haben wir letztlich die entsprechende Kategorie der freien zu *Bürgern gewordenen* Individuen vor uns.

Im Hintergrund dieses Impulses macht sich die Präsenz von Kant bemerkbar, denn in dem Geflecht aus solchen Begriffen und Beziehungen erkennt man leicht seine Beiträge zu einer *Idee der allgemeinen Geschichte*, seine Idee vom *Weltbürgertum*, die Gestaltung der Idee von einem *ewigen Frieden usw.* Ich gestehe, dass mein Blick auf die kantische Präsenz bei dieser unserer heutigen Problematik mich immer wieder zu der Frage führt, wie man in der gegenwärtigen Situation, das menschliche Umfeld zum Ausdruck bringen kann, das Kant in seiner bekannten Schrift über die Geschichte im Auge hatte.

Ich denke an jene Ziele der menschlichen Geschichte, die sich in der *Moralisierung* vollziehen: wir sind *kultiviert* durch Kunst und Wissenschaft, sagt wörtlich Kant, und sogar „*zivilisiert* bis zum Überlästigen. Aber uns für schon *moralisiert* zu halten, daran fehlt noch sehr viel".[1] In dieser Beziehung scheint der Zustand nicht vorangekommen zu sein. Kant hält für „lauter Schein und schimmerndes Elend" jedes Gute, das nicht auf die moralisch-gute Gesinnung gepfropft ist; die Lösung des *impassse* aber wird von Kant auf die „Herausarbeitung des chaotischen Zustandes der Staatverhältnisse bezogen".

Der Plan der Natur in Bezug auf die Vernunft ist, so sagt uns Kant in erster Linie kein anderer als die Entwicklung aller in der Vernunft eingeschlossenen *Anlagen*. Die Vernunft ist das einzige Mittel, das der Mensch hat, um sich irgendeine Glückseligkeit oder Vollkommenheit seiner Natur zu besorgen. *Aber es ist noch etwas mehr:* die vollständige Entwicklung der Anlagen, aus der die Vernunft besteht, überschreitet die Grenzen jedes individuellen Lebens, ist *Angelegenheit des menschlichen Geschlechts*, d.h. sie wird immer in der unkündbaren Gemeinschaft derer vorangebracht, die sich auf dem Weg befinden, die mit dem durch die Vergangenheit Überkommenen rechnen, und die dieses alles aus der Perspektive der Zukunft sehen. *Aber es bleibt noch*

---

[1] Immanuel Kant, *Idee zu einer allgemeinen Geschichte in weltbürgerlicher Absicht* (1784), 7. Satz.

etwas: Die Entwicklung dieser Anlagen durchschreitet einen Antagonismus derselben. Das Bild, das Kant von der menschlichen Kreatur zeichnet, hat Züge einer biblischen Erzählung, eines prometheischen Mythos und einer frohen christlichen Botschaft.

In jedem Fall ist das Subjekt der Geschichte ein kompliziertes und seltsames Geschöpf, weniger durch die anfängliche Tatsache seines Schicksals (eine von der Natur emanzipierte, in die Welt geworfene Vernunft zu sein, ein reines Programm von Dispositionen), als durch die *ungesellige Gesselligkeit,* welche die Entwicklung aufrecht erhält. Und wirklich drückt auch der Streit der Individuen, jedes einzelnen gegen die anderen, die Konkurrenz vieler, damit jeder dasselbe für sich selbst erhält usw., Ungeselligkeit aus. Zugleich aber weckt solcher Streit die Entwicklung seiner Kräfte, die Anstrengung Ziele zu erreichen, tausendfache Anreize, welche die Fortschritte der Kultivierung und der Zivilisierung und schließlich auf eine langsame Weise das Ergebnis einer Moralisierung herbeiführen.

Ich glaube, dass die Herstellung von Verbindungen zwischen den Prinzipien der kantischen Moral als einer Moral oder Ethik der Pflicht und der Bestimmung der „Moralisierung" ein offenes Problem ist; denn die Moralisierung, die den kantischen Blick auf die Geschichte vollendet, ist definitiv auf die politische Handlung bezogen. Der achte Satz der *Idee* ist besonders wichtig: Man kann die Geschichte im Grossen und Ganzen als die Vollziehung des Plans der Natur ansehen, um eine vollkommene Staatsverfassung zustande zu bringen, als den einzigen Vorgang, in welchem die Natur alle ihre Anlagen in der Menschheit völlig entwickeln kann. Dieser logische Schluss –ich sage nicht Zirkelschluss – über die enge Relation zwischen dem Begriff der Menschen als Weltbürger im kosmopolitischen Sinne und der vollkommenen Staatsverfassung legt die Frage nahe, wo und wie, in ihrer realen Wirksamkeit die Quellen der Moralität jenseits des ideal regulierenden Charakters dieser logischen Beziehung zu finden sind.

Also ich frage mich, wie weit die Schlagworte im Laufe der zwei Jahrhunderte, die uns schon von Kant trennen, gepriesen oder breit getreten wurden oder gar problematisch geworden sind. Meine Frage ist durch die zwei Erwägungen, die Kant zu verstehen gibt, bedingt:

Die erste: jede Position, die gegenüber Werten und Normen im sozio-politischen Bereich und Kontext eingenommen wird, schließt letztlich eine anthropologische Position oder einen Kompromiss mit einer Anthropologie in einem möglichst totalen philosophischen Sinne ein.

Die zweite: Diese Erwägungen, die Kant anführt, haben mich veranlasst, meine Reflexion an einer Stelle zu unterbrechen, die es mir erlaubt, Ihnen einen spanischen Denker des 20. Jahrhunderts vorzustellen, dessen Denken völlig in der modernen Unruhe um die strukturelle Einheit des Menschen verwurzelt ist.

Es handelt sich um Xavier Zubiri.[2] Ich glaube, dass der spanische Denker die zentrale Rolle, die Kant bei der Aufklärung dieser Angelegenheit spielt, voll und ganz bemerkt hat. Zubiri durchläuft auf eine ziemlich analoge Weise das kantische System der Vermögen [facultades], wobei er die systematische Einheit überprüft und auf neue Weise heraushebt. Er überspringt aber auch das, was er die kantianische *Apotheosis der Vernunft* nennt, die ihm schließlich zu wenig einheitlich in seinem Menschenverständnis erscheint.

Das alles geschieht mit einem Streben, das in der Nachfolge Kants im Grunde *metaphysisch* sein will. Ich hoffe, dass man erkennen kann, dass die Metaphysik Zubiris auf der einen Seite im Gegensatz zur kantianischen die Versöhnung der Vernunft mit der Realität sucht; und die ganze kritische kantianische Spannung aufrechterhält, wobei er ihrem *innerweltlichen* Charakter einen *positiven* Sinn gibt. Aber irgendwie erweisen sich der Begriff der *Begrenzung* der Vernunft oder der der *Endlichkeit*, den die heideggerianische Interpretation so herausstellte, als ungeeignet, oder unbrauchbar als begriffliche Werk-

---

[2] Eine sehr anspruchvolle Biographie Zubiris ist gerade erschienen. Vid. Jordi Corominas, Joan Albert Vicens, *Xavier Zubiri. La soledad sonora*, Madrid: Taurus, 2006. Besonders interessant scheint mir das Buch in Beziehung auf die Absicht der Autoren zu sein, die spanische intellektuelle Situation während des 20. Jahrhunderts widerspiegeln zu wollen. Der Untertitel „La soledad sonora" ist ein vielfältiges, vielfärbiges richtig erkanntes Wort, das aus dem Gedichte *Cántico espiritual* (Strophe 14) von Juan de la Cruz stammt, das die eigene überlegende Einsamkeit in der Zubiri philosophiert hat, herauszustellen sucht; ein Wort das erst von Zubiri selbst bei seiner Beschreibung unseres heutigen Denk-Zustandes, in dem Alles bzw. Welt, Gott, Ich sozusagen verlorengegangen ist, ausgesprochen wurde.

Vid Infra *Minima* über Xavier Zubiri (1898–1983) in der Schlussanmerkung.

zeuge für ihre Theoretisierung. Was nicht bedeutet, dass sie in einer gewissen anthropologischen Perspektive, der des christlichen Horizonts, nicht legitime und klärende Konzepte sein können.

2. Auf der Suche nach dem Hauptproblem der Philosophie

Es ist schwierig, die philosophische Position Zubiris mit einer gewissen Genauigkeit zu bestimmen. Auf der einen Seite ruft Zubiri bei oberflächlichem Lesen ein Gefühl der totalen Vertrautheit hervor, die auf alte und geschliffene Terminologien die aus der großen lateinischen Scholastik stammen, und auf erkennbare Methoden zurückgreifen wie man an ein Problem herangeht. Nichts von dem was er aufwirft und zur Sprache bringt, ist völlig neu. Seine Verwurzelung in der Geschichte der Philosophie ist absolut und vollständig. In diesem Punkt stimmt Zubiri mit dem Eigensten der hermeneutischen Position überein, die von der heideggerianischen Kritik ausgeht. Jeder von Zubiri gebrauchte Begriff taucht als Resultat einer internen Abklärung eines bestimmten begrifflichen Kerns auf, den Zubiri ans Licht stellt, indem er beim Durchgang durch die Geschichte die Sprache untersucht. Daneben ist der Ort, auf den Zubiri philosophisch abzielt, immer ein *Topos*, in dem alle Regeln der Bestimmung und Stabilität der durchlaufenen *Topoi* zerstört werden, d.h. es wird immer ein neuer Ort erreicht, der keine bloße Alternative im Schoße irgendeiner angenommenen philosophischen Position sein möchte.

Im diesem Sinne zielt Zubiri auf aristotelische Weise auf das immer Problematische, auf das immer Gesuchte und immer überphysische (*metá*) ab. Er schließt dabei aus, dass das, worauf er abzielt, das *Sein* ist. Die Begegnung Zubiris mit Heidegger ist in diesem Punkt entscheidend. Der eigene, letzte, erschließende Ort der Philosophie oder Metaphysik *ist nicht eine Ontologie*. Man könnte sagen, dass Zubiri, indem er weiter gehen wollte als Husserl und Heidegger, die großen philosophischen Wortführer seiner Zeit, den reinen Ort der Philosophie durchzukämmen versucht. Das heisst für Zubiri den zu Grunde liegenden Raum, in dem der Mensch sich mit den Dingen *als*

Realität trifft, zu finden. Ein „Treffen" bei dem sich *alle* Wege der Erkenntnis und der Handlung öffnen. Dieses Treffen bestimmt den Menschen als das einzigartige Tier, das er ist. Tier des Logos? Da-Sein? Nein, sagt Zubiri: „Tier der Realität, oder Realitäts-Tier".

Das scheint sogar gleichgültig, nicht besonders relevant, oder auf jeden Fall sehr wenig originell zu sein, aber wir sind an einem „gefährlichen" Ort angekommen, und zwar an dem Punkt, an dem Zubiri allen Sinn der Philosophiegeschichte konzentriert: in dem Verständnis der *Intelligenz* [denken wir an das alte Wort *NOUS*], dessen, was die Menschlichkeit des Menschen ausmacht. Der Mensch als Tier *der Realität*. Das ist die einfache Beschreibung, von der Zubiri ausgeht, das ist die Angabe, welche das Verständnis des Menschen zusammenfasst. Davon ausgehend wird das moderne Problem der Rationalität durch Zubiri als die strikte Einheit einer *empfindenden Intelligenz* überprüft. Diese Angelegenheit markiert für Zubiri die „Wiedergewinnung" der Philosophie.

Der Mensch ist „Tier der Realität". Realität soll hier die Formalität (Formhaftigkeit) bedeuten, welche das menschliche Leben in Unterscheidung zum reinen tierischen Leben ausmacht, ohne dass dabei dieses menschliche Leben aufhört tierisch zu sein. Realität soll die Formalität benennen, die das menschliche *Empfinden*, in *intelligentes Empfinden* verwandelt. *Realität* ist die Formhaftigkeit des Intelligere, das den Menschen charakterisiert; ein menschliches Intelligere, das auf keine Weise seinen sinnlichen Charakter reduziert. Es geht also darum, eine Wunde zu schließen, die das Verständnis des Menschen spaltete. Die ganze Geschichte der Philosophie ist für Zubiri in diesem Problem der empfindenden Intelligenz zusammengefasst.

> Die Geschichte der Metaphysik – so lesen wir – führt uns zu diesem Problem von *der Wesensart der Intelligenz* als einem vorrangigen und radikalen Problem, welches, so scheint mir, das der empfindenden Intelligenz sein muss. ... In dieser empfindenden Intelligenz muss sich das philosophische Denken niederlassen, hier müssen die Kennzeichen der transzendentalen Ordnung auseinander gelebt werden und hier die Begriffe geprüft werden, welche das System der Metaphysik ausmachen.[3]

---

[3] Vid. Xavier Zubiri, *Los problemas de la Metafísica Occidental*, Madrid: Alianza Editorial, 1994, S. 345.

3. Zubiri, oder ein Modell einer unitarischen Anthropologie

Die These von Zubiri über die Intelligenz lässt erahnen, dass das metaphysische Verständnis der Philosophie, das Zubiri verteidigt, eine deutliche Befreiung einer neuen Anthropologie einschließen muss. Es handelt sich um eine Anthropologie auf der Spur der im Menschen zentrierten Philosophien, aber das ist so seit Zubiri mit voller Entschiedenheit [mit ganzer Radikalität] die fundamentalistische Position der modernen Philosophie verworfen hat, d.h. das reduzierte und dogmatische Verständnis des Menschen als eines Subjekts//Bewusstseins und als Freiheit//Selbstbestimmung.

Solche Konzeptionen der rationalen Besonderheit sind, wie es Taylor so gut beschrieben hat, eine Art und Weise, die Vernunft als „bindungslose Vernunft" zu verstehen. Zubiri spricht auf sehr intuitive Weise von „der Vernunft, die über sie selbst errichtet ist." D.h. eine sozusagen „unsubstantivierte" oder schliesslich un-begründete, oder ganz a-topica (ohne Topos) Vernunft, die unfähig ist,-so sagt Zubiri, sich zu erhalten. Deswegen wählt Zubiri, um zu uns Menschen zu sprechen, und indem er die verschiedenen Philosophien des Bewusstseins zu überspringen beabsichtigt, einen Weg, der am Anfang physisch und biologisch ist, in einer „Kontinuität" mit seinen philosophischen Überlegungen, die uns die aktuelle Wissenschaft und die Evolutions-theorie bestätigen. Zubiri „naturalisiert" und „biologisiert", um „anthropologisieren" zu können, ohne sich in einer Anthropologie des absoluten Heterogenen als Prinzip einzurichten.

Denn analog zu den „Neuigkeiten" bzw. neuen ontologischen Verbindlichkeiten, welche die Biologie der Physik zurückgibt, wird die Anthropologie „Neuigkeiten" bzw. neue ontologische Verbindlichkeiten – der Biologie zurückgeben. Methodologisch aber wird der Weg beschritten, den mit der Hilfe der Formen der Erklärung Schritt für Schritt verwurzelt in der *physis* die Intelligenz erleuchtet hat; so vorläufig das auch immer sein mag und so offen das auch immer für neue Versicherungen und Klärungen sein möge.[4]

---

[4] Der Sprung, den die Menschwerdung bedeutet, ist wirklich spektakulär. Die „Ausstattung" (sic venia verbo) der physischen und biologischen Realität mit Intelli-

Wenn wir von der zubirianischen These der empfindenden Intelligenz Kenntnis genommen haben, und einen Schritt weiter gehen, stellen wir etwas fest, nämlich dass Zubiri damit die bewußtseinsgemäße und selbstgegenwärtige Interpretation des Ichs als Subjekt verlassen hat. Zubiri verwirft den Begriff von Bewusstsein=Substantivität als etwas Sinnloses und beschränkt ihn darauf, Erkennungszeichen für Charaktere einiger Handlungen der Intelligenz zu sein. Gleicherweise verwirft er das Verständnis der Freiheit im leeren Raum als Unsinn, wenn auch natürlich nicht einen gewissen einzigartigen, „abgelösten", d.h. relativ-absoluten Charakter dieser Art von Realität, die der Mensch ist. Eine Art von Realität, die sich in einigen Handlungen bestimmt, die diese Realität als Selbstzugehörigkeit gestalten. Die Skilla der über sich selbsterrichteten Subjektivität zu entkommen, heißt einfach die logische Leere der Rationalität zu entlarven, die nicht mehr in der *Realität* verwurzelt ist.

Vermöge dieser Berichtigung und erneuerten Interpretation des Problems der Intelligenz d.h. des Menschen als des Tiers der Realität, ergibt sich also, dass diese Theorie Zubiris eine entscheidende Bedeutung hat, wenn es darum geht, den Sinn des eigenen menschlichen sich-beziehen auf die Sachen festzulegen.

Der Mensch, der seine vitale Situation als Realität versteht, wird so von Zubiri als jene schon nicht mehr rein tierische Formalität des Lebens gesehen, zu dem in seinem Leben sein eigenes Sein auf dem Wege ist. Ein Schritt weiter und Zubiri vertieft sich in das Problem des Sinnes, indem er uns vom menschlichen Leben als dem System der Möglichkeiten oder der *Aneignung* der Möglichkeiten spricht. *Dies ist die Einzigartigkeit, die a radice von ihrer Naturhaftigkeit her selbst den Menschen moralisch macht.*

Die menschliche Substanzhaftigkeit [Substantivität][5] ist moralische Realität, denn außer den Möglichkeiten, die natürlich aus den

---

genz und Willen ist etwas *mehr* als die reine Erlangung von „neueren systematischen Eigenschaften", d.h. von Eigenschaften, die in Funktion einer Verkomplizierung der Prozesse der *physis* verstanden werden können. Es handelt sich aber um einen Prozess, der eine authentische Erhöhung ausmacht. Aber für Zubiri ist es die Materie, die von sich aus durch Erhöhung den intelligenten Charakter ihres Empfindens erreicht.

[5] Zubiri hat die aristotelische Theorie des Substanz-Subjekt (hypokeímenon) heftig kritisiert und erklärt die Substantivität der Sachen als systematische Struktur von

Substanzen hervorkommen, welche die Substantivität bilden, hat sie andere Möglichkeiten, deren Wurzel nicht das plötzliche Hervorkommen sondern eine „Aneignung" ist, die in einer Art von Selbstbemächtigung ausgeführt wird, die ihr „physisch" zusteht. Ich lasse die Begriffe erscheinen, welche die Analyse Zubiris in der neuen Perspektive ins Spiel bringt.

Zubiri geht hier mit außergewöhnlicher Hartnäckigkeit vor, um den Weg zu öffnen, der diese moralische Dimension des Menschen in Angriff nimmt und zwar auf die in den menschlichen Handlungen begriffliche Dimension der „Rechtfertigung". Er entnimmt diesen Begriff dem ersten Verständnis der Daten, welche die Handlung des intelligenten Tieres anbietet. Das ist das Tier, das die unumgehbare Aufgabe hat, seine Handlungen gegenüber den Anreizen (Stimuli) zu rechtfertigen, indem es die Sachen als Realität versteht. Das menschliche Tier kümmert sich um die „Realität", denn die Sachen stehen ihm gegenüber in einer Distanz und sind ihm nicht mehr bloss Stimuli. Das bedeutet, dass seine Handlungen nicht einfach wie bei den blossen Tieren reine Anpassung sind, sondern dass seine Handlungen Einstellungen sind. Das will heißen, dass sein Tun sich von der blossen Anpassung „distanziert", in der es als reines tierisches Leben sofort ausruhen würde, d.h. es hängt von einer Möglichkeit ab, die den Typus der Anpassung SOZUSAGEN „konstituieren" muss. Das menschliche Leben ist Einstellung, es hat die richtige Anpassung auszuwählen, also muss es *facere justum*, die Anpassung vollbringen, und rechtfertigen. Die Funktion intelligenten Empfindens oder empfindender Intelligenz schließt damit als ihr anderes, neues Gesicht die Dimension der *Aneignung von Möglichkeiten* ein. Darin liegt begründet, dass man dieses menschliche Leben als ein Wollen oder als Wille verstehen muss. Aber es ist jetzt ein Wollen oder ein Wille, den man abhängig oder untrennbar von der Tendenz erklären muss. In dieser Struktur ist die moralische Dimension verwurzelt oder sie besteht in ihr.

Zubiri versucht die Bindung wieder zu gewinnen, die das intelligente Tier mit der moralischen Forderung verbindet, indem er die

---

Noten, wobei die Idee der Respektivität des Realen, die der Noten, und in allgemeinen die der Sachen bedeutet. Dafür hat er lieber das Wort Substantivität (gegen Substanz = Substanzialität) gewählt.

Idee einer Freiheit korrigiert, die sich als *reines Wollen* ohne Verwurzelung in der *Wunschdimension* des Lebens und ohne ein anderes Prinzip der Verbindung mit der Moral als die der Pflicht und der Justiz verstanden hat. Eine solche Moral abstrakt verstanden, die der Pflicht und der Justiz, die in einem sicheren Bereich oberhalb des Lebens angesiedelt ist, hat als Reaktion die Vergeltung des auch reinen Triebes und der Leidenschaft hervorgerufen, die unfähig sind, sich in Verbindung mit einem Wollen zu erkennen.

Die These „der Mensch als Tier der Realität" wird im Kern durch die These „empfindende Intelligenz" erläutert. Aber in Wirklichkeit integriert die anthropologische Analyse zwei andere wesentliche Aspekte: den eines Willens als Prinzip von Handlungen, zugleich Aneignung von Möglichkeiten, wie wir gerade bemerkt haben und auch die Ebene des Gefühls. Das Gefühl als die andere – dritte – Seite: als der Boden, auf dem die Erkenntnis und die Handlung erscheinen. Hier vervollständigt Zubiri seine Theorie von der Verwurzelung des Menschen in der Realität. Er spricht zu uns zugleich sowohl von der „empfindenden Intelligenz" als auch vom „Wollen oder treibendem Willen" so wie auch vom „betreffenden Gefühl" als den drei Dimensionen, die als das Tun des Menschen in der Realität verwurzelt sind und die Realität ausmachen.

Das bloss tierische Leben hat Tendenzen aber es *will* sie nicht, es hat Affektionen aber es *sentimentalisiert* das Affektiertsein nicht, wenn auch unsere Sprache bei den Erklärungen in Bezug auf das tierische Leben zu Anthropomorphismen neigt. Also, die klassische Theorie der Vermögen, die Kant mit den drei Kritiken sanktioniert hat, stellt eine Komplexität bei der Auslegung dar, die Zubiri nicht in Frage stellt. Eine andere Sache ist die Distanz seiner Auslegungen in Bezug auf die kantischen. Damit werden wir uns nicht beschäftigen; aber nach dem Gesagten ist es klar, dass sich uns ein Feld von Contrapositionen anbietet.

Ich werde erneut mein Augenmerk auf das menschliche „neigende Wollen" oder auf die menschliche „wollende Neigung" richten. Wir befinden uns erneut an der Nahtstelle einer Spaltung. In diesem Zusammenhang stellt Zubiri auf entschiedene Weise den Sinn der Selbstbesitzergreifung heraus, den das menschliche Leben in der

Realität einnimmt, dort wo der Wille sagt „ich will" „ich ergreife von
mir Besitz [ich bemächtige mich meiner] in der Besitzergreifung, die
ich von der Realität mache." Das menschliche Leben entfaltet sich in
Aktivitäten oder ist aktiv nicht *allein, weil es real ist,* sondern *um reales
menschliches Leben zu sein.*
Auf den Spuren des Aristoteles vollendet Zubiri eine Verstehens-
arbeit, die der einzigartigen Auszeichnung des Menschlichen – etwas
Unverzichtbares nach der christlichen Erfahrung meinem Verständnis
nach – ohne das Gute am Rande der Güte anzusiedeln, die nur
menschliche Güte sein kann, die durch das Leben erhalten wird. Und
das ist, was man auf der Höhe der philosophischen Forschung *gut*
nennt: *die Realität* als Quelle der radikalen Aneignung, die ich von mir
mache bei meinem Auswählen. Die Realität ist in diesem präzisen
Sinne die Quelle der Möglichkeiten für den Menschen. Darum ist der
Mensch außer der physischen Realität auch moralische Realität gerade durch diese Art und Weise in dem seine Eigenschaften ihn betreffen: als Aneignung der Möglichkeiten. Hören wir Zubiri zu, wenn er
uns einladet, die menschliche Realität als eine moralische Struktur zu
betrachten:

> Gewöhnen wir uns daran, das Problem der Moral nicht mit dem Problem
> des Guten, auch nicht mit dem Problem der Pflicht [Sollen] zu identifi-
> zieren. Das Gute ist ein moralisches Gut und die Pflicht [das Sollen] ist
> eine moralische Pflicht [Sollen], welche die moralische Verfassung des
> Menschen *voraussetzen.*[6]

Wenn Zubiri uns sagt, dass der Mensch moralisch ist, insoweit er
die Notwendigkeit hat, sich die Möglichkeiten anzueignen, indem er
einige auswählt und andere verwirft, richtet er den Blick auf das, was
aus dem Menschen nicht ein Subjekt über und außerhalb des Natürlichen macht sondern auf Sein, in dem das Moralische durch das Natürliche gefördert wird. Die Aneignung (das Ganze dessen, was auf
dem Wege der Aneignung erworben wird) konstituiert die moralische Form oder die moralische Figur des Menschen. Darum ist es
keine Metapher, wenn wir sagen, dass wir (unabhängig von jeglichem

---

6 Xavier Zubiri, *Sobre el Hombre*, Madrid: Alianza Editorial, 1986, S. 143.

Urteil über ein moralisches-unmoralisches Verhalten) in guter moralischer Form oder demoralisiert sind.

Das ist so sehr so, dass so wie der Mensch nicht nicht-bevorzugen
kann und nicht nicht-wollen kann, so kann er auch nicht die moralische Dimension seines Seins nicht ins Spiel bringen, *gerade wenn er
biologisch überleben will d.h. um biologisch überleben zu können*. Denken
wir an diese entscheidende Figur, die wir *Intimität* nennen. Könnten
wir sie betreffend es wagen, den moralischen und den psychophysischen Aspekt übereinander zu legen? Müssten wir nicht besser sagen,
dass der psychisch-physische Aspekt den moralischen Aspekt zer-
trümmert – so wie wir es zu verstehen pflegen –, und der moralische
Aspekt auf den psycho-physischen zurückfällt, und zwar in dem selben Moment, in dem er ihn gestaltet?

Am Beginn, als ich mit meinem Hinweis auf Zubiri begann, be-
merkte ich, dass ich mich der zubirianischen These von der empfindenden Intelligenz annäherte, indem Zubiri sie als eine Berichtigung,
als einen „metaphysischen Schlussstein, einer Interpretation von Vernunft als 'verbindungsloser Vernunft' oder 'über sich selbst errichtete
Vernunft' darstellte. Was Zubiri hier meiner Meinung nach in Gang
bringen will, ist das, was ich die 'Trennung'" der Begriffe der Freiheit
und des Ichs nenne. Denn in Wirklichkeit sind wir allein wirklich ein
Ich und ein Subjekt, allein in der Öffnung zur Realität, und im Ge-
wendetsein auf die Realität, in der die Anderen sich auch befinden.

4. Die menschliche Realität und die Anderen

Die Anderen als das Menschliche sind in unserer Realität, bevor
unsere moralische Dimension ins Spiel kommt. Was heissen soll, dass
unsere moralische Dimension eine soziale Dimension *a radice* ein-
schliesst. Zubiri lädt uns ein, die soziale Realität mehr in ihrer physischen oder real-transzendentalen Dimension zu denken, als als einen
Vertrags-Willen oder ein intentionales Erlebnis. Mit der Langsamkeit
der Analyse, die Zubiri charakterisiert, lädt er uns ein, dieses Problem
des Sozialen von der Wurzel her zu denken. Die Realität, die wir sind
und die uns hat, wir sind sie, und sie hat uns in Verbindung mit dem

menschlichen Haben; etwas, das man *Mentalität* nennen könnte, wobei die Mentalität die Art und Weise des Denkens und Fühlens ist, die jeder Einzelne als ein gerade als Modus durch die Anderen Betroffener hat.[7]

„Mentalität" muss man im nachhinein mit mehr Eigengewicht als „Lebensform" verstehen. Dieses menschliche Haben, diese Mentalität ist auch *Übertragung* = *Tradition*, weil sie einen menschlichen Inhalt hat, der ausgedrückt und veräußert wird. Über dieser Struktur, die das menschliche Haben konsolidiert, eröffnet sich die Vielfalt ihrer Ausdrücke. Zubiri versteht das, *weil* wir eine Vielfalt von Personen in Gemeinschaft sind, und uns auch sozial auf vielfache Weise organisieren; endlich gesagt, *weil* wir Personen sind, *können wir untereinander kommunizieren.* Zwei Dimensionen, die niemals getrennt sind, wenn auch *de facto* eine über die andere die Übermacht haben kann. Aber sie werden begrifflich auf verschiedene Weise gemessen. Sie helfen uns, den Sinn der Fragen, die wir sozial nennen, und den Sinn der Konflikte, die wir in ihnen vorfinden, zu platzieren. „Familie", „Freundschaft", „Liebe" um einige klare Beispiele zu geben, verlangen ihren eigenen Ort in der bestimmten Funktionalität der Kommunion, die unsere soziale Realität trägt.

Zubiri spricht manchmal von der „Gesellschaft" als dem Bereich des Unpersönlichen und von der „Kommunion" als dem Bereich des Persönlichen. Auf jeden Fall handelt es sich um Unterscheidungen, welche die Komplexität des Menschlichen in ihrer Integrität erhellen wollen.

Sowieso hat das Zusammenleben auf allen Ebenen einen strikt psychophysischen Charakter. Die Gesellschaft existiert, insofern der Mensch das Tier der Realitäten ist. Die Bindung [Verbundenheit] taucht auf als eine Einheit, um biologisch zu überleben und lässt den Menschen auf der einen Seite mit einem gemeinsamen Haben und auf der anderen Seite lässt sie ihn in einer kollektiven und persönlichen

---

[7] Gerade beim Bedenken von „Mentalität" als einen erläuterndem Begriffe verwirft Zubiri die heideggerische Analyse des *Daseins* in Bezug auf das *Man* – dem „es", Exponenten der nicht authentischen Existenz, wie wir wissen. Zubiri stärkt hier a radice die soziale Dimension in systematischer Verbindung mit der menschlichen Geschichtlichkeit.

Funktionalität, die den Menschen dazu führt, jeder Einzelne zu sein, der mehr oder weniger in den anderen aufgeht.[8]

In jedem Menschen ist die Gesellschaft eine wesensmäßige definitive Eigenart des Systems der Möglichkeiten, die er von den Anderen erhält. In gewissem Sinne lebt der Mensch in der Andersheit, weil er die Möglichkeiten von den Anderen erhält. Aber in einem anderen Sinn sind ihm diese Möglichkeiten positiv ermöglichende. Diese Möglichkeiten sind in *Lebensformen* festgelegt. Ohne diese wäre jeder Mensch immer am Anfang und das menschliche Leben wäre nie aus dem primitivsten Stadium herausgekommen. Es werden auch nicht alle Möglichkeiten angeeignet, viele bleiben unbefragt. Das System derselben ist fähig, unbestimmt neue Möglichkeiten freizusetzen und andere beiseite zu lassen. So ermöglicht das soziale System das Leben jedes Einzelnen.

> Es sind also die Anderen, insofern sie mich zwingen mir in positivem oder negativem Sinne das System der Möglichkeiten anzueignen, die jeden Einzelnen erlauben oder zwingen jeder Einzelne, der Jeweilige zu sein.[9]

Zubiri untersucht sorgsam den Sinn dieses „Zwingens", wobei er die Frage des „auferlegenden" Charakters des Sozialen angeht. Die Kraft, mit der das Soziale auferlegend ist, wurzelt nach der zubirischen Analyse darin, dass das System der Möglichkeiten unseres Lebens in dieser ausdrücklich sozialen Perspektive ein System der Macht ist. Denn jeder Einzelne verwandelt beim Sich-Aneignen Möglichkeiten für sich und für den Anderen in Macht. Bei jedem Einzelnen bedeuten die Möglichkeiten, die sie ergreifen mehr Macht in der sozialen Struktur als Kraft. Die Möglichkeiten, die ich akzeptiere, sind Macht in mir und haben Macht in dem Leben des Anderen. Deshalb sind die Anderen in meinem Leben nicht als einfaches System von Möglichkeiten sondern als System von Mächten anwesend. Ich kann die Macht nicht akzeptieren, wodurch die Anderen sich in mein Le-

---

[8] Xavier Zubiri, *Sobre el Hombre*, op. cit., S. 271. In diesem Text verdichtet sich, was wir gesagt haben. Stellen Sie den technischen, begrifflichen Charakter in Rechnung, den in der zubirianischen Analyse ein großer Teil der benutzten Termini besitzt. „Bindung", „in gemein haben" – was an anderen Stellen ohne weiteres „das menschliche Haben", „kollektive Funktionalität" „personale Funktionalität" heissen kann.

[9] Ibidem, S. 311.

ben einschalten. In jedem Fall aber ist meine Beziehung dazu keine Beziehung zu einer bloßen Möglichkeit.

Der *Begriff der Macht* erhält auf diese Weise einen „metaphysischen" Ort, insofern er den radikalsten Sinn ausmacht, gemäß dem der Mensch sich in sozialer Gebundenheit [Vinkulation] befindet. Es gibt kein anderes Mittel als gegenüber dieser Macht Position zu beziehen. Wir sind, ob wir wollen oder nicht, Macht für – und miteinander.

Dieser *sui generis* Charakter der *Macht* ist in der Geschichte der Philosophie am stärksten seit Descartes niedergehalten worden. Mit der Idee, dass die Gewalt [potencia] nichts weiter ist, als ein System von Eigenschaften, welche die Dinge haben, setzte sich die Philosophie und die ganze Artikulation des menschlichen Lebens, mit zwei Dimensionen auseinander, mit den Eigenschaften, die der Mensch *hat*, auf der einen Seite; andererseits mit dem, was der Mensch mit diesen Eigenschaften *machen will*. Womit man eine Spaltung auf zwei Ebenen theorisiert hat, deren Kommunikation miteinander ausgeschlossen ist, der physischen und der intentionalen Ebene. Auf diese Weise löst man auf, was die eigene Besonderheit ausmacht, die physisch ist, indem sie das Intentionelle einschließt.[10]

Angesichts einer Ermöglichung eines *Ethos* schließlich, der den Werten eine Verwurzelung bietet, welche die Formen des Lebens in ihrer Dynamik und Geschichtlichkeit rühmen, sagen uns diese Analysen, dass die Tatsache der Gemeinschaft und der Ausstrahlung unseres Lebens den moralischen Alternativen, die sie ausdrücken können, vorhergehen und sie erhalten. Zum Beispiel: Entweder „für die Anderen leben" – „für sich selbst leben", oder die Moral des Egoismus hat allein Sinn als mehr oder weniger ausgezeichnete Möglichkeit in einer unabweislichen Gemeinschaft, in der unsere Realität ist und wird.

Die Strukturen entwerfen uns in den zubirischen Analysen einen Begriff vom Menschen als einem persönlichen, absoluten Zweck, rückgebunden an die Letztheit der Realität, gebunden an sein eigenes Glück [seine eigene Glückseligkeit] und verpflichtet – wozu? *Zu allen Vervollkommnungen, die eine bestimmte Idee des Menschen historisch innerhalb der eigenen menschlichen Realität hat keimen lassen.* Das stimmt mit dem überein, dass der Mensch von sich selbst her, aus einer Form, einer kleineren oder größeren Vollkommenheit gegenüber geöffnet

---

10 Ibidem, S. 318. Die Kursivschrift wurde nicht von Zubiri angewandt.

ist. [Wobei der Mensch trotzdem nicht weiß, was diese Vollkommenheit ist, worin sie besteht.]

Diese moralische „Unsicherheit" ist der Exponent dafür, dass die
Möglichkeiten des Menschen, die Realität seiner Vollkommenheit
etwas konstitutiv Unbestimmbares ist. Aber jeder Mensch muss gerade
durch seine Eigenart als offene Realität durch ein Erwägen die Art der
Vollkommenheit bestimmen, die ihm innerhalb der Gesellschaft und
der Geschichte erreichbar ist. Auch wenn die Moral in ihrer Gestalt
sich ändert, so ändert sich doch nicht der moralische Aspekt dieser
Moral. Denn das letzte Wort hat niemals das System der Konzepte,
die der Mensch gebraucht (wechselnd und differenziert nach Denk-
weisen und Lebensformen), sondern die Realität selbst. In jedem Fall
geben allein das soziale Zusammenleben und die individuelle Situation der Moral ihren letzten konkreten Charakter.

Ich muss schließen. So sehe ich das Denken Zubiris. Indem er lang-
sam alles Gehen und Kommen sichtet, das unsere kulturelle und historische Erfahrung uns beschert hat, legt Zubiri uns eine Struktur vor, die
das Verstehen der Moral realisiert; die Moral verstanden als die
selbstangeeignete Realisierung des Lebens selbst. Das ist der Raum der
Freiheit und der Personwerdung. Die Freiheit ist nicht in der Leere
errichtet und auf den Tod ausgerichtet, wie es bei Heidegger lauten
würde, sondern sie ist der Augenblick meiner Selbstaneignung in der
Realität, die mir Möglichkeiten eröffnet. Der Mensch muss den Sinn für
die Realität zurückgewinnen, um sich wieder einzurichten im Guten
und im Genuss. Dass das geliebte Sein das gewesene Sein sei. Wenn
man das erreicht, dann betritt man wirklich [real] den Boden, den man
betritt; man ist wirklich glücklich. Ein letztes Wort von Zubiri: „Einen
Menschen erkennt man daran, was er an den Festtagen tut."[11]

5. Schlussanmerkung

Xavier Zubiri (1898–1983) gehört zusammen mit Unamuno und
Ortega zu den Referenten des spanischen Denkens des XX. Jahrhunderts. Zubiri war der Jünger, ein wahrer Schüler Ortegas, ein ausge-

---

[11] Xavier Zubiri, *Sobre el sentimiento y la Volición*, Madrid: Alianza Editorial, 1992, S. 81.

zeichneter und unabhängiger Schüler, der dem Einfluss Ortegas seine eigene grosse Ausbildung in einer katholisch-scholastischen Tradition hinzufügte, da er geistliche Studien machte und sein Staatsexamen in Louvain absolvierte. 1926, mit nur 28 Jahren, erhält er den Lehrstuhl für Geschichte der Philosophie der Universidad Central, heute Universidad Complutense. Er zieht in 1928 nach Deutschland, nach Freiburg, wo er seine persönlichen Gedanken über Husserl und Heidegger weiterführen kann.

Nach zwei Jahren in Freiburg zieht er nach Berlin, wo er im Harnack-Hause wohnte, einer Professorenresidenz der Kaiser Wilhelm Gesellschaft. Zubiri, der Physikstudien gemacht hatte, lernt in Berlin Schrödinger und Planck kennen und besucht Einstein in seiner Wohnung, wo sie Gespräche an der Tafel führen. In Berlin lernt er N. Hartmann kennen, dessen gewisse Eingebildetheit ihm missfiel.

1932 ist er wieder in Spanien, bis 1935. In diesen Jahren war er eine der Persönlichkeiten die zum intellektuellen Glanz des republikanischen Spaniens beigetragen haben. 1935 verbringt er ein Jahr in Rom, wo ihm die Säkularisierung, also die Zurückversetzung in den Laienstand gewährt wurde. Seine persönliche Laufbahn macht aus ihm eine Person die in den zwei Fraktionen des damaligen Spaniens schwer einzugliedern war. Er entscheidet sich für das Exil in Paris, wo er bis 1940 lebt. Wieder an der spanischen Universität nach dem Bürgerkrieg – jetzt in Barcelona –, muss er ein Klima von Misstrauen und Unzufriedenheit ertragen, inmitten der ideologischen Kontrolle dieser Jahre, bis er 1942 auf seinen Lehrstuhl verzichtet. Zubiri zieht endgültig nach Madrid um, wo er sich bis zu seinem Tode der stillen Arbeit widmet. Regelmässige Privatkurse (ein Monat mehr oder weniger pro Jahr) geben der Madrider Gesellschaft während der langen Jahre der Diktatur die Gelegenheit, die Grundzüge seiner Arbeit erfahren zu können.

Hauptwerke:

Naturaleza, Historia, Dios (1944), eine Reihe von Arbeiten zwischen 1933 und 1944
Sobre la esencia (1962)
Cinco lecciones de Filosofía (1963)
Inteligencia sentiente (1980), 2. Aufl.: *Inteligencia sentiente/Inteligencia y realidad* (1991)

Inteligencia y Logos (1982)
Inteligencia y Razón (1983)
El hombre y Dios (1984) Opus posthum von ihm selbst vorbereitet

Eine andere lange Reihe von Werken (10 Titel) wird aufgrund seiner zahlreichen Vorlesungen weiter herausgegeben. Gleichzeitig die ersten Schriften, die nicht in *Naturaleza, Historia Dios* ausgewählt worden waren. Alles spricht von einer systematischen Behandlung der Probleme der Philosophie. Vid. z.B.:

Sobre el Hombre, Madrid: Alianza Editorial, 1986
Estructura dinámica de la realidad, Madrid: Alianza Editorial, 1989
Sobre el sentimiento y la volición, Madrid: Alianza Editorial, 1992
Los problemas fundamentales de la metafísica occidental, Madrid: Alianza Editorial 1994
Espacio, Tiempo. Materia, Madrid: Alianza Editorial, 1996
El problema filosófico de la historia de las religiones, Madrid: Alianza Editorial, 1993
El problema teologal del hombre: Cristianismo, Madrid: Alianza Editorial, 1997

Part II
The European Community
as a Community of Values

Peter Kampits
Wien

Europe Is More
than the European Union

I am sure that you do neither expect me to sing praises concerning the development of the European union, nor to add only positive lines to the present situation of education all over Europe, especially at the university level. There are enough politicians and officials travelling around like itinerant preachers and praising the benefits of the common "house Europe", especially after the so-called *Osterweiterung*.

On the other hand there is however a remarkable rise of scepticism and even anxiety concerning the aims and structures of the European Union. What has been welcomed enthusiastically, especially after the decline of the communist system, what has been celebrated as the opening of the road to freedom, welfare and better living conditions turned into disappointment and dissatisfaction. Of course you can enumerate many reasons for this: the horizon of expectation was too high, especially in the former communist countries, and time is too short to judge seriously the advantages and disadvantages. The long-term communist regimes have left traces that cannot be extinguished in a short period. But even among the peoples of "Western European" countries there seems to be no longer a euphoric or enthusiastic agreement regarding the development of the Union.

I want to show with the title of my contribution – "Europe is more than the European Union" – that many of the original tasks included in the idea of a common Europe have been – in the meantime – perhaps not extinguished, but at least minimized or marginalized.

I will try to show this in three steps:
1. The idea (project) of a unified Europe
2. European identity and values
3. The situation of education, especially at the university level

1. The Idea (Project) of a Unified Europe

Concerning the Idea of Europe it would be tempting to begin with the old myth deriving from the Greeks, where Zeus seduced the princess *Europa* living in Asia and brought her to the isle of Crete – obviously by force and by transforming himself into a bull. So violence and crime, force and fraud have been accompanying Europe from its very birth and have been lasting during its entire history. Or as Edgar Morin has put it:

> Europe means on the one hand law, but on the other violence, it means democracy but also suppression, spirituality but also material interests, moderation but also excessiveness; what is more, if it stands for reason, it also stands for myth. Europe is not an exact notion, it is something, born from chaos, it has no fixed borders, it has experienced changes, displacements and ruptures.[1]

If we think of the history of Europe only during the last century, we can only underline this statement: Of course Europe has been the origin of the human rights, of humanism, tolerance, proclamations of freedom, enlightenment, democracy, but it is also the origin of repressions, barbarism, totalitarianism, colonialism and imperialism. Fascism, National Socialism and Communism were not imported to Europe, but were rather European inventions. The history of Europe is a bloody history, full of wars, murder, fraud and religious intolerance. Until very recently, Europe's history never was a history of alliances, of a finding together, but more a story of separation, segregation and losing each other.

It could give us something to reflect on, if we return to the myth and consider the sequel of the story: After she has born three children,

---

[1] Edgar Morin, *Europa Denken*, Frankfurt am Main: Campus Verlag, 1992.

Europa disappears and cannot to be found by her father and her brothers.

Can we take this as a metaphor for the project Europe, especially for the notion of Europe used by the European Community?

Geographically speaking, the borders of Europe are difficult to draw – it is spread from the Atlantic to the Ural Mountains in Russia. But can it be reduced to a geographical notion? Historically speaking, things are even worse. It is neither time nor place for giving even a rough outline of the history of Europe, but we can state that, historically, the roots of Europe are threefoldoues: the Greek-Hellenistic tradition, the Roman-Latin culture and the Judeo-Christian religion. Of course these roots were never in a harmonious interplay, but more in a tension, in a sort of conflict. And we have to consider that these roots were coming from the outside of the continent or at least from its margins. Christianity was introduced from Asia, the Greek Logos and the Roman political and law principles were not coming from the heart of Europe, and over centuries they created a kind of transformation which shaped Europe into a manifold and complex structure.

Through the centuries we can observe many remarkable events that formed a kind of historical constellation: the separation of Roman-Latin and Greek-Byzantine world, starting in the time of the decline of the Roman Empire; the confrontation of orient and occident, including the repulse of the Islamic expansion and then, in the 16th century, the beginning of colonization. But within this historical context the conflicts and tensions were also complex and manifold. The frontiers between the Roman-Latin – we could call it the "Western" tradition of Europe – and the Greek-Byzantine still exist – not only from a religious standpoint. Remember the fact that Byzanz was claiming for decades to be the second Rome, which was replaced by the Russian Tsar who claimed for Moscow to be the third Rome. Only in consequence the fact that Islam had occupied the orient Christianity turned to the occident. Of course the idea or the project of Europe turned up in history rather early, not only in the idea of the "Holy Roman Empire" dominated by the German emperors.

So Europe was never a unity, or more precisely: it was only a unity in difference. Of course history in modern times shows pretty clearly the conflicts and tensions between the states: first between the different dynasties, then, after the origins of the nation-states in the 18th and 19th century, between nations. Politically, Europe was never on the way to unify its different claims and interests. So the claim for a European unity emerged in the last century: firstly as a claim to stop the internal European conflicts and wars. But history provided other answers. The First World War was a European conflict, as was the Second World War. And we should not forget that the phrase "fortress Europe" was invented by the Nazis in order to defend Europe against the East, against Asia, that is, to defend so-called European civilization and culture. As we all know, it ended in blood and disaster.

It was precisely in the last century that the utopias of an idea, of a project of Europe emerged. Just to quote some important steps: the ideas of Victor Hugo or Giuseppe Manzini, longing for a United states of Europe; the ideas of Ortega y Gasset or even of Friedrich Nietzsche; not to forget Coudenhove-Calergi's idea of *Paneuropa*, elaborated 1924, including the slogan "Europe to the Europeans"; and finally of course Winston Churchill's claim for a United states of Europe after the Second World-War. There was no lack of ideas and utopias. But the political reality after 1945 showed a different face: Europe was divided geographically into the east and the west, and politically into democratic systems and communist ones. No wonder that after the decline of the Soviet-Union the idea of Europe began to blossom again. And with the integration in May 2004 of so many former Russian satellites, the project Europe seems to have gained a new and different dimension. But what has really happened to this project Europe?

If we take off all the beautiful rhetoric and if we look to the steps of European integration, we can only state that the main interest was an economic one. Founded as so-called *"Montanunion"*, later expanded to the European Economic Union (*Europäische Wirtschaftsgemeinschaft*), there have been merely economical interests to build up this European Community. And if we refrain from the rhetorical phrases, we only can state that the interests of the community are – within the field of globalization – interests of the market. Of course this is not new. It is not necessary to refer to authors like Viviane Forrester and her book about the terror of economics – even more friendly observers have remarked that the interest to win new players within the game of the European Community is merely an economic one.

So the *Osterweiterung* means primarily the opening of new markets, winning new consumers. Even commentators like *Financial Times* or *Economist* that are in no danger of being called anti-capitalistic, have stated that the meetings and conferences of the high representatives had more the character of a supervisory board of a stock corporation or a Limited Inc. than of a political committee. A quote from *Financial Times* after the summit-meeting in Lisboa can show this very clearly:

> The whole style of the meeting of the leaders of the states resembled more the style of a meeting of a governing board (*Verwaltungsrat*) The final communiqué showed a clear–cut opinion: The model of the free market (*Freie Marktwirtschaft*) has priority on all levels. Successful companies and enterprises are recognised as the driving forces of economic capacity. Governments should only support and the Union's role is that of a catalyst.

This reduction to merely economical interests, combined with the basic principles of economization and the "*Leitkultur*" of the market, transformed the "Project Europe" into an economical factor willing to challenge other economical giants like the United States of America, the "Tigers" in Far East or even China. Especially the United States seem to have become on many levels a shining example for the European Union. Even *The Economist* could ask the other day: "What can Europe be good for, if it turns out to be more and more a copy of the United States of America?"

Of course, this primacy of economics is not a peculiarity of Europe, but rather an effect of globalization spreading all over the world. It includes or seems to include a farewell to many principles in social and political culture, that have been developed in Europe like social solidarity, obligation of the state to care for social security and public health.

Nobody can deny the inclination of Brussels towards technocratic and bureaucratic principles, connected with a certain centralism threatening the very often proclaimed federalism. Of course peanuts like the famous "*Gurkenkrümmung* (the bend of cucumbers)", or the squabble, if jam could be called also "Marmelade" are just jokes, but problems of traffic transit, work permits, visas and immigration policies cannot be solved by centralistic measures, orders or instructions.

Whoever has shared the experience of applying for a scientific project, sponsored by the EU, will agree that even the worst national bureaucracy – and we Austrians are champions in this field – is not nearly as complicated. You get the impression that the application form needs even more work than the project itself.

All these tendencies show clearly enough that the famous European idea or the European identity has shrunk to an ornamental phrase. Also declarations of principles of democracy, of freedom, of traditional constitutions, of a common constitution, of strengthening peace and security are no longer of paramount importance. Clearing the fog of political rhetoric, we find a kind of a social contract, based on economic rationality and also on social rationalization.

Compared to the reality of the European Union, the idea of Europe seems to be replaced by the "*Leitkultur*" of a common market. The Austrian philosopher Rudolf Burger has described this tendency very clearly and without any illusion: The aim of the European unification is not the renaissance of the Christian occident or any other spiritual or intellectual tradition, nor the creation of a common nation or a common state, not even a revitalization of regional cultural structures. The aim is simply the creation of a homogenous market, open to its members with regard to work, products, capital and services.[2]

Let me be clear: of course economical conditions are in themselves very important. But if we reduce the European Union only to its economical basis, we will not find the specific identity of Europe which can only exist in the field of culture.

A European Union reduced to a community of producers and consumers has nothing to do with the project Europe; Europe's specific identity will be extinguished, if we do not enforce its uniqueness

---

[2] Cf. Rudolf Burger, "Kontinentalverschmelzung? Die europäische Frage und die Zukunft der EU", *Merkur. Deutsche Zeitschrift für europäisches Denken*, 57. Jahrgang, 2003, Heft 645-656, S. 187–199.

and its special historical and contemporary situation. It was some years ago, that, in Austria, the Roman cardinal Franz König – who recently died – claimed what he called the "soul of Europe", that is about to be extinguished by the needs of the market. Especially concerning the situation of the new members, the former communist states, Cardinal König, warned of reducing Europe to a simple market unity and underlined the importance of the cultural multiplicity, rooted in particular in the tradition of Middle-Europe and the Danube region.

Europe's identity is not a simple one: it is an identity in difference, in plurality and polyphony. An "unitas multiplex". Paradoxically said: the European identity is an identity in non-identity. This identity can only be found in the multiplicity of different national and regional cultural traditions that have to be mutually respected.

2. European Identity and Values

At first glance, the confusing history of Europe seems to show us an extreme diversity of cultures, nations, regions and ethnics. It was not only the 19th century with its birth of nation-states like Germany or Italy when the different roots and interests have led to conflicts and wars. But as already mentioned this variety was held together in the last instance by the cultural and intellectual traditions: Greek Logos, Roman law and Christian hope for salvation and redemption have been the common sources of a variety of differences.

Of course the perils of nationalism were always present, and are still present, as we can see in the recent wars in Southern Europe and on the Balkan. Obviously the surpassing of the nation-state and its narrow interests is one of the aims of the European Union. But this surpassing must mean integration und not extinction; it must mean recognition of differences and not their subsumption.

The slogan, very often used in the political rhetoric of a Europe of Regions, to preserve the particular character and to protect the cultural pluralism is not only far from the Realpolitik of the European Union, but it is also dangerous.

The replacement of the nation-states by regions has of course brought attention to the fact that nation and state not always coincide, and we have many examples all over Europe that demonstrate that passports do not always show the national identity of a person. Preservation of regions and respect for their historical and cultural differences must avoid many dangers: Firstly a reduction to particularism or even tribalism with the tendency to exclude, if not to extinguish, other ethnical groups. Moreover, regionalism doesn't have to, but can lead to some kind of reservation where picturesque folklore fakes cultural originality. And there is still the peril of a closed provincialism looking only for small-minded interests embedded in group-egoism.

A United Europe and regionalism are not in contradiction with each other, they can be in the best case complementary factors. For it is difficult to find one's identity in a big monster of about 400 millions of consumers. The cold strategy and technocracy of the EU-administrators is very seldom able to develop the feeling of being secure or to feel the warmth of being at home. I cannot image that a Sicilian will ever say "our Copenhague" or a guy from "the Netherlands" our "Kecskemet" – the revival of the long disapproved notion of "home" (*Heimat*), connotated with folklore, narrow-mindedness and provincial thinking and discriminated by the Nazis, is typical for this movement. We can consider it a compensation for the unifying tendencies dominating the European Union and degrading the regional cultural traditions to folklore. Once more the economical main interest suffocates culture and spirit, or as R. Münch has said in his book *The Project Europe*: "The world dominance of modern Western culture ... transformed the cultural multiplicity of species into a multiplicity of commodities."[3]

If we look at this multiplicity of different cultural traditions from the view-point of Americans – especially from the tourist taking part on one of the famous travel programs "Europe in forty days", then of course Europe can seem to be a beautiful Disneyland, full of old churches, castles, Greek or Roman ruins, folklore dancing and music performances. But culture is more than that, even if I do not want to

---

[3] Richard Münch, *Das Projekt Europa*, Frankfurt am Main: Suhrkamp, 1993, p. 287.

enter here a discussion about civilization and culture. If culture is something like the sum of our world of imagination and its spiritual and materialistic realization, then we have to face the fact that the world-wide tendency towards unification has entered the politics of the European Union. I think that we are on a wrong way, if we follow the trend of modernity based on science and technology, on economy and unification. We should avoid one-dimensional thinking.

Postmodern thinkers can teach us to get another view, that is, how to regard and handle difference.

Of course it has also been a long tradition in European philosophy to define identity via the exclusion of the different, of the other. But we have to learn that it is not the exclusion of otherness that leads us to identity, but the recognition of difference. Briefly and a little bit abstractly: identity cannot be found via the demarcation from the other, but rather via the recognition of otherness. The German philosopher Hans-Georg Gadamer has put this in the following manner: In Europe our spiritual fate has taken shape by means of the fact that the most severe tensions were argued between the manifold formations of spiritual creativity.[4]

To live with the other, to live as the other – this human basic task applies to the smallest and the largest example. Here one may find a particular privilege of Europe in so far as it had to learn more than others to live with others, even if these others are different. This vicinity of the other is at the same time mediated with us, despite all otherness. The otherness of the neighbour is not only the otherness to be avoided. It is also an inviting otherness that invites to one's own self-encounter.[5]

Gadamer has always insisted on reminding us that Europe has to maintain its identity by means of a combination of unity and diversity. Not a fight or a clash of different cultures but a dialogue is the chance of Europe. Only then can Europe avoid to become a copy of the United States of America; only then can Europe stop the invasion of a uniform culture, spreading all over the world via World Wide Web, television and other doubtful blessings of globalization.

---

[4] Cf. Hans-Georg Gadamer, *Das Erbe Europas*, Frankfurt am Main: Suhrkamp, 1989, p. 14.

[5] Ibidem, p. 30.

Europe's identity is an identity in difference. We have to learn to say farewell to this uniformity; others speak of a McDonaldization or a Blue-jeanization of the world; against this, we have to preserve the European manifold tradition

If the very often mentioned "European values" can have some importance and significance, this can only be in the field of this intellectual approach that is prepared to respect this unity in difference in a pluralistic society.

I would be very careful in invoking a debate concerning these values, even if many politicians start from the conviction that there are common values and attributes fulfilling the identity of Europe. Let me simply ask whether there are special European values? And what about values in general?

In the wake of the Austrian elections some years ago the Freedom party (*Freiheitliche Partei*) under the leadership of the current Carinthian governor Haider took part in the Austrian government – the European Union reacted very strongly and formulated some – ultimately ridiculous – "sanctions" against the Freedom party's participation. What kind of values are we talking about in this case?

It is always a problem when categories of moral philosophy turn up in political discussions. And the question of values does not even have a long-standing tradition within moral philosophy, but it derived from economics where the value of a good can be defined by many criteria (scarcity, market, supply and demand). Furthermore the question, if values are something independent from our (subjective) demands or if they are objective – so to say eternal – and independent from our wishes and demands, is still under discussion. I do not share the view that there are special European values – if we do not want to go back to global recognised principles, for instance to those written down in the different declarations of human rights. Very quickly: the discussion about values switched to the level of laws and norms that can be elaborated in a common constitution. The basic rights have of course something to do with values, but they are not specifically European, even if they derive from different historical events in Europe – the Enlightenment, French revolution, and so on.

So we find once more that the connection between values and European identity is not as simple as claimed. The different values appearing at the level of ethics and morality of the individual are difficult to be settled within a community dominated by the desire for unification. Anyway, it is remarkable that regarding many issues the members of the Union have different regulations concerning questions of bioethics like euthanasia, research on embryos, abortion, or transplantation. This is a clear sign that the different moral cultures depending on religious and liberal traditions in society cannot be easily settled.

If we are looking for this European identity, we can state that this identity should survive on the basis of its cultural backgrounds and roots and that it should have enough force to challenge the economical and technological unification.

3. The Situation of Education, Especially at the University Level

This trend towards unification can also be observed in the field of education. The different systems in Europe concerning primary schools, high-schools and gymnasiums and of course the universities are the results of different traditions. The school system in Great Britain, for instance, differs from the school system in Austria or in France; the different levels of education have of course different structures and qualities. The declarations and meetings of the representatives of the members of the Union (Pisa, Bologna etc) correspond exactly to the general principles of the Community: unification, compatibility, economization, promotion of vocational training, neglect of cultural and human studies in the tradition of the European mainstream in the last decades.

Like the whole system of education universities need of course to adapt themselves to the changing conditions of the social, political and cultural transformation. They need to re-examine their traditional assumptions and to define a new development. But it seems that, all over Europe, the process of university reforms does not follow the difficult combination of current demand and long-standing tradition.

It seems on the contrary that the university reforms we are currently going through in Austria are completely dominated by economical tasks. Let me just highlight some notions from that reform-rhetoric: competition, service, management, strategic planning, efficiency, best practice, evaluation, bench-marking, synergy effects, controlling performativity are key words, so that one gets the impression that all these terms fit better for a fast-food chain or a factory producing detergents.

The idea of autonomy and independence from state regulation, which is regarded and proclaimed to be the nucleus of the reform, is not as new as it seems. Furthermore the independence from the state is replaced by dependence on economics. The question whether it belongs to the duties of a state to care for public interests like education, health care, social security, or whether the state should give these tasks to private providers, looking for benefits and profit, presents of course a basic decision. The actual university reform proclaims the autonomy of the university: this means that the universities receive a basic sponsoring by the state, but they have full responsibility regarding the distribution of their budgets.

What seems very reasonable at first glance turns out to be in reality a severe restriction and reduction of the money spent by the state. The demand to get sponsorships and money from private investors can work in the fields of medicine and natural science like pharmacy, chemistry and biology, in departments of economics and technology, but hardly in the humanities. This means ultimately that the humanities will be starved out and their importance will be shrunk due to financial pressure.

Precisely this presents a severe danger for the idea of a University. One need not go back to the university reform in Germany in the 19th century where Wilhelm von Humboldt had started a reform dominated by the idea of *Bildung* (education). Of course, the reform of Humboldt was entirely characterized by the philosophy of German Idealism, but it included some ideas which seem to me to have still importance for contemporary university life: educations by means of science, unity of research and teaching, universitas meaning unity and mutual dialogue between the sciences, and last but not least freedom and independence. Let me just give you the definition of education (*Bildung*) of Hartmut von Hentig, recapitulating the thesis of Wilhelm von Humboldt:

> Bildung is a stimulation of all human forces so that these forces develop via an appropriation of the world in mutual limitations and combinations. The aim is an autonomous personality, enriching mankind in its ideal nature and uniqueness.
> (*Bildung ist eine Anregung aller Kräfte eines Menschen, damit diese sich über die Aneignung der Welt in wechselseitiger Be- und Verschränkung entfalten und zu einer sich selbst bestimmenden Persönlichkeit führen, die in ihrer Idealität und Einzigartigkeit die Menschheit bereichert.*)[6]

What Humboldt had in mind was an universal education of the individual with the aim of harmony, and science and philosophy were supposed to function as preservers of the unity of knowledge. This meant at that time an emancipation from the influence of the state which, however, is not exempted from its responsibility to provide the best conditions for society with regard to formation and education. But it is a rejection of regulations and prescriptions from the state concerning the subjects and structures of the different sciences.

We have to consider that even in the time of Enlightenment the influence of the state concerning education and teaching was a very large one. To give you an example of Austrian history: The so called "reform-emperor" Joseph II had declared in 1782 that "there should be nothing taught at the universities, what the students could only use for the sake of the state." If we replace state by economy, it seems that the universities are on the best way to changing their dependence from the state to a dependence on economical factors and interests.

The consequence is of course that education seems to be reduced to mere vocational training. Of course, it has always been one of the duties of universities to provide students and society with vocational training, preparing them for their professional life. But this cannot be the only task of an university, and in the meantime a network of advanced polytechnical colleges (*Fachhochschulen*) has been established offering a special vocational training in a shorter time than the

---

[6] Hartmut von Hentig, *Bildung*, München: Hanser, 1996, p. 40.

universities, more oriented towards practical needs, but also grad-
uating its students. Thus vocational training at the academic level is
offered by different academic institutions which can be in productive
competition with each other.

So what might be the assumptions of a university facing the
changes in society, science and technology?

I think that it is still very important to preserve the essential values of the European universities, as it is of course important to adapt
the universities to new demands.

These essential values are multiple ones: firstly the autonomy and
independence of the universities must be guaranteed concerning
freedom of teaching and research.

We have to preserve the role of the universities as providers of
long-term perspectives upon nature, society and human life.

Moreover, the university has to constitute a place of (ideologi-
cally) independent thinking, of a rational and argumentative approach to our problems.

Then we have to preserve the role of the university as an institution cultivating a free and critical spirit, reflecting even moral values
and accompanying critically the developments in society, sciences
and politics. There is a mutual responsibility between the university
and society: on the one hand, society is responsible for the conditions
of university work; on the other hand, universities have to respect the
needs of society.

I think that the last point is of great importance: for instance in the
year 1968, universities played – however the famous student revolution
might be seen nowadays – the role of a focus of critical thinking; in a
certain way they were a motor concerning new ideas for political, social
and cultural perspectives. Therefore the equilibrium between speciali-
sation and training in the general culture forms something like the
heart of university life. Even if we can admit that the Humboldt university has come into a crisis for many reasons, some of these reasons can
easily be named: the loss of the leading position of philosophy due to
success and diversification especially in science and technology; the
replacement of an unitary outlook at the world by different approaches; the reduction of the function of science by giving up the

orientation towards Bildung; the opening up of universities to a large number of students (the so-called mass-universities) and so on.

But this crisis cannot lead us to a perspective where only applied sciences and so-called useful knowledge (*Verwertungswissen*) replaces general education and culture. If we look at biology, genetics, computer-science or medicine, then we can claim that the development of science and technology has in itself created a lot of general and moral questions. The so-called *Orientierungs-*or *Reflexionswissen* (guiding or reflexive knowledge) has become more important than ever. Of course the humanities are not in themselves a guarantee against the loss of orientation in a postmodern age characterized by so many different and pluralistic approaches. But they have the function of a certain compensation for the one-dimensional way of science and technology, or as the German philosopher Odo Marquard has said: they can help to minimize and correct the damages of modernity. It is out of question that in a specialized world dominated by science and technology the tendency of unification (spread by of Television and World Wide Web) as well as well as the dominance of market and economical criteria are in need of some compensation.

It is interesting that centuries ago Immanuel Kant, in his little treatise "The Conflict of the Faculties", had already claimed autonomy for the faculty of philosophy, as it was devoted to reason (*Vernunft*) and not simply, as the other ones – "medicine, laws and theology" –, to more understanding (*Verstand*).

This very equilibrium between general education and culture and vocational, professional training is in danger. Professional instruction seems to overrun the generalization, the needs and demands of the free-market societies are trying to reduce university studies only to the so-called useful fields and issues. Polemically speaking: it cannot be the aim of a university to produce stooges for the big international companies and enterprises, even if these stooges are key-board artists and digital virtuosos.

Apart from the forgotten balance between general cultural education and vocational training, the tendency towards centralization presents another menace. In all the reform papers and issues there is not only a lack of the idea of the university but also a tendency to disregard the differences of the structures, issues and aims of the different sciences and research topics.

Instead of building up structures for university institutions, faculties or departments in different ways following the special conditions of scientific work, there is a unifying view at the conditions of the university. Precisely the great differences with regard to the needs, the structure and even the working conditions and realms of research are severely neglected. What may fit well for the natural sciences – teamwork in laboratories or under experimental conditions; structuring of a project in different steps with different research emphases – can be the wrong way in philosophy, for instance, where nobody can think for me and where the conditions are completely different. To think that a better organization of science automatically will lead to a better research result or product is also an illusion. Of course the conditions of quality-oriented research and studies can be improved, but it is still the personality of the researchers – his imagination and his scientific qualities – that is decisive. I do not know a better worldwide organization than the organization of McDonalds, but I know much better products.

Another illusion seems to be the demand of raising quality in research and teaching by evaluation and quality-assurance, very often regarded as a fundamental option for all European Universities. If we look at that demand from close up, we have to point out that the set of instruments is not all convincing. Firstly, evaluation is too much concentrated on the quantity of "production", that is, on the number of publications and research results, on the number of collaborators or, concerning teaching, on the number of students, of master's and doctoral theses and so forth. If we look at the criteria elaborated at Bologna (1999), Salamanca (2001) or Prague (2002), we find a bundle of common phrases like curricula quality, academic staff quality, feedback from the students, flexible organization, feedback from the stakeholders, generation of innovative potential and, last but not least, an international organization of accreditation. Once again the trend to create all over Europe a unifying university system comes to the surface. Already in Bologna the uniformity of the university systems all over the European Union was declared: that is, unification of the study degrees (two steps:

bachelor's and master's degree, completely new to most of the traditional degree-systems in Europe and imitating the standards in the United States), standard criteria for planning and evaluation, a centralized credit system and so on. Following the need for professional usefulness in studies, one can ask what the purpose of a bachelor's degree in philosophy or history or even in chemistry or physics should really mean, if not the hidden one of minimising the number of students. The Austrian professor of cultural studies, Justin Stagl, called this tendency a production of academic fast-food, a danger also emerging from the restrictions of the length of studies, as if it were not an important task of the university to grant students some time of reflection and perhaps a glance at different disciplines – a glance that, on the other hand and paradoxically, is demanded by the promotion of the need for more interdisciplinary studies.

Corresponding to the academic fast-food offered through the bachelor's degree and in correspondence with a competitive perspective copying the structure of market-oriented economic companies, there is also a change concerning the position of university teachers and staff. Contracts of a limited period even for professors replace the tenure system (in this case a "false copy" of the universities in the United States where the tenure is still an important instrument to keep highly qualified people at the university), while at the same time the so-called" polyvalent, flexible, mobile Mc-Donald-professor" (Justin Stagl) is on the advance.

Especially the new members (former Communist countries) have generated a real inflation of universities: universities that are sometimes not more than mere vocational management-schools, even if they are private foundations with enormous study fees.

The protest against the reform has been remarkable in quantitative terms – not only in Austria. Over 80% of the comments during the so-called experts' opinion procedure were negative and it was typical that institutions like the Chamber of Commerce (*Wirtschaftskammer*) or the union of industries were welcoming this reform enthusiastically.

In short: the universities in Europe have to accept a reform which carries the labels of centralization, unification (one could ask where the competition is, if everything is compatible), market orientation.

This reform promotes a tendency towards the (economically) useful in alliance with a tendency towards hierarchies and against university democracy; a tendency towards management criteria that does not correspond at all to the "unitas scientiarum et litterarum", the birthplace of the European spirit.

Let me be clear: A combination of education and vocational training constitutes also the task of the university, as it should be the purpose of the "Fachhochschule". I do not think that a clear separation between education and culture on the one hand, and professional training on the other hand corresponds to the actual demands of our situation: what we need instead of a separation are mutual and complementary orientations.

We cannot renounce the needs of society, including the need for specialists trained according to the demands of professional life; but what we cannot renounce as well is the need for culture. Without human beings preserving the spirit and the ideas of our culture and education, our educational system will reduce itself to a mere technocratic monster.

Europe is more than the European Union. In the face of all the needs a technocratic and scientific world poses for us, we need orientation, humanism and the conviction that our life does not find its fulfilment through having professional success, being-up-to-date in the latest computer knowledge, or having complete command of our genetic potential. Where should this guidance come from, if not from the traditions of Europe, many centuries older than the European Union?

Marek Kwiek
Poznań

The Future of the Welfare State and Democracy: the Effects of Globalization from a European Perspective

1. Introduction:
the Welfare State under Global Pressures

The post-war Keynesian welfare state in Europe was sustainable as long as post-war European economies were growing and were relatively closed; however, over the years, as entitlements grew ever bigger and coverage became ever more universal, the proportion of GDP spent on public services rose considerably. With economies becoming more open, the stagnation which started in the second half of the seventies in Europe, following the oil crisis, was perhaps the first symptom that the welfare system in the form designed for one period (the post-war reconstruction of Europe) might be not be working in a different period.[1] In 1960, the average expenditure on social payments was 7.5 percent of gross domestic product in the

---

[1] As Gøsta Esping-Andersen, a leading world authority on the welfare state, put it recently, "most European social protection systems were constructed in an era with *a very different distribution and intensity of risks and needs* than exist today. ... The problem behind the new risk configuration is that it stems primarily from weakened families and poorly functioning labor markets. As a consequence, the welfare state is burdened with responsibilities for which it was not designed" (Gøsta Esping-Andersen, Duncan Gallie, Anton Hemerijck, John Myles, *A New Welfare Architecture for Europe? Report Submitted to the Belgian Presidency of the European Union*, available at www.ccsd.ca/pubs/2002/europe.pdf, 2001; emphasis mine).

affluent countries of Western Europe, as compared to 6 percent being spent in the United States. Already by 1980, though, the average expenditure on social payments in Europe had doubled and reached a level of 14 percent of GDP, while the United States was spending only 9.75 percent. The differencial between the USA and European countries was growing.[2] As a result the social agenda of the eighties and nineties changed radically: after the policies of the golden age of expansion, European welfare states have been shaped by the (Paul Pierson's) "politics of austerity". Consequently, the rhetoric of a "crisis" in the welfare state has been with us since the 1970s. From the 1970s, various theorists have claimed a fiscal crisis, a crisis of government overload, a crisis of liberal democracy or, as Jürgen Habermas called it, a "crisis of legitimacy".[3]

Social scientists have divergent views about the causes of the current pressures on the welfare state; they agree on a single point though; we are facing the end of the welfare state as we know it. Let me quote here three diagnoses leading in a similar direction:

> The welfare state now faces a context of essentially permanent austerity. Changes in the global economy, the sharp slowdown in economic growth, the maturation of governmental commitments, and population aging all generate considerable fiscal stress. There is little reason to expect these pressures to diminish over the next few decades. If anything, they are likely to intensify.[4]

> Throughout Europe, the dominant theme in contemporary social policy is the retreat of the welfare state. ... There is now general agreement that the bulk of the social legislation introduced in recent years in intended to reduce the role of the state in welfare. Policies that lead in the opposite direction play a subordinate role.[5]

---

[2] John Myles, Jill Quadagno, "Political Theories of the Welfare State", *Social Science Review*, March, 2002, p. 34.

[3] For a wider picture of the nexus of globalization and the welfare state, see my book *The University and the State. A Study into Global Transformations* (Frankfurt am Main and New York: Peter Lang, 2006).

[4] *The New Politics of the Welfare State*, ed. by Paul Pierson, Oxford: Oxford University Press, 2001, p. 411.

[5] Giuliano Bonoli, George Vic, Peter Taylor-Gooby, *European Welfare Futures. Towards a Theory of Retrenchment*, Cambridge: Polity Press, 2000, p. 1.

For two reasons, the continued viability of the existing welfare state edifice is being questioned across all of Europe. The first is simply that the status quo will be difficult to sustain given adverse demographic or financial conditions. The second is that the same status quo appears increasingly out-of-date and ill suited to meet the great challenges ahead.[6]

There is no major disagreement, broadly speaking, about the future of the welfare state in its current European postwar form: its foundations, for a variety of internal and external reasons and due to a variety of international and domestic pressures, are under siege today. Major differences are based on different explanations about what has been happening to the European welfare state since the mid-1970s until now, about different variations of restructuring in different European countries, and different degrees of emphasis concerning the scope of welfare state downsizing in particular countries in the future. The question debated today is not whether welfare retrenchment has come to be seen as necessary by the governments of most affluent Western democracies, international organizations (such as the OECD), global organizations and development agencies (such as the World Bank) and the European Commission; it is rather why.[7] As Giuliano Bonoli and his colleagues argue, there are four main factors involved in the current pressures for the retrenchment of the welfare state. They are the following: globalization, an anti-taxation bias, a neo-liberal approach to political economy and the dilemma of "squaring the welfare circle":

The four factors are, first globalization which imposes an international competitive logic which different nation-states cannot escape and which constrains national policies, particularly in relation to taxation and the labour market; secondly, the assumption of politicians and others that

---

[6] Gøsta Esping-Andersen, Duncan Gallie, Anton Hemerijck, John Myles, *Why We Need a New Welfare State*, Oxford: Oxford University Press, 2002, p. 4.

[7] Although it has to be remembered that, as Martin Carnoy put it, "objective data in the economic, demographic and social spheres have greater or lesser impact as focus for welfare retrenchment *according to the way they are politically interpreted and accepted in the country's policy-making process*" (Martin Carnoy, *Globalization and Educational Reform: What Planners Need to Know*, Paris: UNESCO, International Institute for Educational Planning, 1999, p. 153; emphasis mine).

the public will not tolerate increases in taxes and social contributions to finance improvements in welfare; thirdly, the neo-liberal approach to political economy, now dominant in the assumptive worlds of policy-makers, which argues the priority of market freedom over welfare intervention; and fourthly, the dilemma of "squaring the welfare circle", which confronts all welfare states. This refers to the way governments now *experience simultaneous and contradictory pressures from opposite directions*. Increases in the numbers of older people, rising demand for education and training, rising unemployment and the expectations of citizens that social progress will involve higher standards of service press for higher spending. At the same time, concern about the impact of globalization, the logic of liberalism and fears of tax revolt demand the contraction of provision.[8]

European welfare states are confronting differing mixes of the above factors in different countries. Bonoli and his colleagues argue that in deciding how these conflicts are played out in different countries and how they are resolved, a crucial position is held by their respective institutional frameworks to a very large extent (including political institutions, the labor movement, business, finance and the voluntary sectors etc). As retrenchment is difficult to measure, the best way to gain insight into the transformations of the welfare state in recent years is to have a look at the legislative changes adopted in different countries and assess their likely implications for the coverage, level and quality of welfare provision. We need to bear in mind that social expenditure as a proportion of GDP did not decrease but continued to increase during the last decade, even though its rate of growth was considerably slower than in the previous two decades.

Bonoli's more general claims are parallel to those pronounced among the supporters of the idea of the "risk society", especially Ulrich Beck and his British colleagues. The most interesting feature of the new world as described by Bonoli is what he terms shifting the burden of uncertainty to the individual. The expansion of private provision means that individuals will be much more exposed to risks (Bonoli's

---

[8] Giuliano Bonoli, George Vic, Peter Taylor-Gooby, *European Welfare Futures. Towards a Theory of Retrenchment*, op. cit., p. 2; emphasis mine.

example: the market performance of pension funds[9]). The level of security is lower, and the risk-protection is lower.[10] People's dependence on the market is increasing and the burden of social security is being taken off the shoulders of the state. Consequently, the trend is clearly towards the recommodification of society, meaning increasing people's dependence on market forces (and, let us add the complementary picture, towards the desocialization of the economy).[11] The balance between state and market in meeting people's needs (so far met by public sector healthcare and pensions, and possibly including education) is shifting towards the market. This is, in Bonoli's terms, "the reversal of the tendency that dominated social policy-making during most of the post-war period".[12]

---

[9] See in this context the whole idea of multi-pillar pension schemes (consisting of 3 parts: a mandatory publicly-managed tax-financed pillar for redistribution, a mandatory privately-managed fully funded pillar for saving, and a voluntary pillar for people who want more protection for old age) as opposed to traditional "pay-as-you-go" systems. Pure multi-pillar systems only exist in a few countries (and Chile is the flagship example), while the number of countries with blended systems (PAYG and multi-pillar) is growing. Poland is an example of the successful implementation of a blended system. For an overall view see Louise Fox and Edward Palmer's paper on "New Approaches to Multi-Pillar Pension Systems: What in the World Is Going On?" (available at www.issa.int/pdf/helsinki2000/topic3/2fox-palmer.pdf, 1999).

[10] Giuliano Bonoli, George Vic, Peter Taylor-Gooby, *European Welfare Futures. Towards a Theory of Retrenchment*, op. cit., pp. 47–48.

[11] In the classic formulation of Esping-Andersen's *Three Worlds of Welfare Capitalism*, decommodification was the crucial phenomenon referred to in the Keynesian welfare state: "The outstanding criterion of social rights must be the degree to which they permit people to make their living standards *independent of pure market forces*. It is in this sense that social rights diminish citizens' status as commodities". And in a section on "rights and de-commodification" he claims that "in pre-capitalist societies, few workers were properly commodities in the sense that their survival was contingent upon the sale of their labor power. It is as markets become universal and hegemonic that the welfare of individuals comes to depend entirely on the cash nexus. Stripping society of the institutional layers that guaranteed social reproduction outside the labor contract meant that people were commodified. In turn, the introduction of modern social rights implies a loosening of the pure commodity status. *De-commodification occurs when a service is rendered as a matter of right, and when a person can maintain a livelihood without reliance on the market*" (Gøsta Esping-Andersen, *The Three Worlds of Welfare Capitalism*, Princeton: Princeton University Press, 1990, pp. 3, 21–22; emphasis mine).

[12] Giuliano Bonoli, George Vic, Peter Taylor-Gooby, *European Welfare Futures. Towards a Theory of Retrenchment*, op. cit., p. 49.

In this context, I want to discuss the nexus of our understanding of globalization, the future of the welfare-state and the future of democracy as analyzed by Jürgen Habermas, perhaps the most famous living German philosopher, as the author of *The Postnational Constellation*; and Ulrich Beck, perhaps the most famous living German sociologist, as the author of several important recent books including *What Is Globalization?*, *The Brave New World of Work* and *The World Risk Society*.

2. The Postwar Welfare State, Transnational Economy, and Changing Historical Constellations

In Jürgen Habermas' view, globalization heralds the end of the dominance of the nation-state as a model of political organization. It fundamentally challenges the relevance of the nation-state – but at the same time, there seems to be no guarantee that the nation-state will be replaced by anything *better*, as Max Pensky comments in his introduction to *The Postnational Constellation. Political Essays*. The problem we will all face in the 21st century is the following: "can democracies based on social welfare survive beyond national borders?". The answer is a federalist, socially and economically effective European Union.[13] In these essays, Habermas also refers to the "end" and the "revocation" of the welfare-state compromise of the postwar period in Europe as a defining feature of the new situation in affluent Western European democracies. He summarizes past options open to the welfare state in the following way:

> In the mixed economies of the West, states had a considerable portion of the domestic product at their disposal, and could therefore use transfer payments, subsidies, and effective policies in the areas of infrastructure, employment and social security. They were able to exert a definite influence on the overall conditions of production and distribution with the goal of maintaining growth, stable prices, and full employment. In other words, by applying growth-stimulating

---

[13] Jürgen Habermas, *The Postnational Constellation. Political Essays*, transl. by Max Pensky, Cambridge: The MIT Press, 2001, p. xix.

measures on the one side, and social policies on the other, *the regulatory state could simultaneously stimulate the economy and guarantee social integration.*[14]

The golden era of the Western European Keynesian welfare state is certainly over though, and nation-states have fewer and fewer policy options open to them, Habermas claims; there can be no discussion with the data and its interpretation. Habermas, with respect to the future of the current welfare state, is in agreement with Anthony Giddens and Ulrich Beck, Scott Lash and Zygmunt Bauman as well as many other contemporary social thinkers. He has no hesitations when he makes the point that "the welfare state mass democracies on the Western model now face the end of a 200-year developmental process that began with the revolutionary birth of modern nation-states".[15] The idea of the welfare state has so far been realized only in the framework of the nation-state, but the nation-state is reaching "the limits of its capacities" in the changed context defined by global society and the global economy, as he argues in a paper "Crossing Globalization's Valley of Tears".[16]

Traditionally, and especially in the postwar period, the state, society and the economy were co-extensive within *national* boundaries. He dubs the new reality and the radically new historical configuration the *postnational constellation* which justifies the development of a new "postnational" political project accompanied by a transition to a new cosmopolitan law.[17] Generally, Habermas'

---

[14] Ibidem, p. 50; emphasis mine.

[15] Ibidem, p. 60.

[16] Jürgen Habermas, "Crossing Globalization's Valley of Tears", *New Perspectives Quarterly*, Vol. 17, Issue 4, 2000 (Fall), p. 51.

[17] For a strong criticism of Habermas' stance towards globalization, see Klaus-Gerd Giesen's "The Post-National Constellation: Habermas and the 'Second Modernity'" (Klaus-Gerd Giesen, "The Post-National Constellation: Habermas and 'the Second Modernity'", *Res Publica* 10, 2004). His conception of the cosmopolitan law is "fundamentally anti-democratic". Commenting on recent works by Habermas, Giddens, and Beck, he argues that "the political transition towards cosmopolitan law proposed by Habermas corresponds exactly to the move into a second modernity, a 'postnational age' of world governance. If the new Habermas finds enough allies, we should perhaps resign ourselves to living in an age when intellectuals of all

political project presented in *The Postnational Constellation* encompasses the idea that globalization can only be mastered by delegating state prerogatives to a regional supranational organization, in the case of Europe – to the EU.[18] His diagnosis is the following: "the phenomena of the territorial state, the nation, and a popular economy constituted within national borders formed a historical constellation in which the democratic process assumed a more or less convincing institutional form". What is happening today is that developments summarized under the rubric "globalization" *have put this entire constellation into question.*[19] The postnational constellation is bringing to an end a situation in which politics and the legal system intermeshed with economic cycles and national traditions within the boundaries of nation-states.[20] The dilemma national governments face today derives from the zero-sum game into which they have been forced and it is described by Habermas in the following manner: necessary *economic* objectives can be reached only at the expense of *social* and *political* objectives. The dilemma is elaborated in the form of two theses:

> First, the economic problems besetting affluent societies can be explained by a structural transformation of the world economic system, a transformation characterized by the term "globalization". Second, this transformation so *radically reduces nation-states'* capacity for action that the options remaining open to them are *not sufficient to shield their populations from the undesired social and political consequences of a transnational economy.*[21]

Habermas fully acknowledges the significance of the impact of current global transformations on the traditional European welfare state models and on the growing incapacity of national governments

---

persuasions back down one after another in the face of the demands of the strong. After the Age of Reason, it would seem ... we are now well into the Age of Abdication" (ibidem, pp. 6, 13). Strong words indeed.

[18] See ibidem, p. 8 ff.

[19] Jürgen Habermas, *The Postnational Constellation. Political Essays*, op. cit., p. 60.

[20] Idem, "Crossing Globalization's Valley of Tears", op. cit., p. 52.

[21] Idem, *The Postnational Constellation. Political Essays*, op. cit., p. 51; emphases mine.

to conduct national policies, traditionally ascribed to nation-states. His conclusions are clear-cut and reflect a deeply historical perspective from observing the last half a century in Europe:

> no matter how one looks at it, the globalization of the economy destroys a historical constellation that made the welfare state compromise *temporarily* possible. Even if this compromise was never the ideal solution for a problem inherent within capitalism itself, it nevertheless *held capitalism's social costs within tolerable limits.*[22]

What must be especially hard to acknowledge for such a universalistically-minded social philosopher as Habermas is the *contingency* of post-war European social developments (which, incidentally, brings him very close to the general philosophical principles of Richard Rorty among which the notion of contingency plays a crucial role[23]). It was Gøsta Esping-Andersen who made the excellent point that *the contemporary welfare state addresses a past social order.*[24] There was no historical necessity for the appearance and evolution of the European welfare state in the way it actually appeared and evolved; it merely *happened* due to unexpected historical circumstances and most Europeans have already forgotten that these circumstance were related to a particular place and time: the social, political and economic circumstances following the second world war.[25] Habermas thus presents in his essays a historical and

---

[22] Ibidem, p. 52; emphases mine.

[23] See Marek Kwiek, *Intellectuals, Power, and Knowledge. Studies in the Philosophy of Culture and Education*, Frankfurt am Main – New York: Peter Lang, 2004; idem, "Agents, Spectators and Social Hope. Richard Rorty and American Intellectuals", *Theoria. A Journal of Social and Political Theory*, No. 101, June, 2003.

[24] *Welfare States in Transition. National Adaptations in Global Economies*, ed. by Gøsta Esping-Andersen, London: SAGE Publications, 1996, p. 9.

[25] These unusual circumstances in the decades following the second world war – in Fritz Scharpf's formulation in "Globalization and the Welfare State. Constraints, Challenges and Vulnerabilities" – included the conditions "in which *the nation state was able to exercise a historically exceptional degree of control over its own economic boundaries*. As governments were able to regulate capital movements, to determine exchange rates, and to adjust tariffs to imports, external economic factors had little or no influence on domestic policy choices" (Fritz Scharpe, "Globalization and the Welfare State. Constraints, Challenges and Vulnerabilities", ISSA Conference,

political narrative with a beginning (the emergence of the postwar "national constellation" which gave rise to the development of the Keynesian welfare state in Europe) and an end (the emergence of the current, globalization-related "postnational constellation" in which the traditional form of the welfare state is being questioned). Let me quote him here *in extenso*:

> In some *privileged regions of the world*, and under *the favorable conditions of the postwar period*, the nation-state ... succeeded in transforming itself into a social welfare state by regulating the national economy without interfering with its self-correcting mechanisms. But this successful combination is menaced by a global economy that now increasingly escapes the control of a regulatory state. Obviously, welfare-state functions can be maintained at their previous level only if they are transferred from the nation-state to larger political entities which could manage to keep pace with a transnational economy.[26]

3. Globalization as Denationalization – and Europe as a Historical Project

The possible solution to social problems, both for Habermas and for Ulrich Beck, lies in the integrated Europe of the future – that is, at the level of the supranational authorities of a federal European state ("the European Union as the initial form for a postnational democracy" in

---

Helsinki, 25–27 September 2000, p. 1; emphasis mine). Currently, even under the liberal regimes of the WTO, governments have not abdicated their capacity for border control and the freedom of world trade is still constrained. It is different in the European Union where legal and administrative restrictions against the free movement of goods and capital have been completely removed. As Scharpf comments, "as a consequence, the capacity of national governments to protect domestic firms against competitors producing under different regulatory regimes abroad has been eliminated, and their capacity to tax and to regulate domestic capital and business firms is now limited by the fear of capital flight and the relocation of production" (Fritz Scharpe, "Economic Integration, Democracy and the Welfare State", MPIfG Working Paper, No. 2, July, 1996, p. 6).

[26] Jürgen Habermas, *The Postnational Constellation. Political Essays*, op. cit., p. 52; emphasis mine.

the case of Habermas, or as Beck formulates his argument, "without Europe there can be no response to globalization ... There is no national way out of the global trap"[27]). The application of corrective measures to markets and the setting up of redistributive regulatory mechanisms under globalization pressures is possible, Habermas argues, only if the European Union evolves beyond its current form of an interstate alliance towards a "true federation".[28] It is also interesting to refer Habermas' "privileged regions of the world" and "favorable conditions" to the postcommunist transition countries of Central and Eastern Europe today. From a historical perspective, the issue is quite clear: neither the so called "European social model" nor any of the European "welfare state regimes" (Esping-Andersen) available today are valid in most transition countries in question, at least in the full forms discussed or enacted in the West in the postwar period.[29] From a global perspective, the emergence of fully-fledged Continental welfare states there looks merely out of the question. Most new Central and

---

[27] In the context of Robert B. Reich's *The Work of Nations* (Robert B. Reich, *The Work of Nations. Preparing Ourselves for 21st Century*, New York: Vintage Books, 1992), the idea of trust and solidarity between different segments of the population of the nation-state as expressed in the metaphor of being in the same common national boat called the national economy seems endangered too. The emergent transnational capitalist class [TCC] as analyzed recently by Leslie Sklair seems to have different loyalties and follow values other than national; as Sklair argues, TCC "is domiciled in and identified with no particular country but, on the contrary, is identified with the global capitalist system" (Leslie Sklair, *The Transnational Capitalist Class*, Oxford: Blackwell, 2001, p. 10). EU bureaucrats might be another interesting research topic in this context.

[28] Jürgen Habermas, "Crossing Globalization's Valley of Tears", op. cit., p. 55.

[29] I am in full agreement with Zsuzsa Ferge that in the transition countries there is no unique label for emergent welfare systems (except perhaps in terms of their neo-liberal nature) but they share one feature: "the *absence* of a project for a welfare system which would significantly mitigate the costs of the transition in the short run, and would promote the emancipatory dimension of social policy as well as the formation of an integrated society in the long run" (Zsuzsa Ferge, "Welfare and 'Ill-Fare Systems in Central-Eastern Europe", in: Robert Sykes, Bruno Palier, Pauline M. Prior, *Globalization and European Welfare States. Challenges and Change*, New York: Palgrave, 2001, p. 131). Poland, with its unemployment rate reaching 18 percent in recent years, is a good example. The argument of social Darwinists would perhaps be that this is exactly the (necessary) cost for an otherwise mostly quite successful transition away from a command-driven economy.

East European EU entrants do not fit any of the three Esping-Andersen
welfare state regimes – neither the liberal, nor the social democratic,
nor the continental; the closest in the future is probably the liberal
regime as it appears in Australia, Canada, New Zealand, the USA and
the UK).[30] Habermas is very well aware that the economic expectations
of the European population towards the newly enlarged European
Union, especially of new EU members, cannot suffice; what is required
is the "legitimisation of shared values", as he explains in a paper "Why
Europe Needs a Constitution". During the third quarter of the last
century, citizens of Western Europe were fortunate to develop a
"distinctive form of life" based on "a glittering material infrastructure".
Today, under globalization, they are prepared to defend the core of a
welfare state in a society oriented towards social, political and cultural
inclusion.[31] The general thesis of "The Postnational Constellation and
the Future of Democracy" is reformulated in the paper on the
European Constitution:

> The question therefore is: can any of our small or medium, *entangled and
> accommodating* nation-states preserve a separate capacity to escape
> enforced assimilation to the social model now imposed by the
> predominant global economic regime?[32]

The answer to the last question is certainly in the negative, and
hence the growing significance of the European project for Habermas.
For Habermas, the most significant dimension of globalization is
economic.[33] The main questions he asks are which aspects of
globalization could degrade the capacity for democratic self-steering

---

[30] Guy Standing in analyzing welfare transitions in CEE countries notes that
underlying the debates has been the most basic dilemma: "how to provide greater
social protection for the growing number of people in need, while cutting back on
total social expenditure because of actual or perceived resource constraints" (Guy
Standing, "Social Protection in Central and Eastern Europe: a Tale of Slipping Anchors
and Torn Safety Nets", in: *Welfare States in Transition. National Adaptations in Global
Economies*, ed. by Gøsta Esping-Andersen, London: SAGE Publications, 1996, p. 225).

[31] Jürgen Habermas, "Why Europe Needs a Constitution", *New Left Review*, 11.
September–October, 2001 , pp. 8–9.

[32] Ibidem, p. 11.

[33] Jürgen Habermas, *The Postnational Constellation. Political Essays*, op. cit., p. 66.

within a national society and are there any "functional equivalents" at the supranational level for deficits that emerge at the nation-state level. The conventional model of the state is less and less appropriate to the current situation.

The global age introduces a new quality; to quote two memorable phrases Habermas used, "power can be democratized; money cannot" and "money replaces power".[34] Under the pressure of globalizing markets national governments lose their capacity to influence economic cycles, so there remains little room for the effective exercise of legitimized domestic policy.

As markets become increasingly more important than politics, the nation state increasingly loses its capacity to raise taxes and stimulate growth, and with it the ability "to secure the essential foundations of its own legitimacy".[35] "Denationalization" forces societies constituted as nation states to "open" themselves up to an economically-driven world society. Nation-states seem to be losing both their capacity for action and the stability of their collective identities, and hence fears about the disempowering effects of globalization are far from unjustified. The fading away of the "national constellation" brings to the life far-reaching consequences for the Keynesian model of the welfare state – the "compromise" reached after the second world war is over, and so may be the taming of capitalism brought about by the historical circumstances of that period. European states no longer have the necessary resources for the continuation of the traditional European welfare state model, and with globalization forces in operation, the old problem of how to combine the self-regulating nature of markets with the social dimension, especially the changing patterns in the distribution of the gross national product, has reappeared. And in a European context, whenever we mention the welfare state, we also have to mean public higher education and its traditional postwar modes of functioning. The possible reformulation of the welfare state – possibly different in different European economies, or according to some common European guidelines currently being tentatively worked out by the European Commission

---

[34] Ibidem, p. 78.
[35] Ibidem, p. 79.

– are bound to lead to new conceptualizations of how our universities
are going to be functioning in changing social and economic
realities.[36]

4. Globalization and the Second,
Postnational Modernity

In the most general terms, in thinking of radical transformations of
contemporary society, a number of key sociological and philosophical
concepts have been evoked over the last two decades and even from
slightly earlier: the "postindustrial society" as developed for the first
time by Daniel Bell; "postmodernity" as developed by Jean-François
Lyotard, "postmodernity" and "liquid modernity" as elaborated by
Zygmunt Bauman; "late modernity" as presented by Anthony
Giddens; the "postnational constellation" as elaborated in Jürgen
Habermas' political essays; "cosmopolitan democracy" as viewed by
David Held; the "network society" from the Manuel Castells' famous
trilogy on *The Information Age*; as well as "post-Fordism", "post-
Taylorism", "post work" society etc. Also the emergent "knowledge
society" and "knowledge economy" are accompanying concepts from
the international and transnational discourses on the current economic
and political changes in the developed world, especially as
conceptualized by the reports from the OECD and the European
Commission. They usually emphasize different aspects of the rapidly
changing social reality; all of them testify, though, to a sense of
substantial social transformations, in some cases also a sense of a *radical*
rupture with the past. In the case of Ulrich Beck, the key concepts
relating to the present are the "risk society" and the "second,
postnational modernity".

---

[36] See in this context my two papers: "The Emergent European Educational
Policies Under Scrutiny: The Bologna Process From a Central European Perspective",
European Educational Research Journal, vol. 3, no. 4 (December 2004) and "Renegotiating
the Traditional Social Contract? The University and the State in a Global Age",
European Educational Research Journal, vol. 4, no. 4 (December 2005).

For Beck, it is the processes of globalization that define our current social reality. In the paradigm of the second modernity, Beck argues, "globalization is no longer understood as external and additive, but replaces the 'container image' of society and the state. It designates a transnational, despatialized power game whose rules and boundaries, paradoxes and dilemmas, first have to be deciphered".[37] There is a far-reaching parallelism between the social diagnoses with respect to globalization presented by Ulrich Beck and Jürgen Habermas, even though it will be useful to see the differences between them too. The key themes from Beck's recent writings of major interest to us here are the following: the passage from the first, *national*, to the second, *postnational*, modernity; the passage from the work society to the risk society (*Risikogesellschaft*); general uncertainty, insecurity, and unclarity of individual and collective futures[38]; the first, industrial modernization and the second, reflexive modernization; the end of a historical bond between capitalism, the welfare state and democracy; the future of political freedom and democracy in a post-work European society; democracy as work-democracy – the material security of citizens vs. their political freedom; the interplay of transnational and national dimensions of the social; the future of social justice in an age of globality; and certainly the future of European welfare states. All of them are very closely interrelated and together form a coherent sociological and political account of current realities.

Beck in his analyses moves back and forth between the results of empirically-based studies combined with international data and high-level theoretical sociological conclusions (calling his genre of writing

---

[37] Ulrich Beck, *The Brave New World of Work*, transl. by P. Camiller, Cambridge: Polity Press, 2000, pp. 28–29.

[38] John Gray in his *False Dawn. The Delusions of Global Capitalism* (New York: The New Press, 1998) argues that not only individuals but also nation-states must now act "in *a world in which all options are uncertain.* ... National governments find themselves in environments *not merely of risks but of radical uncertainty.* In economic theory, risk means a situation in which the costs of various actions can be known with reasonable probability, while uncertainty is a situation in which such probabilities cannot be known. ... Governments are in a situation in which even the span of options that is available to them is uncertain. This continuing radical uncertainty is the *most* disabling constraint on the power of sovereign states" (ibidem, p. 75; emphasis mine).

"visionary non-fiction"[39]). It is very interesting to see how the two planes reinforce each other and make his claims intellectually convincing. Generally speaking, what is crucial for us here is his emphasis on the *radicalism* of current social transformations in his analyses: in brief, and simplifying his views to the extreme, the picture of society is changing dramatically right before our eyes; the globalization processes are irreversible; the welfare state cannot be revived on a national level (although it might be revived on a regional, European level); the work society based on the territorial nation-states in which we are used to living is right now breaking apart; the social contract between capitalism, the welfare state and democracy is broken[40]; we are living in a world of *endemic insecurity*; and finally there is no way to avoid the emergent *risk society* (whose defining feature is not so much the increased amount of risk but rather the changed nature of uncertainty). All the above processes go hand in hand with, and are direct consequences of, the process of industrial modernization (Esping-Andersen in his report on "Towards a Welfare State for the XXI Century" describes the Gordian Knot we are facing in the following way: "how to sustain Europe's normative commitments to social justice while aspiring to be a truly competitive force in the evolving knowledge economy").[41] The major force at work is globalization. Consequently, the picture of the current social reality is very radical indeed and this reality requires a new

---

[39] Ulrich Beck, *What is Globalization?* transl. by P. Camiller, Cambridge: Polity Press, 2000, p. 8.

[40] Assar Lindbeck rightly claims in "The End of the Middle Way? The Large Welfare States in Europe. Hazardous Welfare-State Dynamics" (*AEA Papers and Proceedings*, Vol. 85, No. 2, May, 1995) that reforming the welfare state is bound to create serious problems for the population, "as welfare-state entitlements may be regarded as long-term contracts between the government and the citizens. A 60-year-old who is told that the government cannot live up to its earlier promises of sick payments, unemployment benefits, or pensions will find it difficult to relive his life for the purpose of saving and buying annuities for himself! Thus, welfare-state policies not only mitigate market risks, but may also create new types of risks in the form of unpredictable changes in politically determined rules..." (ibidem, pp. 13–14).

[41] Gøsta Esping-Andersen, "Towards a Welfare State for the XXI Century". Paper for "European Social Services Conference", Barcelona, 5 June 2002, p. 1.

conceptual framework to be analyzed; in a strong formulation it is the following:

A new kind of capitalism, a new kind of economy, a new kind of global order, a new kind of society and a new kind of personal life are coming into being, all of which differ from earlier phases of social development. Thus, sociologically and politically, *we need a paradigm-shift, a new frame of reference*. This is not "postmodernity" but a second modernity, and the task that faces us is to reform sociology so that it can provide a new framework of for the reinvention of society and politics.[42]

Nothing in the social sphere remains intact at the turn of the 21st century, the world is radically and substantially different. Nothing will be the same, Beck claims. The "second modernity" is a "magical password" that will "open the door to new conceptual landscapes":

At the same time, the whole conceptual world of national sovereignty is fading away – a world that includes the taming of capitalism in Europe by the postwar welfare state.[43]

Beck never uses catastrophic overtones with reference to the interrelated processes of globalization which he sees as unintended but irreversible, harsh but inherent in the development of the world of the first modernity which is now breaking apart. As he puts it dramatically, in the transition from the first to the second modernity, we are dealing with a "fundamental transformation, a paradigm shift, a departure into the unknown world of globality, but not with a 'catastrophe' or 'crisis', if the concept of crisis means that we could return to the status quo ante by taking the 'right' (= usual) measures".[44] (It is important to note that Beck is never a pessimistic visionary who presents a gloomy picture of the new, hostile and hard to understand reality. The theoretical underpinning of his recent books was developed almost two decades ago and presented for the first time in *Risikogesellschaft. Auf dem Weg in eine andere Moderne* in 1986; at that time, in a significant part of his social criticism, the clue to under-

---

[42] Ulrich Beck, *World Risk Society*, Cambridge: Polity Press, 1999, p. 2; emphasis mine.
[43] Idem, *The Brave New World of Work*, op. cit., p. 17.
[44] Idem, *What is Globalization?* op. cit., p. 123.

standing the changing world was provided by the vague concept of "postmodernity", with globalization slowly emerging as the major theoretical concept of the 1990s). Beck in his attempts to revitalize sociological thinking traditionally embedded in the ideas of the nation-state calls for the renegotiation of the basis of the first modernity.

5. The Passage from the Work Society to the Risk Society?

Globalization in Beck's account calls into question a basic premise of the first modernity according to which the "contours of society largely coincide with those of the national state". It is not only new connections and interconnections which come into being: "much more far-reaching is the breakdown of the basic assumptions whereby societies and states have been conceived, organized, and experienced as *territorial units separated from one another*".[45] What is the common denominator for the various dimensions of globalization and what does the changing sense of borders mean for social players today:

> One constant feature is the overturning of the central premise of the first modernity: namely, the idea that *we live and act in the self-enclosed spaces of national states and their respective national societies.* Globalization means that borders become markedly less relevant to everyday behaviour in the various dimensions of economics, information, ecology, technology, cross-cultural conflict and civil society.[46]

Beck's concept of "reflexive modernization" developed for the first time in his *Risikogesellschaft* book of 1986, puts an emphasis on the self-transformation and opening-up of the first, national modernity. What these largely unintended and unforeseen processes signal is a change to the whole of society, a change affecting the "foundations of whole modern societies".[47] "Reflexive modernization" means the possibility

---

[45] Ibidem, p. 21.
[46] Ibidem, p. 20.
[47] Ulrich Beck, *The Brave New World of Work*, op. cit., p. 19.

of a creative (self-) destruction for an entire epoch: for the epoch of the industrial society. "The 'subject' of this creative destruction is not the revolution, not the crisis, but the victory of Western modernization".[48] It is a radicalization of modernity which breaks up the premises and contours of industrial society and opens paths to "another modernity".[49] Modernization annihilates the contours of the industrial society and gives birth to a new historical being. The end of the cold war brought about the political renaissance of Europe but it has not contributed to the revival of Europe's ideas, leading rather to "a general paralysis".[50] In answer to the general agreement of pessimism and optimism that there is only one shape to modernity, that of industrial society (consumer society accompanied by democracy), the theory of reflexive modernization answers: "many modernities are possible".[51]

In the paradigm of the first modernity, globalization is interpreted through the lenses of the "territorial" state, politics, society and culture; in the paradigm of the second modernity, though, globalization changes the relationship between and beyond the nation-states as well as the inner "quality" of the social itself. The very principle of territoriality becomes questionable in an age of globality. From this perspective, the core of globalization is the "deterritorialization of the social". Consequently, in the second modernity:

A territorially fixed image of the social, which for two centuries has captivated and inspired the political, cultural and scientific imagination, is in the course of breaking up. Corresponding to global capitalism is a process of cultural and political globalization which transcends territoriality, as the ordering principle of society.[52]

---

[48] Ulrich Beck, Anthony Giddens, Scott Lash, *Reflexive Modernization. Politics, Tradition and Aesthetics in the Modern Social Order*, Cambridge: Polity Press, 1994, p. 2; see also Giddens' magisterial *Consequences of Modernity*, Cambridge: Polity Press, 1990.

[49] Ulrich Beck, Anthony Giddens, Scott Lash, *Reflexive Modernization. Politics, Tradition and Aesthetics in the Modern Social Order*, op. cit., p. 3.

[50] Ulrich Beck, *World Risk Society*, op. cit., p. 24.

[51] Ulrich Beck, Anthony Giddens, Scott Lash, *Reflexive Modernization. Politics, Tradition and Aesthetics in the Modern Social Order*, op. cit., p. 24.

[52] Ulrich Beck, *The Brave New World of Work*, op. cit., pp. 26–27.

The meaning of this deterritorialization (or despatialization) of the social and the political, Beck argues, can be best illustrated by the example of the future of work. Our work society is becoming a risk society, and accompanying concepts in the academic and public debates are e.g. "post-industrialism", "post-Fordism", "post-Taylorism" or "neo-Fordism". In the second modernity, the risk regime prevails in every field: "economy, society, polity. Here the appropriate distinction is therefore not between an industrial and post-industrial or Fordist and post-Fordist economy, but between the *securities, certainties and clearly defined boundaries* of the first modernity, and the *insecurities, uncertainties and loss of boundaries* in the second modernity".[53] The possible consequence of the free-market utopia is what he calls in *The Brave New World of Work* the "Brazilianization of the West" or the "Brazilianization of Europe" in *What Is Globalization?*[54] The general description of similarities highlights the diversity and insecurity in people's work and life.[55] Beck draws parallels between the changing European work environment and the current realities in Brazil where

> Those who depend upon a wage or salary in full-time work represent only a minority of the economically active population; the majority earn their living in more precarious conditions. People are travelling vendors, small retailers or craftworkers, offer all kinds of personal service, or shuttle back and forth between different fields of activity, forms of employment and training.[56]

---

[53] Ibidem, p. 70.

[54] Ulrich Beck, *What is Globalization?* op. cit., p. 161.

[55] "Insecurity" becomes one of the defining features of both living and working in a post-welfare environment; as Geoffrey Garrett claims, "perhaps the most important effect of globalization is the increase of social dislocations of economic insecurity, as distribution of incomes and jobs across firms and industries becomes increasingly unstable. The result is that *increasing numbers of people have to spend ever more time and money trying to make their future more secure*" (quoted in Torben Iversen, "The Dynamics of Welfare State Expansion. Trade Openness, De- industrialization, and Partisan Politics", in: *The New Politics of the Welfare State*, ed. by Paul Pierson, Oxford: Oxford University Press, 2001; emphasis mine).

[56] Ulrich Beck, *The Brave New World of Work*, op. cit., pp. 1–2.

What Beck calls "nomadic 'multi-activity'" is a rapidly spreading variant in late work-societies where attractive and well-paid full-time employment is on its way out.[57] Consequently, insecurity prevails in almost all positions within society in the West today.[58] Global capitalism in Beck's description is doing away with work and unemployment is no longer a *marginal* fate: it affects everyone as well as our very "democratic way of life".[59] Consequently, Beck's question is how democracy will be possible when the full-employment society is over, or is there a chance for political freedom and democracy *without* material security: in short, "how democracy will be possible without the securities of the work society".[60]

An exclusively profit-driven capitalism that excludes from consideration employees rights, the welfare state and democracy, is a capitalism that undermines its own legitimacy, Beck argues: "the neoliberal utopia is a kind of democratic illiteracy. For the market is not its own justification; it is an economic form viable only in interplay with material security, social rights and democracy, and hence with the democratic state. To gamble everything on the free market is to destroy, along with democracy, that whole economic mode".[61]

Beck proposes a workable antithesis to the work society of the past: a society of *active citizens* – which is "no longer fixed within the

---

[57] Ibidem, p. 2.

[58] What may emerge is what Will Hutton called "the 30/30/40 society" in his "High-Risk Strategy" paper where he describes the emergence of a new stratification of British society, "there is a bottom 30 percent of unemployed and economically inactive who are marginalized; another 30 percent who, while in work, are in forms of employment that are structurally insecure; and there are only 40 percent who can count themselves as holding tenured jobs which allow them to regard their income prospects with certainty" (Will Hutton, "High-Risk Strategy", in: *The Welfare State Reader*, ed. by Christopher Pierson and Francis G. Castles, Cambridge: Polity Press, 2000, p. 337).

[59] Ulrich Beck, *What is Globalization?* op. cit., p. 58. Esping-Andersen summarizes the difference: "The standard production worker and the low-skilled could by and large count on a decently paid and secured job in the welfare capitalist era. This is unlikely to be the case in the twenty-first century" (Gøsta Esping-Andersen, Duncan Gallie, Anton Hemerijck, John Myles, *Why We Need a New Welfare State*, op. cit., p. 3).

[60] Ulrich Beck, *What is Globalization?* op. cit., p. 63.

[61] Idem, *The Brave New World of Work*, op. cit., p. 4.

container of the national state" and whose activities are organized both locally and across frontiers – can develop answers to the new challenges of individualization, globalization, falling employment and ecological crisis.[62] The antithesis to the work society is going to be a multi-active society; the self-active, self-aware, political civil society.

6. A Broken Historical Bond Between Capitalism, the Welfare State, and Democracy?

What is especially interesting is Beck's strongly formulated thesis about the *broken historical bond* today between capitalism, the welfare state, and democracy (that parallels the end of John Gerard Ruggie's postwar "embedded liberalism compromise").[63] As Beck formulates the point, if global capitalism dissolves the core values of the work society, a historical link between capitalism, the welfare state and democracy will break apart. As he argues, democracy in Europe and North America came into the world as *labor democracy*: it rested upon paid employment. Employment breathed life into political rights and freedoms:

> paid labour has always underpinned not only private but also political existence. What is at issue today, then, is not "only" the millions of unemployed, nor only the future of the welfare state, the struggle against poverty, or the possibility of greater social justice. *Everything we have is at stake. Political freedom and democracy in Europe are at stake.*[64]

The association of capitalism with basic political, social and economic rights, in Beck's view, is not "'some favour' to be dispensed

---

[62] Ibidem, p. 5.

[63] To recall briefly Ruggie's idea: "the extraordinary success of postwar international economic liberalization hinged on a compact between state and society to mediate its deleterious domestic effects" (John Gerard Ruggie, "Globalization and the Embedded Liberalism Compromise: The End of an Era?", Max Planck Institute for the Studies of Societies. Working Paper, No. 1, 1997, p. 1), which is what he earlier called the "embedded liberalism compromises" in 1982 (see John Gerard Ruggie, "International Regimes, Transactions, and Change: Embedded Liberalism in the Postwar Economic Order", *International Organization*, Vol. 36, No. 2, 1982, Spring).

[64] Ulrich Beck, *What is Globalization?* op. cit., p. 62; emphasis mine.

with when money gets tight". Rather, such a socially-buffered capitalism was an answer to the experiences of fascism and the challenges of communism, as Karl Polanyi argued for the first time in *The Great Transformation*. Therefore, without material security there is no political freedom and no democracy.[65]

Though in Ancient Greece and Rome, freedom was (among other things) freedom from work, in modern times the citizen was conceived as *a working citizen* (apart from the fact that he was also a citizen of the nation-state). The idea of democracy came into the world as a "work-democracy"; consequently, the issue now is not only chronic unemployment, nor the fate of the welfare state, but also "the future of political freedom and democracy in Europe".[66]

Beck acknowledges the significance of the collapse of communism in Eastern Europe in 1989. This historical phenomenon as seen by those political scientists and sociologists who are dealing with the advent of globalization and the collapse of the welfare state requires separate attention; suffice it to say here, though, that Beck (like e.g. Zygmunt Bauman or Ramesh Mishra) draws a significant connection between 1989, capitalism, democracy and the welfare state. After 1989, Beck argues, basic aspects of the capitalist mode that were covered up in postwar Western welfare capitalism have emerged in a "sharper form".[67]

Most our social institutions are being currently reinvented, beginning with the institution of the state (from "managerial" to "minimalist" to "effective") but the idea of new social contracts is still open. Somehow the plane of thinking about social contracts became altered – from national, confined to single nation-states, to regional if

---

[65] Ibidem, pp. 62–63. As Anthony McGrew formulated the point: "For if state sovereignty is no longer conceived as indivisible but shared with international agencies; if states no longer have control over their national territories; and if territorial and political boundaries are increasingly permeable, *the core principles of democratic liberty –* that is self-governance, the demos, consent, representation, and popular sovereignty – *are made distinctly problematic"* (*The Transformation of Democracy? Globalization and Territorial Democracy*, ed. by Anthony McGrew, Cambridge: Polity Press, 1997, p. 12; emphasis mine).

[66] Ulrich Beck, *The Brave New World of Work*, op. cit., p. 13.

[67] Idem, *What is Globalization?* op. cit., p. 96.

not global (and the EU is a good example here). Consequently, the social sciences may need to substantially revise their fundamental premises and reorient their thinking; sociology, for instance, has traditionally – in today's, retrospective view – been merely a sociology of the first modernity focused mostly, if not exclusively, on the nation-state. As Beck comments, "beyond all their differences, such theorists as Emile Durkheim, Max Weber and even Karl Marx shared a territorial definition of modern society, and thus a model of society centred on the national state, which has today been shaken by globality and globalization".[68]

Beck's political economy of insecurity or his "political economy of world risk society" can be outlined in five points. First, the new power game is acted out between "territorially fixed" political players and "non-territorially fixed" economic players (i.e. between governments, parliaments, trade unions – and capital, finance markets and commerce). Second, the room for maneuver of individual states is limited to the dilemma of either paying with higher unemployment for decreasing poverty rates (as in most European countries) or accepting more poverty in exchange for less unemployment (as in the United States). Three, the work society is coming to an end. Consequently, there are no more "jobs for life" and rising unemployment is due to the success of technologically advanced capitalism. Four, we are currently experiencing what he terms a "domino effect", and finally, five, "labor market flexibility" has become a political mantra. What is especially important for us here is the more general conclusion that "flexibility also means a redistribution of risks *away from the state and the economy towards the individual*". What is evident is one future trend: "endemic insecurity" for a majority of people.[69]

Beck argues that the social consequences of globalization touch on the very *substance of freedom and democracy*. Between political freedom and the new political economy of risk and uncertainty there is "a basic contradiction".[70] Globalization will make possible things which

[68] Ibidem, p. 24.
[69] Ulrich Beck, *The Brave New World of Work* , op. cit., pp. 2–3; emphasis mine.
[70] Idem, *World Risk Society*, op. cit., p. 12.

remained hidden during the stage of the welfare-democratic "taming" of capitalism. Global corporations are playing a key role "in shaping not only the economy but society as a whole".[71] Transnational corporations have launched an attack upon the *material lifelines* of modern national societies.[72] Transnational corporations are bidding farewell to the nation-state and refusing further loyalty to it: "As the national framework loses its binding force, the winners and the losers of globalization cease to sit at the same table. The new rich no longer 'need' the new poor".[73]

While transnational corporations are growing in number and diversity, what is decisive about them is that, in the course of globalization, they are able to play off nation-states against one another. Beck argues that looked at from outside, everything has remained as it was: companies produce, hire and fire, pay taxes. The crucial point, however, is that they *"no longer do this under rules of the game defined by national states*, but continue to play the old game while nullifying and redefining those rules. It thus only *appears* to be a question of the old game of labour and capital, state and unions. For while one player continues to play the game within the framework of the national state, the other is already playing within the framework of world society".[74] The social consequences are stark. What has been re-emerging and growing sharper is the "conflictual logic of the capitalist zero-sum game".[75]

7. Globalization, the Desocialization of the Economic and the Recommodification of the Social

Habermas and Beck agree on one point about the future of the welfare state in Europe: the transformations we are currently witnessing are irreversible, we are passing into a new age with

---

[71] Idem, *What is Globalization?* op. cit., p. 2.

[72] Ibidem, p. 3.

[73] Ibidem, p. 7.

[74] Ibidem, pp. 64–65; emphasis mine.

[75] Ibidem, p. 7.

respect to the balance between the economic and the social. With respect to welfare futures, the emergence of Habermas' "post-natnational constellation" carries roughly the same message as the emergence of Beck's "second, postnational modernity" (and, by the way, Zygmunt Bauman's "liquid modernity"): the traditional postwar Keynesian welfare state, with its powerful "nation-state" component, is doomed, and for them the culprit behind the end of this social project in Europe is globalization, in its theories and its practices. They do not focus on the internal developments of the European welfare state (like changing demographics, including the aging of Western societies; shifts in familial structures; the burden of past entitlements within the inter-generational contract between the old and the young, the working and the unemployed etc), clearly linking the new geography of social risks and uncertainties with the advent of – mainly economic – globalization. They emphasize the role of high levels of taxation and social democratic redestributive policies. The emergence of the "individualized society" (as Bauman called it[76]) is accompanied by the overwhelming power of consumer ideologies, still reinforced by the general neoliberal tendency to desocialize the economic and to recommodify the social. While understandable in a European, including Central European, context, their belief in a future federalist European solution for welfare issues (or for a global scheme of basic income understood as a human right, as Bauman suggests) seems – from a global perspective – very hard to realize under global pressures. They have observed the passage from social solidarity to enhanced individualism, and from the ideals of social cohesion to those of economic competitiveness (even on a regional basis in the enlarged EU) and are not able to accept them on philosophical, social and finally moral grounds.

---

[76] Zygmunt Bauman, *The Individualized Society*, Cambridge: Polity Press, 2001.

Adam Chmielewski
Wrocław

Two Concepts of Unity
in Political Practice

1. Liberty and Unity

For more than a decade now, the famous distinction between two concepts of liberty, introduced by Isaiah Berlin in 1958[1], has enjoyed its second life. It has been revived, though largely for the critical purposes, in the context of the liberal/communitarian debate, especially in Charles Taylor's and Alasdair MacIntyre's critique of individualism, emotivism and atomism in political and social philosophy life of modern societies.

It is worth remarking that Berlin's distinction between two concepts of liberty, negative and positive ones, has been formulated in a very specific historical context. His insistence upon the understanding of liberty as individual freedom from limitations, along with his critique of the historical inevitability, much paralleling, and I think much indebted to, Karl Popper's critique of historicism and totalitarianism, has been put forward at the time when much of the world has been under the sway of the communist regimes which, both doctrinally and practically, aimed at controlling and limiting the freedoms of individuals. Berlin's critique of the positive concept of freedom, just as Popper's defence of the liberal individualism and of the open society, are properly to be understood in the historical context of the dangers liberty had to face at that time.

---

[1] Isaiah Berlin, "Two Concepts of Liberty", a lecture delivered in Oxford on October 31, 1958; in: idem, *Four Essays on Liberty*, Oxford: Oxford University Press, 1969.

Ever since the time of the staunch defence of liberty by Berlin and Popper, the world has undergone dramatic changes. Victorious liberal freedom prevailed in much of the world, most specifically in those parts of it which previously were stifled by non-liberal regimes. At the same time, however, its victory has enticed strong adverse reactions in different regions where the negative freedom is not, and has never been appreciated. The strength of the resistance against globalization of the Western ideology and economy is nowadays leading to dramatic conflicts that contribute to the instability of the post-cold-war world disorder. It is becoming evident that at this particular moment of history, in view of the strength of the resistance against the liberal world, and gravity of the present global conflicts, we should now be addressing not so much the questions of individual liberty, but those of the unity of the world.

It is a common knowledge that, in virtue of the exclusivist nature of human beings, it is easier for people to unite against a common enemy, or against a common threat, rather than around a common cause. There are reasons to believe, however, that essential ineradicability of human exclusivism does not leave us helpless in addressing the question of unity. For there are at least three fundamental attitudes one may adopt toward it. For one may aim at suppressing the agonistic individual need to distinguish oneself from each other, as did Thomas Hobbes and the liberal followers of his para-political[2] concept of society. Alternatively, one may also aim at exciting the agonistic rivalry between individuals and their groups as did, for example, Carl Schmitt in his ultra-political[3] view of mutual relationships between societies, or more recently, Samuel Huntington in his account of the future of the globe as an unavoidable clash of civilizations. What is usually left from sight is a third possible attitude, truly political one, that consists in a continuous attempt at managing the exclusivist rivalries between individuals and their various groupings; this can be achieved not by extinguishing the rivalries altogether, nor

---

[2] For the concept of parapolitics see Slavoj Žižek's *The Plague of Fantasy*, Polish edition: *Przekleństwo fantazji*, transl. by Adam Chmielewski, Wrocław: Wydawnictwo Uniwersytetu Wrocławskiego, 2001, p. 90.

[3] Ibidem, p. 91.

by exciting them into all-out conflicts, but by keeping them alive, yet within limits of respect for life, dignity and well-being of the other.

In order to elaborate on this point, I would like to distinguish, just as Isaiah Berlin did, between two concepts, not of liberty however, but those of unity. For it seems obvious that unity can be understood in two different manners: as the unity of enforced dogma, and the unity of negotiated compromise. The first kind of the unity is achieved through imposition or enforcement, the other is the unity negotiated or hard-won through an argument and through an effort toward mutual understanding. These two concepts of unity differ in the ways of implementing them, as well as in the stability guaranteed by them. The unity imposed may seem firm and durable, yet rarely is; the unity negotiated may seem unstable and fragile, yet is, as a rule, far more permanent. The first kind of unity is usually repugnant to those who are forced to reconcile with it; the other, on the contrary, is by far more respected and treasured by all involved in its achievement and protection; although the first kind unity is likely to win in a short-run perspective, their proponents must be wary of the fact that those who were forced to yield to their will, sooner or later will most likely rebel against it.

One of leading communitarians, Alasdair MacIntyre, has often been misrepresented as preaching a return to the tightly-nit ideal community in which an individual has little scope for his or her individual freedom. This view is far from adequate. In fact, MacIntyre's concept of community enables one better to understand the second concept of unity. Following Alasdair MacIntyre one may say that any community exists in so far as its members are engaged in a permanent debate about what their community is supposed to be. A continuous debate about the identity of a community, conducted within it, is a sign of its life; it should be read as evidence that its members are really concerned about their community, that they identify with it. The death of such an argument would signify that the community has lost its strength and attractiveness, that its members gave up on it and do not wish to take any active part in it; that they refuse to co-determine its future development and do not see anymore a place for themselves within it. A living community builds its unity through a process of a continuously negotiated and renegotiated compromise. It follows from this that a community is never constituted by the unanimity; rather, unanimity is a sign of its atrophy. Unanimity signals that the unity of a community is being built according to an imposed dogma. The concept of a community cannot be understood in abstraction from the two different concepts of unity juxtaposed above.

2. Dimensions and Responsibilities of the European Union

It seems quite obvious that the above distinction between two concepts of unity finds its vivid representation in the recent geopolitics. The American recent policy seems to be an attempt to achieve the unity of the world by imposing upon it, by force, a particular set of values on regions where they have never been at home. By contrast, the European project can be interpreted as an attempt to achieve unity through a process of recognition and respect for the difference embodied in various ways of life and traditions inhabiting this continent.

Recently, however, the European project suffered a series of major setbacks: some elements of the project, especially the Constitution for Europe, have been rejected by some of the nations. In the popular referenda in France and in the Netherlands, the majority of the voters rejected the Constitutional Treaty for Europe. Most recently, the European Union summit in Brussels has failed to produce the Union's budget for the years 2007–2013. The dispute revealed more sharp discrepancies within the Union than anyone would expect just a year ago. In the opinion popular among the European press, these events not only have question the future development of the European Union, but also dealt a severe blow to its present institutions. Some officials and commentators talk even about dismantling the monetary union and abandoning the euro. Few of them, however, bother to remark that the victory of Euro-pessimists, though undeniable, was not a landslide one, few of them also deign to mention that the budget debates have never been any different from the one which we have just witnessed. In the face of the trouble, the European politicians have demonstrated remarkable lack of leadership and seem to be ready to give up on something which may have been the best idea Europe ever had.

Undeniably, however, there is at least one benefit that can be drawn from all this. The rejection of the Constitutional Treaty by two European nations, and other major problems of the European Union, may be understood as a perfect case of a democratic correction to the stifled and bureaucratised procedures characteristic of the European Union, and as a great achievement of the agonistic democracy.[4] For it has opened, more effectively than anything else, the public space to restart the debate on the future of the European unification project. The discussion will hopefully help us to decide whether we, the Europeans, are to save this project, or to abandon it altogether.

Attempting to answer the question of the reasons responsible for recent setbacks in the process of unification of Europe, I would like to

---

[4] Jean Baudrillard, commenting upon the French rejection of the Constitutional Treaty, wrote: „The intriguing thing about the *trompe l'oeuil* Euro referendum is the No that lies beyond the official No; beyond political reason. This is the No that resists. There must be something very dangerous about it to have mobilized all the authorities so determinedly behind the Yes. Such defensive panic is a sure sign of a corpse in the wardrobe. This No is clearly an instinctive reaction to the ultimatum that the referendum has been from the start. A reaction to the complacent coalition around an infallible, universal Holy Europe. A reaction to the Yes as a categorical imperative whose backers did not dream for a moment that it might be seen as a challenge, and a challenge to be met. It does not therefore say No to Europe, it says No to the unquestionable Yes. There is always something galling about the arrogance of a victory assumed *a priori*, whatever the reasons. The outcome has been decided in advance, and all that is sought is a consensus. 'Say Yes to Yes': this now commonplace formula conceals a dreadful mystification. Yes no longer means yes to Europe, or even yes to Chirac, or to the neo-liberal order. It means yes to Yes, to the consensual order; it is no longer an answer, but the content of the question itself. Our Europositivity is being put to the test. And by a reflex of both pride and self-defence, the unconditional Yes spontaneously calls forth an equally unconditional No. The real puzzle is why there has not been an even bigger, more violent reaction against this mindless yes-ism. The No reflex does not require political consciousness. It is an automatic return of fire against the coalition of all those who are on the side of universal good, while the rest are relegated to the twilight of History. What the forces of Good failed to anticipate was the perverse effects of their own declared superiority." See *New Left Review* 33, May June 2005, pp. 24–25.

suggest that it is due to the fact that insufficient recognition of the ineradicably agonistic aspects of human nature. More specifically, the very concept of referenda in which the populations of European Union nations were to decide about the future fate of the Community, has been formulated in such a way as to deprive the individuals of a true choice or a genuine say in the matters in question. The people were treated as a collection of rubberstamps to something which has been agreed and decided beforehand; the Europeans were given a false choice, such a false choice was justly felt by majority as an evidence of the anti-democratic lack of recognition of, and offence to, their judgement, their agency, and their freedom.

3. Three Dimensions

So far the European Union has functioned mainly in two dimensions: the historical and pragmatic one. Both these dimensions implied two major responsibilities the European Union undertook to discharge: preservation of peace and a more just distribution of wealth among the inhabitants of its member states. Both responsibilities involved specific burdens. It is my argument that in order not to crumble under these burdens, especially under the economic ones, the European Union should enter into a third dimension, geopolitical-strategic one.

So far the European Union has shunned from entering into this third dimension. It had its own reasons for that. The burden of the European historical guilt was a justification for it not to engage into any attempts to influence the shape of the world because, in this particular sphere, especially in the first half of the 20th century, Europe has shown its ugliest face. The historical justification for Europe's staying away from strategic matters was for it also, however, a convenient excuse to leave the task of shaping the global world order to America, and, at the same time, to continue its elaborate and popular social policies. The present moment in history should make the Europeans to realise, however, that an active strategic role of Europe in the world is necessary for the sake of safety of the world, and its own, but also may contribute to boosting of its economy. In the view of the accumulating problems created by the unilateralist policies of the United States, and contrary to the supporters of the "atlanticism", a strong and unified European Union is also evidently in the best interest of America as well.

4. The Pragmatic Dimension

Over the past decades the pragmatic aspect of integrative processes in Europe has become more prominent than the historical one. As a result, for the old and new members of the Union, is has had largely, if not exclusively, an economic meaning. Under the pressure of the expectations and claims stirred by the aims the Union undertook to satisfy, it has become largely a social democratic device. This led, however, to the spread of economic demands, lack of creativity, decrease in effectiveness of labour, ossification of the labour market, etc. The old lazy Europeans do not wish to forsake their privileges they won so far. The new hungry Europeans, barred from them for decades, demand them now with a double force, ready to accept far-reaching compromises with morality to win them. The excessive importance of the pragmatic-economic dimension of the European integration causes the Union to falter under the pressure of economy. Moreover, these burdens are unevenly spread, both regionally and socially. When social privileges are in danger, however, the spectres of history are immediately called in to excite horror in the opponents. Recently, since leading nations of the European Union have grown dissatisfied, many spectres have been awoken in the European space, gradually turning the idea of the future European eternal peaceful bliss into a pugnacious nightmare known from the past.

5. Aspirations and Deficiencies

Aspirations are an accurate picture of deficiencies. It is no different in the case of the European Union. The European Union has had an ambition to become, by 2010, „the most competitive and dynamic

economy based on knowledge, able of sustainable development, offering more jobs and more social cohesiveness".[5] The Lisbon Strategy
was designed as an instrument to implement these aims; among them
are the development of education, research and new technologies.
The Lisbon Strategy comprises seven "dimensions of competitiveness"; on the top of the list are „the creation of the information society
for all" and „the European area of research and innovation". The
same ideas can be found in the manifesto of the new social democracy
by Tony Blair and Gerhard Schröder, and in the German Agenda
2010. The direction of the outlined reform stems from a conviction,
largely accurate, that the most efficient way to boost the expanding
Union which now falters under accumulated global and internal pressures, is to develop the scientific research seen as a source of innova-
tiveness and competitiveness of its economy.

This ambition, however, collided with practice. The authors of the
Lisbon Strategy have themselves acknowledged that the implementation of the determined tasks is in a "serious danger". It had become a
laughing matter for the Americans with which Europe tries in vain to
compete. No wonder: nearly a half of the European Union budget is
being spent on agricultural subsidies (actually, at present about 40 per
cent; initially the European community has been spending nearly 70
per cent of its budget on this purpose) whereas, in comparison, the
expenditures on the scientific research are a modest fraction of the
common budget. Discrepancy between the European aspirations and
realities suggests that the European Union has entered the 21st century as a victim of the traditional, largely French, agrarianism, and
will not be able to give life to its modernizing ambitions until it will
not muster the courage to reformulate its priorities.

Both dimensions, historical and pragmatic one, generate, on a
higher international level, new antagonisms. They make themselves
apparent through political quarrels between the advocates of the
Union as a federal super-state and as a community of nations; of the
Europe of solidarity and the Europe of the national egoisms; the
Europe of the spirit and the Europe of book-keepers; between the core

[5] *The Lisbon Review 2002–2003. An Assessment of Policies and Reforms in Europe*,
Geneva: World Economic Forum, 2002, p. 1.

and the peripheries of Europe; between deepening of the Union and its expansion. It seems that acknowledgement of the strategic role of the European Union in the world would present itself as an opportunity to overcome these disputes. Entering the third dimension by Europe would be an opportunity to redefine the community on a different basis in such a way as to enable it to share a large part of the responsibility for the world, the responsibility it avoided in the post-war decades. The European debate between spirituality and accountancy should find its solution in responsibility.

6. The Atlantic Drift

The Autumn of the Peoples of 1989 (quite unjustly symbolised by the fall of the Berlin Wall of November 9, 1989, rather than by the political victory of the Polish "Solidarity" movement in June 1989), which lead to dismantling of the communist bloc; the terrorist assault on the US of September 11, 2001; the expansion of the European Union onto ten new countries; and the conflict in Iraq, are the signposts in the recent rapid transformation of the world. In this unique sequence of events particularly important for the new identity of Europe have been the unilateral action of the United States on the international scene, its aggressive missionary rhetoric, its belief in efficacy of the military action, the lack of respect for international institutions, the United Nations and the International Criminal Court included, and especially the maltreatment of prisoners in the Iraqi prison Abu Ghraib as well as in the Guantánamo Bay military detention centre. Europe, which has began to perceive the world from its own perspective, has found in America a negative point of reference. And vice versa: a high official of the American administration, when asked about US policy toward the European integration, responded: "Disintegration!".

In relation to the latest issue, some Europeans began asking questions about the moral difference between one regime which denigrated, tortured and murdered prisoners in Abu Ghraib, and the other regime which, having abolished the former, denigrates, tortures and murders prisoners in the very same prison. And they are prone to answer that one difference lies in the fact that if the murderers of the former regime tried to hide their atrocities from the outside world and from their own families, the perpetrators associated with the new regime had no qualms about revealing their cruelties to their own families, by sending them self-made photographs depicting their gruesome efforts in Abu Ghraib. Apparently, the feeling of moral rightness of the mission they discharge gave them also a sense of impunity. If that is the case, it is difficult not to ask further questions, e.g.: what does this tell us about the morality of new torturers, and about the morality of their American families, the recipients of the photographs?

7. Two Concepts of Unity: a Moral Aspect

The scorn poured by the United States on the principle of legitimacy of political action, their policy of weakening and humiliating of the UN, the ideology of the pre-emptive strikes, and finally the (un)common American hubris, has provoked a mental breakthrough in Europe. It marked the beginning of a process now interpreted as dissolution of the "West", though it is rather doubtful whether the "West" has ever existed as a unity we grew to think about it. It would be closer to the truth that the increasing coherence of Europe and growing sense of its own identity led to a Gestalt-switch enabling everyone to see the differences within the allegedly unified West which, though have not been noticed before, were there nevertheless.

The Cold War antagonism between the West ("Empire of Good") and the East ("Empire of Evil") has lost its ground some time ago. Ever since we have been witnessing ideological attempts to supersede it by the antagonism between the Occident and the Muslim Orient. This attempt has not been quite successful. The post-Christian Europe and the America-reborn-in-Christ are drifting apart. We do not seem to have one West anymore, but two: one from Venus, the other from Mars; one from Kant, the other from Hobbes. The guilty Europe, forced to forsake its own Europocentrism, gradually gains it back in an another, post-post-modern form. The "innocent" America, however, continues in its outdated Occidentalism, all the more so since it provides it with a well-established justification for its world-domination, and supports its black-and-white-interpretation of the hatred which pushed the terrorists to the attack of September 11, 2001.

The US offers a missionary, unilateralist conception of building the unity of the world according to an Occidentalist dogma, to be imposed onto the world by force. The very existence of the European Union as an independent agent, especially its experience in the peaceful overcoming of historical conflicts and enmities, is becoming an ever stronger promise of a unity of the world built upon the multilaterally negotiated compromise. The European direction in its future strategic course should follow from this transatlantic difference.

8. The EU Must Take Care of Itself

The United Europe must take care of itself, and it must do it urgently. Against the apparent meaning of this expression, it is not meant as a call for more inwardness of which the EU has been repeatedly, and rightly, accused. On the contrary, the EU has a duty to take a proper care of itself in order to be able to take care of others, and be respected by them. This means that the EU has to pull itself together to achieve the agency and power that is necessary for the creation of a new world order in which it would then have to play a leading role. The process of pulling itself together is to be aimed, obviously, against the forces which now, as a result of the latest enlargement, begun immediately to pull it apart.

The forces that pull the EU apart are both external and internal to it. The latter, however, have now become more dangerous to its future. The EU has largely become a social democratic instrument which assumed too much weight on its shoulders and will not be able to deliver everything it promised to an increased number of its citizens. In response, political leaderships of some of the newly accepted countries (though not necessarily their populations) play a populist game of demonstrated discontent. Particularly Poland, the largest of the newly accepted countries, has shown its ugliest (double) face to the UE: following the accession, it begun openly to work to undermine the European unity by aspiring to re-evangelise the irreligious European nations, and to oppose its major policies by standing by the US rather than by the EU, while unashamedly reaching into the common European purse.

Joachim Bitterlich is right in arguing that "the Europeans will have to understand the seriousness of our situation" and that "the need for action is urgent".[6] Similarly, he is right in blaming the situation on the lack of leadership within Europe. So, at the present moment, we have think the unthinkable; that is, we have to think of something which, under the pressure of internal and external enemies of the UE, has become unthinkable to the EU administration. The EU has to reject the arguments that, in the wake of the populist quasi-nationalisms, the countries so far kept at the entrance to the EU, i.e. Bulgaria, Romania and Turkey, should continue to wait for an unspecified period of time. The EU should also abandon altogether its polite though wholly irresponsible play with the idea of the Ukrainian membership. Ukraine, despite its recent orange revolution and despite its being Christian orthodox, should *not* become a member of the EU, whereas Turkey, despite its being Muslim, *should* become its member as soon as possible.

Despite the opposition of some members of the European Union, and despite the hesitant attitude of others, geopolitics shows that accession of Turkey to the European Union is a priority. Evidently, full membership of Turkey in the EU will be mutually beneficial for the EU, Turkey itself, the Middle East, and the whole world. From the strategic point of view, the accession of Turkey seems to open a wholly new perspective for the Union. This country is already one of the world largest economic powers. Yet Turkey is powerful not only economically, but also militarily. The Turkish armed forces, with a troop strength of about 600,000 people, are now one of the most

---

6 Joachim Bitterlich, "Six priorities for tackling the EU crisis", in: *Europe's World*, Brussels 2006, forthcoming. Dr Bitterlich is former German Chancellor Helmut Kohl's foreign and security advisor.

powerful armies in the world. Europeanised Turkey, having at its disposal one of the largest and best trained armies in the world, might play a significant role in stabilising the region. By offering to Turkey the full membership, this formidable force will become a part of the European armed forces which also have urgently to be established. There are reasons to believe that Turkey would work even more willingly and successfully in the interest of the Union of which it will become a part, especially when one remembers that Turkey refused to take part in the American-led "coalition of the willing", aimed at the stabilization of Iraq, the coalition which has been falling apart ever since it encountered first serious troubles in the field. Wielding such a force, the EU will become a power capable of bringing the stability to the Middle East which could not, and will not be brought about by the US misguided policies. By fulfilling this strategic task, the EU will become a respected partner not only for the US, but also China and India. It will also be in a position to extend its helpful hand to the needy Africa.

It is true that 70 per cent of the Turkish population live in poverty, which means that the present European Union countries would have to pay for the increase of the level of their life; it is also true that a significant part of these people are the Kurds who, together with their compatriots on the Iraqi territory, demand an independent state for themselves, and have not been foreign to the acts of terror. In this respect, however, Europe, which for decades has been treating Turkey as a cheap tourist resort, cannot be oblivious to three things, all having to do with oil: one is that some vital pipelines, through which the Iraqi oil is being pumped to the West, are passing through the Turkish territories; the second is the increase of the price of oil; and the third is the fact that in the view of the American failure in Iraq, no one cannot reasonably count on the United States to bring the oil price down. After more than two years of the American attempts to take control of the Iraqi oil reserves, its price doubled, gradually approaching 75 US dollars per barrel, and shooting up even higher. It is thus becoming evident that Europe should not, nor indeed has a right to, count on America in this respect, especially that it did not want to help America to win the Iraqi war, and then it did not want to help it to win the Iraqi peace.

Geopolitics suggests also that Ukraine, despite its recent orange revolution, should not become a member of the European Union in a foreseeable future for the simple reason that, for the time being, Europe, too dependent on the Russian energy resources, has to preserve the best possible relationships with Russia because it cannot afford to disregard the Russian strategic interests. The Polish stubbornness in advocacy of the Ukrainian membership in the Union, visibly lacking in credibility and in altruism, is equally misplaced as the Polish recent anti-Russian hysteria, known in a form of anti-Putinism; there are reasons to believe that it is actually more of an obstacle in opening the window of opportunity for the Ukrainian membership in the UE, than a genuine favour. For now, having enough on its plate, especially its grave internal problems and the rivalry with the US, the Union should not risk a new antagonism with Russia.

Europe has to pull itself together in order to be able to have more inner strength. In the present world this means, above all, more energy, both in the literal and figurative sense. The EU knows quite well that it has not enough energy resources on its own territories; it must realise that the energy resources available to it are located not only in Russia, but also in the Middle East. By *including* Ukraine, the EU will antagonise Russia; even Mr. Gerhard Schröder will not be able, single-handedly, to offset the ensuing harm. By *not* including Turkey, the EU will demonstrate its suicidal political and geopolitical irresponsibility. Either way it will irreversibly jeopardise its future as a global agent. The "identity" criteria – the conjunction of the Greek philosophy, the Christian religion and the Roman law – used now wilfully to delineate the external borders of the EU, are purely ideological and are cynically exploited by the internal enemies of the EU to thwart its strategic, geopolitical dimension. Yielding to these arguments would be a true and final failure of the EU.

Stephan Grätzel
Mainz

Das Verzeihen als Grundlage für das kulturelle Zusammenwachsen von Europa

1. Der moderne Freiheitsbegriff

Der Freiheitsbegriff, wie wir ihn heute moralisch und politisch verstehen, ist nicht nur eine Errungenschaft der Philosophie der Aufklärung, er ist in erster Linie ein Erbe des christlichen Freiheitsbegriffes. Dieser Umstand wird gerade in der Philosophie übersehen, wenn sie die Aufklärung mit der Antike kurz schließt und 2000 Jahre überspringt. Freiheit ist keine intellektuelle Erfindung oder praktische Errungenschaft von Philosophen und Politikern seit dem 17. Jahrhundert, sondern Freiheit ist eine spirituell zu nennende Erfahrung, die im engen Zusammenhang mit dem Sinn des Lebens, der Frage nach gelingendem Leben bis hin zur Sehnsucht nach Erlösung und Heil steht. Sie ist im Abendland das Geschenk einer religiösen Weltanschauung, der es gelungen ist und gelingt, das Bewusstsein der Schuld, das im menschlichen Dasein tief verankert ist und mit dem Wissen um Sein, mit dem Wissen um Existenz, aufkommt, zu bewältigen und zu meistern.

Die Verheißung der christlichen Botschaft, von Sünde und Erbschuld erlösen zu können, kann in seiner Tragweite nicht überschätzt werden. Ein freies Bewusstsein, wie wir es heute als selbstverständlich beanspruchen und zugrunde legen, ist das Ergebnis einer Jahrhunderte dauernden Theologie der Befreiung und Ablösung vom Schuldbewusstsein. Wie weitgehend diese Ablösung gediehen ist, lässt sich allein darin sehen, dass wir heute die tragische Schuld, die uns die griechische Literatur überliefert hat, nicht mehr verstehen. Wir sehen in ihr bestenfalls den bekannten unauflösbaren, tragischen Konflikt, ohne allerdings zu erkennen, dass dieser Konflikt vom Leben selbst und seinen Bedingungen und Notwendigkeiten herkommt. Das Unverständnis gegenüber archaischer Schuld ist das Ergebnis der christlichen Auflösung des Schuldbewusstseins überhaupt vor dem Hintergrund einer Verheißung christlicher Freiheit. Natürlich war diese Verheißung an den religiösen Kult gebunden, aber die Reformation und ihre Theologie der Überantwortung der Schuld in das persönliche Gewissen war der letzte Schritt zu einer vollständigen Profanierung christlicher Freiheit. War die Sühne und damit die Freiheit im christlichen Verständnis noch an den bloßen Glauben gebunden, so ist die Freiheit im modernen Verständnis ganz und gar von der Sühne abgekoppelt. Die Profanierung der Freiheit war nur ein kleiner Schritt, da das existenzielle Schuldbewusstsein, die archaische und im ursprünglichen Sinn tragische Schuld, schon durch die christliche Theologie zur glücklichen Schuld gewandelt war. Das heutige Freiheitsverständnis kommt ganz und gar ohne Schuld aus und kennt nur Freiheit ohne Reue und Sühne.

2. Freiheit ohne Schuld,
aber mit schlechtem Gewissen

Es ist aber zu beobachten, dass diese moderne Freiheit ohne Reue doch ein schlechtes Gewissen hat. Das schlechte Gewissen bekundet sich vor allem in politischen Aktionen, in denen sich eine aggressive Moral zeigt, die in geradezu absurder Widersprüchlichkeit zu den Idealen steht, die vertreten werden, wenn also etwa sogenannte Lebensschützer vor amerikanischen Abtreibungskliniken zur Waffe greifen oder wenn im Namen des Friedens getötet wird. In Deutschland traten unter der Last der Naziverbrechen, die nicht als gesühnt empfunden wurden und bis heute nicht werden, weil solche Verbrechen nicht einfach durch die Bestrafung der Täter aus dem Bewusstsein verschwinden, im Zuge der Studentenrevolution philosophisch verbrämte Gerechtigkeits-Aktionen auf den Plan, die im extremen Fall jene Unmenschlichkeit entwickelten, die sie ihren Gegnern vorwarfen. Auch hier war es die diffuse Schuld, die in einem Deutschland, das gerade mit dem Wirtschaftwunder zur Normalität zurück kommen wollte, die Gemüter gerade der damals jungen Generation belastete, einer Generation, die nicht verstehen konnte, wie ihre Eltern nach solchen Völkermorden ohne weiteres zum Alltag eines bürgerlichen Lebens zurückfinden konnten. Das bürgerliche Leben, die Bürgerlichkeit überhaupt wurde so zum Inbegriff von Verlogenheit und doppelter Moral, zumal die bürgerlichen politischen Kräfte auch den Vietnam-Krieg ohne Skrupel rechtfertigen konnten. Gleichzeitig wurde der Kommunismus und der Sozialismus, trotz seiner Verbrechen für Jahre und Jahrzehnte, zur Gewissensinstanz und für viele im Westen zur guten oder fortschrittlichen, in jedem Fall aber zur gerechten Weltanschauung.

So brach die unbewältigte Schuld der Naziherrschaft gerade bei der jungen Generation hervor, bei Menschen, die selbst weder politisch noch gar kriminell schuldig geworden waren. Hier wurde aber das eigentliche Problem der Schuld deutlich, ihre Nachhaltigkeit über die Bestrafung der Täter und ihrer Mitläufer hinaus. Jede Nation, aber auch jede religiöse Vereinigung oder Kirche und ihre Geschichte, haben offenbar ein Schuldkonto, das solange offen steht, bis die Schuld gesühnt ist. Das Problem der Aufarbeitung von Großverbrechen liegt deshalb darin, die entstandene Schuld zu sühnen. Sühne ist nicht mit Strafe abgegolten, auch nicht mit Bezahlung von Reparationen, die nur Ablasszahlungen sind. Die geforderte Sühne, die wie die Schuld selbst schon unter dem Einfluss der christlichen Vergebung, erst recht aber nach der Profanierung des christlichen Hintergrundes unverständlich geworden ist, muss von der Gegenseitigkeit der Verzeihung und Vergebung her verstanden werden, soll sie zur Aufhebung von Schuld führen.

3. Erkennen und Aufarbeitung der Schuld

Wenn wir heute an die Integration Europas und an die Globalisierung denken, dann sollten wir also davon ausgehen, dass jedes Land ein unbewältigtes Schuldkonto hat, das sich aus Verbrechen und Völkermord in der Vergangenheit herleitet. Die Völker und ihre Regierungen sind schlecht beraten, wenn sie dieses Schuldkonto leugnen und so tun, als hätte die Zeit diese Schuld getilgt. Zwar gibt es gute politische Gründe, mit dem Bekenntnis von Vergangenheitsschuld zurückhaltend zu sein. Das Beispiel des Schuldbekenntnis des ehemaligen amerikanischen Präsidenten Clinton, dessen Entschuldigung für die Verschleppung unzähliger Menschen aus Afrika zur Sklaverei eine Reparationsforderung auslöste, die nicht nur unrealistisch hoch sondern auch unversöhnlich war, zeigt, wie leicht moralische, politische oder metaphysische Schuld als juristische missbraucht werden kann und dadurch den gegenteiligen Effekt hervorbringt. Gerade um diesem Missbrauch entgegen zu arbeiten, ist eine ausgiebige Behandlung der Schuldfrage notwendig, denn in jedem Fall werden die Menschen von diffuser Schuld belastet, die zu unberechenbaren politischen Handlungen führt.

Es ist ein großer Irrtum zu meinen, in der zweiten und dritten Generation nach Großverbrechen, wie sie im 20. Jahrhundert stattgefunden haben, könne zur Tagesordnung übergegangen werden, also zu einer Politik, die das Geschehen als erledigt betrachtet. Gerade in den späteren Generationen der Kinder und Enkel tritt die Schuld der Vorfahren erst richtig heraus, dann also, wenn die Täter und Mitläufer bestraft sind und nicht mehr leben. Denn Schuld verschwindet nicht magisch durch Strafe, Bestrafung ist keine Tilgung der Schuld. Über das Verschwinden von Schuld muss in einem anderen Zusammenhang nachgedacht werden, der uns auf die Problematik von Schuld und Sühne bringt.[1] Nicht Strafe sondern Sühne tilgt die Schuld, wobei auch die Strafe ein Teil der Sühne ist. Aber Strafe reicht eben nicht aus.

Jener Teil der Schuld, der durch Strafe nicht getilgt ist, tritt also überhaupt erst in den folgenden Generationen hervor. Diese Schuld der Kollektive ist aber keine Kollektivschuld, da sie nicht juristisch erfasst und abgegolten werden kann. Sie ist jene existenzielle Schuld, die aus der Solidarität als lebendes und vor allem überlebendes Wesen hervorgeht. Deshalb ist gerade in den folgenden Generationen das Thema der Sühne sensibel zu behandeln.

---

[1] Stephan Grätzel, *Dasein ohne Schuld. Dimensionen menschlicher Schuld aus philosophischer Perspektive*, Göttingen: Vandenhoeck und Ruprecht, 2004.

Wenn wir Völkerverständigung betreiben wollen, müssen wir also ein Verständnis für die Schuld gewinnen, die nicht bestraft wurde und auch nicht und nie bestraft werden kann. Es ist diejenige Schuld, die Jaspers in seiner Differenzierung der *Schuldfrage* 1946 der politischen und der solidarischen, von ihm etwas irreführend metaphysisch genannten Schuld zuordnet. Beide Schuldfragen gehen bei Jaspers über die moralische und persönlich zu verantwortende justiziable Schuld hinaus. Sie betreffen die Mitschuld derer, die durch nationale und solidarische Verbundenheit an die Verbrechen gebunden sind. Diese politische und solidarische Schuld muss gesühnt werden, soll eine europäische Integration vorankommen. Ein wichtiger Teil dieser posthumen Sühne ist aber das Verzeihen und die Vergebung. Verzeihen und Vergebung sind nicht als einmaliger oder symbolischer Akt einer Geste zu verstehen, sondern als kultureller Beitrag zur Integration. Hier hat die Philosophie den wichtigen Beitrag zu leisten, die Dimensionen der Schuld herauszustellen und die Möglichkeiten der Entsühnung und Versöhnung aufzuzeigen. Beides ist bisher nur in einem Maß geschehen, das der Bedeutung dieser Frage nicht genügt. Meine Beschäftigung mit diesem Thema in den letzten Jahre konnte kaum auf einschlägige Arbeiten zurückgreifen, die sich von philosophischer Seite diesem Thema nähern. Zumeist sind die Arbeiten zur Schuld theologisch, kulturwissenschaftlich und natürlich psychologisch orientiert. Die Schuld spielt für die Philosophie offenbar keine wichtige Rolle.

Eine wichtige Aufgabe der Philosophie heute sehe ich also darin, die Dimensionen der Schuld herausarbeiten. Dabei zeigt sich, dass sie in allen Bereichen des Lebens vorherrschend ist, sei es offen oder, wie zumeist, verdeckt. Die verdeckte oder diffuse Schuld ist ein schweres Problem nicht nur in den Praxen der Psychologen und Lebensberater, sie prägt auch den Stil einer Politik, für die bestimmte Themen tabu sind und ausgespart werden. Dabei handelt es sich immer um Völkermorde in der Vergangenheit. Die Beispiele hierfür finden sich schnell, in Amerika ist es der Völkermord an den Indianern, der streng tabuisiert ist, in der Türkei sind es die Armenier, in Russland die Kulaken, in China die Tibeter. Deutschland hat sich jetzt erst nach

60 Jahren dieser Frage gestellt und mit dem Mahnmal in Berlin immerhin ein bisher in der Welt einmaliges Denkmal seiner Schande gesetzt. Solche Zeichen sind aber erst der Beginn einer Auseinandersetzung mit der Schuld, keineswegs die Aufarbeitung selbst oder gar ihr Abschluss. Für die Philosophie stellt sich die Frage, was Schuld ist, wieso sie über die Zeit hinaus wirksam ist und wie sie gesühnt werden kann. Die wissenschaftliche Auseinandersetzung ist die Vorbereitung der persönlichen Aufarbeitung der Enkel und Urenkel von Tätern und Opfern.

4. Die philosophische Behandlung von Schuld und Sühne

Die philosophische Literatur zur Schuldfrage ist spärlich, gleichwohl sind hier gewichtige Autoren zu nennen, allen voran Heidegger, Jaspers und in jüngerer Zeit der Franzose Paul Ricoeur (1913–2005). In seinem philosophischen Testament, seinem letzten Werk *Gedächtnis, Geschichte, Vergessen*[2] hat Ricoeur dieser Frage, die ihn sein wissenschaftliches Leben lang begleitet hat, eine abschließende Fassung gegeben. Schon in dem Projekt unter dem Titel: *Die vergangene Zeit lesen, Gedächtnis und Vergessen* hat Ricoeur das Verzeihen als eigenes philosophisches Problem aufgegriffen. In diesem bis 1996 immer wieder bearbeiteten Text, der auf deutsch in der Sammlung unter dem Titel: *Das Rätsel der Vergangenheit: Erinnern, Vergessen, Verzeihen* (Göttingen 1998) von Burkhard Liebsch veröffentlicht wurde, stellt Ricoeur heraus, dass Verzeihen eine Form des Vergessens sei, bei der nicht der Inhalt, sondern die *Bedeutung* des Vergangenen verändert wird und verschwindet. So sind es nicht die Ereignisse selbst, sondern die Schuld, die vergeben und vergessen wird.[3] Entsprechend fordert er ein neues Verhältnis zur Schuld, das aber nur mithilfe einer „Neuein-

---

[2] Paul Ricoeur, *Gedächtnis, Geschichte, Vergessen*, München: Fink, 2004. Original: *La mémoire, l'histoire, l'oubli*. Paris: Édition du Seuil, 2000.

[3] Paul Ricoeur, *Das Rätsel der Vergangenheit: Erinnern, Vergessen, Verzeihen*, Göttingen: Wallstein, 1998, S. 145.

schätzung des Begriffes der Gabe" möglich scheint.[4] Damit soll entsprechend der Schwere der Schuld auch ein „schweres Verzeihen" möglich sein.[5] Das schwere Verzeihen „ist dasjenige, welches die Tragik des Handelns ernst nimmt und auf Voraussetzungen dieses Handelns zielt, auf die Quelle der Konflikte und der Verfehlungen, die der Vergebung bedürfen. Es handelt sich nicht darum, auf der Ebene einer berechenbaren Bilanz ein Sollsaldo zu löschen. Es handelt sich darum, Knoten zu entwirren."[6] Unter den Knoten versteht Ricoeur einerseits die unauflöslichen Konflikte, andererseits die nicht wiedergutzumachenden Schäden und Verbrechen.[7] Was den ersten Knoten – die unauflöslichen Konflikte – betrifft, so wäre er eigens kritisch zu behandeln, da die Unauflöslichkeit der tragischen Schuld gerade aus antikem Verständnis her mit der Auflösung durch die glückliche Schuld (*felix culpa*) zu verbinden ist. Das ist ein eigenes Thema, das hier nicht behandelt werden kann.[8]

Für das vorliegende Thema ist der zweite Knoten – die nicht wieder gutzumachenden Schäden und Verbrechen wichtig. Hierzu sagt Ricoeur:

> Man muß jetzt mit der infernalischen Logik einer von Generation zu Generation wiederholten Rache brechen. ... Hier berührt sich das Verzeihen auch mit dem aktiven Vergessen: nicht mit dem Vergessen der *Tatsachen*, die wirklich unauslöschlich sind, sondern mit dem Vergessen der *Bedeutung* für Gegenwart und Zukunft.[9]

Ricoeurs Differenzierung zwischen Tatsachen und deren schuldhafter Bedeutung scheint mir aufschlussreich für die Behandlung der Schuld. Die Schäden selbst sind nicht wieder gutzumachen und auch nicht zu rechtfertigen. Die Tatsachen bleiben bestehen, an ihnen ist nicht zu rütteln, sie sind nicht zu relativieren.

Die Relativierung der Tatsachen, etwa ihr Vergleich mit anderen Gräueln oder den Verbrechen der Feinde ist nicht der Weg, Schuld zu

---

[4] Ibidem, S. 148.
[5] Ibidem.
[6] Ibidem, S. 153.
[7] Ibidem, S. 155.
[8] Siehe: Stephan Grätzel, *Dasein ohne Schuld*, op. cit.
[9] Paul Ricoeur, *Das Rätsel der Vergangenheit*, op. cit., S. 155.

beseitigen oder zu sühnen. Die Schuld wird auch nicht durch Rache beseitigt, die auch nur ein weiteres Verbrechen darstellt. Schuld ist ein eigenes Phänomen, das nicht mit den Verbrechen gleichzusetzen ist. Deshalb kann Schuld auch vergeben werden ohne das Geschehene ungeschehen zu machen. Die Unterscheidung zwischen Tatsachen und ihrer schuldhaften Bedeutung ist eine große Einsicht von Ricoeur.

Von hier aus ist auch Ricoeurs Kritik an Vladimir Jankélévitch (1913–1985) und dessen Position des Unverzeihlichen zu verstehen. Jankélévitch setzt Verzeihung mit Verjährung, Rechtfertigung und Relativierung der Tatsachen gleich. War er vor dem 2. Krieg ein glühender Verehrer der deutschen Kultur, so wurde er nach dem Krieg zum fanatischen Hasser. „Die Geschichte des Verzeihens ist in Auschwitz zu Ende gegangen" ist ein weithin kolportierter Satz von Jankélévitch. Sein Aufsatz von 1971 *Pardonner*[10] beschäftigt sich genau genommen nicht mit dem Verzeihen, sondern in erster Linie mit dem Problem der Verjährung von Nazi-Verbrechen. Für die Unvergleichbarkeit von Auschwitz gibt es keine Rechtfertigung und auch kein Verzeihen, es war ein „metaphysisches Greuel" wie Jankélévitch sagt.[11] Trotz des Titels *Pardonner* spricht er nicht von Verzeihen, sondern von der Relativierung von Auschwitz durch Vergleiche mit Verbrechen aus der Geschichte und mit anderen Gräueln des Krieges.

Jankélévitch verwechselt also Verzeihung mit Entschuldigung oder gar mit Rechtfertigung und Relativierung von Schuld. Gräuel von diesem Ausmaß können nicht entschuldigt oder relativiert werden, das ist richtig. Aber Verzeihen ist auch etwas anderes. Verzeihen ist keine Relativierung der Tatsachen. Für die Philosophie stellt sich hier gerade die Aufgabe, eine solche Differenzierung zu ermöglichen. Denn Verzeihen ist keine Rechtfertigung und auch keine Entschuldigung im gewöhnlichen Sinn, es ist ein Akt des Verstehens, durch den eine Aufarbeitung möglich ist. Ohne diese Aufarbeitung führt Schuld zur Rache und zu weiterer Vernichtung.

---

[10] Deutsche Ausgabe: Vladimir Jankélévitch, *Das Verzeihen. Essays zur Moral und Kulturphilosophie*, Frankfurt am Main: Suhrkamp, 2004.

[11] Ibidem, S. 263.

Obwohl also Jankélévitch in dieser Richtung keine Lösung anbietet, lassen solche Sätze aufhorchen wie folgender:

> Wir haben noch das abscheuliche Geschrei der Nürnberger Parteitage im Ohr. Daß ein gutmütiges Volk zu diesem Volk von tollwütigen Hunden hat werden können, ist ein unerschöpflicher Gegenstand der Ratlosigkeit und des sprachlosen Erstaunens.[12]

Dieser Satz steht zwar solitär, er gibt aber immerhin zu erkennen, was die Aufgabe des Philosophen angesichts der Völkermorde sein könnte, nämlich die Unbegreiflichkeit der Nazi-Ära in Deutschland herauszustellen und zu thematisieren. Die Aufgabe der Philosophie ist, die Frage zu stellen: Wie war so etwas möglich in einem Volk, das auch nicht anders war und ist als andere Völker?

Diese Frage ist heute um so dringlicher, auch und gerade in Anbetracht der Tatsache, dass die Völker Europas versöhnt scheinen. Vielleicht liegt hierin die Bedeutung von Jankélévitch' Aufschrei: Großverbrechen vom Ausmaß solcher Völkermorde sind rätselhaft, und sie vergessen sich nicht, auch nicht über Jahrhunderte. Die Zeit allein heilt solche Wunden nicht. Deshalb braucht auch ein vereinigtes Europa eine Kultur des Gedenkens, nicht um die Rachegelüste zu befriedigen oder um die Schande wach zu halten, sondern um überhaupt die Zukunft gestalten zu können. Das gilt vor allem für die jetzt lebenden Generationen. Sie brauchen eine Perspektive, die nicht von Schuld belastet ist.

5. Wie ist Verzeihung möglich

Jankélévitch' Ansatz verwechselt nicht nur Vergebung mit Verjährung und Verzeihung mit Entschuldigung, er gibt auch keine Anstöße darüber nachzudenken, wer um Vergebung bitten kann und wer sie gewähren darf. „Verzeihung? Doch, haben sie uns jemals um Verzeihung gebeten?"[13] Doch wer wird hier genannt, wer sind *sie* und wer ist *wir*? Diese Frage wird dann Derrida und Ricoeur beschäftigen. So

---

[12] Ibidem, S. 267.
[13] Ibidem, S. 271.

stellt sich für beide die Frage, ob und wie eine solche Verzeihung im großen Stil möglich ist. Beide erkennen nur die persönliche Form des Verzeihens und stehen allen kirchlichen und politischen Ritualen der Vergebung skeptisch gegenüber. Alle „Theatralität" der Vergebung sei unwirksam und schade ihrer wichtigen Aufgabe, wie Ricoeur heraushebt.[14] Eine solche Form der öffentlichen Sühne ist unwirksam und eher schädlich. Das bedeutet aber nicht, dass Vergebung nur ein persönlicher Akt des Opfers oder eines nahen Angehörigen sein kann. Die Frage ist und bleibt: Wie ist Vergebung und Verzeihen möglich, an wen richtet sie sich und wer darf sie spenden?

Für Ricoeur bietet die Gabe und der Tausch eine Lösung. Die Problematik einer Annährung vom Tausch her – und dies muss als Kritik an Ricoeur gesagt werden – liegt in der Zeitlosigkeit und Geschichtslosigkeit des Tausches. Die Interaktion zwischen dem Opfer und dem Täter ist aber nicht auf die Betroffenen allein zu reduzieren. Sie betrifft – wie schon gesagt – auch die nachgeborenen Generationen, und dies um so mehr, als hier eine Heilung der Wunden durch die Bestrafung der Täter gerade nicht stattgefunden hat. Dagegen bietet für Ricoeur das Experiment in Südafrika der *Truth and Reconciliation Commission*, die von Nelson Mandela und Bischof Tutu zwischen 1996 und 1998 geleitet wurde, einen konstruktiven Ansatz für die Versöhnung, konstruktiv nicht nur für Schuldigen, die ihre Schuld bekannt haben, sondern auch für die Opfer.[15] Das Bekenntnis und die Vergebung der Schuld sind für beide Seiten hilfreich und heilend. Auch die Opfer und ihre Hinterbliebenen leiden unter der Schuld der Täter, da sie die Taten und Verbrechen noch verstärkt. Schuld kommt zu den Tatsachen und Geschehnissen hinzu und verschlimmert sie nicht nur, sondern macht den Schmerz schwerer und verhindert die Trauer. Solche Zusammenhänge werden aber nur deutlich, wenn die Bedeutung der Schuld von den Tatsachen getrennt betrachtet wird. Dazu ist es wie schon gesagt notwendig, die Schuld als eigenes Phänomen zu erkennen. Was ist Schuld? So muss die Frage lauten. Schuld muss als eigenes Phänomen erkannt werden. Denn wenn die Schuld der Täter bestraft ist, gilt es die Schuld, die sich auf die Kinder und Enkel über-

---

[14] Paul Ricoeur, *Gedächtnis, Geschichte, Vergessen*, op. cit., S. 715.
[15] Ibidem, S. 704 ff.

tragen hat, zu behandeln. Hier bietet ein bemerkenswerter Satz von Jankélévitch einen Ansatz: „Es ist die Verlorenheit und es ist die Verlassenheit des Schuldigen, die allein der Verzeihung einen Sinn und eine Existenzberechtigung geben würden."[16] War dieser Ausspruch von Jankélévitch geradezu das Argument gegen das Verzeihen, so kann er aus heutiger Sicht für das Verzeihen geltend gemacht werden. Denn die Schuldigen sind nicht mehr die Täter, sondern Völker, die mit ihrer Geschichte nicht mehr fertig werden. Hier finden wir diese Verlorenheit und Verlassenheit. Die Verlorenheit und Verlassenheit solcher Gruppen, Völker und ganzer Nationen gilt es zu erkennen und zu behandeln, denn sie geben dem Verzeihen einen Sinn und verhindern, dass ihre Schuld zum Nährboden für neue Aggressionen wird.

---

[16] Vladimir Jankélévitch, *Das Verzeihen*, op. cit., S. 271.

Walter Maria Stojan
Graz, Warszawa

Solidarity – an European Value in an Atomizing World

Solidarity – Solidarność is a key word in Poland in the year 2005. 25 years after the astonishing revolution in Gdańsk and many other cities in Poland the Solidarność – movement, as a working labour union, inspires the fantasy of actual politicians and impresses by the pictures of that time.[1]

Solidarity as a movement became a political power and its dreams of freedom and independence for Poland became reality, hampered for some years of martial law and oppression, but not given up nor destroyed.

The Solidarność – movement reached its goal, but the question to-day is not about the aims of the movement anymore, in a free and independent Poland, member of NATO and the European Union, but about the meaning of solidarity in this new frame of freedom and independence.

A famous word of the Polish pope, John Paul II., states: "What Communism was not able to achieve, Consumism is about to do!" The disintegration of society, the egocentric lust for material goods, the competition of everybody against everybody leads us to question the ways and means of our contemporary achievements.

These achievements are on a broad scale. Looking at our societies we have to recognize that never before the life expectation of the in-dividual was that long as it is now. The living standards of the major-

---

[1] Reference www.solidarnosc.org.pl; www.solidarnosc.gov.pl

ity are higher then ever. Access to education and professional training is open to everybody. Culture and art are enriching the life of an ever growing layer of our societies.[2]

At the same time we have to discern a constant debate in our countries through the last years about the shrinking possibilities to finance the social costs of the social welfare state. The aging society doesn't find the necessary financial basis for the "Contract social", the model of post-war social insurance, anymore. The state, according to the ruling neo-liberal philosophy in every governing party in Europe may it be left or right, should become slimmer, the private engagement towards a "Civic Society" stronger.[3]

So, to my opinion, we are confronted with three major challenges in our debate about our "future Society".

– deregulation and freedom state
– civic society and self-regulating social cohesion
– the fundaments of solidarity.

1. As to Deregulation and Freedom State

Observing the political and social developments in Europe after the Second World War, I can't deny a feeling that all political orientations throughout Europe tend to get closer and closer to the so called American model or way of life. Election campaigns are copied from the US idols. The deep belief in the economy as the essence of society is the pivot of our social system. "Time is money", "Money makes the world go around", "only bad news are good news", "there is no business like show business" are just some of the basic rules taken over from the other side of the Atlantic.

---

[2] Reference www.eu2004.ie; European Social Funds (ESF) www.europa.eu.int

[3] Kurt Biedenkopf, „In Vielfalt geeint: Was hält Europa zusammen?", Transit 26, 2003/2004, Europäische Revue, hrsg. am Institut für die Wissenschaften vom Menschen (IWM) in Wien, Frankfurt am Main; Ernst-Wolfgang Böckenförde, „Die Bedingungen der europäischen Solidarität", Transit 26, 2003/2004, Europäische Revue, hrsg. am Institut für die Wissenschaften vom Menschen (IWM) in Wien, Frankfurt am Main.

An Austrian cultural philosopher, Egon Friedell, stated in his *Cultural history of the New Age*, in 1931:

> There are five possibilities for the future development of the world: Americanism wins in the materiel sense: Ruling of the world by the United States and at the end of this interregnum destruction of the occident through over-mechanization; Americanism wins in the spiritual sense through sublimation of itself: rebirth of Germany, because only there could this happen; the East wins in the materiel sense: World-bolshevism and interregnum of the Antichrist; the East wins in the spiritual sense: renovation of Christianity through the Russian soul. The fifth eventuality is chaos. These five possibilities are given, there are no others: whether politically nor ethically nor psychologically. But I do hope that the intelligent reader is aware of the fact none of these will be realized, can be realized, because the history of the world is no equation, even not with several solutions. Its only real possibility is the unreal one and its only causality the irrationality. Because it is made by a superior spirit then the human one.[4]

We can try to decide whether we are in one of the above mentioned possibilities or if everything is just speculation.

For a better understanding of these very provocative theses, I have to add the Friedell's conception of Americanism. According to him Americanism is based on behaviourism developed by John Watson with the key slogan: "mind is what body does" (very similar to the Soviet-ideology of mechanization and reflexology).[5] This behaviourism leads to the situation of deregulation and freedom state we were confronted with in the United States of yesterday. Free entrepreneurship, agglomeration of capital in the hands of the minority, political power ruled by lobbyism and sound interests led to a wide social gap between the rich and the poor, a bad educational system, problems with drugs and crime Europe did not face yet.

When I outline this picture as the United States of yesterday, I have to take into account the drastic changes in the US after

---

[4] Egon Friedell, *Kulturgeschichte der Neuzeit*, 10. Auflage, München: Deutscher Taschenbuch Verlag, 1993, p. 1516.

[5] Ibidem, p. 1515.

11.09.2001. Freedom turned into protection, the need for security justifies the limitation of human rights.[6]

These observations describe a quite sober picture of the developments and are in contradiction to my everlasting optimism. On the
other hand, I'm deeply convinced that the critical spirit is the basic
conception of the European mind. Critical but not defeatist, we are
able to develop and propose alternatives.

The post-modern human being lives in a pluralistic world with a
multi-polar system of coordinates. Its way of living is in most cases not
straight and streamlined from the cradle to the grave anymore. It is
confronted with a much higher amount of uncertainties about profession, life-partner and centre of its physical living. In order to liberate
the potentials and to strengthen the skills of this human being the
regulation framework should be liberalised in most European countries. A wave of eagerness to put every aspect of life in a law, created a
higher level of security after the Second World War, but led at the same
time to an amount of regulations, even not lawyers can see through
anymore. After the 44th amendment to the ASVG, the Common Social
Security Law in Austria, I quit to count. The degree of bending of a
cucumber or a banana is just the top of the iceberg within the jungle of
regulations within the European Union.[7] My theses to this behaviour
diagnose the remnants of authoritarian and totalitarian belief in the
Western societies, when rule of law is not the same as justice.

Of course, we do need a certain regulation of our complex and di-
versified societies, but we must not forget the potentials of spiritual
freedom of the individual. The strong belief in the dignity and power
of the individual has to be the core of any social model. Deregulation
has to be the answer to the intention of lawyers, as I am by my
studies, trying to define every aspect of life with a tight net of written
rules. To cut regulations, after a process of fostering them, is not an
easy task for the political bodies, but has to be done by visionaries
and not technocrats.

---

[6] Reference „Der 11. September 2001 und die Folgen", „Innere Sicherheit – Demokratie", in: *Aus Politk und Zeitgeschichte*, B 10–11/2002, www.bpd.de

[7] Franz Alt, *Agrarwende jetzt. Gesunde Lebensmittel für alle*, München: Goldman
Verlag, 2001; Horst Siebert, *Der Kobra-Effekt. Wie man Irrwege in der Wirtschaftspolitik
vermeidet*, Stuttgart – München: DVA, 2002.

Freedom is directly connected with uncertainty and has a direct link to responsibility. Freedom is to my opinion also linked to confidence in my neighbour and in society as a whole. The delegation of freedom leads to more security (maybe), but delegates the use of power in order to enforce this security to social structures, which have to be limited themselves by regulations in order to respect the freedom of the individual. Controllers have to control the controllers (of security). Freedom for myself includes the respect for the freedom of my neighbour. This is why I prefer the term respect to the term tolerance. I tolerate something or somebody from the position of superiority, but I respect an equal.

So deregulation will lead to a freedom-state but has to go hand in hand with the according education of its members of society, with the education of consciousness, and I would add, with the education of hearts.

2. Civic Society and Self-Regulating Social Cohesion

Since the fundamental concept of Sir Karl Popper, creating the term "open or civic society"[8], this term is used in many speeches all over the globe. To my opinion we have to make a clear distinction in which context this term is used. George Soros built up his concept of westernisation of the societies in the former communist ruled countries in the world on this basic topic in order to strengthen the consciousness for responsibility for the future developments in these different societies.[9] Starting from a point, where the state or the party used to think for its population, creating a movement of "open society" was a deed of utmost importance. Targeting the youth and the creative potentials of these societies was a bright move, too. But we have to keep in mind that this "new enlightenment" was aimed at the darkness of communism and its remnants.

---

[8] Sir Karl Raimund Popper, *Die offene Gesellschaft und ihre Feinde*, Stuttgart: Broschiert – UTB, 1992.

[9] Reference: www.soros.org

When the term "civic society" is used in the rhetoric of Western politicians, especially in Europe, it means the burden shifting from the Western welfare state towards the individual.[10] According to my beliefs in deregulation and freedom-state not wrong in itself. Only using the example of the United States to underpin this political conception is misleading and based on inadequate presumptions. The development of the societies in the Anglo-American conception is based on freedom without interference of a state, on a puritan economical and social concept with economy as the driving force of social development and the responsibility of the individual for its own sake.[11] I call this the "jungle law" or only the strongest will survive. The aggressive use of force, the material lust for goods, the consumism in its decomposing form are fruits from these roots.

European societies and welfare states developed, quite to the opposite, with the strong belief in centralisation and the benevolent ruler. Not only since the times of Benevolent Despotism the political powers tended towards a stance of not involving to much the common citizen but either relies upon their God given or democratic justification or on the advisory board of specialists and technocrats. The general mistrust in the political fellow citizen (the zoon politikon) led to the various shades of authoritarian and totalitarian ruling in Europe. Therein also the growing lack of interest in democratic procedures of the European voters, in our days, can be found. "Bread and games" to secure the undisturbed policies of the ruler is not a brand new concept. Using the term "Civic society", in order to get rid of unpleasant burdens of government discredits the term itself. To my opinion "civic society" has to emerge in an atmosphere of self-conscious, responsible citizens – either supported by education through the governing groups or even in opposition to the ruling system.[12]

---

[10] Andreas Khol, *Durchbruch zur Bürgergesellschaft. Ein Manifest*, Wien: Molden Verlag, 1999.

[11] „American Values – Living with a superpower", Special Report, *The Economist* (02.01.2003).

[12] Claus Offe, „Europäische Integration und die Zukunft des Europäischen Sozialmodells", *Transit* 28, 2004/2005, Europäische Revue, hrsg. am Institut für die Wissenschaften vom Menschen (IWM) in Wien, Frankfurt am Main.

Directly connected with this conviction of the individual citizen to be the responsible and ruling element of our society the process of reorganization of our social welfare state can take place. If I am convinced to be involved in the creation of my society, I will be ready to think about the future of my personal well-being, the well-being of my relatives and at the end, of society as a whole. This is the moment, when the self-regulating social cohesion can take place. The principle of subsidiarity, introduced by the socialist Jacques Delors into the functioning of the European Union, based upon the Christian-social policies, offers even an organizational system for its functioning in society as a whole. Its implementation in our societies is discussed by the "bottom up – concept" or the "top down – concept". The two definitions: "only the duties, which can not be solved on the lower level, should be delegated to the next higher one" or "every duty, which can be solved on a lower level, should be positioned on this level" (positioned by whom?) reflect these two approaches.[13]

Regarding the actual situation in our social welfare states the "top down – concept" seems more likely to be implemented than the "bottom-up". The responsible politicians have just to keep in mind that this positioning or transferring of duties includes the transferring of rights and loss of tax revenues. Whether governing politicians are willing to limit their own rights and lose political power to civic structures can not be answered beforehand. Personally I am convinced it would be the right way for the evolution of a self-regulating social cohesion system in our societies. An alternative, which can not be excluded, would be the revolution of the broadening impoverished majority of society against the rich minority.

3. The Fundaments of Solidarity

In her speech, delivered on February 25th, 2005, in the frame of the Austrian celebrations for the 10-year-membership in the European

---

[13] *Sozialenzyklika Quadrogesimo anno von Papst Pius XI.*, 15. Mai 1931; Oswald von Nell-Breuning, *Baugesetze der Gesellschaft. Solidarität und Subsidiarität*, Freiburg im Breisgau: Herder Verlag, 1990; Jacques Delors, Rede vor der Friedrich-Ebert-Stiftung in Paris am 29. Juni 2000.

Union, the actual Austrian foreign minister Dr. Ursula Plassnik pointed out:

This continent (Europe) is bound by many longings or yearnings. The yearning:
– for peace
– for freedom and the ruling of law
– for the securing of a specific European social model
– for the possibility to develop in an area without frontiers the colourful concept of pluralism
– for solidarity and living together in the sense of partnership
– also for the concept of "good neighbourhood" with mutual respect and with the common engagement for each other.

She even stressed:

Europe has to and will play its specific role in its responsibility for the world – as a pioneer for democracy, for human rights and solidarity...[14]

Solidarity is a permanent topic in our political life. In spring 2005 a series of debates took place in Warsaw under the synonym of "Tischner debates" discussing with eminent personalities as Lord Ralf Dahrendorf, Charles Taylor or Kurt Biedenkopf the different aspects of solidarity in our societies.[15]

In an article by Anja Ebersbach and Richard Heigl, titled "Click here to protest? About the creation of solidarity via Internet und about the 'theses about the concept of history' by Walter Benjamin", the authors write in their introduction:

Although the notion "solidarity" as a slogan is used almost daily, there is no common definition up to now. Different theories on justice and freedom have been developed in the meantime, but the notion "solidarity" didn't find its adequate definition in theoretical discussions (see Bayertz, 1998). Wildt (1995: 1004) defines solidarity as: "the willingness to engage for common goals or the goals of others, which are recognized as endan-

---

[14] Ursula Plassnik, „Gemeinsame Erfahrungen – Gemeinsame Perspektiven", in: *10 Jahre Österreich in der Europäischen Union*, Wien: Eigenverlag BMaA, 2005, pp. 14–15.
[15] Reference www.erazm.uw.edu.pl

gered and at the same time as valuable and legitimate, especially the support of a fight against endangering".[16]

As a short comment on the definition by Wildt I would like to quote the Austrian cultural philosopher Friedrich Heer:

> Life is conflict and "fight". The metapolitically oriented human being will understand the foreword of the forefather of wisdom Heraklit: Polemos pater panton – the fight, "war" is the father of all things.

But in the concept of Heer this "war" must not be led in the use of physical aggression and destruction anymore, but has to be understood as a "war" of ideas and concepts.[17]

In this sense I would like to ask for other conceptions of solidarity, its roots and its possible realization in society. Solidarity as a sociological topic has to be defined by the conception of its basic element – the human being. I won't come back to point 1 of my presentation "deregulation and freedom state", but there my conception of the human being in its individuality and dignity is based. The individual is the atom of our world. Its unmistakable and unique existence stands at the beginning of every social conception. Personally I even link this atom to a metaphysical level. For the development of a social model this specific detail is not essential. There are other conceptions, which also start from this unique atom called human being, but embody it immediately in the social agglomeration of a group. The individual is nothing without the others (social group, party and others). This conception is possible and historically proved. It is not mine.

The atomizing world is also a proof and a fact, we have to take into consideration, that individualism and its longing for the utmost personal freedom possible lead us to the concept of the unique atom as definer of its existence.

The atom in its freedom has just to take notice that its existence in the world is not a unique one. There are many atoms as the one living, evolving and creating their realities. So my definition states

---

[16] Anja Ebersbach, Richard Heigl, "Click here to protest? Zur Entstehung von Solidarität über das Internet und die 'Thesen über den Begriff von Geschichte' von Walter Benjamin", *kommunikation@gesellschaft* Jg. 6, 2005, Beitrag 1.

[17] Friedrich Heer, *Offener Humanismus*, Bern: Scherz-Verlag, 1962, p. 405.

further: The atom has to realize the fact that it is a social atom surrounded by a universe of other atoms.

On its way of self-reflection and consciousness-building the atom will find out in which way this social connection with the human universe fits the best its own interests. In some way I'm just describing the evolution of mankind.

At this stage let me quote a deep believer in the concept of evolution, Teilhard de Chardin. Deeply misunderstood by his own church, the catholic one, he described his visions of our future during a speech held on March 30th, 1941, in Beijing, as follows:

> Based on my studies of palaeontology I can state two assumptions. a) Mankind is still showing immense reserves for further possibilities of concentration, meaning progress... In an energetic and biological sense the group of mankind is still very young and unspent. b) The earth has not completed its sidereal evolution for a long time to come... What shall we do then with our future, how to behave? I see two possibilities, which can be expressed by five words: a great hope, in community.
>
> a) A great hope: It has to be awakened in every soul; it gives the indispensable move or drive, necessary for progress...
> b) In community. The history of life has decided also in this respect. There is just one way leading to the top: it is the one which leads through a richer organisation to a richer synthesis and union. Away with all the reckless individualisers, the egocentrics, who are just interested in gaining power, but try to exclude or humiliate their brothers, be it as individuals, nations or races. Life is heading towards unification, standardization. Our hope can just be realized if it is expressed by a higher degree of cohesion and a higher degree of human solidarity...[18]

Again, the topic "solidarity" is incorporated in the very centre of the future of society. But let me quote another philosopher in this context, Ernst Bloch. In his masterpiece "The principle hope", written between 1938–1947, first published between 1954–1959, he states:

> Expectation, hope, intention towards a yet unrealized possibility; this is not only an essential feature of the human consciousness, but concretely

---

[18] Ibidem, pp. 183–185.

adjusted and understood, a fundamental philosophy within the objective reality as a whole.[19]

It is the conclusion of his thinking towards a practical oriented philosophy, which intrigues to me the most. On the basis of two material conceptions, the inorganic cosmic matter and the human-historical, historical matter, in the form of life praxis, the "process matter" is developing itself. In the positive look upon this development, the principle hope, the future of society can be shaped. Bloch concludes:

> This is why the big turning, the elevation from the immediate is happening, called the world process: with active anticipation in the subject oriented towards happiness, in a society without master or servant oriented towards a so possible solidarity among all, id est towards freedom and human dignity, towards an "alliance" with nature as an object, which is not tainted by something alien to us, towards "Heimat". [20]

In the two conclusions, made by Pierre Teilhard de Chardin and Ernst Bloch, I find my concept for the possibility of solidarity between the atoms of our societies.

It has politically to be discussed by which ways and means this goal or yearning, as the Austrian foreign minister Plassnik put it, for solidarity can be reached. My concept of deregulation and freedom-state, civic society and self-regulating social cohesion based on solidarity is just one in a universe of many.

It is nevertheless the reason for me, based on my perceptions of the fundamental values of non-European societies, especially the US society, to postulate solidarity as a basic European value in an atomizing world.

---

[19] Ibidem, p. 146.
[20] Ibidem, p. 148.

Part III
Values and Norms
in Contemporary Societies

Tadeusz Buksiński
Poznań

Modernization as a Value and Norm

1. Modernization and the Axiological Structure of Societies

In this article, globalization is understood as a continuation (or further step in the development) of modernization. Today, societies are afraid of the negative consequences of this process, and thus try to regulate them by norms, rules, and values, such as justice, equality, human dignity, recognition and freedom. Philosophers are attempting to provide these norms and values which should be observed. There was a similar situation in the 18th and 19th centuries during the period of industrial modernization. Despite such fears, globalization (understood as technological and economical modernization) is, on the one hand, seen as a value in itself and the aim of societies, and on the other, a necessity. These points will be stressed in this article, with a concentration on the fundamental conditions surrounding the process of technological and economic modernization. The problems are considered from the perspective of post-communist countries, on the basis of the experience of societies in which modernization has been delayed.

The roots and sources of the process of modernization are partly inherent and partly stem from the role of the features of modernization as a means of achieving other values and goods essential to societies. Among the fundamental values which modernization provides to societies and individuals is an increase in prosperity, strength and power, as well as the ability and capability to act independently. This increased ability means increased potential, the freedom to shape oneself and one's environment. These possibilities are created by the institutional, economic, and technological structures that are established. They make it possible for an individual to break free from prejudices, increase the effectiveness of their actions, and become, at least to some extent, independent from natural disasters (such as drought, poor harvest or flood). Nowadays, more and more such phenomena are being brought under control.

All the values today, which philosophers and reformers want to see implemented (dignity, freedom, justice, good standard of living), assume economic and technological modernization and globalization. Modernization is the condition of their realization. Without effective work toward modernization, the above mentioned values and goods cannot be provided and the affected societies would be reduced to a distribution of poverty. This situation was observed during the times of real communism.

However, it must be strongly emphasized that economic and technological modernization only offers **possibilities**, i.e. it **conditions** a greater real freedom, justice and good standard of living, but it is not identical to them. Whether these values are achieved depends on a number of factors: the character of political relations, the type of culture prevailing in the society, the mentality of people, and their ability and capability to act and use the opportunities and possibilities offered by modernization.[1]

The cultural and political systems may function: (1) as a value and direct condition of a good standard of living; (2) as independent factors conditioning (in a positive or negative way) modernization; (3) and as specific phenomena required and extorted by modernization. Modern technologies and systems of organization are not axiologically neutral tools, but they include some normative aspects, namely, they require an appropriate lifestyle, adapted to the requirements of their functioning: discipline, rational behaviour, economic calculation aimed towards an optimal use of resources, invention, creativity, open-mindedness, effective organization of work and cooperation. Only then can they be fully used and function well.

---

[1] Amartya Sen, *Development as Freedom*, New York: Anchor Books, 1999.

The different forms of cultural and political life are either the friendly conditions or the obstacles for continued development of modernization. They facilitate or prevent distortions in the use of the achievements of modernization. They support or prevent their use as tools of aggression, conquest and/or domination.[2]

It seems that it is possible to identify cultures (and societies including their political systems) which favour modernization and which can come to terms with it to a large extent and ones which are not friendly to modernization. The characteristic features of the former are (1) the norms and values they contain assure some equilibrium between aspiration for individual and particular goods on the one hand, and on the other, for the realization of the good of the whole. Extreme particularism and egoism, consisting of showing disrespect to rights, norms, national values, and the creation of Mafia groups, do not favour modernization; (2) they are tolerant, i.e. open to differences, criticism, pluralism; (3) they are flexible, i.e. they permit some internal changes to adapt to the requirements of economic or technological development. Hence, cultures which favour modernization are paradigmatic in T. Kuhn's sense.[3] They have (a) a solid core of basic values and norms, (b) a flexible protection belt of aims, rules and methods of operation, (c) and a sequence of decisions related to typical behaviours, customs and rituals, which are subject to transformation. They are complex and structurally expanded. In these cultures (and in whole societies), changes in their tertiary elements, taking place under the influence of modernization or under the influence of modernization attempts, strengthen their identity (core) because they are an answer to new threats and they adapt them to new situations. In Western cultures, the core consists of individual rights, negative values, social permissiveness, utilitarian rationality, and the custom of compromise. The protective belt consists of norms of

---

[2] Wolfgang Zapf, "Die Modernisierungtheorie und unterschiedlische Pfade der gesellschaftlichen Entwicklung", *Leviathan* 1, 1966, pp. 63–97; M.B. Jansen, L. Stone, "Education and Modernisation in Japan and England", in: *Comparative Modernisation*, ed. by C.E. Black, New York: Free Press, 1976, pp. 214–237.

[3] Thomas S. Kuhn, *The Essential Tension*, Chicago: The University of Chicago Press, 1977.

democratic consensus, compromise, contracts, and peaceful agreements.

On the other hand, the cultures (and societies) which are unfriendly to modernization are usually poorer in structure and content. These are cultures (societies) with a single national identity. They lack relatively autonomous parts. All their constituent parts are equally important for the whole and its identity. They include, among others, cultures (societies) in which religious life has not been separated or even differentiated from other forms of social life or in which the prevailing ideology exists as the sole provider of truth and meaning. These cultures and societies limit their possibilities of modernization due to a lack of political freedoms, non-observance of human rights, lack of negative (civic) freedoms, social and religious restrictions, and/or a lack of subjective abilities allowing the use of the objectively existing opportunities.

Obviously, different cultures (societies) are paradigmatic and uniform in their identity to a varying extent. Therefore, economic and technological modernization must compromise with many lifestyles, with many traditions and many political systems, which can be illustrated by the intensive development of economy and civilization in many countries of Asia, which have a traditional community culture.

The division into paradigmatic cultures (societies) and cultures (societies) with a single national identity, does not coincide with the division into modern cultures (e.g. Western cultures) and pre-modern cultures (e.g. community cultures). Community cultures can also be paradigmatic: Japanese culture from the times of the Meji reforms seems to be a good example of a paradigmatic community culture. The paradigmatic character of culture (society) as a condition for modernization is most important in societies which are at the forefront of modernization (such as England and the USA).

This does not mean that each form of modernization can compromise with any form of culture and any political or social system: in some African and South American countries, more developed forms of economic and political modernization are difficult to implement. The tribal spirit, and particularly the mentality of the people, resist modernization in these regions.

2. Selective Imitative Modernization

Many countries with a single national identity often imitate modernization in a selective way. Such societies import and accept a so-called partial (selective) modernization (usually technological and some forms of economic modernization), for example Russia at the times of Alexander I, some modern Islamic countries, and some South American countries. In countries which imitate modernization, other relations between politics and culture and technological and economic advancement are more possible than in pioneer countries.

In the period of eradicating "backwardness" and catching up with more advanced countries, authoritarian, and even totalitarian forms of government and undemocratic social relations are often effective. They mobilize means and resources, both human and material, to take giant steps toward modernization. And they do it more effectively than countries with democratic systems. Industrialization of the USSR after the Bolshevik revolution, and that of the communist countries after the Second World War can serve as two examples of such modernization attempted by a totalitarian system of an ideological character.[4] However, the effectiveness of such types of modernization is limited to the application of modernising solutions developed elsewhere. So far, no country with an authoritarian or totalitarian system, in which social communities are intolerant, has managed to become a country at the forefront of modernization. They are not capable of creating new forms of modernization on the basis of their own ideological foundations and on their own initiative. It seems that this phenomenon is an expression of some more profound regularity. More and more advanced modernization forms require more democratic political relations and a more open and pluralistic culture.

Partial (selective) modernization, on the one hand, opens up new opportunities, from the other, it creates dangers: (1) It could be treated

---

[4] K. Müller, "'Modernisierung' Eastern Europe. Theoretical Problems and Political Dilemmas", *Archives Europeennes Sociology* 33, 1992, pp. 109–150; Bruno Grancelli, *Social Change and Modernisation, Lessons from Eastern Europe*, New York: De Gruyter, 1995; cf. also *Nationalsozialismus und Modernisierung*, ed. by Rainer Zitelmann, Darmstadt: Wissenschaftliche Buchgesellschaft, 1991.

only as an instrument in the hands of totalitarian or non-tolerant groups and used to exert oppression over people in the country or over foreign nations. (2) It could become fixed, petrified, and persist over a long period (sometimes for hundreds of years) in the shape of half-modernized societies – as in the case of Turkey. (3) Or it could be further developed throughout many sectors of social life, embracing political, public and cultural spheres. In this case, modern economy and technology is unified (combined) with open politics and culture, and the society is developing. Therefore, it is important to influence, from within and without, selective and half-modernization in the direction of developing full modernization in order to avoid the dangers connected with partial modernization. This influence should be consistent with some natural internal tendency present in the process of modernization.

3. The Program of Full Modernization

When I speak about the axiological or normative requirements of modernization, I presuppose that permanent and comprehensive modernization is the "natural" tendency. This tendency appears as the desires and expectations of people to improve their situation: economic, political, and cultural. The fulfilment of these expectations requires the promotion of full modernization. For example, the situation in Poland today requires the abolishment of corruption in public life. Everybody agrees with this desire. It is the precondition of proper functioning of economic and public life. In this sense, it is a natural condition for further "normal" development.

One may put forth arguments against the suggestions concerning the positive value of full modernization by mentioning: colonialism and neocolonialism, wars, manipulation of opinions in fully modernized countries, increase of inequalities, the poverty of many social groups, unemployment, the rules of cliques, the destruction of tradition and identity, the restriction of freedom on account of security, and so on. These are the realities of fully modernized countries.

All these arguments do not weaken the expressed suggestions. Modernization is not only a natural tendency, it is a necessity. It expands from the beginning and spreads from more advanced countries to other nations. To countries left behind, it often brings subordination and exploitation – for example Poland in the 17th and 19th centuries. But the expansion of partly or half-modernized countries (societies) bring worse results than that of fully modernized ones. The only way to avoid negative consequences for less-advanced countries is to fully modernize as quickly as possible.

One cannot neglect these facts. In the last decades, prosperity has been extended to new countries and continents (especially in Asia), and has embraced billions of new people. New, more flexible, more open and more free forms of social and political life are being implemented there. It has already been a long, ongoing process in India, South Korea, Singapore, and it is slowly winning China and Iran. The matter concerns everyday life and public life. More and more people are getting new opportunities to shape their life on their own account.

What is important in this process is the mutual dependence and conditioning of both above mentioned factors (structures): economic, together with technological modernization, from one side and proper norms, values and regulations from other side. Countries which overlook this will collapse just like the communist states of the past. The communists in Central and Eastern Europe strived to intensify modernization (which was an essential part of their programme) using methods of controlling every detail of the social and personal life of its citizens through politics and ideology. At the beginning, this form of politics was successful in imitating Western modernization. More developed forms of modernization could not be adapted to this totalitarian policy, and as a result, modernization stopped altogether. Similar mistakes are made by some philosophers, who criticize unjust international relations and forget about the necessity of creating proper cultural and political conditions for economic and technological modernization in Western and non-Western countries.[5]

It is modernization, together with modern culture and modernized political life, that reveals its value fully. It reveals that it is a condition of real freedom for all. Because only in situations where nega-

---

[5] Nancy Fraser, Axel Honneth, *Redistribution or Recognition?* London, New York: Verso, 2003.

tive freedoms and the rights of man and citizen are assured, as well as in situations of social tolerance and open-mindedness, is it possible to fully take advantage of the possibilities offered by the new means of technology, communication, and accumulated goods. Only then is it possible to use them to form one's own personality, to influence one's environment, to determine one's aims and select the means to achieve them, and to choose one's way of life. Only then, on the one hand, is there the real possibility of choice and the real possibility of achieving one's desired lifestyle, in accordance with one's wishes and values, and on the other hand, are there the conditions for continued efficiency, and by the same token, for the further development of modernization.

In conclusion, we can say that modernity is an idea of responsibility for the development of the world and for the changes taking place within it. World problems should be solved by people. People's responsibility relates to the consequences they have brought about, as well as the phenomena and situations for which they are not responsible but for which they can change or sustain. In modernity, a norm prevails to create conditions (in the form of rights, goods, abilities, qualities, relations, customs) for the increase of the substantial freedom (the freedom of real opportunities) and its accompanying responsibility. In fact, this is a process of self-creation in an open-discussion, in a democratic system.[6]

There are some relations and interrelations between different stages of modernization and respective forms of culture in the development of Western and non-Western societies. Some political systems, cultures and social communities favour the development of respective forms of modernization more than others. Modernization is multifaceted and has many stages. We can identify them in the Western world in terms of a) the manufacturing phase, b) the industrial phase, c) the phase of organized systems, and d) the global phase. It takes a different form in pioneer countries, which are the first to pave the way, and it takes a different form in countries which imitate and try to catch up with the countries at the forefront of modernization.

---

[6] Shmuel N. Eisenstadt, *Modernisation. Protest and Change*, Englewood Cliffs: Prentice Hall, 1996.

Modernization in the industrial phase in the West requires liberal social systems and tolerant cultures for its development, whereas in the industrial and institutionalized phases it forces democratization of political and social life. At present, in the times of globalization, on the other hand, it is accompanied by attempts to organize global legal regulations of economic life, global political systems and some shared norms of global culture. These relations existed in the countries of at the height of modernization.[7]

4. Regulation of Global Modernization

Globalization, as the next step in modernization, is a process of equalisation and compensation of inequalities still present today. Of course, there are too many pathologies in business and politics today, but we are living in a period of hasty transformations and are on our way to introduce proper norms and regulations in global dimensions. We see that modernized countries are attractive for people from countries of a single national identity and from states dominated by ideological systems – immigration is a clear sign of it. The aspirations and actions of people in the world (in Western and non-Western countries) suggest that economic and technological modernity, together with other modern values and norms (personal freedom, rules of law, tolerance), are the most important for them.

The proper regulation of economic and technological modernization is one of the conditions of effective freedom, which is offered by modernization and modern culture. The problem does not consist of opening as many doors for action as possible and liberating the elements. As we know, economic and technological modernization can bring about negative consequences when it is too restricted by culture, ideology and one-sidedly controlled by politics, as well as when it is let to run free, i.e. when its development is beyond the reach or interest of politics and culture. As we mentioned earlier, modernization forces the liberalization of relations for its own sake,

---

[7] Tadeusz Buksiński, *Moderność* [Modernity], Poznań: Wydawnictwo Naukowe IF UAM, 2001.

but often it is too far reaching and over a long period of time it turns out to be detrimental to society and to the processes of modernization. We observed this situation in the 19th century, at the time when industrial modernization was developing in Western Europe, when economic exploitation reduced the working class to poverty and when the particular understanding of the norms of modern culture and politics led to colonization. It is the democratic relations and the welfare state that led to the regulation of modernization in a way which proved favourable for society and for the modernization processes. Societies (and their representatives) must improve modernization processes to ensure real freedom for all. Without these amendments, modernization does not bring real freedom to everybody, nor does it always become effective in the long run.

At any stage of development it is important to see to it that at least two minimum criteria are observed: the effectiveness of modernization (i.e. its continued development) and the avoidance of negative consequences for society. Obviously, for different societies different consequences are negative. This depends on their systems of values and preferences. Some are more community-like and they will take more care to retain the idea of traditional families and religious beliefs, others are more liberal and mainly try to ensure negative freedoms, which should be as broad as possible. Some of these restrictions can have a more or less hampering effect on the development of modernization. So it is not only a problem of adapting culture to the requirements of modernization but often the situation is reversed. If culture cannot be changed or if there is no will to change it, such implementation means for modernization must be found, ones that would be most effective in a given culture. The character of modernization must be adapted to a given culture for it to develop and bring positive results to the entire society, for example when the tradition of free market and contract is lacking, rigorous economic law (including that of contracts), bank law, environmental protection law and an efficient enforcement system of its observance must be created; without that, the market will not function. Stopping the development of modernization because of cultural restraints, however, means the promotion of social stagnation and, as a result, the risk of the eradication of norms, values and cultural goods, which people want to defend; as a result of external competition by more modernized societies, they will be weakened and undermined. On the other hand, modernization which is accepted by a society, i.e. developed with an internal initiative, can lead to the modernization of norms and values which will provide for the continuity of the identity of the society. The criterion for providing as many opportunities as possible for the greatest possible number of citizens to take part in social, economic and political life must be adopted as the desired manner. For that purpose, conditions that favour the strengthening of abilities and people's willingness to improve and use their abilities to work to sustain themselves and others must be created (law, education, health, finance, civilization). Public aid, for example, cannot favour a passive approach. Therefore it must be properly subsidized. Likewise, civic or cultural rights (for the minority) cannot have an absolute character, but must be granted bearing in mind the consequences that they have for the entire society.

At the stage of globalization there is a need to control the spontaneously developing financial markets, goods, and investments. Spontaneous modernization brings about highly destructive consequences for the identity of many traditional societies (and triggers spiritual crises among people), it contributes to the appearance of great areas of poverty in African countries and in South America, it destroys the natural environment, brings about the threat and risk of catastrophes, which could endanger all of Mankind.[8] Control is possible based on the principles of global complex justice and the principles of recognition. It can be implemented by means of institutions and international organizations, both existing ones and newly established ones. On the one hand, ethical norms are needed, which restrict activities that are destructive for others, on the other hand, we need global rights and institutions which will implement them effectively.

---

[8] Ulrich Beck, *Risikogesellschaft. Auf dem Wege in eine andere Moderne*, Frankfurt am Main: Suhrkamp, 1986; Karl-Otto Apel, "Problem uniwersalnej makroetyki współodpowiedzialności" [The Problem of a Universal Macroethics of Common Responsibility], in: Tadeusz Buksiński, *Wspólnotowość wobec wyzwań liberalizmu* [Communities and the Liberal Challange], Poznań: Wydawnictwo Naukowe IF UAM, 1995, pp. 33–50.

Today, microelectronics and computer networks give man new opportunities to shape reality according to one's will and viewpoint. Man must know how to use them to model social reality in order to ensure a sustainable and socially favourable development of modernization. It is no longer enough to respond to the negative consequences of modernization *post factum* and to try to repair them using politics for that purpose. Legal, social, financial, political, and/or institutional frameworks for modernization processes must be established, which would make it impossible to trigger side effects that would be too dangerous for Mankind. In our present times of globalization, the consequences of technological development are too dangerous and a delayed response to them is not acceptable, as it may lead to irreparable damage and destruction. Avoiding the threat of annihilation as a result of the use of modern technologies at the hands of terrorist groups is another problem. Ensuring a multitude of cultures and pluralism of identities is equally important.[9]

These problems can be solved by a global state or a global management system with extensive powers. Only a legislative and executive central office with extensive powers can deal with the nature of a truly global state.

---

[9] Mike Featherstone, Scott Lash, Roland Robertson, *Global Modernities*, London: Sage Publications, 1997; Manuel Castells, *The Rise of the Network Society*, Oxford: Blackwell, 1996.

Rainer Adolphi
Berlin

Wert-Konflikte
– Ein Selbstverständigungstopos
globalisierter Gesellschaften

Denken hinkt vielfach hinterher. Und gerade in Dingen des Moralischen und Gesellschaftlichen häufig in der Weise, daß es kompensatorisch mit überabstrakten Großtheoremen wieder in souveränen Vorlauf zu gelangen sucht. Zuweilen ist die Wirklichkeit schmerzhaft konkreter als alles erreichte Denken.

Unsere gegenwärtige Zeit ist in besonderem Maße eine Phase solcher Diskrepanzen. Manche Entwicklung, die z.B. in Sozialuntersuchungen, in Mentalitäts- und 'Kulturkritik' oder im politischen Journalismus schon längst diskutiert worden war, hatte die theoretische Reflexion einfach nicht wahrgenommen; manches hat sie sich von modisch 'postmodern' auftrumpfenden Gegendiskursen abnehmen lassen; oft zeigte sie sich seltsam hilflos gegenüber dem neuen Zynismus, den wohlfeilen Verdächtigungen, allerwärts alteuropäische Sentimentalitäten, Moralhybris und Denkverbote am Werk zu sehen; und manches, wie etwa der Zusammenbruch des sozialistischen Systems, die Implosion der ganzen einen Hälfte einer ehemaligen Weltordnung und Orientierung, oder der internationale Terrorismus, hat *alle* fast unvorbereitet erwischt. Unsere gegenwärtige Zeit jedenfalls zeigt sich als in besonderem Maße anfällig für den Blick aufs Ganz-Große, anfällig für den verkündeten Neuen Äon, für Theorien der epochalen Wende. Unübersichtlich, produziert die Gegenwart ein Verlangen nach einfachen Problemtiteln, Verlangen nach Hyperübersichtlichkeit. Und, neben der durch Gentechnik und Hirnforschung angestoßenen Problememphase eines 'Neuen Menschenbildes', des Umsturzes all unserer bisherigen altkulturellen humanen Selbstverständnisse, scheint dieses Phänomen sich inzwischen zentral im Thema: 'Globalisierung' zu kristallisieren.

Noch ist kaum entschieden, *was* 'Globalisierung', die Phänomene unter diesem Titel, für das Denken bedeutet. Sicher ist nur das Daß. 'Globalisierung', ohne Zweifel, ist wesentlich auch eine Herausforderung. Nicht allein mit ihren realen Ausprägungen, die uns definitiv auf die Grenzen des Fortschritts stoßen, und überhaupt Grenzen der Steuerbarkeit. Sondern, 'Globalisierung' ist auch die radikale Probe auf die Wirklichkeitshaltigkeit unserer ethischen und politischen Diskurse. Ein binnen kürzester Zeit entstandener planetarischer Horizont, der bislang regelbegrenzte Handlungssysteme aufsprengt und vorderhand nicht überschaubaren äußeren Faktoren aussetzt, scheint eine neue Wirklichkeit, was der Normierung bedarf und wieweit eine Reglementierung dabei überhaupt reichen kann, geschaffen zu haben. Und scheint zugleich in Frage zu stellen, ob die bisherige humane Verwurzelung von Werten und die auf sozialer Begründung basierende *ratio* von gesellschaftlichen Normen, ja überhaupt all unsere gewohnten wie implementiert-gültigen Wertorientierungen und Normierungsstrukturen und Diskurse darüber, damit Schritt halten, noch auf der Höhe des eingetretenen Faktischen sind.

So stehen hier denn auf der einen Seite Erfahrungen, die sich in diesem neuen Problemtitel bündeln, und zugleich immer offenkundiger werdende Schwierigkeiten, diese neuen Strukturgegebenheiten adäquat zu konzeptualisieren. 'Globalisierung', die Phänomene unter diesem Titel, in ihren ökonomischen, gesellschaftlichen, politischen, zivilisatorischen Ausprägungen, bricht herein als ein zunächst praktisch wie theoretisch nicht Beherrschtes – und was gleichzeitig das Problem von Normen und Werten differenzierter sehen läßt, differenzierter zu sehen zwingt. Seit zwei, drei Jahrzehnten wurden Ethik und Politik von *wissenschaftlich-technischer* neuer Lage aus, durch biogenetische Forschung, durch lebensverlängernde Möglichkeiten, durch unabweisbar gewordene ökologische Perspektiven, unter fruchtbaren Druck gesetzt. In einem entsprechenden Umbruch, je-

doch viel radikaler, kommen heute mit 'Globalisierung' die Herausforderungen, in Ethik und Politik alte Abstraktheiten in Frage zu
stellen, mitten aus dem Gesellschaftlichen selber.

Die Gefahr, in unzureichenden Denkschemata zu verbleiben, betrifft dabei beide Pole, sowohl die Konzeptualisierung der Prozesse,
die als 'Globalisierung' vor uns stehen, als auch die Auffassung von
Werten und Normen. Ein überverallgemeinertes Neues steht hier in
Konjunktion mit einer genaubesehen vagen und argumentativ ambi-
valenten Theorieerbschaft. In beiderlei Richtung stehen wir vor den
Lockungen der Nivellierung oder dagegen der Dramatisierung. Aber
das können wir uns eigentlich wohl nicht leisten. – Die folgenden
Überlegungen möchten dazu, in Absicht auf erforderliche Problem-
differenzierung, einige zentrale Aspekte dessen erörtern, mit welchen
Begriffen, Modellen, Denkfiguren wir uns über das Verhältnis von
Globalisierungssachverhalten und der Dimension von Werthaftem
und Normativem zu verständigen suchen. Begonnen sei bei der Frage
der Neuheit des Neuen.

1. Die Wirklichkeit einer Utopie

Neue Begriffe des Denkens bedürfen wohl stets einer gewissen
Zeit der Erfahrungen mit ihnen – Erprobung, Benutzung, Reformulierung bisheriger Fragestellungen –, bevor ihr Gehalt sich zunehmend
herausschält. Bedeutungen, Möglichkeiten und auch Grenzen wie
eventuelle Problematik lassen sich selten a priori wissen. Das trifft für
„Globalisierung" in mehrfacher Hinsicht zu.

Inzwischen gut anderthalb Jahrzehnte der Rede von „Globalisierung" hinter uns,[1] mag heute ein vorsichtiges Bewußtsein aufkeimen,

---

[1] Die Literatur über das Phänomen 'Globalisierung', in Publizistik wie Wissenschaft, setzt etwa 1990 ein (nicht von ungefähr übrigens mit Ende der Ost-West-
Zweiteilung), um dann seither einen exponentiellen Anstieg zu zeigen. – Das Problem
so anzusetzen, daß Globalisierung als ein Geschehen mit lange herkommender Geschichte sich darstellt und in den Linien mehrerer früherer Etappen bzw. Schübe im
Zuge der Industrialisierung, scheint dagegen im Hinblick auf jederlei Frage nach
Wert- und Normaspekten, auch Frage nach den erforderlichen Folgerungen für ad-

daß Aussagen, in denen dieser neue Begriffstitel in Subjekt-Position steht, oft schon zu selbstverständlich von den Lippen gehen. 'Die Globalisierung hat ...', 'Die Globalisierung erfordert ...', 'Die Globalisierung wird ...', 'Globalisierung erzeugt ...', 'bedroht ...', oder auch indirekt: 'Das Zeitalter der Globalisierung verändert ...', 'bringt mit sich ...' etc., solcherlei Aussagen sind aus wirtschaftlichen wie politischen Verlautbarungen, aus Feuilleton und aus wissenschaftlichen Konferenzen kaum mehr wegzudenken. In der Rede von „Globalisierung" kehrt dabei anonym etwas wieder, was man längst überwunden glaubte: ein Hypersubjekt des historischen und gesellschaftlichen Prozesses. Vor Augen stehen Wandlungen, erfahrbare und sinnfällige reale Ausprägungen, die genau das – ohnehin immer schwierige – Verhältnis von Einzelakteuren (bis hin zu Einzelstaaten) und Großprozessen betreffen, und in der Bezeichnung als „Globalisierung", zumal wenn in solch generalisierten Subjekt-Aussagen, erscheint die Veränderung selbst, als Selbsttransformation, Selbstpotenzierung jenes Verhältnisses, tendenziell als Agens und sich prozessierend nach einer eigenen Logik. Das, was *Problem* ist, die strukturelle Veränderung jenes Verhältnisses, erscheint als – und gar nicht mehr befragt im Ob und Wo und Wie und Wodurch – Gesetzlichkeit und universell-finale Tatsache-der-Welt.

Der Diskurs über diese neuentstandenen Gegebenheiten wird, solange ohne Differenzierung, allemal eine prekäre Rede bleiben, prekär aus logischen wie aus sachlichen Gründen. Zunächst ein Begriff der persönlichen Verständigung sowie Rechtfertigung, über neuartige Handlungszwänge und Hereinwirkendes, aus der Perspektive des einzelnen Akteurs und in bezug auf seine je einzelnen, punktuellen Optionsfaktoren, hat sich die Rede von „Globalisierung" eingebürgert in Publizistik sowie in Trendorientierungen in Wirtschaft wie Politik, deren Beschreibungen *über* zu verzeichnende bzw. berücksichtigende oder erwartende neue Phänomene, Beschreibun-

---

äquate Theoriekonzeption, eher entspezifizierend. Das gilt vielleicht für überhaupt alle Bestimmung über 'harte' positive Außen-Indikatoren (aus den Bereichen Wirtschaft, Recht, Verkehr u.a.). Es bedeutet jedenfalls eine ganz neue Potenz, wenn in globalisierter Perspektive *entschieden und agiert* wird; und wenn so (verständigend oder rechtfertigend) geredet wird.

gen über ein Objektiv-Allgemeines – und ist von dort dann als The-
menwort in die Theorie gekommen. Je mehr Theoriediskurs und
Kultur- und Gesellschaftsessayistik, desto mehr indes dabei häufig
mit der Gefahr, die Bezeichnung *für* das Bündel dieser neuartigen
Phänomene und Momente als Subjekt der ganzen Entwicklung zu
nehmen. Dergestalt statt von globali*sierenden* Veränderungen, verschiedenen und je in bestimmten Bereichen sowie Ausprägungen, zu
reden von 'der' Globalisie*rung*, ist da dann, von der Logik und der
Begründung der Aussagen her, in der Tat oft nichts so viel anderes,
als was Karl Löwith in *Meaning in History* am neuzeitlichen philoso-
phisch-metaphysischen Geschichtsdenken kritisiert hatte, oder Popper als „historicism".[2]

Die Komplikation läßt sich nicht einfach wegdiskutieren. Sie
hängt zusammen mit der Struktur des Sachverhalts. In Globalisierung
scheint der universalisierte neuzeitliche Kollektivsingular 'Die-Geschichte'[3] wirklich *real*, scheint finalerweise – d.h. scheint überhaupt
erst – zum objektiven Faktum geworden, und das macht das Problematische in der Tat noch unkenntlicher. 'Die-Geschichte' dabei auch
nicht nur als universeller Geschehens- und Agierenshorizont, sondern als globus- bzw. menschheitsumfassende Gleichzeitigkeit und
Gleichdimensionalität des Aneinandermessens, des Voreinanderbe-
gründens und des zugerechneten Folgenzusammenhangs – daß in
allem, nämlich in jeder je konkreten Hinsicht, das Nicht-im-selben-
Maße-Gute dem Besseren, Effektiveren und Erfolgreicheren weichen
muß. Es ist die einstige Theorieidee des: gilt für alle, mißt sich an allem, wettstreitet mit allem, allseitige Immanenz ohne Auslagerung
von Konsequenzen, Lateralfolgen oder Nichtintegrierbarem, Theorieidee der Durchlässigkeit und des *Vis-à-vis* in bezug auf ein betref-
fendes endliches Gut resp. Ressource und Theorieidee des im großen

---

[2] Vgl. Karl Löwith, *Meaning in History. The Theological Implications of the Philosophy
of History*, Chicago/London: University of Chicago Press, 1949; Karl R. Popper, *The
Poverty of Historicism* [1944/45], London/Boston: Routledge, 1957; idem, *The Open
Society and Its Enemies*, vol. II, London: Routledge, 1945.

[3] Reinhart Koselleck, *Vergangene Zukunft. Zur Semantik geschichtlicher Zeiten*,
Frankfurt am Main: Suhrkamp, 1979; bes. „Über die Verfügbarkeit der Geschichte",
ibidem, S. 264–277.

Gesamt (durch eine *invisible hand*) auf einen 'vernünftigen' Fortschritt hin Ausgeglichenen, nun als *Wirklichkeitszustand*.[4] Doch in Umkehrung der Perspektive der alten Philosophie und Gesellschaftsreflexion nicht als ein handlungsmächtig, durch Vernunft herbeigeführtes oder herbeizuführendes Eines-Ganzheitliches, vielmehr als Schicksal, Verhängnis und Zwänge des Sich-anpassen-müssens. Nachdem noch wenig zuvor mit dem groß verkündeten 'Ende der Geschichte', Übergang in die 'Postmoderne' und ähnlichen Titeln eines finalen Umbruchs die Problematik von ideologischen, ideen-fixierten Wertsystemen die Zeitwahrnehmung dominiert hatte, ist es gegenwärtig geradezu umgekehrt, und dies im Problembewußtsein 'Globalisierung' verdichtet: der Tatbestand einer objektiven Eigenlogik, Herrschaft einer trans-menschlichen *ratio* in den Prozessen der Geschichte, und dagegen die Frage der Werte, Normen, Ideen als das, um der gesellschaftlichen Lebensmöglichkeiten willen, Eingreifen-*Müssen*.

Eine erforderliche Konturierung des Sachverhalts wird darum gut daran tun, von der Betrachtung der globalisierenden Veränderungen auszugehen, jenen Veränderungen, die die Frage nach Wertungs- und Normierungsbeständen neu, und verschärft, aufgeworfen haben. Das Problem wird vorsichtiger angegangen werden müssen. Scheint es

---

[4] Eine erste Vorkehrung, dem nicht unbesehen ausgeliefert zu sein, wäre wohl, die bewährten (auch mit durchaus skeptischer Verwendungsgeschichte angereicherten) sozialwissenschaftlichen Begrifflichkeiten nicht leichtfertig über Bord zu werfen. Was 'Gesellschaften' als ganze betrifft, d.h. unser etabliertes neuzeitliches Verständnis – auch die Institutionenstruktur, und die Diskurswege wie Identitäten der Wir-Gemeinschaften –, wäre bis auf weiteres, statt eines neuen übergeordneten Geschichtssubjekts, besser und präziser von 'globalisierten Gesellschaften' zu sprechen. 'Globalisierte Gesellschaften' meint: sowohl die Veränderungen der Durchlässigkeit wie des erweiterten Horizonts als auch der Vergleichsdruck von außen. Geschichtliche Herkunftsordnungen sind in all ihren Funktionsdimensionen unten den Druck der – und global – anderen neben ihnen geraten; und was einst als die Prozesse eines geschichtlichen (Zusammengehörigkeits-) Ganzen gedacht war: politische Macht, 'Gesellschaft', Bürger-'Gemeinschaft', Ökonomie, Weltbild, deckt sich nicht mehr schlechthin. – Ohnehin ist die zu berücksichtigende Vielfältigkeit am besten offengehalten, wenn die neuartigen Phänomene und davon ausgehenden Probleme in adjektivischer und verbaler Weise bezeichnet werden und das substantivische 'Die Globalisierung' allenfalls der (bewußten) abkürzenden Rede dient.

zunächst, als ob mit exponentiellem Zuwachs nahezu *alles* in den Sog der neuen Gegebenheiten und Determinationsmächte hineingerissen werde – und die Rede von 'der' Globalisierung würde dies zementieren –, so zeigen sich doch, sobald der Blick darauf geht, *was* eigentlich neuartigen, spezifisch globalisierenden Entwicklungen unterliegt, durchaus ganz verschiedene Dimensionen. 'Globalisiert' werden nicht nur Produktionsprozesse, Dienstleistungen, Finanzmärkte, internationale politische Aktionen; sondern auch Informationen, zivilisatorische und 'technische' Errungenschaften; ferner Ausprägungen der Alltagskultur, in ihrer Bedeutung als umgebender sozialer Kosmos, von Kleidung über Ernährung (Fastfood, Coca-Cola, ...) bis zu Musik und Sprache (Anglizismen, aber auch sonst Herausbildung von jeweiligen Einheitssprachen durch Radio und Fernsehen); freilich ebenso das ganz andere von regionalen Konflikten und die infolge dessen ausbrechenden Migrationsbewegungen; sowie schließlich auch zum Beispiel Krankheiten, Lebensgrundlagen und natürliche Umwelt, das gemeinsame ökologische Schicksal.

In allem hat sich etwas unaufhaltsam und mit zunehmender Beschleunigung verändert. Und verändert nicht allein in quantitativen Belangen, sondern einschneidend qualitativ. Doch dies *Was?*: was jeweils der Globalisierungsvorgang bzw. die Ausprägung fundamentalen Wandels ist, worin das dabei Folgenproblematische liegt, und wodurch der Prozeß bewirkt wird, woraus sich speist – dies Was ist sicherlich nicht überall dasselbe oder gar überhaupt ein eines großes Geschehen. Es ist nicht einmal alles wirklich problembeladen; zum Beispiel wohl kaum die Globalisierung von Informationen durch Satellitenfernsehen, Satellitentelefone und Internet, oder daß man (falls man will) in Beijing Pizza essen kann oder in Südafrika (falls man es bezahlen kann) Krankheiten mit Penicilin behandeln. Neben der Frage nach dem *Wer?* gilt es darum auch stets den Aspekt des *Inwiefern?* abzugleichen: nicht nur wer-konkret-betreibt-Aktionen, die Globalisierungsfakten setzen bzw. einen weiteren Globalisierungsschritt definitiv machen? – das ist der Vorbehalt der sachmaterialen sozialwissenschaftlichen Untersuchung –, sondern auch inwiefern kommt es tatsächlich zu einem neuartigen Verhältnis von Einzelakteuren und Großprozessen, macht sich hier ein qualitativ neuartiges

Verhältnis geltend? Die umrissene Breite des Phänomens im Blick, läßt denn auch wohl schnell deutlicher werden, daß man *strukturell unterschiedene Bewandtnisse* dessen, was man mit dem übergreifenden Titel „Globalisierung" faßt, differenzieren muß.

Der Überkomplexität des Sachverhalts wegen wird man dabei kaum ohne Eingrenzung auskommen. So empfiehlt sich, um die *philosophisch-theoretisch* relevanten Probleme prägnant zu halten, abzusehen, gewissermaßen 'nach unten', von dem, was schlicht die höhere Dichte des Austauschs und In-Kontakt-Tretens macht,[5] und was die großen Migrationen; und, 'nach oben', von dem, was man das Sittenwächter-Problem nennen könnte – aus Angst um die alten Bräuche und Pietäten und die innere Hoheit der angestammten Autoritäten das Eigene schon gegen *chewing-gum* und Internet-*news* meinen schützen zu müssen. Ebenso wäre vom überhaupt ganz Generellen abzusehen, das all jene Veränderungsphänomene zum Gegenstand einer 'kulturkritischen' Essayistik ('E-Mails/Handys verändern unsere Welt!') qualifiziert. – Dies jeweils eingeklammert, lassen sich wohl dreierlei zentrale Bewandtnisse voneinander abheben:

Die *Eine-Welt*-Bedeutung von „Globalisierung". Sie reicht von dem, was vor allem eine mentale Frage, Frage eines umspannenden Welt-Bildes, ist – und was im Grunde mit Entdeckungsreisen und Erdumrundung beginnt –, bis zu den faktischen Prozessen des zunehmend globus-übergreifenden Zugangs-zu-... (einschließlich des nicht mehr lokal gebundenen Optierenkönnens-für-vielerorts-Gegebenheiten) und Betroffenseins-von-... Sinnbild dieser Bedeutung mag vielleicht das eine Bild sein, das wohl der größte, der relativ größte, Teil der Menschheit kennt: das Foto von der kleinen Erde, aufgenommen vom Mond aus. In ihm und vielem Entsprechendem seither kommen die alten 'philosophischen', alten denkerischen Ideen von 'Menschheit', 'Weltbürgertum', Zugehörigkeit zu einem gemeinsamen Sein und Geschichte, 'Verantwortlichkeit' zur realen Anschaubarkeit.

---

[5] Ein wesentliches Feld der mit diesem zusammenhängenden Problematik liegt im *Wirtschaftlichen*: dort diese eingetretene Dichte mit dem Effekt, ein Über-Übergewicht des Großen und Global-disponieren-Könnenden hereinzubringen.

Dann zweitens die Bewandtnis, mit „Globalisierung" und den durch globalisierende Veränderungen erwachsenen Problemen das zu meinen, daß bisherige, tradierte, in einem bestimmten Kreis *herrschende* Standards und Normierungsweisen mit dem Blick auf andersgeartete gelebte *Möglichkeiten* konfrontiert werden. Durch einen weiter werdenden Horizont erfährt bislang jeweilig (lokal) Gültiges, bislang unbefragt Herrschendes und Geübtes eine gewisse Verfremdung. Oder gerät evtl. unter nachhaltigen Begründungsdruck.

Schließlich drittens, daß mit Globalisierung auch unser ganzes bisheriges Denken und Sich-Verständigen über Gesellschaft, Moral und Politik in Frage gerät – die Modelle und Idealisierungen, mit denen wir bisher Handeln, gesellschaftliche Institutionen und gültigrationale Normen begriffen haben. Die *Einheiten* – relativen Einheits-Gebilde –, in denen die bisherige Orientierung stets gedacht hat, und was normativ integrierte Zusammenhänge sind, erscheinen plötzlich immer fraglicher. Zwei – die zwei wesentlichen klassischen – Probleme der normativen Grundlagen moderner Gesellschaften sind mit Globalisierung wieder ins Manifeste herausgetreten: gegen die Fiktion, die theoretische oder ideologische Idealisierung, der Gesellschaft als eines weithin geschlossenen, zusammenwirkenden Gefüges – nach dem Modell des 'Organismus' – zeigen Gesellschaften sich in folgenerheblicher Hinsicht als offene Systeme; und gegen die Idee der Selbststeuerung, nicht allein sozialtechnologisch und administrativ, sondern vor allem nach 'wertenden Prinzipien' des 'Guten Lebens' und der *res publica*, zeigt sich zunehmend die Grenze der Eingriffsmacht. Beides sind nichts Geringeres als Grenzen auch der neuzeitlichen Idee gesellschaftlicher Rationalität. So sind unter dem Phänomenkomplex 'Globalisierung' – mit den Veränderungen, für dieser neue Titel steht, Veränderungen, die unter diesem Begriff aktuell verhandelt werden – heute alte Fragen zu Ethik, Wirtschaft und Staat, zu normativen Regelungen, Recht und Gerechtigkeit – nämlich: was das alles eigentlich *ist* – noch einmal in verschärfter Form aufgebrochen.

Nicht all dies berührt in selber Weise Fragen unserer werthaften und normativen Bestände, setzt durch qualitativ und überhaupt strukturell neuartige Gegebenheiten einen offen heraustretenden Problemdruck. Neben der ersten Bewandtnis könnte man die zweite allgemein die *Verfremdung-von-Traditionen*-Bedeutung der normativen Problematik von Globalisierung nennen – nicht notwendig ein Relativismus, aber eine unweigerliche Relationalisierung von Traditionen; und die dritte allgemein die *Was-eigentlich-ist-eine-Gesellschaft?*-Bedeutung und *Wie-eigentlich-funktionieren-reglementierte-Prozesse?*-Bedeutung – verbunden mit der Frage, ob wir es uns nicht bisher zu leicht gemacht haben, ob nicht 'Globalisierung' uns auf noch gänzlich Unbegriffenes hinweist. Und während bei der ersten Bewandtnis die globalisierte Wirklichkeit den Triumpf der Philosophie zeigt, das Wir-hatten-recht der alten denkerischen Ideen, ist es bei der dritten, gewissermaßen umgekehrt, ein fundamental antiphilosophischer Effekt, Faktizitäten, die überhaupt jederlei Theorieskepsis nähren. Ja, diese dritte Bewandtnis ist als solche vorrangig eine Frage vor allem an die Theorie. Die intellektuelle Diskussion über 'Globalisierung' und ihre Probleme betrifft denn auch offenkundig vor allem diese dritte Bewandtnis, in Verschränkung mit Aspekten der zweiten. Und hier auch erst scheinen die Faktizitäten von Globalisierungsprozessen eventuell mit Erfordernissen grundlegend *neuer* Wertungsperspektiven, oder gar neuer Werte, unseres Handelns und Deutens einherzugehen.

Der neuartige Problemdruck dergestalt differenziert, läßt dann in der Tat auch das Modell des Normativen und seiner Wurzeln präziser fassen. Die Differenzierung weist zurück auf die normativen Grundlagen sozialer Ordnung. Am Faktum Globalisierung offenbart sich, wie unsere bisherigen Denkfiguren in zentralen Modell-Annahmen überhaupt *zu einfach*, weil zu 'fundamentalistisch' waren. Das betrifft allgemein den Punkt, daß das Verständnis reglementierter Gesellschaftsprozesse einseitig von einer bestimmten traditionellen Begrifflichkeit der „Werte" absorbiert ist.

2. „Die Werte" – Zur Theoriekarriere eines Begriffs

Dem Begriff der „Werte" haftet von Anbeginn eine gewisse Unschärfe an, verglichen mit anderen entsprechenden wie etwa „Präferenzen", „Maximen", „Normen", „Ideale" oder auch „Prinzipien". Bei

„Präferenzen" sind Handlungsmodell und Sachverhalt einigermaßen
klar umrissen; in Frage stehen vor allem Folgerungs- und Anwen-
dungsprobleme, wie Rationalisierbarkeit von Präferenzen, Optimier-
barkeit von Präferenzgemengen (oder Angleichungs-, Ausgleichungs-,
Kompromiß-Möglichkeiten), Kalkülisierbarkeit.[6] Und Normen: zeich-
nen sich aus durch gültig/ungültig; durch Sanktionen (in irgendei-
nerlei Weise); durch funktionale Institutionalisierung im jeweiligen
sozialen Gefüge, dabei in der Tendenz Reglementierung in *Verfahren*;
durch in nicht unerheblichen Bereichen in der Tat Erklärung durch
Genesis oder gesellschaftsevolutionär – ihr Sein und Status dadurch,
was (konkret) der Regelung bedurfte (bzw. wo nicht mehr: ihr
Verblassen, ihre Dysfunktionalität, ihr Rudimentcharakter, ihr Ata-
vismus begreiflich werden); und häufig auch durch einen Normen-
Verbund, in dem die einzelne im Verhältnis zu *anderen* verortet und
umzirkelt ist. Durch all dies ist der Begriff der „Norm" sozusagen
eingehegt, erfährt von dort her seine prägnante Bedeutung. Hinzu,
daß der Terminus (praktische) „Norm" in Alltags-Verständigungen
üblicherweise nicht auftritt, sondern ohnehin – weitestgehend –
speziellen intellektualisierten Diskursen, juridischen und philoso-
phisch-ethischen, zugehört, Diskursen, die auf eine relativ klar umrissene bestimmte Funktion dieses Terminus zugeschnitten sind bzw.
er in ihnen geradezu definiert ist. – Aber Werte? Dabei hat das Konzept der „Werte" eine bemerkenswerte Karriere in der neueren Philosophie wie auch sozialwissenschaftlichen Theorie gemacht; und ist
wesentlich von dort ausgehend, repräsentierend dieserart Betrach-
tungshinsicht – Reflexionsvergegenständlichung und Reflexionsver-
allgemeinerung –, in unserer normalen Redeweise heimisch geworden.[7]

---

[6] Sowie dabei dies alles sich stellend in bezug auf komplexere ('gesamtgesell-
schaftliche') Theoriebildungen, d.h. als Verallgemeinerungs-Probleme.

[7] Auch im *Grimmschen Wörterbuch* ist, bevor es dann zu Belegen aus der philosophischen Fachliteratur aus dem beginnenden 20. Jahrhundert kommt, von der heute
längst selbstverständlichen substantivischen Verallgemeinerung „Der Wert" oder gar
„Die Werte" nichts verzeichnet; allenfalls die eingeschränkte ökonomische Bedeutung
und partielle Analogisierungen damit. Vgl. *Deutsches Wörterbuch*, von Jacob Grimm
und Wilhelm Grimm, Bd. XIV/I,2, Leipzig 1960, Sp. 460–470.

1. Heideggers Diktum 'Niemand stirbt für Werte' mag in dieser polemischen Apodiktizität[8] falsch sein. Man denke etwa an die inszenierten Selbsttötungen im japanischen Militär nach der Kapitulation 1945 durch den Tenno, oder an manche frühchristlichen Märtyrer.[9] Aber es deutet darauf hin, daß im gewöhnlichen, funktionierenden Alltagsleben 'Werte' – ein Faktor 'Werte' – zunächst einmal so nicht vorkommen. Menschen – wo nicht ohnedies weithin gelernt-imitierend oder schlicht gewohnheitsmäßig – erstreben Dinge, Menschen schätzen dies oder jenes, Menschen bewerten-beurteilen Gegebenheiten, mögliche Ziele, Optionen; aber das 'Haben' von (in Handlungsorientierung) geltenden bzw. zueigen gewordenen Werten, als Verständnis und Selbstverständnis der Aktoren und als sozialer Zugehörigkeitsindikator, – eine solcherart Subjekt-Struktur, wie Theorie dies gegenstandsfeldkonstituierend ansetzt – ist wohl stets eine sekundäre Herausbildung und, je allgemeiner 'die Werte', desto mehr, Produkt einer relativen Spätzeit. Erst wenn Weltbilder und Lebensweisen intellektuell interpretiert, ausgelegt werden, vor allem in Abhebung von anderen sozial kursierenden (oder vormaligen) Reglementierungs-Mustern, Abgrenzung gegen anderes, erst wenn ein Diskurs *über* die normativen Grundlagen einer Gemeinschaft in deren Alltag hereinkommt, oder dann bei expliziter Kultur- und Werte-Erziehung, können Menschen überhaupt – vor anderen und auch vor sich selber – thematisieren, was ihre essentiellen Wichtigkeiten und vollends dann 'ihre' Werte sind (bzw. vermeinterweise seien): können solch Thematisierung und Wissens-Punkte des Mich-Leitenden und Mir-Unabdingbaren bei Bedarf mobilisieren. So gehört z.B. sicher, seit es Menschen gibt, zu den Urerfahrungen die der Freundschaft. Aber hier wurden, als man sich mit dieser Erfahrung

---

[8] Vgl. Martin Heidegger, *Holzwege*, Frankfurt a. Main: Klostermann, 1972, S. 94 („Keiner stirbt für bloße Werte" [1938]). Was Heidegger im Blick hat, ist, obwohl unmittelbar auf den großen denkgeschichtlichen Umbruch des 19. Jahrhunderts: H. Lotzes werttheoretische Reformulierung des Platonischen Idealismus und dann Nietzsche verweisend, die breite wertphilosophische Strömung seiner Zeit.

[9] Das angesichts des Terrorismus unserer Tage am nächsten liegende Beispiel dagegen, der Selbstmord-Attentäter, ist wohl eine noch einmal ganz andere Motivations-Struktur.

auseinandersetzte und sie ins Verhältnis zu anderen Gegebenheiten des (sozialen) Lebens brachte, in mythischen Geschichten, Liedern, Gedichten und Epen hohe *Beispiele* solchen Verhaltens und solcher Gesinnung gerühmt. Doch daß 'Freundschaft' ein *Wert* ist, ist wohl erst ein sehr, sehr spätes Verhältnis dazu.[10] Dies vollends bei anderem, das mit allgemein-'anthropologischen' Verwurzelungen in vermittelteren Linien zusammenhängt. Die selbstverständliche Rede von den geltenden bzw. zu erstrebenden Werten der 'Objektivität', des 'Gebildetseins', der 'Frömmigkeit', der 'Authentizität', des 'geschmackssicheren Lebensstils', ja auch dem der 'Familien*ehre*' oder selbst denen des 'Erfolghabens', 'Machthabens' ist allemal ein durchaus *gewordenes* Verhältnis der inneren Reflexion sozialer Gemeinschaften, und bis zu dem für Verständigungs-, auch Selbstverständigungsprozesse zureichenden prägnanten Bedeutungsumriß ist es normalerweise ein langer Weg.

Theorien jedoch, in Philosophie wie Sozialwissenschaften, haben seit der Mitte des 19. Jahrhunderts 'Wert' zu einem Ur-Begriff gemacht, 'Werte' von vornherein als Urphänomen genommen. Seit Hermann Lotze, Nietzsche, neukantianischer Wertphilosophie und phänomenologischer Wertethik ist der 'Wert'-Begriff auf breiter Front in die Philosophie hereingebrochen; es kam zum Übergreifen der 'Wert'-Terminologie und mit ihr des ganzen entsprechenden semantischen Felds auf immer mehr traditionelle philosophische Gegenstände.[11] Desgleichen, leicht zeitversetzt, in sozialwissenschaftlichen Theorien.

---

[10] Das hätte wahrscheinlich nicht einmal Aristoteles, dem wir bekanntlich die Einführung des Paradigmas 'Freundschaft' in die Ethik verdanken, so prononciert. Obwohl bei Aristoteles erstmals klar die Differenzierung, die in Mythen usw. noch kaum im Blick ist, vorgenommen ist: die Abhebung der 'Freundschaft' im eigentlichen ethischen Sinne von der für die Sozialstruktur wichtigen Gestalt entsprechenden Verhaltens und entsprechender Bindung, wo 'Freundschaft' mit Treue, Loyalität, Gefolgschaft usw. in eins verschmilzt. Vgl. Aristoteles, *Nikomachische Ethik*, Buch VIII–IX.

[11] Vgl. Fritz Bamberger, *Untersuchungen zur Entstehung des Wertproblems in der Philosophie des 19. Jahrhunderts*, Halle 1924; August Messer, *Wertphilosophie der Gegenwart*, Berlin: Junker & Dünnhaupt, 1930; Jürgen Gebhardt, „Die Werte. Zum Ursprung eines Schlüsselbegriffs der politisch-sozialen Sprache der Gegenwart in der deutschen

Mit diesen schon binnen kurzem kaum mehr reflektierten Veränderungen im Denk-Gefüge sind dabei im selben Grade ihrer Etablie-
rung zugleich auch ihr Hintergrund, ihre Voraussetzungen ins Un-
bewußte abgesunken: daß zu dieser Karriere der 'Wert'-Begriff-
lichkeit eine ganz bestimmte Theoriebildungs-Konstellation gehört.
Denn in genau dem Maße, wie die Welt zur: objektiven Tatsache
wurde, streng und geschlossen kausalistisch, zu empirischen Positi-
vitäten, neutraler Seinswirklichkeit – in dem Maße wurde, auf der
Gegenseite, die *Einstellung dazu* dem Subjekt anheimgegeben. Erst wo
für den Seins-Zustand der Welt das Ideal der Sachlichkeit – der Objektivität des 'So-ist-es' – eingefordert, wurden, als Gegengewicht,
'Die Werte' zur Dimension des wahrhaft Subjektiven. 'Die Werte'
wurden zum Refugium des Humanen – des Allgemeinen in unserer
Individualität und (sozialen) Erfahrungslage, einer Subjektivität, die
gleichwohl nicht nur situationell-affektiv ist, sondern die Eigen-
Identität, das Allgemeinheits-Niveau der alten philosophischen Begriffe von Personhaftigkeit, Geist, Lebenssinn, Glückseligkeit, Ge-
meinschaftszughörigkeit usw. wahrt. 'Werte': definierten, ja retteten
das Subjektive in einer bedeutungs-entleerten, einer sinn-los gewordenen, einfach nur noch kausalgesetztlich ablaufenden Wirklichkeit.
Tatsachen-und-Werte: dieses seitherige, scheinbar so reflektiert-
selbstevidente Denkmuster, ist auf beiden Seiten gleicherweise eine –
hoch theoriehaltige und entsprechend spät dazu gewordene – Stilisie-
rung. Ein spezielles Problemthema des *Wissenschafts-*, des Verwissen-
schaftlichungs-Prozesses, die 'Wertfreiheits'-Debatte am Beginn der
Verfachlichung der Sozialwissenschaften, hatte dies vollends fixiert.[12]

Philosophie des späten 19. Jahrhunderts", in: *Anodos. Festschrift für Helmut Kuhn*, hrsg.
von Rupert Hofmann, Jörg Jantzen, Henning Ottmann, Weinheim 1989, S. 35–54. – Zu
einer kritischen Erörterung vgl. Herbert Schnädelbach, „Werte und Wertungen",
Logos. Zeitschrift für systematische Philosophie, Bd. 7 (2001), S. 149–170.

[12] Zur langen Wirkungsgeschichte dieses Themas, das, unter dieser Struktur, bis
heute unabgeschlossen als Dimension der Reflexion steht vgl. *Werturteilsstreit*, hrsg.
von Hans Albert, Ernst Topitsch, Darmstadt: Wissenschaftliche Buchgesellschaft,
³1990; Theodor W. Adorno et al., *Der Positivismusstreit in der deutschen Soziologie*, Neu-
wied – Berlin: Luchterhand, 1969; *Mythos Wertfreiheit?*, hrsg. von Karl-Otto Apel,
Matthias Kettner, Frankfurt a. Main – New York: Campus, 1994.

Nicht völlig von ungefähr ist das Problemfeld in der ganzen vormaligen Theorie *nicht* als das der 'Werte' (oder unter anderen strukturell entsprechenden Titeln) verhandelt worden. Was die Philosophie betrifft, so ist das Thema erst dann zur eigenen, und grundlegenden, Bewandtnis herausgetreten, als die zwei – komplementären – Theorie-Voraussetzungen zur nicht mehr begründungsbedürftigen Struktur des ganzen Denkens und Phänomenblicks sich durchgesetzt hatten: die Objektivität der 'Welt' als neutrale Fakten, als enteigenwertet, und alle Wichtigkeiten und Rangordnung dem Subjektiven anheimgestellt, was bis dato *allein* im (modern) Ökonomischen so angesetzt war – 'Werte' wurden dadurch zum Gedanken einer neuen Gegenstandshaftigkeit des Subjektiven (eine neue Allgemeinheit spezifischer Art);[13] und als hinzu ein Bewußtsein von ganz verschiedenerlei Dimensionen solcher möglichen Wichtigkeiten des menschlichen Lebens zur Selbstverständlichkeit geworden war (z.B. 'der künstlerische Wert' einer Sache oder Handlung, in Abhebung von ihren anderen Aspekten; 'der technisch-ingenieursmäßige Wert'; usw.).[14] Daß 'Werte' ein Urphänomen des Menschlichen seien, die Universalität, ja der Metastatus der 'Werte' im Kosmos der menschlichen Subjektivität, als

---

[13] In derselben Phase wie der Aufstieg des Themas 'Werte' finden sich darum zugleich die vitalistischen und die mit 'Energie'-Begrifflichkeiten experimentierenden Strömungen einer ontologischen Hinterschreitung des (modernen) Naturbegriffs, überhaupt der objektivistischen Naturphänomenalität.

[14] Für letzteres bedeutete Nietzsche den Einschnitt: indem er, gegen die (wiederum naturalistische) Engführung von Wertungen mit sozialer oder humaner Evolution, in zweiter Potenz die Frage nach dem Wert der Werturteile, d.h. des Werturteilens seinerseits bzw. überhaupt, aufwarf. – Dazu, daß 'Wert' in eine fundamentale Position einrücken konnte und es zu einer elementar *werttheoretischen* Konzeption der Theoriebildung kommen konnte, mußte das Denken nicht allein über die angestammte Wert-/unwert-Polarität (welche im letzten noch am Modell 'Güter' orientiert ist) hinausgehen; es mußte vor allem auch über eine einfache *2er-Struktur* hinausgehen: über die Struktur von einerseits einem unmittelbaren Subjekt-Bezug – das mir natürlich bzw. existentiell Bedeutsame – und andererseits *einem noch anderen* (Indirekten, Höheren, Vermittelten). Das war die Struktur des ökonomischen „Wert"-Begriffs gewesen (direkter Gebrauchswert / und daß darüber noch ein indirekter Tauschwert existiert), und es dominiert auch noch ausschließlich den „Wert"-Begriff der vormaligen philosophischen Klassiker (etwa Kants Denkstück vom „moralischen Werth" einer Handlung, „absoluten Werth" der Person usw.).

Ursprungspol alles human Sinnhaften und menschengewirkter
Schöpfungen, ist denn auch mit Begründungen eingeführt, die
genaubesehen höchst voraussetzungsvoll sind: entweder ist das Phänomen 'Werte' aus dem Schätzen-Vorziehen abgeleitet, d.h. abstrakt
verallgemeinert; oder es meint im Grunde ein Mir-Wertvolles; oder in
den psychologisierenden Theorien (Ehrenfels, Meinong, Brentano) als
Kennzeichen (des Aufbaus) unserer Strebemotivierungen überhaupt;
oder im Blick auf soziale Praxis: als Expression des 'ich!' (Ich-
Besonderer) oder des normativen 'Sollte!'; oder phänomenologisch als
eigentlich eine (im Zeichen des Subjekt-Faktors reformulierte) Theorie
der *Güter*; oder im Neukantianismus als eigentlich Wertungs*strukturen*; und dgl. mehr. Mit dem historistischen Umbau des idealistischen
„Geistes", und je mehr auch der Begriff der „Kultur" historistisch
relativiert, war im Thema der 'Werte' zugleich eine innere Reflexion
des Historismus erwachsen, ein 'Halt!' gegen das Abgleiten in bloßen
Relativismus oder gar Subjektivismus. 'Werte' so als Erläuterungsbe-
griff für 'Kultur', hatte, im Zeichen des Kulturellen, all jenes definitiv
ineinanderfließen lassen.[15] – Eine nicht weniger prekäre Problemge-
neralisierung verzeichnen die sozialwissenschaftlichen Theoriebildungen. Wo nicht ohnehin, aus empirischem Gestus heraus, 'Werte'
als abfragbare *attitudes* gleich anderen Subjektüberzeugungen verstanden, haben sie in ihrer Frage nach Gesellschaft 'Werte' als die
letzten normativen Haltungspunkte angesetzt – als das, wovon alle
konkreten Reglementierungskriterien und auch 'Institutionen' sich
letztlich ableiten bzw. worauf fußen, 'Werte' als die Steuerparameter
in Funktions- und Integrationsprozessen, und 'Werte' als das Eigentliche in Prozessen der Internalisierung.[16] Auch der sozialwissen-

---

[15] So nimmt es denn auch kaum Wunder, daß die angeführten *Beispiele* für 'Werte'
häufig die beanspruchte Allgemeinheit nicht tragen. Etwa wenn beim Aspekt Gefal-
len/Mißfallen ein eigentlich Soziales ins Ästhetische, Geschmacklich-Inkommensu-
rable verschoben ist.

[16] Die rigideste Konzeption eines Zur-Theorie-Bringens, die Theorie von T. Parsons, zeigt diesen strukturellen Ansatz und seine problematischen Abblendungen und
Kontaminationen vielleicht am deutlichsten. Vgl. *Toward a General Theory of Action*,
hrsg. von Talcott Parsons, Edward A. Shils, New York: Harper and Row, 1951 (darin
vor allem den Aufsatz von Clyde Kluckhohn, "Values and Value-Orientations in the

schaftliche Zugang behandelt, wo nicht mehr große gesellschaftliche Einheitscharakterisierungen, sondern er in die materiale Erforschung eintritt, 'Werte', je distinkt und zu einem ganzen Systembündel sich fügend, als die Konkretisierungsphänomene von 'Geistigem' und 'Kultur'. Seine Modelle changieren dabei durchweg zwischen Präferenzen-Agieren und Anerkannte-soziale-Güter und einfach Code-Verhalten.

2. Auch in der Sache, der sozialen Wirklichkeit, ist das Phänomen genaubesehen keineswegs eine Urtatsache menschlichen Existierens, Urtatsache des Sich-Orientierens, Sich-Verhaltens und Sich-Verstehens. Jedenfalls nicht, solange man nicht, so vor allem in 'kulturanthropologischer' Wissenschaftsperspektive, Perspektive eines um der Wissenschaft willen gewollten kulturellen Neutralismus-Relativismus, den Begriff des '*Be*wertens' – qua Bedeutsamkeit-überhaupt und des Mehr-und-Weniger, nämlich gegenüber einer per definitionem nichts-weiter-besagenden empirischen Seinswirklichkeit, auch empirischen Sozialfaktizität – inflationär aufbläht. Auch in der Sache, als soziales, ist das Phänomen 'Die Werte', in dieser Allgemeinheit, relativ jung.

Erst als der Einzelne *nicht mehr* durch: Status, Alter, Geschlecht, 'Kaste', ethnische Herkunft, Religion, gesellschaftliche Funktionsposition ('Rolle'), Teilhabe am Bildungskanon usw. spezifiziert wurde, erst dann konnte eine neue Sozialwahrnehmung und neue soziale Diskursweise sich herausbilden, in der der Einzelne als soziales Mitwesen (zuletzt) durch 'seine Werte' (und *in praxi*: seine daraus fließende 'Moral') qualifiziert wurde und auch sich selber so qualifizierte. Erst als die (tradiert geltenden) Zuschreibungen, die sich an natürlichen oder sozialfunktionalen Merkmalen festgemacht haben oder/und die aus Legitimierungs-'Weltbildern' abgeleitet waren, nicht mehr alles vorausfestlegten, erst als manches – und zunehmend – zur (sozial akzeptierten oder anerkannten) individuellen Entfaltung *freigegeben* war, konnte dies Charakteristische auf die (ein Denken, Verhalten und Gemeinschafts-Zugehörigkeit ausmachenden) 'Werte'

Theory of Action", S. 388–433); Talcott Parsons, *The Social System*, New York: Free Press, 1951.

verallgemeinert werden.[17] Statt der Vor-Spezifizierungen, der Auf-
spaltung des Mensch-seins durch solche *klassifizierenden* Zuschreibungen konnte sich allererst ein neues Strukturmuster entwickeln –
und unumkehrbar, sich selber stablisierend etablieren –, worin zunächst in gewisses Menschen-Allgemeines angesetzt ist – und dann
die *Differenz* in einer, einer neuen, Ebene von *Merkmalen des Geistig-
Willentlichen*, der geistig-willentlichen Optionsspielräume (Einstel-
lung-*zu*-... und Dezision) verortet ist: mein Interaktions-Gegenüber,
meine Referenz-Gruppe der (rechtfertigenden) Zugehörigkeit, und
auch ich mich selber dann, verstanden als jeweils eine basale Gemeinsamkeit universell-humaner Empfindungen und Regungen und ansonsten 'das' Individuum, das für seine ganz persönlichen Beurtei-
lungs- und Wichtigkeits-Überzeugungen steht. An die Stelle äußerer
Merkmale (natürlich oder sozialfunktional) treten Zuschreibungen,
auch Selbstzuschreibungen des mental *Innen*. Die gesellschaftliche
Lage der Zeit hatte dies obendrein aufgeladen, indem auf der einen
Seite mit zunehmender Komplexität und zunehmendem Wandlungs-
druck das Verlangen nach dem wahrhaft Wertvollen, die Polarisie-
rung von wertvoll-vs.-unwert, sowie die Drohung der identitätsauflö-
senden Zersplitterung durch die vielen in mich hineinragenden
„sozialen Kreise" (G. Simmel) eine dominante Bedeutung bekam; und
indem auf der anderen Seite, von einem idealisierten relativ festen
Normensystem und seiner Institutionenverkörperung – Kirche und
autokratischem Staat – aus, jeder Zweifel, jedes Abweichen fast so-
gleich als 'hat-gar-keine-Werte-mehr' erschien. Der Nihilist wie sein
politisches Pendant, der Anarchist, sind Gestalten aus der Mentalität
des 19. Jahrhunderts.

So haftet der Rede von 'Den Werten' sowohl als theoretischem
Begriff wie innerhalb der sozialen Verständigung sein durchaus be-
stimmter geschichtlicher Index an. Theorien – Theorien eines bestimmten Typs – und gesellschaftliche Entwicklung, gesellschaftlicher
Zustand haben die Phänomene allererst auf dieses Eine: 'Werte' ver-

---

[17] In einer parallelen Entwicklung übrigens mit der Herausbildung der Konzeption und Begrifflichkeit des 'Weltanschauungshaften'. Vgl. dazu Helmut G. Meier,
'Weltanschauung'. Studien zu einer Geschichte und Theorie des Begriffs, Münster 1970.

dichtet. Verhaltenserfahrung, Verhaltensorientierung und Verhaltens-verständigung auszurichten zuletzt an einem Faktor 'Werte' ist ein Spätphänomen einer individualisierten Gesellschaft. In ihr erst hat das Denken die Anschauung eines diesen Phänomens, Anschauung einer, auch wo nicht mehr Status-Gebührendes, Standes-Pflichten, 'Rollen'-Verhalten usw., doch allemal bestimmten – regelmäßigen und festen – Profilstruktur subjektiver Akteure und von Akteurs-gruppen. 'Werte': von spezifischen geistig-kulturellen Optionen ge-leitet zu werden oder solche zu eigen zu haben, schienen das letzte Gemeinsame, um *im* Prozeß der Enttraditionalisierung, der Pluralisie-rung und Individualisierung das Selbstsein und die Zurechenbarkeit des Subjekts nicht an die Mächte naturaler Bedingtheiten zu verlieren; und zugleich das letzte Relativ-Allgemeine, um nicht ins schlechter-dings inkommensurabel Subjektivistische abzurutschen, sondern ge-wisse Grundbezüge des Sozialen und Geistigen (Geistig-Vertret-baren) zu wahren. In *terms* von 'Werten' – und dem ganzen damit verbundenen semantischen Feld – schien sich überhaupt noch von Subjektivem und Humanem reden zu lassen.[18]

Die Entwicklung der gesellschaftlichen Prozesse und Beziehungen hatte, indem immer mehr Profanes, Alltagsweltliches, Privatlebens-haftes freigesetzt bzw. freigegeben, welches aber gleichwohl gewissen offenkundigen normativen Reglementierungen gehorcht, die sozialen Gültigkeits- und Wichtigkeits-Positionen unter einen Hierarchie-Druck gesetzt – auf ein Oberstes-Letztes hin, welches dann als 'die (betreffenden) Werte' umrissen wurde resp. erschien. Indem immer mehr Kreise des Profanen, Alltagsweltlichen, Privatlebenshaften her-eingriffen – offenkundig reglementiert, aber nicht mehr nach hei-lig/göttlich-vs.-notgedrungen/weltlich oder nach einander umgrei-fender Dignität wie Staatlich-Dorfgemeinschaft-Häuslich ordenbar –, bedurfte es eines solchen neuen Hierarchisierungs-Musters, das Ab-grenzungen gegen das Un-Werte, Nicht-Eigentliche, Sozial-und-Kul-tur-Entkoppelte, Sub-Geistige usw. erlaubte. Ohne dies, was der Dis-

---

[18] Daß mit der als fundamental angesetzten 'Wert'-Begrifflichkeit in Theoriebil-dung wie sachmaterialer Untersuchung auch überhaupt ein bestimmtes *Handlungs*-Modell einhergeht, bedürfte noch einmal einer ganz eigenen Erörterung.

kurs dann auf den Titel 'Werte' des Einzelnen und von Interagierens-Gemeinschaften brachte, mußten die sozialen Personen, Agenten, Mechanismen, *innestehend zwischen* den verschiedensten Normierungsfaktizitäten, als sonst profillos, ohne eigene Identität, zersplittert-zerstreut, ein Spielball des gesellschaftlich gewordenen Pluralen und der prähumanen Bedingtheiten, ohne Widerstand gegen die situativen Mächte erscheinen.[19] 'Werte': wurden so in letzter Konsequenz überhaupt zu dem, was die Persönlichkeit ausmacht im Meer der naturalen Welt, die Kontur des Subjekts; 'Werte' wurden zu dem, was Menschen (im Sozialen) teilen; und 'Werte' wurden auch zu dem, worüber (woran festgemacht) ein ansonsten befremdendes Verhalten ggf. 'verstehbar' wird – 'Werte' als das Eigentliche in Prozessen des 'Verstehens'.

Damit aber wurde der Kategorie 'Wert' wohl unversehens zuviel aufgeladen. Als diese Phänomeneinheits- und Letztkategorie *geworden*, geworden in Theorie wie in sozialer Verständigung und Selbstverständigung, ist 'Wert' nicht zu trennen von dem, was, dieses Eine und Allgemeine überhaupt erst profilierend, damit ersetzt und umbesetzt wurde. Und all solches unreflektierte Zuviel – wofür „Wert" alles stehen soll, welche Phänomenstruktur damit angesetzt ist – ist auch heimlich mitgeschleppt, wenn wir heute von „Wertproblemen", von „Alten Werten", von zu etablierenden „Neuen Werten", die wieder Orientierung zu geben vermögen angesichts der gewandelten ('globalisierten') Wirklichkeit, usw. sprechen. Faktoren der Idealisierung, vor allem Theorie-Kriterien – Kriterien der Eindeutigkeit und des Mentalen, der mentalen Präsenz – und entsprechende weithin gleiche Kriterien der sozialen Zuschreibung in einer Spätphase gesellschaftlicher Verhältnisse, sind hier in den Gegenstand projiziert. Mit dem Begriff 'Wert' – etwas als Frage von „Werten" zu verstehen – sind, und zwar ganz gleich, ob dann als transzendentale Gültigkeitsstrukturen ausbuchstabiert oder als phänomenaler Ausdruck meiner menschlichen Strebestruktur oder als subjektive Expression oder als

---

[19] Und erst wenn so der subjektive Faktor überhaupt so eigens herausgehoben ist und dergestalt besetzt, kann „Wert" sich vor die anderen klassischen Themenbegriffe der menschlichen Praxis, wie: „Güter", „Tugenden", „Pflichten", oder auch Vernunft, schieben: kann sich ihnen, theoriestrukturell grundlegend, vorordnen.

soziale Anempfehlung oder Verbindlichkeit, bestimmte erhebliche Voraussetzungen verbunden: Bewußtheit (oder doch Bewußtheitsfähigkeit), 'Selbstheit', gefügte Einheit bzw. Harmonie; hinzu, daß 'die Werte' der Menschen und ihre betreffenden anerkannt-geübten Sozialformen einander wechselseitig entsprächen. Das sind Voraussetzungen, hinter denen, wie heimlich auch immer, doch gerade ein sehr klassisch-'idealistisches' Denken steht. Der soziale Diskurs und die Selbstwahrnehmung der Akteure in einer individualisierten Gesellschaft haben diese ursprünglich von der (philosophischen) Theorie her hereingekommene terminologische Form zusätzlich zementiert. Auch die soziale Verständigung selbst produziert unvermittelterweise solch 'idealistische' Vorstellungen ihrer Akteure.[20] Das Individuum moderner Gesellschaften, desgleichen die institutionellen Akteure und integrierten Subgruppen, schien in der Orientierung an 'Werten' zu agieren und schien auch nur so, als überhaupt geistig bzw. nicht-natural, verstehbar. Auch im sozialen Prozeß selbst steht so, mit dem Emergieren der Begrifflichkeit der leitenden oder zueigenen 'Werte', ein gut Stück der Substantialisierung und der Selbstidealisierung – 'idealistische' Handlungsbegriffe und 'idealistische' Sozialerfahrungs- wie Selbstbeschreibungen. Ein 'Idealismus', der gleichwohl ein *Faktum* ist, Faktor einer bestimmten avancierten Struktur der (mehr denn fundamentalnaturalistischen) Theoriebildung und Faktor des Selbstverständnisses wie Orientierungsraums der Akteure, und insofern nicht einfachhin eliminativ zu hinterschreiten.

Ein Blick auf das, wie so etwas wie „Werte" – die Rede von „Werten", Berufung auf „Werte" – effektiv fungiert im Sozialen, und welcher Art verwoben in historische Prozesse, mag einen Weg jenseits der ererbten heimlichen Denkhypotheken dieses 'Idealismus' weisen. Er läßt das Thema 'Werte' etwas weniger grundsätzlich erscheinen. Und wird dann auch die heutige Herausforderung 'Globalisierung' reflektierter einordnen lassen.

---

[20] Für die verschiedenen sozialwissenschaftlichen Konzeptionen im 20. Jahrhundert cf. die luzide Darlegung bei Hans Joas, *Die Entstehung der Werte*, Frankfurt am Main: Suhrkamp, 1999. Bei etlichen der Konzeptionen wäre jedoch zu fragen, wie selbstreflexiv sie wirklich sind – und ob sie nicht, auf der Suche nach 'sozialen Tatsachen' höherer ('kultureller') Art, ihren Themengegenstand reifizieren.

3. Die Zumutung der Werte

1. *Rückbau von Theorieidealisierungen.* Vielleicht wird man dereinst sehen, daß so, wie im Bereich des Theoretischen zuvor der Begriff des 'Selbstbewußtseins', im Praktischen der der 'Werte' einer Läuterung seiner idealistischen Erbschaften bedurfte,[21] Läuterung in logischer Analyse seiner Begriffsverwendung und seines semantischen Gehalts. Heute jedenfalls steht seine kritische Reflexion noch weithin bevor. Einige Eingrenzungen lassen sich jedoch skizzieren.

Zunächst einmal: 'Werte', als Begriffswort, und das, wofür es gemeinterweise steht, stehen in einem eigentümlich gegensinnigen Verhältnis. Über „die Werte" redet man, nach „Werten" fragt man immer erst dann, wenn das – die Verhaltensweise, Verhaltensorientierung –, wofür sie stehen, *nicht mehr* sicher gegeben ist. Und zwar solches Nicht-mehr-sicher nicht lediglich als Denker-Problem – *theoría*-Intellektualität und Aufklärung –, daß Infragestellungen des Muß-es-so-sein?, Warum-eigentlich? und Woran-Begründungen-festmachen? intellektuell in den Horizont der Reflexion treten, sondern erst wenn es tatsächlich sozial als Problem erfahren wird.[22] Das, was mit „Werte" gemeint ist, kommt erst in den Blick, wenn die betreffende Verhaltenstypik, Orientierungsressource oder Lebensform schwindet oder an Kraft verliert; wenn „die Werte" genau sich wandeln; oder neu mit anderen machtvollen Kriterien konfrontiert werden. „Werte" werden immer dann beschworen, wenn funktionierende Regelungs-Praktiken, wenn ein Hintergrundkonsens *nicht mehr* genügend erforderliche Bindungskraft besitzen. Mit einem *Inhaltlichen* – den jeweiligen „Wert"-Gehalten – wird hier auf eine brüchig werdende oder sonst als nichtselbstverständlich bewußtgewordene *Form* – Form der funktionierenden Interaktion, des funktionierenden Ineinandergreifens bzw. Anschlußhaftigkeit – geantwortet.

---

[21] Nach den – gerade in ihrer Kritik – noch weitgehend am theoretischen Subjekt-Objekt-, Ich-Welt-Modell orientierten kursierenden Klärungen über 'Wollen', 'Freiheit' ('Freiwilligkeit'), 'Willensschwäche', 'Unbewußtheit'/'Selbsttäuschung' usw.

[22] Oder anders gesagt: erst wenn der 'Sophist', die 'sophistische' Aufklärung, aber auch der Tugend-Fanatiker oder 'nihilistische' Regungen in breiterem Rahmen Resonanz finden.

Die Prozesse machen sichtbar, wie viel implizite Regelungsselbstverständlichkeiten einmal *waren*. Zum Beispiel beim Ruf nach „Wert"-Bindung der globalisiert-entfesselten kapitalistischen Logik und 'Zwänge' (Anpassungs-, Mitmachens-Notwendigkeiten): wieviel eingewöhnt-funktionierende Verhaltensweisen – Verbindlichkeiten, Verpflichtungen und Wertvoll/unwert-Beurteilungsmuster – in den alten noch irgendwie (und sei's auch nur ideellerweise) persönlichen Verhältnissen, wo die Einzelnen, auf keiner der Seiten, eben niemals nur als 'Charaktermasken' agierten. Und bei allem das mit „Werte" als prekär Bewußtwerdende oder mit „Werte" thematisiert Entschwindende nicht als Totalzweifel, drohende gänzliche Reglungsanarchie (in der betreffenden Hinsicht, dem betreffenden Feld des Lebens) – dies ist immer ein Philosophen-Konstrukt –, sondern stets ist etwas (jeweils) Gemeinsames gerade nicht infragegestellt. Positiv wie negativ, setzt sich in der Rede von „Wert" so die eigentümliche Struktur fort, die seine Entstehungskonstellation als Begriffstitel kennzeichnet: unthematisch das Nicht-mehr eines anderen, wofür es eintritt, an sich zu tragen. In den Blick – und in Rede – kommende „Werte" sind, in der sozialen Wirklichkeit wie in der Verständigung, immer ein *relativer* Faktor, relational zu einem, ggf. sehr weiten, Bereich betreffender unthematischer eingewöhnt-funktionierender Reglementierungen.

Ein Zweites beträfe die genannte, vorderhand vor allem der Theorie-Perspektive geschuldete, Idealisierung, daß 'die Werte' einer Gesellschaft, nämlich die die Subjekte leiten bzw. zueigen sind, und die (für diesen gesellschaftlichen Verband) adäquaten Sozialformen einander geradewegs entsprächen; daß die tradierten, verbreiteten 'Werte' und die institutionalisierten, geübten Formen des sozialen Lebens – im ganzen: die Sozialordnung – eben die *zwei Seiten* der sozialen Integration sind. Die 'Werte' wären demzufolge die subjektive, in den Einstellungen und Typisierungen der Akteure im Wortsinne ver-körperte Innenseite des sozialen Normierungssystems, in Tradierungsformen weitergezeugt und per Erziehung internalisiert.

Das aber ist schon allein phänomenal schwerlich haltbar. Von all dem schlicht historisch Bedingten und 'Unordentlichen' dabei einmal noch abgesehen, decken Sozialformen und 'die Werte' sich sicher niemals ganz. Nicht nur weil das Soziale gewissermaßen 'nach unten' flüssiger wird oder ausfranst – es im Konkreten ganz unterschiedliche Motivationen des Mit-machens, Sich-einfügens gibt.[23] In einer Gesellschaft ist darüber hinaus auch sicher nur in kleiner Teil 'der Werte' einigermaßen einheitlich übers Ganze. Entweder vielmehr sind die betreffenden Kriterien-*cluster* ohnehin *aufgeteilt* nach Interaktionskreisen oder konkret eintretenden Kontakt-Bewandtnissen; die Menschen eines ländlich-bäuerlichen Umfelds, die so gut wie nie mit Verwaltungs-Prozeduren, mit (autonomer) Kunst oder mit Wissenschaft in Berührung kommen, *'brauchen'* sozusagen auch nicht betreffende 'Werte' – gar keine –, müssen ihre Verhaltensweisen und -orientierungen nicht mit solchem für sie Irrelevantem belasten. Oder wo übers Ganze, sind 'die Werte' der Menschen im meisten zum Beispiel *komplementär-doppelt* (und gerade je weiter modern, desto mehr) verteilt[24] – als die von Herrschenden und Beherrschten, Priesterschaft (bzw. Mönchsleben) und Laienmasse, Kapital und Arbeit, Künstler und 'Bewunderer' usw., die jeweils auch bei ggf. großer Diskrepanz ein funktionierendes Gespann abgeben.

Beide gleichsam 'harten' Manifestationen regelmäßigen Verhaltens, subjektiverseits das, was die Haltungspunkte des Verhaltens sind, und objektiverseits die Ordnungsgestalt des Gesellschaftlichen, lassen sich mithin auf keinen Fall umstandslos mit dem Fungieren entsprechender dominanter 'Werte' identifizieren. Es *gibt* Regelmäßigkeiten und Mechanismen der Bindung wie Reglementierung, doch nicht einfachhin und schlechterdings *wegen* 'Werten'. – Damit fällt aber auch eine dritte Voraussetzung: nämlich daß genauso (jedenfalls relativ) ausgeglichen und funktionierend, wie das soziale Gefüge sich darstellt, auch die Menge 'der Werte' der betreffenden Gemeinschaft untereinander ein stimmiges, gar harmonisches Ganzes bilden. Es ist kaum wahrscheinlich, daß die Kriterien des ökonomischen Verhaltens und 'die Werte' des Familialen (einschließlich Dorfgemeinschaft und

---

[23] Vgl. dazu meinen Aufsatz Rainer Adolphi, „Fügsamkeit. Max Weber über die Grenzen der Legitimität von Herrschaft", in: *Law. Power. Sovereignty*, hrsg. von Roman Kozłowski, Karolina Cern, Poznań: Wydawnictwo Naukowe UAM, 2004, S. 41–81.

[24] Auch wo scheinbar nicht, wo scheinbar vielmehr eine Einheit, so doch jedenfalls das im Realen Relevante der *Interpretation* der 'Werte'.

Clan), oder Wissenschaft und die Anforderungen politischer Herrschaft, *jemals* in völlige Einheit oder gar Harmonie zu bringen sind. Hier liegt vielmehr die Versuchung, daß unsere wissenschaftliche Erkenntnis ihrerseits dafür, ganz hoch gelagert, ein geschlossenes 'Weltbild' konstruiert, das alles Verhalten durchprägte. In der kulturellen Realität jedenfalls sind die verschiedenen Dimensionen sicher auch beim Buddhisten oder beim Hopi-Indianer nicht in schlechthinniger 'werte'-gesteuerter Harmonie.

2. *'Werte' im sozialen Geschehen.* Das Ergebnis dieser erforderlichen Eingrenzungen ist nicht nur negativ. Sondern es gibt vor allem den Blick frei über substantiale, gar ontologische Verständnisse von 'Werten' hinaus. Je konsequenter die daraus fließenden Folgerungen, vor allem Folgerungen der Komplexität des Phänomensachverhalts geltend gemacht, desto deutlicher. Es läßt sehen, wie „Werte" allemal überhaupt Konstrukte sind, Konstrukte in Orientierungs- und Verständigungsprozessen. „Werte" stehen stets als abkürzende Titel für ein ganzes Bündel von sehr konkreten und typisierten Verhaltensweisen[25] – abkürzend für das Gesamt, *wie* man sich verhält, wenn man diesen Wert 'hat', er einem (als anderem vorgeordnet) bindend 'gilt'; und vor allem auch abkürzend für das, was Anzeichen sind, daß er einem *mangelt*, nichts bedeutet. Und dabei sind die bezeichneten 'Werte' – außer vielleicht gewissen ganz basalen Primar-Werten, die aus unserer anthropologischen Ausstattung erwachsen und unmittelbar (universalmenschlich) verstehbar sind, wie 'Liebe', 'Verläßlichkeit', 'Ehrerbietung' gegen Ältere, 'Gastfreundschaft' usw. – wohl ohne ihre konkreten *Deutungen*: Deutungen jener Verhaltensweisen, weithin nur Hülsen.

In beidem, als abkürzende Titel und der Füllung durch ihre Deutungen, sind die leitenden, zueigenen, tradierten, geteilten Wertpositionen verflochten in den sozialen Prozeß, wie eine Gesellschaft sich

---

[25] Freilich: bei ausgebildetem gesellschaftlichem Diskurs dann, innerhalb dieser Diskursformen, mit sich präsentierender substantialer Gegenständlichkeit, Objekt-Festigkeit. – Die Frage nach dem 'ontologischen' Ort dieser Konstrukte – ob im Geist, der Kultur, der Gefühlswelt, den Lebensinteressen, den sozialen Praktiken usw. – sollte, weil dabei jeweils eine Dichotomie aufgemacht wird, nicht allzu grundsätzlich veranschlagt werden. Allemal aber sind auch Konstrukte eine *Wirklichkeit.*

interpretiert – dabei zumal: wie ihre Probleme bewältigt, in geregel-
ten Wegen hält –, und die historische Dynamik dessen. Da aber sind
die „Werte"-Deutungen – was als dominante solche Interpretationen
steht – schon unter sozusagen normalen, nicht-globalisierten Verhältnissen durchaus unordentliche Hervorbringungen, unordentlich und
auch weithin profan. – Ich möchte dazu nur stichwortartig fünf
Punkte ansprechen. Alle fünf zeigen, wie 'Werte' sozusagen nicht aus
irgendeinem 'Kultur'-Himmel stammen;[26] oder auf der anderen Seite
einfach als die Verfaßtheit der psychischen (Strebe- und Beurteilungs-)
Struktur der Subjekte genommen werden könnten, als quellend aus
deren (selbstidentischer) 'Persönlichkeit'.

– Die Entwicklung gesellschaftlicher Praktiken, Herausgestaltung
sozialer Formen ist stets, daß Muster des Agierens, Reglementierungen betreffenden Verhaltens entstehen und sich – gegen anderes und
zumal das vormalig Herrschende – etablieren. Diese sind allenthalben
mit Zumutungen des Mitmachens und Sicheinfügens verbunden, mit
erzwungenem Sichkompatibelmachen und 'Sanktionen' (aktiven
oder, durch sonst drohendes Ins-Abseits-Geraten, Relatives-Zurück-
fallen usw., nicht minder wirksamen passiven). Und aus dieser *Wirklichkeit des Geregelt-Geübten* heraus wird dann ein Teil der jeweiligen
Funktionserfordernisse als Begründungs-Punkte, und überhaupt als
sprachliche Bezeichnungen für Motivierungsaspekte des Handelns, in
Reflexionsvorstellungen formuliert. Anders gesagt, in den allerweite-
sten Bereichen stehen als erstes: Praktiken, Muster, Reglementierungen; und stehen auch als alles Subjektive und Geistig-'Geltende'
übergreifend.[27] Die *Formen*, den Einzelnen als die machtvolle Wirklichkeit des Mit-einander-lebens zugemutet, und jeder zunächst einmal darin hineinwachsend, schaffen sich die 'Menschen' dazu, die
Akteursprofile und -voraussetzungen des darin Integrierten. Und
diese Agierenssubjekte dann – als Ausübende-Eingefügte – werden
interpretiert als betreffende 'Werte' habend, betreffende 'Werte' als

---

[26] Vielmehr allenfalls umgekehrt: als ihr (je) bestehendes Gefüge, dessen Stand
bzw. Stadium, dies 'Kulturelle' *sind*, repräsentieren.

[27] Dies gilt wohl auch bei neuen (relativ zum Bisherigen) 'experimentellen' Weisen des Lebens.

ihnen gültig, sie davon geleitet: 'Werte' als normativ bedeutungsvolle Zuschreibungen und Selbstzuschreibungen ihres So-Agierens. 'Werte' stehen so vor allem als verdichtete Überschriften für bestimmte (insonderheit lebensbereichspezifische) herausgebildete Sozialinterpretationen des normativen Gehalts eines faktisch Herrschenden[28] – abgesunken in die kursierende Handlungssprache, zur Vorstellbarkeit, Kommunizierbarkeit und Abgleichbarkeit dieses Faktischen.

– Der Prozeß der Interpretation ist sicher kein reiner oder etwa funktional ein emergierender Bestandteil des gesellschaftlichen Funktionsgefüges, das Funktionieren der funktionalen Interaktion abbildend – und als dieses hinwiederum dies Gefüge reflexiv stabilisierend –, sondern wird sich in erheblichen *Eigenwegen* entwickeln; diese Eigenwege freilich angestoßen von und bezogen auf die gesellschaftliche 'Erfordernis'-Lage – die aufgebrochenen erfahrbaren 'Probleme' (des sozialen Miteinander) und Un-Selbstverständlichkeiten – solcher interpretativen Fixierung, Verdeutlichung, Thematisierbarmachung. So gibt es denn zweifellos Bandbreiten der Interpretation und Bandbreiten der herausfiguriert-etablierten 'Werte'-Arten. Dies reicht von zum einen der Ausformulierung jener basalen anthropologisch gewurzelten, universalmenschlichen 'Werte' wie 'Liebe', 'Gastfreundschaft' usw.;[29] über so etwas, was man Charakter-'Werte' nennen könnte, wie etwa 'Förmlichkeit' ('Schicklichkeit', 'Contenance') oder dagegen 'Authentizität', 'Selbstlosigkeit' ('Altruismus') oder 'Stärke', 'Prinzipientreue' oder 'Flexibilität'/'Geschmeidigkeit', und was wohl in starkem Ausmaß eher Lebensstil-*Ideale* sind; dann solcherart 'Werte', die tatsächlich mehr oder minder für ausdifferenzierte und stark „eigengesetzlich" gewordene gesellschaftliche „Sphären" (M. Weber) stehen, Sphäre und betreffender spezifischer 'Wert' (oder Wertcluster) einander wechselseitig definierend, so etwa 'der religiöse Wert', 'der künstlerische Wert', 'der technische Wert', 'der Wert der Selbstaufklärung, Bewußtheit über sich selbst', u.a.m. – sie dienen oft der

---

[28] Und erst *an diesem* können sich dann, in einem Spätstadium der intellektuellen Auseinandersetzung und Durchdringung, evtl. Vorstellungswelten eines Anders-Agierens, weil ganz andere 'Werte' als gut und richtig eingesehen, abfigurieren.

[29] Dort vor allem ein strukturelles Kontinuum zwischen 'Werten' und *'Tugenden'*.

Heraushebung eines Agierens oder eines Handlungsergebnisses
oder einer menschlichen Schöpfung aus deren anderweitigen (relativ
'uneigentlichen') Bedingtheiten und Phänomenaspekten; ferner
'Werte', deren Gehalt bzw. Bewandtnis gerade eine (betreffende)
Nicht-mehr-Normierung ist, ein Freigeben des Bewertens[30] – exem-
plarisch dafür 'Werte' wie 'Toleranz', humaner 'Respekt', das *nil
admirari*, oder der Vorbehalt gegen jederlei Fundamentalismus sowie
Fanatismus; und schließlich jene, die etwas Substantialistisches (sowie
eine geschichtliche Prozeßmacht) vorstellen-projizieren und die als
tendenziell Ideologie-'Werte' zu bezeichnen wären, wie 'Fortschritt',
'Nation'/'Volkstum'/'Rasse', liberalistische 'Freiheit'/'Markt', 'Klas-
seninteresse/-bewußtsein'. – Desgleichen wird es stets verschiedene
Interpretations-Linien geben, jeweils meist aus singulären histori-
schen/sozialen Konstellationen entstanden und dann verfestigt und
fortgeschrieben. Nur *eine* davon, in bestimmten Phasen freilich dominant, ist die Interpretation-Reinterpretation, in der sich ein gewisser
Vereinheitlichungs-Druck kristallisiert, eine 'Systematisierung'. 'Systematisierung' – Kriterien der 'Systematisierung' – ist hauptsächlich
sekundäre Systematisierung. Die von ihr interpretierten 'Werte' bzw.
'Werte'-Bedeutungen fungieren bes. dort und dergestalt, wo es um
Legitimierung von sozialen Strukturen, Positionen und Rechten, um
rechtfertigende 'Weltbilder' und um oberste Gesellschaftsziele geht.

– Bandbreiten wie Interpretations-Linien, oder allgemeiner gesagt:
das Nicht-Festgelegte der 'Werte'-Formulierung bzw. -Figurierung,
bewirken zwangsläufig, daß es schon deswegen allemal auch dys-
funktionale 'Werte' geben wird, Mehrfachbesetzungen, ein bleibendes
Unausgeglichenes, ja Widersprüchlichkeiten.

– 'Werte', die Vorstellung ihrer Wichtigkeit und Vorstellung der
exemplifizierenden Handlungsweisen, erfüllen, so jedenfalls in kom-
plexeren sozialen Verhältnissen,[31] eine zentrale sozialintegrative Funk-

---

[30] So vor allem in den – dabei als 'privat' deklarierten – Bereichen der Lebensge-
staltung, der 'geschlechtsspezifischen' Interessen, Aufgaben und Rechte, des Sexual-
verhaltens, oder in den religiösen Gefühlen und Praktiken.

[31] Das heißt: dort, wo es das Phänomen 'Werte', einen Faktor 'Werte' im strengen
Sinne auch nur 'gibt'; in den Verhältnissen, die sie auch haben herausformen lassen.

tion – als Punkte des Zugehörigkeits-Gefühls, dieses Affektiven ('ich gehöre dazu, weil ich diese Werte teile ...'), als Titel der Verständigung, als Bezugsargumente (des akzeptierten Kreises) der Rechtfertigung. Dies Subjektiv-Bedeutsame festzuhalten, muß man nicht Konstruktionen eines klassisch-'idealistischen' Denkens bemühen. Doch genau daraus ergibt sich eine weitere Problematik sozial etablierter 'Werte', die das Unordentliche und durchaus Profane offenkundig macht. Denn im gesellschaftlichen Prozeß werden sich zunehmend *sekundäre Koordinierungen* von Akteursgruppen – eine zweite Dimension eines Sekundären – herausbilden sowie 'zivilisatorische' Neutralisierungen des Mir-Werthaften: Gruppen mit differenten 'Wert'-, auch Lebens-Wichtigkeiten, die in erfahrene (nicht weiter durch andere Kriterien wie Status, Prestige, Alter u.ä. reglementierte) Handlungsverflechtungen treten, und – aus den eintretenden Anlässen bzw. Notwendigkeiten zu solchem heraus sukzessive – Koordinierung, die zwischen oder 'über' diesen steht, relativ 'neutral'; sowie Funktionserfordernisse des Gesellschaftlichen, von meinen mich ausmachenden eigenen 'Werten' abzusehen, sie hintanzustellen oder sie als gänzlich irrelevant behandelt zu sehen. Beides mit *Zumutungs*-Charakter: Zumutung der Abschleifung des Kreatürlich-Anarchischen, des Ungefügen, des Inkompatiblen; relatives Zurückstellen des Nicht-Allgemeinen; und in allem, um sozial erkennbar, rubrizierbar und 'verstehbar' zu sein, die Zumutung der Bewußtheit/Klarheit, Abschleifen des Nicht-Erklären-Könnens, Nicht-Rechenschaft-geben-Könnens, Zumutung werte-*gemäßen* Sichverhaltens. Was dem nicht nachkommt, nicht mithält mit diesen sich akkumulierenden Zumutungen, wird zum relativ Zurückbleibenden in der Dynamik des gesellschaftlichen Prozesses. – Für diese Entwicklungen aber kann es zudem auch keine irgend reinen Lösungen geben. Allemal wird allgemein ein Zwiespalt bestehen zwischen einerseits der darüberstehenden relativen Neutralität sozial etablierter Koordinierungs-Reglementierungen, sowie subjektiv der Internalisierung oder Akkomodation an diese zugemutet-erzwungenen Indifferenzierungen, und andererseits den – gleicherweise zugemuteten – 'Wert'-Wichtigkeiten, 'Werte'-Bewußtsein: dem gerade spezifischen 'Werte'-Profil, an dem meine Gemeinschaftsbezüge und meine ('geistige') Identität hängen, 'Werte'-Profil, um ein Individuum zu sein und zurechenbar. Im Gesellschaftlichen kann es dafür nur 'politische', abwägend-kompromißhafte Festlegungen geben; im Globalisierungs-Großen betrifft es die möglichen Wertperspektiven und Normierungserfordernisse selbst, indem es stets um eine labile Austarierung zwischen Anpassungsdruck und dem, die in kursierenden 'Werten' verkörperte Identitätsressource (auch Kommunikationsressource) nicht zu verlieren, geht; und auch individuell steht der stets – in einer je faktischen Weise – neu zu stiftende Abgleich zwischen den mich ausmachenden 'Werten' meiner menschlichen Herkunft, Zugehörigkeit, Bindungen und andererseits meinen Verhaltenskompetenzen der (gemessen am Stand der gesellschaftlichen Formen) Funktionstüchtigkeit.

– Und schließlich: Je moderner Gesellschaften: je komplexer die Handlungsverflechtungen und Normierungsformen, je pluraler die gesellschaftliche Teilung und die sozialen Lebensentwürfe, je vielgestaltiger die Erfordernisse an Funktionsangepaßtheit, Flexibilitäts-Opportunität und gleichzeitig Prinzipien-Klarheit, je differenzierter Reglementierungssphären, herangetragen-etablierte Gültigkeiten und Erfahrungswelten, desto mehr werden divergente Gruppierungen und Zugehörigkeiten, hinzu auch divergente Anforderungen, bewußt. Bewußt werden Faktizitäten des Nicht-Einheitlichen, bei gleichzeitiger höchster Formalisierung, höchster Reflexionsallgemeinheit für solch Divergenzen. Und „Werte", zusammen mit „Interesse", werden zur *Sprache* dafür. „Werte" und „Interesse" werden unter dieser fortgeschritten modernen Konstellation zu den Basiswörtern der Sprache des Sozialen – der Verständlichmachung und der Rechtfertigung. 'Werte' und 'Interesse' stehen als das, was, im sozialen Diskurs, hinzunehmen ist im schlichten Daß ihres 'Habens'. Je unübersichtlicher dann die Zusammenhänge und gesichtsloser die realen Agenten, desto mehr werden darum *Struktur*-Konflikte des *Ganzen* – Konflikte der Ordnung wie als verschiedenartige in mich hineinragende Handlungskreise – als 'Werte'-Konflikte (sowie 'Interessen'-Konflikte) wahrgenommen und verhandelt. Mehr und mehr gehört es zur Logik des sozialen Austauschs, Struktur-Konflikte, wo immer nicht handfeste 'Interessen' namhaft zu machen, *als* 'Werte'-Konflikte zu verstehen und auszuagieren.[32] Angefangen bei den Konflikten von verschiedenen eigen-konstituierten Sphären des gesellschaftlichen Handelns (Ökonomie, Recht, Technologie, Moral, Kunst, Wissenschaft, usw.); und festge-macht oft daran, daß viele 'Werte' (freilich keineswegs alle) sich in weitem Maße genau durch *Abgrenzungen* definieren, ihre Abgren-zungen gegen anderes Kursierendes oder vormalig Gültiges.[33] – Das läßt den Bogen zurück zum Anfang schlagen und damit zur Leit-motivierung unserer Problemfrage: dem Faktum Globalisierung.

3. *Wendezeit? (Globalisierung und 'Neue Werte').* In welcher Hinsicht ist die Lage von Globalisierungs-Entwicklungen ein Problem dessen, daß wir neue Werte brauchen, neuartige Werte leitend machen müs-sen, nach neuen Werten suchen müssen? Ja, auch ein Problem von neuen 'Werte'-Vorstellungen, neuem Bewußtsein, was wir mit 'Wer-ten' und Fragen von 'Werten' eigentlich meinen, Bewußtsein, worum es dabei geht?

Zunächst einmal steht vielmehr, von aller Dramatik, auch Drama-tisierung, leicht überstrahlt, in vielerlei Hinsicht die umgekehrte Be-deutung, umgekehrte Bewandtnis einer Entselbstverständlichung. 'Globalisierung', als neues Faktum und neue Erfahrung, macht, näm-lich in breitem Bewußtsein, *aufmerksam* auf lange verdrängte Fragen der gesellschaftlichen Modernisierung. 'Globalisierung' läßt unüber-

---

[32] Vielleicht gilt schon für das oben erwähnte 'Freundschaft', daß es erst dann als *Wert* auftritt, wenn ein betreffender *Konflikt* zum Horizont des Bewußtseins gehört – wenn ein Bewußtsein, was jetzt 'Freundschaft' gebühren würde statt eines anderen Handlungszwangs, Handlungsverstrickung, Handlungsopportunität; wenn ein reales Freundschaft-*oder*-... bewußt ist.

[33] Diese 'Wert'-Konflikte reichen einerseits weiter, sind aber andererseits weniger fundamentalistisch-dramatisch, als sie von der alten Wert-*Philosophie* gefaßt wurden. Was etwa der Neukantianismus und die Phänomenologie hier als Phänomen be-schrieben hatten, ist eine Vermengung von Form- und Inhalts-Aspekten. Die Dramatik macht sich bei ihnen fest an dem, was eigentlich nur die Herausbildung eines Wer-tungs-*Sensoriums* ist – zum Beispiel über ein Sensorium für Aspekte von ange-nehm/unangenehm oder schön/häßlich zu verfügen –, aber noch gar kein Was und Wie, gar keine inhaltliche 'Wert'-Festlegung betrifft. – Ohnehin gilt wohl nur bei einer bestimmten 'Werte'-Art, nämlich den Charakter-'Werten' (s.o.) wie 'Förmlichkeit'/ 'Authentizität', daß sie zumeist in *Paaren*, und durch logische Abgrenzung gegenein-ander, auftreten.

sehbar heraustreten, etwa daß, mit Sicherheit jedenfalls in der beste-
henden ungesteuerten Weise und bestehendem Modus des Umge-
hens-mit-..., Güter und Möglichkeiten nicht für alle reichen werden,
ja sogar Lebensgrundlagen wie Wasser und gesunde Umwelt. Mit
'Globalisierung' – dem Komplex von Phänomenen, die unter diesem
Titel vor uns stehen und in unseren neuen Diskursen verhandelt
werden – kehren alte Fragen der Verteilungs-Gerechtigkeit, die am
Anfang der Industrialisierung zunehmend durch 'Fortschritt' und
staatliche Maßnahmen als sich aufgelöst habend schienen, in verschärfter Form wieder.[34] Daneben liegen in 'Globalisierung' auch im
positiven Sinne *Chancen* einer besseren Problembewältigungsstruktur:
nicht nur überhaupt eine sukzessive, habituell werdende Erweiterung
der Horizonte, sondern auch, schlicht unter dem Ansturm, dem Druck
der Entscheidungs-Notwendigkeiten und Entscheidungs-Möglich-
keiten ein zunehmend nüchternes, unaufgeregtes, weniger rigoristi-
sches Umgehen mit Uneindeutigkeiten und Vorläufigkeiten; dann der
fremde Blick, das Hereinreichen, Hereingreifen, auch schrittweise
Verinnerlichen eines Von-anderswo-her – denn natürlich kann man
sich auch über die eigene Welt recht massiv täuschen, über das Eigene und dessen 'Werte'; und schließlich als Chance: einfach die *Notwendigkeit* zu Kooperation.

Auf der anderen Seite stehen das in der Tat Beängstigende des 'Ist
nicht mehr durchschaubar'; die Uniformierung der Lebenswelten,
Marginalisierung der kulturellen Spezifik; umgekehrt das Brüchig-
werden der Traditionen, Überlieferungen, Bindungen. Doch in all
dem verfängt sicher weder die Beschwörung des Alten noch eine Pa-
thetik des neuen Äons und anstehender ganz neuer menschlicher
Denkens- und Handlungsweisen. All diese kalt ins Leben eingreifen-
den Veränderungen sind wohl kaum *wegen* eines Megaprozesses
'Globalisierung', sondern sind Teilphänomene und Begleiterschei-
nungen – jeweils mit sehr konkreten sachspezifischen Faktoren, sehr
benennbaren Geschehensmechanismen und Auswirkungen – eines
Gesamts der erfahrenen Wandlungen der gesellschaftlichen Welt,

---

[34] Zu einem Panorama der aktuellen Debatten cf. *Globale Gerechtigkeit – Global
Justice*, hrsg. von Jean-Christophe Merle, Stuttgart: Frommann-Holzboog, 2005.

welche unsere sozialen und politischen Diskurse (heutigentags) unter diesem Begriff zusammenfassen. Alles darf nicht den Blick dafür verstellen, daß bei dem, was unter dem Großtitel 'Globalisierung' an uns herantritt, die hauptsächlichen werte- und normenbetreffenden Probleme allemal weithin *interne* der jeweiligen Gesellschaften sind: die Erfahrung der *Entwertung*, Erfahrung, daß etwas lebensweltlich sehr Konkretes real *entwertet* wird – sowohl soziale Kompetenzen als auch entsprechende Lebenswege, sowohl Produktionsweisen als auch angesammeltes geistiges wie ökonomisches Kapital-für-die-Zukunft werden real entwertet, in Prozessen, die einen gesichtslosen, schleichend sich allem anhaftenden und scheinbar unsteuerbar hereingreifenden Auftritt haben; funktionierende Regelungs-Praktiken und ein bestehender Hintergrundkonsens – beides sozusagen der Boden, auf dem man steht – werden, weil durch eintretende Entwicklungen mit massiv *ausgedehnten* Erfordernissen konfrontiert, die die zugehörigen *Mechanismen* der Adaption bzw. des Nachfolgens überfordern, brüchig und verlieren darüber sukzessive ihre Bindungskraft, vor allem auch Macht als sozialer Kitt; die Zumutungen an Anpassung, Unsituiertheit und ein allgemeines Funktions-Leben bei der Teilhabe am 'Öffentlichen' haben sich potenziert; und die Anforderungen wie Möglichkeiten an 'Gerechtigkeit' zeigen sich immer dramatischer.

Transformationsgesellschaften sind von all dem in besonderem Maße betroffen. Doch auch für bereits relativ 'flexible' Gesellschaften gilt, daß genau diese Probleme eben nicht durch 'die Globalisierung' *verursacht* sind, am Verursachungsursprung dieser Probleme jenes neue Große 'Die Globalisierung' stünde. Solcherlei Aussagen (Kausalperspektiven) sind, neben dann auch der Folge bequemen Feuilletonismus und fahrlässiger Theoriesimplifizierungen, lediglich populistische Schuldzuweisungen in politischen Machtkämpfen, Ablenkungen bei den Grenzverschiebungen gesellschaftlichen Terrains. Durch Globalisierungsentwicklungen ist zu den internen Problemen vielmehr vor allem eine zusätzliche Brisanz, und zusätzliche Unüberschaubarkeit, hinzugekommen. Hinter den Problemen steht zunächst einmal die – gemeinhin lange herkommende – Dynamik von exponentiell sich aufstufenden (gesellschaftsinternen) Modernisierungsprozessen. Das Faktum 'Globalisierung' hat da vor allem die – gestaltend-eingreifenden, korrigierenden, gegensteuernden – Handlungsspielräume, auch Handlungsklarheiten noch zusätzlich eingeengt.[35]

Die Gefahr ist, daß das erfahrbar Bedrängende – das scheinbar anonym Hereingreifende, mit undurchschaubarer Macht unser Handeln und unsere Lebenswelt Verstrickende, wie verhängnishaft sich Vollziehende, Globus-Umspannende, faktische Prozesse ohne entsprechende Instanzen und Agenten ohne Gesicht – ins so Fern-Übergroße gesteigert ist, daß statt in vielem durchaus benennbarer Mechanismen, 'Interessen', betreibender Akteure, und vor allem lokalem Strukturwandel, lokalen Lebensweltumbrüchen, lokalen Krisen, nur noch das Bild der einen riesenhaften, unfaßbaren Schicksalsmacht steht, der einen allesverschlingenden, über allem siegenden Ananke. Vielmehr umgekehrt: Was unter dem Großtitel 'Globalisierung' steht, ist wesentlich auch ein – ein erzwungenes – Experiment darauf, wieviel Verzicht z.B. auf 'Gerechtigkeits'-Maßstäbe wir uns leisten können, wieviel Verschleuderung von Generationen-Wissen und angesammelten kulturellen Erfahrungen, wieviel Zwang zu Unsicherheit und Unselbstverständlichkeiten des Lebens. Wie viel von all dem, damit unser soziales Zusammenleben noch human bleibt, damit das Miteinander noch sein humanes Antlitz bewahren kann.

Und auch die 'Wert'-Orientierungen, die wir angesichts von Globalisierungs-Tatsachen zu mobilisieren versuchen: Solidarität, Verantwortung, Blick auf zukünftige Folgelasten, Verstehen und Toleranz gegenüber dem Fremden, oder auch 'Verzeihen' u.a.m., sind ja nicht eigentlich *neue* Werte. Sondern es sind weithin durchaus bekannte *alte* Werte – nur eben solche, die aus dem neuzeitlichen Verständnis von Staat und Recht (rahmengebenden Rechtsnormen) und Gesellschaft bisher draußengehalten, oder herausdefiniert, waren.[36]

---

[35] Mit 'intern' vs. 'Globalisierung', desgleichen 'Modernisierung' vs. 'Globalisierung' soll nicht ein Unklares gegen ein anderes Vages ausgetauscht werden, eines gegen das andere ausgespielt werden. Es soll hier lediglich der Verdeutlichung der erforderlichen Fragerichtung dienen. Es will nichts, was wir ontologisch als sichere Kausalitäten einstreichen könnten, unterstellen.

[36] In dieser Hinsicht ist die Erfahrung des Faktums 'Globalisierung' nicht zuletzt auch das, daß in dem Moment, wo Staat und Recht und 'Gesellschaft' ihre sozialen Aufgaben nicht mehr zureichend wahrnehmen können, sich der Preis der funktiona-

Hegel hatte das Bild von der „Eule der Minerva" geprägt, die erst bei einbrechender Dämmerung vom Boden des Alltäglichen und Nächsten abhebt, sich ins freie Höhere aufschwingt und ihren Flug der Weisheit beginnt. Die theoretische Reflexion komme immer zu spät; freie Klarheit erlange sie erst, wenn ein Tag des Lebens sich dem Ende neigt. Bis dahin gehört sie selber viel zu sehr dem Gewöhnlichen zu, als daß sie belehren oder klärend eingreifen könnte. Doch zugleich ist in dem Bild eine Verwobenheit von Leben und Denken im Übergang zu neuen epochalen Stufen des Geistes und der Kultur festgehalten, die dem Zuspätkommen noch eine Rolle im Sinngeschehen der Geschichte abgewinnen will.[37]

Vor Augen ablaufende erfahrene Prozesse eines Neuen, das Umgehen mit dessen aus sich heraus produzierten Vorstellungen-von-sich und schlicht die *Notwendigkeit* des reflektierten Eingreifens sind in dem Modell nicht vorgesehen. Und vollends nicht ein Neues des Überall und des Gesichtslos-Nirgends. Unsere heutige Rede über 'Globalisierung', die einen eingetretenen Wandel, nämlich zugleich Wandel ganz neuer Art und ganz neuen Ausmaßes, wieder ins Begreifen zu bringen sucht, ist daran gemessen sowohl tendenziell zu spät *als auch* schief in vielem. Aus fehlendem Abstand verdoppelt sie häufig nur das ohnehin Faktische, generiert überabstrakte Großtheo-

---

len Ausdifferenzierung und Separierung von Politischem, Ökonomischem, Rechtlich-Geregeltem, Moral, Gemeinschaftsbindung usw., die den Weg der Moderne kennzeichnet, zeigt. Aus den (sozial verankerten) Wert-Ressourcen anderer Lebensbereiche schöpfend, treten nachgeordnete Sozialbezüge und -prinzipien wieder herein, um das, was der Staat, Recht und das Gesellschaftsganze einst geleistet (oder doch zu leisten versprochen) hatten: Gerechtigkeit, Frieden, Arbeit, soziale Sicherheit, mit zu übernehmen oder zu komplementieren – zu 'humanitären' Erfordernissen, durch 'Patenschaften' für Projekte, durch Initiativen der Bildung und neuer Formen der Beschäftigung, durch kulturelle Verständigung, durch allgemein NGOs, aber auch ganz banal durch Gesprächskreise, spirituelle Sinn-Angebote und dgl. mehr. Es gibt sicher stets so etwas wie 'unzeitgemäße' Werte. Mit den Entwicklungen der 'Globalisierung' stehen wir vor der Konstellation, daß was bislang auf Weg der Moderne 'unzeitgemäße' Werte im Bereich des Politischen und Gesellschaftlichen waren (oder dergestalt abgedrängt, bereinigt waren), indirekt in Aktualität rückt.

[37] Georg Wilhelm Friedrich Hegel, *Grundlinien der Philosophie des Rechts*, Berlin 1821, Vorrede.

reme. Das vor allem, wenn dies große geschichtliche, gesellschafts-strukturelle und zivilisatorische Geschehen um die Frage nach dem Schicksal der *Werte*, gar Frage nach 'neuen Werten' zentriert ist. Denn das Primäre und Hauptsächliche ist doch sicher, daß etwas Lebens-weltwichtiges – und insofern: Mir-Wert*volles* – nicht mehr standhält; daß es für einst hoch geschätzte Kompetenzen – auch Ziele und Ideale – keine Verwendung mehr gibt, sie außer Dienst gestellt werden; daß kulturelle werthafte Praktiken relativ *entwertet* werden; daß dadurch auch ganze Gesellschaftsgruppierungen und Lebenspositionen de-gradiert werden; ferner die radikale Verschiebung in der Zusammen-gehörigkeit der Generationen – und den dadurch gestifteten Identi-täten –, Hereinbrechendes in die Kontinuität von Älteren und Nach-wachsenden, ein radikaler demographischer Selektionsdruck des Nicht-mehr-Mithaltens; dann daß Wertfestigkeiten, die Eindeutigkeit normativer Kriterien, unter der Dynamik überhaupt verschwimmen; daß gesichts-lose Prozesse und Zwänge, in denen 'Werte', gleich wel-che, *gar keine* Rolle mehr zu spielen scheinen, einen immer breiteren Raum einnehmen, anderes unter sich begraben, und daß Mechanis-men dominant werden, in denen, um überhaupt teilzuhaben, statt 'Tugenden' und 'charakterlicher', Bildungs- oder 'Persönlichkeits'-Eigenschaften – also sozusagen subjektseitiger Eigenqualitäten – nur noch Funktionalität und Opportunität *gilt*. Dies alles, zweifellos zum großen generellen Phänomenfeld der menschlichen Bedeutsamkeits-gebung und des Erstrebens-, Beurteilungs- und Sinnhandelns gehö-rig, doch sachlich wie in seinen Prozeßfaktoren ganz different, grup-pierte sich als solches allenfalls unter klassisch philosophisch-idealistischer Sicht unter das eine Schicksalsthema 'Die Werte'.

Die einst komplexe Sozialphilosophie, deren Theoriebewußtsein wie Muster nicht zuletzt von Hegel, die Erfahrungen der gesell-schaftlichen und kulturellen Moderne reflektierend, auf die Bahn gebracht war, hatte sich mit Aufkommen des Themas 'Die Werte' zur Wertphilosophie gewandelt. Ihre Sachfragen und Problemeinsichten waren binnen kurzem vom werttheoretischen Diskurs, der werttheo-retischen Begrifflichkeit absorbiert. Vielleicht ist heute allem voran ein klares Bewußtsein erforderlich, daß angesichts der neuen Heraus-forderung, für die der übergreifende Terminus 'Globalisierung' steht, am allerwenigsten *dieser* Weg noch einmal begangen werden sollte. Sonst ist die Reflexion über das *Problem* nur: die allerneueste 'Große Erzählung'.[38] Das erfahrbare Problem 'Globalisierung' mit einer neuen 'Werte'-Debatte allzusehr engzuführen, gar 'Globalisierung' statt sozialtheoretischer Untersuchung wiederum einem Überthema 'Die Werte' zu subsumieren, als dessen Teilfrage oder als Aspektphänomen von dessen Geschichte, dürfte eher kontraproduktiv sein. Die realen Ausprägungen sind drängend genug. Das sollte man nicht auch noch durch eine schief oder jedenfalls unangemessen gebaute Theorie überfrachten.

---

[38] So wie einst die alte Metaphysik der Geschichte, die Vorstellungen von Emanzipation der Menschheit oder die Konstruktionen des Vernunftfortschritts und der hermeneutischen Freilegung des Sinns. Vgl. Jean-François Lyotard, *La condition postmoderne. Rapport sur le savoir*, Paris: Minuit, 1979.

Erwin Bader
Wien

Das Problem
der weltweiten religiösen Pluralität
aus der Sicht des Weltfriedens

Religion wird in der Philosophie heute wieder als ein – wenn auch noch nicht gerade *das* – Kernphänomen des Menschseins entdeckt. Die Publikationen[1], auch aus der Feder bekannter Autoren[2] über Religion nehmen deutlich zu. Die Klassiker der Philosophie von Platon bis Hegel hatten schon festgestellt, daß sie den Menschen gegenüber anderen Lebewesen auszeichnet. Die Vernunft ist schon nach Aristoteles das Kennzeichen des homo sapiens, aber damit ist freilich nicht das Denkvermögen im bloßen Sinn der funktionalen Intelligenz gemeint, denn diese unterscheidet, wie die moderne Zoologie sagt, den

---

[1] Auswahl, v.a. aus Wiener Sicht: *Orte der Religion im philosophischen Diskurs der Gegenwart*, hrsg. von Klaus Dethloff, Berlin: Parerga-Verlag, 2004; *Recht – Geschichte – Religion. Die Bedeutung Kants für die Philosophie der Gegenwart*, hrsg. von Herta Nagl-Docekal, Berlin: Akademie Verlag, 2004; Gianni Vattimo, Richard Schröder und Ulrich Engel, *Christentum im Zeitalter der Interpretation*, hrsg. von Thomas Eggensperger, Wien: Passagen-Verlag, 2004; Thomas Auinger, *Das absolute Wissen als Ort der Ver-Einigung. Zur absoluten Wissensdimension des Gewissens und der Religion in Hegels Phänomenologie des Geistes*, Würzburg: Königshausen und Neumann, 2003; Erwin Bader, *Dialog der Religionen*, Münster – Wien: LIT-Verlag, 2005; etc.

[2] Jürgen Habermas, *Zwischen Naturalismus und Religion. Philosophische Aufsätze*, Frankfurt a. Main: Suhrkamp, 2005; Norbert Hoerster, *Die Frage nach Gott*, München: Beck, 2005; *Der leidende Gott. Eine philosophische und theologische Kritik*, hrsg. von Peter Koslowski und Friedrich Hermanni, München: Fink, 2001; Jacques Derrida, *Über den Namen. Drei Essays*, hrsg. von Peter Engelmann, Wien: Passagen-Verlag, 2000; Richard Swinburne, *Gibt es einen Gott?* Frankfurt: Ontos, 2005; etc.

Menschen weniger prinzipiell als graduell von den Tieren. Daher ist es eher die Religion, welche etwa in der prähistorischen Anthropologie den frühen Menschen, etwa durch spezielle Begräbnisse und besonders Grabbeigaben, als solchen identifiziert. Ist dies nicht mehr gültig, da heute nach statistischen Erhebungen weltweit „nur" etwa 86% der Menschen – in manchen Völkern mehr, in anderen weniger – einer religiösen Gemeinschaft angehören? Immerhin besteht seit der Aufklärung der Verdacht, daß Vernunft und Religion nicht gut vereinbar seien, ganz zum Unterschied von Johann Gottfried Herder, der den Begriff Vernunft – auch vom Sprachlichen her – als die Fähigkeit des Vernehmens der göttlichen Weisheit verstand. Kaum zu bezweifeln ist, daß die meisten Menschen, die bisher auf dieser Welt lebten, einen Bezug zu irgendeiner Form von Religion hatten. Abgesehen vom gegenwärtigen Phänomen des Säkularismus, welches ein welthistorisch kurzes, geographisch beschränktes und – im Gegensatz zu dem von Zeitgenossen vertretenen Anspruch einer angeblichen Endgültigkeit – bestimmt unzureichend aufgearbeitetes Phänomen darstellt, ist über alle Zeiträume der Geschichte hinweg kein Volk bekannt, das nicht auch irgendeine Form von Religion entwickelt und dieser in der Regel auch einen hohen Stellenwert zuerkannt hätte. In den Industrieländern kommt es zwar zur Abnahme der kirchlichen Bindung, aber nicht generell zum Verschwinden jeglicher Religiosität, und diese Entwicklung trifft auch nur für die meisten Länder Europas, aber nicht für Amerika oder andere Kontinente zu. Der Säkularismus[3] stößt sich zwar am vermuteten Gegensatz zwischen traditioneller Religion und Vernunft, da Religion pragmatisch unter der Vernunft steht, wenngleich sie existentiell als deren Fundament erfahren wird. Aber an die Stelle der traditionellen Religion tritt heute häufig eine – bisweilen mit Wissenschaft und Logik schwer vereinbare – esoterische Weltanschauung. Religion ist, zum Unterschied von seinerzeitigen marxistischen Erwartungen – offenbar nicht zum Absterben verurteilt und auch sicher nicht definitiv abschaffbar. Aber die Religion durchlebt Krisen. Das bedeutet, die Menschen durchleben Krisen, die sie von der Perspektive ihres positiven oder negativen

---

[3] Cf. Hermann Lübbe, *Säkularisierung. Geschichte eines ideenpolitischen Begriffs*, Freiburg i.Br. – München: Alber, 1965.

Verhältnisses zur Religion her interpretieren. Eine besondere Herausforderung wird an die Religion speziell in der globalisierten Welt gestellt, wo eine Diskrepanz der einander widersprechenden Glaubenssätze der unterschiedlichen Religionen auftritt. Das heißt, wenn die Annahmen der Religion A richtig sein sollten, so schließt dies formal oft die Richtigkeit der Annahmen von Religion B aus. Dies ist einerseits eine Herausforderung an den Verstand und die Religiosität, andererseits auch eine Herausforderung an die Gruppenidentität der sich zu Religionen bekennenden Menschen. Von den drei genannten Aspekten ist der letztere am ehesten verantwortlich für kollektive Konflikte. Religionskonflikte sind primär Konflikte zwischen Personengruppen, die jeweils anderen sozialen Großgruppen und Kollektiven angehören, wobei sich diese sozialen Gebilde hinsichtlich ihrer religiösen Vorstellungen definieren und unterscheiden. Die soziologische Betrachtung wird bei Konflikten, wie sie Samuel Huntington[4] beschreibt, einen großen Teil bereits erklären können. Der österreichische Soziologe der Zwischenkriegszeit (in der Nachkriegszeit in den USA) Ernst Karl Winter[5] erkannte freilich, daß auch unterschiedliche Denkstile für Gruppenkonflikte verantwortlich sind. Das heißt, es spielt auch die intellektuelle Herausforderung durch die Diskrepanz zwischen stark divergierenden religiösen oder sonstigen Sinnantworten eine Rolle bei der Gefahr von Konflikten.

Manche Konflikte breiten sich in der globalisierten Welt über breite Teile der Erdoberfläche aus, weil sie Probleme betreffen, welche die globale Ordnung oder deren Mangel betreffen. Richtig ist, daß heute die plurale Welt der Religionen mit der Ausbildung von globalen Konflikten zumindest insoferne zu tun hat, als die Rechtfertigungsmodelle für Aggressionen sich der Betonung religiöser Diskrepanzen bedienen. Falsch scheint aber die These zu sein, daß die Pluralität der Religionen per se zu Konflikten führe und führen müsse.

---

[4] Samuel P. Huntington, *Der Kampf der Kulturen. Die Neugestaltung der Weltpolitik im 21. Jahrhundert*, 5. Auflage, München – Wien: Europaverlag, 1997.

[5] Erwin Bader, „Ernst Karl Winter und die Versöhnung der politischen Lager", in: *Konservative Profile. Ideen und Praxis in der Politik zwischen FM Radetzky, Karl Kraus und Alois Mock*, hrsg. von Ulrich E. Zellenberg, Graz – Stuttgart 2003, S. 363–378.

Um möglichst objektive Urteile über die Grenzen der jeweiligen Religionen hinaus fällen zu können, eignet sich die Methode des Rekurses auf Positionen der philosophischen Aufklärung, weil in ihr ein gleichsam außerhalb der Religionen stehender Fixpunkt gefunden wird, von dem aus die Religionen mehr oder weniger neutral betrachtet werden können. Aber das Urteil über die Religion von einer außerreligiösen Warte und in Distanz zur Religion könnte auch leicht zu einem gleich negativen Urteil über alle Ausformungen der Religion und damit zu einem unbrauchbaren Ergebnis im Sinne des Erfassens des Wesens der Religionen führen.

Die im Rahmen der christlichen Kultur entstandene, wenngleich formal mehr oder weniger gegen die christliche Religion gerichtete Aufklärung[6] hat sich nicht immer starr gegen die Religionen gewendet, sondern schon früh die Formel der religiösen Toleranz und Pluralität entwickelt, um Konflikte zwischen religiösen Gruppen zu entschärfen. Ohne den bekannten massiven Religionskonflikt, so möchte ich behaupten, wäre es in Europa nicht zur Aufklärung gekommen. Aber ich meine nicht, daß die Religion in sich die wesentliche Ursache für die Konflikte war, sondern ich meine, daß gerade in der Religion auch schon die Lösung der Konflikte vorgezeichnet war. Interessant ist dazu eine These von Erich Fromm. Er sagt, daß sich die religiöse Großgruppe der Christen von anderen Gruppenbildungen in einem wichtigen Punkt unterscheidet: Wenn alle Gruppenbildungen dazu führen, daß der Einzelegoismus zugunsten eines Gruppenegoismus zurückgestellt wird und somit an die Stelle von Einzelkonflikten Gruppenkonflikte treten, so gibt es im Christentum eine Bremse gegenüber dieser Wirkung, indem die Zugehörigkeit zu dieser Großgruppe sich selbst ausdrücklich damit definiert, daß auch die anderen, nicht dazugehörenden Menschen zu achten und zu lieben sind. Auch wenn dies nicht durchgehend wirksam wird, so wirkt sich diese Besonderheit als Bremse gegenüber der Ausbildung von Gruppenegoismen aus. Damit war ein wichtiger Schritt in die Richtung von Toleranz und Pluralität gegeben, auch wenn die Gruppendynamik und deren autoritärer innerkirchlicher Vollzug eine Realisierung die-

---

[6] Cf. Hermann Lübbe, *Religion nach der Aufklärung*, 3. Auflage, München [u.a.]: Fink, 2004.

ser Werte lange verhinderte. Die Aufklärung postulierte diese Werte nun als unabhängig von Religionen und war somit, weil sie eine neue Erscheinung in der Weltgeschichte war, vom Vorwurf der Nichtbeachtung derselben Grundsätze in der Vergangenheit losgesprochen, wenngleich inzwischen die Versuche, die Werte der Aufklärung zu realisieren, nicht nur in der französischen Revolution auch zu manchen intoleranten Auswüchsen führte.

Es ist ein unbestreitbarer Zug der geistesgeschichtlichen Entwicklung, daß in Folge der Aufklärung Philosophie und Religionsgeschichte im allgemeinen die Aussagen der Religionen relativieren und versuchen, diese überhaupt rational zu erklären. In der Regel wurde von den klassischen Vertretern der Aufklärung zunächst weniger der Gottesbegriff schlechthin, sondern die christliche oder sonstige Besonderheit der Antworten in Frage gestellt.[7] Das Besondere steht unter dem Allgemeinen, daß dies auch für die Religionen gelte, zeichnete die Auffassung von Nikolaus Cusanus ebenso aus wie die von Lessing und Goethe. Damit wird freilich noch keine Relativität im Sinne einer angeblichen Egalität ausgesagt. Aber es fällt in der Tat nicht schwer, die geschichtlich gewachsenen Religionen als besondere Ausformungen der Beziehung zu den jeweiligen Betrachtungsweisen Gottes oder des Heiligen zu deuten, der (das) zwar in jeder Religion anders betrachtet wird aber doch derselbe ist. Die Aufklärung kommt hier eigentlich nicht weiter als die schon von Cusanus behauptete Koinzidenz der Religionen im Unendlichen. Der Dialog der Religionen, wie er heute geführt wird[8], obwohl er von Karl Jaspers noch nicht für möglich gehalten wurde, beruht damit nicht nur auf der Aufklärung, sondern zumindest indirekt auch auf den im Rahmen

---

[7] Ich denke dabei an François-Marie Arouet, genannt Voltaire, der einerseits sagte, wenn es keinen Gott gäbe, müßte man ihn erfinden, weil ihn die einfachen Leute bräuchten, andererseits aber gegen das Christentum sinngemäß meinte, ein Religionsstifter, nach dessen Aussage eher ein Kamel durch das Nadelöhr käme als ein Reicher in den Himmel, sei für ihn nicht akzeptabel, und da jener selbst zugegeben habe, sein Reich sei nicht von dieser Welt, sei klar, daß dessen Religion auch nicht für diese Welt tauge.

[8] *Dialog der Religionen. Ohne Religionsfrieden kein Weltfrieden. Mit Beiträgen von Religionsvertretern, Theologen und Philosophen*, hrsg. von Erwin Bader, Wien – Münster: LIT Verlag, 2005.

der (speziell christlichen) Religion vorbereiteten Ansätze zur Überwindung der aus den Verschiedenheiten resultierenden Konflikte.

Wenn wir heute die Religionen in ein Gespräch miteinander führen, geht es also nicht primär um die divergierenden Besonderheiten, weil die Religionen diese jeweils brauchen, um ihre Identität zu wahren. Sondern es geht – bei aller Achtung der Besonderheiten – primär um eine gewisse Gemeinsamkeit, welche unter anderem im gemeinsamen Ethos und der Suche nach dem inneren und äußeren Frieden liegt.

Dem scheinen aber die von mehreren Religionen vertretenen Ansprüche der Alleingültigkeit ihrer jeweiligen konkreten Ausformung des Religionsverständnisses zu widersprechen. Das Christentum sieht seine Botschaft als die nicht mehr überbietbare „Frohbotschaft" an, daß Christus die Güte Gottes offenbarte. Der Islam sieht die Richtigkeit seiner Religion darin bestätigt, daß diese die letzte Offenbarung Gottes sei. Der Hinduismus sieht im Gegenteil die Richtigkeit seiner Religion in ihren besonders hohen Alter bestätigt und meint, alle anderen Religionsstifter als spätere Emanationen der Hindu-Gottheiten interpretieren und damit auch die Religionen integrieren zu können. Der Buddhismus geht davon aus, seine besondere Toleranz zeichne ihn aus, möglicherweise wegen des wenig fixierten Gottesbezuges. Der Konfuzianismus wieder meint, keine andere Religion sei so philosophisch-rational wie er und sei auch so wenig auf religiöse Wundererzählungen angewiesen. Das Judentum sieht sich schließlich von Gott in dessen geschichtlich wirksamer direkter Zuwendung aus besonderer Gnade sozusagen wundersam auserwählt. Dabei gilt der Monotheismus in seinen drei großen Ausprägungen vielen Beobachtern als anfälliger für politischen Extremismus. In der Geschichte wurde auch häufig – global betrachtet – eine stärkere Affinität von monotheistischen Religionen zu kriegerischen Handlungen beschrieben als von anderen Religionen. Die Vorstellung der Einzigartigkeit Gottes könnte zu gewissen, mit Aggressionen leicht zu verknüpfenden, Ausschließlichkeitsansprüchen der einen oder anderen Religion führen. Dies ist aber nur die eine Seite der Betrachtung, denn zweifellos eignet sich gerade die Annahme eines einzigen Gottes besser dazu, auch eine integre Einheit der Welt – sei es im physischen oder im politischen Sinne – zu postulieren. Auch muß man verstehen, daß der Krieg speziell im Raum des alten Orients der vorklassischen Periode, aber auch in Zentralasien sowie von den germanischen Völkern als der Naturzustand schlechthin angesehen wurde.

Die Annahme des einen Gottes kann wie gesagt besser die Einheit der Welt erklären als die Annahme vieler Gottheiten, von denen die Alten der Antike bekanntlich nicht wussten, wer letztlich wofür zuständig war und wieso sie nicht eher gegeneinander als zusammen regieren sollten. Aber auch aus der Behauptung der Einheit lassen sich unterschiedliche, ja konträre Folgerungen ableiten: Entweder der Friede durch die Einheit in Vielfalt oder die Forderung nach einer streng-einheitlichen Anschauung für alle Menschen auf Erden. Letztere widerspricht freilich völlig dem im Westen hochgehaltenen Wert und Anspruch des Pluralismus. Was den Pluralismus betrifft, könnte dieser bisweilen in Beliebigkeit abgleiten, inwiefern unterschiedliche Wahrheiten nebeneinander für gleich gültig angesehen werden und folglich der Mensch gegenüber der Wahrheit selbst gleichgültig wird. Außerdem können gerade vom Anspruch einer (religiösen oder säkularen) Wahrheit, die den Anspruch der Allgemeingültigkeit erhebt, auch Forderungen abgeleitet werden, die mit repressiven Mitteln durchgesetzt werden, aber nicht nur im religiösen, sondern auch im säkularen Bereich, etwa zur Verteidigung der Demokratie und der Menschenrechte, was natürlich dem Anspruch der Demokratie und Menschenrechte widerspricht. Demokratie ist in sich zwar pluralistisch, aber duldet eigentlich neben sich keine anderen obersten Werte, ähnlich wie der Gott des Judentums keine anderen Götter neben sich duldete. Dahinter verbirgt sich also nicht nur eine Parallele zwischen Religion und Politik, sondern auch ein wirklich schwer lösbares Problem. Die Politik kennt die ungelöste Frage, ob die Demokratie gegen undemokratische politische Tendenzen allein mit demokratischen Mitteln verteidigt werden kann oder ob die Demokratie streng genommen nicht zu schwach ist, um sich gegen ihre Widersacher zur Wehr zu setzen. In dieser Frage wiederholt sich aber jene alte Frage, die sich vorher auch schon insbesondere der christlichen Religion gestellt hatte. Der Islam hatte im Laufe seiner Geschichte diese Frage für sich durchaus anders als das Christentum beantwortet, denn für ihn war die kämpferische Komponente bei der Verteidigung der eigenen Interessen kein erst mühsam zu rechtfertigender Selbstwiderspruch wie im Christentum und heute auch in der Demokratie. Frühere europäische politische Vorstellungen haben aber trotzdem ein ziemlich unproblematisches, nicht nur positives, sondern oft sogar extrem expansives Verhältnis zur Gewalt gepflegt und diese Tendenzen wirken bis die Gegenwart weiter.

Die Idee der Pluralität der Meinungen ist zwar auch in anderen Kulturen wie in denen Asiens schon sehr früh vorhanden gewesen, hat sich aber in seiner rational begründeten Form erst in Europa entwickelt, indirekt aus christlichen Wurzeln heraus, wenngleich zum Teil im Gegensatz zu diesen. In der religiösen Christentumsgeschichte spielte die Abwehr von sogenannten Irrlehren stets eine große Rolle und Gewalt war dabei immer im Spiel. Aber die meist von oben her inkriminierten divergierenden Interpretationen haben sich andererseits gerade an einer Materie wie dem christlichen Glauben besonders gern und leicht entwickelt und so ist die soziologische Geschichte des Christentums eine Geschichte von Spaltungen, also von Anhängern einer These und einer Antithese. Es war eine Geschichte der – wenn auch durch obrigkeitliche Gegenmaßnahmen erschwerten – dialektischen Entwicklung einer von unten her wachsenden Auseinandersetzung mit Glaubensfragen. Trotz der von der Obrigkeit erlassenen Verbote gab es genug virulente Widersprüche und Konflikte im europäischen Denken, nicht nur zwischen den jeweils Rechtgläubigen und abweichenden Glaubensrichtungen, sondern auch etwa zwischen den unterschiedlichen, damals gesellschaftlich wichtigen Ordensgemeinschaften. Aus mittelalterlicher Sicht waren die Orden keineswegs ein Einheitsgemenge desselben Glaubens, sondern es gab hier faktisch einen Pluralismus sehr unterschiedlicher, in manchen Fragen widersprüchlicher, oft genug auch einander anfeindender mächtiger Sondergruppen innerhalb der einen Kirche.

So ist auch die Demokratie eine hinsichtlich der Meinungsfreiheit pluralistische politische Institution mit Grenzen der Toleranz, worin sich die Analogie zur früheren Kirche durchaus zu wiederholen scheint. Eine Beliebigkeit hinsichtlich der Infragestellung der Demokratie und der Menschenrechte wird verständlicher Weise nicht leicht hingenommen. Die Demokratie hat also die mit der Pluralität der Meinungen verbundenen Konfliktpotentiale in einigen Punkten ähnlich, wenngleich tendenziell wohl besser gelöst als die mittelalterliche Kirche. Es handelt sich sowohl um ererbte Probleme als auch um ererbte Lösungsmuster.

Nun ergibt sich aber heute im Zuge der Globalisierung die neue Situation, daß die moderne westliche Zivilisation zu einer Durchdringung der gesamten Welt und somit mit Kulturen mit völlig anderen religiösen Denkmustern führt, wofür die alten Lösungsmodelle nicht mehr ohne weiteres geeignet sind. Bisher wurde die Pluralität immer unter einem gemeinsamen Dach anerkannter Werte praktiziert. Ist die Pluralität in einer pluralistischen globalisierten Welt ohne gemeinsamem Dach überhaupt praktizierbar? Oder bietet sich die westliche Zivilisation und mit ihr ein Kompendium globaler Werte als gemeinsames Dach an?

Angesichts der letzten Terroranschläge erhebt sich immer dringender die Frage: Ist der Weltfriede bei einer Pluralität der religiösen Anschauungen überhaupt praktizierbar? Und wenn, auf welcher Basis?

Fest steht, daß der unvoreingenommene Dialog, der nicht nur als Brücke zwischen Menschen und Gruppen, sondern auch als Mittel zur Wahrheitsfindung verstanden wird, als ein Mittel zur Herstellung des Friedens zwischen den Religionen fungieren kann und daß es ohne Frieden zwischen den Religionen keinen dauerhaften Weltfrieden geben kann.[9] Außerdem kann man davon ausgehen, daß auch eine gewisse – dem Denken der Aufklärung durchaus nahestehende – Fähigkeit zur Infragestellung der jeweils eigenen Position, sei diese religiös oder nichtreligiös, eine mögliche Voraussetzung zur Überwindung der Barrieren eines Friedens zwischen den Religionen sein kann, wenngleich dies keineswegs so zu verstehen ist, daß damit eigene Positionen im Interesse des Friedens und der angestrebten Gemeinsamkeit in willkürlicher Weise aufgegeben werden sollten.

---

[9] Cf. Hans Küng, *Projekt Weltethos*, 6. Auflage, München: Piper, 2001; *Dokumentation zum Weltethos*, hrsg. von Hans Küng, München: Piper, 2002; *Weltfrieden durch Religionsfrieden. Antworten aus den Weltreligionen*, hrsg. von Hans Küng u. Karl-Josef Kuschel, München: Piper, 1993; *Ja zum Weltethos. Perspektiven für die Suche nach Orientierung*, hrsg. von Hans Küng, München: Piper, 1995.

Ein Kriterium sollte bei allen Bemühungen immer als wichtiger Maßstab zur Beurteilung der Richtigkeit herangezogen werden: Die Frage, ob und auf welchem Wege ein bestimmtes Merkmal der vorgefundenen Überlieferungen einer Religion mit dem für Religionen im allgemeinen charakteristischen Weg zum inneren und äußeren Frieden kongruent ist. Es gilt, diesen inneren Kern mit allen den Menschen zur Verfügung stehenden Mitteln der Vernunft zu suchen, denn wo ein Ziel mit voller Kraft angestrebt wird, dort finden sich die Mittel zur Realisierung. Ähnlich ist es ja den Menschen – nach langem Ringen – gelungen, so viele bedeutende Schritte des technischen Fortschritts zu entwickeln, nachdem der franziskanische Mönch und Wissenschafter Roger Bacon in Oxford schon im 13. Jahrhundert eine Reihe technischer Entwicklungen der Zukunft für realisierbar hielt, zum Beispiel: „Wagen werden auf den Straßen zu sehen sein, die sich fortbewegen, ohne daß Zugtiere vor sie gespannt sind."[10] Was man sich vorgenommen hatte, wurde letztlich erreicht; in ähnlicher Weise sollte es den Menschen heute das Anliegen sein, die Mittel zur Erreichung des weltweiten Friedens (untereinander, aber auch mit der Umwelt) zu suchen. Wenn dies die Menschen unterschiedlicher Religionen und auch jene ohne Religion gemeinsam mit allen ihnen zur Verfügung stehenden Kräften anstreben, dann sollte es auch gelingen. Mit einer Abwandlung eines Satzes von Karl Marx will ich schließen: Die Menschen haben die Welt schon viel verändert, nun kommt es (auch) darauf an, sie zu erhalten.

---

[10] Zitiert nach: Hans Bauer, *Der wunderbare Mönch. Leben und Kampf Roger Bacons*, Leipzig: Koehler & Amelang Verlag, 1963, S. 163.

Barbara A. Markiewicz
Warszawa

Politic as a System of Education[*]

> *Zwei Erfindungen der Menschen kann man wohl als*
> *die schwersten ansehen die der Regierungs- und die*
> *der Erziehungskunst nämlich, und doch ist man selbst*
> *in ihrer Idee noch streitig.*
>
> I. Kant, *Ueber Pedagogik*[1]

The awareness of connection between the political order and the model of education has been present in philosophy since its birth, also becoming one of the major topics of political philosophy. Even today this connection evokes great interest and anxiety among philosophers despite the fact that pedagogy has long been isolated from philosophy and granted the status of a separate discipline, and despite the development of modern democracy and political institutions connected with it. This is why I started my considerations quoting Kant who considers this association of education and politics from a new perspective, in the conditions when it became questionable. I refer to Kant here not only because every self-respecting philosopher should write a few words about Kant, but also, and first of all, because I highly respect accuracy and permanent validity of his statement quoted above and of all other ideas he discussed and developed in his

---

[*] The main theses of this paper were presented on the international Symposium "Philosophy and Education in Contemporary Society" (Croatia, September 2004) in the lecture "The New Education and Virtual Humankind".

[1] Immanuel Kant, „Ueber Pedagogik", in: *Kants Werke Akademie-Textausgabe*, Berlin: Walter de Gruyter & co., 1968, p. 446.

lectures on pedagogy. I consider them particularly important, especially in the context of new conceptions arising within political philosophy, its new images and their implications in the sphere of education. And in this sense only I shall discuss here the new model of education.[2] Since the most expressive modern image of political order has been presented by the representatives of liberalism, I shall use modern liberalism as a basis for reflection on the contemporary way of harmonising the norm and values of "the art of politics" and "the art of education".

The debate connected with *The Theory of Justice* by John Rawls, which was first published in 1970, was the most important event within contemporary political philosophy. The language as well as the level of discourse proposed by Rawls has established a new canon of liberal thought, thus enlivening theoretically liberalism itself and enforcing a new definition of trends remaining in opposition to liberalism like, e.g., communitarism. Influenced by these debates, Rawls revised some of his ideas and developed them in his subsequent work, i.e., in *Political Liberalism*.[3] And it is this work that constitutes the basis of my considerations. I wish to stress, however, that I am not going to criticise Rawls's conception or argue its point. Rawls's system is exceptionally consistent logically and has an extremely dense conceptual structure. Thus, if its criticism and polemics were to be honest, they would require a comprehensive approach, preferably in the form of a competitive system. My project is much more modest. My goal here is to express certain anxiety that I experienced while reading Rawls's work and whose source is accurately described by Kant's thought quoted as the motto. My anxiety resulted from an attempt at reconstructing the model of education that, in my opinion, is implicitly included in the project of political order offered by Rawls. Or rather, it resulted from my trying to discover its anthropological assumptions.

---

[2] I would like to stress here that referring to the conception of "new education" does not mean that I refer to any definite historical form of education, e.g., the reform of education introduced in America by Benjamin Franklin, which is often given this name. Neither shall I discuss here the conception of education connected with postmodernism commonly criticised as the new model.

[3] John Rawls, *Political Liberalism*, New York: Columbia University Press, 1996.

It must also be stated at once that this kind of operation is beyond the theoretical frames determined by Rawls himself. In his programme he isolates his theory of justice from considerations of metaphysical or anthropological nature, recognising autonomy of political philosophy in this respect. He states that political philosophy, as he conceives it, is autonomous, because in order to characterise its basic concepts that are to serve "to express ourselves in it in our moral and political thought and action that suffices" to adopt certain normative system without reaching to its base, assumptions or foundations. This philosophical minimalism links Rawls with realism: "We strive for the best we can attain within the scope the world allows".[4] Also another eminent representative of liberal thought, Stephen Macedo, warns against transferring the criticism of liberalism to an excessively abstract level because, according to him, liberalism "is most directly a way of organising political life that stresses the importance of freedom, individual rights, law, limited government and public reasonableness".[5]

However, despite these warnings and declarations, the solutions offered by modern liberalism, including those discussed by Rawls in *Political Liberalism*, many a time evoke in the reader (or rather in some readers) the need for their deeper justification. Obviously, Rawls is prepared for this situation too. He honestly takes into account all readers' worries and needs of this kind, though he removes them beyond the boundaries of studies he conducts. To explain this, we must refer here to an extremely useful, not to say sophisticated, methodological solution that Rawls offers in *Political Liberalism*. Though it was developed for the needs of the theory of justice as fairness, mostly to determine the conditions necessary to enable its common acceptance, it can also be used in theoretical discussions.

Well, according to Rawls, the essential feature of a contemporary democratic society that is able to apply the idea of justice that he worked out is "reasonable pluralism".[6] This means that it is a society

---

[4] Ibidem, p. 88.

[5] Stephen Macedo, *Liberal Virtues. Virtue and Community in Liberal Constitutionalism*, Oxford: Oxford University Press, 1990, p. 207.

[6] Cf. John Rawls, *Political Liberalism*, op. cit., pp. 36 ff. As Rawls himself claims, he owes this distinction between ordinary pluralism and "reasonable pluralism" to

in which various comprehensive doctrines, "all completely rational," are alive.[7] Among those reasonable comprehensive doctrines Rawls includes, i.a., religions and ideologies as well as philosophies. Just because citizens promote various rational comprehensive doctrines of this kind, which shows their rationality, they are also able to achieve a consensus regarding the "political conception of justice". This, however, can be achieved only at the price of "putting aside the question how these comprehensive doctrines, being alive in the society, are connected with the content of the political conception of justice". In this way the consensus is not achieved in the process of harmonising those rational comprehensive doctrines, but through ignoring them. They are transferred behind the "veil of ignorance" which, in this way, becomes even tighter than it was in the *Theory of Justice*.[8] Rawls hopes to achieve full political consensus as regards the idea of justice through minimisation of its scope and neutralisation of the procedure of achieving it.

Taking this into consideration we must also accept the fact that other than normative philosophical objections and doubts addressed at Rawls's theory of justice are situated beyond it, that is, within the sphere of the reasonable comprehensive doctrines. I am full of admiration for this methodological solution that resembles to some extent

---

Joshua Cohen's work "Moral Pluralism and Political Consensus", in: *The Idea of Democracy*, ed. by David Copp, Jean Hampton, John E. Roemer, Cambridge: Cambridge University Press, 1993.

[7] Cf. John Rawls, *Political Liberalism*, op. cit., in particular Lecture II, pp. 58 ff.

[8] It is important to remember that "the veil of ignorance" is a very specific theoretical construct, which in the *Theory of Justice* is to warrant to the parties of social contract a univocal choice of a definite theory of justice as fairness in a definite original position. As Rawls states: "Somehow we must nullify the effects of specific contingencies which put men at odds and tempt them to exploit social and natural circumstances to their own advantage." Among these specific contingencies he includes, i.a., position in the society, social background, natural dispositions and gifts, particular conceptions of good, life plans and psychological traits as well as membership in generation. All particular knowledge remains behind the veil of ignorance. Still, Rawls does not deprive the parties of social contract of general knowledge, e.g., that regarding the conception of good or essence of humanity. (Cf. John Rawls, *Theory of Justice*, Cambridge, Massachusetts: Harvard University Press, 1995, pp. 136 ff.) As we can see, in *Political Liberalism* even the general knowledge is oust behind the veil of ignorance.

Alexander the Great's cutting of the Gordian knot. However, since – as I have already stated – I am not going to argue with Rawls or criticise him, I do not mind my being situated beyond the theoretical sphere he determines. Considering the anthropological assumptions of the educational model that arises from Rawls's conception, I consciously remain within the reasonable comprehensive doctrine called traditionally understood philosophy, the more so, that here I am accompanied by Kant.

After all these explanations it is necessary to describe the outline of Rawls's conception of the new political order constructed as an idea accompanying his basic political concept, i.e., the idea of justice as fairness. In Rawls's words this order is described as a "well-ordered society". If a given society, i.e., "a just system of cooperation through generations" is to be recognised as a well-ordered society, it must satisfy the following conditions:

1. Publicly recognised conception of justice: "everyone accepts, and knows that everyone else accepts, the very same principles of justice";

2. Effective regulation of such conception of justice: "its basic structure – that is, its main political and social institutions and how they fit together as one system of cooperation – is publicly known, or with good reason believed, to satisfy these principles";

3. Effective sense of justice of the citizens: "its citizens have a normally effective sense of justice and so they generally comply with society's basic institutions, which they regard as just".[9]

Again I shall emphasise that according to Rawls's political liberalism in a well-ordered society, the conception of justice that can be accepted by all citizens is limited to the "sphere of what is political", and its value is just tenuously connected with their views, religious beliefs or philosophy (reasonable comprehensive doctrines). It is so because the ultimate task of the idea of justice turns out to be the limitation and correction of social processes. What is more, in a well-ordered society there is no room for this kind of utopian – in Rawls's opinion – view that all citizens accept the same comprehensive doc-

---

[9] John Rawls, *Political Liberalism*, op. cit., pp. 35 ff.

trine. They only publicly recognise the same conception of justice. The main idea of this conception of justice is the idea of society as a system of just cooperation complemented by the idea of well-ordered society and an idea of citizens as free and equal persons. We should also notice that Rawls does not want to link these ideas in any fixed and necessary way, claiming that the two latter ones merely "accompany" the idea of justice.

Let us now look what traits should mark the citizens able to generate a well-ordered society. Their rationality proves to be a necessary condition. The first two of the above mentioned conditions of a well-ordered society can be fulfilled only in this way. Only a rational citizen is able to understand the procedures of fundamental agreements and observe their conditions. It is also important for this construction to recognise that being a citizen is not a man's function, role or dignity, concordant with his specific essence (like, e.g., in Aristotle). Similarly to Hobbes, Rawls refers here to the concept of person:

> In the present case the conception of the person is a moral conception, one that begins from our everyday conception of persons as the basic units of thought, deliberation, and responsibility, and adapted to a political conception of justice and not to a comprehensive doctrine. It is in effect a political conception of the person, and given the aims of justice as fairness, a conception suitable for the basis of democratic citizenship. As a normative conception, it is to be distinguished from an account of human nature given by natural science and social theory, and it has a different role in justice as fairness.[10]

To characterise rationality that distinguishes citizens Rawls uses two categories, which, in fact, were first distinguished by Kant, that is, the reasonable and the rational.[11] However, the rational itself is not able to make citizens observe the principles of justice or, first of all,

---

[10] Ibidem, note from p. 18.

[11] For Rawls, rationality and reasonableness are two complementary ideas. Within the idea of just cooperation reasonableness and rationality are complementary ideas, but they cannot be connected with each other or infer one from another. They act as a couple and each of them is connected with a corresponding moral power: reasonableness with justice and rationality with the conception of good. Cf. John Rawls, *Political Liberalism*, op. cit., pp. 48 ff.

make them recognise the need of justice. Hence, Rawls endows them also with moral powers. This means that citizens are not merely "carriers of desires", i.e., persons appropriately motivated to act, but they are also responsible for their choices and aims, tastes and preferences. It is the form and aims of these desires that can make social cooperation either more effective or impossible. It is obviously one of the most difficult problems of social and political philosophy, for we touch here the question of a proper model of such choices and preferences. Rawls tries to avoid considering this problem. However, recognising that being incapable of just social cooperation is pathology, he makes this very capacity for just cooperation a norm, and not merely an ethical one.[12]

Let us also notice that according to Rawls a citizen, being reasonable and rational, possesses two moral powers, namely 1) the capacity for the sense of justice and 2) the capacity for a conception of good.[13] As we can see, in this case the already known to us division into the idea of justice and comprehensive doctrines is applied as well. The sense of justice makes us capable of a consensus regarding the political conception of justice. On the other hand, as regards the conception of good, it is shaped within our comprehensive doctrines. In this way Rawls gets rid of the classical debate of political philosophy, namely the debate regarding common good. What is more, he also separates the idea of good from the idea of justice.

As we remember, in Rawls's conception the idea of citizen is complementary to the idea of society as a system of just cooperation through generations. To make this cooperation possible, the citizens

---

[12] Ibidem, p. 184. Within political liberalism it is a norm biding for the model of a citizen. Though in the *Theory of Justice* this incapability of social cooperation that Rawls identifies as the lack of the sense of justice allowed for the statement that "one who lacks a sense of justice lacks certain fundamental attitudes and capacities included under the notion of humanity". John Rawls, *Theory of Justice*, op. cit., p. 488.

[13] Cf. John Rawls, *Political Liberalism*, op. cit., p. 81. Moreover, to make use of these powers a citizen must also possess: (1) the intellectual powers of judgement, thought and inference and (2) at any given time a determinate conception of the good interpreted in the light of a (reasonable) comprehensive view. We must also assume "that citizens have the requisite capacities and abilities to be normal and cooperating members of society over a complete life".

must be free and equal persons. According to Rawls, the citizens' freedom is conditioned by their rationality and reasonableness. On the other hand, the citizens are equal, at least to the minimum, necessary extent, just because they possess moral powers. This connection between the citizens' rationality and moral powers is very important here. It is moral sensitivity characteristic of reasonableness that should determine the citizens' desires, and their desires are the basis of their activity. Hence Rawls devotes so much room to "moral psychology". It is very important, because if a well-ordered society is to be stable, not only should all citizens know and accept its principles, but, most of all, exercise them, that is, apply them in action. This means that the principles should regulate people's actions in their mutual relations (community, society, etc). It is this very element that is essential to Rawls's conception of education, and particularly of moral education.

This characteristic of a citizen includes one more element important for the liberal and republican tradition. After Kant, we can describe it as a requirement of civility. The principle of legitimization of democratic order adopted by Rawls requires that the ideal of citizenship binding for it imposes one more moral duty, namely the duty of civility. In Rawls's approach this means that citizens should be able to explain one another, taking into account basic issues,

> how the principles of policies they advocate and vote for can be supported by the political values of public reason. This duty also involves a willingness to listen to others and a fair-mindedness in deciding when accommodations to their views should reasonably be made.[14]

I hope that I managed to indicate in Rawls's conception those elements, which compose the picture of his political project, of his political liberalism. This project is drawn as a political image of a society that, thanks to common acceptance of the idea of justice and partly due to reasonable consensus, is able to build constitutional democracy.[15] Thus, it is time to reconstruct the image of education that would be in accord with this political construction.

---

[14] Ibidem, p. 217.
[15] Cf. ibidem, pp. 38–39.

My concern here is with education understood as a process of upbringing and teaching. Upbringing means controlled shaping of various personality features while teaching means transmitting definite
knowledge and skills. With the passage of time, in modern states,
both the contents of upbringing and teaching (though to a different
extent and on different levels) have been subjected to the control of
political institutions. Recording this trend in the development of education, classical liberalism recognised it mostly as a threat to individual freedom. This regarded particularly upbringing, i.e., moral education, which, according to, e.g., John Locke, should be first of all left
to parents and remain in the private sphere.[16] As regards teaching,
and especially professional teaching, Locke was ready to leave it to
the state. In his opinion, however, when the political authority tries to
assume the responsibility for the formation of the citizens' character,
it reaches beyond the sphere of activity that is appropriate for it,
namely, the public sphere. And trespassing the private sphere it
threatens the fundamental individual rights to freedom and the individual's striving for happiness.

As regards Rawls, in the educational process he is first of all interested in the way of acquiring the competence necessary for the citizens to be able to participate in the political sphere:

> Society's concern with their education lies in their role as future citizens,
> and so in such essential things as their acquiring the capacity to under-
> stand the public culture and to participate in its institutions, in their be-
> ing economically independent and self-supporting members of society
> over a complete life, and in their developing the political virtues, all this
> from within a political point of view.[17]

The latest reservation means that according to Rawls the goal of education should consist in preparing children for their becoming

> fully cooperating members of society and self-dependent persons; it
> should also promote political virtues so that the children were willing to

---

16 Cf. John Locke, *Some Thoughts Concerning Education. The Harvard Classics 1909–14*;
see also *The Columbia Encyclopedia*. Sixth Edition 2001–05: http://www.bartleby.com/65

17 John Rawls, *Political Liberalism*, op. cit., p. 200.

observe fair conditions of social cooperation in their relations with the rest of the society.[18]

Thus, the process of education should include elements like development of intellectual powers, transmission of knowledge and professional skills as well as moral formation. Limited to this inventory, the contents of the discussed model of education do not include, as it seems, any new elements as compared to the model adopted today by democratic states. However, when Rawls speaks here of "society's concern", he makes it clear that this model of education cannot be imposed or forced by political authorities. It should emerge in effect of the citizens' actions taken in the public sphere, which, as we can remember, is distinguished by Rawls from the political sphere, constituting its background or, rather, base.

Again we can notice here the distinction that is noticeable on every level of a well-ordered society, i.e., the division into the political sphere (the sphere of common consensus regarding the idea of justice), and vast, comprehensive doctrines differing from one another. It should also be remembered that Rawls's distinction between the public sphere and the non-public one does not correspond with the traditional division into the public and private spheres, because it regards different areas of rationality and, according to Rawls, there is nothing like private reason.

In Rawls's conception, initial education including moral education remains in hands of the parents, and its shape is determined by their chosen comprehensive doctrines that also determine their lifestyle. Admitting that children's upbringing depends on their parents' lifestyles, Rawls refers to one of the most important elements of classical liberalism. Once more we shall quote here Stephen Macedo:

> Liberalism holds that reasonable persons properly pursue a wide variety of lifestyles, goals, projects, and commitments. Indeed, one of the great attractions of liberal politics and its view of man is that they liberate persons from inherited roles, fixed hierarchies and conventions that narrowly constrain individuality and the scope of choice. Liberal reasonableness must be broad enough to encompass variety: it must accommodate liberal diver-

---

[18] Ibidem, p. 199.

sity, public reasonableness, and critical reflection on personal roles and allegiances.[19]

However, a basic difficulty appears here. In what way can these diverse models of education rooted in different comprehensive doctrines, i.e. in different lifestyles and systems of values, and therefore connected with different conceptions of man, compose a common model of a citizen of a well-ordered society? While explaining this, we can reject the idea of the "invisible hand of the market" in advance as it does not take into account the idea of justice, and the conception of "prearranged harmony" since it issues from a very definite philosophical doctrine (Leibniz).

Let us notice here that as early as in the *Theory of Justice* Rawls offered the solution to this problem, which evokes comparisons with another great philosophical system, namely with the Plotinus's theory of emanation. He admitted that the sense of justice as the goal of moral education couldn't occur within us as a result of coercive indoctrination or psychological training. Rawls also rejected moral education conceived as simply a casual sequence, whose final result would be the occurrence of proper moral bonds. In this situation he suggests gradual, adjusted to the stage of education, adoption of the idea of justice on the basis of permanent contact with it:

> As far as possible each stage foreshadows in its teaching and explanations the conception of right and justice at which it aims and by reference to which we later recognise that moral standards presented to us are justified.[20]

This emanative model of moral education was valid in the situation in which the parties of social contract were equipped with a certain amount of general knowledge, because it was only through reference to it that they could determine subsequent levels of the acquired knowledge and subsequent moral standards. However, when

---

[19] Stephen Macedo, *Liberal Virtues*, op. cit., p. 207.

[20] John Rawls, *Theory of Justice*, op. cit., p. 515. As regards the importance of moral education for political education cf. Thomas L. Pangle, *The Ennobling of Democracy: The Challenge of the Postmodern Age*, Baltimore: The John Hopkins University Press, 1992, particularly part IV.

Rawls made his requirements regarding the original position of the parties of this contract more radical, rejecting also general knowledge, the problem occurred again. What is more, an additional difficulty arose, connected with Rawls's political liberalism understood as general knowledge, its place and function in moral education and in political education in general.

As Rawls himself noticed, it is mostly the area of education that houses the danger of transforming political liberalism into one of the numerous comprehensive doctrines striving to rule over the greater part of life or even the complete life (as he claims to be the case in Kant's or Locke's liberalism). It might be, as Rawls regretfully admits, a certain "unavoidable consequence of reasonable requirements regarding children's education". However, in Rawls's opinion, political liberalism does not strive to encompass all life. Its goal is different and its requirements much smaller.

> I will ask that children's education include such things as knowledge of their constitutional and civic rights, so that, for example, they know that liberty of conscience exists in their society and that apostasy is not a legal crime, all this to insure that their continued membership when they come of age is not based simply on ignorance of their basic rights or fear of punishment for offences that do not exist.[21]

Again it turns out that political liberalism itself does not offer any definite model of education. It only addresses certain demands at public education and its different forms, so that it is able to educate proper citizens. Also, as it becomes liberalism, the formulation of these demands cannot be hard nor have the nature of command. Rawls advocates soft solutions. This is why he suggests that the "idea of justice as fairness" itself can perform this unifying role in the political sphere, allowing for organization of different conceptions of education so that they can serve stability of a well-ordered society. For he is convinced that a proper political idea is also equipped with educational function:

> Thus, the account of justice as fairness connects the desire to realise a political ideal of citizens' two moral powers and their normal capacities, as

---

[21] John Rawls, *Political Liberalism*, op. cit., p. 199.

these are educated to the ideal by the public culture and its historical traditions of interpretation. This illustrates the wide role of a political conception as educator.[22]

It is thanks to this identification of the image of political order with the order of education that we can find in Rawls this "system of education" I heralded in the title of this work.

If we now put together all these diverse elements of Rawls's political construction, it will turn out that a well-ordered society, in effect of respecting the idea of justice as fairness, creates a pattern that determines possible forms of social and political activity. The model of a citizen and person also issues from it. And this is why it can also perform educational function for the citizens, advocating definite actions and personality models. This kind of statement, exposing or even overexposing certain fragments of Rawls's reasoning still remains within its range. As I have already mentioned, I want to discern here also what model of a man can be fitted in this model of education and what are its anthropological assumptions. This kind of question, however, makes it necessary to transcend the theoretical range determined by Rawls while constructing political liberalism.

Thus, consciously placing myself beyond this construction I can look from a new angle at the original position, fundamental for acceptance of the idea of justice. I appreciate novelty and theoretical elegance of the solution adopted by Rawls. Instead of arduously searching for common points of view and areas for possible compromise he undertakes an individual action consisting in rejection of all differences that could make this original compromise difficult. Therefore, in order to become parties in this original contract regarding the idea of justice men have to be able to reduce themselves to mere "parties" of this contract. This means that they must reduce to the extreme not only their knowledge, but also themselves, their individuality and uniqueness. Looking from the outside we can perceive the veil of ignorance merely as a shadow theatre. Is it possible, however, that a contract made between shadows can preserve its validity also for the owners of the shadows? It is not by chance that Rawls

---

[22] Ibidem, p. 86.

denies autonomy to the parties of the contract, connecting it with the whole political sphere. This is why I am also worried by the new conception of political education offered by Rawls. For me it seems like programming an individual rather than educating him. It is so even if Rawls selects a very noble programming language, the language of justice, and even if the programming itself is limited to defining the original position behind the veil of ignorance.

Accordingly with the rules of the language used by Rawls, a citizen in the political sphere, if he is to be always ready for actualization of the original contract, i.e., if he is to retire again behind the veil of ignorance, seems to me "a man with no characteristics". He should, first of all, control himself, be able to self-reduce his individuality, be polite in relations with other, identical persons and, last but not least, be rational. Therefore, we must realise that programming will always result with a virtual person. It will always be a man who is distinctly idealized, not through his perfection or outstanding personality, but rather through his ordinariness achieved on the basis of some statistical mean. That the educational product of political liberalism is not a rich diversity of lifestyles but rather a mediocre commonness of a virtual man is practically manifested today by the model of "political correctness" observed in certain spheres and places. Programmatic rejection of a definite system of values and strict philosophical assumptions becomes the basis for justification of ethical shallowness as well as formlessness of mass democracy.

I must again stress that the above doubts and objections to the Rawls's conception and the model of education connected with it comes from beyond his own system. They also result from my attachment to another model of education. It is a model in which, contrary to Rawls's views, one consciously makes his original choices and the goals of education remain in the undetermined perspective of the future. For, like Kant, I am convinced that stabilization of an already achieved political state of things, even if it is recognised as perfect, is not the proper dimension of education. Education is always directed at the future. And in regard to the future our knowledge can be merely approximate. This is why Kant placed his project of education in a more general perspective of philosophy of history. According to it one can only cherish a justified hope for constant improvement of humankind. This regards also its political dimension, namely the idea of global republic warranting permanent world peace.

According to this model, education itself is a process that consists in evoking changes inside a human being and stimulating his creative efforts in this direction. And this can only be achieved through influence of other human beings, paragons (educators) and not through simulation of an ideal form of a society that will program such changes within him. The situation that I described as programming Kant would probably perceive as conditioning, which he recognized as incompatible with the idea of education. According to him education should first of all teach a child to think, i.e., it should lead a child to the principles that give an impulse to action and not impose the form of this action.

Knowing how much Rawls respects Kant, I can assume with high probability that he would accept these remarks, at least some of them, referring them, however, to the area of a comprehensive doctrine, i.e., to the area of philosophy. Yet, I do not expect that he could manage to cope in this simple way with Kant's thought that I am going to quote at the end of this paper. In a way it shakes the fundamental intention of the conception of political liberalism in which the model of education is understood as a consequence of the political model (even if they are identical). Namely, it shows that we will only be able to determine a proper political model when we find the proper model of education:

> Vielleicht daß die Erziehung immer besser werden und daß jedes folgende Generation einen Schritt näher tun wird zur Vervollkommnung der Menschheit; denn hinter der Education steckt das große Geheimnis der Vollkommenheit der menschlichen Natur.

Dariusz Dobrzański
Poznań

The Problem of Justification
of Political Obligations.
A Civic Solidarity Argument

1. Introduction

Problems related to *political obligations* and their justification have been increasingly brought up by various kinds of normative reflection on politics in philosophy (A. John Simmons, Andrew Mason, George Klosko). It seems that one of the reasons – though most certainly not the only one – why philosophers are interested in the problem of political obligations of citizens of liberal democratic societies is the recognized crisis of the *quality of participation* in public institutions.

In the current policy of democratic states, participation is essentially realized in the paradigm of instrumental rationality, rarely communicative rationality (civil society/NGO's).

In my article, I am going to discuss the issue of justification of political obligations. The main focus will be on the reconstruction of civic solidarity argumentation.

I am going to look for arguments in the tradition of modern civic republicanism, in works by such scholars as Cass Sunstein, Charles Taylor and Andrzej Walicki reflection on patriotism.

This selection seems particularly fitting in view of the fact that republicanism not only emphasises the importance of solidarity – based deliberative activity of citizens for political order in the republic, but is currently experiencing a renewed interest of scholars – caused by the emergence of the information society which discards the traditional republican belief that a system based on active participation can only function effectively on small territories, e.g. on the level of cities, regions, considering it a relic of the past.

2. Four Types of Justification of Political Obligations

Political obligations are usually understood as obligations stemming from different social roles or voluntary duties assumed by citizens. They are usually taken to include at least the obligation to obey the laws of the land and are often thought to include also further obligations of loyalty and "good citizenship". Political obligations are moral obligations of citizens to support and comply with the requirements of their political authorities and the problem of political obligation is that of understanding why (if at all) citizens in various types of states are bound by such obligations.

The problem discussed by us here has its history in literature pertaining to this area of study. Among a number of proposals put forth by different scholars, four are most often invoked, including:

Locke's consent argument
Socrates' gratitude argument
Hart's fair play principle
Rawls' fairness argument

The justification of political obligations by consent is linked to the argumentation proposed by John Locke[1] (*Second Treatise on Civil Government*). Locke writes that an individual leaving the state of nature and giving an autonomous *consent* to living in a political community[2]

---

[1] John Locke, *Two Treatises on Government*, Cambridge: Cambridge University Press, 1960 [Polish edition: *Dwa traktaty o rządzie*, transl. by Zbigniew Rau, Warszawa: Wydawnictwo Naukowe PWN, 1992].

[2] The political society is constituted of members who are independent and reached the age of reason. Locke lists the "chief end" of the political society as "preservation of property". Property includes for Locke "Life, liberty, and estate". Another defining feature of political society is that the power to judge is transferred to public institutions in the civil society". Locke provides for both: express a tacit consent, but there is considerable ambiguity about what constitutes express consent. The

at the same time consents to being subject to the law of this community and fulfil obligations towards its government. The social contract concluded by individuals with their government imposes limits of mutual obligations and rights for both parties. This consent can be either express (for example direct agreements, elections) or tacit – the only obligation expected of a foreign visitor. Voluntary intention consent of some sort is necessary for political obligation, while government without popular consent is tyranny. Locke provides for both express and tacit consent.

Another type of justification of obligations is based on gratitude.

Authors who invoke this argument, often use an illustrative analogy, comparing the relations between citizens and the state to the relationship between children and parents. Claims are made that just like children are grateful to their parents, so citizens owe gratitude to the state for the benefits and advantages they receive from it in the course of their lives, including, for example, security, upbringing or education.

It is argued that each citizen receiving benefits from the state is obligated to reciprocate them.

Proponents of this argumentation often invoke Socrates from Plato's dialogue *Crito*[3] and the reasons he gives explaining why citizens should abide by the state law, unjust though it may be. This version of the argument is controversial. Quite apart from the many points of dissimilarity between political and familial relationships which weaken the analogy, a crucial flaw in the argument is its assumption that a child's obligation to obey its parents is an obligation of gratitude.[4]

---

seventeenth century did not have regular election or universal suffrage, he is more precise as to the tacit consent, which is the only the obligation expected of a foreign visitors.

[3] *The Apology, Phadeo and Crito of Plato*, New York, 1961 [Polish edition: *Kriton*, Warszawa, 1982].

[4] The argument runs as follows: (1) The person who receives benefits from X has an obligation to requite or make a suitable return to X. (2). Every citizen has received benefits from the state. (3) Every citizen has an obligation to make a suitable return to the state. (4) Compliance with the law is a suitable return. (5) Every citizen has an obligation to comply with laws of his state.

The argument runs as follows:

(1) The person who receives benefits from X has an obligation to requite or make a suitable return to X.

(2) Every citizen has received benefits from the state.

(3) Every citizen has an obligation to make a suitable return to the state.

(4) Compliance with the law is a suitable return.

(5) Every citizen has an obligation to comply with the laws of his state.

Yet another type of justification of political obligations is the well-known argument proposed by a lawyer J. Hart and called the fair play principle. Hart assumes that the society is an association of co-operating citizens who, entering into cooperation, mutually restrict their liberties (e.g. freedom of privacy) in order to achieve a previously formulated public objective that will yield them mutual benefits. Participation in benefits resulting from cooperation, with a simultaneous mutual restriction of liberties, is sufficient to generate obligations.

The basic aspects of this argumentation were taken up and developed by J. Rawls.[5] Rawls claims that citizens should not use the co-operative effort without having a fair share in it, which means that a beneficiary of the cooperation scheme is obligated to perform his part of the tasks, not only take advantage of the benefits of cooperation without participating in costs.[6]

---

[5] John Rawls discusses the problem of obligations and their justification e.g. in his "A Theory of Justice" and earlier in his article entitled "Legal Obligation and the Duty of Fair Play", in: *Law and Philosophy*, ed. by Sidney Hook, New York: New York University Press, 1964.

[6] J. Rawls principle of fair play may be defined as follows: "1. Suppose there is a mutually beneficial and just scheme of social cooperation, and that the advantages it yields can only be obtained if everyone, or nearly everyone, cooperates. 2. Suppose further that cooperation requires a certain sacrifice from each person, or al least involves a certain restriction of his liberty. 3. Suppose finally that benefit produced by cooperation is unstable in the sense that if any one person know that all (or nearly all) of the other will continue to do their part, he will still be able to share a gain from the scheme even if he does not do his part. Under these conditions a person who has accepted the benefits of the scheme is bound by a duty o fair play to do his part and

It must be added that Hart's "fair play principle" and Rawls' "fairness principle" are conditional, which means that obligations arise when rules laid down by institutions and practices are fair (a necessary precondition) and cooperation is organized on a voluntary basis.

Critics of this argumentation emphasise its voluntaristic and individualistic nature.

3. Civic Republicanism

For civic republicans (Sunstein, Pettit, Taylor)[7] solidarity is an element of civic virtue. What are the civic virtues[8] defining a model good citizen in modern republicanism?

---

not to take advantage of the free benefits by not cooperating". John Rawls, "Legal Obligation and the Duty of Fair Play", op. cit., pp. 9–10.

[7] I realize that the picture of civic republicanism I am presenting here is idealized, since historically it was not free from faults, e.g. it excluded African Americans, women and poor people from political debate, while the tradition it referred to glorified military-heroic bonds that were hardly useful in times of peace. A claim can be made that republicans were linked by their interests and negative solidarity. On the other hand, contemporary American Revolution historians stress that the period of development of the American constitution should not be analyzed exclusively in terms of Locke's concept of consent. On the contrary, the role of republican thought in developing the principles of the so-called American constitutionalism is frequently emphasized nowadays. See Michelman, *Supreme Court*, vol. 100; *Harvard Law Review* 4, 1986; Bruce A. Ackerman, "The Storrs Lectures: Discovering the Constitution", *93 Yale Law Journal* 1984; Charles Taylor, "Cross-Purposes: The Liberal-Communitarian Debate", in: *Liberalism and the Moral Life*, ed. by Nancy L. Rosenblum, Cambridge: Harvard University Press, 1991. The Constitution and its integrating role determine constitutional republicanism which, next to civic virtues, makes the Constitution the common space for identification and consciousness of republicans.

[8] J.G. Pocock, defining the modern – Renaissance-originated – notion of "virtue" found e.g. in Machiavelli, uses the terms "nature", "essence" or "essential characteristic" and states that it can be understood as the "capacity to act in confrontation with fortuna". The notion, elaborated in the republican lexicon, meant "a devotion to the public good, it could signify the practice, or the precondition of the practice, or relations of equality between citizenship engaged in ruling and being ruled; or an active ruling quality – practicing the active line". John Greville Agard Pocock, *The Machiavel-*

An answer to this question can be found in the works of Cass R. Sunstein[9] who formulated a model of basic tenets of modern republicanism referring directly to civic virtues. According to Sunstein,[10] republicanism is defined by the following principles.

a. The first principle is that of deliberation. The virtue of public debate is understood not only as a character trait, but more broadly, as a rule perfected in political debate, a precondition for the achievement of social justice.

Deliberative government[11], points out the author, is both an end in itself and a means to achieve external goals. Politics is a domain in which private interests are disclosed and a balance in debate is attained. The deliberating parties are to achieve a sense of measure and a critical distance both towards their own expectations and practices and those of their interlocutors.

Republicans express a conviction that in public debate desires, expectations and interests can be reconsidered in the course of discussions. Debaters can change their initial stance under the influence of rational persuasion and arguments. It is known that the process of political decision-making can take the form of bargaining, with different groups attempting to defend or gain particular benefits. Prior to bargaining, bargainers rationally define their preferences before starting a discussion. By contrast, in the case of debate-based decision-making postulated by republicans, debaters construe – in the course of debating – the meaning of preferences, having regard to their goal, i.e. the previously assumed common good.[12]

---

lian Moment. Florentine Political Thought and the Atlantic Republican Tradition, Princeton: Princeton University Press, 1975.

[9] Cass R. Sunstein, "Beyond the Republican Revival", *Yale Law Journal*, vol. 97, 1987–1988.

[10] Ibidem, p. 1539. Sunstein stresses that it is hard to come up with a definition of politics that would be universal for republicanism, however believes that the constituents he lists are typical of this political attitude.

[11] The good example of deliberative government we can find in Madison letter (*The Federealist* no. 39) – a republic is the government which derives all its powers directly or indirectly from the great body of the people, and is administered by persons holding their offices during pleasure, for a limited period or during good behaviour". Alexander Hamilton, James Madison, John Jay, *The Federalist Papers*, New York, 1961.

[12] Cass R. Sunstein, "Beyond the Republican Revival", op. cit., p. 1541.

In this perspective, deliberation is a criticism rather than a description or celebration. Republicans are often viewed as critics of liberal institutions, individual rights, e.g. the right to property, since they treat private ownership as a product of public decisions, not natural laws.

b. Another principle is that of political equality, understood as an equal access of individuals and groups to the political process. The principle is tightly linked to economic equality.

c. Yet another principle concerns universalism. Republican thinking is imbued with universalism rejecting ethical relativism and scepticism. Republicans believe that different lifestyles in the course of deliberation, communicative mediation controlled by practical reason, will achieve a consensus, an agreement. Republicans regard the concept of common good as a coherent and cohesive idea, while questioning the pluralism of opinions on what in fact is common good. They also believe in the effectiveness of the so-called political empathy, whose tool is practical reason, i.e. situations in which actors stand a chance of a mutual recognition of their right arguments. It must also be added that republicans do not consider universalism a starting point, but a result of debate.

d. The final principle is the above mentioned participation and citizenship.

Republicans attach a great importance to participation and citizenship. They seek control mechanisms of national institutions and possibilities of decentralization of power. One area (or dimension) of participation is, for example, the monitoring of actions undertaken by representatives selected for their involvement in political institutions. They not only treat participation instrumentally, but also, they claim, participation is where the above-mentioned empathy, virtues and a sense of belonging to a community are construed. The belief and conviction about the role of citizenship demonstrates the critical attitude of republicans towards individuals, which they sharply disapprove of.

Historically speaking, the meaning of citizenship[13] has undergone major transformations accompanying changes in the type of sover-

---

[13] For a number of researchers, the modernization of societies entails a decline of solidarity-based bonds, which is why a debate on citizenship, not solidarity, is fre-

eign power. The direction of changes can be closed in the formula: from the King-sovereign to the Nation-sovereign. For republicans, present-day sovereignty of a nation means a genuine possibility of self-government.

Civic republicans often prefer to talk about virtues, rather than obligations or duties, but it is clear that they regard the fulfilment of obligations as partially constitutive of what it is to be "good citizen".[14]

The concept of solidarity, though postulated in republicans' works and positively valorized, linked – from example by Charles Taylor[15] – with the concept of patriotism, is not conceptualised. At this point, I would like to devote some time to discussing the concept of solidarity.

Admittedly, there exist a plethora of descriptions and definitions of solidarity and I will refer here only to those which seem the most typical and which render the sense of the term to the fullest extent.

Solidarity is understood as an attitude of an individual towards other individuals and the community, a significant component of which is the feeling of being connected, belonging to a certain whole together with the remaining members of the community – or at least a declarative readiness to help and co-operate. Other descriptions treat

---

quently proposed. In its historic development, citizenship was discussed by Thomas H. Marshall in his *Citizenship and Social Class* (1950), London: Pluto Press, 1992, a work presenting the history of the evolution of the idea of citizenship in England: the first stage, in the 18th century was marked by the emergence of the right to acquire rights and caused a consolidation of civil rights related to freedoms, i.e. freedom of speech, freedom of religion, right to ownership, right to a fair trial. The second stage, in the 19th century, saw the emergence of the institution of political rights, e.g. the right to participate in the political process of holding power, in the Parliament and associations. The 20th century marked the beginning of yet another type of right – social rights, i.e. the right to education or the right to social welfare. A question that is currently brought up in relation to citizenship in the context of global emigration problems, multiethnicity and multiculturalism pertains to the criteria of citizenship acquisition. Politics understood as self-government, Philip Pettit points out, stems from the republican understanding of freedom as non–domination. See Philip Pettit, *Republicanism. A Theory of Freedom and Government*, Oxford: Oxford University Press, 1997.

[14] Compare Stephen Macedo, *Liberal Virtues: Citizenship, Virtue, and Community in Liberal Constitutionalism*, Oxford: Clarendon Press, 1990.

[15] Charles Taylor, "Cross-Purposes: The Liberal – Communitarian Debate", in: *Liberalism and the Moral Life*, ed. by Nancy L. Rosenblum, Cambridge: Harvard University Press, 1989.

solidarity as a sentiment and as a moral obligation of members of a group with respect to each other, based on a community of shared interests, values and traditions. Still other descriptions, to be found in the social teaching of the Roman Catholic Church, recognize solidarity as a perfect expression of Christian Love (Agape) – i.e. as a virtue. Generally, one can list four necessary and sufficient elements constituting the notion of solidarity. These include:

– altruistic attitude
– feeling of belonging
– willingness to help and co-operate
– moral obligation

It should be added that it is not easy to find an antonym to the word and to the idea of solidarity. Steven Lukes[16] proposes the term fluidarity, by which he means "a lack of stable social relationships or bonds, or connections, an absence of community or fellow feeling".

4. Argument from Civil Solidarity

It is worth discussing the problem of justification of political obligations with civic solidarity in a broader context of issues that make up the notion of modern republican political patriotism. It seems that – without depreciating the legitimacy and the force of argumentation of previously discussed "cold" and rational justifications of political obligations (i.e. consent, gratitude, fair play and fairness) the one important aspect they lack is a reference to feelings intrinsic in political patriotism. Without embarking on any complicated analyses of the very concept of patriotism and its intricate metamorphoses (e.g. patriotism seen as ethnocentrism, nationalism), it should be noted that patriotism tends to be understood as the feeling of love towards one's homeland, nation and family cherished by citizens, which manifests itself e.g. in being loyal towards them.[17] By discussing Polish political

---

[16] Steven Lukes, "Solidarity and Citizenship", in: Kurt Bayertz, *Solidarity*, Dordrecht: Springer Verlag, 1999.

[17] Alasdair MacIntyre, "Is Patriotism a Virtue?", in: John Arthur, *Morality and Moral Controversies*, Upper Saddle River, NJ: Prentice Hall, 1981 [Polish edition: "Czy

tradition, we want to demonstrate the community of views – the universalism of opinions – of seemingly different political cultures, an area covered by modern republicanism.[18] On the other hand, it appears that the feeling of solidarity deprived of emotional exaltation that is inherent in love can, in its civic form, be an element of the modern notion of patriotism.

The simplest answer to the question why someone should be involved in any political obligations is that the person identifies with the tradition of the political culture of their country that includes – in addition to competing political schemes – an institutional field for the achievement of the common good. Each citizen creates the common good and is shaped by it.[19] It seems that without conscious civic identification it is neither possible to establish a community of property, nor to achieve human ambitions whose natural agonistic field is political involvement understood in Aristotelian terms. In the end, the focus is not on "wide-access" patriotism, the "practical wisdom" (phronesis) of which was already undermined by Socrates in *Crito*, but the patriotism of principles which assumes rational argumentation and feelings.

The problems of civic identification with state institutions, national tradition and other communities, and the definition of the

---

patriotyzm jest cnotą?", in: *Komunitarianie*, ed. by Paweł Śpiewak, Warszawa: Aletheia, 2004].

[18] The issue of the heritage of the republican tradition, as well as its topicality in the political thought of Europe and North America is discussed by authors of the work: *Republicanism. A Shared European Heritage*, ed. by Martin van Gelderen, Quentin Skinner, Cambridge: Cambridge University Press, 2002.

[19] The notion of political culture is related to the sphere of attitudes referring to the public life, standards regulating it, as well as ideas of the society. The concept was first introduced into Polish historiography by Józef Siemieński who, referring to Aristotle, evaluated various forms of rule. Contrary to Aristotle's views, Siemieński saw democracy as "the best form of rule". In his opinion, in the period of Noble's Democracy, Poland had a truly democratic political system and was well ahead Western Europe e.g. in the development of political institutions. Arguments listed by Siemieński include: a greater proportion of the population (10%) that had their share in wielding power and used political liberty; equality of all the nobility before the law, regardless of their financial status; a greater scope of powers exercised by representation bodies in relation to the king's authority (elections). See Józef Siemieński, *Kultura staropolska* [Old Polish Culture], Kraków: Polska Akademia Umiejętności, 1932.

common good, due to their "inbuilt" ambiguity and rhetorical nature, pose a number of difficulties for a theoretical analysis. Ongoing global integration processes that are currently taking place (e.g. in Europe) create new frames of reference entailing certain practical consequences. What institution does one owe their political duties to in the first place? Is it an institution of "their state" or perhaps an international institution? Is a person lodging a complaint with the European Court of Justice against an institution of "their state" committing an act of utter disloyalty or just exercising their civic rights? Are well-educated people leaving the country which offered them free education in search of better economic opportunities committing an act demonstrating their lack of solidarity with institutions and fellow citizens?

Let me postpone venturing an answer to the above questions and discuss the notion of patriotism as it was understood in the tradition of noble republicanism – a tradition that seems very distant from the one invoked above after C. Sunstein. Noble's Democracy is generally understood by historians as a tradition of Polish republicanism of the 17th century.[20] The typology of patriotism that I will be using in my argument – though deeply rooted in the history of Noble's Democracy and its historic institutions – is universal in character.

Andrzej Walicki distinguishes three typologies of patriotism. The first one can be defined as faithfulness to the national will and manifests itself in the pursuit of internal and external sovereignty (republican model). Another typology defines patriotism as faithfulness to the national idea that is conveyed by tradition and supposed to become reality in the future (romantic model). The final typology perceives patriotism as a defence of realistically understood national interest (national democratic model).[21]

On account of the extensiveness of the material and – above all – the topic discussed here, I am going to develop the main aspects of

---

[20] I refer here to the typology of patriotism formulated by Andrzej Walicki in his *The Three Traditions in Polish Patriotism and Their Contemporary Relevance*, Bloomington: The Polish Studies Center, 1988 [Polish edition: "Trzy patriotyzmy", in: Andrzej Walicki, *Polskie zmagania z wolnością*, Kraków: Universitas, 2000].

[21] Andrzej Walicki, "Trzy patriotyzmy", op. cit., pp. 225–226.

the republican typology that constitute elements of the justification of political obligations proposed in this paper.

Republican patriotism[22] understood as faithfulness to the national will[23] is based on the foundation of positive freedom that was basically political in nature. A free person, i.e. a patriot, is someone participating in political decision-taking and law-making, and subject to these laws. Using the distinction proposed by Benjamin Constant,[24] positive freedom is the "Liberty of the Ancients", actions in the public sphere, liberty in the state and for the state. The spirit of this freedom is sovereignty. The subject of this freedom in Noble's Democracy was the sovereign nation – in Poland it was the nobility that jointly defended the right to exercise positive freedom, considering it their patriotic duty. The opposite of positive freedom is modern negative freedom, i.e. freedom from the interference of the state, pertaining to the private domain. The latter tended to be regarded by the nobility as a secondary sphere of life. The spirit of this freedom is the restriction of all sovereignty, including the sovereignty of the nobility, by the rights of the individual. The subject of this freedom is an individual endowed with pre-political rights. The nation (nobility) is the subject of sovereign will, equipped with procedures and principles, creating institutional rights and, at the same time, being an originator of an essential element of democracy, namely the public opinion, an element of control of particular interests and their articulation. The ethos of Noble's Democracy was anti-authoritative, for all the decisions were taken after all parties had been heard and voices counted. Parliamentary debates in the Seym were governed by the controver-

---

[22] Theorists of the idea of Polish republicanism included, among others, Andrzej Frycz Modrzewski (Andreus Fricius Modrevius), Hugo Kołłątaj and Maurycy Mochnacki.

[23] The basic category of this typology is the category of the nation, the role of which in the Polish history is linked to the history of the nobility, their privileges and obligations. Walicki emphasizes that it was a political category rather than an ethnic one and points to the period of the Polish-Lithuanian Union as the period in which the political interpretation of the category of nation was taking shape.

[24] Benjamin Constant, *O wolności nowoczesnej w porównaniu z wolnością starożytnych*, 1819 [Benjamin Constant, *Political Writings*, Cambridge: Cambridge University Press, 1980].

sial procedure of *liberum veto* (I forbid)[25] closely related to the rule of unanimous voting of resolutions. Analysed against the background of political customs in other European states at the time, the *liberum veto* principle was a curiosity, since the parliamentary voting systems in France and England were based on the majority vote. I am not attempting to resolve the historians' dispute over the role of the *liberum veto* procedure which – used irresponsibly – paralysed the decision-taking process. Suffice it to say that the one advantage of *liberum veto* was that the threat of using it forced different political parties to seek compromise, taught them the culture of political argument and was an instrument of demonstrating the "public will". In this case, democracy was not merely procedural, but was a "living" debate. On the other hand, a basic disadvantage of the *liberum veto* principle was that – as the Seym practice showed – it was prone to manipulations and protected the interests of the strongest conservative political circles. The *liberum veto* was based on the "collective wisdom of the nation" rather than individual courage and responsibility.

Claude Backvis[26], a friendly critic of this voting procedure, emphasizes that the *liberum veto* principle, giving priority to discussion

---

[25] The first use of *liberum veto* is commonly attributed to Władysław Siciński, a representative at Seym in 1652. *Liberum veto* was abolished by the Constitution of 3rd May in 1791. *Liberum veto* has a long and interesting bibliography in which a common point is the shared relief that the procedure evolved from a principle expressing liberty from monarchy and political responsibility for the future of the state into a procedure demonstrating collective interests. It is worth adding that it was favourably evaluated by J.J. Rousseau, who referred to it as a "beautiful law", since he views an act of political decision as an act of self-knowledge and moral self-determination, not merely a formal procedure – see Jerzy Michalski, *Rousseau i sarmacki republikanizm* [Rousseau and Sarmatian Republicanism], Warszawa: PWN, 1977. Claude Backvis claims that the majority voting system fails to make different parties search for a third alternative, it is a sham discussion, for different parties are not interested in truth but a temporary majority. He believes that unanimity makes it possible to determine "the will of the general public", i.e. the main assumption of democracy. See Claude Backvis, "Wymóg jednomyślności a 'wola ogółu'" [The Unanimity Requirement and the "Public Will"], *Czasopismo Prawno-Historyczne*, vol. XXVII, 2, 1975. An unambiguously critical opinion of the *liberum veto* principle is expressed by Władysław Konopczyński in his extensive monograph: *Liberum veto* (1918), Kraków: Universitas, 2002.

[26] Claude Backvis, "Wymóg jednomyślności a 'wola ogółu'" [The Unanimity Requirement and the "Public Will"], op. cit., p. 167.

over decision-taking, created political knowledge, humanized politics, overshadowing its formal and legalistic aspects. Backvis writes that:

> the British Minister pretends to be addressing Members of Parliament, Members of Parliament pretend to be addressing the Minister, in full awareness of the fact that the whole richness of argument has no bearing on the result of subsequent voting. Ultimately, political speeches are only given for the press that prints or summarizes them in order to persuade the limited number of voters that are undecided between both parties.[27]

A number of researchers analyzing modern public life[28] claim that a contemporary individual living in the Western culture is politically homeless and essentially interested in cultivating privacy and difference – a phenomenon that Taylor terms "expressive individualism".[29] Following the decline of the "great millenaristic and communist utopian scheme", the crisis of participation of liberal democracy, contemporary Western individuals do not identify with any political tradition in fear of another "political bite". This may be the reason why political populism, growing with media strength, has gained such extensive public space. An alternative for this option can be joint and several self-government, participation, citizenship and a debate on the organization of the Republic of Poland – an alternative, let me add, aware of the fact that patriotism, a virtue of civic solidarity, emerges in the course of practice (habitus).

---

[27] Ibidem, p. 167.

[28] Richard Sennett, *The Fall of Public Man*, New York: Knopf, 1974; Hannah Fenichel Pitkin, "Justice: On Relating Private and Public", *Political Theory* 9, 1981; Jurgen Habermas, *The Structural Transformation of the Public Sphere: An Inquiry Into a Category of Bourgeois Society*, transl. by Thomas Burger, Cambridge: MIT Press, 1989; James S. Fishkin, *The Voice of the People*, New Haven: Yale University Press, 1995.

[29] Charles Taylor, *The Ethics of Authenticity*, Cambridge: Harvard University Press, 1991 [Polish edition: *Etyka autentyczności*, Kraków: Znak, 2002].

Danuta Sobczyńska
Poznań

Motherhood:
a Timeless Value for Humankind,
a Choice for Her?

1. Introduction

Many a time when motherhood is referred to, the same thing or a similar thing could be said about fatherhood or, more generally, about parenthood. However, in this text I choose the convention of deliberations related to motherhood exclusively: its specific features such as the biological certainty of motherhood and the accompanying psychophysical commitment of a woman surely support my choice. It is also substantiated by an enormous change in the social and economic situation of women in the 20th century that has also affected their attitude towards motherhood. Today, motherhood is no longer perceived as „destiny", the major determinant of women's fate, but instead it is, to a large extent, the subject of their conscious choice. The possibility of choice, in turn, triggers thought and responsibility.

The article is divided into two parts. In the first of them, which applies to the universal and the timeless values related to motherhood, I ponder on its role in the cosmic phenomenon of Life and in the giving of meaning to the existence of Humankind and individuals. I also consider motherhood as a gift and a sort of a social institution. I draw attention to the mythic, religious and mystic elements of motherhood: in all human cultures, even those remote, it was perceived as a miracle and a mystery, as *a sacrum* of human life.

The second part discusses a few tendencies characteristic of the present day: motherhood as a consciously made choice and the underlying rationale. Talking about the motherhood of famous women in public has become a social standard, and many of them are willing to disclose this aspect of their privacy and intimacy to the media. Women "regained voice" in speaking about their great and personality transforming experiences, as pregnancy and child birth are, as well as breastfeeding and attending a son or daughter in their development. In this part I also raise, though out of necessity – very briefly, the question of a few trends in the contemporary procreative medicine which, in the opinion of some groups of people, reflect the social needs and, in the opinion of others, men's "attack" on that aspect of procreation that by the law of nature remains the exclusive domain of women. I also underline the spiritual aspect of motherhood. In the closing part of my article I conclude that there are conflicting approaches to the perceiving of motherhood in the globalizing contemporary world: despite appearances of appreciation of motherhood, too many times it is talked about before TV cameras, and too little attention is paid to motherhood by thinkers, including women philosophers. The lifestyles found in wealthy western countries are not rather conducive to joyful and happy motherhood, since the contemporaries focus on "today" and not "tomorrow". In world that rewards successes and quick careers motherhood means a withdrawal and a professional regression. In political life and at different levels of power much too often lip service is paid to motherhood, including that "difficult"; whereas women feel that there is too little friendly atmosphere, social safety and certainty about a further professional career after coming back from their maternity leaves.

2. Motherhood as a Universal, Autothelic and Timeless Value for Humankind

2.1. Motherhood as Part of the Phenomenon of Life

How did life begin on Earth? Does it exist anywhere else in the universe? Is it a prevalent or a unique phenomenon? Do we have "brothers in reason" somewhere in outer space? Questions of this type were asked by people from the very flash of their intelligence, and in the 20th century, when the representatives of humankind left their mother planet for the first time, they became even more popular. Surprisingly, these questions are even raised by contemporary theology. To those who are not satisfied with religious explanations science offers a range of hypotheses and more or less likely speculations which are far from being certain.

Regardless of the fact whether or not we will ever have a chance to find an answer to these questions, the existence of an intelligent and self-conscious Life being represented by Humankind is a value, if we can acknowledge the soundness of a metaphysical thesis about the predominance of existence over non-existence. The existence of humankind is certainly of essential and autothelic importance, and Hans Jonas[1] is right in announcing his imperative: „Humanity should last". Jonas's book is a picture of the philosopher's struggle with attempts to justify the "shouldness of being" of humanity. This imperative probably gives voice to the archetypal "collective unconsciousness" being expressed in the instinct of self-preservation and care over progeny. It seems primary and obvious in terms of common human feelings and various political pacts being concluded after the production of weapons of mass destruction. The existence and survival of humanity is an autothelic value: humankind as a medium of Reason being created by the universe is precious and valuable in itself. For humankind to last and retain the light of Reason it has to reproduce.

Those individuals who think highly of the religious message of human procreation are told in a similar manner by the Holy Bible to: „Be fruitful, and multiply, and replenish the earth". Also here there is no justification of that procreative imperative, except one that is implied by religious intuition: apparently, it is God's will to have further and more numerous generations of people speaking of His honor.

As beautifully put by H. Arendt[2], human beings survive thanks to their power of rebirth and natality. New people continue to inhabit

---

[1] Hans Jonas, *Zasada odpowiedzialności* [The Imperativ of Responsibility], transl. by Marek Klimowicz, Kraków: Wydawnictwo Platan, 1996.

[2] Hannah Arendt, *The Human Condition*, Chicago: University of Chicago Press, 1958.

Earth to undertake yet new activities transforming the world. Humankind revives because of human parenthood, motherhood and fatherhood. However, it is motherhood that has a bigger role assigned that is more biologically and mentally involving. Thus, the mission of women can be treated as a universal and a timeless value and as the fulfillment of the imperative „humankind must survive". Motherhood is a struggle for the preservation of our species and as such it has always been *a sacrum* of humanity.

2.2. Motherhood as a Mainstay
of Biological Duration of Humanity

Generations of mothers create the corporeal history of humankind. The next human generations see offspring feed on the juices of the bodies of their mothers, leave them by force during birth, feed on their milk, grow in their arms and become mature with their patient love, wisdom and sacrifice.

Human parenthood means bringing out increasingly new treasures from the biological heritage of humankind and from the genetic heritage. This specific gamble with the potential of Nature is a genetic roulette that is "played" by individuals on the unmeasured space of biodiversity. These games have a dual aspect: individual and global. In the individual aspect, the touch of "destiny" encoded in genes may be painful or tragic. In the global aspect, the individual genetic mutations and tragedies are something banal and somehow incorporated in the "rules of the game" and they fade in the history of generations as a drop in the ocean.

The written history of humankind generally refers to the history of men. Inheriting the names, estates, titles and powers as well as family trees are permanent traces of patriarchal history of our species. Yet, human bodies and each cell in them contain within their genome a trace that cannot be erased or obliterated: the mitochondrial DNA, a witness and a participant of the "female history" of each of us, passed by the Great Mother and her successive daughters. B. Sykes[3]

---

[3] Bryan Sykes, *Siedem matek Europy* [Seven Daughters of Eve], transl. by Krzysztof Kurek, Warszawa: Wydawnictwo Amber, 2001.

was the manager of a group of geneticists examining, under a 10-year scientific program, the genetic past of the European peoples and relations between them. This extremely interesting research covered 100 thousand years back to the times from which no material evidence of culture is available. It turns out that almost every European can find traces of a genetic tie only with seven women! They are ancestors of 650,000,000 Europeans in the female line. These Great Mothers of Europe were given symbolic names: Ursula, Xenia, Helena, Velda, Tara, Katrine and Jasmine. Further research by Sykes's team based on the concept of examining the "fate" of mitochondrial DNA applied to the times about 150 thousand years ago and led to the symbolic Eve living in Africa. It was the people from her "clan" that initiated expansion world-wide.

The human genetic heritage is a magnificent deposit inherited from our remote ancestors, human and prehuman. It reflects the mysterious powers of nature being active for billions of years that we do not fully understand and probably will never do. Here we stand in the face of Mystery that can be approached in many ways: in the religious, pantheistic or deep ecologic spirit. It is also possible to comprehend it on scientific grounds. But then even a rational approach, which is so close to our times, leaves many questions unsolved. This transcendent and mystic dimension of motherhood was well recognized by primeval peoples and cultures. Motherhood was the subject of reverence and cult; each strong religion had its Great Mother and minor deities and fertility patrons.

Reveling in our knowledge about the human genome and celebrating our first successes in genetic engineering, today we do not quite share the humility of our ancestors towards the powers of nature related with reproduction. We do not want to trust them, but we would like to manage them, forgetting the fact that human actions more often than the forces of nature entail the possibility of errors and tragic mistakes. Also, it is hard for us to decide what our attitude should be towards the genetic heritage that we are heirs of: lords and masters or humble and fair depositaries and guards of a treasure with endless possibilities.

2.3. Creating the Meaning of Life

When thinking about the category of motherhood in its global dimension, we can be struck by the scarcity of philosophical deliberations about this issue, in particular, about that determinant of the human fate, the experience of which is given to the female half of the humankind. Motherhood has both ontic and axiologic, sense generating dimensions. With motherhood the human generations are exchanged, the biological and the spiritual "tissues" of humankind are renewed and the history goes on. And owing to the fact that we have someone to pass our material and spiritual legacy, the history of humanity acquires sense.

Let us conduct an experiment, an extreme and a sinister one, but, fortunately, only in our mind. Imagine a world without any children: a mature generation has suddenly suffered from the pandemics of infertility, or women announce, as ancient Lisistrata did, a general strike: no more discomforts and suffering related with pregnancy, labor, breastfeeding, baby-related home slavery; they want to be free like men. The human world would have to end with the death of the last human being. Who then and to whom would prove that any world has existed at all?

Bringing next human generations to the world has then at least a dual meaning: it creates witnesses to the world in its natural dimension, it creates conscious observers of space and it creates aware participants of history. It gives an aware, intelligent, sensitive and sympathetic proof of Being. It gives each generation existing at a given time meaning to their actions, an incentive and a motivation to carry on. The lasting of human civilization, be it a moment in nothingness or in eternity, permeates the emptiness of space with a conscious thought and feeling and calls the beings emerging from that nothingness to last transiently or longer.

Bringing the next human generations to the world also makes much sense for the human social existence on the third planet from Sun. During a day, we do not realize well enough that we do everything for Descendants, for Children, even if we do not have our own. We do it for the future generations that we will never meet and that will have our genes and our "mems". They will be provided with any goods and legacies, material and spiritual, because only in the perspective of further collective existence do all our efforts make sense. We can hope for the future, maybe very remote, to show that our efforts are not in vain.

Also in the individual lots of people, the relations of parents with children belong to the strongest and the most significant. A. Rich[4] notes that a relation of a child with mother is the determinant of the sense of existence to both of them.

> The child receives the first confirmation of the sense of his or her own existence from the mother's appropriate gestures and facial expression. As if the mother's eyes, smile and caressing touch gave the child the first message: *You are here!* And the mother also discovers her existence anew. She is related with that other being by the most earthly and invisible ties in a way that she cannot be related with anyone else, except for her own relation with her mother in the remote past.[5]

In all human cultures a long-lasting visual contact between the mother and the child during the first few days after the birth is of utmost importance. The biological value of this act of getting to know each other is clear: the mother learns the face of her child, and the child exercises his or her sight and learns how to recognize from the chaos of indistinct spots the face that is most important during that time, the face of a carer and feeder. In psychological terms, it is the case of the imprinting of faces of two people that are mutually important to each other. In philosophical terms, in turn, it is the case of meeting the Other, Second: to the woman it is meeting a defenseless and a trusting entity that needs affection and care. To the child it is meeting a person that will help, after the shock of birth, regain the prenatal warmness and peace and learn, as the mother's milk, drop by drop, a new unknown world.

People have always had strong feelings about the formidable and mysterious miracle of the birth of a new entity. Philosophically, we

---

[4] Adrienne C. Rich, *Zrodzone z kobiety. Macierzyństwo jako doświadczenie i instytucja* [Of Woman Born. Motherhood as Experience and Institution], transl. by Joanna Mizielińska, Warszawa: Wydawnictwo Sic! 2000.

[5] Ibidem, p. 76.

deal in fact with transcendence, when during the labor a new human being crosses the boundaries of the body of the mother being.[6] This is a great miracle important to all humankind in terms of culture, important in terms of family. How many husbands accompanying their wives at the birth of their child, unless fainted, give voice to their deep spiritual experiences! And in the history of humanity how big a respect was shown to the oldest profession and woman's function – midwife!

Thanks to our Children we gain comfort in our final days, at the moment of passing away and confronting the Doomsday. If children suddenly disappeared from the world, if only one last man remained, who would mourn his or her death? Who would bury his or her body? And if that man died, would not the world have to die, too?

2.4. Motherhood as a Gift

In the contemporary humanities the problem of a gift is recurrent. The deliberations about the phenomenon of a gift spread from anthropology and ethnology (B. Malinowski, M. Mauss), but also, to a certain extent, from the heritage of Christian thought. The contribution of philosophical reflections, for instance, by Heidegger, P. Ricoeur, E. Levinas, M. Buber, J. Derrida is also considerable. The issue of a gift was also considered (R. Girard) in the context of the issue of sacrifice.[7] The analyses conducted by philosophers, though subtle and complex, omit the question of motherhood and, to the best of my knowledge, feminist writers have not undertaken any analyses of motherhood from this point of view, either.

Motherhood is then a special gift. The situations of giving and taking gifts, as considered by the said (and other) thinkers, take place within the communities of adults, equivalent entities in the act of giving; the goods being mentioned are generally of a material nature,

---

6 Jolanta Brach-Czaina, *Szczeliny istnienia* [Gaps of Existence], Kraków: Wydawnictwo eFKa, 1999.

7 Cf. *Fenomen daru* [The Phenomenon of the Gift], ed. by Anna Grzegorczyk, Jan Grad, Rafał Koschany, Poznań: Wydawnictwo Naukowe UAM, 2004.

though deeper symbolism can be associated with them. But it is not the case for motherhood. Firstly, the "subject" of the gift has an autothelic value: it is a human child presented with life, entering the world. Is it possible to think of a greater gift than giving the child to the world and giving the world to the child? Secondly, from the very beginning this gift is marked with the situation of fate and randomization: the gift is addressed to a potential person, not known to us, who only through the prenatal phase will become our child. Thus, we take a first step towards a situation, the paradox of which was pinpointed by H. Jonas[8]: responsibility towards beings that will come. The features mentioned above that distinguish the gift of motherhood are sufficient to claim that it is transcendent.

Let us take a look at a few other aspects of that transcendence related with the giving of life to a child:

- It is evident in the aforementioned relation between a new human entity and World (according to Heidegger's convention – Being). Simultaneously, this relation becomes reciprocal: World is also made available to the new human entity and his or her developing cognition.
- Thanks to motherhood, humanity regenerates; with the exchange of generations, as in the entire natural world, continuous presence of humankind on Earth is maintained. With such exchange it is possible to preserve and multiply material goods and cultural goods.
- There are also elements of multi-level "crossing" in the personal relation between the parents of a child. With their own child a couple crosses the boundaries of their bodies to weave their genes into a living tissue of the biological "substance" of humanity. Each of the parents crosses also an individual potential: cultural, educational, economic, and the like.
- With their own child a human couple also crosses the boundaries of this limited period of historic time during which they were meant to live. This last factor of transcendence is time related. It means a hope of existence in children and grand-

---

[8] Hans Jonas, *Zasada odpowiedzialności* [The Imperativ of Responsibility], op. cit.

children, a hope of continuity of history of their family. Tempo-
rality is also a factor that distinguishes a gift.
– Theoreticians and thinkers dealing with the question of a gift
underline its spontaneous, disinterested and somehow excessive
nature. Only a spontaneous outburst of positive feelings is what
creates the gift and allows it to be distinguished from presents or
gifts expected by the convention. The same goes (or should go)
for motherhood.

A common human intuition is expressed in the phrase that a child
is a fruit of love and that only loving parents can provide optimum
conditions for the child's development. The Catholic Church talks
about it in the strong normative sense referring to the beginning of
human life (John Pope II). Today, this option is not convincing to
everyone. Many people, while seeing the need for love as a source
of life, reserve the right for married couples to choose the number of
children that they want (and can) raise.

2.5. About the Institution of Motherhood

We owe the „discovery" of the institution of motherhood to Adrienne Rich, born in 1929, an American poet and philosopher. When we
think about institution, claims Rich[9], we can usually see it embodied in
a building: Vatican, Pentagon, Sorbonne.... Whereas when we think
about the institution of motherhood, no symbolic architecture crosses
our mind nor any visible embodiment of authority or power. This may
be the reason why the notion of the institution of motherhood, as a
social institution, occurs, on the one hand, so late (in the book referred
to in this article that was first issued in 1976) and, on the other hand, as
a result of feminist reflection on the condition and the fate of a woman.

The institution of motherhood is not tantamount to giving birth
and raising children just as the institution of heterosexuality is not the
same as intimacy and love. They both establish terms and conditions,
under which certain behaviors and choices are accepted or abandoned. The institution of motherhood is simply a set of socially le-

---

[9] Adrienne C. Rich, *Zrodzone z kobiety. Macierzyństwo jako doświadczenie i instytucja*
[Of Woman Born. Motherhood as Experience and Institution], op. cit.

gitimized rules and directions how to properly fulfill the role of a mother. It is a product of specific social structures and conditions and it completely ignores both the individual experiences of women and the way they themselves perceive their motherly roles and behaviors.

The institution of motherhood, being thoroughly analyzed by A. Rich, imposes standards on women so high that they cannot be fulfilled by real women. What is expected of mothers is an absolute moral purity, total devotion to children, omission of their own needs, gigantic physical powers and angel's patience... What is worse, it is mothers (and not fathers) that are made responsible for their child's health, development, intelligence, good behavior, good grades at school, and the like. It is father's duty to demand and punish, while mother's to love and suffer. This pattern is followed by hundreds, if not thousands, of literary works that, beyond any doubt, reflect the standards existing in the patriarchal society.

Without reference to the criticism leveled at the said institution by A. Rich, I would like to draw your attention to the possibility of interpreting it socio-biologically. The institution in question is certainly, as many others, a cultural component of human behavior that emerged through evolution. Motherhood plays the major role in the struggle for the preservation of humankind. The forms of practicing it socially are conditioned by the fact that a great deal of time must pass before a human newborn reaches adulthood. Feminist writers are tending to depart from evolutionist and socio-biological components, but still these can be seen in a similar manner, as seen by S.B. Hrdy[10] in her analysis of the development of human customs related with sexual life.

3. Contemporary Dilemmas about Procreation

3.1. Motherhood as a Question of Choice

For ages the biblical procreative imperative and the institution of motherhood developed in the Christian culture of the West have guarded the growth of new human generations. There was much

---

[10] Sarah B. Hrdy, *Kobieta, której nigdy nie było* [The Woman that Never Evolved], transl. by Marcin Ryszkiewicz, Warszawa: Wydawnictwo Cis, 2005.

point in it, when humankind formed species that was not yet very numerous, and survival in adverse natural conditions was not easy. There was also much point in having many children (especially sons) in families that made a living out of farming or tending flock. It also made much sense to a ruler to have a successor. Many children were considered as a blessing, while infertility (particularly, of women, since it was easier to disclose) as a curse and shame. Also, the religious aspect of parenthood was underlined: it is God that gives children to parents, blesses woman's womb and sends a child an immortal soul.

A number of factors can be distinguished that have caused various types of procreative imperatives to diminish and decline in the reality of life of contemporary western societies. Firstly, people have already sufficiently "replenished the earth" and have become a species that dominated the biosphere. Only in the 19th century Malthus diagnosed that the reproduction of humankind was faster than the production of food and this state of affairs was likely to invite a disaster. Today, in a number of countries such as China drastic measures have been taken to curtail the population. At this point, a question arises whether it is not necessary to make a global attempt to stabilize the number of human beings at a certain optimum level so as to ensure all the inhabitants of Earth a fair value of life.

Secondly, the characteristics of contemporary societies have changed essentially, as compared with previous ages. People no longer produce mainly food and things necessary for living. We are a "third wave" generation (Toffler) and we produce increasingly huge resources of any type of information, be it scientific, publicist, artistic, economic, commercial, and the like. Accordingly, other priorities have emerged and a different hierarchy of values has come into being: many people dismiss procreation in favor of values that are perceived as higher. To the previous generation parenthood was still an unquestioned obviousness linked with marriage. At present, a social standard is a considerable reserve in undertaking matrimonial commitments as well as greater ease in breaking those already made. The relationships that are willfully childless proliferate. The role of a child is taken over... by a dog.

Thirdly, the relations between the sexes have changed radically. The emancipating processes going on from the 19th century became reality in the majority of industrial societies in the 20th century. This meant, first and foremost, that women became entities in the sense of receiving full citizen rights, freedom of views and feelings, access to education and professional careers.

Finally, in the 60's last century a contraceptive pill was introduced on the market. Women became free to decide about their body and motherhood, which, to a large extent, shaped a new partner type relation with men and strengthened the liberation of women. Motherhood could become a choice and a responsible decision. At the same time, it was a first step to separate sex from procreation. Sexual revolution was carried out, the signs of which can be observed now.

3.2. Motherhood as a Valuable Individual Experience

A characteristic feature of our times is individualism, creation of one's own personality and revaluation of former standards of decency that prohibited discussing various private matters in public, particularly of an intimate nature. A specific social aura is also formed around motherhood. It is affected by diverse factors that, in terms of significance, could be classified as follows:

– Motherhood has been clearly appreciated as both the contribution of women in the "renovation" of humankind and their task, experience, individual "adventure with child"; in the feminist trend of activities the problem of motherhood is addressed broadly enough.

– Literary works have been developed in this area with a wide scope: philosophical, psychological, sociological, medical, guides, specialist magazines, TV programs for parents, etc.

– Fathers tend to be more active and aware in sharing the parents' roles and tasks: they often accompany their wives during birth, take care of the child from the first hours after birth.

– New fashions and customs are established: it is trendy to proudly exhibit (and not "mask") pregnancy with clothes, to give birth at home or video-record the delivery (!), publish interviews with famous women held during the first few days of their motherhood, and the like.

– Social favor with and interest in motherhood, unfortunately, cannot be transposed to professional lives. Newly employed young women often have to sign statements that they do not plan to have any children; pregnant women are not always transferred to easier work and after maternity leaves they are frequently dismissed from their jobs.

Many of these changes result from the circumstances referred to in the preceding paragraph: motherhood ceased to be the destiny of a woman, her major role and duty, but instead it became the subject of her choice. This means that women can give up motherhood and pursue a different model of life. With several emancipating factors a woman became an entity in relations with a man in private, professional and social spheres. And with the specific "coeducation" of the social life being observed on many planes, both sexes have become much closer to each other, also mentally. Being often inspired by feminist literature, women explore its role in the miracle of birth, contemplate their experiences related with pregnancy and childbirth, their first contacts with child in biological and mental terms, and they exchange their views. New standards and social customs have developed and motherhood has become the subject of specific fascination also to men.

3.3. Procreative Medicine and Its Prospects

When in 1978 Luise Brown was born in Great Britain, her birth stirred emotions not only in the Brown family, but also in the world of medicine. Little Luise was the first tube-test baby in the world that was conceived from the gametes of her parents through *in vitro* fertilization. Research on the external fertilization was carried out from the 50's in the 20th century and in the 70's it was widely applied in the raising of pedigree breeds of cattle. When doctors decided to apply it to people, a powerful taboo of cultural and religious nature was broken. Exhibiting the fertilization and making it the subject of experimental manipulation seemed to many individuals an attack on *sacrum* of the very beginning of human life. The methods of supported procreation were persistently criticized particularly by successive popes of the Catholic Church, which is understandable in the light of its moral education (John Paul Pope II).[11] Some of the representatives of the medical world and even the pioneers of this method, such as J. Testart[12], also publicly shared their moral and social doubts.

In the medical profession the method of *in vitro* fertilization aroused much disturbance and resistance, mainly due to possible complications for the health of mother and child. The following years of generally successful results dispelled this sort of fears and now *in vitro* method is a routine method to treat infertility that is used when conventional medicine is ineffective. At the same time, the said method became something else: another step, following contraception, on the way to the separating of sex from procreation.

Undoubtedly, we are living in the interesting period of history, when humankind begins to steer its own evolution. This is conspicuous with examples of new techniques of human reproduction. While looking, e.g. after Baker[13], at the possibilities offered by modern medicine, we cannot help our extreme feelings: on the one hand, admiration or even fascination and, on the other, concern, fear and sometimes terror or shock. Well, different variants are possible in reproduction: homologous fertilization (gametes from both spouses) and heterologous (gamete donation) and substitute motherhood, pregnancy after menopause, application of deposits of gametes from the dead, etc. Critics of these methods accuse them, among others, of violating a clear structure of affinity, attacking the sanctity of motherhood, complicating the line of genetic transfer. Here, however, in a biological sense, each child has a father and mother, but, much to the resentment shown by traditionalists, single women or lesbians also use the services of procreative clinics.

Even more concern and anxiety is connected with the genetic engineering techniques, including cloning, that are available "just round

---

[11] Jan Paweł II, *Evangelium vitae*, Poznań: Księgarnia Św. Wojciecha, 1999.

[12] Jacques Testart, *Przejrzysta komórka* [L'oeuf Transparent], transl. by Janina A. Żelechowska, Warszawa: PIW, 1990.

[13] Robin Baker, *Seks w przyszłości* [Sex in the Future], transl. by Tadeusz Chawziuk, Poznań: Dom Wydawniczy Rebis, 2002.

the corner". It will be then possible to asexually copy already existing human beings and reproduce in a manner entirely unknown to nature: with a properly prepared genetic material a woman could have a baby with another woman and a man with another man! As a result, the sex and the style of sexual life will become even more "accidental" and will even to a lesser extent determine the choice of social roles, lifestyle and possibility of procreation. It is hard to deny that the notion of father-hood and motherhood will lose their biologically and socially legit-imized sense. Only a labile notion of parenthood understood in its broadest sense will remain. The author of the cited book depicts even a wider perspective of genetic engineering in the area of procreation by writing about the possibility of creating inter-species hybrids, including hybrids of a man and an animal. At that time, probably the last biologi-cal stand would fall that bans crossing the species, as well as the social and cultural stand that bans sexual relations with animals.

These new genetic engineering methods are yet followed by the dynamically developing inventiveness in the area of "ordinary" engin-eering. I mean the so-called ectogenesis, raising a human pregnancy in a synthetic womb. Work of this type continues and it can head in two directions:
– create a conventional device – a technical analog of a woman's womb, or
– breed its biological tissue replica with the use of knowledge about so-called mother cells.

In both cases motherhood would be reduced to the donating of egg cells and a human embryo would develop outside a woman's body. To feminists such as Firestone, who considered pregnancy and delivery to be an oppression of women, this indisputably would be a convenient and a simple solution. But then would such a technologization of hu-man procreation not make its profound and humanistic sense void?

3.4. Spiritual Dimension of Motherhood

The biological and medical dimensions of reproduction incorpor-ate quite a heavy load of tradition: the majority of people want to have a child that will be genetically their own. We cannot see that humankind, also in the genetic sense, forms a large family of individuals that are related more than we have thought. Also, we cannot see, or we appreciate too little, the spiritual dimension of parenthood. Man, as an entity capable of transcending and living in communities that make up cultures, develops close ties not only with biological parents and children. Quasi-parental relationships also occur between adults and adopted children or children under temporary guardianship and also, for instance, between teachers and students. These relationships, despite the fact that they lack "blood ties", further the spiritual dimension of motherhood and/or fatherhood associated with developing the personality of a young person and providing that person with the cultural heritage.

Committed teacherhood is an example of an intellectual and emotional relationship that from the times of Plato was called the "fertilization of beautiful souls". This kind of relationship existed not only for Socrates and Plato or Plato and Aristotle, but also Saphona and a few of her students or Hypatia and selected students. Similar relationships based on the acquisition of artistic skills also existed in painting, sculpting and other schools. Analogous emotional engagement could also be seen between Jesus Christ and His disciples; a few of them were called "beloved disciples", which is referred to in the Gospels.

The tradition of cultivating the spiritual and educating aspect of parenthood has lasted to this time, but not only in the professions associated with science and art. It appears in every place, where a teaching person shows commitment and passion and a learning person smartness and diligence. This happens between older women and girls in learning certain types of profession. The "spiritual mother" can be a woman teacher during singing, dancing or playing classes, a woman coach in sports, the matron of nurses, the boss during tailoring, hairdressing or cooking apprenticeship. The "Master" not only introduces the technical arcana of profession, but also teaches professional ethics and pays much attention to the practical and the social contexts of the existence of a young person in a professional group. Similar relations are established, of course, between adult men and their students. The fact that relationship between the tutor and schoolchildren can be truly strong and lasting to the end is described by Janusz Korczak, who stayed with children from a Jewish orphanage until they died in death chambers in Oświęcim (Auschwitz).

Therefore, man, as a transcending entity, was provided with extra-biological means to fulfill parental functions. Only few of them are mentioned here; however, in various types of motherhood or fatherhood the biological parenthood does not have to necessarily be conducive in the spiritual sense.

3.5. Conflict of Individual and Global Dimensions of Motherhood

The qualities of motherhood being highlighted in the first part of this text, such as timeless and universal values, status of the *sacrum* for humanity, sense generating aspect, a gift of life given with love, all these features and circumstances seem to fall into oblivion today. Still, wealthy societies of the West, preoccupied with the pursuit of success, seem to be satisfied with themselves. The notion of the "quality of life" being coined in the circles of utilitarian ethics makes a smashing career. But then its interpretation is definitely too narrow. It is defined, on the one hand, as good health and physical fitness and, on the other hand, as access to consumer goods. The pattern of life is determined by advertisements and trends promoted by popular color magazines. Thus, we have a pattern of "life from a supermarket". It is dominated by a professional career, cozy house, fashionable sports and nice and easy exchange of things, and exchange of life partners. A responsible thoughtful motherhood and fatherhood fall within these patterns somehow with difficulty.

It seems indeed that humanity has forgotten about Being as the being of its own species. In lieu of a great common idea that would unite it, humankind wastes its efforts in mundane hustle and bustle. Children are considered and talked about in the context of the "quality of life" of a given married couple. Accounts of financial costs of leading a child to maturity are kept, different strategies of motherhood are promoted (child to be born after studies, then career or conversely or otherwise late motherhood). No one is going to say that childbirth may follow from the strong feelings for another person and/or gratitude for the gift of one's own life given to next generations.

Contemporary generations have forgotten about the gift; it is too much associated with sacrifice or sacrificial blood, and maternity is the gift of flesh and blood. The world, in turn, belongs to enterprising and strong people who can only exchange gifts prescribed by conventions, but not make a gift of half of their lives. Maternity requires sacrifice, hardship of hearts, minds and hands. And the power of mothers, how illusory it is: it happens to be a sign of mental frustration and rarely the manifestation of a real power changing the world.

The situation of mothers and children is not the best in the present-day world focused on "today and now". Overworked women find it hard to further the spiritual message of motherhood in the world dominated by the consumer-oriented culture. Still, it seems that this lacking reflection on the human procreation is conducive to the emerging of a dissonance between the global and the individual dimensions of motherhood. We are excellent in our promises and special occasion activities: we care about offspring, we raise funds for starving children, once a year the Polish people become generous and offer donations to the Great Orchestra of Christmas Charity. *Pro Life* organizations operating worldwide in favor of unborn children seem not to remember those already born. Also, color magazines would rather talk about happy motherhood of famous and well-to-do women than about the individual, lone mothers that have just lost their jobs or helpless parents of a handicapped child. Poverty and suffering are photogenic so little… and they sell badly…

4. Summarizing Notes

Contemporary times offer us an ambivalent treatment of motherhood. On the one hand, it has become the subject of a conscious choice among women and married couples. Generally, women prepare for their new role and experience their motherhood with awareness and commitment. More than ever children have a chance for a happy childhood. On the other hand, the political transformations in the countries of the Central and Eastern Europe sometimes become the source of serious social pathologies that affect impoverished families, minor mothers and children deprived of due care. For this reason, the problem of motherhood and concern about the future generations should become a focus for political decision makers. This also entails the question of economic decisions, namely what funds from the present state budget should be invested in a good future for those generations which will come after us and that we will not meet personally.[14]

The economic account should cover the axiological "account". Our life experience shows that our strongest feelings are evoked by what we have put most effort into – effort of our mind, body, heart, and hardship and tears. There is no true motherly love without this sort of "investment", since it is the foundation for daily life of families and for the valuable and important archetype of mother and her love that is universal throughout human culture. What would humankind be, when deprived of its Great Mother as the archetype of motherly love? What surrogate would replace her love to millions of children who do not feel special and loved only for the sake they are here? Motherly love is a great wealth, a great treasure of humanity and the best investment in the future.

Translated by Magdalena Janas

---

[14] Cf. Dieter Birnbacher, *Odpowiedzialność za przyszłe pokolenia* [Verantwortung für zukünftige Generationen], transl. by Bolesław Andrzejewski, Przemysław Jackowski, Warszawa: Oficyna Naukowa, 1999.

Elżbieta Pakszys
Poznań

Value-Neutrality or Gender Bias in Research on Human Relationships Globalization

Today women's movement is far from being unanimous in its general attitude towards globalization, seeking quite often to revindicate itself rather than take its rightful place within the widespread anti-globalization movement.[1] Consequently, its institutional and intellectual agencies or representations, like gender/women's studies, are either (1) seeking a "recognition of the other" within feminist scholarship,[2] or (2) discussing "the Capabilities Approach", a humanitarian/humanist position addressed some years ago by Martha C. Nussbaum[3] to Feminist Liberalism. In both cases, directly or indirectly, these proposed discourses/projects raise the problems of women's human rights. However, it seems that only a combination of these two strategies/stances is likely to be effective when seeking possibly global solutions for the most striking effects/examples of multicultural patriarchy. Let us here take the opportunity to outline what this might mean.

---

[1] Catherine Eschle, "'Skeleton Women'. Feminism and the Antiglobalization Movement", *Signs*, vol. 30, no 3, 2005 (Spring), pp. 1741–1769.

[2] Bruce Baum, "Feminist Politics of Recognition", *Signs*, vol. 29, no 4, 2004 (Summer), pp. 1073 –1102; *Międzykulturowe i interdyscyplinarne badania feministyczne. Daleki – Bliski Wschód: współczesność i prehistoria* [Cross-cultural and Interdisciplinary Feminist Research. Far to Near East: Contemporary and Prehistory], ed. by Elżbieta Pakszys, Poznań: Wydawnictwo Naukowe UAM, 2005.

[3] Martha C. Nussbaum, *Women and Human Development. The Capabilities Approach*, Cambridge: Cambridge University Press, 2000/2001.

Reflecting then rather on the potentially positive aspects of global-ization, e.g. unification, we shall take a look at the chances for cross-cultural/-national influences on the particular patriarchal codes that have hitherto been recognized as discriminating against women in different parts of the world.

This perspective/objective aims at the possible empowerment of women through the replacement of such codes with the adoption of those norms and values worked out in Western cultures, which can not only serve as patterns/models of acquired gender equality, but have proved their applicability for the rest of the world.

In spite the often justified skepticism concerning the real power of any legal regulations aimed actually or potentially at global institu-tions and their social policies,[4] the recognition and implementation of women's human rights seems to be the most promising tendency in this direction regarding its scope/dimension for the time being. Over half century has passed since the announcement of the Universal Declaration of Human Rights in 1948, which[5] should be considered as a warrant for further action in this direction assuming, however, its continued development through the implementation of the women's agenda,[6] which is quite new.

In order to approach these general/global goals, i.e. the improve-ment of women's position in societies through the projects/agendas indicated above (1–2), one of the main criteria of modern scholarship as well as within social policy; i.e. value-neutrality: impartiality or "objectivity"; should undergo serious reconsideration. In many in-stances it should be suspended and/or replaced/exchanged by a so called gender mainstreaming attitude, focusing clearly on women's and other minorities' oppression. As for social policy – affirmative

---

[4] Magdalena Środa, "Rozmyślania roztropne. Równość, wolność, kobiecość" [Reasonable thinking. Equality, liberty, femininity], *Ośka*, 4, 1998, pp. 64–65.

[5] Mary A. Glendon, *A World Made New. Eleanor Roosevelt and the Universal Declara-tion of Human Rights*, New York: Random House, 2001.

[6] Shanhi Dairiam, "Wyzwania związane z promocją praw kobiet" [Challanges connected with the promotion of women's rights], *Ośka*, 4, 1998, pp. 45–48; Susana T. Fried, „Żądajcie praw człowieka kobiet! Od analizy do działania" [Demand Human Rights for Women! From analysis to action], *Ośka*, 4, 1998, pp. 43–48.

action or quotas/parity – appear to be the most valuable, though still controversial, instruments. For academe this postulate especially concerns those disciplines in the humanities within which and with help of which we can attempt to cope with the acknowledged most 'toxic' stereotypes of gender roles in order to possibly eradicate and replace them with humanitarian and egalitarian ones. This only seems possible when following both tracks, the results of women's/gender studies and NGO's recognition. In any event what is indispensable is knowledge of the "others", the exotic cultural codes responsible for supporting patriarchy and expressed in visible domination of men over women, [even in the less painful (civilized)[7] instances.]

However, the well known historical examples of women's stigmatization and oppression; like chastity belts (Europe in the Middle Ages), female foot binding (in China), or *sati* – widow burning (in India); which have been overcome through the ages prove that the most cruel customs can be condemned and finally eliminated.[8]

Hence, in order to follow the mainstream direction indicated, old and new instances of women's (children and adults) oppression which are recognized but not yet acknowledged in law have to be named and denounced as a violation of the specific human rights of women, and should forthwith be implemented on a really global scale.[9]

---

[7] Elżbieta Pakszys, „Platforma działania – Pekin 1995: główne cele światowego ruchu kobiecego w perspektywie polskiej" [The Platform for Action – Beijing 1995: the main aims of the world women's movement in the Polish perspective], in: *Humanistyka i Płeć III. Publiczna przestrzeń kobiet. Obrazy dawne i nowe* [The Humanities and Sex/Gender III. Women's public space: pictures old and new], ed. by Elżbieta Pakszys, Włodzimierz Heller, Poznań: Wydawnictwo Naukowe UAM, 1999, pp. 259–274.

[8] Certainly we could discuss here contextual or side images, like connecting this process with post-colonialism or interpreting it as complex result of actual intra/transcultural and economical exchange or perhaps even the domination of the Western cultures umbrella.

[9] Charlotte Bunch, „Prawa w ujęciu feministycznym" [Transforming Human Rights from a Feminist Perspective], *Ośka*, 4, 1998, pp. 40–42; *Human rights are women's rights*, Warszawa: Amnesty International Publ., 1995. Here should be mentioned possibibile debate with the text by Christoph Menke (in this volume) on the relationship between "human dignity and human rights", especially those versions including gender as a factor of difference especially in a multicultural context. Since neither the

Among the best known and relatively mild instances of women discrimination today are 'clothing and dress restrictions', like the Muslim chador/veil, with the headscarf/*foulard*/*Kopftuch* affairs coming recently into general conflict with educational and legal systems (in France, Germany and Netherlands). In the light of the various ways of solving this problem it is possible to treat them as possibilities helpful in testing international communities resistance and tolerance towards the 'other'.[10]

These examples of free or forced (?) 'Muslim women coming back to tradition' should also be considered with regard to their own female recognition of the possibilities to act within highly patriarchal and fundamentalist societies.

More difficult to interpret, though especially vital, are the various examples of direct (as well as indirect) pressures in violation of the reproductive rights concerning women. Among them is the 'lack or limited choice in entering the marital state by women'; including premature marriages, polygyny and polygamy which are mostly sanctioned by Koranic law, but in the light of recent research[11] reflecting mainly the growing economic prosperity of men leading their tribes[12]. The so called 'crimes of honour' that aim to extort the bride's dowry, now recognized following many BBC TV documentaries, is

---

Stoics, nor Puffendorf and Kant can help us in the matter of women's dignity and women's human rights, the discourse will certainly not be an easy one.

[10] *Tolerancja i wielokulturowość – wyzwania XXI wieku* [Tolerance and Multiculturalism – the challenges of 21th cent.], ed. by Agnieszka Borowiak, Piotr Szarota, Warszawa: Akademia, 2004; *Tolerancja i jej granice w relacjach międzykulturowych* [Tolerance and its limits in cross-cultural relationships], ed. by Aleksander Posern-Zieliński, Poznań: Wydawnictwo Poznańskie, 2004.

[11] Longina Jakubowska, „Paradoks nowoczesności: poliginia wśród zurbanizowanych Beduinów" [The paradox of modernity: polygyny among urban Bedouins], in: *Międzykulturowe i interdyscyplinarne badania feministyczne. Daleki – Bliski Wschód: współczesność i prehistoria* [Cross-cultural and Interdisciplinary Feminist Research. Far to Near East: Contemporary and Prehistory], ed. by Elżbieta Pakszys, op. cit., pp. 161–193; Katarzyna Kurzawa, „Urodzić się muzułmanką. Między religią a tradycją świecką" [Being born a Muslim woman: between religion and secular tradition], ibidem, pp. 195–227.

[12] From a Western point of view these customs mainly reflect the serious limits concerning laws relating to an individual in many tribal societies/nations.

subject to legal penalties in India and Pakistan.[13] While 'stoning as a punishment for female adultery' (in Nigeria) has only recently achieved recognition/fame through successful Internet interventions, hence global!, on behalf of the victims.[14]

Both examples above confirm that the media (and new technologies) can engage in energetic interventions, and with the weight of international public opinion have proved to be very effective. The problem is, however, that these cases are also very effectively hidden and are never usually seen outside of the local government's jurisdiction.

The least examined remain those abuses belonging generally to the section of indirect women's reproductive rights. Among them is the 'lack and/or violation of human bodily integrity' through so called 'ritual female (also male) circumcision', which appears to be in fact the mutilation/maiming of women's genitals (FGM), hidden behind Islamic as well as several other cultural/secular rites.[15] While another direct one, euphemistically called 'selective abortion', i.e. female foetus elimination after prenatal (USG) examination, is nowadays performed on such a scale that it has created a serious imbalance in the sex ratio, a factor being crucial in the demography of the most overpopulated countries (China, India). Over recent decades this 'gendercide' is estimated to have cost the lives of nearly 100 million women.[16]

---

[13] Monika Browarczyk, „Wybrane aspekty sytuacji kobiet w Indiach współczesnych" [Selected aspects of the situation of women in contemporary India], in: *Międzykulturowe i interdyscyplinarne badania feministyczne. Daleki – Bliski Wschód: współczesność i prehistoria* [Cross-cultural and Interdisciplinary Feminist Research. Far to Near East: Contemporary and Prehistory], ed. by Elżbieta Pakszys, op. cit., pp. 63–98.

[14] Safiya Hussaini Tungur Tudu, Raffaele Masto, *Safiya. Żyję dzięki wam* [Io, Safiya], Warszawa: Świat Książki, 2005. The case of Safiya Hussaini Tungur Tudu some years ago, condemned to death by stoning and rescued of the Internet action.

[15] Rebecca J. Cook, Mahmoud M. Fathalla, „Prawa reprodukcyjne: poza Kairem i Pekinem" [Reproductive rights: beyond Cairo and Beijing], *Ośka*, 4, 1998, pp. 49–53; Waris Dirie, Corinne Milborn, *Przełamać tabu* [Schmerzenskinder], Warszawa: Świat Książki, 2005; Katarzyna Kurzawa, „Urodzić się muzułmanką. Między religią a tradycją świecką" [Being born a Muslim woman: between religion and secular tradition], op. cit.

[16] Nicolas D. Kristof, "Stark data on Women: 100 Million are Missing", *Population and Development Review*, 11.09.1991; Maria Kruczkowska, „Świat bez kobiet" [World without women], *Gazeta Wyborcza. Wysokie obcasy*, 27, 325, 09.07.2005, pp. 30–33.

We may again ask: why should the neutrality/relativity idiom undergo reconsideration, hence not be obeyed, or suspended in contemporary and future anthropological research as well as in humanitarian action? [which may give rise to resistance among not only Polish cultural anthropologists[17]]. The answer seems to be clear though not simple; to make our world more human, for both genders in fact.

This hope rests on an extension of the human rights policy standards over a globalizing world. And these demands express women's (NGO) and feminist communities (W/G Studies) in their appeals for mainstreaming or genderization, i.e. the implementation and execution of direct and indirect reproductive women's human rights into the executive documents of all globally operating organizations and institutions.

"You may say that I'm a dreamer, but I'm not the only one..."

---

[17] Ryszard Vorbrich, *Tolerancja racjonalna czy subiektywna? Europa wobec okaleczania narządów płciowych* [Tolerance rational or subjective? Europe towards the mutilation of genitals], in: *Tolerancja i jej granice w relacjach międzykulturowych* [Tolerance and its limits in cross-cultural relationships], ed. by Aleksander Posern-Zieliński, Poznań: Wydawnictwo Poznańskie, 2004, pp. 155–176.

Sven Sellmer
Poznań

Neo-Hinduism
as a Response to Globalization[1]

When discussing the philosophical problems connected with the notion of universal values and the process of globalization one should never lose sight of the concrete cultural conditions in which these problems pose themselves – conditions that often differ quite markedly from the situation in Europe. Therefore I will now pick out one particular non-European case and sketch the approach some Indian thinkers have taken to tackle the challenge they have been confronted with, ever since the Europeans – especially the British, of course – gained influence on the subcontinent.

Colonialism can be regarded as one of the early stages of globalization. The very fact that Europeans appeared on the scene put a hard stress on the world views and value systems of many traditional societies. And the following conscious attempts to westernize the colonized societies have led, in most cases, to the disappearance or marginalization of the native cultures. Only in a few instances, where the non-Western cultures have been big and powerful enough, were they able to stand their ground and to react in a creative way to the European challenge. One of these examples is India.

The reactions of Indian thinkers to the ideas brought to their country by the new British rulers were manifold. Here I have to confine myself to a rough outline of one, although very important current

---

[1] For technical reasons I have to employ a simplified transcription for Sanskrit terms.

of thought: the so-called Neo-Hinduism.[2] It must be noted that Neo-Hinduism is by no means a monolithic doctrine, and the difference to traditional Hinduism is not always very clear.[3] In this paper I will be thinking mainly of influential figures like Swami Vivekananda (i.e. Narendranātha Datta, 1863–1902) and Sarvepalli Radhakrishnan (1888–1975), all the time staying on a rather general level. Nevertheless, in spite of all the internal differences in Neo-Hinduism, one may safely say that the main aim of its exponents was both to preserve the heritage of Hinduism (as they understood it) and to adopt those of the Western ideas that seemed fruitful and important to them. But before I will take a closer look at some of the strategies employed in pursuing this goal, it is necessary to sketch in a few words the basic structure of traditional Hindu ethics.

The central notion of traditional Hindu ethics is denoted by the Sanskrit word *dharma*.[4] Because there is no word in English that would match its whole range of meanings – as is the case with most central concepts of foreign cultures – one cannot simply translate it.[5] To put it very roughly, *dharma* denotes firstly the whole of the duties regulating Hindu society (and this includes legal as well as moral and religious duties – according to Western terminology, because in the

---

[2] Probably the best introduction to Neo-Hinduism is chapter 13 of: Wilhelm Halbfass, *India and Europe*, Albany: SUNY Press. 1988. Indeed, this whole paper is highly indebted to Wilhelm Halbfass' groundbreaking work.

[3] In a certain sense, a purely traditional Hinduism may have become impossible, at least for intellectuals. As Creel puts it: "For philosophers to talk about *dharma* is thoroughly modern, and reflects the breakdown of traditional *dharma*" (Austin B. Creel, "*Dharma* as an ethical category relating to freedom and responsibility", *Philosophy East and West* 22, 1972, p. 162).

[4] It must be noted that the usages of *dharma* in Buddhist contexts, where the word also plays a very important role, are for the most part quite different and specific. But in this paper I am talking solely about Hinduism.

[5] It is significant that Kane begins his monumental work on Sanskrit dharma literature with the statement: "*Dharma* is one of those Sanskrit words that defy all attempts at an exact rendering in English or any other tongue" (Pandurang Vaman Kane, *History of Dharmaśāstra*, vol. 1, part 1, Poona ²1968, p. 1). Of the vast secondary literature on dharma, the reader's attention is once more drawn to W. Halbfass, *India and Europe*, op. cit., chapter 17: "*Dharma* in the Self-Understanding of Traditional Hinduism".

Indian tradition there is no such distinction). Therefore both "law"[6] and "religion" are common, albeit one-sided translations of *dharma*. Secondly, inside the one over-arching dharma there are also partial dharmas, as it were. Every social group has a special dharma. Even every individual has a particular *dharma* that is rigidly determined by gender, social position, membership of caste etc. The content of all those duties is, according to the traditional treatises on dharma, derived from four sources (in some texts only the first three are mentioned): (1) Revelation (i.e. the Vedic texts), (2) Tradition (particularly the specialized treatises on dharma called *dharmasūtras* and *dharmaśāstras*), (3) Good Custom (*sadācāra*, i.e. the way exemplary people live), and (4) self contentment (*ātmatushti*, a freer translation would be: "good conscience"). In practice, Tradition and Good Custom were the most important sources; self contentment comes into play only when all the other sources are quiet.

The concept of *dharma* is closely linked to the theory of *karman* according to which compliance with or violation of one's dharma leads to reward or punishment in future births. Furthermore, there is also a cosmic aspect to it, for sometimes dharma is seen as a kind of all-encompassing force that is lending structure and support to the universe. The priests, and especially the king,[7] must see to it that this structure is kept intact.

It is a point of special importance for our present task that, originally, this system of dharmic duties was exclusively restricted to Hindu society. Foreigners were without exception regarded as barbarians *(mleccha)*, who did not belong to this community and *could not even* become its members because this was a question of birth. (In practice, things were not always handled so strictly, but this is a different problem.) In a word, the traditional values of Hindu society

---

[6] The traditional Indian legal system is a complex structure in which dharma is only one of the main components, the other two being custom and royal ordinance, whose mutual relationship is quite different from the situation in Roman law; see Robert Lingat, *The Classical Law of India*, New Delhi: Thompson Press, 1993, esp. part II: "From Dharma to Law".

[7] Cf. Gavin D. Flood, *An Introduction to Hinduism*, Cambridge: Cambridge University Press, 1996, pp. 67–69.

were extremely ethnocentric, anti-global, so to speak. This is nothing exceptional: The value systems of most pre-modern societies are (or were) ethnocentric. But it means that the confrontation with the European cultural challenge was a double one: There was not only the fact that technically superior invaders gathered more and more political power; in addition, the new rulers, convinced that they were acting in the name of universal values, were actively propagating these values. (At least most of them, to be precise: There was also a number of so-called "Orientalists", who highly estimated the traditional culture of India.)

In the face of this situation the Indian thinkers basically had three possibilities:

1) to adopt the values of their British lords in a more or less wholesale fashion, in other words: to westernize themselves;
2) to ignore the challenge;
3) to accept the challenge and grapple with the new ideas on the basis of traditional Indian thought.

Let us have a short look at all of these possibilities in turn:

1. More or less conscious westernization is the prevalent strategy among the upper and middle class. That does not exclude the preservation of certain traditional values – which in quite a few cases may lead to problematically incongruous identities. But nevertheless, one can surely call a person westernized if her value system is for the most part Western. According to one vision of globalization, this is the way the future will look like: A largely unified Western style value system all over the world, with certain minor local variations and additions.

2. To ignore the European challenge seems to be almost impossible, at least for an intellectual. (I am not here concerned with the masses. They were and, to a certain extent, still are able to continue their traditional ways of life and thinking, as long as they do not transgress certain legal boundaries.) But that ignoring is indeed a real possibility is shown by the fact that Hindu thinkers – at least as far as we can judge from the literature – largely ignored Islam though, from the 13th century on, Muslim rulers had been the lords of most of Northern India.[8] Still, the impact of Western ideas proved to be even

---

[8] Cf. Wilhelm Halbfass, *India and Europe*, op. cit., p. 182.

stronger, so Indian scholars who are thoroughly traditional and totally uninfluenced by Western ways of thinking are nowadays hard to find.

3. Of the greatest interest for our topic is the third possibility: the attempt to preserve the most important elements of traditional Indian ethics by combining them with modern Western ideas. If such attempts proved to be successful and produced a stable and widely recognized value system, it would mean that the result of the process of value globalization would not be so simple as it is sometimes expected.

The traditional Indian social framework – with its most characteristic trait: the caste system – was not only, as already pointed out, ethnocentric and in this sense isolated, but also extremely static. Dharma was considered eternal and unchangeable.[9] Upward social motion could (at least in theory) only occur by way of rebirth, according to the rules of karmic retribution. In a way, this conception is exactly opposed to the ideology of progress, that many of the British 19th century colonialists were attached to, and to the zeal of spreading the Word, so characteristic for the accompanying missionaries.

Under these circumstances, it is clear that in order to enter into any form of dialogue or to put up active resistance the orthodox Indian self-centredness had to open up. This opening up took place, indeed, and its main symptoms are characteristic reinterpretations of the concept of *dharma*. Here, a twofold development took place that can be brought under the headings of (a) individualization and (b) universalization.

(a) Individualization

Dharma had always had an individual dimension in so far as every single person had to fulfil his dharmic duties that result from his being a member of such and such a caste, having a certain age etc.

---

[9] At least, this is true on the highest level. The actual application of dharma in the different world ages (*yugas*) is considered to differ in strictness. We live in the worst world age, the *kaliyuga*, therefore the requirements are fairly low.

But these duties did not have their origin, as it were, in the individual. Rather, the individual found himself in a social position that was *objectively* characterised by these duties.[10]

Neo-Hindus, on the other hand, tend to see a person's dharma in the context of his individual development. Each person has a very personal, his very "own" dharma (*svadharma*)[11] that he has to realize in order to progress on his way to better births and, eventually, to final liberation (*moksha*). Such an individualistic, or personalistic, view of dharma is quite different from the traditional perspective and reminds one of Western theories of self realization. To try to directly derive it from the source texts of Hinduism is, in my estimation, a hopeless endeavour. Nevertheless, various arguments can be brought forth to defend this modern understanding of dharma against the accusation that it is nothing but a *mis*understanding. Instead, one may see it as a new conception on the basis of several motives, already present in traditional texts. Firstly, in Indian philosophy there is a quite common terminological usage of *dharma* in the sense of "essential property".[12] To be sure, this usage has little or nothing to do with the usage of *dharma* in the sphere of morality and religion; still, it facilitates the move to take my personal duty as depending on my own essence. Secondly, according to the karman theory I am not "thrown" into the world by some inscrutable fate; rather, my present situation is the direct consequence of my deeds, not only in this, but – most importantly – in former lives. So my dharma is, in a certain sense, of my own making and is definitely very closely linked to my future development. Thirdly, the highest goal of Hinduism – liberation – has always been understood in a very individualistic way. Its relation to dharma is quite problematic and different attempts were

---

[10] Creel rightly underscores the absolutely determining role of birth: "Birth is the determinant of social status as of individual endowment, the two being fused" (Austin B. Creel, *"Dharma* as an ethical category relating to freedom and responsibility", op. cit., p. 157).

[11] This word does already appear in ancient texts (most prominently in *Bhagavadgītā* III 35), but with a much more objective sense.

[12] Cf. Wilhelm Halbfass, *India and Europe*, op. cit., p. 334 f. – One may compare the usage of *phúsis* in Greek philosophy.

made to harmonize them.[13] One of these attempts consists in understanding life in accordance with dharma as a kind of preparation to final liberation. And in this light, dharma may indeed be seen as part of an individual way to a most personal goal.

b) Universalization

In spite of the importance of "one's own dharma" (*svadharma*) for Neo-Hinduism, the conception of one "master dharma", so to speak, that encompasses all particular dharmas has never been lost. Quite on the contrary, its scope has been vastly extended. While for traditional Hinduism it was restricted to Hindu society and, therefore, geographically to the Indian subcontinent, many Neo-Hindus regard Dharma as a universal Rule and Law that applies to all human beings in the world.[14] Radhakrishnan even used the expression "dharma of humanity".[15]

This is a radical move with far-reaching consequences that proves the thinkers of Neo-Hinduism to be forerunners of a kind of spiritual globalization. To use an old communist slogan (ascribed to Walter Ulbricht), they managed to overtake their positivist and Christian challengers without catching up with them. This was possible because they made use of a fighting means that is omnipresent in Indian history of thought: inclusivism. This expression, coined by Paul Hacker, denotes a certain strategy in intellectual struggles between seemingly opposed convictions: One side claims that the position of the other side is already included in its own position which is, however, superior, because more comprehensive.[16] In the present case this gives the following picture with regard to the areas of religion and ethics:

---

[13] See Daniel H.H. Ingalls, "*Dharma* and *Moksa*", *Philosophy East and West* 7, 1957, pp. 41–48; J.A.B. van Buitenen, "*Dharma* and *Moksa*", *Philosophy East and West* 7, 1957, pp. 33–40; and, especially, Gerald James Larson, "The *trimūrti* of *dharma* in Indian thought: Paradox or contradiction?", *Philosophy East and West* 22, 1972, pp. 145–153.

[14] The pioneering figure in this regard was Bankim Chandra Chatterji (cf. Wilhelm Halbfass, *India and Europe*, op. cit., pp. 335–337).

[15] Quoted ibidem, p. 338.

[16] For a discussion of this conception see *Inklusivismus. Eine indische Denkform*, ed. by Gerhard Oberhammer, Wien: De Nobili Research Library, 1983.

In the view of the Neo-Hindus, Hinduism (or the Eternal Dharma, *Sanātanadharma*, as they often call it) is no religion on an equal footing with Christianity, Islam etc., but a kind of meta-religion that encompasses and transcends all others.[17] This claim is often under-pinned by the metaphysical position of the most influential sub-school of Vedānta philosophy: the school of unqualified monism (*advaita*), which assumes the ultimate identity of God (philosophically speaking, the universal principle, *brahman*) and each individual self (*ātman*).[18] Moreover, it is a typical strategy of Neo-Hindus to "prove" their monistic metaphysics by alleged meditation experiences. These strategies are, in my estimation, highly problematic, but this is not the place to discuss them.[19]

Similarly, in ethics it is believed that the principle of non-violence (*ahimsā*) implicitly contains all other, more specific ethical principles and is itself directly grounded in monism. Basically, the argumentation runs as follows: If – in accordance with the main assumption of monism – all is one, then you are, in a way, me (and vice versa); and if I really understand this, it would be absurd for me to do you any wrong, because nobody wants to hurt himself. At first, this argumentation might seem convincing, but two things should be noted. Firstly, the principle of non-violence undoubtedly plays an important role in traditional Hindu ethics but, from a historical point of view, its connection to monism seems to be secondary.[20] Secondly,

---

[17] To illustrate this point, here are a few quotations culled from an interesting, though widely forgotten Neo-Hindu publication with the telling title: *The World's Eternal Religion* (publ. by The Publication Department of The Sri Bharat Dharma Mahamandal, Benares 1920). "But the Indian Dharma ... is a universal spiritual system, recognizing the goal of humanity's true life, and explaining and guiding its course to that goal" (p. 2 f.). "The Hindu Dharma is Nature's inexorable Universal Law" (p. 11). "But the Sanâtana Dharma of India is not marked by any such spirit of narrowness or exclusiveness. It is not a particular 'creed' promising Salvation to its followers alone, it is the Universal Dharma for all mankind for all times" (p. 13).

[18] There are several organisations in the following of Vivekananda that operate under the title of Vedanta Society in different countries.

[19] For a critical assessment of the role of the "Concept of Experience in the Encounter Between India and the West" cf. Wilhelm Halbfass, *India and Europe*, op. cit., chapter 21.

[20] For a critique of Vivekananda's "Practical Vedānta" cf. Wilhelm Halbfass, "Practical Vedānta", in: *Representing Hinduism*, ed. by Vasudha Dalmia and H. von Stietencron, New Delhi etc 1995, pp. 211–223.

the very step from the objective proposition "All is one" to the subjective one "I am you" is far from obvious and contains many problems.[21]

All of these convictions are often found combined with an almost missionary zeal because among the Neo-Hindus, Western civilization is generally considered materialistic and fatally lacking of a spiritual dimension, so that it bitterly needs the insights of the holy sages of India. (At least the first part of this diagnosis probably is shared by many Westerners, too.)

So we see how a closed and ethnocentric ideology has been turned by a group of thinkers into an emphatically universal religious and ethical world-view (according to itself: the most universal world view possible). Their aim in doing so was twofold: They wanted both to learn from the West and to preserve what was valuable in their own tradition. Did they succeed?

To the second part of the question – Did they manage to preserve the core of their tradition? – it is impossible to give an objective answer. It depends on the members of a given tradition if they accept changes and additions as enrichments, or if they reject them because they feel they would lead to a loss of identity. Among the followers of Hinduism Neo-Hindu ideas have been quite successful, to be sure – which may be, to a large extent, just due to their Western flavour. But there are also many conservative Hindus for whom the ideas of thinkers like Vivekananda are so "Western" that they consider them to be a betrayal.[22] The discussion is going on, and in the end only the Hindus themselves will have to decide about the identity of Hinduism.

The answer to the first part is easier: Neo-Hinduism certainly took over a great many ideas from European philosophies that were en

---

[21] The distinction between objective and subjective propositions is taken over from Hermann Schmitz; see e.g. Hermann Schmitz, *Der Spielraum der Gegenwart*, Bonn: Bouvier, 1999, pp. 37–42 and 75–84. For an application of Schmitz' notion of subjectivity to Indian philosophical traditions, see Sven Sellmer, *Formen der Subjektivität*, Freiburg/München: Alber, 2005.

[22] The influential ideology of "Hinduness" (*hindutva*), while undoubtedly heavily influenced by Neo-Hinduism, seems to take quite different positions in certain respects. Most importantly, it is extremely "Indocentric"; cf. C. Ram-Prasad, "Hindutva ideology: extracting the fundamentals", *Contemporary South Asia* 2, 1993, pp. 285–309.

vogue around the middle of the 19th century, especially from positivism and utilitarianism. But the inclusivistic way in which they are used often leads to substantial changes in meaning and makes a rational discussion difficult.

My aim in this paper has been to sketch an Indian perspective on globalization. If this perspective, and other non-European ones, will stay different or lose their originality completely and end up as minor additions to the main stream, remains to be seen. A prognosis is difficult because the future of values in a globalizing world does not depend on the strength of rational arguments alone but also on the mighty influence of – both Western and non-Western – cultural traditions and religious beliefs.

Anna Seweryn
Łódź

Consumer Choice:
Petit Bourgeois Tautology
and Bourgeois Individualism
in the Age of Globalization

1. Introduction

In the humanities and the social sciences the issue of globalization has dominated contemporary academic debates dedicated to the condition of modernity. From an anthropological perspective, the heart of these disputes can be described in terms of: intercultural dialogue, a widespread relativism undermining an authority of inherited systems of values and norms, a progressive erosion of traditional forms of common coexistence, and the pervasive influence of western popular culture that is repeatedly accused of causing standardization, only to mention the most crucial.

In this paper an attempt will be made to consider the question of choice which is frequently raised in the context of individual autonomy as well as the rationality of the decision-making process or human action in general. Hence, we will be forced to exceed the limits of classic anthropological topics in order to discuss puzzling issues commonly raised by philosophers, sociologists or economists. However, certain general remarks aimed at outlining the background of our core analysis must come first. The same holds true for the tentative explanation of terms which will be used in the course of a more detailed inquiry namely: globalization, consumerism, petit bourgeois tautology and bourgeois individualism. In addition, it seems crucial to specify the approach we will adopt the essence of which is embodied in the expression "thick description".

2. Globalization

When the question of the contemporary meaning of "choice" is considered, reference to the issue of globalization seems inevitable. Despite long-standing feuds over formal and definitional issues, most authors unanimously agree that the fact that we witness and are involved in the socio-cultural process under study is a serious obstacle to a detailed and profound analysis of the problem of globalization. Under these circumstances we cannot keep the safe distance characteristic of an objective and neutral observer for which we are indebted to scientism. On the other hand, however, methodological assumptions of the postmodernist paradigm are rightly accused of a lack of cohesion, careless eclecticism and subjectivity, a rejection of scrupulous academic investigation into social phenomena in favor of experimental textualization.[1] Let us now, then, specify the approach to be employed further.

It should be emphasized that, the principal aim of this inquiry can be defined as a systematic attempt to give a so-called "thick description" of particular communication produced by the media.[2] We will, therefore, focus on a specific case (adopting the crucial expressions: petit bourgeois tautology and bourgeois individualism) in order to undertake a systematic examination of a particular aspect of the phenomenon to which the label "consumer choice" will be applied below.

In consequence a revolutionary and all-embracing theory of modernity will not be developed here. Instead every effort will be made to provide a deep insight into a single yet significant issue. We wish

---

[1] The reason we highlight these issues is that they remain in the background of widespread discussions centred on the problem of globalization as well as the challenges of modernity, owing to the fact that they strongly influence this debate provoking acrimonious controversies around methodological and epistemological issues.

[2] Cf. Clifford Geertz, *The Interpretation of Cultures*, New York: Basic Books, 1973.

to consider the particular dimension of the process of globalization, namely, the Western European and North American model of consumerism disseminated on a global scale thanks to the means of mass communication.[3] Within the model a cardinal role is played by the realm of international mass media that creates a specific symbolic, semantic and communicative sphere. This unique sphere becomes an ultimate contemporary source of accepted behavior patterns in nearly every possible domain from fashion to mores and religion. More to the point, within the described realm elements of various and remote cultural environments coincide and fuse. This "global flea market" is the arena where form and content, sign and meaning, artifact and mechanism generating it, which determines its significance in a specific cultural whole, all exist separately.

Let a single but spectacular example suffice to illustrate the thought expressed above. The inglorious failure to export a precious invention of the West namely, liberal democracy, is a good case in point. The fundamental issue here is that democratic institutions and procedures are transferred without the set of values which supports them within the western tradition. Therefore, this project can be compared to the replanting of a crop without its roots. Thus, speaking of democracy in general (either in New York, Cairo and Beijing) is completely unjustified if we consider the divergent traditions and systems of values in distant parts of the globe.[4] Both "our" and "their" world has been "crayoned" (to use the term invented by Roland Barthes), trivialized and reduced to the level of folk souvenirs – nothing more than the sum of captivating articles of trade: i.e. regional delicacies,

---

[3] From the perspective of this essay the issue of "McDonaldization" in itself is irrelevant. For further details on this subject reader may refer to: George Ritzer, *Makdonaldyzacja społeczeństwa* [The McDonaldization of Society], Warszawa: Wydawnictwo Literackie Muza, 2003. Cf. Tomasz Szlendak, Krzysztof Pietrowicz, "Konsumpcja i stratyfikacja w kapitalizmie bez kapitału" [Consumption and Stratification in Capitalism without Capital], in: *Na pokaz. O konsumeryzmie w kapitalizmie bez kapitału* [On Display: On Consumerism in Capitalism without Capital], ed. by Tomasz Szlendak, Krzysztof Pietrowicz, Toruń: Wydawnictwo UMK, 2004, pp. 7–28.

[4] Cf. Edmund Wnuk-Lipiński, *Świat międzyepoki – globalizacja, demokracja, państwo narodowe* [The World of Interage: Globalization, Democracy, National State], Kraków: Wydawnictwo Znak, 2004, pp. 10–11.

ethnic music, water pipes, and meditation practiced merely as a stylish form of relaxation.[5]

These remarks describe the situation at the level of a "clash of civilizations" that will not be our main concern here. However, this is worth mentioning because in the age of globalization nations, local communities and ethnic minorities face difficult choices that exert a strong influence on their cultural identity as well as international policy.

The mass media realm is a "natural environment" within which the rules of consumerism operate. These rules themselves will be the main context of our further argumentation. Let us then discuss this problem carefully.

3. Consumerism

The vast majority of authors put a negative slant on the word "consumerism", presenting it as a splendid triumph of economic standards and the "mentality of a salesman" responsible for a widespread decline in true values.[6] Yet, consumerism is not merely a western model of acquisition, aggregation and acceptance of the generous offer of the world market whose destiny is to penetrate, hand in hand with the World Wide Web, every nook and cranny on the face of the Earth including desert islands and virgin forests. More to the point, what consumerism is not is a contemporary version of an ancient dilemma: "to be or to have?" The same holds true for the maxim: "I consume. Therefore I am". Keeping these remarks in mind we may now emphasize that for the purposes of this paper consumerism will be taken to mean the idea embodied in the formula: **"buying is an appropriate mode of acquisition not only within the material**

---

[5] Cf. Roland Barthes, *Mitologie* [Mythologies], Warszawa: Wydawnictwo KR, 2000, p. 25.

[6] Cf. Radosław Kossakowski, "Spacerowicz i pucybut, czyli słów kilka o polskim społeczeństwie konsumpcyjnym" [A Shoeblack and A Stroller: Some Comments on the Polish Consumer Society], in: *Na pokaz. O konsumeryzmie w kapitalizmie bez kapitału* [On Display: On Consumerism in Capitalism without Capital], ed. by Tomasz Szlendak, Krzysztof Pietrowicz, op. cit., pp. 165–167.

sphere". In this connection it is vital to highlight the fact that from a perspective of an individual, consumerism is a realm within which certain conditions that determine self-identification[7] are in force. These very conditions will be further designated as "**consumer choice**" and interpreted using two main categories, namely: **petit bourgeois tautology** and **bourgeois individualism** (terms coined by Roland Barthes and Leszek Kołakowski respectively). In order to make this interpretation let us now focus on the analysis of the phenomenon of globalization in terms of significant transformations in the socio-cultural sphere described as a transition "from fate to choice".

4. Fate *versus* Choice

According to some authors we are nowadays obliged to live in a culture of excess and abundance causing general confusion and perplexity, whereas others stress that a successful study of modernity must be based on the concept of "the end of metanarratives" (to mention history, science, religion and, last but not least, tradition). These diagnoses when brought together express and illustrate the content of the phrase "transition from the society of fate to the society of choice". More relevantly, they support the notion that the golden age when a stable social order established unfailing standards of indisputable self-identification has long been gone. In the light of this and similar statements the pre-modern world exists as Garden of Eden where Adam, blessed with innocence, ignorance and a precise place in a definitive social hierarchy, can undoubtedly rely upon rigid mores as well as authoritative conventions and traditional norms and thus he is not prey to temptation to become an adherent of cultural relativism or cable TV, the Internet and a free market enthusiast. By contrast, an

---

[7] In further discussion the terms "self-identification" and "personal identity" will be used. For the purposes of this paper the former and the latter will be taken to mean an answer that an individual gives to the question: "Who are you?" (as it is understood in a *Twenty Statements Test*). This definition is sufficient from the perspective of our inquiry.

alternative tendency is for every aspect of contemporary human activity to be characterized in terms of individual choice: "(...) more and more choices determined merely by my own will, (...) choices without absolute or even significant sanctions".[8] Therefore, from one extreme, we go to the other: **each step** from the cradle to the grave is to be reckoned as a **consequence of autonomous choice**.

With respect to the comments let us express one additional remark. Some authors are convinced that if seen in the light of relations between choice, personal autonomy and human dignity within the western tradition, the phenomenon we now observe (i.e. expansion of the domain where decisions of independent individuals remain in force) should be regarded as highly desirable. Indeed, to take the argument a step further, it may seem that the transition "from fate to choice" is a manifestation of human emancipation. On balance, however, it ought to be highlighted that fate or a rigorous social order cannot be entirely blamed for the enslavement of an individual any more than a mobile phone may be enthusiastically praised as a "tool of liberation". Yet it should be admitted that significant changes have taken place in the way we perceive ourselves and our interactions with socio-cultural environment. These transformations are implicit in the contemporary notion of the term "choice" that in itself has evolved over time. In this connection it would be illuminating to analyse this issue diachronically. However, this inquiry into the widespread model of consumer choice will be limited to a synchronic interpretation based on ideas embodied in the two expressions coined by Roland Barthes and Leszek Kołakowski. For this reason, we will not focus on complex problems connected with personal autonomy and the dignity of man. Nevertheless, we hope to demonstrate below that if the categories of petit bourgeois tautology and bourgeois individualism are employed it will be possible to surpass the limitations of the interminable debates concentrating on the infantilization of cultures, or mass standardization and the common rejection of traditional values.

---

[8] Sławomir Magala, *Między giełdą a śmietnikiem. Eseje simmlowskie* [Between Stock Exchange and a Garbage Dump: Essays on Simmel], Gdańsk: słowo/obraz terytoria, 1999, p. 25.

5. Consumer Choice

At the very outset let us formulate the main thesis which we aim to advance in further argumentation. The model of consumer choice as defined above (in the context of a certain sense of consumerism) embodies the fundamental ideas expressed in phrases: **petit bourgeois tautology** and **bourgeois individualism.**

According to Roland Barthes the former refers to a particular mentality, the true essence of which lies in:

A. **the total negation of qualitative properties,** and

B. a definite reduction of diversity in the whole human domain to the sum of **quantitative properties.**[9]

The latter was illustrated earlier using the example of the "global flea market" where cultural values exist merely as articles of trade whereas the former will be a focus of our further investigation. Let us now refer to the second category in the light of which the contemporary model of consumer choice will be examined and subjected to rigorous criticism: i.e. bourgeois individualism. According to Leszek Kołakowski this is based on a specific false impression, let us quote: **"When I choose things I experience an illusion that I choose myself; and that holds true in a certain sense: I choose myself as a combination of commodities".**[10] As will be argued below these concepts characterize essential aspects of the model of consumer choice in the context of consumerism and the global realm of the mass media. This brings us to a consideration of one significant aspect of this peculiar marriage.

Firstly, it seems crucial to emphasize that the very notion, for which we are indebted to Leszek Kołakowski, reflects the fundamental principles of petit bourgeois tautology. With regard to this, the elimination of qualitative differentiations[11] should be understood as a determination of personal identity in terms of a final aggregate of

---

[9] Cf. Roland Barthes, *Mitologie* [Mythologies], op. cit., p. 117.

[10] Leszek Kołakowski, *Kultura i fetysze* [Toward a Marxist Humanism], Warszawa: PWN, 2000, p. 114.

[11] Let us stress that only if there is a qualitative difference between X and Y, are X and Y incomparable.

material goods purchased by an individual and at the same time it is the *sine qua non* of such a definition. In this connection it would be vital to analyse other prerequisites for this characterization of personal identity. As will be argued below only a particular conception of socio-cultural reality meets the requirements for such a representation of an individual. This conception describes a world delimited by excess as well as a disintegration of the established social order and other significant collective points of reference. Both the excess and the disintegration, as will be demonstrated below by way of an example, make the establishment of a certain pattern of self-identification based on the formula "choose yourself" possible. That brings us to a concrete instance of consumer choice influenced by the standards propagated in the realm of consumerism by means of mass communication.

Let us then give a "thick description" of the television advertisement for the Ericsson mobile phone. A very attractive and seductive looking female wearing a highly unusual green dress resembling grass is holding a photo of an Ericsson mobile. And there is also the slogan: "Choose yourself" with the comment: "Shouldn't your mobile be just like you?".[12] When we focus on these two slogans and present a plausible interpretation of their content, the solution to the main problems will present itself. Let us begin by depicting the general impression evoked by the advertisement, the heart of which is an illusion of exceptionality and uniqueness. As it can be seen due to the unusual female clothing, the center of our attention is an **extraordinary** mobile phone (let us notice: the attractive member of the weaker sex is to emphasize uniqueness of the product, not vice versa). The anonymous author of the advertisement seems to address the potential customer: "Doesn't it strike you that today there is plenty of everything including beautiful women and trendy mobiles? Look at the crowd of people in the street. Every single day you pass them without noticing. Do you really want to

---

[12] Cf. Aldona Jawłowska, *Wizerunek ciała w reklamie* [Image of the Body In Advertisement], in: *Homo eligens – społeczeństwo świadomego wyboru. Księga jubileuszowa ku czci Andrzeja Sicińskiego* [Homo Eligens – The Society of Conscious Choice: Essays in Honour of Andrzej Siciński], ed. by Dariusz Gawin, Warszawa: Wydawnictwo Instytutu Filozofii i Socjologii PAN, 1999, pp. 36–37.

share their sad fate and remain average and ordinary for the rest of your life? Oh no, you just can't let this happen!" In this context it seems necessary to acknowledge once again that these statements can be formulated only with respect to a certain conception of socio-cultural reality which must be described in the light of all the aspects of modernity that were considered before.

Passing on now to a systematic examination of the conception mentioned above let us highlight the relevance of the slogan "choose yourself". On brief reflection: such an expression would be absolutely nonsensical in reference to a social order within which indisputable and everlasting standards of self-identification are in force as in the case of "society of fate". This can be confirmed as follows: if determination of X's personal identity is based on a valid pattern of social affiliations or set of roles that X plays within both formal (e.g. university) and informal (e.g. family) interpersonal structures, then the appeal "choose yourself" would either:

1. require a transformation at one of the interactional levels mentioned (e.g. if X gets married then he/she can be defined as somebody's husband/wife, or to take another example, if X quits his/her job at the university and decides not to take any other then he/she can be described as, let us say, an unemployed philosophy professor); or

2. be impossible to make for the obvious reason that if X occupies a number of positions within the social hierarchy founded on a final authority of tradition, then holding these positions is simply not a question of individual choice.[13]

Turning now to the content of point one. Firstly, let us place a special emphasis on the lack of any interpersonal context in the advertisement here analyzed. Surely, in the light of the slogan used in this advertisement we may suspect that other people should notice that both I and my brand new Ericsson are unique but this is the only role, though important, they ought to play. Neither they, nor any interpersonal relations, are the base or at least a significant point of reference as far as the model of self-identification founded on the appeal

---

[13] This issue, however fascinating, will not be discussed in this paper as it demands a diachronic interpretation which will not be presented here.

"choose yourself" is concerned. It is, therefore, hard to escape the obvious conclusion: other people are treated instrumentally (i.e. merely as means to an ultimate end – they **are to be a background** that highlights my exceptionality). Moreover, they are described in a purely negative way (i.e. I am extraordinary and **they are not**). These comments will be developed further and now let us consider the statements expressed in point one using a different perspective.

A potential customer may be tempted to consider the Ericsson mobile to be advertised as a symbol of social rank or the material status of an individual. As widely acknowledged the former and the latter can be represented in material goods (esp. luxury goods, to mention for instance *The Theory of the Leisure Class*, by Thorstein Veblen), therefore, the notion is attractive. However, doubts arise when the evidence is carefully scrutinized. Let us begin by stating that:

a) The anonymous author of the advertisement does not imply that X ought to buy an Ericsson mobile in order to become a member of a certain prestigious or respectable group (if such was the case, the advertisement slogan would be, e.g.: "Shouldn't your mobile be as befits a prominent dentist?"); **and, moreover**

b) in itself, being in possession of particular material goods symbolizing a high social status, has never been sufficient for changing X's position in the social hierarchy. From the very nature of common coexistence it follows that a transition of this kind requires something more. In this context it suffices to point to one undisputed aspect: X's contribution and participation in a certain system of social interactions **and** his/her awareness of that fact, **and** the acceptance shown by others are the essence of X's social rank.[14]

This line of argument need not be pursued further as it may be easily deduced that an Ericsson mobile is not a symbol of self-identification the requirement of which is membership in a particular social whole

---

[14] Let us clearly exemplify these statements. I do not automatically become a doctor just because I have bought a stethoscope. Being in possession of that instrument confirms my identity as a doctor only if I am accepted to a specific group of people (i.e. doctors in general).

(e.g. a prestigious association). As mentioned before the model of personal identity we wish to consider can be properly interpreted only if we understand the true meaning of the appeal "choose yourself". Therefore, let us now move on to another connected aspect.

Although it may seem surprising, let us stress the heart of the slogan "choose yourself" **is not a choice of exceptionality**. In order to support this statement let us once again return to the example. In the light of the Ericsson advertisement slogan, a potential customer may be unable to escape the conclusion that the extraordinary mobile phone will manifest the uniqueness of its owner. However, serious doubts arise when this opinion is examined scrupulously. Firstly, it is undeniable that today those who **do not have** a mobile phone are the minority so it is they who should be considered exceptional. Moreover, it is indisputable that the target of the advertising campaign is by definition mass, and therefore, far more than one person is expected to buy Ericsson's product (the true intention of the company is to gain as many customers as possible and in a perfect situation persuade every potential buyer to acquire this mobile). Hence, X's uniqueness, as demonstrated by Ericsson's product, is nothing more than a nonsensical day-dream. This noteworthy observation will let us reveal the real essence of the model of consumer choice we analyzed above. The heart of this concept can be rightly characterized only in terms of petit bourgeois tautology and bourgeois individualism. To put it more directly, in a certain sense the qualitative difference between customer and commodity becomes invalid.

This may be defined as a three-stage process of reduction:
1. The determination of a potential customer's personal identity is devoid of positive references to interpersonal or social context

Firstly, it should be noticed that Ericsson's slogan is framed using the second person and singular and thus it is addressed to an individual and not a group of people. More importantly, a potential customer is not described in terms of particular interpersonal relationships which he/she builds and sustains as an irreplaceable[15] person,

---

[15] More detailed inquiry into this kind of relations can be found in the essay by Leszek Kołakowski quoted here.

or a set of roles played within various interactional systems. This stage is indispensable for the creation of the category "be yourself" (and therefore not be e.g. somebody's lover, husband, friend, mother, neighbor or simply pianist, doctor or teacher).

2. Disregard for the distinctive features or attributes of an individual

In the light of the illusion of exceptionality cherished by the advertisement this statement may seem contradictory as "uniqueness" is commonly understood to mean something that is by definition connected with the elements mentioned in point two. Nevertheless, it should be noticed that the category "be yourself" cannot be correctly defined as for example to "be a tall blonde with blue eyes who likes swimming, horse-riding and painting", because no such expression is used in the Ericsson advertisement. From this it can be concluded that the second stage of reduction is the creation of a situation in which the choice of **the same product** would equally manifest the uniqueness of e.g. an introvert **and** an extrovert, a football fan **and** a ballet lover, an honest brunette **and** a bald gambler. Thus, none of these characteristics may be constitutive of the structure of self-identification that is embodied in the category "be yourself". Moreover, the advertisement does not even refer to a customer's discrimination or taste and preference (let us note that the slogan does not say: "Choose this mobile because this is the product for a true connoisseur" or "Only this mobile integrates indisputable aesthetic qualities with functionality"). And so this phase of reduction paves the way for next stage.

3. "Choose yourself"

As a result of previous stages in the process of reduction the slogan "choose yourself" cannot be determined either in terms of any transformation at the level of interpersonal relationships or even in the context of individual features. As was argued the Ericsson advertisement presents a model of personal identity which is not based on social roles and positions or intimate relationships. Just as in the case of individual characteristics, a choice of the same product is to demonstrate that doctor, judge, widow, atheist, Buddhist, best friend and worst enemy of Mrs. Robinson – each and everyone has already "chosen him/herself". In this connection the slogan "choose yourself" cannot be taken to mean any possible modification within the system of social interaction or interpersonal relations (e.g. as a decision to change profession, confession or life partner). Let us stress this once more other people are treated like objects – merely as means not ends in themselves. They are to supply a background thanks to which my exceptionality (confirmed by my mobile) is emphasized. It is obvious that others will notice my uniqueness but that is not the most significant aspect (if such was the case the advertisement slogan would be e.g. "Let others see that your mobile is just like you"). As far as this model of self-identification is concerned all references to interpersonal context are irrelevant. Approval (or any other response) expressed by other social actors is not truly meaningful in this case. What actually is both vital and sufficient is my own awareness of the fact that I have "chosen myself".

We will now pass on to another probable interpretation of the slogan "choose yourself". Let us for the sake of discussion suppose that X defines him/herself as follows, e.g. "I am a hard-working woman" or "I am a brave and honest person". Using this perspective to depict a process of self-identification, we may reach a conclusion that the slogan "choose yourself" can be taken to mean X's decision to reduce, replace or improve traits that he/she has (for the sake of argument we presume this kind of transformation is possible by virtue of X's will and regular practice). In other words, if analogous characteristics were the most important in constituting the structure of personal identity, X could "choose him/herself" by "choosing" the attributes desired and in consequence one day his/her answer to the question: "Who are you?" would be, e.g. "I am a patient person". However, as we demonstrated above, in the context of the model of self-identification presented in the Ericsson advertisement no specific combination of individual features is relevant. Consequently, the appeal "choose yourself" as formulated in the advertisement cannot be defined as a request for the realization of some personal ideal because that is always connected with the improvement of certain individual qualities. Therefore, we must ask once again: what does the appeal "choose yourself" really mean? In the light of the whole discussion the absurdity of this slogan reveals itself. The advertisement does not offer any close or more detailed description of the customer. It is evident that the slogan is so formulated that every single customer is under the illusion that s/he belongs to the category of people who can respond to Ericsson's appeal. And that holds true because in the sense expressed in the slogan every X already is "him/herself" by virtue of the banal fact that no one except X him/herself is, was, will be or ever could be X **and** that X him/herself is not somebody else.[16] Accordingly, everyone is by definition unique, extraordinary and exceptional. However, as we demonstrated above uniqueness of a potential customer cannot be manifested by a mobile phone produced on a large scale for the very simple reason that more than one person will buy an Ericsson mobile (and as far as we all know no phone has the miraculous ability to adapt itself to an individual owner, e.g. change its shape or color automatically). But since every single X already "is him/herself" (because X firstly is someone simply on account of his/her existence – if s/he were no one s/he would not exist **and** secondly is no one else **and** thirdly no one else is X) what does the slogan "choose yourself" mean?

In the light of the whole previous discussion the answer is now obvious, it purely means "choose a mobile". However, in this context it is vital to consider the other slogan, namely "shouldn't your mobile be just like you?" It is widely acknowledged that any mobile phone cannot be reasonable, patient, sensitive or cheerful not to mention that it can never be a mother, friend, lover, fireman or pianist and thus, it is X who should be like his/her mobile. And yet this is in fact possible by virtue of the category "be yourself". In other words, X is to become similar to his/her mobile and this is possible only on the grounds of the elimination of qualitative difference between the uniqueness of a person and the uniqueness of a thing, as well as between an individual and a commodity. The profound meaning of this elimination should be comprehended as description of a self-identification which is devoid of any reference to interper-

---

[16] Let us stress: in the foregoing argumentation we consider the case of those who do not suffer from personality disorders or mental illnesses (e.g. schizophrenia).

sonal context. To put it more simply, X's personal identity is not determined in terms of social affiliations, intimate relationships or even his/her traits but it is defined as combination of commodities purchased. **The choice of material objects is constitutive of the self-identification of Ericsson's customers.** Moreover, X's "choice of him/herself" is determined only by his/her own will (by definition, no one but you can "choose yourself" or "be yourself" on your behalf) and it is nothing more than a choice of a thing. To formulate such a definition of the slogan "choose yourself" the first two stages in the process of reduction we analyzed above were necessary. By virtue of this reduction exactly, the qualitative difference between customer and commodity is erased because if a **full** description of X's self-identification and exceptionality can be given **merely** in terms of material objects X decides to buy then, yes indeed, by choosing a mobile X chooses a certain identity.

Let us mention one more aspect of consumer choice. It should be noticed that the Ericsson advertisement ignores all the aspects that are usually considered essential as far as mobile phones are concerned (e.g. functionality or advantageous price). According to the previous conclusions, uniqueness is a nonsensical illusion and the true attraction is the fact that for the price of a mobile a potential customer gets a particular self-identification (to choose a phone is to buy a phone). In addition it is worth mentioning that when X purchases Ericsson's product he/she also gains a fixed form of self-expression (i.e. his/her being in possession of a mobile expresses "being him/herself"). This brings us back to the definition of consumerism presented at the beginning of the paper. Let us repeat: the idea that "buying is an appropriate mode of acquisition not only within the material sphere" determines the context of the model of consumer choice. It is by virtue of this fact that an advertising campaign can be based on a deception that buying a mobile phone is beneficial for the personal identity and self-expression of a customer.

Finally, it is worth noting that our discussion is a prerequisite for a detailed examination of the models of self-identification and self-expression grounded in the conception designated "consumer choice".

6. Conclusions

In the context of the contemporary culture of excess and abundance the illusion of a uniqueness which can be purchased seems an appropriate marketing tool. In the context of "the end of metanarratives" (i.e. undeniable hierarchies, ultimate sanctions and categorical standards) the appeal "choose yourself" can be formulated and determined merely by the consumer's will. Finally, it is worth noting that the idea of petit bourgeois tautology and bourgeois individualism embodied in the slogan "choose yourself" is connected also in regard to other aspects of consumer choice (e.g. range of choice). These issues ought to be examined systematically as should further implications of the terms coined by Roland Barthes and Leszek Kołakowski (esp. in the context of personal autonomy, morality and existence within a community). In order to highlight these implications at the level of "clash of civilizations" the "global flea market" was mentioned. In this connection it would be illuminating to analyse the problem of choice of cultural identity. The above questions will be considered in some of my future papers.

Part IV
Science
and Globalization Processes

Marek Sikora
Wrocław

On the Role of Science
in the Global Society

Science is created by people.
This fact understandable in itself is easily forgotten.
W. Heisenberg, *Der Teil und das Ganze*

My considerations shall begin with the picture of modern science that Edmund Husserl presented in *The Crisis of European Sciences*. In opposition to this picture, though preserving certain similarities, I shall discuss the role of science in the global society, i.e. a society that consciously sets itself specific goals and strives to attain them. Science shall be reflected upon through the prism of laboratory sciences, for I believe that they determine the present-day notion of science to the greatest extent.

1.

Husserl asserts plainly that, for our vital needs and difficulties "science has nothing to say to us". From his area of interest, he excludes any questions concerning the "meaning or meaninglessness of the whole of this human existence". He offers no reflection on man, who is "free in regard to his capacities for rationally shaping himself and his surrounding world". From researchers, he demands that they

"carefully exclude all valuative positions". Scientific truth is "exclusively a matter of establishing what the world, the physical as well as
the spiritual world, is in fact".[1]

Furthermore – Husserl adds – this factuality remains markedly
limited due to the way of comprehending nature assumed by the
ideal of modern science. Galileo, who is generally recognized as an
originator of this ideal, claimed that nature should be treated as a
world external to the subject exploring it – a world that can be presented using the language of mathematics. The formulas of this language are supposed to make it possible to describe nature truthfully,
i.e. offer a truthful description of the external world itself. A result
of such a description is a thematically and methodically reduced
abstract representation of the world. Nevertheless, it is an "objective" representation, founded exclusively on exact and essential
judgements of the "pure mathematical sciences" that lead to knowledge equal to "the God in objective certainty".[2] A mathematical
scheme of nature accommodates all concretely experienced phenomena. As a consequence of mathematical idealization, they take
the form of mathematical models, i.e. "pure ideal limit-concepts".
Hence a new method of observing phenomena and a necessity to
reduce them, by means of direct or indirect mathematization, to
quantitative characteristics. As such, they are related to various
mathematical interpretations, thanks to which there emerges a possibility to demonstrate general relationships between them, i.e. an
opportunity to determine the "natural laws" of the world.

The world that is subjected to the reflection of natural sciences is
not – Husserl argues – the only world. Things that really exist may
not be identified with those arising due to the application of idealizing laws. A methodological error is made if results obtained from
idealizing assumptions are considered autonomous with regard to
these assumptions. Physicists and representatives of other so-called
positive sciences, heavily mathematically-oriented, often commit the

---

[1] Edmund Husserl, *The Crisis of European Sciences and Transcendental Phenomenology*, Evanston: Northwestern University Press, 1970, p. 6.

[2] Galileo Galilei, *Dialogue Concerning the Two Chief World Systems: Ptolemic and Copernican*, Berkeley: University of California Press, 1989, p. 104.

error nevertheless. They should rather assert that nature is subjectable to mathematization, not that it is a mathematical universe.[3]

Beside the world that is a product of objectivizing science, there is – Husserl emphasizes – "the actually intuited, actually experienced and experienceable world, in which practically our whole life takes place".[4] It is precisely the everyday life-world (*Lebenswelt*) that determines the foundation for natural attitudes of "real people". It is also a basis for the meaning of natural sciences, however a forgotten basis. The source of geometry of ideal objects was an ability to measure areas (totally free from the concept of ideal objects). However, following its constitutionalization, the main focus of geometry became "ideal limit-shapes". The moment these were recognized as the main objective of its pursuits, geometry departed from its initial objective. This marked a fundamental transformation from the "real *praxis*", encompassing real and realistically possible empirical entities, to the "ideal *praxis* of pure thinking", operating exclusively with ideal geometric shapes. Real being thus gave way to "mathematical existence". In effect, reality became expressed simply as a mathematical construct.

Meanwhile – Husserl writes – "in everyday sense-experience, the world is given in a subjectively relative way".[5] Even though there is always just one life-world, it appears to us in a variety of ways. Everyone perceives the same things and phenomena through their senses; however – at the same time – everyone does this from a different viewpoint, i.e. subjectively. Subjectivity does not mean freedom, but rather diversity, multiplicity of aspects. In a process of mutual communication, human subjects make themselves aware of what then becomes accepted as valid. A starting point for them is the world understood in relative terms, in which the identity of things or phenomena is merely an approximation and which lacks unambiguous strict classifications that are a domain of positive sciences striving for "objectivization".

---

[3] Aron Gurwitsch, "Husserlian Perspectives on Galilean Physics", in: *Phenomenology and the Theory of Science*, ed. by Lester Embree, Evanston: Northwestern University Press, 1974, p. 56.

[4] Edmund Husserl, *The Crisis of European Sciences and Transcendental Phenomenology*, op. cit., pp. 50–51.

[5] Ibidem, p. 23.

A criticism of the concept of these sciences embarked on by Husserl is aimed at demonstrating that it is merely a "residual concept", in which the everyday life-world has ceased to be a focus of attention. A crisis of science is related precisely to this very process. An orientation towards the *Lebenswelt* is supposed to bring science back to its meaning, i.e. reason, conceived of as a basis for "absolute", "eternal", "supertemporal", "unconditionally" valid ideas and ideals.[6]

2.

The analyses of the author of *The Crisis* regard science that is conceived of as a certain whole. It seems, however, that they should rather refer only to some disciplines that are accommodated within broadly understood science, i.e. those shaped by the "mathematical tradition". The tradition dominated modern science and established its **"classical"** model, whose major aim is to describe and explain reality with theories. Beside this model, however, it is also possible to distinguish yet another model – determined not by mathematical but experimental tradition.[7] Disciplines accommodated within this model are referred to as Baconian sciences, based on the name of their initiator. In these sciences, a basic structural unit is an experiment, not a theory. Experiments are conducted not in order to confirm something that is already known or to define a certain detail in order to extend an existing theory – as in the "classical" model of science – but to answer a question of how nature will behave in circumstances that have not been studied before. The aim of experiments is "**twisting the lion's tail**", i.e. force nature to reveal its properties in such conditions in which nature would never find itself without the forceful **intervention** of man: "he men who placed grain, fish, mice, and various chemicals seriatim in the artificial vacuum of a barometer or an air pump exhibit just this aspect of the new tradition".[8]

---

[6] Ibidem, p. 9.

[7] Thomas S. Kuhn, "Mathematical versus Experimental Traditions in the Development of Physical Science", in: idem, *The Essential Tension. Selected Studies in Scientific Tradition and Change*, Chicago: The University of Chicago Press, 1977, pp. 31–65.

[8] Ibidem, p. 44.

The "classical" model dominated the development of science – argues Ian Hacking – until roughly the first half of the 19th century. Until that time science studied natural phenomena, i.e. those found in pure nature. Science described and explained them as occurring in accordance with the objective laws of nature formulated as part of scientific theories. In contrast, modern science focuses mainly on the phenomena created by humans. It cannot be reduced exclusively to exploring and representing the world, for it is also – if not first and foremost – focused on acting, interfering in the world. Science is thus practice rather than knowledge.[9] Hacking, though excessively disregards the role of theory in scientific study, aptly expresses a pragmatic inclination of this type of study, under which description and intervention, knowledge and power, knowledge and modification become from the very outset, a means and an end.[10] This trend is particularly conspicuous in laboratory sciences that – using apparatuses of a specific type employed in isolation – interfere in the natural course of nature and not only discover new phenomena, but also generate them.[11] Spectacular examples of such phenomena are supplied mainly by biological laboratory sciences and theoretical physics. The current stage in the development of biology, the Human Genome Project, gives rise to assume that an object that is to be studied will be examined in such a way as to allow for its change, i.e. created according to previously adopted assumptions. Similar practice is frequently adopted in physical laboratories, where procedures assuming artificial states or objects are often employed, e.g. those resembling atoms, the so-called "quantum dots", and others. This dimension of knowledge is characteristic of the entire modern science, defining modern rational thinking.

---

[9] Ian Hacking, *Representing and Intervening. Introductory Topics in the Philosophy of Natural Science*, Cambridge: Cambridge University Press, 1983, p. 146.

[10] Paul Rabinow, "Artificiality and Enlightenment: from Sociobiology to Biosociality", in: *Incorporations*, ed. by Jonathan Crary and Sanford Kwinter, New York: Zone Books, 1992, p. 236.

[11] Ian Hacking, "The Self-Vindication of the Laboratory of Sciences", in: *Science as Practice and Culture*, ed. by Andrew Pickering, Chicago: The University of Chicago Press, 1992, p. 33.

Experiments conducted in laboratories consist mainly of stabilizing, purifying and generating phenomena. As Knorr-Cetina notes: "the laboratory is an enhanced environment which improves upon the natural order in relation to the social order".[12] The improvement means basically that laboratory studies assume the **malleability of natural objects**. They are not regarded as unchanging objects defined beforehand. They are very rarely used in their natural state and are often subjected to manipulation. They are combined taking into consideration only some of their properties. Knorr-Cetina sets the laboratory against the notion of **reconfiguration**, i.e. an establishment of a new "phenomenal field" in which a peculiar interaction between the natural order and social order occurs. As a consequence, a particular laboratory order emerges. The particularity of this order stems from the possibilities offered by the laboratory. It can *"transcendent mundanity"*, i.e. alter the properties of natural objects with respect to particular components of social life that draws its inspirations predominantly from the domain of the world experienced every day.

We have already indicated above that Husserl also pointed to a deep and inseparable rootedness of science in the life-world. The author of *The Crisis* ascribed to this world the role of a general basis of science, common for itself and everything else. He also recognized science as a new type of venture related to everyday life. However, the relation was not meant to be anything more than *"a relationship of ultimate dependence"*. Meanwhile, Knorr-Cetina argues that currently transformations of the natural and social order triggered by particular laboratory orders, i.e. those that have their source in daily life, are not ultimately – as in Husserl – open only to philosophical reflection. They do not link the eidetically perceivable universe of everyday world to some abstract concepts which are thought to lie at the core of science, but remain concrete and omnipresent within its working. They lie hidden under cover of technical jargon; they are entrenched in cognitive aspirations and situated in methodological procedure. Considered jointly, from the point of view of transformations they

---

[12] Karin Knorr-Cetina, "The Couch, the Cathedral, and the Laboratory: On the Relationship between Experiment and Laboratory in Science", in: *Science as Practice and Culture*, op. cit., p. 116.

provoke, they bring a significant contrast to the established orders, both natural and social, demonstrating their malleability.[13]

Laboratories, whose importance has been steadily growing since the successes of Louis Pasteur[14], are becoming a central element of the global society. Thanks to them, humanity as a whole is becoming increasingly aware of the fact that it can set itself certain goals and realize them.[15] In this sense, history will have exactly the shape that will be given to it by people themselves. However, the process of thus practiced history is only just beginning and the direction it will take is not – obviously – predetermined. The risk of various threats is high, though, pertaining both to the production of new types of weapons (nuclear, laser, chemical or biological), as well as accidental uncontrolled side-effects related to the implementation of new scientific and technical solutions for peaceful purposes.[16]

Irrespective of these threats, the development of laboratory sciences, particularly within the domain of biology, reveals the inevitability of relating results obtained in the course of study to the sphere of axiology. The results confront the researcher and, through him, the total human community with numerous ethical dilemmas. The thesis that there is no relationship between science and values, and that science as such bears no social responsibility, is another dogma that

---

[13] Ibidem, p. 136.

[14] The success of L. Pasteur was not predominantly the fact that he was able to discover the mechanism of attenuation of pathogenic microbes in the laboratory, but the fact that he chose as a subject of his research a question that was the most vital from the point of view of the early French society. He was able to translate social expectations into the language of laboratory research practice. The problem is discussed in detail by B. Latour (Bruno Latour, *The Pasteurization of France*, Cambridge: Harvard University Press, 1988, pp. 65–67).

[15] Hacking compares his position to the aspirations of K. Marx: "Both say – he writes – that the point is not to understand the world but to change it" (Ian Hacking, *Representing and Intervening. Introductory Topics in the Philosophy of Natural Science*, op. cit., p. 274).

It is worth emphasising that when Marx wrote about changing the world in his *Eleven Theses on Feuerbach*, what he meant was philosophy, while Hacking meant science.

[16] Tadeusz Buksiński, *Moderność* [Modernity], Poznań: Wydawnictwo Naukowe Instytutu Filozofii UAM, 2001, pp. 229–231.

cannot – in our opinion – be defended. Developing clear relations between scientific aspirations and values seems one of the most important, if not the *most* important, task of contemporary culture. The threat of eugenics is an excellent example here.[17] Jürgen Habermas makes an outright warning against the perspective of the future in which today's contentious practices may turn out to have broken new ground for *"liberal eugenics"*, regulated by the market, which – conceivably – will lead towards a fulfillment of the metaphor of "breeding of humans".[18] Jeremy Rifkin argues that a consequence of the development of biotechnology may be a Second Genesis on the Earth.[19] With its coming, the concepts of humanity, human freedom, equality, dignity, responsibility and other basic existential categories will have to be defined anew.

On account of the achievements of modern science, Francis Fukuyama revised his controversial thesis about the end of history.[20] He recognized that it was not possible to talk about the end of history yet, for the end of science had not occurred and – what is more – we were facing one of the most break-through periods in its development. A dramatic progress in biotechnology and sciences studying mechanisms governing the human brain is not only triggering off increasingly reverberating moral dilemmas, but also making us aware of critical political consequences, as it opens up new possibilities in social engineering. It enables – as never before – an implementation of

---

[17] In professional literature, two types of eugenics are distinguished: "positive" and "negative". The first type means that using genetic manipulations attempts are undertaken to produce "improved babies", which – considering the state of our knowledge of life and social evolution – usually leads to nothing more than racist and Nazi-like madness. Nevertheless, in many cultures such manipulations still enjoy huge popularity. In the second type steps are taken in order to prevent the birth of babies that, based on prenatal tests, are known to be seriously ill or disabled. For a discussion of the problem of eugenics cf. e.g. L. Graham (Loren R. Graham, *Between Science and Values*, New York: Columbia University Press, 1981, chap. 8).

[18] Jürgen Habermas, *Die Zukunft der menschlichen Natur. Auf dem Weg zu einer liberalen Eugenik?* Frankfurt am Main: Suhrkamp Verlag, 2001.

[19] Jeremy Rifkin, *The Biotech Century. Harnessing the Gene and Remaking the World*, New York: Jeremy P. Tarcher/Putnam, 1988, p. 67.

[20] Francis Fukuyama, *Our Posthuman Future. Consequences of the Biotechnology Revolution*, New York: Farrar, Straus & Giroux, 2002, chap. 1.

various political projects. When, for example, a correlation between specific genes and human abilities such as intelligence or aggression becomes known, a temptation arises to use this knowledge to shape concrete social institutions (universities, the police, the military, etc). Until now, projects designed to restructure this type of institutions, together with – as in Karl Marx – a change of the entire social and political system have been, to a lesser or greater extent, in the sphere of ideology. Currently, they can be realized in the laboratory.

3.

The relationship between laboratory sciences and the global society is, naturally, mutual. One of its effects is a question concerning the values inherent in the traditional culture of scientific practice. These values – as Robert Merton proposes – make up the normative structure of science. They form a basis for principles of a particular type, governing the functioning of the autonomous community of scientists – in other words, they are a foundation of the so-called **ethos of science**. The ethos of modern science consists of four groups of institutional orders defined by Merton as: universalism, communism, disinterestedness and organized scepticism. **Universalism** believes that

> truth claims, whatever their source, are to be subjected to *preestablished impersonal criteria:* constant with observation and with previously confirmed knowledge. The acceptance or rejection of claims entering the lists of science is not to depend on the personal or social attributes of their protagonist.[21]

Communism establishes that

> substantive findings of science are product of social collaboration and are assigned community. ... Property rights in science are whittled down to a bare minimum by the rationale of the scientific ethic.[22]

---

[21] Robert Merton, "Science and Democratic: Social Structure", in: idem, *Social Theory and Social Structure*, London: The Free Press, 1964, p. 550.

[22] Ibidem, p. 555.

Disinterestedness requires scientists to interpret the findings of their study without taking into consideration personal gain, ideology or any objectives other than the pursuit of truth.

> The demand for disinterestedness has a firm basis in the public and testable character of science and this circumstance, it may by supposed, has contributed to the integrity of men of science. There is competition in the realm of science, competition that is intensified by the emphasis on priority as a criterion of achievement, and under competitive conditions there may well be generated incentives for eclipsing rivals by illicit means. But such impulses can find scant opportunity for expression in the field of scientific research. Cultism, informal cliques, prolific but trivial publications – these and other techniques may be used for self-aggrandizement. But, in general, spurious claims appear to be negligible and ineffective.[23]

Organized scepticism is this norm that one must practice the suspension of judgment *"until the facts are at hand"* and that the "detached scrutiny of belies in terms of empirical and logical criteria" come into play.[24]

Sheldon Krimsky in his book with the suggestive title *Science in the Private Interest*, following an analysis of the scientific process in biomedical sciences in the USA, voices a need of revising the Mertonian view of the ethos of science.[25] He begins his argument with postulating a need to change the way the university is treated, suggesting that it should be referred to as an **"academic-industrial complex"** rather than a place of pursuit of truth. This new concept is necessary, as it helps to describe social relations that occur more and more frequently between commercial institutions and scientific establishments. In the period from 1980 until 2000, the industry's financial outlays on science rose by 875 percent, from 0.26 to 2.3 billion USD. Close entanglement of science and industry has now become a fact of life.

---

[23] Ibidem, p. 560.

[24] Ibidem, p. 561.

[25] Sheldom Krimsky, *Science in the Private Interest. Has the Lure of Profits Corrupted Biomedical Research?* Lanham: Rowman & Littlefield, 2003, p. 73.

They are aptly illustrated with the term "**postacademic science**", coined by John Ziman.[26] It combines elements of academic and industrial science intertwined and mutually affecting each other. The classical distinction between science and its applications, sustained in science for a long time, is now becoming gradually blurred. An academic laboratory is in reality little different from a laboratory in an industrial plant. Both of these establishments conduct versatile studies aimed at realizing socially set goals. In a race to realize these goals, laboratories – contrary to what Merton claims – rather compete with one another, instead of cooperating. An example of his phenomenon is a growing number of instances in which researchers are denied access to data related to the results of research presented in scientific circles.[27] The traditional ethos of practising science is thus changing.

4.

By way of conclusion, let me return to Husserl again. He criticized modern positivistic science mainly because of the fact that it

---

[26] John Ziman, *Real Science*, Cambridge: Cambridge University Press, 2000, p. 116.

[27] Krimsky quotes a report published in 2002 by Eric Campbell, from which it follows that as much as 47 percent of geneticists surveyed throughout the previous three years were denied access to data that they were going to use in their research (Sheldom Krimsky, *Science in the Private Interest. Has the Lure of Profits Corrupted Biomedical Research?* op. cit., p. 83).

The problem of a deficient free flow of information between researchers was already signalled by Paul Feyerabend in the 1970s, when he wrote that "increasing amounts of theoretical and engineering information are kept secret for military reasons and are thereby cut off from international exchange. Commercial interests have the same restrictive tendency. Thus the discovery of superconductivity in ceramics at (relatively) high temperatures, which was the result of international collaboration, soon led to protective measures by the American government. Financial arrangements can make or break a research programme and an entire profession. There are many ways to silence people apart from forbidding them to speak – and all of them are being used today. The process of knowledge production and knowledge distribution was never the free 'objective', and purely intellectual exchange rationalists make it out to be" (Paul Feyerabend, *Against Method*, London: New Left Books, 1988, pp. 130–131).

Marek Sikora

"decapitates philosophy".[28] In the global society, with laboratory sciences interfering in the world more and more boldly with a view to changing it, philosophical reflection deserves attention as – perhaps – never before. A good example is the problem of human nature. Philosophers have explored the issue for ages. Meanwhile, when it becomes a "concrete real construct" and as such appears in the laboratory, philosophers are very rarely asked for their opinions and their role in the media-dominated public debate is now seriously marginalized. Philosophy as a type of knowledge is disappearing even from university curricula.[29] Pragmatically-oriented modern science is, in principle, governed only by utilitarian aims. In this context, the voice of Husserl in defence of philosophy and, to be more precise, reasoning that it postulates, is now a very topical one.

[28] Edmund Husserl, *The Crisis of European Sciences and Transcendental Phenomenology*, op. cit., p. 9.

[29] Allan Bloom, *The Closing of the American Mind. How Higher Education Has Failed Democracy and Impoverished the Souls of Today's Students*, New York: Simon & Schuster, 1987.

Piotr Leśniewski
Poznań

Values in Social Structures. An Outline of a Formal Study

1.

The aim of the paper is a short presentation of the foundations of my research program. The program is devoted to the problem of justification of questions in moral debates and it is conducted within the framework of erotetic logic. But there are two general and non-formal presuppositions of the aforementioned program. First, following the famous Whiteheadian passage it is assumed that "A clash of doctrines is not a disaster – it is opportunity".[1] Does logic have something in common with moral debates?[2] The answer is straightforward: yes. But

---

[1] Cf. Alfred N. Whitehead, *Science and the Modern World*, New York: The Free Press, 1967, p. 186.

[2] Let me quote late Łukasiewicz's opinion here: "Logic is not a science of the laws of thought or any other real object; it is, in my opinion, only an instrument which enables us to draw asserted conclusions from asserted premises. The classical theory of deduction which is verified by a two-valued matrix is the oldest and simplest logical system, and therefore the best known and widely used. But for some purposes, for instance in modal logic, an n-valued system, $n > 2$, might be more suitable and useful. The more useful and richer a logical system is, the more valuable is." Cf. Jan Łukasiewicz, *Selected Works*, ed. by Ludwik Borkowski, Amsterdam – London: North-Holland, and Warszawa: PWN [Polish Scientific Publishers], 1970, p. 333. For a different point of view, see: "All kinds of statements have indirect references to the here, the now, the I (first person). And these statements have a logic; it is possible to say that some of them are true by virtue of their syntactical form. Thus in view of the commonness and simplicity of these statements, we are certainly obliged to investigate their intrinsic logic". Cf. Dana Scott, "Advice on Modal Logic", in: *Philosophical Prob-*

let me remind the following fragment of Peter Singer's fascinating and popular book:

> If we were put the case against abortion as a formal argument, it would go like this:
> *First Premise*: It is wrong to take innocent human life.
> *Second Premise*: From conception onwards, the embryo or fetus is innocent, human and alive.
> *Conclusion*: It is wrong to take the life of the embryo or fetus.
> As a matter of formal logic, the argument is valid. If we accept the premises, we must accept the conclusion. Since the abortion does take the life of the fetus, we would then have to agree that abortion is wrong. Conversely, if we want to reject the conclusion, we must reject at least one of the premises. (For simplicity, in what follows I shall use "fetus" to refer to the embryo or fetus, and I shall leave out the word "innocent", since there is no debate over the claim that the fetus is innocent in the required sense.). Those who do not think abortion is wrong generally attack the second premise. They deny that a new human life comes into existence at conception, and suggest instead some other point, at or before birth when a new human life comes to existence. But human development is a gradual process, and it is not easy to see why any particular moment should be *the* moment at which a human life begins.

Singer asks the question:

> Why should the location of the fetus/infant, inside or outside the womb, be so significant that it marks the beginning of a new human life?[3]

It is obvious then that at least some fragments of contemporary moral debates consist of arguments which include questions. Such a situation involves a good (i.e. logical) theory of questions. Of course, there are various versions of the logic of questions.[4] There are several methodological controversies connected with each of these theories. After Wiśniewski it is worth emphasizing that

---

lems in Logic, ed. by Karel Lambert, Dordrecht: D. Reidel Publishing Company, 1970, p. 150.

[3] Cf. Peter Singer, *Rethinking Life and Death. The Collapse of Our Traditional Ethics*, New York: St. Martin's Griffin, 1994, pp. 100–101.

[4] Cf. David Harrah, "The Logic of Questions", in: *Handbook of Philosophical Logic*, ed. by D. Gabbay and F. Guenthner, 2nd Edition, Vol. 8, Dordrecht – Boston – London: Kluwer, 2002, pp. 1–60.

... a question Q of a formalized language represents a question Q^* of a natural language constructed in such way that the possible and just-sufficient (i.e. direct) answers to Q^* have the *logical form* of direct answers to Q.[5]

But a very special theory is the *inferential erotetic logic* (IEL, for short).[6] Let us note that in the IEL the non-reductionistic approach to questions is assumed:

> The controversy about the "nature" of questions is not only a conceptual one. If the radical reductionist view is correct, no logic (in the very sense of "logic", as opposed to "logical theory") of questions is possible. If the moderate reductionist view is correct, logic of questions should be developed only within the framework of some other philosophical logic. But if we accept the non-reductionist approach, the problem of building (or discovering, as a platonist might say) of the logic of questions remains open.[7]

It is obvious that my studies belong to ethics if, according to the classical work of R.M. Hare, it is considered as a logical study of the language of morals.[8] The second presupposition of my study is represented by the question (a) "How to talk with barbarians?" or/and the question (b) "How to stop talking with barbarians?".[9] Most of contemporary moral debates suggest that (1) there is a conflict between sets of moral commandments, and, (2) that a choice between these sets has to be made. Singer states "It is time for another Copernican revolution", and he compares two such sets.[10] Hence, there is no doubt that the studies of such principles as the Golden Rule and/or the Universal Law, for example, in the sense of Gensler, are of the greatest import-

---

[5] Cf. Andrzej Wiśniewski, *The Posing of Questions. Logical Foundations of Erotetic Inferences*, Dordrecht: Kluwer Academic Publishers Group, 1995, p. 87.

[6] Cf. ibidem.

[7] Cf. ibidem, p. 42.

[8] Cf. Richard M. Hare, *The Language of Morals*, London: Oxford University Press, 1964, p. iii.

[9] This time however the barbarians are not waiting beyond the frontiers; they have already been governing us for quite some time. We are waiting not for a Godot, but for another – doubtless very different – St. Benedict. Cf. Alasdair MacIntyre, *After Virtue. A Study in Moral Theory*, Notre Dame, Indiana: University of Notre Dame Press, 2003, p. 238

[10] Cf. Peter Singer, *Rethinking Life and Death*, op. cit., pp. 189–206.

ance.[11] But I reject both (1) and (2). Most of all there is only one choice – the theory (or theories) of virtues should be developed and introduced into some new model of moral education. Moreover, I am convinced that the question: "Which moral code should be chosen?" is improperly posed. So is the question "Which moral code did you choose?". I call these questions *improperly posed* since they are simply unanswerable – i.e. neither true nor a false answer could be given to each of them. Just because "Knowing how to act virtuously always involves more than rule-following".[12] It does not entail the moral relativism or the moral nihilism in the sense of Rescher.[13] By the way, a dangerous result in the practice of moral absolutism should be noted:

> The true lesson of the Jacobin Clubs and their downfall is that you cannot hope to reinvent morality on the scale of a whole nation when the very idiom of the morality which you seek to re-invent is alien in one way to the vast mass of ordinary people and in another to the intellectual elite. The attempt to impose morality by terror – the solution of St. Just – is the desperate expedient of those who already glimpse this fact but will not admit it. (It is this and *not* the ideal of public virtue which, so I would argue, breeds totalitarianism.)[14]

Then a fruitful theory of questions has to be presupposed, and the problem of justification of such questions as (a) and (b) should be

---

[11] Cf. Harry J. Gensler, *Formal Ethics*, London – New York: Routledge, 1996, pp. 93–148, and idem, *Introduction to Logic*, London – New York: Routledge, 2004, pp. 229–252.

[12] Cf. Alasdair MacIntyre, *Dependent Human Animals. Why Human Beings Need the Virtues*, Chicago – La Salle, Illinois: Open Court, 2002, p. 93.

[13] Cf. Nicholas Rescher, *Moral Absolutes. An Essay on the Nature and Rationale of Morality*, New York/Bern/Frankfurt am Main/Paris: Peter Lang, 1989, p. 37. Cf. the following fragment from John Dewey & James H. Tufts, *Ethics*, New York: Henry Holt and Co., 1959, p. 313: "Only if some rigid form of institutionalism were true, would the state of culture and the growth of knowledge in forms usually called non-moral, be without significance for distinctively moral knowledge and judgment. Because the two things are connected, each generation, especially one living in a time like the present, is under the responsibility of overhauling its inherited stock of moral principles and reconsidering them in relation to contemporary conditions and needs. It is stupid to suppose that this signifies that all moral principles are so relative to a particular state of society that they have no binding force in any social condition. The obligation is to discover what principles are relevant to our own social estate".

[14] Cf. Alasdair MacIntyre, *After Virtue. A Study in Moral Theory*, op. cit., p. 238.

studied within the theory. But if we want to introduce some theoretical framework for the dialogue in our new dark ages, we need a formal theory of social structures, too.

2.

By the *MacIntyre's questions* I mean these two questions:

(Q_1) 'What am I to do?';
(Q_2) 'Of what story or stories do I find myself a part?'.[15]

There are other interesting questions formulated by MacIntyre, for example:

(Q_3) 'Why is it important for us to attend to and to understand what human beings have in common with other intelligent animal species?';
(Q_4) 'What makes attention to human vulnerability and disability important for moral philosophers?'.[16]

But I believe that there is a very interesting kind of the *generalized* reducibility which is connected with the questions (Q_1) and (Q_2). The main intuitions concerning the generalized reducibility of questions are as follows. Let Q be a question (called an *initial* question). Let Φ be a (non-empty) set of questions and X – some set of declarative sentences. According to Wiśniewski[17], we can formulate these intuitions as follows: (i) the initial question Q which is reducible to the set of

---

[15] Cf. ibidem, p. 216.

[16] Cf. Alasdair MacIntyre, *Dependent Human Animals. Why Human Beings Need the Virtues*, op. cit., p. vii. The following remark on some erotetic relations between questions of some kind and their answers is placed in *After Virtue*: "It is now possible to return to the question from which this enquire into the nature of human action and identity started: what does the unity of an individual life consist? The answer is that its unity is the unity of a narrative embodied in a single life. To ask 'What is the good for me?' is to ask how best I might live out that unity and bring it to completion. To ask 'What is good for man?' is to ask what all answers to the former question must have in common". Cf. Alasdair MacIntyre, *After Virtue. A Study in Moral Theory*, op. cit., p. 218.

[17] Cf. Andrzej Wiśniewski, "On the Reducibility of Questions", *Erkenntnis* 40, 1994, pp. 266–267.

questions Φ on the basis of the set X has a true direct answer if and only if each question in Φ has a true direct answer provided that all the sentences in the set X are true; (ii) each "combination" of direct answers to questions in Φ enables us – together with the set X – to answer the initial question Q, but the set X alone does not entail any direct answer to the initial question; (iii) the questions in Φ are not more complex than the initial question. The generalized reducibility of this kind was investigated by Leśniewski.[18] In fact, one may say that the MacIntyre's question (Q_1) is reducible to the question (Q_2). But I think that the concept of the *'historical' reducibility* should be investigated: the MacIntyre's question (Q_1) is reducible to the question (Q_2) relative to the history H. For formal approaches to histories, see for example Montague's *Deterministic Theories* and Wójcicki's *Topics in the Formal Methodology of Empirical Sciences*.[19] Some formal concept of the history is proposed below.

Yet the problem of the justification of MacIntyre's questions should be investigated in details. In the IEL the concept of the relative soundness of a question is introduced in the following way. We say that the set X of declarative well-formed formulas (d-wffs for short) of a formalized language L entails a d-wff A of L if and only if A is true in each normal interpretation of the language L in which all d-wffs in X are true. Following Wiśniewski[20], the concept of *multiple-conclusion*

[18] See also Piotr Leśniewski, *Zagadnienie sprowadzalności w antyredukcjonistycznych teoriach pytań* [The Problem of the Reducibility of Questions in Non-Reductionistic Theories of Questions], Poznań: Wydawnictwo Naukowe Instytutu Filozofii UAM, 1997; idem, "On the Generalized Reducibility of Questions", in: *Rationality, Realism, Revision. Proceedings of the 3rd International Congress of the Society for Analytical Philosophy (September 15–18, 1997, in Munich)*, ed. by Julian Nida-Rümelin. *Perspectives in Analytical Philosophy*, vol. 23, Berlin – New York: Walter de Gruyter, 2000, pp. 119–126; Piotr Leśniewski, Andrzej Wiśniewski, "Reducibility of Questions to Sets of Questions: Some Feasibility Results", *Logique & Analyse*, No 173-174-175, 2001, pp. 93–111.

[19] Cf. Richard Montague, "Deterministic Theories", in: idem, *Formal Philosophy. Selected Papers of Richard Montague*, ed. by Richmond H. Thomason, New Haven, CT – London: Yale University Press, 1979, p. 310, and Ryszard Wójcicki, *Topics in the Formal Methodology of Empirical Sciences*, Dordrecht – Boston – Wrocław: D. Reidel/Ossolineum, 1979, p. 35.

[20] Cf. Andrzej Wiśniewski, *The Posing of Questions. Logical Foundations of Erotetic Inferences*, Dordrecht: Kluwer Academic Publishers Group, 1995, p. 108.

entailment (*mc-entailment* for short) is introduced. We say that a set of d-wffs X of L *mc-entails* a set of d-wffs Y of L if and only if the following condition holds: whenever all the d-wffs in X are true in some normal interpretation of L, then there is at least one d-wff in Y which is true in this interpretation of L. In other words, X mc-entails Y if and only if each interpretation of L which is a model of X makes true at least one d-wff in Y. A question Q is said to be *sound* in an interpretation M of L if and only if at least one direct answer to Q is true in M.[21] A question Q is said to be *sound relative to* a set of d-wffs X if and only if the set X mc-entails the set of direct answers to Q.[22] In a very natural way several concepts of 'historical' soundness may be proposed (a question Q is sound relative to a history H).

3.

The best motto for this part of the paper is: "Evaluative questions *are* questions of social facts"[23]. But there is a better one: "It is not such a bad image, the brain as an ant colony!".[24] By a *social structure* I mean a structure of the form:

(*) $S = (A, R_1, ..., R_m)$,

where A is a non-empty set and $R_1, ..., R_m$ are relations over A. Each relation R_k (for $k \leq m$) is a set of ordered n-tuples. Let $S = (A, R)$ be a social structure, where A may include not only men but chimpanzees, and R be some binary relation over A. Let us call the set A a *social group*. An *a priori* reasoning can be developed in different directions. For example, if the social group A is given, then $S_1 = (A, R_1)$ and $S_2 = (A, R_2)$, where $R_1 \neq R_2$, are two different social structures. But the most interesting case arises when formal properties of relations in social structures are discussed. Let $S_1 = (A_1, R_1)$, $S_2 = (A_2, R_2)$, and $S_3 = (A_3, R_3)$ are

---

[21] Cf. ibidem, p. 113.

[22] Cf. ibidem, p. 118.

[23] Cf. Alasdair MacIntyre, *After Virtue. A Study in Moral Theory*, op. cit., p. 123.

[24] Cf. Douglas R. Hofstadter, *Gödel, Escher, Bach: an Eternal Golden Braid. A Metaphorical Fugue on Minds and Machines in the Spirit of Lewis Carroll*, Harmondsworth: Penguin Books, 1984, p. 350.

social structures and let R_1, R_2, R_3 are relations "a controls b" in the unusual sense "a is responsible for (at least) one b's action".[25] Suppose that R_1 reflexive, symmetric, transitive and connected in A_1, i.e.:

(*) $\forall a \, (a \in A_1 \supset \, <a, a> \, \in R_1)$;

(**) $\forall a \forall b \, ((a \in A_1 \wedge b \in A_1 \wedge \, <a, b> \, \in R_1) \supset \, <b, a> \, \in R_1)$;

(***) $\forall a \forall b \forall c \, ((a \in A_1 \wedge b \in A_1 \wedge c \in A_1 \wedge \, <a, b> \, \in R_1 \wedge \, <b, c> \, \in R_1) \supset$
        $\supset \, <a, c> \, \in R_1)$;

(****) $\forall a \forall b \, ((a \in A_1 \wedge b \in A_1 \wedge a \neq b) \supset (<a, b> \, \in R_1 \vee \, <b, a> \, \in R_1))$.

Then, suppose that R_2 is irreflexive, antisymmetric, intransitive but it is not connected in A_2, i.e.:

(#) $\exists a \, (a \in A_2 \wedge \, <a, a> \, \notin R_2)$;

(##) $\forall a \forall b \, ((a \in A_2 \wedge b \in A_2 \wedge a \neq b \wedge \, <a, b> \, \in R_2) \supset \, <b, a> \, \notin R_2)$;

(###) $\exists a \exists b \exists c \, (a \in A_2 \wedge b \in A_2 \wedge c \in A_2 \wedge \, <a, b> \, \in R_2 \wedge \, <b, c> \, \in R_2 \wedge$
         $\wedge \, <a, c> \, \notin R_2)$;

(####) $\exists a \exists b \, (a \in A_2 \wedge b \in A_2 \wedge a \neq b \wedge \, <a, b> \, \notin R_2 \wedge \, <b, a> \, \notin R_2)$.

Finally, suppose that R_3 is asymmetric, transitive, connected in A_3, i.e.:

(+) $\forall a \forall b \, ((a \in A_3 \wedge b \in A_3 \wedge \, <a, b> \, \in R_3) \supset \, <b, a> \, \notin R_3)$;

(++) $\forall a \forall b \forall c \, ((a \in A_3 \wedge b \in A_3 \wedge c \in A_3 \wedge \, <a, b> \, \in R_3 \wedge \, <b, c> \, \in R_3) \supset$
        $\supset \, <a, c> \, \in R_3)$;

(+++) $\forall a \forall b \, ((a \in A_3 \wedge b \in A_3 \wedge a \neq b) \supset (<a, b> \, \in R_3 \vee \, <b, a> \, \in R_3))$.

Obviously, R_3 is then nonreflexive in A_3, i.e. $\forall a \, (a \in A_3 \supset \, <a, a> \, \notin R_3)$.

Let us note that binary relations of controlling which hold between two social groups and those which hold between an individual and some social group may be studied within this framework. It is possible to investigate n-ary relations of controlling too.

---

[25] It is assumed that relations of giving and receiving are uncalculated. Cf. Alasdair MacIntyre, *Dependent Human Animals. Why Human Beings Need the Virtues*, op. cit., p. 117.

If $S = (A, R)$ is a social structure, then each change in S is described by means of the concept of *social transformation* of the form:

(t) $S = (A, R) \Rightarrow S^* = (A^*, R^*)$.

A *history* of the social structure S is an infinite sequence of social transformations:

(s) $H(S) = S_0, S_0 \Rightarrow S_1, S_1 \Rightarrow S_2, ..., S_n \Rightarrow S_{n+1}, ...,$

where $S_n \neq S_{n+1}$. It is obvious that each history has a set-theoretical limit. It is worth emphasizing that according to Wójcicki's approach, a system can be identified with its history.

4.

Let V be a finite, at least a two-elements set, called *a domain of values*. Let E be a relation x *is of the same value as* y in V. So, E is an equivalence relation in V, i.e. it is reflexive, symmetric and transitive in V. Let us put it formally as follows:

(e_1) $\forall x\, (x \in V \supset <x, x> \in E)$;

(e_2) $\forall x \forall y\, ((x \in V \wedge y \in V \wedge <x, y> \in E) \supset <y, x> \in E)$;

(e_3) $\forall x \forall y \forall z\, ((x \in V \wedge y \in V \wedge z \in V \wedge <x, y> \in E \wedge <y, z> \in E) \supset$
   $\supset <x, z> \in E)$.

For every $x \in V$, let $[x]_E$ denote the set of all $y \in V$ such that $<x, y> \in E$. The sets $[x]_E$, where $x \in V$ are called *the equivalence classes* of E. By the way, let us remind that for each $x, y \in E$: (i) $x \in [x]_E$; (ii) $<x, y> \in E \supset [x]_E = [y]_E$; (iii) $<x, y> \notin E \supset [x]_E \cap [y]_E = \varnothing$. Thus the equivalence relation E determines *a partition* of the set V into disjoint non-empty sets (i.e. into the equivalence classes of the relation E) such that two elements $x, y \in E$ belong to the same subset of V if and only if $<x, y> \in E$. For $x_1, ..., x_n \in V$, where $n > 1$, let $[x_1]_E, ..., [x_n]_E$ are the equivalence classes of E. The sequence of the form $[x_1]_E, ..., [x_n]_E$ will be called *a basic sequence* for V. Each element of the equivalence class $[x_i]_E$ is of less value than each element of the equivalence class $[x_{i+1}]_E$, where $i+1 \leq n$. Let $x, y \in V$. We say that x *is of a less value than* y (in symbols

$<x, y> \in R$) if and only if in the basic sequence $[x_1]_E, ..., [x_n]_E$ there are sets $[x_i]_E, [x_j]_E$ such that $x \in [x_i]_E, y \in [x_j]_E$ and $i < j \leq n$. The triple of the form $<V, E, R>$ will be called *a hierarchy of values*. R is irreflexive, asymmetric, and transitive in V of the hierarchy of values $<V, E, R>$. Formally speaking:

$(r_1) \forall x (x \in V \supset <x, x> \notin R)$;

$(r_2) \forall x \forall y ((x \in V \wedge y \in V \wedge <x, y> \in R) \supset <y, x> \notin R)$;

$(r_3) \forall x \forall y \forall z ((x \in V \wedge y \in V \wedge z \in V \wedge <x, y> \in R \wedge <y, z> \in R) \supset$
$\supset <x, z> \in R)$.

If the social structures are introduced as values of such hierarchies not only different concepts of changes but also several concepts of development and progress may be defined.

Moreover, on the basis of appropriate collective epistemic logic several models of collective rationality may be developed.[26]

5.

After systematic investigations into 'historical' soundness of Mac-Intyre's questions, and in 'historical" reducibility, the results should be applicable to the theory of the practical reasoning. Moreover, according to MacIntyre:

---

[26] For collective epistemic logic, see Piotr Leśniewski, Zbigniew Tworak, "Collective Epistemic Logic", in: *Erotetic Logic, Deontic Logic, and Other Logical Matters. Essays in Memory of Tadeusz Kubiński*, ed. by Andrzej Wiśniewski, Jan Zygmunt, Wrocław: Wydawnictwo Uniwersytetu Wrocławskiego, 1997, pp. 89–102 (*Acta Universitatis Wratislaviensis No 1890*, Seria: *Logika*, t. 17). For a critical exposition of the collective rationality see for example Nicola Yeates, "Social Politics and Policy in an Era of Globalization: Critical Reflections", *Social Policy & Administration*, Vol. 33, No. 4, 1999, pp. 376–377. For an experimental approach to the dynamics of hierarchies of values in social structures, see for example Thomas E. Nelson, Jennifer Garst, "Values-Based Political Messages and Persuasion: Relationships among speaker, Recipient, and Evoked Values", *Political Psychology*, Vol. 26, No. 4, 2005, pp. 494–501. See also Marina F. Barnea, Shalom H. Schwartz, "Values and Voting", *Political Psychology*, Vol. 19, No. 1, 1998, pp. 18–21.

Practical reasoning is by nature, on the generally Aristotelian view that I have been taking, reasoning together with others, generally within some determinate set of social relationships. Those relationships are initially formed and then developed as the relationships through which each of us first achieves and is then supported in the status of an independent practical reasoner.[27]

Assume that the practical reasoning consists of the four parts: (i) a presupposition on preferences of an agent ("There are first of all the wants and goals of the agent, presupposed by but not expressed in, his reasoning. Without these there would be no context of the reasoning, and the major and minor premises could not adequately determine what kind of thing the agent is to do."[28]); (ii) the major premise, "an assertion to the effect that doing or having or seeking such-and-such is the type of thing that is *good for* or *needed by* a so-and-so (where the agent uttering this syllogism falls under the latter description)"[29]; (iii) the minor premise "... wherein the agent, relying on a perceptual judgment, asserts that this is an instance or occasion of the requisite kind."[30]; (iv) the conclusion – the action.[31] It should be noted that following MacIntyre: "The conclusion of sound and effective practical reasoning is an action, that action which it is best for this particular agent to do in these particular circumstances".[32] But there is the other side of the practical reasoning, namely its connection with explanations in humanities. According to Poznań Methodological School, the goal of an action is produced of the agent's knowledge of the conditions of action, and of the sys-

---

[27] Cf. Alasdair MacIntyre, *Dependent Human Animals. Why Human Beings Need the Virtues*, op. cit., p. 107.

[28] Cf. idem, *After Virtue. A Study in Moral Theory*, op. cit., p. 161.

[29] Ibidem, pp. 161–162.

[30] Ibidem.

[31] It should be noted that Aristotle's practical syllogistic was formalized in Jerzy Kalinowski, "Théorie des propositions normatives", *Studia Logica*, I, 1953, pp. 147–182.

[32] Cf. Alasdair MacIntyre, *Dependent Human Animals. Why Human Beings Need the Virtues*, op. cit., p. 92. See also Karen L. Myers, David E. Wilkins, "Reasoning About Locations in Theory and Practice", *Computational Intelligence*, Vol. 14, No. 2, 1998, pp. 153–156.

tem of values of the agent.[33] The agent's knowledge entails that action should yield the preferred result. It is presupposed that the agent is a rational person at least in the general, or a subjective sense. That is the assumption of rationality. The appropriate reasoning concerning the action of a given agent consists of the following steps: (i) if the agent is rational, then in order to attain his goal he undertakes a given action in accordance with his knowledge and his system of values; according to the knowledge such an action is to bring the preferred result (called also the *sense* of an action[34]); (ii) since the agent is rational, he/she shall undertake this action; (iii) the agent undertakes this action.[35] More formally, the assumption of rationality is formulated by Kmita as follows:

(+)   If the agent x at time t is to undertake one of the complementary and mutually exclusive – to his knowledge – actions $a_1,\ldots,$ a_n, unambiguously associated – to his knowledge – with results $r_1,\ldots,$ r_n ordered in turn – according to his norms – by an appropriate relation of preference, then x at time t will undertake the action a_i ($i = 1, \ldots, n$, or a_i is the objective equivalent of the logical disjunction of members of a proper subset of the set $(a_1, \ldots, a_n)$, when all elements of this subset correspond to the same result of maximum preference.[36]

Since the reasoning of this kind is deductive by its very nature, it serves the request for an explanation of the agent's action. Then it is possible to maintain that the answer to the question 'Why is agent x at time t undertake the action a_i?' consists of: (i) the assumption of rationality; (ii) a description of the actions $a_1,\ldots, a_n$; (iii) a description of results $r_1,\ldots, r_n$ as they are associated with these actions; (iv) a de-

---

[33] The agent's knowledge may be represented as a belief set in the sense of Peter Gärdenfors, *Knowledge in Flux. Modeling the Dynamics of Epistemic States*, Cambridge, Mass., London: The MIT Press, 1988.

[34] See Jerzy Kmita, *Problems in Historical Epistemology*, Warszawa: PWN [Polish Scientific Publishers], and Dordrecht/Boston/Lancaster/Tokyo: D. Reidel, 1988, p. 97.

[35] Cf. Jerzy Topolski, "Historical Explanation in Historical Materialism", in: *Narration and Explanation. Contributions to the Methodology of The Historical Research*, ed. by Jerzy Topolski, Amsterdam – Atlanta: Rodopi, 1990, p. 75.

[36] Cf. Jerzy Kmita, *Problems in Historical Epistemology*, op. cit., p. 97.

scription of the preference relation.[37] But I have to raise a point about the *why*-questions against the above statement. If the non-reductionistic approach to why-questions is adopted, then the problem of logical forms of answers to such questions remains open.[38] I am hard at work on the theory of such explanations in which the assumption of rationality is removed. Instead of the rational agent the MacIntyre's *tragic protagonist* is introduced.[39] It results in several models of 'historical' reducibility of questions.

---

[37] Cf. Jerzy Topolski, "Historical Explanation in Historical Materialism", op. cit., p. 75.

[38] Cf. Sylvain Bromberger, *On What We Know We Don't Know: Explanation, Theory, Linguistics, and How Questions Shape Them*, Chicago: The University of Chicago Press, & Stanford: The Center for Study of Language and Information, 1992; Theo A.F. Kuipers, Andrzej Wiśniewski, "An Erotetic Approach to Explanation by Specification", *Erkenntnis* 40, 1994, pp. 377–402.

[39] Cf. Piotr Leśniewski, *On the Justification of Questions in Dialogue Systems* [in preparation].

Part V
Law and Politics
in the Context
of the Challenges of Globalization

Werner Krawietz
Muenster

Beyond Methodological and Theoretical Individualism – Are There Collective Actors or Collective Subjects in Modern Legal Systems?

1. On Understanding and Explaining Legal Communication

1. Conventional theories of norms and action are usually based on individual human behaviour. They examine whether and to what extent certain intentions of the actors correspond to their legal actions.

– Actions are understood as the intentional behaviour carried out by certain subjects of action, that is, by a 'human being', an 'individual', a 'person' or a 'legal subject'.

– Legal actions appear as the expression of a will (so called *theory of will*) declared by a legal subject (*subject theory*).

– From the point of view of legal and social theory we can, therefore – here in agreement with Georg Henrik von Wright – speak of deliberative intentionalism.[1]

2. There can be little doubt that both legal practice and legal theory require not only normative standardization and patterns of behaviour but also socially adequate theories which enable us to attribute individual (concrete) behavior to certain persons as factual action.

---

[1] See, for example, Georg Henrik von Wright, "An Essay on Door-Knocking", *Rechtstheorie* 19, 1988, pp. 275–288; see also idem, "Das Verstehen von Handlungen", *Rechtstheorie* 20, 1989, pp. 3–34; idem, *Erkenntnis als Lebensform*, Wien – Köln: Böhlau, 1995, pp. 62 f.

– To observe and reconstruct, i.e. to describe, interpret and explain these processes of attribution[2] is one of the tasks required of a theory of norms, especially of law.

– Legal communication which is, of course, the means of producing and imparting normative information appears nowadays as the crucial operation in this task both from the point of view of legal practice and legal theory.

– The distinction between communication and action allows us to develop and expand systems of normative meaning, especially those of the law.

– Concrete legal actions which in the normatively structured communication procede in accordance with the rules of law without being inescapable determined by them do, however, have to be differentiated from the communication structure of legal facts and normative premises.

3. It is one of the most important tasks of contemporary legal and social theory to develop a theory of norms and action[3] which takes account of the requirements of the modern information- and communication society.

– According to Georg Henrik von Wright we can only gain a proper, socially adequate *understanding* of the relationship between legal norms and actions if – and only if – we are also in the position to *observe, describe and explain empirically* the opera-

---

[2] Discussed in Werner Krawietz, "Brauchen wir eine neue Theorie der Verantwortung? Voraussetzungen und Folgen rechtlicher Verantwortungsattribution", *Internationales Jahrbuch für Rechtsphilosophie und Gesetzgebung* 1992, pp. 49–86; idem, "Theorie der Verantwortung – neu oder alt? Zur normativen Verantwortungsattribution mit Mitteln des Rechts", in: *Verantwortung. Prinzip oder Problem?* ed. by Kurt Bayertz, Darmstadt: Wissenschaftliche Buchgesellschaft, 1995, pp. 184–216; Ludger Heidbrink, *Kritik der Verantwortung. Zu den Grenzen verantwortlichen Handelns in komplexen Kontexten*, Weilerswist: Verlag Velbrück Wissenschaft, 2003, pp. 60, 62 f., 294 f.

[3] Georg Henrik von Wright, *Norm and Action*, London 1963; transl. *Norm und Handlung*, Königstein 1979, Kap. 3, Abschn. 4, pp. 49 f., Kap. 5, Abschn. 7, pp. 83 f.; Werner Krawietz, "Recht als normatives Kommunikat in Normen- und handlungstheoretischer Perspektive", in: *Normative Systems in Legal and Moral Theory*, ed. by Ernesto Garzón Valdés, Werner Krawietz, Georg Henrik von Wright, et al., Berlin: Duncker & Humblot, 1997, pp. 369–390, 371 ff., 374 ff.

tions involved in the processing of information by which all legal action and all legal communication take place.

- It is my central thesis here that we can understand what we can explain from the point of view of legal and social theory. On the other hand, we can only explain what we have already previously understood juridically – in whatever way.

- In terms of methodology and theory of law that does not mean that we are dealing here with the validity of law and juridical hermeneutics in the traditional sense, but with a new kind of analytical-empirical legal hermeneutics[4] and the construction of an information- and communication theory of law.

2. Are There Global Players, Collective Actors or Collective Subjects?

1. An information- and communication theory of law must be based on collective human behaviour. A classical formulation for that which is described here as 'collective actor' or 'collective subject' can be found in Georg Henrik von Wright's investigations of *Norm and Action*.

- Significantly here the author does *not* refer to collective *subjects* or collective *actors* but only to „collective *action*".

- Neither does he contrast „personal agent" with collective agents but speaks instead only of „impersonal agents". As for the addressees of the normative prescriptions they are always conceived of as „individual men".[5]

- The *locus classicus* is to be found on page 85 of his famous work *Norm and Action*:

---

[4] See generally Werner Krawietz, „Sprachphilosophie in der Jurisprudenz", in: *An International Handbook of Contemporary Research,* ed. by Marcelo Dascal, et al., Berlin – New York: De Gruyter, 1996, Vol. 2, Nr. 102, pp. 1470–1489, 1486. For an instructive overview see *Beobachtung verstehen, Verstehen beobachten,* ed. by Tilmann Sutter, Opladen: Westdeutscher Verlag, 1997.

[5] See the comments of G.H. von Wright, referred to in note 3 above.

> If acts of impersonal agents are reduceable to acts of personal agents, and collective action to the action of individuals, then prescriptions whose subjects are individual men hold a basic position relative to all other prescriptions. ... Here we shall consider only individual men as subjects of prescriptions.

These words encapsulate the problem to be discussed in the following.

2. In all those attempts of constructing a theory of norms and action which restrict themselves to an individualistic approach the far more complex, highly organized, genuinely social 'collective actors' or 'collective agents' are excluded from the picture. This must be seen as a major deficit in basic legal research that has to be addressed.

- We are told again and again that only 'human beings', 'individuals', or 'persons' exist in reality – whatever that may mean –, while the existence and effectiveness of social actors or collective subjects is denied or refuted.
- This raises the question – to be addressed to Georg Henrik von Wright, in my opinion – what the social situation is and how it has to be reconstructed theoretically when the agent is not an individual but a so called collective subject, state or non-state legal system or transnational global player.

3. Human actions are considerably influenced and determined within the legal system by collective subjects like, for instance, *the* school, *the* local authority, *the* regional government or *the* state. This is my second thesis.

- These do, in fact, exert a significant and determining influence on human behavior or action, as will be shown in the following, and can, at the very least, be seen as social agents.
- I am sure, there is no need for me to expand on that. In terms of legal and social theory I am referring here to all these institutions, organizations and social systems.
- It is vital, therefore, that an information- and communication theory of law seeking to understand the nature of organized social actions should aim to make good the deficits of an individualistic theory of action which is focussed on the actors and individual subjects, and to compensate for these.

4. We are talking here about a *transindividual* normative attribution of responsibility to collective subjects (*the* local authority, *the* state, *the* church etc!).

- The legal and social reflection of the attribution or ascription and imputation of collective rights and duties has been largely missing from the point of view represented by legal dogmatics, or at least neglected by it.
- It is precisely for this reason that it requires a thorough analysis from the standpoint of legal and social theory.
- An information- and communication theory of law which seeks to include organized *social action* must, therefore, attempt to balance and compensate potential deficits of an entirely agent- and subject-based, individualistic theory of action.

3. Concept of Legal Communication and Legal Communities in Outline

1. The questions I asked above also arise from my doubts as to whether it is appropriate to assume with von Wright that it is „always human beings" which – „be it individually or collectively, – always function as the normative authorities". I am also in doubt about the suggestion that – from the point of view of a theory of norms and action – „acts by non-personal actors" must be „reduceable to acts performed by personal actors and collective actions to the actions of individuals".[6]

a) In view of the traditional, merely conventionally applied or implicitely presupposed concept of action which is used by dogmatic jurisprudence, anyone examining the communication of law from the perspective of a theory of norms and action must be prepared for some long overdue corrections and necessary rearrangements in the design of the theory.

---

[6] See Georg Henrik von Wright, *Norm und Handlung*, op. cit., Kap. 3, Abschn. 4, pp. 84 f.

– The latter appear to me to be essential today although the legal concept of action in the legal and social sciences had previously appeared thoroughly and securely established.

– In contrast to the traditionally individualistic concept of action my thoughts on the subject in the following take their orientation from the realization that all communication of law and all legal actions in the daily life of a community have always been guided and steered by normative associations, institutions and social systems.[7]

– Basically they form an emergent legal phenomenon which is not totally covered by our intentions, possibly not even touched by these, due to the fact that the actor's capacity for consciously dealing with legal problems is extremely limited.

b) The challenge facing us is this: we have to formulate a theory that will describe and explain how legal communication and decision-making really works.

– The key idea advanced in contemporary philosophy of law is that a legal and social theory must be based on communication.[8]

– And in doing so we are then no longer engaged in legal hermeneutics in the traditional sense but we are establishing the beginnings of an information- and communication theory of law.

2. In the following I intend to outline a theory of legal communication which rests on integration of legal and social theory.

---

[7] Discussed in Werner Krawietz, *Recht als Regelsystem*, Wiesbaden: Steiner, 1984, pp. 155 et sequ.; idem, "Paradigms, Positions and Prospects of Rationality – The Changing Foundation of Law in Institutional and Systems Theory", in: *Festskrift til Torstein Eckhoff*, ed. by Anders Bratholm, et al., Oslo: Tano, 1986, pp. 152–465, 456 et sequ. See also idem, "Towards A New Institutionalism in Modern Legal Thinking. Facets of Rationality", in: *Reason in Law*, ed. by Carla Faralli, Enrico Pattaro, Milano: Giuffrè, 1987, Vol. 1, pp. 313–325; Florian Simon, *Assoziation und Institution als soziale Lebensformen in der zeitgenössischen Rechtstheorie*, Berlin: Duncker & Humblot, 2001, pp. 83, 89, 101 et sequ.

[8] See here and for what follows Werner Krawietz, "Legal Communication in Modern Law and Legal Systems. A Multi-Level Approach to the Theory and Philosophy of Law", in: *My Philosophy of Law. The Law in Philosophical Perspectives*, ed. by Luc J. Wintgens, Dordrecht – Boston – London: Kluwer, 1999, pp. 69–120, 98 et sequ. For a detailed account see Werner Krawietz, "Gemeinschaft und Gesellschaft", *Rechtstheorie* 35, 2004, pp. 579–652, 607, 616 et sequ.

a) From the point of view of a juridical communications- and systems theory[9] the normative communication of law consists of a *tripartite selection process*. This process binds together (i) information, (ii) utterance and (iii) understanding in a single *emergent legal unit*.
- Separately these components have no independent existence. It is only when they coincide with each other that a normative communication actually takes place.
- The following may serve as an *example*: the legislator (1) passes a law by setting down the normative information required for it in form of an *if-then* regulation, (2) he publishes the law in the usual form by addressing and communicating it to those whom it concerns, so that (3) the addressees of the law who have to comply with it, – that is, a) the citizens and legal subjects, and b) the legal staff of the state – have knowledge of it and understand it.

b) Legal communication is, then, successful if the addressee and recipient have understood the factual/normative utterance directed to him by the lawgiver and has thereby been placed into the position of finding his own orientation by conforming with or deviating from the norm.
- The ensuing behaviour which expresses the acceptance/rejection is, however, already to be regarded as the *beginning of a further, new communication*.
- It produces a new (factual and normative) information from which may follow further communications and actions – be they conforming or rejecting.

c) The most fundamental unit in social interactions and transactions spanning a variety of organized social systems is, therefore, *not the human being, the individual, the person or the subject* as the voluntarist agent of human action but the normative-socially structured *juridical communication* or *interaction* which interlinks with other juridical communications and interactions and thereby invests the social order of law with a concrete content, binding character and normative stability.

3. It is the communicative relationship between the setting of the rules and the following of rules that is always central to legal communication. This is my third thesis.

---

[9] See for details Werner Krawietz, "Information and Normative Communication in Modern Legal Systems", *Rechtstheorie* 34, 2003, pp. 27–38.

a) The continuous *correlation of norms and facts* which takes place *case by case* must not be narrowed down to an approach that is purely normativist, merely voluntarist or even positivist in respect of the legislation and law – which is what happens not infrequently in legal methodology and jurisprudence in general. Instead, we must comprehend the legal systems of modern society as information- and communication systems.

b) When investigating such communication systems it appears particularly important to make a thorough analysis not only of the social relations of the 'personal' or 'non-personal' (collective) agents which in the eyes of sceptics may not even exist. One has to analyse the 'knots' in the communication networks of legal relations in society, as it is these – both from the anthropologist's point of view and of that of the theory of action – that are occupied by the respective *actors* (or, more precisely, by the *legal subjects*, as it is seen from the point of view of legal dogmatics).

– In any case, we must distinguish between the normative communication of law and the intentions or interests of 'individuals' who participate in the politico-legal selection processes, either as their originators or as figures of influence without being themselves part of the network.

– One might say, therefore, if one were to exaggerate a little – *legal interaction interacts* or *legal communication communicates*[10] – and not its authors, in other words, not any human beings, individuals, persons, subjects or legal subjects.

– If this interpretation of communication in law were to prevail it would *pro futuro* have considerable consequences of the analysis and description of the way legal norms, legal order and legal systems function.

c) The conventional understanding of the law which regards legal norms as expressing the will of a particular legislator (*theory of will!*)

---

[10] See Walter Kargl, "Kommunikation kommuniziert? Kritik des rechtssoziologischen Autopoiesebegriffs", *Rechtstheorie* 21, 1990, pp. 352–373. Comprehensively treated in Werner Krawietz, "Jenseits von national und staatlich organisierten Rechtssystemen – Normative Kommunikation von Recht in der modernen Weltgesellschaft", *Rechtstheorie* 34, 2003, pp. 317–331.

and in so doing follows the traditional *subject theory* and its voluntarism would no longer be tenable in this form, not, at least, at the level of legal and social theory.

4. Linguistic or Non-Linguistic Conceptions of Legal Norms, Legal Order and Legal Systems?

1. In their form, structure and functions the legal systems of modern society – considered from the point of view of the theory of norms and action – constitute *a single information- and communication system* for the whole of society and with a world-wide influence.
 – The normative net-works of this system, fixed by the language of law and founded on socially generalized expectations[11], serve the whole of society by providing orientation and by guiding behaviour in all kinds of experiences and actions.
 – It is the social function of legal systems to ensure that the addressees of the law act in accordance with their rules, i.e. to induce them to comply with the norms.
 – This occurs when the latter fulfil the prescribed behavioural expectations set down and generalized by means of the language of law.
 – A great deal of detailled research is still needed, however, to determine how legal communications are made legally binding and socially effective.

2. In the following I make the distinction between legal order and legal system.
 – By legal systems I mean largely but not exclusively state legal systems in the context of modern society. They are characterized by

---

[11] Werner Krawietz, "Legal Norms as Expectations? – On Redefining the Concept of Law", in: *Law, Morality, and Discursive Rationality*, ed. by Aulis Aarnio, Kaarlo Tuori, Helsinki: University of Helsinki, 1989, pp. 109–140, 121 et sequ. See also idem, "Taking Legal Systems Seriously: Legal Norms and Principles As Expectations", in: *Sprache, Symbole und Symbolverwendungen in Ethnologie, Kulturanthropologie, Religion und Recht*, ed. by Werner Krawietz, Leopold Pospišil, et al., Berlin: Duncker & Humblot, 1993, pp. 361–384, 376 sequ.

their bureaucratic and procedural apparatus and their organization of persons (legislatures, courts, lawyers etc) who enact, apply, administer and otherwise deal with the rule of law.

– The legal order can be understood as an unpeopled, abstract entity that has comprehensively determined all legal rights, duties and powers within a society. As a result it needs careful structuring and systemization.

a) Legal action is defined as social behaviour governed by normative or factual information. However, legal actions are constrained to limited alternatives by institutions and social systems.

– The term „information" has a particular meaning. There are two types of information.

– The first is practical (prescriptive) information, or knowledge of what ought to be done and of what is better or worse.

– The second is descriptive information, or knowledge of what is.

– Practical information has always to do with a norm, an ought proposition. These normative propositions include rules, principles, goals, values and interests, etc.

– The information, both practical and descriptive, that one communicates and processes in making a decision comes from learning through experience in one's cultural environment.

b) The second major determinant of human action is the scope for action permitted by institutions and social systems.[12] Human beings operate within frameworks or structures or rules that both enable them to achieve certain ends and prevent them from achieving others.

3. From the point of view of a socially based theory of legal institutions and social systems legal communication can now be defined in terms of function as I have already implied at the beginning of this paper.

– The legal system is a system of communication that serves to secure normative expectations.

[12] See Werner Krawietz, "What does it Mean 'To Follow an Institutionalized Legal Rule'? On Rereading Wittgenstein and Max Weber", *Archiv für Rechts- und Sozialphilosophie* Beiheft 40, 1991, pp. 7–14, 12 et sequ. Compare idem, "Recht und moderne Systemtheorie", *Rechtstheorie* Beiheft 10, 1986, pp. 281–309; *Kritik der Theorie sozialer Systeme. Auseinandersetzung mit Luhmanns Hauptwerk*, ed. by Werner Krawietz, Michael Welker, Frankfurt am Main: Suhrkamp, 1992.

- New communications are regularly produced by the system, but the system is programmed to steer legal communications to the legal circuit, economic communications to the economic circuit, etc.
- Which communications belong to which circuit is a question determined by each circuit itself according to its own code.

a) The legal system processes legal communications internally. The content of law and the legal order can change through legislation and judicial application.

- In reducing complexity, the legal system limits itself to certain kinds of communications, that is, only certain kinds of communications generate further communication and thereby continue the operation of the system.
- Somewhat like a digital computer, the legal system does this by selecting communications according to a binary code.

b) The coding is what gives communication within the legal system its legal meaning and excludes from the system other meanings.

- This code could be translated as law (and not: non-law), legally valid (and not: legally invalid), legal (and not: illegal), right (and not: wrong), just (and not: unjust).
- Only legally relevant communications are operative.

c) Obviously in today's society many communications can have legal, political, economic, religious and other meanings.

- Because of the binary coding system, however, the communication will have only one meaning within each system. Thus a system of legal meaning is created.
- There is no starting point and no final point (unless the system disintegrates).
- One communication leads to another, which leads to another, and so forth.

5. Résumé

The growing criticism directed nowadays against the *subject- and will theories of law* means, in fact, that nobody analyzing the reconstructions of legal order – whether from an analytical-conceptual or an empirical point of view – can any longer start from atomistically conceived 'individuals' or 'subjects' without clarifying the social premises and the hidden societal underpinnings of these legal relations and juridical communication systems.

In terms of an information- and communication theory of law it seems to me that associations, institutions and social systems do not consist of individual actors, or rather their intentional actions, but that they are self-referentially constituted and can be understood as social systems of action and interaction linking communicative acts, in other words, directives and norms to former directives and norms and so on.

If we were to regard the single human being, the individual etc. as an element or last unit in social communications and in the formation of communication systems we would lack any socially adequate basis for dealing with the existing social relations or interactions, since neither interactions nor relations are human beings. We have to conclude then that the theory of norms and action itself must be replaced or substituted by a new pattern of interpretation if we want to understand and explain organized action carried out by 'collective agents' or collective subjects of any kind, including the state and non-state legal systems.

Roman Tokarczyk
Lublin

Global Meaning Values
and Norms of Biojurisprudence

1. The Outline of the Problems

The moment of conception is the undeniable beginning of all deliberations on human life as the supreme good that conditions the
utilization of other goods. Human life, no matter how explained and
justified, is unanimously regarded as the value of values. Human
birth is the natural entry into the social and natural environment just
as inevitable human death is also a natural way out. Man's biological
nature alone determines, by conception, birth and death, the objective
boundaries of deliberations on his life.

The uniqueness of human life consists in the entwinning of man's
biological nature and rational nature, and of the two with social nature. One-sided descriptions of human nature led to the formulation
of one-sided paradigms that did not show all its sides: biologism,
naturalism, evolutionism, rationalism, culturalism, sociologism, psy-
chologism, legalism etc. The interconnections of all sides of human
nature are manifested more fully when its descriptions are subjected
to evolution and regulation in particular normative systems.

The experience of all history of humankind demonstrates that different sides of human nature can be permeated both by good and evil.
Good, unlike evil, does not require any normative regulation. Evil,
which hurts the body with pain, can arouse evil in human rationality
witch in turn provokes evil in man's social interactions. Other directions of evil penetration are also possible. Conceived in the rational or

social layer of human nature, evil can affect its bodily side. Normative systems aim at preventing evils resulting from different sides of human nature or at least at minimizing their effects.

Descriptions, evaluations and norms concerning different aspects of human nature are the object of cognition consolidated through scientific knowledge. The vast knowledge of man forces narrow specialization wherein fragments of the particular sides of the rich and interesting human nature can be known. Scientific specialization hampers a comprehensive and coherent description of human nature. There is therefore considerable truth in the words of Edgar Morin, a well-known French philosopher, that the last continent not yet explored by man is man himself. The comprehensive and coherent cognition of human nature is hindered by rapid development of technology, which interferes in the life of man situated in the life of the natural environment. Scientific knowledge and resultant technology raise both great expectations and just as great fears. This is particularly evident in the development of human nature and the natural environment.

The aiming at an overall and coherent understanding of human life leads to the formation of new currents of thought and the resultant new branches of knowledge. These holistic trends of thought belong to anthropology in the broadest sense. They produce new branches of knowledge that integrate the knowledge of different sides of human nature, segmented by narrow specialization. The most interesting branches of scientific knowledge concerned with that goal are at present those which, basing on the descriptions of human life discovered by the biological sciences, formulate new value judgment derived from the ethical sciences, for the possible application of the medical and technological sciences regulated by the legal sciences. We can thus discern the contours of bioanthropology, anthropoethics, anthropopolitics, bioethics, biopolitics, biomedicine and other branches of science.

Investigating the problems that combine the achievements of biological sciences in describing human life and the environment with their evaluation by the ethical sciences, for their frequently risk-laden (since experimental) application in medicine and technology, I find

sufficient grounds to present the outline of a new current in jurisprudence called biojurisprudence that accounts for the comprehensive
and coherent treatment of some new problems.

2. Characteristics of Biojurisprudence

I derive the name of biojurisprudence from the Greek word *bios* or
life and the Latin word *jurisprudentia* – legal knowledge and wisdom.

Biojurisprudence as the name of new current in jurisprudence directly points to the connection between its subject matter and biology
and jurisprudence. However, it does not directly indicate the existing
links with medicine and ecology. These are manifested primarily in
the application of technological achievements, sometimes hazardous
for human life and harmful for the life of the environment. Biojurisprudence does not cover the whole subject matter of the aforesaid
branches of science. It embraces only those parts that relate to human
life and the life of the environment, often threatened by the risk –
laden (since experimental) application of technology and thereby requiring legal protection.

The subject matter of biojurisprudence covers all threats to human
life from the moment of conception until death, requiring legal protection on account of frequent risk-laden experimentation. It also covers the protection of the life of the natural environment as the obvious
condition of human life. In view of the natural rhythm of human life:
birth proceeded by conception, life and death, three segments of
biojurisprudence can be distinguished: biojusgenesis, biojustherapy
and biojusthanatology.

Biojusgenesis deals with threats to human life that require legal
protection from the moment of conception until death. The origins of
the legal protection of this stage of human life (*nasciturus*) go back to
early Roman law, which, using legal fiction, treated the nasciturus as
the born child whenever his or her good was involved (*nasciturus pro
iam natu habetur quotiens de commodis eius agitur*). The development of
the legal protection of the nasciturus in Roman law and the related
systems was characterized by the scattering of regulations in various

branches of law. It is currently included in international law as part of human rights. It is confirmed by national constitutional law. It is further specified by civil law within the scope of being a carrier of rights, legal capacity, and in property and non-property relations. It is consolidated by family law. It is broadened by contract laws to especially include the law on offenses arisen during fetal life. Contract laws, to especially include the law on offenses arisen during fetal life, broaden it. It is recognized by succession law, which treats the nasciturus as a potential heir. It is protected by criminal law against unjustified annihilation. The catalog of situations that demand the intervention of the law during the period from the moment of conception to man's birth is widened by the dilemmas accompanying the conceptions of the right to life, genetic engineering, eugenics, assisted fertilization techniques and techniques preventing conception and birth. All those manifestations of the protection of the nasciturus, rather uniform but artificially scattered in legal systems, are comprehensively and coherently embraced by biojusgenesis as a segment of biojurisprudence.

Biojustherapy can be extended to cover both human life and the life of the natural environment. With regard to the protection of human life, biojustherapy deals primarily with highly controversial problems of transplantation of some cells, tissues and organs in order to improve the quality of and save human life. No less controversial is the complex of doubts about the advisability and scope of the legal regulation of euthanasia. The problem of suicide belongs to the subject matter of biojustherapy insofar as it stems from factors outside human nature that can be regulated by law. A highly specific character is displayed by the normative and legal aspects of population policy. The normative and legal aspects of population policy display a highly specific character. The scope of biojustherapy also includes the issues of the protection of the life of the environment. Since this has been comprehensively regulated in environmental law, they need not be dwelt upon. It must, however, be stressed that environmental law can be treated as a special model for an overall and coherent solution as described by ecology and evaluated by ecological ethics. A similar comprehensive and coherent treatment would be desirable in the case of the scattered legal norms that protect human life. The conceptions of the right to life provide the conceptual ground for an overall treatment of the legal protection of human life and the life of the environment.

Biojusthanatology is especially concerned with the regulation by law of the end of human life: man's death. Descriptions of death symptoms are provided by the advances in the biological, medical or even sociological sciences. The advances in the biological, medical or even sociological sciences provide descriptions of death symptoms. The biological sciences treat of biological death, medical sciences of clinical and brain death and finally sociological sciences deal with man's social death. Each of these kinds of human death can arouse a number of doubts that require, nevertheless, unequivocal solutions by law. The doubts are mainly as to whom, on what condition and for what ends decides about another man's death. Unequivocal legal solutions, with definite legal consequences caused by human death, belonging to bio-justhanatology, could be developed on a broader plane of thought: that of biojusgenesis and biojustherapy as segments of biojurisprudence. The legal norms protecting human life from its conception until death could make up a branch of law called the human life protection law.

The characteristics of jurisprudence is further deepened and enlarged by showing its links with the biological, medical, ethical and legal sciences.

3. Biology and Jurisprudence

The juxtaposition of biology and biojurisprudence cannot miss the question about what unites and divides the two realms of scientific knowledge. For one thing, they are united by the first and divided by the second constituents of their names.

The common subject matter of biology and biojurisprudence is manifested in the interest in human life as a continuous process in the natural environment, yielding to adaptation, accommodation and assimilation factors. However, while biology mainly describes human life and the life of the environment, jurisprudence, on these grounds and following selected axiological criteria, postulates the protection of life. The more precise the biological description of life and the more lucid the criteria of axiological evaluation of life, the easier it is for biojurisprudence to formulate postulates of regulating it.

An extreme form of biology is biologism or even panbiologism as a preferred way of explaining the world, both natural and social, from the biological viewpoint. Certainly, biologism, even less so panbiologism, does not leave much room for traditional jurisprudence, or even modern biojurisprudence in explaining the dilemmas of the protection of human life and the environment. Biologism, reinforced by spectacular achievements in genetics, embryology, genetic engineering, physiology, and bionics, developed peculiar worship of the biological sciences. Biologism, reinforced by spectacular achievements in genetics, embryology, genetic engineering, physiology, and bionics, developed peculiar worship of the biological sciences. Biological strands penetrated some currents in jurisprudence, notably in the form of evolutionism, racism, psychoanalysis, and behaviorism. However, biologism is most markedly felt in those doctrines of natural law that recognize the biological side of human nature as the proper source of moral and legal duties. Those doctrines, often without good reason, have in a way included the sphere of ethos in the sphere of bios. Biojurisprudence, while emphasizing the importance of advances in the biological sciences for the protection of life, does not reduce them to the extremes of biologism.

An extreme form of biojurisprudence would be total legalism consisting in the attempts to regulate by law the whole of human life and the whole of the natural environment. Although the history of mankind has known such ideas, they should be decidedly rejected in view of the objectives of jurisprudence. For jurisprudence postulates regulation only of that scope of human life and the life of the environment that is threatened by the often risk-laden (since experimental) application of scientific discoveries through technology. For jurisprudence postulates regulation only of that scope of human life and the life of the environment that is threatened by the often risk-laden (since experimental) application of scientific discoveries through technology. Total legalism, as confirmed by the tragic experience of mankind, admitted arbitrarily of criminal exceptions, despite declarations of the total protection of human life and the life of the environment. Following political criteria, total legalism deprived of such protection the lives of the whole groups of people exterminated for racial, national, religious or other reasons. Biojurisprudence firmly dissociates itself from the extremes of total legalism.

Unlike biologism influencing jurisprudence, the impact of jurisprudence on biology has never been very great. This impact can be felt, probably not very distinctly, through the connections of the philosophy of law with the philosophy of biology. For the two philosophies meet on the common ground of the philosophy of life also encountered under different names: practical philosophy, philosophy for everyone, wisdom of life, the art of life and the forming of life.

4. Medicine and Biojurisprudence

The word medicine, derived from Latin *mederi*, has had many meanings in its long history. Two of them, however, are the most important: (1) the science of health and disease, (2) the art of healing as a practical skill of preventing disease and treating the sick. It was largely the second meaning that contributed to the formation of the subject matter of biojurisprudence. Medicine alone as a science does not have a direct influence on human life. This influence is only evident in the practice of treating disease, the more so if it utilizes techniques that are often risk-laden as they are experimental. Therefore, biojurisprudence attaches less importance to the art of healing in accord with medical canons or *lege artis*, as lawyers call it. For biojurisprudence far more important is the opposite of the art of healing called medical malpractice. However, biojurisprudence is primarily concerned with defining the legal grounds for risk-laden experimentation in the art of healing.

Risk-laden experimentation in medicine became possible due to the advances in biological and technological sciences. The advances in the former define for medicine the range of risk-laden experimentation while the advances in the latter provide the means: medical techniques. Risk-laden experimentation in medicine certainly raises great expectations and equally great fears; it challenges the existing norms of the protection of human life and calls urgently for the making on new norms. The main task of biojurisprudence is thus to comprehensively and coherently present the conditions of the scope of regulation by law that provides the legal grounds for risk-laden experimentation in medicine. This is the task of the state authorities, which regulate and control medicine with the help of the law. Here, too, the extremes are possible: from full liberalism based on complete trust in the professional and moral competence of physicians to total legalism, which we reject, that tends to regulate by law everything that can be regulated.

The two extremes are a theoretical model rather than a solution that could be consistently applied in medical practice. Medical practice, manifested through the art of healing, will probably remain, as always, in the sphere of various compromises trying to balance divergent interests. Biojurisprudence, in its comprehensive and coherent treatment of that problem, can assist medicine in balancing divergent interests. This is possible provided that biojurisprudence itself attains such normative equilibrium that will be situated on the changing points between the protections of human life as the supreme value of risk-laden experimentation in the art of healing. In determining these points, we can apply the taxonomy of the ways of legal regulation and medical techniques. The taxonomy of the ways of legal regulation can concentrate on the values protected (human life), medical techniques, motives for the protection of values and application of techniques, organizational structures of the protection of human life, admitting the use of these techniques. The taxonomy of medical techniques alone can be reduced to evaluations of technology that remain the object of intensive scientific investigation. The right combination, in the area of biojurisprudence, of the results of the two kinds of taxonomy can become an alternative both for groundlessly fatalistic and uncritically optimistic views.

5. Morality and Biojurisprudence

The sense of term 'morality', close to the Latin term *moralitas*, denotes the whole of judgments, norms, models and rules of conduct that protect the values of good, rightness and justice binding through social acceptance. Theoretical views on morality are called ethics, but it is not only in scientific discourse that the term morality embraces both morality and ethics. Morality together with ethics is of paramount importance for biojurisprudence because not only does it judge and evaluate the objects of legal regulation but also provides models of such regulation in the form of moral norms. The crucial importance of morality for biojurisprudence can be expressed by means of two questions: (1) what is the connection of the legal status of norms with the moral status of norms? (2) what is the scope, if any, of the necessity and admissibility of enforcing moral norms by means of legal ones?

Question one prompts a search for the answers in ethical thought, which is home to extremely divergent views but in respect of the protection of human life it remains exceptionally unanimous. The connection of the legal status of norms with the moral status of norms is a reflection of the vast problems of the relation between morality and law. The existence or non-existence of this connection is justified by the thought essential both for ethics and jurisprudence. It is clearly substantiated by the thought of natural law and the accompanying thought of natural rights, whereas its existence is strongly denied by the thought of legal positivism. In the thought of the social contract (contractualism) this connection is manifested indirectly while in highly influential utilitarian thought it is immaterial. All those currents of thought, however, are important for biojurisprudence, which seeks justification for the scope of regulation by law of the protection of human life and the life of the environment against the threat of risk-laden experimentation.

Morality, also on account of its multiplicity of currents of thought, comprises the broadest scope of the protection of life. This is expressed by morality in general and by particular ethics built upon it, for example the ethics of the protection of life, ecological ethics, medical ethics etc. The scope of the protection of life by law is narrower because the scope of regulation by law is narrower. The task of biojurisprudence lies in comparing the ranges of regulation of the protection of life and indicating the scope that deserves to be regulated by law. There are thus instances of the scope of the protection of life regulated both by morality and by law, exclusively by morality or by law, and possibly neither by morality nor by law. The agreement between legal regulation and moral regulation is favorable to both of them with respect to their social acceptance. Disagreement of that kind weakens first of all the effectiveness of the law because the ineffectiveness of morality is less measurable and thereby less conspicuous.

Another question leads to the answer that biojurisprudence has grown from a conviction of the necessity to enforce some moral norms that protect life by means of legal norms. This answer is too general: it should be developed on the vast scale of moral judgments ranging from moral skepticism (which expresses doubts in the possibility of knowing and rationally justifying moral judgments) to different varieties of moral relativism (referring judgments to relativized facts rather then to the criteria of universal rationality) to moral absolutism (which maintains that only one moral structure is acceptable: the divine command) and moral egoism (which seeks praxeologically effective means to realize the ends of subjective interests, not necessarily contradictory to moral altruism). The choice of particular moral judgments as the grounds for justifying a legal regulation belongs to the realm of politics, which formulates its law-making decisions in the broad systemic spectrum from democracy to dictatorship. Biojurisprudence is probably unable to overcome the antinomy, especially evident in newer moral systems, between the conceptions of the sanctity of life and those of the quality of life. The conceptions of the sanctity of life are included in religious moral systems, notably in Catholicism, demanding the extension of legal protection over the whole of human life from the moment of conception to natural death. They uphold, like all moral systems, the prohibition to kill a human being and the duty to protect, sustain and save human life without any exception. However, the secular conceptions of the quality of life, while they likewise uphold the prohibition to kill, yet they admit of numerous exceptions in respect of the protection of human life ('justified' war, the state of necessity, self-defense, death penalty, euthanasia, experimentation risk, inevitable traffic accidents). Biojurisprudence cannot and will not compete with the religious conceptions, therefore it relates to the secular conceptions.

6. Jurisprudence and Biojurisprudence

Biojurisprudence is one of the currents in jurisprudence that reflects some effects of advances in the modern biological and technological sciences and in medicine, demanding regulation by law. The subject matter of biojurisprudence is the whole of legal thought, legal norms in force and postulated and legal practice concerning the protection of human life and of the natural environment. Like all other currents in jurisprudence it is incapable of promoting good directly. It can indirectly consolidate well by endeavors to prevent evil or, when this proves to be unsuccessful, to minimize its effects.

Jurisprudence embraces the whole of legal thought, legal norms and practice, derived from the term *ius* used by Roman lawyers as unmatched masters in the art. Biojurisprudence primarily relates to that sense of the term *ius*, that, which Celsius, an eminent Roman lawyer, formulated in a maxim: *law is the art of applying that which is good and right* (*ius est ars boni et aequi*). Jurisprudence has always been influenced by other branches of knowledge in its scope of the catalogs of protected values and their justification, less so with respect to the legal constructions and procedures themselves. These influences come from the older trends in jurisprudence, mainly natural law and legal positivism, and from its newer currents, for example jurisprudence of concepts and interests, and analytical and sociological jurisprudence.

It would be difficult to overestimate the vital importance of the conception of natural law for the whole of jurisprudence and also biojurisprudence. Based chiefly on philosophical and ethical assumptions, the conceptions of natural law construct universal norms of the protection of man under rationalized freedom. It would hardly be possible to say the same thing about the conceptions of legal positivism. Relating primarily to philosophical and politological voluntarist thought, the conceptions of legal positivism resolve conflicts between the protection of man and the protection of the state's interests in favor of the latter. Although the conceptions of natural law are decidedly closer to the assumptions of biojurisprudence (one can even say that it exhibits some features of natural law), yet the latter cannot ignore the conceptions of legal positivism characterized by greater realism.

Biojurisprudence should also be generally situated among the newer currents in jurisprudence. Jurisprudence of concepts (*Begriffsjurisprudenz*), developed in the circle of German thought, points to the crucial or even law-making sense of legal concepts. This indication remains important also for biojurisprudence because precision of concepts is an immanent value of the whole of jurisprudence aiming at the univocality of concepts, strict formulations and clarity of constructions. A similar relationship obtains between biojurisprudence and Anglo-Saxon analytical jurisprudence, recognized as a variety of legal positivism based on the experience of the practice of common law. If jurisprudence of interests, having European origins, treats law as a means of resolving conflicts of interests in society, then biojurisprudence is entirely jurisprudence of interests but concentrated on the 'interest of interest' – the protection of human life and the life of the environment. Finally, sociological jurisprudence, developed on North American soil, and other possible currents in jurisprudence: economic, politological, psychological, anthropological, and integrative, reflect primarily those contexts of law that are signaled by their names. All those contexts are found together in biojurisprudence since the protection of human life and the life of the natural environment are entangled in the whole complex of social relations.

7. Filiations between Sciences

Biojurisprudence, like every current in science, cannot claim a monopoly of the subject matter with which it deals. It has numerous and more or less complicated filiations with other branches of knowledge. Besides the problems that belong exclusively to its subject matter, it includes topics that partly overlap, intersect with or border the subject matter of other branches of science. As most branches of knowledge are interested in human life and many of them in the life of the natural environment, these filiations are extremely well developed. In order to mark the contours of the subject matter of biojurisprudence more clearly it is enough to mention its direct filiations with, on the one hand, two branches of knowledge with an ethical character and on the other hand, also with two branches with a jurisprudential character. In the former we touch upon some filiations of biojurisprudence with bioethics and medical ethics, and in the latter some filiations with medical law and forensic medicine.

Bioethics derives its name from the combination of the Greek word *bios* or life and *ethos* or custom in the sense of morality. It is a new branch of knowledge, developed only since the 1960's. Like biojurisprudence it deals with the normative knowledge of the protection of human life and of the life of the environment against the threats accompanying risk-laden experiments in utilizing the achievements of the biological sciences. In that sense, together with jurisprudence, it is included in the 'science of survival' of man and the environment. However, while bioethics strives for that survival by means of sanctions arising out of moral norms, biojurisprudence tries to do so with legal sanctions. And it is at that point that the main differences between the two should be discerned.

Medical ethics is a set of principles and moral norms that should bind physicians in the practice of their profession. As the ethics of one profession it is a specific concretization of the principles and norms of general ethics. Biojurisprudence relates both to particular medical ethics and general ethics. Numerous codes of medical ethics, worked out for millennia, contain universal contents accepted by biojurisprudence. In most general terms, they focus on the patient's good, taking into account the interests of society. There are, however, fundamental differences of principles and norms between different kinds of medical ethics about whether it is advisable to endow them with legal sanctions. According to the conceptions of the autonomy of medical ethics the regulation by law of the professionalism of physicians brings more harm than good because it restricts their freedom of decision. According to paternalistic conceptions, however, the law should determine the limits of the physician's freedom of decision-making because this follows from the state's function towards medicine. Biojurisprudence favors the paternalistic conceptions but at the same time it emphasizes the necessity to limit to the necessary minimum the legal regulation of the professional practice of physicians.

Medical law has marked its separate character mainly in the Anglo-Saxon countries. As a separate branch of law it does not reflect those divisions of legal systems into branches of law that are preserved in traditional jurisprudence. Therefore medical law contains legal norms that are, on the one hand, so much homogeneous as to be of interest for medicine, and, on the other hand, so much heterogeneous as to belong to various branches of law: from civil law to contract law and tort law to criminal law. It must be pointed out that this solution is very close to the assumptions of biojurisprudence. For its aim is to break the existing ties of the legal norms protecting human life with various branches of law and to collect them, following the model of the law on the protection of natural environment, into a uniform and coherent whole. In its most general terms, medical law regulates the relations between physicians and patients and the organization of medical institutions. It includes the legal criteria of distinguishing between good medical practice (*lege artis*) and medical malpractice. Important rules of medical law concern the patients' consent as to the form and range of therapy, the confidential character of information on his condition, the treating of the dying persons and the pronouncing of death. Medical law treats of these norms from the medical point of view while biojurisprudence mainly from the standpoint of law. Moreover, the treatment by biojurisprudence of the problems of the protection of human life is more universal than their treatment by medical law.

Forensic medicine is a branch of medical science whose objective is to apply it practically for the needs of the administration of justice. While biojurisprudence, bioethics, medical ethics and medical law have a normative character, forensic medicine is more of a descriptive nature. Forensic medicine is even indispensable in some civil cases (for example to establish paternity) and most often in criminal cases (to establish the cause of death). It thus plays an important role in lawsuits and criminal proceedings in discovering the objective truth, which is the basis of just adjudication. While the normative branches of knowledge create the norms of the protection of human life, forensic medicine serves to help in their practical application.

8. Summary

Biojurisprudence, whose concepts I present, is a new current in jurisprudence concentrated around the problems of the legal protection of human life and the life of the natural environment. This current seeks to integrate both the law-making thought scattered by narrow specialization and the law-making practice concerning the protection of human life and the life of the environment. Biojurisprudence provides a scientifically well-grounded foundation for new branches of law that bring to the fore, emphasize and protect human life and the life of the environment.

The subject matter of biojurisprudence embraces all threats to human life and the life of the natural environment. Taking into account the natural rhythm of human life from the moment of conception to birth, and life until death, I distinguish three segments of biojurisprudence: biojusgenesis, biojustherapy and biojusthanatology. This tripartite division, with appropriate modifications to avoid anthropomorphism, can also apply to the protection of the life of the environment.

I show the connections of the subject matter of biojurisprudence with the subject matter of many branches of knowledge, primarily with biology, medicine, ethics and jurisprudence. Biological knowledge provides biojurisprudence with descriptions of life. Medical knowledge arouses the interest of biojurisprudence in the ways of utilizing the biological knowledge about human life and the life of the environment, sometimes requiring regulation by law. Ethical knowledge, with its judgments of life and the ways of saving it, provides the ground for legal regulations. The knowledge of jurisprudence is to some extent the source and broader background for biojurisprudence.

I also indicate the interesting filiations of biojurisprudence with some other sciences, whose goal is also the protection of human life and the life of the environment: bioethics, medical law and forensic medicine. I see the urgent need to develop a new branch of law, after the model of environmental law, which could be called human life protection law. This law would collect into one uniform and coherent whole all legal norms concerning the protection of human life that are now scattered in many branches of law.

I find it peculiar paradox that law created by man for man has pushed man himself into the background in its systems. In the traditional systems of law prominence is given to property and non-property law, substantive and non-substantive law, proprietary and non-proprietary right, private and public law etc but there is no law on the protection of man. There is an urgent need to change the situation by for example instituting the code of the protection of life (of man and of the environment), which would assert the primacy of life in the hierarchy of values protected by law. Biojurisprudence gives the impetus to the indispensable changes, for example in the legal systems, by the all-round treatment of the whole of problems concerning the legal protection of life.

Otmar Höll
Wien

The Global System between Integration and Fragmentation

1. Introduction

Undoubtedly the whole international system has undergone dramatic structural changes since the end of the 1980s, marking a paradigm shift. To a large extend this transformation after the end of the Cold-War-period to a large extend was a consequence of the unforeseen rapid demise of the communist regimes in East European countries and primarily in the Soviet Union, with a pivotal forerunner role played by the Polish political opposition. As a further result these changes brought about major structural transformation not only for Europe but for the global system as a whole, much deeper and more far-reaching than during the whole Cold-War period before. And this process of transformation is still going on. We are still within this rapid and multi-dimensional transformation and adaptation process of the whole international fabric, and from today's perspective we can not say, where this process will finally lead us to. During the first post-cold-war-years of euphorism and high expectations, many (including the former president of the USA, George Bush sen.) thought we were entering a new phase of a "New World Order" or of a "New Multilateralism", the world heading towards a more peaceful and cooperative, more integrated, stable and prosperous community of Nations. Forecasts then seemed to be obvious and highly positive especially for the Western countries, and read approximately like this: While those countries and societies in the

European East – and also in the world's South – would have to adapt to "Western standards", eventually to completely change their economic, social and political systems to the new given environment, societies in the West (Western Europe, USA, Japan and all the others, organised within the group of OECD-States) would remain quasi as they were, stable and "integrated". Thus there seemed to be no need for deeper changes or adaptations in this part of the world.

In the beginning neither politicians nor larger part of the scientific community realised that with the demise of communism and its consequences, the reshuffling of the whole "Second World", both former parallel systems, East and West, had just started being transformed into one completely new, comprehensive and interdependent global socio-political entity. With the effect that also those countries and societies in "the integrated West", later on called the "old Europe" by Donald Rumsfeld, found themselves thrown into a completely new system together with the "new Europe", the former countries of Eastern Europe, now the new members of the EU since May 2004. In the middle and longer term this new situation brought deep socio-economic and political changes for the West in almost all dimensions, economic, political and social, too. Today both sides, and together with the countries in the South, the whole community of States find themselves in a completely different world, where traditional national policies and political measures on a national scale do not apply any more as they did before. Consequently the same is true for security and threat scenarios and subjective perceptions of the overall security situation[1], they all have undergone deep changes too.

What had happened, however? *Not much!* *Not much?* We have started from the remnants of a long and familiar period of the Cold War, and we have ended up in a new large and comprehensive sys-

---

[1] Most important is to recognize the altered character of "threats" in the post-Cold-War period. Although it's true that those kinds of threats have been known to human kind for centuries, however, their interlocking character and new dimensions added through increased interdependence are of crucial importance. Local problems and crises may, more often than ever, have global consequences: threats people far from here have to face are threats to all of us. And they are closely linked to each other. As a consequence of globalization: national borders have become much more permeable, and provide less protection for nationals.

tem, where almost all countries and all their sub-systems are torn together, interfere and relate to one another, at a certain level, being even more dependent on one another than before, especially, but not exclusively, on the economic level.[2] Interdependence of states and societies has become not only an accepted theoretical concept years ago (cf. Keohane/Nye's famous book on that issue and the notion of "complex interdependence" has been published back in the late 1970s) but a fact of daily life. And – as we know – interdependence means also: more vulnerability, for rich and poor, small and big states, also for societies, even for the individuals at economic, societal and political levels. The horrifying attacks of 9/11 in New York and Washington is only the proof and has become a symbol of all that. Discussions on theoretical and academic levels had started already in the gone 1990s of last century: Security policies and doctrines since then had become a broad, comprehensive matter – not only military – issue in real global politics.

Subsequently this new situation brought about even more change and further dynamics into new, much more deregulated, flexible and unstable structures for all countries and societies, at a much higher pace, not only in real/material terms, but also fundamentally in the way people, i.e. citizens perceived these changes with senses of insecurity, anxiety and fear.[3] Within only a few months or so after the break-down of the bi-polarity system a new notion began to make a global carrier through international media: "globalization", under-

---

[2] One explanation among others that almost no scholar of IR foresaw the possibility of fundamental change of parameters of the international system may be due to the fact that IR-scholars belong to the most conservative groups of social scientists worldwide. Most of them are sceptical not to say cynical about major structural changes. And a great majority of them holds the opinion that major change could bring greater chaos or destruction than a realistic acceptance of the sometimes grim reality of international politics. So during the whole of the Cold-War period a justifiable cynicism concerning the then traditional international system could have contributed to neglecting significant changes. However, these fundamental changes were of course not the first in the history of the international system, and it might challenge the whole of what we had so often referred to as the "Westphalian System", the system of "sovereign" and closely definable single states.

[3] See Anthony Giddens, *Beyond Left and Right – The Future of Radical Politics*, Cambridge: Polity Press, 1994.

stood as an ever-expanding process of integration, interconnectedness and interdependence, based on scientific and technical revolutions in the fields of technology and communications during the decade(s) before, which led to the apparent shrinking of distances, and most important, an ever-increasing rate of transnational economic exchange and competition between economies.[4] But, however, globalization and increased interdependence (which, and again this is important to understand, means also increased vulnerability for all the nation states and their people involved) have not led to a higher degree of overall homogenization, but also to several forms of economic and social fragmentation. It can be observed in many different ways to varying degrees and in many different contexts, and has led to different kinds of societal and "civil society" reactions throughout the world, since globalization tends to shift the balance of power towards business, which becomes increasingly global and flexible, whereas political reaction remains rather national.

2. The Perspectives of Globalization and Interdependence

To define the nature of the international system as of today does not simply mean to account for the conditions created by the more or less non-violent (self)defeat of the Soviet Union and its ideological, cultural and political superstructure. The end of the Cold War and the re-arrangement of Russia in the ranking-order of the hierarchically organized international global system are just two of the many elements of present world changes. Besides, it is also important to understand the rapid transformation of the international system under the effect of the acceleration of the globalization process, also as a consequence of the communist demise. Economic interdependence of national markets seemed much more promising than political measures on national level.

---

[4] Cf. among others James N. Rosenau, *Turbulence in World Politics. A Theory of Change and Continuity*, New York: Harvester-Wheatsheaf, 1990.

According to George Modelski[5] and others globalization[6] is a process of growing interdependence, and by no means not a new phenomenon. It has already started centuries ago, and is likely to continue well into the future, beyond the 21st century, in case we experience no break-down or catastrophic events that could bring this process to an end.

International interdependence is often said to have rapidly increased during recent past decades. Often international trade is taken as a main indicator of interdependence. Its high and, with two deep interruptions by the two world wars in the 20th century, rapidly growing values are commonly accepted as strong evidence of the increasing interdependence of states and societies. So as an example during the period between 1820 and 1992, world population increased five-fold, income per head eight-fold, world income 40-fold, and world trade even 540-fold.[7] For quite some time international financial flows have been taken as another meaningful measure of permanently growing interdependence.

However, the notion of "globalization" has been unveiled, massively and critically studied recently because of its growing pace over

---

[5] George Modelski, "Evolutionary paradigm for global politics", *International Studies Quarterly*, vol. 40/3, 1996, pp. 321–342.

[6] "Globalization" is not only and foremost an economic phenomenon, although it was in the economic-financial, technological, transport and communicational fields that were so to say at the forerunners, globalization has also become an environmental, cultural, and, above all and highly important, a mind-setting phenomenon (people everywhere in the world, even in the most remote places today think in these terms and realize the consequences!), which had started already decades before. 1989 was only a boost-up in pace, and 9/11 – and what followed – was, as it seems, its cruel proof. 9/11 was not only the proof for many theoretical analyses done in the 1990s, "asymmetric conflicts" (terrorism, ethnic or religious conflicts, organised crime, private proliferation of weapons, ...) will be one or **the** most important form of the "new images of conflicts" in the 21st century. But 9/11 could have been a real watershed: for governments' new understanding of "security", for the future of globalization and for "nation states", in so far as more trans- and international cooperation is – badly – needed for all states; perhaps with the exception of one state, the single hegemonic power, the USA. But: could the USA really follow a policy of "going it alone"? One can seriously doubt that.

[7] Cf. Angus Maddison, *Monitoring the World Economy 1820–1992. Development Centre Studies*, Paris: OECD, 1995.

the last ten to twenty years or so, and there seems to be good reason to argue that today's process of globalization is unprecedented, large, comprehensive and increasing.[8] For this reason, we can subsequently talk of our times as of "the era of globalization". The world in this era has become a world of easy and intense mobility and communication, persistent demands for implementing individual and collective human rights, recurrent waves of democratization, fast imitation and, at least to a certain extent, pressure on uniformization of societies and cultures. We have arrived at a state of affairs where new problems ("interdependence-problems" as we call them in the discipline of International Relations) have emerged that cannot be solved by single states alone like that of ecological pollution, migration, terrorism, proliferation of weapons of mass destruction, trafficking people and other forms of trans-national organized crime and – last but not least – epidemics, diseases, and natural catastrophes.

But the world of the globalization era is much more complex like all this. It is also contributing to structural fragmentation, discontinuity, decentralization and individuation.[9] It is the world of the autonomy and auto-organization of the individual (person, group, society, region) which has been "released" from the absolute conditioning determination of its origins and personal and physical environment. It is the world of the untiring and even violent reaction of the individuals, single women and men, groups, cultures and regions, to the risk of being overwhelmed by the rest of the world for their lack of ability to seal national borders, protecting and separating them from "the others", the foreigners.

---

[8] Some authors point on at least five qualifications that make today's globalization unprecedented: first the rapid growth of the ratio of international trade to national income, second approx. a dozen developing countries have benefited from trade and foreign investment, third and paradoxically, direct foreign investment today constitutes a smaller portion of total investment than before 1914 (the bulk flows into the USA), fourth there is less international migration than during 1870 and 1913, barriers to immigration are higher now, and fifth and finally it would be foremost the damage to consumers and producers if trade would be eliminated, which indicates the high degree of global interdependence, which, however, means that markets in some way become more important than states. But it does – by no means – indicate "the end" of the nation states, at the contrary.

[9] On such a term see *Globalisation and Territorial Identities*, ed. by Zdravko Mlinar, Aldershot: Avesbury, 1992.

In such a globalized world, the ability of states to control their territorial borders and protect their citizens has been highly put in question. The power to stop ideas and movements of any kind across state borders got lost, even the ability of the most effective governments to keep all kinds of cross-boundary flows under their firm control has been markedly reduced. At the same time, the states discover themselves as deprived of the material and political conditions and instruments to continue "making" foreign policy more or less autonomously as they did before such changes took effect. Moreover, the states realized how unable they were to provide for the security of their citizens with traditional political means in any field, from territorial to economic, from cultural to environmental security.[10]

Structural interdependence, however, is just the other side of the coin of globalization, which means that only states and societies cooperating closely which each other can come to terms with problems they all share, and which they cannot effectively solve alone anymore. But it needs strong, sustained political will and communicative skills that are necessary for long term cooperation, although on the other hand a great number of forces work in favor of integration: the growth of economic interdependence and even the spread of multinational corporations, the proliferation of functional international institutions at both the regional and global levels, the overall homogenizing effects of modernization, the spread of Western media and popular culture, the growing global embrace of shared standards of human rights and democratic politics, the international flow of scientific ideas, and the effects of cheaper and more efficient modes of transportation and communication contribute immensely to enhanced cooperative development. These forces take political expression in the form of actors who benefit from, welcome and seek to further the growth of political, economic and social interdependence. But at the same time, it produces also losers of this process, excluding a greater part of societies not only in the South and (former) East, but also in "the West" from progress and gains also connected with globalization.

---

[10] Cf. Josef A. Camilleri, Jim Falk, *The End of Sovereignty? The Politics of a Shrinking and Fragmenting World*, Aldershot: Edward Elgar, 1992; and *Global Politics. Globalisation and the Nation-State*, ed. by Anthony G. McGrew, Paul G. Lewis, Cambridge: Polity Press, 1992.

The forces of growing fragmentation are just as varied as the dimensions of globalization and integration. They include ethnic warfare, religious and nationalist cleavages, the backlash of local cultures against modernization and Western penetration, conflicts generated by resource scarcities or environmental strains, economic protectionism, and the struggle between the haves and the have nots. States, groups or actors harmed and effected by various forms of interdependence will seek to stop or even reverse its spread. However, there is the North-South conflict, which is one of the major macro-social problems of our time. Scholarly views and opinions of scientists and experts on this problem are quite divergent.[11] Questions of how to evaluate the level of development of a society, as well as differing visions of possible interactive mechanisms among societies, play crucial roles in the analysis of this topic.

3. Politics in a World of Mutual Dependence, Globalization, and Fragmentation

All these ingredients were already present before the end of bipolarity, but were not in the focus or foreground of the international agenda, but already embedded in the over-arching East-West- mega-confrontation structures. But under the surface, the information revolution of the 1970ies and 80ies has fostered a sense of mutual sensitivity and vulnerability. Television today displays to people what is occurring around the world or, at least, someone's version of it. Selectivity and individual or collective perception may be a bigger issue than objectivity, since there is so much more information available today. Telephones, faxes and the internet enable people to exchange views about what is happening worldwide and discuss how to respond. Networked computers, as all know, allow people to plan concerted action at an entirely different level of effectiveness and effi-

---

[11] For a creative new perspective on how to bring "development" about cf. the recently published book by the 1998 Nobel Prize-Winner in economics, Amartya Sen, *Development as Freedom*, New York: Knopf, and Oxford: Oxford University Press, 1999.

ciency. This is as true throughout the „interconnected world" as within, and between governments, companies and civil society.

In a study published in the early 1990ies by the Canadian International Development Research Centre, Ivan Head and Jorge Nef correctly observed that there is now a reality of „mutual vulnerability."[12] Others developed this concept of vulnerability further and advocated the need for a strong commitment to social solidarity. Religious leaders have been searching for parallel references in the Bible and in the teachings of other religions, like Hans Küng and his "Project World Ethos". The ethics of sustainability, as brought forward by the World Commission on Environment and Development (WCED), chaired by the former Prime Minister of Norway, Gro Harlem Brundtland, propelled an enlightened and secularized view of our common global interests.[13]

There has also been an increase in mutual sensitivity, a sense that even though events may not physically or substantially touch someone far away, that person feels affected or even involved mentally or emotionally. So, e.g. citizens in Europe and North America demanded an end to the genocide in Bosnia-Herzegovina, eventually pushing their governments to intervene. The underlying reasons were only partly the danger of the conflicts spilling over. We have seen the same process only some years ago in Kosovo, although with uncertain results till date. Back in the 1990ies, there was strong pressure on governments to alleviate the developing disaster in the refugee camps of Eastern Zaire or then in Somalia. The greater part of the public had only a vague idea of what had happened there. What the remarkable effect about this episodes is that the arrivals and subsequent departures of the international media, under the leadership of CNN, determined the willingness or lack thereof to participate in similar international interventions. But, fortunately, so the same „mutual sensitivity" also pushed a number of governments to act to ban anti-

---

[12] Ivan Head, *On the Hinge of History: The Mutual Vulnerability of South and North*, Toronto: University of Toronto Press, 1991; and Jorge Nef, *Human Security and Mutual Vulnerability: An Exploration into the Global and Political Economy of Development and Underdevelopment* (2nd ed.), International Development and Research Centre, 1999.

[13] *Our Common Future*, Report of the World Commission on Environment and Development-WCED, edited 1987.

personnel land mines or to donate to the victims of the Tsunami-catastrophe in late December 2004.

Analysts of global issues today are facing two simultaneous yet only apparently contradictory processes: those of increasing global interdependence connected with integration and increasing fragmentation. James Rosenau[14] has correctly described these processes as not contradictory but instead fundamentally linked. Indeed, he has invented the term "fragmegration" for it.[15] New technologies made globalization (defined here as growing interconnectedness throughout the world) possible, indeed inevitable. That reality consequently leads to fragmentation, a human response to what some see as overwhelming and homogenizing pressures that looks for differentiation, distinctive identity, and group expression. Moreover, and very important, globalization is occurring at the same time as increasing stratification in the whole world, almost in all societies, as noted by many authors. This too contributes to fragmentation. Benjamin Barber and Robert Kaplan have both also addressed these issues in their books, published back early in the 1990ies.[16]

4. The Changing Global Agenda

The implications of the transportation, communication, and information revolutions and the growing impact of interdependence and globalization can be fully understood only in the context of the changing agenda of global issues.

The international agenda, simultaniously to the developments mentioned, has obviously deeply changed over the past two centuries

---

[14] James N. Rosenau, *Turbulence in World Politics. A Theory of Change and Continuity*, Princeton: Princeton University Press, 1990.

[15] For Rosenau "fragmegration" is a decentralized fusion of global and local interests. It juxtaposes the processes of fragmentation and integration occurring within organizations, communities, countries and transnational systems in such a way that it is impossible not to treat them as interactive and causally linked. This leads to decrease authority of states, and increase the role of transnational networks.

[16] Although Barber focuses on the cultural dimension and Kaplan focuses on the evidence for fragmentation; both received a great deal of attention.

too. Looking into the "longue duree" the main task of the nineteenth-century European agenda was to represent the respective states' interests in the maintenance of peace, the process of alliance building, and the conduct of wars. During the relatively long period in which the Concert of Europe prevailed, diplomats and leaders initially met at regular congresses in order to establish a set of rules, norms, and institutions that maintained the European balance of power and minimized the risks of war.[17] The agenda of the states' representatives was dominated by typical topics of traditional national security: state survival, the pursuit of power, and the balance of power. This diplomatic routine continued well into the twentieth century.

It was only until the 1970s that politicians and diplomats maintained this focus on political and security questions. Increasingly, in the years after, they gradually have turned their attention more and more to economics, trade and other matters. Although, in a number of countries, trade matters (economic political measures) are handled by separate and often competing national ministries. This contributed to a process, described by some authors of the International Relations discipline of the gradually breaking down of the distinction between domestic and foreign policy. In more recent years this has changed even more, insofar as national agendas and interests have reflected the ascendance of human security issues and the dilution of traditional national security concerns.[18]

---

[17] Kalevi J. Holsti, "Governance without Government: Polyarchy in Nineteenth-Century European International Politics", in: James Rosenau, *Governance without Government*, Cambridge: Cambridge University Press, 1992, pp. 30–57.

[18] Cf. the relatively new human security concept, which has been widely used to describe the complex of interrelated threats associated with civil wars, genocide, natural disasters and the displacement of people. While "national security" focuses on the defence of a state from external attacks, human security is about protecting individuals and countries from any form of violence or natural catastrophes. Human Security threats are strongly interrelated with poverty, socio-economic and political inequity and the lack of functioning states. Cf. among others: *Human Development Report*, ed. by United Nations Development Program – UNDP, New York 1994; Jorge Nef, *Human Security and Mutual Vulnerability: The Global Political Economy of Development* (2nd ed.), Ottawa: IDRC, 1999; and Cristobal Kay, *Globalisation, Competitiveness, and Human Security*, London: Cass Publishers, 1997.

To demonstrate the changing nature and function of the traditional foreign policy agenda, one needs only to compare the agenda of the Great Powers at the Concert of Europe Congresses in the 19th century with that of today's G7/8 summits. At the Concert of Europe meetings, the Great five European Powers concerned themselves primarily with the maintenance of peace and overall societal stability. Things today are highly different. While growth in trade and of global capital flows is, on a highly aggregated balance, desirable and adds to global economic growth and welfare to a greater extent for middle classes and the rich, it has at the same time led to serious problems of managing increased interdependence. For example, banks and individuals today channel much more capital in an attempt to benefit from fluctuations in exchange rates then they do for productive investment and trade purposes. The cross mentality of these operations, with the attendant risk of financial market overstretch and instability, offer some crises from the 1990s onward has become clear to many. The inadequacy of transparency, supervision, and regulation in emerging markets is now quite widely accepted. It has led to initiatives to improve the "international financial architecture", the idea of the "Tobin tax" being one of many, however, soft counter measures that emerged.[19] The increasing importance of global trade and capital flows, underlining our mutual dependence and vulnerability, have given rise to the emergence of global Economic Summits.

Now the agenda is changing again and, interestingly, this is reflected in the preoccupation of the G7/8 leaders with a broader global

---

[19] The "Tobin tax" was first proposed in 1978 by James Tobin, Nobel Prize-Winner and US-professor of economics. His idea was a tax on foreign exchange transactions that would be applied uniformly by all countries. A tiny amount (less than 0.5%) would be levied on all foreign currency exchange transactions to deter speculation on currency fluctuations. While the rate would be low enough not to have a significant effect on longer term investment, it would cut into the yields of speculators moving massive amounts of currency around the globe in seeking profit from short term differentials in currency fluctuations. Interest has grown rapidly in such a mechanism, as the pace of foreign exchange transactions and financial deregulation has accelerated over the past decade. Today approximately US-$1 trillion volume of currency is traded every day in unregulated financial markets. Only 5% of this activity is related to trade and other real economic transactions. The other 95% is simply speculative activity as traders bet on exchange rate fluctuations and international interest rate differentials.

agenda. Indeed, the G7/8 has turned over most of the international economic coordination issues to their finance ministers, and now the leaders in a G8 configuration concentrate more on issues such as the environment, health, and crime and, – if we take the last summit in Scotland in summer 2005 security and developmental issues – fighting poverty in summer 2005 Africa.[20] The changed global agenda, now increasingly influenced by human security concerns, has had and will have a fundamental impact on the overall international agenda in the future.

6. The Concept of Human Security

In the past there were few if any foreign ministries who have spent much time worrying about infectious diseases, and the same is true, although perhaps to a lesser extent, about climate change, terrorism and organized crime. Yet already in the past recent years politicians nonetheless had to discuss how to better collaborate transnationally to deal with major issues of global concern, not to leave them to national or international bureaucrats only.

Human security issues refer to a variety of threats to human well-being, whether from violence or from other nontraditional threats such as environmental degradation, "natural" disasters as hurricanes, Tsunamis or climate change, or other transnational events endangering human health. Above all, with respect to former casualities, conflicts now are much more frequently, and even so primarily, intra- than interstate[21] borne. What is important in acknowledging the value of the concept of human security is not to deny the fact that the classic problems of security have disappeared. And they are unlikely ever to disappear in a world in which the destruction of all weapons of mass destruction, be they nuclear, biological or chemical, is highly improbable, since the "old" ones still exist and new generations of that kind (some of these very small in size, but highly efficient) are under construction.

---

[20] See the program of the meeting of the G8 in Gleneagles, Scotland, in July 2005.

[21] Kalevi Holsti, *The State War and The State of War*, Cambridge: Cambridge University Press, 1996, especially chapters 1, 2, and 4.

Global issues are now being dealt in almost all national ministries. These issues call for global public policy and for better transnational or "global" governance. The concept was the research subject of a major international UN-commission headed by the former prime minister of Sweden Ingvar Carlsson, and Sonny Ramphal, the former secretary-general of the Commonwealth and was published in 1993.[22]

The likelihood is that the prominence of climate change as a global issue will increase further in the next few years as it has become evident (even in the USA) that it is not just an environmental issue but one of human security. The International Panel on Climate Change – IPCC itself is an interesting example of new forms of governance in the world, has predicted that average surface temperature will warm by 1 to 3.5 degrees C in the next quarter century. The increase will not be the same in all regions, but the result will be among others more extremes in weather, already noted as a risk by the insurance industry. Rising sea levels, which will cause serious flooding in low-lying places, and an increase in diseases, and – as a possible consequence for Europe the melting of the Arctic ice belt and consequently the conversion of the Gulf Stream with major consequences – a sharp decrease of the overall temperature level could follow later on. The need for better governance, including a "grand bargain" among the various stakeholders, new policies, new instruments (both domestic and international), and perhaps new or radical reforms of existing institutions, will be unavoidable.

At present worldwide there are approximately 14 million international refugees (as to the Geneva-Convention) and around 50 million internally displaced persons, if not more. Many, perhaps most, of

---

[22] The global population will grow from 6 to 8 billion people in the next quarter century. More than one-quarter of the world's population today lives in absolute poverty. Their highest priority is economic opportunity, and few political leaders in developed countries, let alone in countries with annual per capita incomes under $100 US, are prepared, for example, to say they will compromise on economic growth to avert the risk of contributing to a future warming of the planet. Energy demand could therefore increase by 50 percent. It is imperative, in deciding how to respond to these needs, that political leaders act with full awareness of the implications for climate change. This means we must significantly reduce fossil fuel emissions from present levels, and certainly not allow them to increase.

these people have moved, not on free will, because of concerns about their security. There are critical shortages of fresh water in certain world regions already existing or looming ahead. Already it has become evident that poor water quality has been a major factor in the rise in infectious diseases, underlying the linkages among many of the issues described as global. There is a highly uneven distribution of fresh water resources, regionally as well as socially. The willingness to share between the haves of the world and the have-nots is not a given, it is rather doubtful. In some areas, consumption of fresh water is more rapid than replacement, with negative effects on water supply. All in all, one-third of the world's population lives in countries suffering from water shortage or pollution. Climate change is likely to add to the problem. The consequences for human security in all these cases are clear and figure among others as root causes of international terrorism.

Population growth will occur almost exclusively in already overcrowded cities in the poorer countries of the world. Overpopulation will cause problems of shelter, food, and waste disposal, with implications for health and human security. Breathing dirty air is obviously a danger to human health. The challenge of bad air quality is likely to become even greater in megacities such as Beijing, New Delhi, Jakarta, and Mexico City. Today, the World Health Organization estimates that almost one and a half billion people breathe substandard air. The annual mortality rate estimation is 500.000.

Declining biodiversity is not just an issue for nature freaks. It is a consequence of population growth and development, and it will be aggravated by climate change. Fifty plant species are becoming extinct every day. By 2050, half the species alive today could be extinct. Loss of habitat is one of the major reasons. The consequences include a serious risk of reduced resiliency for the remaining living organisms. Again, the implications for (lack of) human security and for subsequent spread of violent political movements are obvious, although this issue is too often seen as an environmental rather than a security concern, but both threats are mutually reinforcing each other.[23]

---

[23] See *Human Development Report 2003: Millennium Development Goals*, ed. by United Nations Development Program, New York: Oxford University Press, 2003.

Deforestation still remains a serious regional and global problem. At a time when the capacity to absorb carbon dioxide should not be decreased, that is precisely what is happening. Organizations and NGOs active in saving rainforests need to be encouraged, since they offer opportunities to substitute for cutting down trees, like e.g. the International Network for Bamboo and Rattan, with a species that can be harvested after five or six years and which can absorbe carbon as it grows.

Eight hundred million people today suffer from chronic malnutrition. Two hundred million of them are children. While there is sufficient production globally, there are major local failures, often because of transport or distribution problems. The countries with food security problems are often those with shortages of fresh water and a great number of people concentrated in cities with bad air quality. This covers all aspects of the human security problem. It leads to migration pressures and increases the risk of uncontrollable violence. Once again the linkage among the global challenges is more than obvious.

Other global issues that have an important human security dimension are international terrorism, transnational organized crime, consisting of a variety of activities including money laundering, trafficking in stolen or illicit goods as well as people, computer crimes, and theft of intellectual property. Criminals today are becoming better equipped with high-tech means. They have learned how to network and to form alliances of convenience. These alliances can run a variety of strategies from cooperation between ethnically based criminal cartels to links between criminal and terrorist groups.

Citizens today in many parts of the world see their security jeopardized not only, and probably in most cases not primarily, by the threat of pending wars, whether inter- or intrastate. But, however, there is a need to address a much broader agenda. This is the case not simply because lives are in danger from other threats than traditional violent conflicts, but because many of the risks described above, if not adequately addressed, could and likely will lead to an increase of classic security threats and violent conflicts. Only the sources and roots of potential conflicts are changing.

Policies and strategies therefore need to be re-considered and, if necessary, reinvented, and set on new, transnational, basis. These global issues as of today have not traditionally been in our usual purview, but now they should be there, without any doubt. The citizens of our countries need to understand the substance, not simply relying on the experts, but applying their creative senses and practical skills to responding to this new problems. The global environment is changing rapidly in different ways, however, beyond the impact of technological changes and the new international agenda.

7. Conclusions and Perspectives

It is always risky to claim that the whole global system is in a process of fundamental transition. But at certain times in history there is enough evidence to make such strong statement. Many scholars worldwide today agree that we live in a time where this international system is in a process of fundamental change, from a system of rather autonomous or more or less "sovereign" states to one in which they are increasingly involved in growing mutual interdependencies and networks. These interrelations are multi-dimensional.

In addition to economic interdependence – esp. trade, finance and direct investment dimensions – also educational, technological, ideological, and cultural, as well as ecological, environmental, legal, military, strategic, and political crucial topics are now rapidly interconnected throughout the world. Financial capital and goods, images and people, sports and religions, guns and drugs, and diseases and pollution can now be moved (or move) quickly across national borders. When beginning in the 1970s new global communications systems were established, instantaneous communication from any part of the world to any other became possible. It is not only the creation of a 24-hour capital market that became possible but also the flashing of pictures of statesmen and all kinds of local events across the globe, making these faces more familiar to us than those of our next-door neighbors.

Although it is true that states today are more constrained than they were used to be during the decades before – from above by

global economic forces and from below by citizens and peoples asking for rights, participation, or independence – reports of states' immediate or eventual demise, as suggested by the titles of such books
such as *Sovereignty at Bay* by Raymond Vernon (1972), *The Twilight of
Sovereignty* (Walter Wriston, 1997), and *The End of the Nation State and
The Borderless World* (Kenichi Ohmae, 1990), are somewhat premature.
The perspective of rapidly and permanently increasing globalization
and decay of nation states arises from a short time frame covering
only the last 30 or 40 years, at the beginning of which countries
seemed to be rather well protected and sealed up as a result of the
experiences of the great interwar depression period and further on
World War II.

Scholarly views differ on the gains or costs global mobility of such
things as goods and services, finance, technology, and ideas might
bring. In an often-quoted passage, John Maynard Keynes[24] wrote that
„Ideas, knowledge, art, hospitality, travel – these are things which
should of their nature be international. But let goods be homespun
whenever it is reasonably and conveniently possible; and, above all,
let finance be primarily national." Today it is more fashionable to
deplore „cultural imperialism" or the „homogenization" of the film
and TV-industry, the mass media and the global spread of mass culture, and to attempt to confine culture to local tradition, activities, and
products while advocating free trade in material goods and services.

Neoliberals usually advocate completely for free trade and a good
deal of laissez-faire but not the free movement of people. In the eight-
eenth-century French economist François Quesnay added to "laissez-
faire" the concept of "laissez-passer". This is forgotten today, perhaps
because contemporary neoliberals fear that it would accelerate population growth especially in the low-income countries providing new
floods of emigrants and therefore not contribute to raising their welfare, or that it would interfere with economic objectives, especially
concerning the level and distribution of income, or cultural values, or
social stability and cohesion, or societal security, in the countries receiving the migrants. But all these objections also apply to the free

---

[24] John Maynard Keynes, "National Self-Sufficiency", *Yale Review* 22/4, 1933,
pp. 755–776.

movement of goods and services. In any case, there seems to be some inconsistency of "progressive" and critical reflexion.

For many globalization is considered to be an uncontrollable force that destroys states, communities and traditional ties of solidarity. Others consider globalization a consequence and a value of modernity, individual freedom and an important root of wealth. I would argue that globalization is neither a catastrophe nor a value per se: it is primarily an economic and financial process that, with the rise of new transnational and non-governmental actors, it is constantly redefining the options of people, the role of the state and the space of action left to national governments in domestic and international affairs. Consequently globalization demands permanent change and learning for people, new forms of governance at national and international levels in order to transform its challenges. Included are also different kinds of fragmentation and conflicts within and between states, regions or continents, and the exclusion of at least parts of the less equipped individuals' communities and countries. The process may bring new opportunities for greater democracy and for individual and collective freedom, it may also mean peripherization.

"Governing" or regulating globalization is not about stopping the growth of global markets or bring the process to an end, but is about searching for rules and institutions capable of giving globalization a "human face", of enhancing the advantages of global markets and making them adequately work for people at local, national, regional and global levels.[25] The impact of globalization poses great challenges for national politics, especially with regard to the role of the state. Some have announced the withering away of the state, with the transformation or even demise of welfare systems, the uncontrolled power of multinational enterprises, the regional and local fragmentation of communities. There is no doubt that the trend in nationalizing the means of production that characterized the post-war period and the building of welfare states is undergoing a reversal. But the process of privatization does not mean that governments are at the mercy of profit seeking private enterprises exclusively: the competencies of the

---

[25] Dirk Messner, Franz Nuscheler, „Das Konzept Global Governance. Stand und Perspektiven", *INEF-Report* 67, 2003 (Duisburg).

state are being transformed into regulation rather than ownership. The role of governments is to ensure that the wealth produced by increasingly global economic processes – reaches all sectors of society and does not produce a gap between the „haves" and the „have-nots". Welfare systems need to be reformed to become more just and inclusive. Education systems need to be strengthened to create new knowledge and creativity, to improve employment opportunities and invest on the most important source of the wealth of nations: human "capital", i.e. in human beings.

The transformation of the role of the state is not without conse-quences for the people. While levels of governance have moved "upwards", becoming increasingly multi- or supranational, even well established nation-states have experienced a certain degree of internal fragmentation and regionalization of interests. Accountabil-ity, democratic representativity, and transparency are key concepts that have recently become objects of debate. Subsidiary, devolution and federalism are some of the answers that states and governments have found to preserve peaceful societies and to ensure democratic participation of all groups of societies. Information technology, in many ways the metaphor or symbol of globalization, also provides some instruments to ensure the relation between local, regional, national, cosmopolitan and global identities.

This applies for the internal governance of developed and well-established, "functioning" states. In the sphere of international politics, growing political and economic interdependence between states has reduced the possibilities of inter-state conflict. Yet the end of the Cold War and of the politics of deterrence, has opened a Pandora's Box of nationalism and ethnic conflicts within the boundaries of states. While it is arguable that the violent and in certain cases dramatic fragmenta-tion of states and societies witnessed in the past decade is somehow a consequence of globalization, it is clear that global interdependence makes it even more imperative for the strong and peaceful states to find ways to govern centrifugal and destructive forces and to provide the possibility of integrating peacefully in the international community.

Stronger regionalism could help significantly to govern globalism: the example of the European Union, as a form of regionalism, makes a strong case in this direction. UN-General Secretary Kofi Annan once argued, that nowadays we must not only provide democratic structures within states, but also between our states and within the communities that form states. The same is true for the active protection of human rights and human security: We have to defend and promote them even if this means overcoming the traditional sphere of national sovereignty with peaceful means. Here lies the greatest challenge that the international community faces in the post-Cold War era: promoting democracy and human security beyond the borders of the states that have achieved peaceful democracies during the past fifty years.

But we must not forget that we live in a period in which trends run counter to strengthen democracies and the rule of law. So a strong focus of legitimacy and accountability in global governance must still be with good governance of states, International Law and the United Nations whose role as a decision making forum for global responsibility and sanction capacity must be enhanced and whose institutional structure needs to be reformed and revitalized.

Thomas Nowotny
Wien, Washington

Security and Power through Interdependence – on the Morality of Globalization

Inscribed over the portal of the town hall of Luxembourg is the city's motto: *We want to remain what we are.* The wish strikes us as extraordinary only because of its being expressed with such naive frankness. Nowadays, in an era of life-long learning, when a premium is being put upon adaptability and readiness to change, it might not be wise to admit to it that openly. Yet nonetheless and in truth, that is what most humans aspire to; as do most organizations; and most politically organized communities. The wish to remain unchanged even corresponds to what sociobiology assumes to be the driving force behind all organic life: namely the genetically imbedded drive to transmit into the future the unchanged genetic code that defines the nature of this or of that specific animal or plant.

And in fact a good many papers at this conference deal with that issue: of identity being under siege; and of the need to preserve and re-assert it. These papers thus continue a long tradition and a well entrenched discourse of Western culture. It is the discourse on the autonomy of the individual and its legitimate quest for a maximum of freedom.

To remain what we have chosen to be, or been made to be; and to defend this condition against all outside pressures is thus seen as the foundation of Western morals. A prominent Catholic theologian – Teilhard de Chardin – was even persuaded that the continued widening of this realm of personal autonomy would correspond to a scheme god himself had devised for the human race.

The urge to live and the urge to replicate unchanged into the future is primeval. It implies the desire to preserve ones identity, and the autonomy to define it and assert it. As mentioned, this holds true not just for individuals but for states too – as is reflected in the motto above the entrance to the Luxembourg City Hall.

Yet it is evident that within societies, that drive towards individual autonomy must have become tempered by some other force. Were it otherwise, societies would not exist. With everyone being sufficient unto himself or herself, there would be no place or base for common efforts to reach common goals. Yet civilization is something that is shared and common. It is a collective creation.

How then was it possible to bridge the gap between this yearning for a maximum of autonomy on the one hand, and the need for collective efforts and for cooperation on the other? Because by their very nature, such collective efforts infringe upon the freedom of each individual to do as she or he pleases. How did mankind escape being programmed for a never ending, mortal fight of everyone against everyone?

Some process must have run its course which had instructed humans that they would be better off maximising cooperation instead of each of them maximising his or hers unfettered freedom to follow every whim regardless of the effects this would have on people around.

There are many theories or metaphors on that bridging of the gap between the search for individual freedom and the need for collective action: from Rousseau's metaphor of humans of a specific group signing – so to say – between them a "contrat social"; to Karl Deutsch's theory of communication establishing the trust as the base for reciprocity; to Adams Smith' theory of moral sentiments – that is obligations to the community resulting spontaneously from the search for individual benefit.

All these theories have one thing in common. They all explain the transition from a "state of nature" towards a civilization based on mutual obligations. They do not explain it by claiming a wholesale transformation of human nature. They explain it by humans having undergone a learning process. Humans remain as they have been;

driven by the urge to secure their continued existence. What they have learned though, is that this goal is best served not by maximising independence and autonomy, but by co-operation. This is reflected in our view of humans and of society. We no longer see as natural a "state of nature" with everyone distrusting everyone, with bloodletting and mutual slaughter being the normal state of affairs; and distrust and suspicion being the best guide in human encounters.

Surprisingly the same does not hold true for our view of the global order and of relations amongst states. Here, we still believe a "state of nature" to prevail, with wars or the threat of war being ever present, and being, so to say, the only currency to count in the transactions between states. True – alternate visions and explanations are being provided in the realm of academia. But amongst those that actually practice statecraft, this is still the explanation that has gained the widest currency. This shows in their discourse. American politicians tend to see and pronounce the world as being *"unipolar"*. Some European gladly accept that. Others with greater courage or ambition wish to define the world as being *"multipolar"*; and they are joined in that by Russians and Chinese.

Now – what makes for such a "pole" (be it the only one, or just one among several others)? Is it the capacity to force others – against their will and inclination – to do as one likes them to do? Surprisingly, this still is the prevailing view. It is surprising because this view is so starkly at odds with reality. For if that view were correct, military power would be the only thing to count. This would imply that, over times, the big fish would have eaten the small ones. Smaller states would have become extinct. But this is not what we find. The vast majority of the states are small. Small states even seem to be more resilient than larger states or empires. The latter have tended to disappear. But the smaller political units endure. Luxembourg is still around while the Soviet Union, the Ottoman and the Austro-Hungarian empires have vanished.

If those were right who saw wars and military might as the only currency to count in international relations, we also should expect wars to have become more numerous. After all, more states have come into existence, and with them more players. According to theory, all of them should have been eager to join in the game of military rivalry. But such has not been the case either. In fact, wars between states have become rare (while violence *within* states has become more frequent).

Table 1. International (2) and national (1) violent conflict 1945–1998

1 = internal conflicts
2 = international conflicts involving, at least on one side, a state as such

Source: Heidelberger Institut für Internationale Konfliktforschung; www.hiik.de

Among mature democracies, wars have ceased altogether.

This does not imply that states would have suddenly changed their innermost nature; and would not longer be driven by the same desire as all large organizations, communities or even individuals; by a drive which, as mentioned, seemed to be the quasi biological one of preserving the imbedded distinctness and individuality. Yet – obviously – what has changed is the strategy employed to this end.

Before the onset of the industrial age, victory in war was apt to result in both greater prosperity and greater security. Then, the economic base of the society was still mainly agricultural. The bigger the country and the wider thus the agricultural surface, the greater this base of national wealth; the greater also the base for recruiting soldiers; the more distant too from the capital the frontiers of the state and the wider thus the terrain an enemy would have to conquer before unseating a ruler.

Small wonder then that rulers perceived relations amongst state to be a "zero sum game" and to define these relations in a way the so called "realists" still do. The gains of one state would automatically translate into an equally large loss by another state. Given these views and circumstances, it made sense for any ruler to strive for a maximum of independence so as to preserve and secure for his state and society identity and permanence, and to cut, to the extent possible, reliance on the external world. By its very nature, this outside world could not be anything but hostile; and thus apt to use any such liens as tools to pressure a state to do things he would not have done on its own free accord.

Today's though, this notion of gaining security by minimising relations to the outside world no longer provides useful guidance. In its pure and unadulterated form, this notion still informs the foreign and security policies of a few aberrant states – such as North Korea and its "Juche" philosophy of utter independence. Yet even beyond the realm of such aberrant exceptionalities, similar notions linger on. Again and again, they shine through the veil of common platitudes that politicians and diplomats use when hard pressed to define the position and aims of their states in the global order of things. Doing so, they signal a failure to come to terms with the world as it actually exists today.

This failure might or might not have serious consequences. It might reflect no more than that perceptions still lag behind actual realities and the failure to grasp the nature of changes that have occurred in the international order. Such a failure might be corrected for later, when such erroneous perceptions are cast aside and are being replaced by some more congruent with reality. Or, on the other hand, such erroneous picture of global realities might be taken at its face value and serve as guide for actual policies that will have the effect of transforming the reality and return it to a prior, more primitive stage of global order, closer to the state of an anarchic fight of everyone against everyone. Let me quote an example for the first of these two alternatives.

In the time between 1970 and 1975 – thus just a generation ago – I had been private secretary to the Chancellor of the Austrian Republic. Holding contacts with the ministry of defense was among my duties. Both this ministry and the chancellery were involved in the drafting of a new security doctrine for Austria. This doctrine was intended to take proper account of Austria's geopolitical situation as a neutral state at the outer edge of the "Western" camp; as well as of the difficulties in creating in Austria a military density comparable to the one that existed beyond both its Eastern and at its Western borders. The new doctrine was also intended to provide a comprehensive definition of security, of the threats that could undermine it, and of the tools available to thwart such threats. Maintaining a maximum of self sufficiency in the production of food became defined as one of the tools to safeguard this external security.

Notoriously, farmers worldwide will use any excuse or pretext to claim exemption form international competition. But it is noteworthy that a mere forty years ago this their claim was still accepted as valid in terms of external security. In the meantime, though, it has become difficult to ignore that the international exchange of goods has become intense even in this protected realm of agriculture. Overall, such an exchange is beneficial to both sides. Austria itself imports much of the high – protein feed – stuff for its herds of cattle. On its turn, it exports quite some cattle and beef. Fortunately thus, one had not heeded this injunctions of the new Austrian security doctrine as it had been drafted in the Seventies. The warped world-view encoded in this doctrine had thus not caused any lasting damage to either the international order or to Austria itself. It simply was proof of the well known tendency of our collective cognitive facilities being deficient by always lagging behind the reality they should grasp. Thirty years ago we thus failed to see then that interconnectedness, mutual interdependence was less of a threat, and more of a safeguard of peace.

But the consequences of such a failure might be more ominous. For our view of reality has consequences. Even if erroneous and even where the result of nebulous ideologies and unfounded prejudice, inevitably our view of what the world is about is the base of our actions and of our policies towards this world. Such views then become reality by transforming and shaping reality.

Our world views are based on past experience; often on experiences that date far back and that thus have come to shape the prevailing culture. Views emerging from distant memories prompt us to base our reaction to the outside world on the experience of a reality as it existed at some far – back time; and not on a view of the world as it exists today. This would condemn us to repeat the past – with all of its inefficiencies, tragedies, monstrosities. It would impede addressing the issues of today, to combat the risks and use the chances emerging from a new order of global affairs.

To point to the obvious: the progress of civilization has implied an ever broader division of labour. Were it otherwise, we still would be clad in furs and live in caves. The town is dependent on the countryside; the smith on the farmer to give him bread; the farmer on the smith to forge his ploughs. This mutual dependence has taught towns to cooperate with the countryside; farmers with craftsmen; traders with producers; and so on.

As many other mammals, humans still in a "state of nature" were basically territorial. The solidarity, formal hierarchy and cooperation was within a very small pack of individuals only. All outsiders were enemies, to be driven away, to be killed and even to be eaten. There was a rationale to this programming of behaviour. In a "state of nature" humans live as hunters and gatherers. Their livelihood depends on their having exclusive right to exploit a stretch of land for its fruits and animals. Any outsider intruding threatens to reduce the scope of this their exclusive property and thus endangers the survival of the pack.

The six billion humans that populate the globe today could not exist as hunters and gatherers. The globe could even hardly sustain a population of a mere billion of hunters and gatherers. But the earth can now carry six billions because these do not live in forests but in cities mainly. They do not eat snails and roots, but rice and wheat that come from fields ploughed by tractors, and made productive by artificial fertilizer. Six billion live in today's world because they have learned to rely in their existence on much that is not produced by themselves; but that is being produced by others and that is being delivered to them in a predictable and efficient manner. At least in merely material terms, even the poorest among those global city dwellers is better off – than those still living from hunting and gathering in the obscurity of a forest.

In this process, patterns of behaviour, norms, morals have co-evolved with growing wealth. The virtue of the proud alpha male defending his territory and his right to exclusive insemination of the females of his pack still is being celebrated in some of the popular culture and lore. But actual behaviour follows other rules. One practices birth control and shares the fruits of labour with others so as to profit, on the other hand, from the work of others. In short, one works for wages and has learned to cooperate with others and to be dependent on others in both the professional and the more private life.

Over times, the circle of cooperation and of mutual dependence and trust had expanded together with the division of labour and with the wealth it produced. The tribe evolved into the city state; the city state into the feudal state; later into the modern state; and now into the postindustrial state.

The circle of cooperation and the liens of interdependence now span the globe.[1] Citizens of one state have come to depend on the citizens of other states to a degree not known before. An increasing share of what is produced in one state is being sold to, and is being consumed in another one. An increasing share of what we consume on our side, is being produced abroad. As a consequence, world trade is growing faster than the world's overall wealth. And Foreign Direct Investment is growing faster still than international trade.

It has become difficult for instance to say where an automobile has been produced. Fifty years ago one could be certain that a GM car had been made in the United States. Nowadays it might hail from Romania or Korea; whereas many of the Toyotas come from United States. For big firms and even for a number of medium sized ones, the world has become not just their market place, but their production site too.

---

[1] This does not imply that all participate; or that all participate equally; just as not all citizens of a modern state had all profited from, and had shared in the fruits of industrialization. But that is an issue we neglect at this juncture.

Table 2. Growth of world production and of world trade 1951–2000 (Index 1951 = 100)

Source: WTO

Source: World Trade Organization, annual report; www.wto.org

Six billion humans depend on that system of interdependence being stable and predictable. Yet our world views, laws, institutions and morals have not co-volved together with this further expansion of the circle of mutual dependence.

While having learned the lessons of interdependence and solidarity for the purpose of arranging the internal functioning of a state, nations are mostly still amiss in drawing similar lessons for their policies towards the rest of the world. There, in fact, the underlying notions are still those of hunters and gatherers. Among these notions is the one of gaining security by being as independent as possible; as well as the notion of a "zero sum game" being played on the world scene, with anyone's gain implying an equally large loss by some other actor on the international scene. Nations still aim to be "powerful", that is on top of others and able to force those below to bend to their will even if those thus pressed would have preferred to act otherwise.

There is much discussion on what makes for this power or the lack of it. More often than not, though, power is seen as "emanating from the mouth of a gun". While there are certainly many ways to have one nation obey to the injunctions and wishes of another nation, military power is seen not just as the ultimate means of pressure. It is also perceived to indicate a nation's rank in the global pecking order. The greater this biceps of military might, the higher the standing, the firmer the expectation that the whims and wishes of this muscular nation will be heeded. The biggest alpha male with the biggest club would rule the roost.

Search the discourse of practicing politicians and you will find that below the veneer of platitudes on peace and motherhood, this notion of states living in a "state of nature"[2] still prevails. For what concept of the global order lurks behind the US claim of being "the last surviving super power"? And what world-view is implied in the promise of the 2002 US security doctrine to never permit the rise of any competing superpower? What does president Chirac imply when opposing these notions of untrammeled US supremacy, he proposes a model of a "multipolar" world, with the European Union being one of these "poles"? And what do Russians imply when joining the French they also wish for a world that would be "multipolar"? Anything else than that a multitude of thugs is better than a single one?

Why is military might held in so high an esteem? Because it is said to provide the only true guarantee for a nation's security and to its continued existence. Yet, the reverse seems closer to reality. States that invest too heavily in the military lose rank and might even go under. The heavily armed Soviet Union had the world's best, or at least second best fighting machine. Nevertheless, it no longer exists. After being defeated in 1945, Japan and Germany[3], on the other hand, invested little in their military. Nonetheless they became prominent on the global scene. Costa Rica is one of the few examples of democratic and economic success in Central America. It has no army[4];

---

[2] In terms of political science: in a "state of anarchy".

[3] With Germany, for example, exporting more than all of the United States.

[4] I do not promote this as an example to be emulated. In other places of the globe that might not be feasible. Most nations would like to retain an army so as to be prepared for the worst; just as one invests in a fire brigade to be prepared for the worst. But then having a larger or smaller fire brigade will not establish the rank of a township amongst its peers. Nor will it define the well being of the inhabitants of this town.

whereas those nearby countries that relish military power (such as Nicaragua) have fared poorly. Finally, it is worth recalling that in the last century, all those who took the initiative in offensively using military power have come to regret it. In all cases, the final-result of their wars turned out to have been different from the one that the instigator of hostilities had planned for.

Little is thus gained – as it seems – from being able to inflict on people of other nations things they do not want – such as aerial bombing or occupation armies. But much is gained by offering them things they need and want; such as – for instance – disc drives for computers. Taiwan and South Korea together produce most of the world's disc drives. These products have become what economists call "commodities". The term stands for goods produced in high quantities; where competition is via the price mainly. Yet while this production is not at the cutting edge of innovation, potential other producers would still find it difficult to penetrate this market dominated by the two Far – Eastern nations. For some time at least, these two countries will have the world market for disk drives more or less to themselves. These drives might be "commodities". But as such they have become as essential to the continuity – the security – of our everyday lives as bread and water. What if Korea and Taiwan ceased exporting them? What if for that reason no new computers could be produced – at least not for some time?

Now compare South Korea to its sister state in the North. North Korea maintains one of the world's largest armies. If it does not already have them, it soon will have nuclear weapons. It has the missiles too, to carry those weapons far beyond its borders across the Sea of Japan. What will North Korea gain in return for having produced these weapons, and for maintaining an outsized army; and for paying for all of that by starving millions of its people to death? Security from military attack and invasion? Hardly – for its security is not threatened by such an attack. No volunteers are in sight to take on the job of battling a million of North Korean soldiers, ready to die. Few nations too, would relish a role as occupiers of this impoverished country with its downtrodden, traumatized society. Not just for its own miserable citizens, for the world at large, the North Korean regime is a menace and an irritant. It is something to be wished away. And vanish it will sooner or later. Even nuclear arms and missiles will not secure its future. They endanger it.

South Korea and Taiwan, on the other hand are not a menace to the rest of the world. They are useful to it as they supply a large quantity of proven and cheap disk drives. Should Taiwan or South Korea disappear, the consequences for the world would be troublesome. No ready, alternate source for the production of disk drives exists, and today the world can not do without them.

So what makes for the security of states like South Korea or Taiwan? What makes for the continued existence of small states such as Austria and Luxembourg, which – if the so called "realists" were correct – should long since have disappeared, being swallowed up by some mightier neighbour wielding superior military power?

Such wealthy but small countries can feel secure – I claim – because they are so densely woven into the fabric of global interconnectedness. This interdependence enhances security. It does not reduce it. In a world where states seek to obtain a maximum of independence and security by being autonomous, size matters of course. In such a world, each state would be well advised to produce all the things it consumes. Yet, in order to be autonomous for example, in the production of automobiles, states would have to have at least a market of 200 million customers. Fewer potential customers would make for shorter production runs in the national auto-factory. Such short production – runs would be inefficient. The cars would become outrageously expensive. Smaller states would also lack many of the basic inputs into production – as for example and notably – oil and natural gas.

So if states were to become truly addicted to the search of maximum independence, they would have to expand their territory so as secure for themselves markets that are big enough to sustain an economically efficient production; and a territory varied and wide enough to contain at least most of the basic raw materials they consume. In such a world, small states would find it difficult to survive.

Neither could small states survive in a world where military might would be the only "currency" to count, and in which the threat of war is constant. Size would again correlate with viability. Only greater size would provide a state not just with the necessary demographic and economic base of military power; but also with the required "strategic depth".

Yet, nonetheless, small states are still around. In many ways, they even do better than bigger ones. This clearly shows that something is amiss in the view of the world offered in academia by the so called "realists"; and in the philosophy still underlying most of the actual "strategic" pronouncements of statesmen.

I realize that it might not seem proper to pursue this argument here in Poland which, in the last three hundred years, had been the victim of superior military power directed against it from mightier states or empires in both the East and the West (and, as Austrian, I should add: also from the South).

But while it might be unwise not to heed the lessons of history, it would be unwise too, to ignore how history has changed. For now and for the foreseeable future, Poland's territorial integrity is not threatened by any outside invader. Its security will be enhanced by integrating into Europe and into the rest of the world. And it would be dimished by the failure to do so. On the other hand, Europe's security as a whole will be enhanced by a Polish success in inserting into the web of interdependence; and Europe's security would be impaired by a Polish failure to accept this interdependence with the rest of the continent and by Poland instead coming to chase the chimera of self-sufficiency.

Success and failure in accepting and using this global interconnectedness depend less on outside factors; and more on the internal situation; on a society's mores and values, its social set-up; its political institutions and traditions; its economic culture; etc. That is, of course, an analysis that sits uncomfortably with much of the world's political class. This class has always found it expedient to blame outsiders for this or that ill afflicting a society. They found it even more expedient to picture other powers and nations as a mortal threat to the security of their country.

Blaming outsiders is convenient. It spares one addressing those issues that do indeed enhance a nations well being and security; such as growing wealth, democratization or social cohesion.

Humans are genetically programmed, as it seems, to subordinate all other goals to the goal of mere physical survival once their survival is seen as being threatened. Given a reason or a prompt to fear for this survival, they will automatically subordinate all other ambitions and goals to the single aim of averting a looming threat of their annihilation. They will no longer hold political leaders accountable for delivering to them an effective public administration free of corruption, basic infrastructure, decent schools and – finally – a say in how things should be run. Opposition to rulers evaporates. National cohesion is established in societies otherwise riven by deep – seated conflicts.

Now what if rulers the world over are no longer given that easy excuse for manipulating the public into acquiescence to their selfish and inefficient rule? What if the notion of an outside threat became too implausible? What if rulers were thus no longer able to invoke it so as to secure their own position? Societies would then feel free to address their true problems. They could then search for ways to make them truly secure, able to survive into the future. They and the world would benefit from such a re-ordering of priorities.

Two examples to make that point obvious.

For sixty year now, Arab leaders have rallied their people around the notion of a mortal threat emanating from Israel. And though all of the Arab – Israeli wars had been started by the Arab side[5], this notion had been widely accepted. Resistance to, and defeat of Israel became the priority goal, uniting an Arab world otherwise torn by unresolved external and internal cleavages and conflicts.

Uniting around an alleged threat emanating from Israel has not impeded the steady decline of the Arab World.[6] It had declined because Arab leaders have failed to have their states deliver what modern states should be able to deliver: prospect of material betterment, equal justice for everyone, freedom from fear and suppression, access to culture, and – last not least – the hope of governance becoming

---

[5] If one exempts the somewhat ambiguous case of the Israeli invasion of the Lebanon.

[6] Including those who should have profited from soaring revenues from exports of oil.

more democratic. This failure of Arab states[7] endangers their internal security. Even while posing as defenders of national security against Israeli threats leaders have lost legitimacy. Civil society is fragile. Where it exists, it does so as a network of Muslim institutions that are hostile to, and incompatible with the modern world. Arab states have missed out on the chances of export driven economic growth such as it becomes manifest in the soaring growth rates of India and China. They have largely missed out on the "information revolution", with not only computers and Internet access being rare; but even books.

This failure of Arab states to connect with modernity and to meet the needs of their citizens is also reflected in a retarded state of their international relations. All attempts have come to naught to forge greater coherence among the Arabs themselves either through political unions, economic unions or free trade agreements. Even among Arab neighbours, many borders are being contested.[8]

Such failures have repercussions far beyond the Arab world. It is difficult, for example, not to assume that this weakness and inefficiency of Arab states would not be connected to their having become the main nod and crucible in the network of world-wide terrorism. For the rest of the globe, Arab states do not "produce" security. They produce an inordinate amount of insecurity.

There is another example of the failure to accept interdependence. It is even more portent of future troubles: increasingly, the United States tend to opt out of the system of mutual dependence instead of sustaining and stabilizing it. The process is underway since some time already. But it has accelerated dramatically under the presidency of George W. Bush.

The United States were essential in shaping and preserving a global order which over sixty years, has spared us a new world war;

---

[7] Certainly, there are exceptions – as least in parts: Some tender shoots of political pluralism have sprung up in some of the Arab states. A few too, have become more integrated into the system of world wide economic interdependence by diversifying production and exports. But as the "Arab World Development Reports" demonstrate, these are the rare exceptions. Overall, the picture is gloomy; with the prospect of that the gap still widening that separates the Arabs from the rest of the world.

[8] Examples: borders between Mauritania and Morocco; between Morocco and Algeria; between Saudi Arabia and Yemen; between Kuwait and Iraq.

and which has permitted a tripling of global wealth. They did this by creating and upholding a "regime" that benefits most (though not all equally). This their role was supported by their prominent position in the network of global interchange. They are the hub, or at least the most prominent nod, in the network of information that spans the world. Theirs is the main reserve currency for central banks all over the world. They are the center for the trading of stocks and bonds. They thus set the rules for these markets. It was mainly on their initiative that world wide international organizations such as the United Nations have been created and that these have made at least some headway in establishing and implementing rules to make relations between states more predictable and stable. And by their example the US had guaranteed that such international norms would be heeded and thus would be effective.

By now, however, the United States have become delinquent in fulfilling these roles. Instead of stabilising it, they endanger the world financial system by unilaterally pursuing a fiscal and monetary policy that is bound to end in a financial crash that will reverberate all over the world. Eighty percent of all of the world's disposable savings are being used to compensate for the lack of savings in the United States and for filling the "double deficit" in both the current account (near 6% of GDP), and in the federal budget (near 5% of GDP). This will not continue and the asset bubble created by the inflow of foreign capital is bound to burst.[9] On the political side, the United States have failed to uphold their part of a bargain that sought to prevent the further proliferation of nuclear weapons. Instead of downscaling their nuclear armory, they are developing it. With that intent, they fail to ratify the treaty that would ban all tests of nuclear weapons. Small wonder that others with nuclear ambitions find good excuse to proceed in efforts to join the rank of nuclear powers as soon as possible.[10] Having once fought for the wider application of international law and for the world-wider respect for human rights, they now ridicule such

---

[9] As it did in the Nineties in Southeast Asia and in Russia.

[10] This is just one example of the US absconding from prior engagement that were essential parts of the world political regime. The list could be prolonged: treaty that banned an arms race in outer space; Kyoto protocol on global warming; etc etc.

efforts and pointedly wage an all out campaign against an International Court established to persecute crimes against humanity. Ever more often too, they tend to act against the principle of free trade. As we have seen, free trade is the main vehicle of global interconnectedness, and thus the main pillar of global security. If a mighty nation like the US defects; other might be tempted to do the same.[11]

I have pointed to two examples of states or groups of states trying to defect from the system of global interconnectedness. The Arab world, quoted as the first example, might still be seen as simply laggard; not fully up to date; not there yet where other nations and regions have arrived, and thus not ready yet to seek security by cooperation.

The Arab example might point to a deficiency not yet fully overcome; or – on the other hand – it might point to troubles still ahead, with others emulating Arab attitudes. So the implications of this example are ambivalent. They are less so and more ominous in the second example we had chosen. Nobody could claim the United States being backward in the traditional sense of the term. They certainly see themselves as being an example for others to follow. And as mentioned, as upholder of the "regime" they have a central, irreplaceable function in the world order of interconnectedness.

So this turn of the US policies implies a serious warning. A trend that has carried the world forward might be reversed. But let us first ask the simple question as to whether such a reversal would really be so bad a thing? Certainly, overall wealth would be lower in a world that would again become less interdependent, with less international trade, less foreign direct investment, less exchange of information, and with less of what is shared world wide as (natural or created) "global commons".

One other result of such a reversal is certain too. As we have argued, external security would also suffer of such a change in the in-

---

[11] Countless pressure groups all over the world are always eager to provide thousand of excuses for why they should be exempted from international competition. Their single-mindedness makes it tempting for politicians to yield to this their pressure.

ternational "regime". Interconnectedness promotes peace amongst nations. It safeguards the external security of even smaller states and punishes hostile policies. Rupturing the liens of interdependence would thus weaken this base of peacefulness.

Yet frequently, humans are moved by motives more powerful than the ones for greater wealth and firmer security. Neither of these two motives, can, for example explain the world-wide surge in religious fundamentalism. Often therefore, the drive for wealth and security takes second place behind the drive for autonomy, identity and for the certainty of unchanged moral rules.

The rise of global interconnectedness is widely feared to threaten autonomy, identity and with it the base of traditional morality. Is there substance behind such fear? Is globalization really nothing but the steamroller that crushes everything and everyone into the submission of a flat, low existence of a "McDonald" world; that deprives him or her of cultural distinctness and of moral autonomy?

In answer to that question – let's first look at the obvious. Yes – Hollywood dominates the television screens not only in Europe. Yet India turns out more films than California; and, increasingly, these too find a world wide audience. So do films from China, but also from states far less populous such as Australia and New Zealand. Yes – Americans and the English language dominate in publishing. But major contributions to recent world literature have come from other parts of the world – such as from Latin America. Yes the fast food chain McDonald and the "hamburger"[12] is American and McDonald outlets are to be found all over the world. But so are Pizza parlors that sell Italian type of food; Taco Bells that acquaint us with Mexican food; restaurants that print their menus and wine cards in French; and Sushi bars which are the Japanese contribution to global gastronomy.

Much of the local has indeed been crushed underneath an onslaught of international brand names and of globalized patterns of consumption. But this does not automatically translate into a reduced personal or collective autonomy; as a trade off exists between such losses and the widening scope of choice as it is brought about by

---

[12] Though it owes its name not to "ham" but to the German city of Hamburg.

globalization. If some indigenous cultures have been forced into extinction, other formerly merely national or regional cultures (as – for example the above mentioned Latin America literary tradition) have been given a global presence.

It is also argued that sitting atop the pyramid of economic interchange, America dominates the world economy, reducing others to an inferior state. The US would take the lion's share of the increase in world-wide wealth, with the tentacles of its transnational firms wrapped around and suffocating all potential alternate sources of wealth. While simple and emotionally appealing, such presentation refers to a part of the picture only. Doubtlessly, the Unites States do benefit from their special economic position. They do so – for example – by being able to keep the Dollar the world's main reserve currency[13]; or by their being able to impose upon the rest of the world many of the rules that underpin their specific form of "share – holder – capitalism". But nonetheless, the main beneficiaries of the present world economic order have not been the United States, but the Far Eastern countries with their astounding rates of economic growth.

As in the realm of culture, in the economy too, global interconnectedness has increased the volume of output and the number of relevant players. Here too, we are faced with a trade – off. Some type of apples that once were produced for local consumption might have disappeared from the markets. But we now may chose from countless other types of apples, many of which are imported. We, on our turn, might also export quite some quantity of apples for others to eat.

So – if seen from a global perspective – the number of different sort of apples might have decreased. Without doubt, many distinct small cultures have vanished. But for each individual and for each political community the scope of choice has widened. For them, the world of today does not present itself in terms of a flat sameness, but as a – sometimes puzzling and unsettling – variety, implying a vast scope of choice.

---

[13] And thus having the rest of the world finance their deficits in the current account and in the federal budget. The US may claim even can claim that their doing so is beneficial, as they thus provide a liquidity to the world monetary system that otherwise would not be available.

This still leaves us with two of the most serious objections against global interconnectedness. The first objection is that it does not benefit all equally. It even would actively exclude and marginalize some. The second objections concerns morals. The dense global interconnectedness and the vast scope of choice would promote a culture of consumerism; would put a premium on selfish behaviour; and it thus would estrange humans from their communal roots and thus from the base of their morality.

Let us first deal with objection number one. It is true that global interdependence does not benefit all equally. It even actively marginalizes some parts of humanity. This becomes evident by rising inequality both within nations and between nations. Among the nations that once were poor, some – like Korea – have managed to develop rapidly. Doing so, they have surpassed some countries which previously had been wealthier than they. By and large though, these were the exceptions. Most of those that once had been poor, remain poor; whereas those wealthier continue to become wealthier still. The graph on the following page provides proof of these developments. The lines show how the wealth of various nations has evolved over two centuries.[14]

There were only a few "Koreas" that once were very poor yet who have overtaken others that once were even a bit wealthier than they. In that graph only few of the lines cross that show this economic development of nations. The majority of lines spread out in the form of a fan. This indicates that the distance has widened that separates today's wealthy countries from the poor ones. In fact, the gap has grown into an abyss with the per capita income in the wealthiest country being 200 times larger than the per capita income in the world's poorest countries. In history, this is unprecedented.[15]

---

[14] The graph is on a logarithmic scale. What are lines on these graphs are thus curves in actual life.

[15] But within nations too, the gap between the rich and the poor has become wider. This is against all prior predictions forecasting that this gap would narrow as the economies matured in the most advanced countries. In those advanced countries the rich became richer still. And the poorer – mainly unqualified labour – sank deeper into poverty. Changing technology is the main cause of this slide into poverty. But the surge of international trade and international investment has also contributed to it, with many labour intensive products being imported instead of being created at

Table 3. Over the long run, (most) poor countries stay trapped in poverty (Vertical axis: ratio of income to subsistence income; log 2 scale)

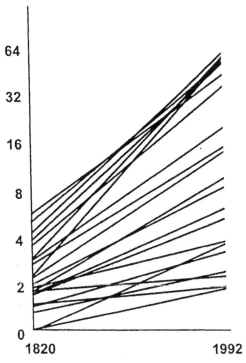

Source: William Easterly, *Inequality Does Cause Underdevelopment: New Evidence*, Washington, DC: Center for Global Development, 2002.

This glaring and still growing inequality[16] poses a serious challenge to the notion that greater interdependence should be welcomed

home; and with some of the labour intensive production migrating overseas where wages and thus costs to the producer were lower.

[16] There are different ways of assessing inequality as it exists among nations. We have given each country equal weight in the above graph. Using that method, the finding is unambiguous indeed. Differences are widening. But giving each country equal weight is not unproblematic. Is it right to give equal weight in such a comparison to China on the one hand, and to Niger on the other? So if we change this method and adjust for the uneven size of the population of each country, the differences become smaller. Some claim that by using this gauge, differences in wealth would shrink

by all; and that it would contribute to greater global security and stability. The salient question to ask is thus the following: is this inequality *caused* by this growing global interdependence?

The trivial answer is: "of course". Evidently, some would not be poor if there were no rich against whom they could compare their fate. But less trivial arguments are also harnessed to support the claim that rising wealth on one side causes growing poverty on the other[17]. Once a production has become established in one country, potential entrepreneurs in another country will find it harder to start production in the same field. He who comes first certainly has an advantage. But more generally too, wealth creates incentives for further accumulation of wealth. And poverty creates conditions that tend to make poverty endure.

Obviously, this does not transform into an iron law, as a number of formerly very poor countries had managed to break out of the vicious circles of poverty and to cast free from the ensuing disincentives to growth. Some of these disincentives reside in the external economic relations of poor countries. But the overwhelming number of them emerge from internal factors. By and large, it is thus not justified to hold external relations, as they exist in a regime of world wide interdependence, responsible for the sorry state of poor countries. Quite on the contrary – globalization in its various aspects still offers them the best chance to exit from poverty and climb on the train of economic growth. Basically, poverty is still caused by the absence of economic growth and not by others having become wealthier before.

We thus can not object to global interdependence because it would be the cause of stark inequality on earth. It might have made such inequality more visible; and it might have increased the negative fall – out from such inequality. But as statistics demonstrate, it has not caused inequality.

Yet no statistics are readily available to help us in dealing with the other challenge raised against global interdependence: namely that it

---

instead of growing. But this still leaves us with the fact that such differences as they exist today are indeed bigger now than ever before in human history.

[17] Finding expression in various theories on "neo-colonialism" and in the theory of "dependenzia".

destroys human autonomy and that it has this noxious effect not just on individuals but also on whole communities and states, depriving them of their unique identity and undermining their cohesion.

One does not identify that closely with goods and services one has not produced on one's own. If such services and goods are needed, one has come to expect that these may be bought and will be delivered in a reliable fashion.[18] In a way, much of a persons life is thus "outsourced" today. Much of what we need and consume is not something we ourselves had created before. Instead, it is being purchased on the market. We have come to even routinely "outsource" in realms that were once considered very personal. The education of children, for example, is being entrusted to paid teachers.

One has come to expect that paying for something is the only exertion demanded from the "outsourcer". And one has come to expect to receive in return and without doing much, not just the necessities of life; but – increasingly – even such intangibles as good health, sexual satisfaction, excitement, amusement, and happiness. Even these emotions are thus no longer directly connected to what one does for oneself. They have become entitlements, purchased on the political or on the economic market. We thus have become removed from responsibility even for things that affect us very closely. And we have come to feel little responsibility for, or identification with the complex arrangements that provide this input into our daily lives.

I still remember faint echoes from a time when things were different. A mere sixty years ago, in my childhood, people and small communities in Austria were still more self-sufficient. They carried greater responsibilities for their well being. The liens between their own exertion and the ensuing rewards were more direct; as were the liens that tied people together in these smaller communities. In the village where I lived during the Second World War, farmers still used to build, repair and maintain their own houses; bake their own bread; slaughter themselves their pigs; make their own cider; knit their own underwear and stockings; sew their own clothes; heat their homes with wood they themselves had hewn; man the fire brigade and care for the villages infirm; create themselves the things that entertained

---

[18] Either directly of through my taxes.

and amused them. Even rather small communities had their pub, their general store and post office, their blacksmith and tailor, their theater group and their village celebrations.

It is easy to fall prey to the charms of such reminiscences. And indeed, societies as different as the Arab and the American both seem tempted by the illusion of being able to return to the past. In both of these societies, the illusion of being able to turn back the clock is one of the main motives behind[19] their rejection of global interdependence. A good number of conservative Americans dream about, and yearn to resurrect the United States of small towns, of intimate communities, of the self reliant and self sufficient yeoman farmer. On the other side, a good number of Arabs actively work for a return to even more distant a time when the Caliph ruled Muslims the world over and when the certainties of Koran had not yet found their challenge in the complexities and contradictions of a modern, varied and interdependent world.

Such reminiscences are irrational in the narrow sense of this term. But while they conflict with, and contradict present realities, they are powerful and even primordial and they thus can affect and change this present reality. They have done so in the past when similar yearnings had prevailed over the more tangible goals of preserving world-wide wealth and security.

While intense today, world-wide interdependence is nothing unprecedented. Much of it already was present in the late Nineteenth Century. Then too, a rapid rise in global wealth went together with, and was connected to a vast expansion of international trade, of global foreign investments and to a broadening and acceleration of the international exchange of information. Then as now, one expected that this rise in global interconnectedness would induced nations to behave to another in a more responsible manner. They would shy from waging wars. Cooperation would prevail over hostility.

---

[19] In the US such dreams find their most salient expression in the sub-culture of the "survivalists", who believe that for one reason or an other, the US society will crash and each one will return to a state where he alone is responsible for his or her survival.

But this was not the case. Desires other than the ones for wealth and security proved stronger. The outbreak of World War One rang the death knell to this bygone era of worldwide cooperation. This death was accompanied less by mourning than by jubilation. In all the countries that entered it, the public welcomed the war. People rejoiced in the demise of the old, stable order. They were eager to exchange their personal moral responsibility to national euphoria and to transfer ethic autonomy to military commanders and political ideologues. For fifty years thereafter, cooperation between nations was in decline.

Table 4. The decline of interdependence in the First half of the Twentieth Century

Merchandise trade as % of GDP[6]

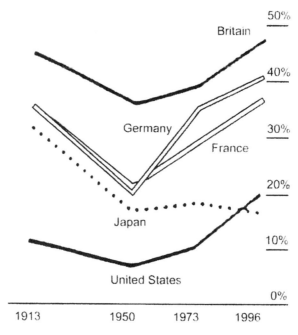

Source: A.Maddison 1997

Source: Angus Maddison, *Monitoring the World Economy 1820–1992*, Paris: Development Centre Studies, OECD, 1995.

Surely, it was no coincidence that this period of decline in co-operation came to be known as the "Terrible Twentieth Century", with democracies on the defensive; with new totalitarian ideologies having their sway; with a deep world economic crisis creating armies of poor and unemployed; and with a second world war arriving as if by necessity.

We should assume these were not the results intended by those who rejected the global interdependence at the turn from the Nineteenth to the Twentieth Century. What they yearned for was greater autonomy and unchallenged, secure identities. Somehow they wished to return to a magic past in which these things were in place still. But even if they would have been able to turn back the clock of history, would they have recovered the paradise they yearned for? Would they have truly gained greater self determination and autonomy? Would they have become imbedded in environment more suitable for teaching and for sustaining morals?

The notion or the "moral" implies the possibility of choice. Where no choices can be made, moral does not rein but simple necessity. The notion of moral also implies the existence of the "other". Moral is a quality in the relationship with others. Where none of them exist, the notion of moral becomes void.

In the pre-modern conditions we left behind, necessities were pressing, the choices were few; and the number of "others" was limited. What we left behind therefore is not an era of greater morality. What we left behind are the certitudes of limited options and the security of living in small groups of close kin. Those longing for a return to this past do not opt for greater personal responsibility and choice. On the contrary, they wish to escape the present conditions where choices are wide. They wish to return to when things were more preordained and when moral responsibilities were more reduced.

We have to accept of course, that this present widening in the scope of choice does indeed heighten insecurity. It does indeed shatter the permanence of our identity and it forces us to re-define it daily. But, at the same time, it dramatically widens the number of persons, institutions, nations we have to rely on and have to cooperate with. We have to trust that they will continue to deliver the goods we can not do without. We, on our turn have to prove trustworthy to them.

One might object that this is a rather rosy and idealistic definition of what essentially are commercial transactions. These transactions would not be conditioned by someone being trustworthy or not; but by whether the right price is being offered and accepted. Morals would not enter this transaction. On the contrary – the purely commercial nature of such relationship would void it of any moral content that it might have embodied in earlier times and in societies less affected by the onrush of modernity.

But such harsh view does not penetrate the surface of commercial relationships. It does not shed light on the mechanisms that built them, that underlie them, that sustain them. For underlying these transactions that seem no more than merely commercial is a complex of expectations, norms, traditions and institutions. Those have to be built in an evolutionary process that teaches reciprocity, honesty and responsibility. Commercial networks and markets do not suddenly come into existence merely because of material benefits and because money is being offered. Take as a proof the example provided in places and times where such an evolution had not yet taken place, and where persons, communities or states[20] were suddenly afloat with money. In such cases, the money evaporated quickly without the affected having been able exchange it for things that permanently would have improved their position. Far from destroying the moral base of our society, this necessity to cooperate strengthens it.

In a world where nations prevailed by having the stronger armies and the more resolute and brutal generals to lead them, the virtues of reciprocity, honesty and reliability were not much in demand. Obedience and subordination was. But reciprocity, honesty and reliability are in demand when cooperation becomes the base of world order. The wider the scope of choice, the greater the number of participants in the potential exchange, the wider the sphere where truly moral judgments have to be made; and where moral virtue is rewarded by material benefit.

There is no way of avoiding the fact that the word "interdependence" contains the word "dependence". And there is no way we can

---

[20] As example for states: income from oil. It now is seen more as a curse than a valuable gift; as it rob affected states from all incentives to evolve and modernize.

change the meaning of this term. We have to accept that growing global interdependence will deprive us of some of the autonomy of deciding alone and just for ourselves on our personal affairs. But, on the other hand, autonomy had been enhanced by a wider scope of choice and by having gained broader access to others. Global interdependence forces us to seek the other and thus to add to the stock of values that are widely shared.

Global interdependence is not the enemy of freedom. But fear of freedom is the enemy of global interdependence. What has become lost in the process of global interdependence is less the freedom of choice; but more so the certainty of an unchanging identity.

So is the motto of "remaining what we are", the motto inscribed of the portals of on the town hall of Luxembourg, really nothing more than a reminder of how this goal has become impossible to reach? Is the deep instinct misguided of holding on to such an identity?

As morals, identity too, has two poles, so to say: the "me" and the "other". Without the "me" I could not see the other as "other". Without the "other" I could not distinguish myself from him as "me". Both poles are contingent upon each other. The wider and the more challenging the realm of the "other", the more urgent the need to also broaden the "me". To be secured, identity has to evolve. Global interdependence does not obliterate the need for a "me". It even makes it more urgent. But at the same time it engages identity to become something broader. In olden times of unbroken Nineteenth century optimism one has called that process "civilizational progress". Perhaps we should revive that notion.

Luxembourg, by the way, is the wealthiest country on earth. This is not because the country could command vast armies. Its wealth – and its global presence (which is not commensurate with its small size) do not stem from Luxembourg pursuing the goal of being self-sufficient. They are grounded in the capacity to cooperate with, and being useful to, a vast number of states, communities, persons. Looking into the future, I hope and believe it to lie more with Luxembourg than with the nostalgic ambitions of both the Arab World and of the United States.

Zeinep Shaimergenova
Bischkek, Wien

Aussenpolitik und Globalisierung am Beispiel der Kirgisischen Republik

Die heutige Kirgisische Republik gehörte zu den 12 Sowjetrepubliken in der ehemaligen UdSSR – Union der Sowjetischen Sozialistischen Republiken – und hieß mit dem vollen Namen Kirgisische Sowjetische Sozialistische Republik.

Nach dem Zerfall der Sowjetunion entsprechend der Proklamation vom 31.08.1991, erhielt sie ihre Unabhängigkeit und wurde in die Republik Kirgisistan umbenannt.

Kirgisien, Kyrgyzstan, Kirgistan, oder Kirgisistan? Wie heisst heute das Land nun wirklich? Diese Frage ist nicht selten zu hören. Der volle richtige Name lautet seit 1993 Kirgisische Republik oder kurz – Kirgisistan.

Die Kirgisische Republik liegt im Herzen Zentralasiens (ZA). Die Fläche beträgt 198.500 km², Einwohnerzahl: 5.004.000 (2003), Bevölkerungsdichte: 25 Ew/km², Hauptstadt: Bischkek (ehem. Frunse), Staatsform: Präsidialrepublik, seit 1991 Verwaltungsgliederung: 7 Regionen und Hauptstadtbezirk.

Die Fläche des Landes ist den gesamten Flächen von Portugal, Schweiz, Belgien und Niederlanden gleich.

Kirgisistan grenzt im Osten an China (Territorium: 9,6 Mio. km², Bevölkerungszahl mehr als 1 Mlrd. Menschen), im Süden an Tadschikistan (Territorium: 143 100 km², Einwohnerzahl: 6,5 Mio (2003)), im Westen an Usbekistan (Territorium: 447 400 km², Einwohnerzahl: 25,03 Mio (2002)), und im Norden an Kasachstan (neuntgrösstes Land der Erde mit der Fläche 2 717 300 km², Einwohnerzahl: 14,8 Mio. (2002)).

Schon seit Jahrhunderten war Kirgisistan eine Art Brücke zwischen Orient und Okzident, zwischen Norden und Süden. Das Land liegt in der Kreuzung von verschiedenen Kulturen. Durch das Gebiet von Kirgisistan ging die berühmte Grosse Seidenstrasse.

Internationale Beziehungen der Kirgisen in der Vergangenheit haben eine lange und ereignisreiche Geschichte. Mehr darüber könnte man im Buch *Internationale Beziehungen der Kirgisen und Kirgisistans: Geschichte und Gegenwart* von Univ. Prof. Dr. Dr. Kaana Aidarkul finden.[1]

Die Ausrufung Kirgisistans als unabhängiger und souveräner Staat hat ein qualitativ neues Niveau der Entwicklung seiner internationalen Beziehungen eröffnet.

Obwohl in der vergangenen Zeit die Verfassung der Republik die Selbstständigkeit in den auswärtigen Angelegenheiten festgelegt hat, trugen die Regelungen dennoch deklarativen, propagandistischen Charakter. In der ehemaligen Kirgisischen Sowjetrepublik gehörte das Amt des Aussenministers eher zu den Ehrenfunktionen, das zusätzlich zu einem Hauptposten verliehen wurde. Nicht zuletzt bekamen dieses Amt Frauen, was für die ausländischen Delegationen auch als Beispiel der Frauengleichberechtigung galt. Aufgrund der Gegebenheit, dass die Entwicklung der internationalen Beziehungen „von oben" diktiert wurde, blieb für Kirgisistan damals nichts anderes übrig, als sich zurückzuhalten. Die Beziehungen entwickelten sich nur mit den Staaten des gleichen oder ähnlichen politischen Staatsaufbaues.

Der Zerfall der Sowjetunion und die Proklamation von Kirgisistan als unabhängiger Staat, so wie seine Bereitschaft in die Weltgemeinschaft einzutreten, haben die Republik vor neue Aufgaben gestellt. Dementsprechend bekam das Ministerium für auswärtige Angelegenheiten einen neuen Status. Früher erfüllte es eher rein protokol-

---

[1] Kaana Ajdarkul, *Meždunarodnye otnošenija kyrgyzov i Kyrgyzstana: istorija i sovremennost'* [Internationale Beziehungen der Kirgisen und Kirgisistans: Geschichte und Gegenwart], Biškek 2002.

larische und konsularische Aufgaben. Von nun an verlangte die Selbständigkeit des Landes die Ausarbeitung einer eigenen Strategie im aussenpolitischen Bereich und deren konzeptuale Verwirklichung. Statt der Politik des Isolationismus wählte die Republik die Politik der Offenheit. Im Ausland war die Kirgisische Republik damals noch völlig unbekannt. Anfang der 90-er Jahre entdeckte nicht nur Kirgisistan die Welt, sondern auch die Welt entdeckte für sich dieses zentralasiatische Land. Alle Menschen aus der ehemaligen Sowjetunion waren bis zu dieser Zeit „Russen". Das Interesse für Kirgisistan konnte die Autorin dieser Zeilen selbst 1992 in der Bundesrepublik erleben, damals unter den ersten Lehrlingen aus den Neuen Unabhängigen Staaten von Mittel- und Osteuropa an der Diplomatischen Akademie des Auswärtigen Amtes. Dieses Interesse haben zahlreiche Gespräche und Interviews gezeigt. Gleichzeitig wirkte die Tatsache, im Auswärtigen Amt eine Praxis auszuüben, die Kommission der EU und sogar die NATO Zentrale zu besuchen, für die Vertreter des ehemaligen Ostblocks sensationell.

Für Kirgisistan und für die Kirgisen war es die Zeit der Wende. Grosse Veränderungen standen bevor. Dazu gehörte die Umwandlung eines autoritären Staates zu einem Rechtsstaat, die Demokratisierung der Gesellschaft und die Ersetzung der Planwirtschaft durch die Marktwirtschaft. Einerseits sollte die Mentalität des Volkes geändert werden, andererseits wollte man zu nationalen Traditionen und zu eigenen Identität zurückkehren.

Am Anfang betrachtete man alle zentralasiatischen Länder und deren Völker als homogene Gebilde. In der Tat gibt es viel gemeinsames in der Geschichte und Kultur. Gleichzeitig verfügen diese Völker über spezifische Momente in ihrer geschichtlichen, wirtschaftlichen und kulturellen Entwicklung. Die Startpositionen dieser Länder und auch ihre ersten Schritte als unabhängige Staaten waren nicht gleich.

Ohne über den Begriff und die Geschichte der Globalisierung zu diskutieren, könnte man sagen, dass die Unabhängigkeit Kirgisistans mit der Beschleunigung der Globalisierung zusammenfiel. Sehr oft verbindet man Globalisierung mit den wirtschaftlichen und sozialen Prozessen in der Welt. Der Begriff beinhaltet aber auch eine politische

Seite. In den letzten Jahrzehnten erfolgte eine stürmische Verbreitung von internationalen Organisationen, Unionen und Verbindungen. Anfang des XX. Jahrhunderts gab es 37 zwischenstaatliche Organisationen und 170 internationale NGOs, Ende des XX. Jahrhunderts gab es schon 6415 zwischenstaatliche Organisationen und fast 44 Tausend internationale NGOs. Die Gesamtheit der zwischenstaatlichen Beziehungen, Verträge und Abkommen überzieht die Welt. Das Netz der politischen Beziehungen entwickelt sich mit globalen wirtschaftlichen und sozialen Vorgängen.

Die Globalisierung stellt auch die Frage: wie sind wir mit den anderen verbunden? Auch in Kirgisistan kamen Internet, Satelliten TV, Mobiltelefon usw. dazu. Neue Informationstechnologien öffneten neue Kommunikationsmöglichkeiten. Die Welt wurde transparenter und die Staaten wurden öffentlicher. So entstanden neue Chancen aber auch neue Bedrohungen und Gefährdungen. Früher waren sie vorwiegend nationale oder lokale, jetzt sind sie auch globale.

Laut der Verfassung ist Kirgisistan ein säkularer Staat. Sie garantiert auch Religions- und Glaubensfreiheit. Politik und Religion sind getrennt. Ein ehemals offiziell atheistisches Land wurde in der globalisierten Welt ein Interessensfeld vieler religiöser Strömungen und Sekten.

Neu war für die Republik auch die Entstehung vieler politischen Parteien und Bewegungen anstelle der ehemaligen alleinregierenden kommunistischen Partei. Die Zahl der Parteien ist von 20 am Anfang der Unabhängigkeit bis gegen 60 angewachsen. Politische Parteien religiöser Prägung gibt es nicht. Starke Bedeutung gewann die sogenannte Zivilgesellschaft. Es gibt über 6000 NGOs.

Kirgisistan ist ein kleines Land. Es bedroht niemanden. In seinem Selbstverständnis hat es keine Gegner. Entsprechend den Nationalinteressen waren die grundlegenden Aufgaben Bewahrung der territorialen Einheit, Gewährleistung der nationalen Sicherheit, Demokratisierung der Gesellschaft, Durchführung der Reformen und Integration in die Weltmarktwirtschaft.

Für die kirgisische Politik war es klar, dass die Verwirklichung der inneren Umwandlungen ohne aktive aussenpolitische Tätigkeit unmöglich ist.

Die Aussenpolitik wurde auf friedliche Koexistenz und internationale Sicherheit ausgerichtet. Wesentlich waren Anknüpfung und Entwicklung fruchtbarer bilateraler und multilateraler Beziehungen mit allen Ländern der Welt.

Im ersten Jahr der Unabhängigkeit haben Kirgisistan 120 Staaten anerkannt, mit 67 Staaten wurden diplomatische Beziehungen aufgenommen.

Die Weltgemeinschaft zeigte ihr grosses Interesse für die wirtschaftliche und politische Zukunft der GUS Länder, darunter auch Kirgisistan.

Eine wesentliche Rolle wurde auch den in der Weltgemeinschaft vorhandenen Instrumenten globalen und regionalen Charakters beigemessen.

In kurzer Zeit wurde Kirgisistan Mitglied vieler internationaler und regionaler Organisationen, wie z.B. UNO, OSZE (KSZE), IWF, IBRD,UNESCO, WHO, ILO, ESCAP, ECO, ICO, EBRD.

Die Teilnahme an diesen Organisationen hatte neue politische, kulturelle, wirtschaftliche und wissenschaftliche Beziehungen zur Folge. So bestimmte die Unterzeichnung der Schlussakte von Helsinki am 8. Juni 1992 den Weg der Republik zu einem demokratischen Staat und konzipierte die Grundprinzipien ihrer Entwicklung. Anfangs 1992 wurde Kirgisistan Mitglied der OSCE, damals KSCE. Der Teilnahme an der Arbeit der OSCE wird eine grosse Bedeutung zugemessen. So wurde im März 1993 die Botschaft der Kirgisischen Republik in Wien gleichzeitig als Ständige Vertretung bei der OSCE eröffnet. Sie war die erste Botschaft von Kirgisistan in Europa.

Der UNO kommt in der Zeit der Globalisierung eine besondere Rolle bei der Ausarbeitung der strategischen Richtlinien in der Politik der Staaten zu. Kirgisistan wurde Mitglied der UNO am 2. März 1992. Die ständige Mission der UNO in der Republik wurde im Jahre 1993 eröffnet. Heutzutage haben ihre ständigen Vertretungen in der Kirgisischen Republik die sechs dem UNO System angehörenden Organisationen. Darunter solche wie UNFPA, UNHCR, UNICEF, UNDP, WHO. Durch die regionalen Vertretungen besteht eine gute Zusammenarbeit auch mit UNDCP, UNESCO, dem UNO-Programm UNAIDS und der ILO. Ebenso besteht eine aktive Zusammenarbeit auch mit IOM, deren Mission in der Republik zusammen mit den UNO Institutionen verschiedene Programme und Projekte realisiert.

Wie in der ganzen Welt gewann die Frage der Frauengleichberechtigung eine besondere Bedeutung. So wurde in der Republik die Koordinationsgruppe „Gender in der Entwicklung" gebildet. Zu ihr gehörte neben UNO Institutionen wie UNDP, UNFRA, UNIFEM, UNESCO, auch IOM. Diese Gruppe hat eine grundlegende Rolle in der Ausarbeitung eines Nationalen Aktionsplanes der Genderpolitik in Kirgisistan gespielt.

Alle in Kirgisistan akkreditierten UNO Agenturen sind Mitglieder des Hauptkoordinationskomitees für ausserordentliche Situationen. An der Spitze des Komitees steht der Vize-Premierminister.

In allen sogenannten UNO Städten, New York, Genf und Wien, hat die Kirgisische Republik diplomatische Missionen errichtet. Dieser Sitz in den UNO Zentren der Welt hat die Zusammenarbeit des Landes mit der UNO, deren Agenturen und Kommissionen gefördert. Neue Bedeutung erhielten die Fragen der Menschenrechte. Unter diesen Bedingungen war die Zusammenarbeit mit UNCHR wichtig. Ökologische und soziale Probleme forderten die enge Kooperation auch mit der Atombehörde (IAEA) in Wien.

Kirgisistan hat als erste unter den ehemaligen Sowjetrepubliken die Beitrittsverhandlungen mit der Welthandelsorganisation (WTO) erfolgreich abgeschlossen. Offizielles Mitglied dieser Organisation ist die Republik seit Dezember 1998. Mehr als 140 Staaten sind Mitglied der WTO. Ihre Zahl wird noch wachsen. Heute strebt praktisch jeder Staat nach dem Aufbau einer effizienten Wirtschaft und gleichberechtigter Beteiligung am Welthandel.

Das globale Ziel der Gegenwart besteht im Aufbau einer friedlichen, sicheren und freien Weltgemeinschaft. Die Kirgisische Republik leistet dazu vielfältige Beiträge.

Besondere Bedeutung bei der Sicherheitsfestigung und Stabilität wird der Entwicklung der Zusammenarbeit mit China, Kasachstan, Russland, Tadjikistan und Usbekistan (Indien, Pakistan, Iran – Beobachterländer) in der Shanghaier Organisation für Zusammenarbeit und in der Organisation des Vertrages für Kollektive Sicherheit mit Armenien, Belarus, Kasachstan, Russland und Tadjikistan beigemessen.

Kirgisistan ist kein NATO Mitglied. Eine Kooperation erfolgt im Rahmen des Rates für euroatlantische Zusammenarbeit (EACC) und Partnerschaft für den Frieden (PfP).

Kirgisistan ist bestrebt, freundschaftliche Beziehungen auf politischer, wirtschaftlicher und kultureller Ebene mit allen Ländern zu entwickeln. Besondere Beziehungen verbinden die Republik mit Russland, China und USA.

Eine neue Prägung haben auch die Beziehungen mit den unmittelbaren Nachbarn bekommen. Die zentralasiatischen Staaten haben gemeinsame Grenzen, tiefe historische und kulturelle Wurzeln, Verkehrs- und andere Kommunikationen, reiche Wasserenergie- und Rohstoffvorräte. Dadurch sind sie miteinander eng verflochten. Aber die alten Kooperationssysteme gelten nicht mehr. Heute funktionieren zwei regionale Kooperationsvereinigungen: die Organisation der Zentralasiatischen Zusammenarbeit und die Eurasische Wirtschaftsgemeinschaft. Die beiden Vereinigungen wurden mehrmals umgeformt, umbenannt und erweitert. Die erste geht zurück auf den Vertrag über den Gemeinsamen Wirtschaftsraum, den die Präsidenten von Kasachstan, Kirgisistan und Usbekistan am 30. April 1994 unterzeichneten. Die zweite geht zurück auf den Vertrag von Russland und Belarus vom 6. Jänner 1995 über die Zollunion. Am 20. Januar 1995 wurde der Vertrag von Kasachstan und am 29. März 1996 von Kirgisistan unterzeichnet. 1998 trat Tadjikistan in die Gemeinschaft ein. Die Bemühungen der Mitgliedsländer umfassen eine breite Palette der Zusammenarbeit. Die Aktivitäten sind vor allem auf die Förderung der Integrationsprozesse und des weiteren wirtschaftlichen Zuwachses gerichtet. Die Gewährleistung der regionalen Sicherheit und die Erhaltung der Stabilität gehören auch zu den vorrangigen Aufgaben.

Für Kirgisistan ist die Entwicklung der Beziehungen zu den europäischen Ländern besonders wichtig. Das öffnet den Integrationsweg für die Entwicklungsländer in die Gemeinschaft der alten Demokratien. Einen neuen konkreten Inhalt bekam die Kooperation mit der EU und deren Institutionen. Prioritäre Bedeutung hat die Vertiefung der Zusammenarbeit mit Deutschland, Frankreich, der Schweiz, Grossbritannien und der Türkei. Ein besonderes Augenmerk erfordert die Entwicklung der Beziehungen mit den Ländern Osteuropas.

Kirgisistan ist für gegenseitig vorteilhafte Beziehungen mit Japan, der Republik Korea, Malaysien, Indien und Pakistan. Es tritt auch ein für die Entwicklung der allseitigen Verbindungen und gegenseitig vorteilhaften Zusammenarbeit mit den Staaten der islamischen Welt. Kirgisistan unterhält freundschaftliche Beziehungen mit den islamischen und arabischen Ländern. Die Achtung des gewählten Entwicklungsweges ist Grundlage dieser Beziehungen.

Die geopolitische Situation hat die Zentralasien-Region sowie auch Kirgisistan in die Interessenkreise der führenden Welt- und Regionsmächte hineingezogen.

Die Situation in Afghanistan, die verstärkte Politisierung der religiösen Organisationen in ZA, Drogen und Waffenhandel usw. bestimmen die Lage in ZA als Zone der potenziellen Instabilität.

Grundlegende Veränderungen der Weltlage in den letzten Jahren, insbesondere nach dem 11.09.2001, haben die Aussenpolitik weltweit vor neue Herausforderungen gestellt. Kirgisistan sollte entsprechend diesen neuen globalen Risiken reagieren.

In diesem Zusammenhang unternimmt die Republik konkrete Schritte. Als einer der ersten ist Kirgisistan aktiver Teilnehmer der internationalen Anti-Terror-Koalition. Für die humanitäre Hilfe für Afghanistan leistete Kirgisistan sein Möglichstes.

Die politische Position des Landes wurde nicht nur in verschiedenen internationalen Konferenzen artikuliert, es wurden auch entsprechende Vereinbarungen auf bilateraler und multilateraler Ebene abgeschlossen.

Seit Ende 2001 befindet sich in Kirgisistan ein Militärstützpunkt der US-geführten internationalen Anti-Terror-Koalition. Die Stationierung ist durch die Situation in Afghanistan bedingt. Seit Ende 2003 ist in Kirgisistan ein Stützpunkt von Teilen der schnellen Eingreiftruppen der Länder des Kollektiven Sicherheitsvertrages eingerichtet.

Heute ist Kirgisistan anerkanntes Mitglied der Weltgemeinschaft. Grosse Unterstützung fand unsere Initiative zur Durchführung des Jahres der Berge.

Unsere 2200 Jahre alte Staatlichkeit fand Anerkennung seitens der UNO, ebenso das 1000 Jahrjubiläum des kirgisischen Epos Manas, des grössten in der Geschichte der Menschheit. Das Beibehalten des Kulturerbes und der nationalen Identität aller 80 in Kirgisistan lebenden Volksgruppen ist immer auf der Tagesordnung unserer Politik.

Nach den Ereignissen des 24. März 2005 und nach dem Machtwechsel blieb das Land allen seinen früheren Verpflichtungen auf der internationalen Ebene treu. Die grundlegenden Prinzipien der Aussenpolitik, ihre Ziele und Aufgaben sind unverändert. Sie widerspiegeln die Interessen der multinationalen, polykonfessionellen Bevölkerung der Republik.

Part VI
Democracy and Globalization

Klaus Müller
Kraków

Globalization and Democracy. Progress and Paradoxes

Globalization and democracy, two encompassing and ambitious concepts, are commonly used to characterize secular processes, which have been unfolding over long periods of time, perhaps several centuries, but only most recently developed to full display. Today, it is said, we live under the conditions of globalization, which can be felt almost everywhere. Certainly in economic affairs, where globalization is associated with the liberalization of capital markets since the late 1970s, but also in every-day live, from world music to tourism and fashion, globalization is present. Even more impressive changes are assigned to the political sphere: Today, more countries than ever before are classified as electoral democracies. The worldwide diffusion of democracy seems to have pushed the "age of extremes" which was overshadowed by nazism, communism and third world dictatorships of all kinds back into history: Over the two last decades the sky cleared up and opened the prospect of a coming "Democratic Century".[1] Since globalization *and* democracy are omnipresent in the media, in politics and in the social science discourse, since both processes became intertwined and nearly coextensive, the widespread impression emerged that we more or less know the implications of both processes and how they interact.

---

[1] Seymour Martin Lipset & Jason M. Lakin, *The Democratic Century*, Norman: University of Oklahoma Press, 2004; cf. Larry Diamond, "Can The Whole World Become Democratic?", *Center for the Study of Democracy*, Paper 03–05, University of California, Irvine, 2003.

Unfortunately this is not the case. Especially the relation between globalization and democracy remains ambivalent and essentially contested. Broadly speaking, there are two opposed camps. The liberalist school explains the flourishing of democracy by economic growth and rising prosperity. If globalization is "spreading the wealth", as David Dollar and Aart Kraay from the World Bank suggest, then it comes hand in hand with liberty, a rising world middle class and democratic institutions.[2] When, on the other side, Branko Milanovitch, another World Bank economist, is right, then globalization aggravates inequality on the national, regional and global level.[3] Under these conditions globalization may lead to global instability, a backlash against free trade, slowed economic growth und right wing nationalism; exporting Western free market capitalism to the rest of the world risks to provoke violent upheavals of impoverished masses against market-dominating minorities, especially if these are recognizable as outsiders or ethnic groups.[4] All this would reduce the chances of a democratic future, as feared by sociologists like Ralf Dahrendorf.

What this controversy underlines – irrespective of which side may prove right – is that the prospects of democracy have become a critical dimension of globalization and a crucial reference point to assess its implications. How then, one may ask, is it possible at all that social scientists can hold such contrary opinions on the future of democracy?

I propose to approach this question in three steps. At first I will outline the common understanding of globalization. My diagnosis will be critical and short: much of the literature on globalization is theoretically naive and empirically misleading – especially the vision of a borderless communication which is said to have dissolved the territorial base of political domination. My second point gives a short overview over the recent history of democratization, since – like global-

---

[2] David Dollar & Aart Kraay, "Spreading the Wealth", *Foreign Affairs*, Jan./Feb. 2002, pp. 120–133.

[3] Branco Milanovic, *Worlds Apart. Measuring International and Global Inequality*, Princeton: Princeton University Press, 2005, p. 149.

[4] Ami Chua, *World On Fire. How Exporting Free Market Democracy Breeds Ethnic Hatred and Global Instability*, New York: Double Day, 2003.

ization – democratization arrived in historical waves. The recent decades are usually characterized by Samuel Huntington's famous 'Third Wave of Democracy', which started in the mid-1970s and merged in the late 1980s with the liberalization of markets.[5] So one may assume an "electoral affinity" between economic and political liberalization. But: Correlation is not causation. In my third and last point I will revisit the debate on the future of democracy under global conditions which touches some far reaching questions: Is democracy actually spreading around the globe? Are there chances to widen its scope: to a post-national space, to a global civil society or even to a global democracy? In addressing these questions we should remember that in the course of its long history the concept of democracy itself underwent several transformations. If we live in a time in which globalization and democracy interfere it is well possible that democracy is changing its meaning again. Could this imply that democracy is in danger to be reduced to decision-making modelled on the market?

1. Globalization – Concepts and Illusions

(1) Coming to globalization, the standard concepts prominent in the literature usually refer to vanishing borders, the shrinking of time and space, the free flow of capital, ideas and people. According to this view we are experiencing a de-territorialization of politics, the economy and also of society. Globalization is defined, in the words of David Held and colleagues as:

a process (or set of processes) which embodies a transformation in the spatial organization of social relations and transactions – assessed in terms of their extensity, intensity, velocity and impact – generating transcontinental or interregional flows and networks of activity, interaction, and the exercise of power.[6]

---

[5] Samuel P. Huntington, *The Third Wave. Democratization in the Late 20th Century*, Norman: University of Oklahoma Press, 1991.

[6] David Held et al., *Global Transformations*, Stanford: Stanford University Press, 1999, p. 16.

These are quite abstract terms – and abstract they have to be, since conventional social science concepts, it is said, have lost their referents. National economies were dissolved into globalized markets, nation states are loosing their capacity to rise taxes and to provide social security at the same levels as in earlier times. National cultures give way to multicultural encounters and hybrid identities. In this sense, many globalists think that we are living already in a new age, characterized by post-sovereign states operating under post-national conditions. Thus, the formal jargon of many globalization theories may be interpreted as an act of saying farewell to good old modernity – or again in the words of David Held:

> As with the idea of modernization, which acquired intellectual primacy within the social sciences during the 1960s, so today the notion of globalization has become the *leitmotiv* of our age.[7]

What are the forces driving this development? The first trend commonly associated with globalization is communication. News satellites, the internet, and the media are said to have fostered exponential growth in the exchange of ideas, information and life stiles. This has brought life to a whole new infrastructure of communication, making interaction across long distances possible in real time. Also the second driving force of globalization depends on communication – the free flowing of capital around the globe. Today the amount of money on "short-term financial round-trip excursions" (J. Tobin) surpasses the combined reserves of all central banks by far. This comes together with a third trend – the rising of new powerful actors, namely transnational corporations commanding more resources than medium sized states.

In all of these contexts communication, a central concept of social science theory since a few decades, became the key metaphor of the global age. And from here a direct linkup is made to democratization. Not only according to Anthony Giddens, television played a decisive role in the fall of the Berlin Wall and, more generally, in the fall of

---

[7] *The Global Transformations Reader*, ed. by David Held & Anthony McGrew, Cambridge: Polity Press, 2000, p. 1.

communism. It also spread the power of anti-authoritarian movement to South Africa and to other parts of the world.[8] From this the impression arises that globalization is not only something new, but comes as a revolution. Since communication in times of the World Wide Web is borderless, since global capital markets are beyond the control of any single state, since globalization is carried by the most advanced technologies, it also seems irreversible.

(2) This account is perhaps well-meaning but also dangerously naïve in that it suggests that we live under the conditions of democratic peace, where democratic states have no longer enemies and authoritarian regimes are televised away. So it is important to see why this approach is misleading – in terms of globalization as well as in terms of democracy.

As regards globalization – despite all the talk of the communications revolutions and global capital markets – both trends are not unknown. According to a now widely held view, there have been earlier waves of globalization, earlier periods of expanding markets and of worldwide political activities: Colonialism, the "golden age of liberalism" or, more precisely: imperialism, and the Cold War era, when the globe was in a perverse sense united by the threat of mutually assured nuclear destruction. And there had been considerable movements of people. European countries, just now trying to come to terms with being immigration societies, were in the past characterized by emigration. In fact, emigration into the settler colonies in North America, Australia and New Zeeland spread the seeds of democracy beyond its North-west European countries of origin.

Taken together, the three common indicators of globalization, namely trade, capital flows and migration (indicated by immigration to the USA), draw the following picture of three waves of globalization.[9]

From this graph two conclusions can be drawn: *First*, earlier globalizations were reversible, though by a price. The 'golden age of liberal-

[8] Anthony Giddens, *BBC Reith Lectures*, London: LSE, 1999, Lecture I.
[9] From *Globalization, Growth, and Poverty. Building an Inclusive World Economy*, World Bank Publication, Oxford: Oxford University Press, 2002, p. 23.

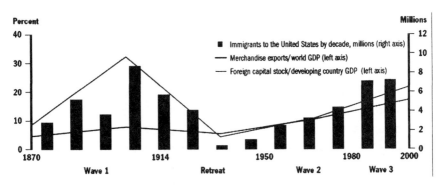

Fig. 1. Three Waves of Globalization

ism' was wrecked by trade warfare, the Great Depression, and the rise of economic nationalism. In Germany it paved the way for nazism and World War II. *Second*, technological trends alone did not play a decisive role: Costs of sea freight, air transport and telecommunication actually fell from 1920 to 1940 without marking a difference in the volume of trade or investments into foreign countries. In the middle of last century world export had fallen back to the level of 1870; the retreat to nationalism came along with rising inequality between countries and world regions. To make a long story short: If there have been earlier reversals, then, a future backlash against globalization is possible, too.[10] Some economist fear that the failure of the last round of trade talks may lead to trade-bilateralism, perhaps preferred by the United States. A trade war between the US and China seems possible. Nobody exactly knows the implications of the global imbalances marked by the US deficit and what the consequences of the steep fall of the Dollar would be.

Let me add a third point: If we take a look at the world map of wealth production, we don't see the "spreading of wealth", as suggested by Dollar & Kraay. Rather, we can note a highly concentrated distribution of incomes and foreign direct investments in regional terms. "Globalization" is a highly uneven process, which has become

[10] Harold James, *The End of Globalization: Lessons from the Great Depression*, Cambridge, Mass.: Harvard University Press, 2001.

the subject of a "new economic geography", which clearly operates within time-space categories.[11]

To be sure, to recognize that there have been earlier episodes of globalization does not imply that there is nothing new under the sun. Quite on the contrary, the history of previous waves of globalization provides the background for seeming more clearly the new qualities of the current time. And these new qualities are to be found in the political arena, signalled by the rise of International Organizations with a global mandate and by the fact that the current wave of globalization happens under the conditions of democracy. This second new quality of current globalization brings me to my second point – the globalization of democracy itself.

2. Unsolved Problems of Global Democracy: Widening – Deepening – Upgrading

Compared to the concept of globalization, the concept of democracy seems to be less controversial. There is a long tradition of theories of democracy, there are some well established definitions of the concept, and, in normative terms, democracy as a principle of government seems not to be contested any more. But, as indicated above, democracy also came in historical waves, and went through several breakdowns and reversals. The meaning of democracy thereby experienced several transformations, changing its content as well as its scope. Presently we are living through a time in which democracy is challenged from three different sides, all related to globalization, but having quite different implications. In this sense, the globalization of democracy can mean very different things: namely the *widening*, the *deepening* or the *upgrading* of democracy. Taking these dimensions together, not only progress but also some paradoxes come into view.

(1) *Widening* seems to be the least controversial aspect. In fact, most of the literature since the 1990s, certainly the bulk of quantitative

---

[11] Peter Dicken, *Global Shift. Transforming the Global Economy*, London: Sage, 2003.

research on democracy working with different scales and correlations, is devoted to the diffusion of democracy across more and more countries. From this perspective, democracy since its early days has been part of a broader spectrum of processes of worldwide significance. Already the first wave of Huntington's scheme started in two continents, with the Revolutions in France and America, and then progressed over some West European countries, the European settler colonies in Australia, Canada and Chile up to the newly proclaimed democracies in Central Europe after Word War I. A second, shorter wave reached Western Germany, Italy, Japan and South Korea under allied occupation after 1945; along with this second wave the worldwide process of decolonization set in, leading to democracy in India and the Philippines. The recent period of time is commonly characterized by a famous "Third Wave" which rolled over Southern Europe in the second part of the 1970s, taking Latin America and parts of Asia and Africa in the 1980s to culminate in the Eastern European Revolutions of 1989.

From an empirical point of view, the impression of a world wide progression of democracy can hardly be denied. The facts seem self-evident. In the beginning of the last century only 25 of the then 55 states (next to another 55 imperial or colonial entities and 20 protectorates) could be called democracies of some sorts. In 1950 the governments of 24 countries in a world of now 80 states were elected democratically. Since the start of Huntington's Third Wave the set grew continuously: from 39 countries in 1974 to 117 in 1995. In 2004, 119 of the 194 states of the world are governed by elected leaderships – or are at least formally democratic.[12]

A significant progress indeed. Adherents of this approach, at least in retrospect, are celebrating a century of democracy. "Today everyone is a democrat", writes Anthony Giddens. As a general explanation for this amazing outcome he cites globalization – in his eyes "the emergence of more reflexive populations across the world", illuminated by an "emerging globalized information order", relying on sat-

---

[12] Adrian Karatnycky, "Civic Power and Electoral Politics", in: *Freedom in the World 2005*, New York: Freedom House, 2005.

ellite communication and the internet.[13] The main causes Huntington is referring to are the economic growth of the last decades and "snowballing", i.e. demonstrations effects televised from one country to another. An eminent political scientist like Martin Lipset – one of the authors of the *World Development Report* of 1997 on the role of the state in a changing world – even suggests, that the International Monetary Fund (IMF) and the World Bank may have played a positive role – or more generally that "international agencies and foreign governments are more likely to endorse pluralistic regimes".[14] As in classical political sociology, well prospering and well informed global middle classes are the agents of democratization. And this seems also to be the political background and explanation why the already mentioned overoptimistic paper by Dollar & Kraay on the welfare benefits of globalization appeared in the journal *Foreign Affairs*. "Spreading the wealth" by globalized trade, thereby creating a global middle class as a standard bearer of democracy is stated as the cardinal normative principle of US foreign policy since the 1990s.

(2) Sceptics, on the other hand, point to the fact that globally stretched concepts of democracy may sacrifice some of its qualities. Therefore, the *quality of democracy* and not the widening should be the primary concern for the next decades.[15] The reason for this sceptical view is that quite a few of the "New Democracies" are at best 'democracies with adjectives',[16] some are thinly disguised 'electoral dictator-

---

[13] Anthony Giddens, *BBC Reith Lectures*, op. cit., ch. 5. This is a remarkable swing of opinion, since before 1989 Giddens draw intimate connections between modern state power, industrialised warfare and sophisticated techniques of surveillance, which could easily lead to a new totalitarianism (s. Anthony Giddens, *The Nation-State and Violence*, Cambridge: Polity Press, 1985, pp. 295–312).

[14] Seymour Martin Lipset, "The Social Requisites of Democracy Revisited", *American Sociological Review*, Vol. 59, No. 1, 1994, p. 16. More generally on the ideas of "regime change" and "promoting democracy" see Jon C. Pevehouse, "Democracy from the Outside-In? International Organizations and Democratization", *International Organization*, Vol. 56, No. 3, 2002 (Summer), pp. 515–549.

[15] Dieter Nohlen, "Political Participation in New and Old Democracies", in: *Voter Turnout Since 1945. A Global Report*, Stockholm: International IDEA, 2002.

[16] David Collier & Steven Levitsky, "Democracy with Adjectives: Conceptual Innovation in Comparative Research", *World Politics*, Vol. 49, No. 3, 1997, pp. 430–451.

ships'. Thus, during the 1990s some events and development brought
to mind, that, like globalization, democratization may very well be
reversible.

May even a third "reverse wave" like those dated from 1922 to 1942
and 1958 to 1975 be a real danger? In fact, most of the literature dedicated to hybrid regimes, is addressed to the "New Democracies" of the
last fifteen years. And there are many different classifications of various
subtypes of imperfect democracies in use. There are dubious cases like
the Russia's 'illiberal democracy': a democratic constitution is in place
and more than a hundred elections on all levels of the state led to
numerous changes of leadership. On the other side, there is no integrative party-system, the media are back under state control, elections in
many places where obviously rigged, outside interventions could be
observed in the case of Ukraine. In Eastern Europe we have at least two
countries, for which the phrase of a transition to democracy makes no
sense at all: Belarus und Moldova. In some countries, where elections
took place, civil war is still a possibility: Albania and Macedonia. The
post-communist countries in Central Europe and the Baltics seem to
fare better than many thought in the early 1990s. In this case Lipset's
allusion to an international actor surely was right: the EU functioned as
an external anchor which prevented most of the post-communist
countries from drifting into authoritarian waters. Nevertheless, even in
this region civil societies are weak, party systems not well connected to
social interests, governments not really representative, voter turnout
low – only 40 percent during the Polish elections in 2005. On the other
hand, corruption in the 'new democracies' in Eastern Europe is well
above west European levels.

Contrary to Lipset's hopes, in other world region foreign governments or international agencies, were not of great help to establish
political pluralism at all. The geographical neighbourhood to the USA
did not prevent Honduras or Nicaragua from being downgraded
in the Freedom House Index. Pakistan, named as the biggest setback
in 1999[17], as well as the newly consolidated autocracies in Central

---

[17] Adrian Karatnycky, "A Century of Progress", *Journal of Democracy*, Vol. 11,
No. 1, 2000.

Asia became closed allies of the United States during the "war on terror". War, as was made evident in this context, is the worst possible environment for promoting democracy in foreign countries or to secure freedom at home.[18] Almost always civil liberties are the first victims – patriotism becoming an easy excuse to restrict criticism and opposition. Taken these heterogeneous cases together, it is difficult to come to general conclusions. But a few things seem clear. First: liberal democracy has *not* become, as proclaimed by Giovanni Sartori 15 years ago, "the only game in town".[19] Second: a minimal definition of democracy risks what Juan Linz and Alfred Stepan[20] termed "electoralist fallacy": to take elections, a necessary condition, for a sufficient one. Even if there is no third wave of a breakdown, the substance of democracy has been hollowed out in many countries. There are, as Larry Diamond observes, "elections without democracy".[21]

Given this heterogeneous scenery, does it make sense to look for a common causality called "globalization"? Surely, globalization is a too complex and ambivalent process to be praised – or blamed – for all and

---

[18] As Baker observes: "soaring rhetoric has often clashed with geopolitical reality and competing U.S. priorities" (Peter Baker, "The Realities of Exporting Democracy", *Washington Post*, January 25, 2006, A01). On the contradictions of this approach see Thomas Carothers, "Promoting Democracy and Fighting Terror", *Foreign Affairs*, January/February 2003.

[19] Giovanni Sartori, "Rethinking Democracy: Bad Polity and Bad Politics", *International Social Science Journal*, No. 129, 1991, pp. 437–450.

[20] Juan J. Linz and Alfred C. Stepan, *Problems of Democratic Transition and Consolidation*, Baltimore: John Hopkins University Press, 1996, p. 4.

[21] Larry Diamond, "Elections Without Democracy. Thinking About Hybrid Regimes", *Journal of Democracy*, Vol. 13, No. 2, 2002, pp. 21–35. A few years earlier Larry Diamond ("Is the Third Wave over?", *Journald of Democracy*, Vol. 7, No. 3, 1996, pp. 20-37) already had speculated that the Third Wave of democracy may be over. Carothers concludes that the "transition paradigm" also failed on a theoretical level and diagnosed an "authoritarian rebound" (Thomas Carothers, "The End of the Transition Paradigm", *Journal of Democracy*, Vol. 13, No. 1, 2002, pp. 5–21; idem, "Democracy's Sobering State", *Current History*, December 2004, pp. 412–416). McFaul rejects the concept of a "Third Wave" because quite a few "transition countries" entered the path towards a postcommunist dictatorship (Michael McFaul, "The Fourth Wave of Democracy and Dictatorship. Noncoopera-tive Transition in the Postcommunist World", *World Politics*, Vol. 54, January 2002, pp. 212–244).

every thing. Nevertheless, there are some dimensions, which make globalization more a part of the problem than of its solution. Many of the new democracies of the 1990s tried to modernise their societies according to a globalized policy: the notorious "Washington Consensus" – a "consensus" of business and political elites on supposedly universally applicable principles of economic reform. Radical marketization was a condition of loans from the IMF and the World Bank. "Drowning the state" was part of an ideological climate which entrusted markets not only to restructure the economy, but also to reorganise the fabric of society. Politically, this led to "state desertion" in many and a "stateness problem" in some cases: a lack of governability and rule of law. Economically, it made the liberalized markets vulnerable to a new type of financial crises, spreading around the globe by "contagion" – as demonstrated by the Russian and Asian Crisis in the late 1990s. Sociologically, rising inequalities often go hand in hand with a bias against political participation on the side of socially deprived groups and with distrust in political institutions.[22] A "vicious circle of inequality" undermined confidence in the public institutions especially in Latin America where societies are generally perceived as unjust.[23]

(3) But, how relevant are these observations *globally*? If the democracies of the "Third Wave" are in danger of being hollowed out by internal weakness and external pressures, do the old democracies of fare better? This is an acute question, since nearly all comparative accounts of democratization take the 28 Western democracies as benchmarks, not as possible problem cases themselves. This seems to be inappropriate for two reasons. First: better criteria to evaluate new democracies may be their respective status quo ante and the comparative situation in countries of similar stages of development. Seen this way, e.g. Russia despite all justified concerns is politically better off than two decades earlier[24]; better also than China, the poster-child

---

[22] Dieter Nohlen, "Political Participation in New and Old Democracies", op. cit., p. 15.

[23] Terry Lynn Karl, "The Vicious Cycle of Inequality in Latin America", in: *What Justice? Whose Justice?: Fighting for Fairness in Latin America*, ed. by Susan Eva Eckstein & Timothy P. Wickham-Crowley, Berkeley: University of California Press, 2003.

[24] Andrei Shleifer & Daniel Treisman, "A Normal Country: Rethinking Russia", *Foreign Affairs*, Vol. 83, No. 2, March/April 2004, pp. 20–38.

of globalization, where no democratic reforms have been tried at all. Second: there is another branch of sceptical literature on the erosive effects of globalization on the democracy in Western societies as well.

And this may be the real challenge to the very core of the concept of democracy. Some disturbing signs point into a direction opposed to a "third transformation" which Robert Dahl envisaged in his "Sketches for an Advanced Democratic Society".[25] Instead a deepening a regression to a minimalist understanding sees to be in the making, which rolls back those historical extensions of democratic rights which have been taken for granted since T.H. Marshall's[26] classical sociological concept of citizenship.

The conceptual background of this development was laid a few decades ago, when a "New Political Economy" generalized the liberalist conception of individual choice to the political sphere. If, according to this view, politicians were 'political entrepreneurs' maximising votes and voters were making their choices in the 'political market place', then in fact the whole procedures of democracy could be treated and streamlined like a business firm. What started as a sectarian branch of political theory, mimicking the more prestigious economic discipline, became a mainstream. More important, the "economic theory of democracy" entered the self-interpretation of acting politicians. While leaders in the New Democracies often justify austerity measures by the assertion, that "the IMF made us do it", governments in Western countries "explain" tax cuts and welfare reductions by referring to the forces of globalization.

The consequences are well known. Economic policy is subordinated to monetary stability irrespective of its consequences for growth and employment. Regarding the domain of politics, decision-making on more and more matters is "outsourced" from parliaments to so called expert commissions. Conformity to market sentiments is elevated to a general meta-criterion for political decision-making.

---

[25] Robert A. Dahl, *Democracy and Its Critics*, New Haven: Yale University Press, 1989, ch. 23.

[26] Thomas H. Marshall, "Citizenship and Social Class" (1949), in: *Citizenship and Social Class and other Essays*, Westport: Greenwood Press, 1973.

Now, if all governments are doing the same in the name of "no alternatives" this pre-empts the very sense of democracy, namely to deliberate alternatives to the just given state of affairs. Socially, in nearly all old democracies we see a big U-turn of rising income inequality, which started in the early globalizers, Britain and the United States, and now also arrived in France and Germany.[27] And from here a feedback loop leads back to the quality of democracy well described by Craig Murphy in the following words:

> Increasingly unequal incomes mean increasingly unequal market power. In a world in which we let the market do much of our collective business, increasingly unequal market power means increasingly less democracy.[28]

The formal procedures of party politics, voting, representation, division of power, legislation, etc. stay in place. In practice, democratic participation and parliamentarian decision-making become severely restricted, elections turn into a matter of marketing, opinion polls and 'video-politics'. Advanced societies, then, would enter a "post-democratic" stage.[29]

(4) If these observations capture the trend in mature democracies, how could this development be countered? In the first place, it is helpful to point to the difference between real forces of globalization and the generalized myth of a powerless state. There is a lot of empirical evidence on alternative strategies to respond to the challenges of global integration. Comparative research on the dynamics of welfare reform suggests that the level of social protection as well as the level of inequalities and taxation depends more on country-specific political constellations than on the level of economic liberalization.[30]

---

[27] Arthur S. Alderson & Francois Nielson, "Globalization and the Great U-Turn: Income Inequality Trends in 16 OECD Countries", *American Journal of Sociology*, Vol. 107, No. 5, 2002, pp. 1255–1299; Anthony B. Atkinson, "Income Inequality in OECD Countries. Data and Explanation", *CESifo Working Paper*, No. 881, 2003.

[28] Craig Murphy, "Political Consequences of the New Inequality", *International Studies Quarterly*, Vol. 45, 2001, p. 350.

[29] Colin Crouch, *Post-Democracy*, Cambridge: Polity Press, 2002.

[30] Walter Korpi & Joakim Palme, "New Politics and Class Politics in the Context of Austerity and Globalization. Welfare State Regress in 18 Countries 1975–95", *American*

As Dani Rodrik has outlined in several papers, successful strategies of globalization require strong integrative institutions to avoid damaging social conflicts and political instabilities.[31]

Nevertheless, there are also new challenges, which can not simply be broken down by traditional political means, since they surpass the power of single states. Many of the imperatives of globalization which allegedly overcharge politics per se, are in fact collective action problems that would require cooperation. Regional integration is one of the approaches to come to terms with this type of problem. In fact, regional integration agreements are the most significant trend in global politics, the EU being the most advanced project of this kind and the widely acclaimed role model for a democracy stretching beyond national borders.

And this the place, where an *upgrading of democracy* would have to come into play – or in the language of Dahl's approach "a change in the *scale* of political life, (which) once again alters the limits and possibilities of the democratic process".[32] In the most general terms this would mean to lift democratic procedures to a higher level of decision making. There are many proposals how to upgrade democracy beyond the scope of the nation state and many different associated aspirations. Some approaches seem utopian – others quite realistic.

To discuss the prospects of upgrading democracy would to a large degree mean to debate the democratic credentials of the EU – on which opinions, again, are divided. So far the most ambitious attempt towards a democratic Europe on a supranational level has been the draft constitution for Europe from July 2003. A European constitution – be it in the weaker sense of a "constitutional treaty" – seemed to be the logical consequence of an 'ever closer union' and, at the same time, the only way to civilize the unfettered forces of globalized mar-

---

Political Science Review, Vol. 97, No. 3, 2003; Edeltraut Roller, *The Performance of Democracies*, Oxford: Oxford University Press, 2005.

[31] Dani Rodrik, *Has Globalization Gone Too Far?*, Washington, DC: Institute for International Economics, 1997.

[32] Robert A. Dahl, *Democracy and Its Critics*, op. cit., p. 312; cf. Jürgen Habermas, *Die postnationale Konstellation*, Frankfurt am Main: Suhrkamp, 1998, ch. 4.

kets.[33] But, characteristically, the drive towards a democratically constituted EU is usually formulated in terms of a normative functional-
ism which easily confuses desirable state of affairs with political realities. Reality was brought back in when put to referendum in
France, the constitutional treaty did not pass the public expectations
of a social Europe and was shelved for the foreseeable future.[34]

A more modest approach is being debated in recent years under
the headlines of *Global Public Policy* and *Global Governance*. In these
cases states pool their sovereignty to solve specific problems and may
invite, case by case, the private sector or civil society groups for consultations. This idea is taken serious by several procedures to "demo-
cratise" the multilateral institutions, which in practice means to improve and to co-opt non-government organizations of different types.
Even the IMF and the World Bank have been receptive to this idea by
installing civil society forums to enhance transparency. Thus the UN
has postulated a governance by the "international public domain"
which would include "civil society organizations, the private sector,
parliamentarians, local authorities, scientific associations, educational
institutions and many others".[35] The opening to outside observers, to

---

[33] Jürgen Habermas, "So, Why Does Europe Need A Constitution?", Robert
Schumann Centre, European University Institute, Florence, 2001.

[34] For good reasons: contrasting to high hopes in a post-national Europe, it was
highly doubtful if the draft of a "Treaty on a Constitution for Europe" of 2003 would
have enhanced the democratic legitimacy of the EU-system. On the one hand, it elevated the status of the European Council, i.e. the central arena of national interests, to
the sole institution beyond control by the European Court of Justice and the European
Parliament. On the other hand, even the composition of the European Parliament does
not follow the principle of "one person, one vote" but is based on nationally weighted
electorates. So far at least, the EU has done more to foster democracy in its member
and neighbour states than on the supranational layer of its own institutions. For a
critical evaluation of the draft treaty see: Olivier Beaud et al., *L'Europe en voie de
Constitution*, Bruxelles: Bruylant, 2004; Ralf Dahrendorf ("Making Sense of the EU. The
Challenge for Democracy", *Journal of Democracy*, Vol. 14, No. 4, 2003, pp. 110–114) and
Philippe Schmitter ("Democracy in Europe and Europe's Democratization", *Journal of
Democracy*, Vol. 14, No. 4, 2003, pp. 71–85) are doubting if the EU is the proper place to
expect democracy in the common understanding or even in a "post-national" sense at all.

[35] Kofi Annan, 2000: *We, the Peoples. The Role of the United Nations in the 21st Century*, New York: United Nations Department of Public Information, 2000, p. 13.

those affected, to concerned or advocacy groups can improve the responsiveness and accountability of international organizations, which may occasionally give in to the soft power of moral persuasion. But as long as decision-making is monopolized by state-representatives, this is only a very rudimentary precondition of democratization.[36] At the same time, the unaccountability and often undeclared funding of many civil society organizations may even obscure real interest and power structures, "good governance" being a cheap surrogate for real participation.[37]

The most ambitions approach aims at a global democracy in the full sense of the term, resting on transnational institutions. The UN-General assembly would, in the long run, develop into a system similar to the European Parliament. In this sense, David Held and Anthony Giddens think, a *cosmopolitan democracy* would be a precondition to re-regulate the globalized world economy, to reduce ecological risks and economic inequalities – and also to give new life to democracy on the lower levels.[38] Giddens is cautious enough to present this perspective as "utopian realism". This seems fair enough. But to answer the question how to weight the "utopian" and the "realist elements" in this formula would require another discussion. So for it seems that globalization is posing more problems for democracy than solutions.

---

[36] „Global bodies tend to be either irrelevant if representative, or, if relevant, to be dominated by the rich", as Milanovic (*Worlds Apart. Measuring International and Global Inequality*, op. cit., p. 150) observes, cf. Robert A. Dahl, "Can International Organizations be Democratic? A Sceptics View", in: *Democracy's Edge*, ed. by Ian Shapiro & Casiano Hacker Cordón, Cambridge: Cambridge University Press, 2000.

[37] Jim Whitman, "Global Governance as the Friendly Face of Unaccountable Power", *Security Dialogue*, Vol. 33, No 1, 2002, pp. 45–50.

[38] Anthony Giddens, *The Third Way and it Critics*, Cambridge: Polity Press, 2000, ch. 6.

Jarema Jakubowski
Poznań

Preconditions of Democracy

It is hard to see even a narrow path

Tu Wei-Ming

1. Introduction

The few simple thoughts proposed below will be primarily of a theoretical nature. However, since they are formulated within a specific historical context, it is hard not to see their relation to social and political activity.

Only for a decade did we delude ourselves thinking that liberal democracy, while it is not the constitution of each country, has no competition at the level of ideas. The Muslim world's waging war on the West and the tempestuous mass demonstrations advancing slogans such as "We want Islam, not democracy" have offered an opportunity for a more sober reflection on our own civilization and the rest of the world. However, this more sober scrutiny hits the barrier of noble idealism and the moral mission of spreading the values we deem objective and universal, both characteristic of Western spirituality. The values in question are justice, truth, and goodness, features initially identified with Christianity and then with civilization as such; today it is primarily democracy and human rights that are regarded as the fulfilment of the ideals of humanity. Therefore, the long and ruthless war waged on us – even if we know it first needs to be resolved in a military manner – can in the long run lead to the peace and well-being of the world only with the introduction of democracy.

Such pervasive is the power of the moral mission that it results in delusions, in persistently claiming that a country whose one more province has introduced the death penalty for professing Christianity is a near-model version of democracy or that a state where only a man, authorised by religious authorities at that, can stand for election is a democratic country, etc.

Just like there are people who speak about democracy in ancient Greece failing to see the existence of slavery there, there is a not-so-small group of present day intellectuals who, combining a moral mission with an intellectual impotence, see democracy where it is non-existent. Some of them, excited by the ideals of community and concerned about the phenomena of individualization and atomization, willingly look at definitely community-based Islam countries who have introduced something that for some may resemble democracy. In order to have a view on the social and political reality of the best-known Islam states, let us look at them not so much through ideological glasses and wishful thinking but rather through the prism of bare facts:

> More than 300 million Christians are either threatened with violence or legally discriminated against because of their faith. Across the Islamic world, Christians are systematically discriminated against and persecuted. Saudi Arabia bans churches, public Christian worship, the Bible and the sale of Christmas cards, and stops non-Muslims from entering Mecca. Christians are regularly imprisoned and tortured or trumped up charges of drinking, blaspheming or Bible-bashing. ... The Copts of Egypt make up half the Christians in the Middle East, the cradle of Christianity. They inhabited the land before the Islamic conquest, and still make up a fifth of the population. By law they are banned from being president of the Islamic Republic of Egypt or attending the Al Azhar University, and severely restricted from joining the police and army. By practice they are banned from holding any high political or commercial position. ... It is illegal for Muslims to convert to Christianity, but legal for Christians to convert to Islam. Christian girls are abducted and forcibly converted to Islam. ... In the Islamic Republic of Pakistan, most of the five million Christians live as an underclass, doing work such as toilet cleaning. A Muslim can testify against a non-Muslim in court but a non-Muslim cannot testify against a Muslim.[1]

---

[1] Anthony Browne, "Church of Martyrs", *The Spectator*, No 9216, vol. 297, 26 March 2005, pp. 12–13.

These examples indicate that the introduction of democratic procedures in states which are completely different from the West as far as their civilization is concerned will turn democracy into sometimes a pathetic and more frequently a horrible caricature.

The reflections that follow aim at defending four main assumptions. (1) Democracy is not something that can be freely, at will, introduced anywhere. Western-type democracy[2] as an active and robust constitution is a result of an inner development of this civilization; (2) in other societies it is something external, artificial, purely formal, and in time totally foreign; that is why democracy will not be the constitution of the global world; on the contrary – each society must find its own system, accordant with its culture and religion, social structures, patterns of the economy, and psychological attitudes of the people. (3) In particular we would like to point out that the economic modernization of the capitalist type does not directly yield only one pattern of political life; capitalism in itself does not directly generate social and spiritual values. It is the cultural and social factors that are an obstacle for the establishment of the Western-type democratic system. (4) We will also endeavour to show that in the Western world, too, the old form of democracy is becoming exhausted and must undergo fundamental changes.

At first we will present (a) the current state of social change related to globalization, since it is these changes that make the questions about world democracy so urgent; subsequently (b) we will enumerate the key elements of the cultural, social, and economic development of the West, which in the twentieth century led to the development of a mature form of democracy; then (c) with a reference to randomly selected Confucian and Islamic civilizations, we will try and show the factual impossibility of democracy as a system that makes up a harmonious and substantial whole with the other elements of a society; finally, (d) we will map out the directions of the destruction of electoral democracy in the Western world and the

---

[2] We fully realise that there are different normative models of democracy. These reflections are based on the assumption of the liberal-democratic model which has actually developed in the vast majority of Western societies.

emergence of its new forms. Changes within society call for new institutions and new principles to enhance and stabilize them, rather
than for a simple attachment to old structures, even if we regard them
as the most valuable and desirable.

2. The Information Age and Globalization

Since the very beginning of its development, the Western world
has exhibited its fundamental systemic characteristic: **exteriorization**,
"reaching out", not only in the purely formal territorial sense, but first
of all in the areas of culture, society, and civilization. The West can be
symbolized by an **ocean**, an endless space, a space that does not pose
a threat but rather constitutes an opportunity and hope. Transgress-
ing its own borders, the Western world met with the civilizations of
the **wall**, immersed in their own world, treating anything other as
foreign, dangerous, and threatening their inviolable identity. The
West adopted new elements, transforming itself, constantly developing spiritually and socially, not endangering the essence of its own
identity, invariably remaining the same civilization. The wall societies, while they sometimes did expand territorially, their expansion
was a simple and direct negation of the other; they either did not
adopt any foreign elements at all, or – conversely – the external influences were so powerful that they led to changes resulting in an in-
fringement of identity and the emergence of a new, different whole,
which was neither a continuation not a sublation, but rather an
autonomous form of a mixed type.

Ancient Rome constantly exteriorized its institutions, its law, and
its way of life; freeing other peoples of barbarity, it incorporated them
into the circle of civilization. The world willingly accepted the universal Roman patterns, finding fulfilment in objective structures, values,
and the vision of a good life. Processes of advanced universalization
took place.

In the modern era, after the full development of the Latin civilization, we have witnessed three basic waves of exteriorization. First of
all, the spread of Christianity by the Spanish and the Portuguese, sec-

ondly, attempts made by the British and the French at making civilization as such universal, and thirdly, today we are witnesses to the process of globalization whose active centre is located primarily in the United States.[3]

Since the demise of the Middle Ages and the decline of the agrarian era, where society was organized around agriculture, the West entered a transformation process unique for it, i.e. the stage of multidimensional (cultural, economic, social, and political) modernization. In its fundamental form it was a transition to the industrial age, where the centre of social organization moved to big industry, with coalmines, ironworks, and factories employing thousands, and not infrequently tens of thousands of people. Such a division of labour led to the formation of social classes with their own class culture and economic and political interests. In the twentieth century modernization led to high living standards and to the wide participation of citizens in political life, especially by means of the institution of electoral democracy which allowed all adult citizens to participate in the decision making process.

In the second half of the twentieth century the modernization processes in their old forms were petering out, and the existing structures, institutions, and social life proved an obstacle for further development. Technological advancement, and primarily the emergence of new "high technologies", new means of communication and transport, computerization and the Internet have led to a radical systemic transformation in the West, i.e. to re-modernization. A transition from the industrial age to the information age has occurred. The traditional heavy industry is being edged out by the high technology industries. Because of computerization we deal today with information economy and the network society; as manual labour gives way to mental activity, education is becoming the prime focus. These processes are not a mere continuation of the old model of development; we are dealing here with a principally new phenomenon, a **bifurcation of modernization.**

---

[3] Cf. Walter D. Mignolo, "Globalization, Civilization Processes, and the Relocation of Languages and Cultures", in: *The Cultures of Globalization*, ed. by Fredric Jameson and Masao Miyoshi, Durham and London: Duke University Press, 1998, pp. 32–53.

The transition to the information age requires the exteriorization of the industrial world, which is becoming a ballast for the West. This phenomenon is taking the form of globalization. Globalization is a process of disseminating not only economic patterns, but also institutions, social structures, culture, way of life, and political patterns of electoral democracy. Today's transformations: the re-modernization and the transition to the information age in the West and the narrower globalization in other parts of the world, must be viewed as principally connected yet systemically divergent.

In many cases the exteriorization of the West is faced with vehement opposition, as it is encroaching on cultures and societies which for structural reasons are not able to accept new patterns without an attendant loss of the very essence of their identity.

A systemic feature of globalization is not so much the homogenization, unification, and universalization of modernization but rather its particularization, or **hybridization**. The dissemination of the Western patterns of modernity outside its territory does not consist in a replacement of local structures by other ones, but rather leads to the establishment of a new hybrid whole. The universal forms which within the Latin civilization form a substantial whole with particular social practices, since they are something internal and "natural" so to speak, when external and abstract for local social practices result in the establishment of a new whole of a mixed type. Sometimes the universal forms, as in the case of the differentiation of the system, are not accepted at all or are strongly contested. These phenomena accompanied each wave of the exteriorization of the West. The spread of Christianity to peoples who have not yet separated themselves from nature and remain at the level of animist consciousness results in the generation of a bizarre hybrid, which even the zealous missionaries would hesitate to call Christianity. One can point here to African states where half the local "Christians" combine their religion with voodoo practices.

The human world is not composed exclusively of objects and exclusively of abstract patterns, but of human understanding of these objects and patterns. What defines the human world is not so much an object, but an attitude and intentionality related to this object.

A purely physical "object" like a zoo is understood by the Western man as an area to be visited with a view to acquiring knowledge about nature, while the same zoo in South America is treated (and actually used) by local Indians as a hunting ground.

The phenomenon of hybridization refers also to the spread of democracy. The current changes trigger two questions: about the feasibility of Western-type democracy on a global scale and about a new shape of democracy in the West.

3. Democracy in Western Civilization

Naturally, abstract reflections on the question of the best constitution raised in present-day debates are nothing new. There have always been people who believed that the political constitution is something that can be isolated at will and used anywhere, in any society, irrespective of its uniqueness. While there is a note of something noble in these opinions, they are totally unrealistic. Each social system has its own inner rationality, each society must constitute a harmonious whole. Formal democratic procedures cannot be transplanted at will since it is only in Western civilization that democracy is a result of an inner and natural development; it is here that is constitutes a substantial whole with the other aspects of society and it is here that it is live and active.

The absurdity of formal and abstract reflections on the best constitution was unambiguously and convincingly pointed out by Hegel:

> The inquiry into the best constitution is frequently treated as if not only the theory were an affair of subjective independent conviction, but as if the introduction of a constitution recognized as the best, – or as superior to others, – could be the result of a resolve adopted in this theoretical manner; as if the form of a constitution were a matter of free choice, determined by nothing else but reflection. Of this artless fashion was that deliberation, – not indeed of Persian *people*, but of the Persian *grandees*, who had conspired to overthrow the pseudo-Smerdis and the Magi, after their undertaking had succeeded, and when there was no scion of the royal family living, – as to what constitution they should introduce into

Persia; and Herodotus gives an equally naive account of this deliberation. In the present day, the Constitution of a country and people is not
represented as so entirely dependent on a free and deliberate choice. The
fundamental but abstractly (and therefore imperfectly) entertained conception of freedom, has resulted in a Republic being very generally regarded – in theory – as the only just and true political constitution ...
This representation is founded on the distinction which the reflective understanding makes between an idea and the corresponding reality;
holding to an abstract and consequently untrue idea; not grasping it in its
completeness, or – which is virtually, though not in point of form, the
same – not taking a concrete view of a people and a state. We shall have
to show further on that the constitution adopted by a people makes one
substance – one spirit with its religion, its art and philosophy, or, at least,
with its conceptions and thoughts – its culture generally.[4]

The democracy we know from the Western world of the twentieth
century did not appear as a gunshot in the middle of the night; it is an
effect of a process whose beginning may and must be sought at the
very source – when the pivotal point of spiritual progress was transferred from the despotic monarchies of the ancient East to Greece,
giving rise to what is the best, most noble and most just in humanity,
i.e. the Latin civilization.

It was the Greeks who in a spiritual sense left the enchanted walls
of the palace of the Eastern despot-God and entered the open space of
the *agora*, thus exposing political and social issues, making them open
and available to a group of citizens. In the *agora* the dictate and obedience to the will of the despot is replaced by a debate – the *logos* is
born, a concept fundamental for our civilization, one which epito-
mizes its genius. In its ambiguity, the *logos* – as a word and as a discursive reason – shapes the form of social life, based on rational argumentation conducted by means of words. In this sense it
crystallises one of the basic features of the Western man: a desire for
informed knowledge based on arguments, preceded by discussion,
argumentation, and critical judgement. The Greeks exhibited additional features which have become permanent characteristics of the

---

[4] Georg Wilhelm Friedrich Hegel, *The Philosophy of History*, transl. by J. Sibree,
Kitchener: Batoche Books, 2001, pp. 60–61.

structures of civilization: they favoured rivalry and construed political life precisely in terms of competition. The Greeks developed a public sphere agonistic in character, i.e. one where political life is understood as competition. Thus they were the first to see society through the prism of competing individuals, which has become of paramount importance in the modern era.

We may visualise an image of debating Greek citizens. Debate and argumentation, unlike dictate, must rest on the assumption of the equality of the debating parties: the Greeks overcome the Eastern consciousness of the despot-God and understand society as composed of a group of free and equal citizens. If we look closely at the arguments and the competition related to what are supposed to be just principles of conduct for the *polis*, we can see that this argument calls for a resolution. We may also hypothetically imagine the disputants to be accompanied by an audience who are to resolve whose vision of society is better; they no longer decide by means of magic or religious formulae, nor do they take up arms in order to indicate the winner, but simply cast their vote on who is right in a debate.

The Greeks inaugurate the fundamental features of Western consciousness: the principle of persuasion, argumentation, and critical judgement; they understand that a society is contingent on the rivalry and competition of (a limited number as yet) equal citizens. Freedom and equality evolve as cultural values.

Rome, in turn, adds its invaluable treasure of universal law and institutions to spiritual and social development. It is law and institutions that would effectively allow a separation of successive peoples from nature, raising them from barbarity and subordinating to objective social principles.

Rome makes a significant step forward with respect to Greece, namely it separates citizenship from birthright. Being a slave is no longer an ontic property but acquires a social and institutional character; one can be freed from slavery by means of legal instruments and acquire a status equal to that of the Romans, not infrequently achieving a prominent social position.

Rome will give birth to its own negation in the form of Christianity. The new religion awakens the final awareness of equality, freedom and the identical dignity of each human person, first in a religious perspective, as the creation of each man in God's image and likeness, and in more recent times in a secular form.

Since Christ's times we have had no division into owners and slaves or into women and men; nor have we had racial differences. Naturally, the institutional implementation of this cultural awareness was a matter of many centuries to follow.

The Christian religion brings with itself significant elements of inner dynamism: a reference not only to the Bible, but also to tradition, which allows a departure from the strict dogma and a constant reformation. The key decisive element for the continuation of the evolution of the civilization is the principle "render to Caesar the things that are Caesar's, and to God the things that are God's". Even if it was a reference to a particular historical context, it nevertheless originated in Christianity and was later present in the works of eminent thinkers. The sense of the existence of two orders, the religious and the secular one ultimately led to the separation of the *sacrum* and the *profanum*, the Church and the State, a fundamental process of modernization. Finally, a thought of the salvation of each individual soul, which will not be dissolved in the ocean of the "universal soul", or the salvation of the Church as a whole, will be an embryo of subjectification, individualization, and the granting of rights to each human being on account of his or her being a person equal to others.

The process of modernization and rationalization began with the decline of the Middle Ages. Slightly earlier we can notice the occurrence of at least two facts of primary importance. In the year 800 AD the pope crowns Charlemagne emperor, thereby "sealing" the existence of two orders, the secular and the religious one, the state authority and the ecclesial one. Second of all, we can observe the emergence of universities, which – with their culture-engendering function of critical thinking – are not confined solely to the provision of standard knowledge. Thanks to universities, which have survived in this form until the threshold of the twenty-first century, the West has not become a swarm of human termites, each of which acts, thinks and speaks exactly the same as the rest. Only recently have we seen in Europe the emergence of an idea that everyone should become an engineer.

Modernization has influence on fundamental social, economic, and ideological characteristics which condition the birth of democracy. Social bonds and the character of social integration undergo a profound transformation. Traditional communities of the *Gemeinschaft* type, as tribes and estates, are in decline, while we can witness a simultaneous rise of the *Gesellschaft* type society, first in the form of social classes, today also as free and independent associations. The era of modernization is a transition from normative integration based on a shared consciousness, to functional integration, where important bonds and social interdependencies are formed around the division of labour. The transition to the industrial age means, apart from the development of social classes, the emergence of a mass society. The Peace of Westphalia for the next couple of centuries set the pattern of social organization as existing within nation-states, with their own borders, territories, and internal sovereignty. A factual separation of the *sacrum* and the *profanum* is taking place. The one in power is gradually losing the status of God's anointed one and becomes a ruler (later on a president, prime minister) by the will of the people – a nation. Religion, while present at the level of faith and ritual, ceases to directly impact daily practical activities connected with everyday life, economy and politics; an autonomous secular sphere is being born.

As we know from Hegel, philosophy is the apprehension of its time in thoughts. Civilizational transformations are accompanied by intellectual reflection, which is a witness to its times and which, as is frequent in the case of philosophy and social theory, enhances and directs progress.

From among the thinkers who made a significant contribution to the development of the modern mind and today's vision of society, Thomas Hobbes is in many respects a breakthrough person. We owe to him a vision of the human being who does not follow in his actions the higher ideas of justice, goodness, and harmony but first and foremost falls back on his natural passions, such as fear. Hobbes explicitly presents a conflict-ridden vision of society: there are too few goods to be distributed among everyone and as a result fierce rivalry ensues, which poses a hazard to human property and life. Out of fear, people being in conflict with one another lay down principles of peaceful cooperation, which principles no longer arise from any traditional bonds but from a convention in the form of a social contract. Ever since, we have understood society as resting its stability on the law and contracts concluded between egoistic individuals aiming at satisfying their particular self-interests. Hobbes's entire construct signals the persistence of the question about how to assure the best ways of integration and conflict-resolution under such a vision of a society.

Through his principle "I think therefore I am" Rene Descartes establishes the focal point of rationality in the human mind. Ever since, it is no longer an objective and transcendental being but my inner subjective conviction that has been a source of rationality. In addition, Descartes effects a destruction of the understanding of religion: God ceases to be a transcendental being and becomes confined to the individual consciousness and ever since has held his prime position there. As a further consequence of this approach, God is only a subjective experience of the world, and as such cannot be singled out from among other kinds of experience.

John Locke provides a modern conceptualisation of the civil society as an association of sovereign citizens rather than, as before, subjects of a ruler. For Locke and the entire liberalism, being a citizen means first of all being able to participate in political life. And while in the course of time the civil society was understood as organized around a free market (Hegel), and today is seen mainly as free associations independent from the economy and politics (Habermas), it is widely believed that it is precisely the civil society that is a precondition of democracy. No wonder today's criticism of the marked deterioration of civil activity constitutes further proof of the ever weaker condition of democracy as we know it today.

At the same time J. Locke makes a clear distinction between religion and the civil society and the public sphere and makes religion the private matter of each human being. This separation points to the development of an autonomous political community, independent first of all from a religious community. Ever since, a political community understood in this way has become the centre of transformations leading to the foundation of a mature form of democracy. In addition,

John Locke furnishes a vision of a good society as an association of individuals endowed with subjective rights, developing over the next centuries from civil rights through political to social ones. Property rights hold a special position among these rights; for Locke it was literally a natural right since it arose from the hunger that could only be assuaged by claiming possession over food.

In some aspects Immanuel Kant supplements the discussions and conceptualizations of modernizing transformations. Kant points out that religion is exclusively a question of faith rather than rational knowledge. In principle, until Kant's times there was a general conviction that God may not only be believed in but also apprehended, e.g. His existence might be proved. For Kant religious issues cannot be resolved rationally, and as such they do not belong to theoretical reason, but to the practical sphere, such as that of morality, a good life, etc.

In his ethics and social philosophy, where he indicates no particular ideal of a good life, Kant subjects the participation in a community solely to formal rather than substantial conditions.

This is tied with the transformation of the social hierarchy and a shift from the notion of honour to the notion of dignity. Honour clearly points to one's being distinguished on account of social status (therefore some are eligible for it whereas others are not), while dignity is something that everyone possesses on account of being human, and in Kantian categories – on account of being a rational agent.[5]

The few selected intellectual witnesses of the modern era pave the way which leads directly to the development of today's form of democracy. The progressive separation of the Church from the State and the relegation of religion into the sphere of private and subjective experience result in the emergence of a sovereign political community. The "privatisation" of religion and values means the removal of the most abrasive, rationally intractable elements from the public sphere and the direction of human activity towards business and economy, where a reasonable agreement is far easier to obtain.

---

[5] Charles Taylor, *The Politics of Recognition*, in: idem et al., *Multiculturalism: Examining the Politics of Recognition*, ed. and introduced by Amy Gutmann, Princeton: Princeton University Press, 1994, pp. 26–27, 41.

The decline of traditional structures, the shift in the position of religion, and the growing complexity of the system all lead to the emergence of independent activity in the form of a civil society. After the acquisition of the basic rights, the struggle for political participation and, in time, for material and social well-being begins.

The dissolution of communities, an individual as the subject of rights, and religion as but a way of experiencing the world and an element of practical life, are in fact different yet interconnected aspects of alienation processes, inseparable from modernization. Here we may therefore paraphrase Peter Berger's compelling remark[6] and say that there is no democracy without alienation. Alienation is one of the factors that are the strongest elements propelling the dynamism of a social system; in the modern era it has led to institutional subjectification, i.e. to the granting of rights to the subject and to an ever growing number of people, while today it occurs in the form of social individualization and leads to the emergence of a network sociality.

The process of industrialization, taking place in particular throughout the nineteenth century and the first half of the twentieth century, led to the development of social classes, with their unique culture, awareness, as well as economic and political interests. The most fundamental social conflict is the one between great groups – classes. Democracy, whose second major function consists in an efficient and non-violent rule, provides a tool for the resolution of this conflict. Democracy as we know it was developed relatively late, i.e. in the twentieth century, along with the inclusion of all adult citizens, even if women were usually the last to benefit in this respect.

---

[6] "This issue brings to my mind a conversation I have recently held with the sociologist Peter Berger. He advanced a strong – and most likely correct – thesis that in the liberal and democratic tradition of the West the sense of freedom would not be possible without the attendant sense of alienation. Then, from his point of view, the awareness of being alienated is a major element of the apprehension of freedom. Individuals must feel alienated from their own communities in order for the sense of freedom to be born." Tu Wei-Ming, "Humanizm konfucjański a demokracja" [Confucian Humanism and Democracy], in: *Europa i społeczeństwo obywatelskie. Rozmowy w Castel Gandolfo* [Europe and Civil Society. Conversations in Castel Gandolfo], ed. by Krzysztof Michalski, Kraków: Wydawnictwo Znak, 1994, p. 209.

A welfare state which minimizes inequalities arising from the competition of the market is being born in the West as a result of the democratic process. Democracy functions within the territory and organizations of the nation-state, which has enough power to impose democratic decisions.

In this way, the spiritual, social and economic process that has continued over three millennia has given rise to today's democracy in its fullest and most perfect form. In Western civilization democracy is a result of an inner and all-encompassing development; it is something substantial rather than a formal "best constitution" transplanted from outside.

4. Democracy versus Confucian and Islamic Civilizations

One has to admit that a wide road is for the time being out of the question; in other words, a fruitful exchange between Confucian humanism and the ideals of democracy is a matter of the future. What is more, it is hard to see even a narrow path.[7]

We have begun this paragraph with a lucid quotation for two reasons: first of all, it puts forth the thesis of the reflections that follow; secondly, it indicates that authors scrutinizing other civilizations, in this particular case the Confucian one, from within are capable of a far more realistic and sober analysis than some Western thinkers, who delude themselves with their wishful thinking.

In the present paragraph, apart from illustrating the thesis that democracy is a system principally alien to the cultures and societies of non-Western civilizations, we wish to point out indirectly that the economic modernization of the capitalist type does not naturally entail the emergence of the political life and political culture of a democratic type.[8]

---

[7] Ibidem, p. 202.

[8] Incidentally, it is in order to point to a fact which, strangely enough, is little noticed by the advocates of unification and homogenization, namely that there is no such

First of all, let us note that democracy in the proper sense of the word exists in societies which meet the fundamental cultural prerequisite, i.e. those that have developed an awareness of the dignity and freedom of each human being. In reality, such awareness is for the time being present exclusively in the Latin civilization. Despite extended democratic procedures, accompanied by state-of-the-art technologies, it is difficult to speak about fully-fledged democracy in the country where the annihilation of two cities by means of atom bombs was far less shocking than the attempt to inform the general public that the emperor is no god.[9]

Not only can the introduction of democratic procedures not lead to the establishment of a living and active democracy, but may have truly harmful consequences. In the case of peoples who remain at the level of normative integration, where the basic form of community life is either a tribe or a religious community, democracy becomes a negation of its fundamental function of conflict resolution. In tribal societies, which are not themselves capable of self-objectification in the form of social and political institutions, democratic procedures do not lead to the resolution of conflicts, but rather to their intensification, deepening, and enhancement! In such a case democratic procedures, similarly to so-called identity politics, may lead to the explosion of fanaticism, chauvinism, racism, and in some cases also to genocide.

While we do realise that this can be formulated differently, let us assume that there are four principles in the Confucian civilization that impart order to the universe, society, and man's place within them; these four principles are the following: holism, harmony, family, and self-cultivation. The above principles are totally different from, if not contradictory to, those that have helped develop the Atlantic civilization, with democracy as its major element. All the principles are

---

thing as a uniform and universal pattern of global capitalism, which is alleged to be sweeping over the world. See e.g. Charles Hampden-Turner, Alfons Trompenaars, *The Seven Cultures of Capitalism*, New York: Doubleday, 1993.

[9] "Even Japan – a fully democratic society – has in principle a single-party political system, with factions within one party". Tu Wei-Ming, "Humanizm konfucjański a demokracja" [Confucian Humanism and Democracy], op. cit., p. 204.

firmly interconnected, they are contingent on one another and their separation is possible only at the analytical level.

The Confucian vision of the world is of a profoundly **holistic** character, in a cosmic dimension at that. The universe, society, authority, and the individual make up one interconnected whole, where elements that would violate this whole are either nonexistent or eliminated as completely foreign, useless, and worthless. The vision of man is a totally social one; the subject can be defined only as a plexus of social relations, and never as an isolated individual, with no reference to the family, friends, local community, nation, etc.

Such an understanding of the world has profound ramifications when compared with the totally divergent vision of Western civilization. Holism is alien to the fundamental elements that have led to the development of today's world. Holism is incompatible with the principle of the multidimensional differentiation of the system, the pivot of modernization and democracy, which manifests itself for instance in the separation of the sphere of private and family life from the public sphere, in the separation of the religious and the secular, or finally in the establishment of separate, often antagonistic, structures of the state and the civil society.

The Confucian vision excludes the autonomy of the subject and rules out Western individualism which is invariably the source and foundation of democracy. There is no room here either for a vision of the subject who, as far as the principles of social co-existence are concerned, enters into free contracts with others and in so doing is motivated by his own egoistic interests.

The perspective of an all-embracing whole must be finally pitted against the democratic vision of multiple world outlooks and views on good life, with the attendant plurality of competing political and social groups.

Naturally, the principle of **harmony**, encompassing the organization of the social structure and the relations between an individual and a society, is at variance with the Western vision of a competitive society centred around the realization of the personal interests of individuals. This has a direct impact on the understanding of the democratic process, which in the perspective of the Confucian spirituality is seen as struggle, competition, and argument which pose threats to the harmonious whole. The existence of opposition groups is an unnecessary and dangerous destruction. We may phrase the above aspects even more categorically: if there are no elements of conflict and struggle at the foundations of society and the vision of the world, then Western-type democracy *de facto* loses its sense since its principal function is precisely the integration and reintegration of the system in a situation of internal tensions and conflicts.

Confucian societies are deeply particularistic, with an extensive network of community bonds, and as such they are an antithesis of the universalistic countries of the West. In the Confucian reality and social structure it is the **family** which provides the pattern for all relations. It sets the standards of social, political and economic organization. Japan, an economically developed country, has developed a model of capitalism which is significantly different from the one present in Europe and the United States. It is rooted in familiarism, in family ties and relations of friendship, i.e. in those elements that from the Western perspective would be called "unwholesome arrangements", being at variance with universal and objective legal contracts.

A community understood in such a way is fundamentally different from the contractual vision of a society. Patriarchal family patterns have impact on the authority model with its hierarchy, authoritarianism, and obedience. A society is headed by a king-sage, who is simultaneously a leader, thinker, paragon of virtues, and a political, intellectual, and moral authority. Authority is all-powerful and almighty, and these are precisely the normative expectations of the population towards it. It is authority that is supposed to know and care about everything. Authority is to be trusted and obeyed.[10] Western-type democracy is, in contrast, governed by a free interplay of political forces, by an incessant (and desirable) critique of authority, finally by the distrust towards this authority. The liberal democracy of the West has the minimum-state as its model; it is transferring

---

[10] It is hard not to notice that the above qualities, as well as a number of others, may be easily found also in Russian civilization.

more and more powers to the citizens, who can take initiative, plan their own lives, and develop society; finally, the minimum-state legitimises the right to civil disobedience. Authority is not expected to be omnipotent but rather to confine itself exclusively to the functions which citizens are unable to perform on their own.

Last but not least – the Confucian ideal of **self-cultivation** clearly shows that the starting point for the stabilization of the system is not law, as it is true about the West, but the perfection of the subject as well as its grasp of morality and virtuousness. Such a vision is alien not only to a society based on coercion, but also to a society that pre-serves order despite the "amoral clash of competing interest groups".[11] Confucianism lays stress on active upbringing and edu-cating a human being in accordance with community values; allowing a great degree of freedom of choice is foreign to this civilization. "For the Neo-Confucian, freedom is not the 'freedom to choose'".[12] The idea of personal liberty cannot be thus seen as a top-priority issue, hence the natural weakness of the notion of the civil society as a free association which one "enters and leaves" at will.[13] Hence, also, the sense of inner social duty replaces or attenuates the significance of positive law as a regulator of interpersonal relations. We can safely say that familial, social, and political harmony is a function of inner order. All the above elements belittle the idea of subjective rights, with the attendant freedom of creed and of the press, freedom of as-sociations and the choice of moral principles and the possibility of "leaving society", while the subjective rights with their extended con-cretisations are the foundation of Western democracy.

The aforementioned social and spiritual factors and the entire vi-sion of the world make the "democratic movements of East Asia re-

---

[11] Richard Madsen, "Confucian Conceptions of Civil Society", in: *Alternative Con-ceptions of Civil Society*, ed. by Simone Chambers, Will Kymlicka, Princeton and Oxford: Princeton University Press, 2002, p. 196.

[12] Ibidem, p. 202.

[13] William Theodore de Barry, "Konfucjanizm i społeczeństwo obywatelskie" [Confucianism and Civil Society], in: *Europa i społeczeństwo obywatelskie. Rozmowy w Castel Gandolfo* [Europe and Civil Society. Conversations in Castel Gandolfo], ed. by Krzysztof Michalski, op. cit., p. 187.

main in permanent conflict with the native culture";[14] Western-type democracy remains something external and principally alien to Confucian societies.

Let us begin our considerations on the incompatibility of the patterns of Western democracy from a quotation by an author connected with Islam: **"religion in Islam is a political system, an economic theory, and a social structure"**.[15] This sentence requires but a brief word of comment. In reference to Islam one may reiterate the sentence used before: "it is difficult to see even a narrow path". What is more, the path in general seems unlikely to be found since the Islamic civilization has no inner developmental "embryos" of the Western type, or even their approximation.

Islamic societies have not developed an awareness of the equal dignity of each person. Only a Muslim is a fully-fledged human being, and still, even within Islamic societies it would be hard to speak about the equality of men and women.

These societies are integrated not so much by functional principles, but by a shared religious identity, which encompasses the entire human world. Islam is a non-diversified religious and political community where there is no separation between religion and the state; in fact such a separation is impossible. This is because Islam does not know an institutional Church of the Christian type. To put it simply, there are no two things here to be separated from each other. A leader is at the same time a political, religious, and moral authority. These aspects constitute a non-diversified whole. Religion legitimises authority and is the source of law. Islamic societies, to use Western terminology, are contingent on natural law of religious origin, rather than on contracts. "In the oldest preserved Muslim record from the British House of Commons, an author who was visiting England at the close of the 19th century expresses his concern with the fate of the

---

[14] Tu Wei-Ming, "Humanizm konfucjański a demokracja" [Confucian Humanism and Democracy], op. cit., p. 216.

[15] Hasan Hanafi, "Alternative Conceptions of Civil Society. A Reflective Islamic Approach", in: *Alternative Conceptions of Civil Society*, ed. by Simone Chambers, Will Kymlicka, op. cit., p. 187.

nation which is lacking in the revealed divine law, like the Muslims, and is thus forced to resort to the pathetic practice of proclaiming its own laws".[16] Religion determines the way of life and relations within a family and between individuals.[17] A lack of a division into secular and religious authority, or *regnum* and *sacerdotium*, makes the formation of an autonomous political community, a pivot of democratic discourse, impossible.

What is lacking in Islam is not only the idea of the autonomy of the political sphere, but also the idea of the autonomy of the individual with respect to religion and a religious community. Islam is morally rather than cognitively oriented. A Muslim is bound by a moral duty with respect to religion. Hence the emotional vehemence of the believers of Islam and their violent, unconditional, and uncompromising actions. Greece and Christianity have contributed to a cognitive orientation of the Western man; even in a purely religious sense, man is duty-bound to get to know God, and in a secular dimension to get to know and transform the world.

Finally, as in the case of Confucianism, also here the idea of individual rights, a key concept of liberal democracy, is nonexistent.

> Traditional Islamic culture may be based on the idea of duties rather than the idea of rights (duties of man and rights of God), while modern Western culture is essentially based on the idea of rights rather than duties (rights of man and maybe duties of God).[18]

We can point to a few attempts at modernizing Islamic countries the Western way. The world vividly remembers how such an attempt

---

[16] Bernard Lewis, "Europa, islam i społeczeństwo obywatelskie" [Europe, Islam, and Civil Society], in: *Europa i społeczeństwo obywatelskie. Rozmowy w Castel Gandolfo* [Europe and Civil Society. Conversations in Castel Gandolfo], ed. by Krzysztof Michalski, op. cit., p. 156.

[17] "Sometimes conservative judges rule for them and declare the thinker accused to be an apostate who should suffer penalties, including divorce from his wife, because a Muslim woman cannot be legally married to an apostate". Hasan Hanafi, "Alternative Conceptions of Civil Society. A Reflective Islamic Approach", in: *Alternative Conceptions of Civil Society*, ed. by Simone Chambers, Will Kymlicka, op. cit., p. 187.

[18] Ibidem, p. 188.

developed in Iran and is concerned about the results of a return to a purely Islamic state there.

Let us call to mind, however, the most lasting example of partial modernization, i.e. Turkey, where there are democratic procedures in place and where the army must function as a stabilizing agent. It is the army, more or less openly, for instance through the delegalization of some parties, that cripples any and all attempts at introducing a constitution chosen by the majority. One may predict with a fairly high degree of accuracy that a decision of the majority could lead to the abolition of the majority rule and to the introduction of a funda-mentalist Islamic constitution.

In general, we may observe that internal attempts at halting fun-damentalism are not democratic in nature but are based on a military dictatorship or quasi-dictatorship.

In conclusion, let us refer to a question which for centuries has been alien to the West, namely the death penalty for religious dissent. While within a democracy the freedom of creed is one of the inalien-able rights, some Islamic countries combine elements of democratic procedures with the death penalty imposed on religious grounds. What is greatly surprising, however, is the fact that there are people in the West who go into raptures and speak about those countries as democracies; it is as if one said that an electric chair is but a chair.

The few comments sketched above were meant to exemplify the thesis that Western-type democracy is something principally foreign and external to other societies and that the introduction of democratic procedures into those latter countries leads to the formation of a cari-cature hybrid rather than a wholesome and natural constitution.

5. Decline of Electoral Democracy in the West

The radical transformations of the human world associated with the transition to the information age and with globalization trigger questions about the form of democracy in the West. No social, politi-cal or institutional form is eternal; they evolve along with the changes of other elements. There are no good reasons to suppose that the above applies to everything else apart from democracy.

Today we are faced with a crisis of democracy, observable in our daily experience. However, we are also witnesses to far more significant systemic processes, which allow us to speak about the decline of democracy and the emergence of new democratic institutions. One of the most conspicuous manifestations of the above **crisis** is the **cracking of democratic space**. The perfection of procedures and their encroaching on ever new territories, the expanding intellectual reflection and the cult of democracy are accompanied by the ever diminishing impact of citizens on the decisions taken, which results in the decline of their activity and participation in democratic practices and in the withdrawal into the private sphere. Attempts aiming at counteracting this phenomenon, such as the demand of the introduction of mandatory voting, only prove the general sense of hopelessness and helplessness.

The democratic procedures, which have so far been a path leading to a consensus and conflict resolution with a positive impact on reality, have turned into their opposites and have become today tools of **privileged interest groups** who, taking advantage of the existing institutions, cripple progress (incidentally, this is responsible for the ever frequent attempts at making governance independent from democracy, for instance through the conclusion of contracts establishing "a grand coalition" for a few successive terms of office, irrespective of the election results).

Democracy today has transformed into **a democracy of the margins**, where public space is being invaded by minority groups and their activists. What is at stake here is not so much the recognition of minority groups as fully-fledged participants of social life, but rather their domination of democratic discourse and the withdrawal of "the silent majority" from this discourse.

A shift towards **marginal democracy**, where "the worse is edging out the better", has become an inherent and natural feature of democracy today. This is closely related to the relegation of morality from political life and its replacement with a formal law, where no one is guilty unless they have disobeyed the written code and have not been proven guilty until the very last instance. In Poland this doctrine was expressed directly a decade or so ago, when the presidential candidate who won the election in a fraudulent manner, when asked whether he has the moral right to hold his office, responded as follows: "in democracy the result of a vote is the only moral right". This leads to the withdrawal of the most valuable and respectable persons from public life and their replacement by mediocre individuals, or those who see the existing institutions exclusively as tools for furthering their own interests.

The above remarks are part of the critique of everyday reality. It seems, however, that a systemic process is taking place which leads to the **decline** of the form of democracy we know, as the present-day comprehensive transformations undermine the two principal functions of democracy: the function of integration and that of holding authority.

The **integrational function** seen as, first of all, the provision of equality through granting each and everyone the same vote and, second of all, as a resolution of conflicts between big social groups, is losing its importance. In the information age equality perceived in this way is becoming obsolete. Social inequalities will be conditioned by other factors, such as the level of education as well as access to knowledge, information, and new technologies. This, however, provides a totally different platform for the discussion of the question of social unity and social exclusion.

The processes of individualization and the emergence of network sociality lead to a situation when it is no longer big groups but individuals that will be the subjects of the information age. The Western world is moving away from the era of nations and nation-states. Contrary to what some may think, what is at issue here is not so much psychological sentiments, but really important institutional processes. We are witnessing a systemic and fundamental process, especially in the European Union, consisting in the **separation of individual rights from participation in a national community**. These transformations shift the pivotal point of a conflict from the opposition between social classes to the opposition between individuals and groups which have so far enjoyed a privileged status. As such, it will no longer be resolved in traditionally democratic ways, but rather by courts, often international ones, who first of all defend the rights of individuals.[19]

---

[19] Cf. Richard Münch, "Otwarte przestrzenie: integracja społeczna w ramach państwa narodowego i ponad jego poziomem" [Open Spaces: Social Integration

The **function of holding authority** and of an actual influence on the decision-making process has so far been implemented through the organizations and social institutions of the nation-state. The information age and globalization change this state of affairs dramatically. The decision centre moves away from the nation-state to such transnational factors as corporations, institutions like the World Bank, networks of associations of a global civil society, or transnational political bodies, such as the European Union. On the other hand, national governments are ceding ever-greater competences top-down, i.e. to local governments and non-governmental organizations. The decisions of nation-states are becoming less and less tied with the implementation of the will of the nation as expressed in a vote but are increasingly an implementation of the policy of transnational institutions.

The above factors have to be supplemented with the visible decline of the welfare state, which over the last decades has made up a cohesive social whole with the political form of electoral democracy. The dwindling importance of national solidarity and the declining power of the state that could impose democratic decisions contribute to the erosion of this form of social organization.

A new era and a new social whole require new institutions and new principles, which will provide stability, point out a direction, and enhance progress. The new time-context, then, calls for a redefinition of the form of democracy, which cannot be treated as sacred. As today we can point to different normative models of democracy, over the years there have been different institutions that defined it. Electoral democracy, which in the past few decades has been the fullest manifestation of social and political ideals of the West, seems at the end of its tether. What has remained immutable and will continue unchanged, though, is the democratic values, first and foremost equality and liberty; what will no doubt change is their particular interpretations and institutional implementations. It seems that it will

Within and Above the Nation-State], in: *Postkomunistyczne transformacje* [Post-communist Transformations], ed. by Tadeusz Buksiński, Poznań: Wydawnictwo Naukowe IF UAM, 2002, pp. 150–158.

be judiciary democracy and educational democracy, as well as poly-centric network governance that will be increasingly responsible for the provision of equality and liberty. What these institutions and these principles will look like in concrete terms will remain a question to be tackled on another occasion.

We have endeavoured to show in this essay that the democracy that we, people of the Western world, regard as one of the most valu-able achievements, will not be a constitution of the global world and that the concrete form of democracy known to the last generations is subject to radical change. These are the functional requirements of the present day; as nearly all new elements, they might be treated with opposition, reluctance, or regret. However, we might as well adopt a different approach, namely that of looking at an ocean as an invita-tion, hope, opportunity, and an endless road that can be embarked on with caution, yet without fear.

Stanisław Zyborowicz
Poznań

Alternation of Power
as an Important Condition of Democracy

1. Introduction

Democracy cannot function if there is no alternation in power. Alternation is an important factor of contemporary democratic systems as a political duality in public sphere. This thesis is accepted but mainly on the legal level. There are many political theorists who understand democracy on the Schumpeter's level only – a formal institutionalization of electoral process according to democratic standards. Of course, we must agree it is *sine qua non* condition but it is not a complete meaning of democracy. The main aim of this paper is to broaden the logic of democracy about alternation of power. It is possible to understand this notion on different levels: 1. Normative one – legal standards of a democratic election; 2. Empirical one – real changes of ruling subjects.

If we treat democracy in Schumpeter's understanding, it is when we have a minimum two opposite political subjects which compete with one another. There are theoretical chances to win but it does not mean that a change must take place. In a normative view a minimum condition is fulfilled. Anyway, there is a question in an empirical view: if there are regular elections but there are not real changes of ruling political parties (coalitions), can we call this country a democratic one?[1]

---

[1] Andrzej Antoszewski, Ryszard Herbut, *Systemy polityczne współczesnego świata* [Political Systems of Contemporary World], Gdańsk: Arche, 2001, p. 17.

2. Some Remarks on Democracy

Since the every beginning of human civilization the notion of democracy has caused emotions thus expressing one of the psychological needs of human being as an individual. Democracy has many shapes. It is an equivocal notion, both with respect to its content and form. Democracy refers to many things at the same time: a mode of organization and administration, a set of institutions, an intellectual discipline, a code of ethics, an ideal of individual and collective behaviour, a developing historical reality.[2]

The origins of democracy date back to the reforms from the 6th century BC *What is democracy?* It is undoubtedly, one of the most difficult questions to answer satisfactorily. Linguistically, the word *democracy* means, *government by the people*. A question arises here – who are the people? No political system at any time, democratic or not, has ever provided for *all* the people even to choose the government. Usually, citizenship has been restricted to a number of grounds: age, sex, literacy, property, social status and sometimes colour and religion have all at one time or another barred certain people from the enjoyment of political rights enjoyed by others.[3] If the term *government by the people* is taken to mean formulation of the national policy *by the whole* electorate, then it has never existed. It is difficult to answer about the future, but probably also not in the future. It has always interpreted in practice to mean government by some or by a few on behalf of the rest.

The nineteenth century tradition, democratic government was seen mainly in terms of equality of political and legal rights, of the right to vote, to express differing political opinions and to organize political opinion through political parties, of the right of elected representatives to supervise or control the activities of the government of the day. Today, there are some different interpretations. Much more stress is laid upon the need for the state to guarantee everybody certain economic and social rights. Obviously, we must not identify

---

[2] Alain-Marc Rieu, "Scientific revolutions and ideas of democracy", in: *European Democratic Culture*, ed. by Alain-Marc Rieu, et al., London – New York: Open University Press, 1995, p. 15.

[3] Dorothy Pickles, *Democracy*, New York: Putnam, 1970, p. 9.

democracy with majority rule only. Democracy has complex demands, which certainly include voting and respect for election results, but it also requires the protection of liberties and freedoms, respect for legal entitlements, and the guaranteeing of free discussion and uncensored distribution of news and fair comment.[4]

Let's try to describe democracy as a minimum. It is a set of institutions, which fulfill at least two essential requirements: 1. Be able to elicit as accurately as possible the opinion of as many people as possible on who their representatives shall be. How should the country be governed? It means: universal suffrage, political parties, and organizations of free voting in uncorrupted elections; 2. It must provide ways of ensuring that those chosen by the public do in fact what the electorate wants them to do otherwise they might be replaced if they do not even between elections. There must be a dialogue between rulers and those ruled. Of course, all the time one question must be kept in mind, which in ancient Rome was as follows: *Quis custodiet ipsos custodes?*[5] We ought to take for granted that dictators can achieve power by use of the regular, electoral machinery. They can therefore, maintain themselves in power throughout taking the unfair advantage of the whole public opinion, or by ignoring or repressing its free expression. There are some important principles of liberal democracy: 1. Popular control of the governors: choosing governors at the periodic elections. The concept of popular sovereignity is central to the need to control those in power; 2. Equality: in a democratic sense, equality implies establishing equal political rights, equal voting rights, equality of opportunity, and equality before the law; 3. Political freedom: the voters must be able to freely express their opinions and be given a choice of candidates and parties. They should also be free to, if they desire, form alternative or new parties; 4. Majority decision making: policies are decided by a majority of representatives voting for them.[6]

---

[4] Amartya Sen, "Democracy as a Universal Value", *East European Politics and Societies*, Vol. 12, No. 3, 1998 (fall), pp. 9–10.

[5] It means: Who will guard against those who themselves are guards?

[6] Keith Pye, Richard Yates, *British Politics. Ideas and Concepts*, Cheltenham: Thornes, 1992, pp. 113–115.

Anyway, there are also different attitudes. The Islamic tradition for instance, contains a number of key concepts that are presented by Muslims as the key to *Islamic democracy*. Iran's President Mohammad Khatani, in a television interview in June 2005 before that country's presidential elections, noted that *the existing democracies do not necessarily follow one formula or aspect. It is possible that democracy may lead to a liberal system. It is possible that democracy may lead to a socialist system. Or it may be a democracy with the inclusion of religious norms in the government.*[7]

3. Alternation as a Democratic Mechanism

To the ancient Rome question: *Who will guard the guardians?* There has been one well-known answer for centuries *those who choose the guardians*.[8] But there is also another possibility – alternation of power, which provides a minimum control of the rulers. The term alternation of power is closely related to *popular participation*. The hopes for participation derived from and renewed a long historical evolution of theories and practices of democracy. The conception with the longest history and widest acceptance has focused on participation as the ideal functioning of pluralist representative democracy. Political parties competing within codified rules of the game then become the main channels through which the whole adult population can have a voice in the selection of leaders and policies. This conception has supposed free competition in ideas and criticisms, protection of the rights etc. Pluralist democracy has been formally endorsed by majority of states since World War II. It is a basis for creation of alternation.

There are some levels of alternation in power: ideological, political, legal, psychological etc. On an ideological level, there are norms and values accepting ideas of a group/personal change among the political elites governing a state. On a political level, real possibilities of change must be established. Political parties and organizations

---

[7] John L. Esposito, John O. Voll, "Islam and Democracy", http://www.neh.gov/news/humanities/2001-11/islam.html

[8] Gerald M. Pomper, *Elections in America*, New York: Dodd Mead, 1968, pp. 262–263.

which have a different attitude to general political question must exist. In practice, there must be a possibility of representing different groups and showing different programs. It must be a real political market of programs, not just a formal artificial political game. Pluralism developed as a way of explaining that liberal democracies were basically organized around the activities of organized groups and not individuals. The major principle in pluralism is that political power is dispersed amongst many groups and that political decisions are reached as a result of bargaining and interaction between groups. For the groups to act effectively people had to have complete freedom of access to them and other basic freedoms became necessary: freedom of speech, freedom of assembly and freedom of association. Pluralism came to be viewed as a way of securing an open political system which would tolerate competing viewpoints and produce guarantees for basic political freedom. Pluralism generates a base for introducing alternation of power into public life. On legal level, some essential factors of free elections must be introduced to social life: 1. Elections must take place regularly within set time limits, and may not be postponed indefinitely by public officials whenever they wish; 2. In order to exercise effective control of their public officials, voters must have a choice between at least two candidates for each office to be filled. Of course, it must be a real competition, it just must provide a significant choice between minimum two quite different points along each spectrum – and, equally important, between minimum two quite different human beings. All agree that a truly free election must furnish the voters meaningful choices; 3. No substantial group in the population denied the opportunity of forming a political party and putting up candidates; 4. If two candidates for an office are allowed to run but only one is permitted to present his/her views publicly and to have his/her name printed on the ballot, then he/she is effectively the only candidate. There must be a complete freedom for all candidates and their supporters to publicize their names and policy positions, so that the voters can hear what they have to say. There is a question: how can we manage it, effectively? Probably there is a need, that every candidate must be guaranteed at least some financial support, so that all candidates, rich and poor alike, have at least minimum opportunities to publicize their views and appeal for popular support. We can add some other conditions of free elections: universal adult suffrage, equal weighting of votes, free registration of choices, accurate counting of choices and reporting of results.

Political leaders throughout the world have succumbed the pressure for elections, and even those who came to power through non-democratic or extra-constitutional ways have tried to legitimize their regimes through elections. In established democracies, elections are a basic mechanism for ensuring accountability, in that the possibility of being voted out of office acts as an incentive to respect rules. In fledging democracies however, they can play a more ambiguous role, and in some instances flawed elections have severed to undermine public confidence in the electoral process.

Throughout the world, those with political power want to retain it. A central issue is whether the institutional basis for political alternation exists. Lack of genuine opportunities for alternation presents a problem to political development and to the consolidation of democracy. It is often both a cause and a consequence of the predominance of personality – driven politics. Orderly, political succession through the ballot box and peaceful alternation of power are the hallmarks of effective democratic system.

Alternation in power is an essential concept in a democracy. Samuel P. Huntington has proposed that electoral alternations of power – measured by what he calls the *two turnover test* – signal the consolidation of democracy.[9] In the wake of two cycles of political replacement, most political actors have lived as both, winners and losers without revolting. Thus, they signal their acceptance of the rules of the electoral game. Huntington reduced consolidation to alternation. Is Huntington right? Surely, more than any other political event, a peaceful electoral transfer of power from one group of governors to another symbolizes *rule by the people*. In the public imagination, electoral alternation helps to broadly legitimize democracy.

Newly democratizing countries are not well served if ruling parties are so predominant that other views are not heard, or if political

[9] Samuel P. Huntington, *The Third Wave: Democratization in the Late Twientieth Century*, Norman: University of Oklahoma Press, 1991, pp. 266–267.

alternation and sharing of power are all but impossible. Coalition governments, strong and responsible parliamentary oppositions, or the election of presidents from one party and the majority of parliamentarians from another are quite common features of a number of established democracies.

Elections are a basic mechanism for ensuring accountability, in that the possibility of being voted out of office acts as an incentive to respect rules. Otherwise, there is a chance that elections will return the same people to office, regardless of performance, or will be won by those who can distribute the greatest amount of gifts and political favors at election time. Civic education would, over time, help to change the expectations of the electorate and create a normative environment which encourages and rewards accountability and transparency. However, poverty and underdevelopment can make individuals and communities susceptible to campaign gifts and election promises.

4. Role of Electoral Systems

We must agree that free elections are certainly not all there is to democracy but in every modern nation that is generally called democratic free elections are the basic device that enables the people to control the rulers.[10]

In setting up their electoral systems all democratic countries have tried to satisfy all the requirements of free elections mentioned at the beginning of this paper, but they have chosen a wide variety of means for doing so. The main types of systems are: single-member district systems and multi-member proportional systems. Among single-member district systems are: 1. The First-past-the Post; 2. Absolute majority systems. Multi-member proportional systems are: 1. Party-List Systems (No Choice Among Candidates and Some Choice Among Candidates); 2. The Single-Transferable-Vote System.

Both the first-past-the post and proportional systems have strong partisans among present-day democratic theorists. There are some

---

[10] Austin Ranney, *Governing. A Introduction to Political Science*, New York, Chicago, San Francisco: Hold-Rinehart and Winston, 1982, p. 138.

popular conclusions of Douglas Rae: 1. Every electoral system tends to award parties with large share of the popular votes more than their proportional shares of parliamentary seats. On the other hand, the smaller parties get even smaller shares of the parliamentary seats than their shares of the popular votes; 2. Single-member district systems tend to produce two-party competition except where minority parties are especially strong in particular areas; 3. Proportional systems discriminate against small parties without strong local bases less than do majority systems, and consequently they tend to produce multiparty systems rather than two-party systems; 4. In order to achieve a legislative majority capable of ruling, more parties willing to join coalitions are necessary in proportional than in single-member district systems; 5. The most important single factor affecting the degree of proportionality – that is, the closeness between the shares of the popular vote and the shares of the legislative seats – is the size of its electoral districts. The more members that are elected from each district, the more proportional are the seat shares to the vote shares.[11] These are some of the most notable facts. As yet, no ideal electoral system has been found.

5. Conclusion

Democrats are committed to the rule of the people. They insist that no aristocrat, monarch, bureaucrat, expert, or religious leader have the right to force people to accept a particular conception of their proper common life. People should decide for themselves, by appropriate procedures of collective decision, what their collective business should be.[12] Anyway, it sounds like an idealistic political ideology. There are limited possibilities of the direct democratic procedures. So, there is a need of alternative solutions.

---

[11] See: Douglas W. Rae, *The Political Consequences of Electoral Laws*, Rev. ed., New Haven: Yale University Press, 1971.

[12] Ian Shapiro, *Democracy's Place*, Ithaca and London: Cornell University Press, 1996, p. 224.

In fledging democracies alternation of power plays more important role, than in consolidated ones. The lack of alternation of power, even in a stable democracy, usually led to corruption, arrogance and ignorance. In the future, democratic political system could be changed into dictatorship. Dictators can achieve power by use of the regular, electoral machinery. They can therefore, maintain themselves in power throughout taking the unfair advantage of the whole public opinion, or by ignoring or repressing its free expression.

Political alternation is a democratic mechanism and it is difficult to practice democracy without it. It is one of the main features of electoral competition. There is a very close connection between alternation and issue voting. It is something like a natural *breathing* of democracy.

Krzysztof Brzechczyn
Poznań

Paths to Democracy of the Post-Soviet Republics: Attempt at Conceptualization

1. Introduction

From the perspective of fifteen years after the collapse of the Soviet Union, it is possible to distinguish five basic developmental paths the post-Soviet republics followed. The societies in which an independent civil revolution took place, enter the first developmental path. However, this path of development bifurcates into two further sub-variants. Namely, civil revolutions in the Baltic republics (Lithuania, Latvia and Estonia) resulted in their independence and stable democracies. On the other hand, civil revolutions in the Caucasus republics (Georgia, Armenia) proved only partially successful. Civil movements in these countries managed to gain independence, yet they were unable to build stable democracies. Countries such as Azerbaijan, Belarus, Moldova, and Ukraine achieved sovereignty and followed the next developmental path, seceding from the Soviet Union. However, it was mainly local communist nomenclatures that initiated establishment of independent states. Democratization – characteristic of the first period of their independent existence – was counterbalanced by the subsequent emergence of autocratic tendencies that surfaced with different force and from different reasons. And again, this path of development bifurcates into two developmental variants. In the former, growth of power regulation was hampered by successful civil resistance (Ukraine), whereas in the latter, growth of power regulation did not encounter such strong civil reaction (Azerbaijan, Belarus, Moldova). Finally, the countries of Central Asia (Kazakhstan, Kyrgyzstan, Tajikistan, Turkmenistan and Uzbekistan) followed the fifth developmental path. In these societies, independence permitted to preserve dictatorship of local communist nomenclatures.

Therefore, naturally, a question arises how to identify social mechanisms leading to this developmental differentiation of the post-Soviet republics. It seems that an answer to this problem lies in the nature of real socialism in the Soviet version and the way of its collapse. This view will be systematically presented in this paper which is divided into five sections (including *Introduction*). In the second section, main theses of non-Marxian historical materialism, establishing a theoretical base for made analyses, are presented.[1] This approach is extended in the third section. Political development of the post-Soviet republics is described in the fourth section. In the last section, the paper closes with a summary of presented conceptualization and concluding remarks that place this developmental differentiation of the post-Soviet countries in the global context.

2. The Legacy of Soviet Socialism

According to theoretical categories of non-Marxian historical materialism real socialism in the Soviet Union may be characterised by three basic features. Firstly, it was a social system where one social class, disposing means of coercion, production and indoctrination, controlled politics, economy and culture. Secondly, the main interest of this class of triple-lords consisted in the maximisation of power regulation. Thirdly, this social system built up an empire consisting of the Russian metropolis and the external provinces: Latvia, Lithuania, Estonia, Armenia, Georgia, Azerbaijan, Belarus and Ukraine. Let us briefly characterise the three above-mentioned aspects of real socialism in the Soviet version.

2.1. On Three Class Divisions

Class divisions, in accordance with non-Marxian historical materialism, exist not only in economy, but also emerge spontaneously

---

[1] Full presentation of this theory is in: Leszek Nowak, *Property and Power. Towards non-Marxian historical materialism*, Dordrecht: Reidel, 1983; idem, *Power and Civil Society. Towards a Dynamic Theory of Real Socialism*, London: Greenwood Press, 1991.

in other spheres of human activity, such as politics and culture. In each sphere of social life it is possible to distinguish a material level consisting of means of coercion, production and indoctrination. Relation to the means of coercion in politics determines the division of society into two social categories: the class of rulers, which controls the use of means of coercion, and the class of citizens, deprived of such possibilities. In economy, the material level is made up of the means of production, which determines the division into the class of owners and the class of direct producers. In the cultural domain, the material level consists of the means of spiritual production – for example printing presses, radio, and television. Between these pairs of social classes: priests and the indoctrinated, owners and direct producers, rulers and citizens, a contradiction of interests arises. In the cultural domain, the class of priests enhances its spiritual domination over the indoctrinated at the expense of their spiritual autonomy. In economy, the class of owners maximises its profits limiting income of direct producers. In the sphere of politics, the class of rulers enlarges power regulation at the expense of citizens' autonomy. Social antagonisms, resulting from unequal access to the material means of society (means of coercion, production and indoctrination) in each of these three domains of social life have an autonomous character. Class divisions in other domains of social life can only strengthen antagonisms in a given domain or conversely, weaken them.

Thus control over the material means provides the basis for typology of societies in non-Marxian historical materialism. Applying this criterion it is possible to distinguish class societies, where existing classes are separated, and supra-class societies where, for example, one social class, keen on increasing the range of its social influence, may seize control over the means of coercion, production and mass communication. A society with a triple class of rulers-owners-priests, monopolising control over politics, economy and culture, exemplifies a type of supra-class systems. This social system refers to the structure of real socialism. The apparatus of the Communist Party, which controlled not only political life, but also economy and culture, was the counterpart of the triple-lords class.

2.2. On Political Nature of Socialism

Real socialism was the system of triple-rule in a political version because possession of the means of production and indoctrination by the class of rulers-owners-priests was subordinated to the enlargement of power regulation. In order to present the dynamics of social systems of this kind, dynamics of power should be described in the first place. Now, the main theses of the first model of power in non-Marxian historical materialism will be presented in brief.[2] Theses

---

[2] Theory of power in non-Marxian historical materialism applies methods of idealization and gradual concretization (Leszek Nowak, *The Structure of Idealisation*, Dordrecht: Reidel, 1980). Presented theory consists of a sequence of models. The first model of power considers only those factors which are regarded as main ones for the phenomenon of political power. That is why, among other, in the first model, the influence of cultural and economic domain, institutional structure of power, social consciousness of political classes, internal relations, technological growth of means of coercion and faction competition is omitted in the analysis of the evolution of a purely political society. In the process of concretization, some idealising assumptions are cancelled out, transforming the original approach into a multi-model theory of power whose level of realism increases (Leszek Nowak, *Power and Civil Society*, op. cit.). Among numerous contributions made to the theory of power in non-Marxian historical materialism, it is worth mentioning, papers refining the concept of revolution in that theory (Krzysztof Brzechczyn, "Civil Loop and the Absorption of Elites", in: *Social System, Rationality and Revolution*, ed. by Leszek Nowak, Marcin Paprzycki, Amsterdam: Rodopi, 1993, pp. 277–283; Katarzyna Paprzycka, Marcin Paprzycki, "How Do Enslaved People Make Revolutions?", ibidem, pp. 251–265; G. Tomczak, "Is It Worth Wininng Revolution?", ibidem, pp. 265–277) and analysing influence of such factors as: unsuccessful aggression and subordination (Krzysztof Brzechczyn, "Unsuccessful Conquest and Successful Subordination. A Contribution to the Theory of Intersocial Relations', ibidem, pp. 445–456), different types of political systems (T. Banaszak, "Problem autokratyzacji ustroju politycznego" [The Problem of Autocratisation of Political System], in: *Marksizm, liberalizm, próby wyjścia* [Marxism, Liberalism, Attempts of Exit], ed. by Leszek Nowak, Piotr Przybysz, Poznań: Zysk i S-ka, 1997, pp. 381–399), secret police (Krzysztof Brzechczyn, "Władza a tajna policja polityczna. Próba modelu" [Power and Secret Political Police. An Attempt at Model], *Przegląd Politologiczny* 1–2, 1999, pp. 81–97), generational divisions (Krzysztof Brzechczyn, "Pokolenia a demokracja" [Generations and Democracy], in: *Filozofia a demokracja* [Philosophy and Democracy], ed. by Piotr W. Juchacz, Roman Kozłowski, Poznań: Wydawnictwo Naukowe IF UAM, 2001, pp. 215–241), different types of institutional change (Lidia Godek, "Wprowadzenie demokracji kontraktowej w Polsce. Próba interpretacji" [The

(i–iii) concern static assumptions of such a model, whereas thesis (iii–viii) dynamic ones.

(i) Every citizen has a set of preferences, which direct his or her actions. Among citizens' actions it is possible to distinguish those that are autonomous and regulated. Regulated actions are undertaken under threat of repression from the ruler, but autonomous actions are not restricted by similar sanctions taken by those controlling means of coercion. This distinction should not to be conceived too simply because citizens' actions regulated by rulers comprise also administrative ones. Their regulation by power is a base of social order; therefore regulation is profitable for both parties[3]. The ratio of the number of regulated actions to the number of actions undertaken by citizens (universe of action) is called *civil alienation*. It is assumed that intensity of civil resistance depends on the level of civil alienation and can be presented as follows:

– when the number of regulated actions is low (and thus civil alienation is also low), social peace prevails as citizens have no reason to resist;

– when the level of civil alienation is high, the level of resistance is low as declassed and atomised citizens are unable to resist;

– a political revolution breaks out when civil alienation is moderately high; which means it is painful enough to evoke political reaction, yet not so painful as to paralyse citizenry;

(ii) There are two basic methods to subordinate social life: bureaucratization and terror. Bureaucratization replaces

---

Introduction of Contract Democracy in Poland. An Attempt at Interpretation], in: *Rola wyborów w procesie kształtowania się społeczeństwa obywatelskiego w Polsce* [The Role of Elections in the Formation of Civil Society in Poland], ed. by Sebastian Drobczyński, Marek Żyromski, Poznań: WSNHiD, 2004, pp. 117–133) and class compromise (Krzysztof Brzechczyn, "Porozumienie przy Okrągłym Stole w świetle koncepcji kompromisu klasowego. Próba modelu" [The Round Table Agreement in the Light of Concept of Class Compromise. An Attempt at Model], ibidem, pp. 27–47) on the evolution of a political society.

[3] Krzysztof Brzechczyn, "Unsuccessful Conquest and Successful Subordination", op. cit., p. 447.

autonomous social relations (citizen – citizen type) by etat-
ized ones (citizen – ruler – citizen type). This way, power
gradually permeates into the structure of social life making
it impossible to undertake any social action without its
permission. Resorting to terror, rulers physically 'eliminate'
from social life (death, long-term prison or isolation, etc)
those from the class of citizens who are centres of independent social relations;

(iii)   However, the state of declassation does not last forever. It is
assumed that when bureaucratization of social life passes a
certain threshold, there appears a tendency for revitalization
of autonomous social bonds among citizens. It means that
etatised social bonds are replaced by autonomous ones, social relations controlled by authorities shrink and the sphere
of autonomous social life enlarges;

(iv)   It is supposed that at the starting point of dynamic relations
between rulers and citizenry, peace prevails. In *the phase of
increasing civil alienation*, as a result of the mechanism of political competition between disposers of means of coercion an
average ruler is forced to enlarge his/her sphere of regulation. Those, who do not compete, are eliminated from the
political structure of power or, by process of trials and errors, learn to enlarge their sphere of control. In consequence,
social autonomy shrinks and the sphere of power regulation
enlarges;

(v)   According to static assumptions, growth of power regulation
intensifies citizens' resistance, which gradually transforms
into a mass civil revolution. Possible victory or failure of a
civil revolution opens the way to bifurcation of political development;

(vi)   Let us suppose that citizens have won. Then, from a purely
materialist point of view, nothing of consequence changes,
because inside the class of citizens, a division into (new) disposers of means of coercion and those who are deprived of
such clout, is spontaneously reconstituted. Now, the crowds,
not to mention armed civil guards, form the means of co-

ercion. Therefore, a revolutionary elite structures the core of a new class of rulers. The mechanism of political competition among them leads once more to the growth of power regulation. This, in turn, leads to the growth of civil resistance and an outbreak of the next political revolution. When this revolution wins again, the mechanism of a civil loop repeats once more. However, civil loops cannot repeat endlessly and some revolution in a row will lose;

(vii) The defeat of citizens' movement enables the rulers (new or old ones) to use post-revolutionary terror. It afflicts those from the class of citizens who are the centres of independent social bonds. In *the phase of enslavement*, atomisation of the class of citizens makes it possible to control an increasing number of social fields. When all domains of social life are subordinated, the system reaches the state of total enslavement. In such circumstances, the only means to stop power disappears. Under such social conditions, there are no social spheres to regulate. Because the mechanism of political competition forces typical rulers to enlarge their sphere of regulation, further competition proceeds at the expense of social spheres already controlled by other rulers. Periodic purges, which make a clean sweep of surplus candidates for power, solve the problem of political over-competitiveness. This way, enslavement of citizens turns into self-enslavement of rulers which, starting at the bottom of power apparatus, gradually reaches the centre of power;

(viii) However – according to static assumptions – in an analysed political society, there appears a tendency towards a gradual revitalization of independent social bonds, which increases citizens' ability to resist. This leads to a revolution, which initiates *the phase of cyclical declassation* and gradual reduction of power regulation. This revolution is crushed, but rulers – in order to avoid a follow-up, reduce the scope of their control. Yet, mechanisms of political competition lead once more to the growth of power regulation, triggering an outbreak of the next revolution on a greater scale. This forces rulers to make larger concession and makes it more difficult for them to repress rebels. Thus a political society evolves according to the following scheme: civil revolution – repression – concessions – growth of political regulation – next political revolution with a wider social base;

(ix) Finally, in *the phase of a cyclical revolution,* mass protests erupt and their scale is so widespread that authorities instead of starting off with repression, have no choice but allow sweeping concessions, which reduces control of the rulers to the level acceptable by the class of citizens.

One may, roughly speaking, distinguish counterparts of developmental phases of the presented model of a purely political society in the history of the Soviet society. The overthrow of the tsarist regime in February 1917 can be perceived as a civic revolution leading to a civil loop. The Provisional Government tried to regulate economic life concentrating in its hands more and more power. This, however, stirred social unrest, which culminated in the October Revolution, commanded by the Bolsheviks, and levelled against the Provisional Government. Very soon, however, the Bolsheviks began to concentrate power for the sake of power. Nationalization of banks, introduction of "war communism" or formation of secret police, enjoying a wide scope of competencies over citizens' lives, may serve as a confirmation of the above. It brought about a new wave of social unrest with peasantry at the oppositional forefront. Finally, social disturbances spread to cities: seamen and workers in Kronstadt – closest supporters of the Bolsheviks rebelled against them. Pacification of the Kronstadt revolution ended the second civil loop and led to the imposition of total political control over people. The Stalinism period, from 1929 to 1953, can be perceived as a phase of enslavement. Stalin's purges in the 30s are a counterpart of a sub-phase of self-enslavement of power.

The prisoners of Gulag, transforming themselves from atomised individuals into self-organized masses, initiated a series of prison riots. The first uprising broke out in July 1950, in the labour camp near Vorkuta. First half of 1953 marked the apogee of the Gulag uprisings, resulting in a certain liberalization of the oppressing political system, manifested by Khrushchev's condemnation of Stalin's Cult at the 20th Congress of the Communist Party. These events can be interpreted as the transition of the whole system to the phase of cyclical declassation. Recurrent civic revolutions included: worker's strikes in Novocherkassk and fourteenth towns of central Russia in the 60s, national revival in the Baltic countries in the 70s, strikes at the beginning of the 80s. They led, on the one hand, to repressive measures towards rebellious citizens, but, on the other hand, forced those at the helm of the Communist Party to make political concessions so as to avoid an outbreak of the next revolution. The Gorbachev's reforms comprised the most serious attempt to avoid social revolution similar to the Solidarity movement in Poland. However, this reformism policy, increasing social autonomy of people, stimulated, in fact, revitalization of autonomous civil bonds and lead to the growth of civil unrest, precipitating the final decline of the triple rule.[4]

2.3. Dynamics of the Soviet Empire

However, presented model of a purely political society and its historical operationalization does not take into consideration internal relations of the Soviet Union and the very fact that this country played the role of an aggressor in relations with the neighbouring societies. Therefore, it is necessary to concretise the first model. The main theses of the 4th model are presented in an analogous way. Theses (i)–(ii) describe static whereas, and (iii)–(v) its dynamic part.

(i) Successful aggression ousted the authority of a conquered country and enslaved its citizens. The ruling class of aggressor's society gained extraordinary growth of external power regulation. Aggressiveness conceived in such a way occurs in certain phases of development of an analysed society. It is possible to distinguish two ranges of aggressiveness. The society enters *the first range of aggressiveness* in the late stage of

---

[4] More on this: Leszek Nowak, "The Totalitarian Approach and the History of Socialism", in: *From a One-Party State to Democracy: Transition in Eastern Europe*, ed. by Janina Frentzel-Zagórska, Amsterdam – Atlanta: Rodopi, pp. 45–67.

the *phase of increasing civil alienation*. Owing to an extraordinary increase in power regulation, the class of rulers stabilizes relations with its own class of citizens and averts the threat of revolution. In *the second range of aggressiveness*, a political society enters *the phase of enslavement*. Than, external growth of power regulation allows for averting the threat of self-enslavement of the class of rulers;

(ii) It is worth characterising social consequences of aggression for its victim. The class of rulers of an attacked society is removed and the whole country is incorporated into the empire. The class of citizens of a conquered society becomes enslaved, irrespective of the developmental phase it achieved. A successful conquest has the same consequences as a lost civil revolution – it leads to the enslavement of the class of citizens;

(iii) Let us suppose, at the starting point of our analysis, that social peace prevails. In the initial stage of development rulers enlarge their domestic spheres of regulation. It leads to the growth of civil alienation and social resistance. In order to avoid an outbreak of a revolution, rulers conquer another society, entering the first range of aggressiveness. This takes place when civil alienation passes the threshold of class peace. Enslavement of citizens from conquered societies stabilizes social peace in the metropolis. Not for a long time, however. Political profits reaped from aggression run out and rulers have to undertake subsequent aggression or enlarge spheres of regulation at home. However, the second solution intensifies resistance of metropolitan citizens. Subsequent conquest of another society leads to the formation of an empire consisting of a metropolis and external provinces. Finally, after some time, at a given technological level of the means of coercion, cost of conquest and control of provincial citizens exhaust possibilities of empire's growth;

(iv) From that moment on rulers have to enlarge their spheres of regulation at the expense of the autonomy of metropolitan citizens, which intensifies their resistance. The growth of civil alienation leads to an outbreak of a revolution in the me-tropolis. If – *in the phase of a civil revolution* – social disturbances in the metropolis co-occur with similar events in provinces, it offers the best chance of victory for the latter and separation of rebellious provinces from the empire. During revolution the level of aggressiveness of the empire decreases because rulers are busy struggling with own citizens;

(v)   Let us suppose that the revolution of metropolitan citizens is defeated. In *the phase of enslavement*, the level of aggressive-ness of a considered society is still low because rulers enlarge the sphere of regulation at the expense of the autonomy of metropolitan citizens. The aggressiveness of the empire in-creases in *the sub-phase of self-enslavement of authority*. At that time aggressiveness reduces the threat of self-enslavement of power structure because successful conquest provides new vistas for power regulation;

(vi)   In *the phase of cyclical declassation*, the level of aggressiveness again decreases because metropolitan class of rulers has to deal with the resistance of own citizens. Simultaneously, the process of revitalization of autonomous social bonds com-mences also in the provinces of the empire. The provinces, which were conquered earlier, initiate this process. Provinces conquered later are still enslaved. However, this phase of de-velopment is prolonged because possession of external provinces allows to maintain different factions of citizenry at different levels of enslavement. The class of rulers, instead of dealing with protests of the whole class of citizens, deals with isolated citizen protests, occurring at different time and in different parts of the empire;

(vii) In *the phase of a cycling revolution*, the level of aggressiveness increases again. However, this grow is morbid because metro-politan citizens are less and less willing to fulfil the social role of an imperial gendarme. Civil revolutions in provinces enjoy greatest chances of victory when they coincide with revolutionary occurrences in the metropolis, which brings the existence of the empire to an end.

In the political history of the Soviet Union and its neighbouring societies one may find, roughly speaking, counterparts of two waves of aggressiveness. The first range of aggressiveness took place in the years 1917–1921. At that time the Caucasus republics were conquered and the Soviet domination in Central Asia was restored. The second range of aggressiveness took place in the years 1939–1941. Then, Western Belarus and Ukraine, Moldova, Lithuania, Latvia and Estonia were incorporated into the borders of the Soviet Empire. High level of Soviet aggressiveness was still maintained during hot confrontations (Berlin crisis, Korean War) and the Cold War with the capitalistic world. The level of aggressiveness decreased after 1956 when the model of peaceful co-existence of the two military camps was promulgated. Again, the growth of aggressiveness appeared when the empire was approaching its end, which was testified by growing engagement in the Third World or invasion on Afghanistan.

3. Collapse of the Empire.
Attempt at Conceptualization

However, the final years of the Soviet Union history hardly fall under the 4th model of a purely political society as a result of an emergence of a new political phenomenon, which was not captured in this model. Namely, in the face of increasing weakness of the central authority, local fractions of the class of rulers, making or refusing to make concessions to own citizens, seceded from the Soviet Union and established independent states, which preserved the whole power.

In order to conceptualise this phenomenon, the final stadium of the development of an imperial society should be concretised. In a society of a political type, rulers can enlarge their sphere of regulation at the expense of the autonomy of own citizens (i) and/or by conquest of other societies (ii). In the first case, rulers have to overcome growing resistance of own citizens. In the latter, they have to crush the resistance of subordinated rulers and enslaved citizens. In both cases, under force of tacitly accepted assumptions, the universe of citizens' actions remains constant.

However, when this assumption is waived, rulers enjoy another possibility of maintaining civil alienation at a constant level. Namely, local factions of rulers can enlarge the universe of political actions. Let us remind that civil alienation is a ratio between the sum of actions regulated by rulers to the overall number of actions undertaken by citizens. Therefore, even in spite of the growth of power regulation, civil alienation remains at a constant level. In an exceptional situation, when the growth of the universe of citizens' action is higher than the growth of regulated action, the level of civil alienation may even decrease.

One way to enlarge the universe of citizens' actions consists in the separation of a new society S' from a mother-society S. In such a way the society S' is established and separate classes of rulers and citizens are constituted in it. Independent existence of a given society generates in it a set of new domains of social life, e.g.: military policy, diplomacy, internal security etc, which can be regulated by the class of rulers. Moreover, rulers of the society S' take control of these domains of social life which were regulated by metropolitan rulers.

As a result of gained sovereignty, rulers of a new society S', instead of reducing citizens' autonomy, subordinate new spheres of social life, which are formed in the course of separation from the previous metropolis. As a consequence of the enlargement of the universe of citizen's action, civil alienation decreases, even in spite of the growth of power regulation. Civil alienation also decreases as a result of concessions made by rulers who strive to stabilise independent existence of their society. In order to ensure support of own citizens, which is needed to confront the authorities of the empire, rulers make concessions to own citizens. In the model of a purely political society, the growth of citizens' political autonomy is the perquisite to win civil support. Jointly, reduction of civil alienation occurring thanks to the enlargement of the universe of citizens' actions and/or concessions made by rulers is named *the independence effect*.

Let us consider who it to gain profits and who to bear costs of the formation of a new political society S'. It is obvious that secession is politically profitable for the local faction of rulers because separation from the empire allows for further growth of power regulation without the risk of civil resistance. New authorities control new domains

Krzysztof Brzechczyn

of social life, which emerged as a result of independent existence. Also, the class of rulers seizes control over these spheres of public life that were dominated by the class of metropolitan rulers.

Whether successful secession is profitable for citizens depends on the degree of concessions made by provincial authorities and on the advancement of liberalisation processes in the metropolis. When the level of civil alienation, as a result of the independence effect, becomes lower than the level of civil alienation of metropolitan citizens, then secession is profitable for provincial citizens. However, when, in the spite of the independence effect, the level of civil alienation is still higher than the level of civil alienation in the metropolis, then independence is unprofitable for provincial citizens.

However, rulers from the metropolis are to bear most substantial costs. Successful secession weakens their position inside the empire and encourages citizens from the metropolis and other provinces to further political resistance. Additionally, shrinking of the territory and population of such an empire weakens its international position. It is natural that imperial rulers usually undertake actions leading to a subsequent incorporation of rebellious provinces into the structure of the empire.

If an insurgent province is threatened with a military intervention, in a newly independent society the phenomenon of *regulational credit* occurs.[5] Because conquest would deteriorate citizens' position, they accept without demur introduction of stricter disciplinary rigours, which are considered as administrative actions of the authority. For that reason, civil alienation remains at a constant level and may even become lower. In the latter case, growing citizens' support for the authority of an attacked country is witnessed.

It is possible to distinguish two kinds of secession conceived in such a way: *progressive* and *regressive*. Progressive secession occurs in those provincial societies where the level of power regulation is lower than that of a metropolitan society. In such societies, enlargement of the universe of citizens' actions and concession made by rulers lead to the reduction of civil alienation. As a result of relations between the class of rulers and citizenry, class peace is introduced. Thus, inde-

---

[5] Krzysztof Brzechczyn, "Unsuccessful Conquest and Successful Subordination", op. cit., pp. 447–450.

pendence stabilises civil peace in the province and protects 'civilised' provincial society against the intervention of a 'barbarian' metropolis.

When authorities consolidate their position, the mechanisms of political competition lead to the growth of power regulation. Its results may be twofold. If a decrease in civil alienation stimulates revitalization of citizens bonds and promotes civil self-organization, then readiness of civil masses to resist is a sufficient guarantee of class peace and stabilization of democracy. If a decrease in civil alienation does not stimulate revitalisation of civil society strongly enough, then the growth of power regulation leads to the open autocratization of a political system.

Regressive secession occurs in these provincial societies where the level of power regulation is higher than that of power regulation of a metropolitan society. Passivity of citizen masses makes restoration of sovereignty an initiative of local faction of rulers, who this way may maintain their political domination. In this type of secession the independence effect also appears, but its range is circumscribed. Although, the level of civil alienation decreases, it does not introduce class peace in rulers – citizens relations. Paradoxically, independence retards the decrease in power regulation in the province of the empire, protecting it against the wave of liberalization coming from the centre. In this case, sovereignty protecting a 'barbarian' province against intervention of more 'civilised' metropolis allows to preserve the political *status quo*.

To sum up, in the conceptual apparatus of non-Marxian historical materialism, it is possible to distinguish the following basic paths of disintegration of a political empire:

(i)   victorious civil revolution;
(ii) progressive secession;
(iii) regressive secession.

4. Political Development of the Post-Soviet Republics: A Survey

This chapter aims to present an introductory categorization of political development of the post-Soviet republics from 1985 to 2004. The description is organized around the following criteria:

- size and range of civil resistance and forms of its institutionalization;
- political concessions made by republican authorities;
- level of control over republican structure of power exercised by the class of citizens;
- way of gaining independence;
- fate of democratic systems in newly independent states.

Bearing in mind striking similarities in the political evolution of Lithuanian, Latvian and Estonian, the development of the Baltic societies will be presented jointly, in one narrative. The same strategy of description is adopted with regard to the societies of the Central Asian countries: Kazakhstan, Kyrgyzstan, Tajikistan, Turkmenistan and Uzbekistan. Yet, political development of other republics: Armenia, Azerbaijan, Belarus, Georgia, Moldova, and Ukraine is presented separately.

4.1. Victorious Civil Revolution

4.1.1. Victorious Civil Revolution Leading to Stable Class Peace (Political Development of the Baltic Societies)

In the Baltic countries political protests began from ecological discontent (Estonia) and celebrations of forbidden historical anniversaries (Lithuania, Latvia).[6] In 1986 Estonians protested against construction of phosphorus mines. These protests had a political context because implementation of new investments meant migration of Russian workers. Finally, the ecological demur made central authorities in Moscow resign from the construction of new mines. In Lithuania, civil revival commenced from an independent celebration of the 600th

---

[6] This subsection is based on empirical research conducted by: Grzegorz Błaszczyk, "Partie polityczne Litwy w latach 1988–1992" [Political Parties in Lithuania from 1988 to 1992], *Obóz* 25/26, 1993, pp. 57–77; Jerzy Krawulski, *Estonia, Litwa, Łotwa. Przeobrażenia polityczne i gospodarcze* [Estonia, Lithuania, Latvia. Political and Economical Transformations], Warszawa: CBW UW, 1996; Jan Lewandowski, *Estonia* [Estonia], Warszawa: Trio, 2001; Anatol Lieven. *The Baltic Revolution. Estonia, Latvia, Lithuania and the Path to Independence*, New Haven: Yale University Press, 1994.

anniversary of Lithuanian Baptism (1986) and in Latvia – from independent commemoration of the 1940 deportations. Also, Estonians commemorated tragic anniversaries of the Soviet-Estonian relations. One of the largest demonstrations took place at the time of the Molotov-Ribbentrop agreement commemoration, on 23 August, 1987, in Tallinn, capital of Estonia.

Very soon, these demonstrations gained momentum and acquired a massive following. For example, at that time in Estonia from 150 to 300 thousand people used to participate in different kinds of manifestations and forms of protest (Estonia had 1.5 million inhabitants). The largest demonstration was held on 23 August 1989. Then, 2 million people (the 2/3 of the population of the Baltic republic) formed a human chain from Tallinn to Vilnius to protest against the results of the Molotov–Ribbentrop agreement.

Mass civil movement in the Baltic republics was organized in the form of Popular Fronts that officially supported Gorbachev's *perestroika*. First organization of this type in the Soviet Union was founded in April, 1988 in Estonia. In Lithuania, the Popular Front (*Saiudis*) was established in June, 1988, in Latvia – in October, 1988. Apart from these structures, there emerged other independent organizations and political parties that overtly called for restoration of full state independence and complete political freedom.

Self-organized civil movement took control over some legally existing organizations and enforced political concessions from the authorities of the Baltic republics that had to enlarge their sphere of autonomy from Moscow.

In Estonia, at the beginning of April, 1988, the participants of a joint session of the Boards of Writers and Artists Associations demanded the dismissal of Karl Vaino, first secretary of the Estonian Communist Party, and of Brunon Saul, Prime Minister of the republican government. Moreover, the participants of this assembly wanted to have full rights to the Estonian language granted and punish those guilty of crimes against the Estonian nation committed during the Soviet occupation. Under social pressure, K. Vaino was dismissed in late spring 1988 and B. Saul resigned from his post in autumn.

The Supreme Council of the Estonian Socialist Soviet Republic restored the traditional flag of the Estonian pre-war independent state.

In October and November 1988, the Popular Front collected 800 thousand signatures under a petition for amendments in the Estonian republican constitution. Under civil pressure, on November 16, 1988, the Supreme Council passed amendments to the republican constitution and admitted 'The Declaration of Sovereignty' granting, in practice, priority of the republican law over the federal (Soviet) one. In January 1989, the republican parliament also bestowed on the Estonian language the status of the state language of the republic.

Also, in Lithuania grass root members of different official republican organizations became more independent in their support of civil movement. In November 1988, members of the Lithuanian Union of Artists dismissed own authorities, loyal towards the Communist Party, and choose democratically more independent representatives. On October 18, 1988, the Supreme Council of the Lithuanian Socialist Soviet Republic granted the Lithuanian language the status of the state language and restored traditional symbols of the independent state (flag and national anthem). Over half a year later, on May 18, 1989, the Supreme Council declared sovereignty of the Lithuanian Republic.

On April 1986, the official Union of Latvian Writers claimed more rights for the national language. One year later, the same demands were restated by the organization of the Latvian teachers. Under increasing civil pressure, the Supreme Council of the Latvian Socialist Soviet Republic proclaimed sovereignty of Latvia on 28 July, 1989 and granted to its national language the status of the state language.

Growing civil movement was one of the most important causes of divisions in republican Communist Parties. The Communist Party of each Baltic republic split into a faction remaining loyal towards Moscow and a faction supporting greater republican autonomy from the centre of the Soviet Union. In Estonia, this division revealed in the first half of 1989, during the 20th Congress of the Estonian Communist Party. In Latvia, the Communist Party had just declared that it is not part of the Communist Party of the Soviet Union. This declaration was an impulse to establish a faction that still remained obedient to Moscow. In Lithuania, in December 1990, the Lithuanian Communist Party renamed into the Lithuanian Democratic Labour Party and openly supported republican sovereignty, which brought about the rise of a pro-Moscow faction.

As a result results of elections held in the first half of 1990, citizens' movement took control over the legislature of the Baltic republics. In Lithuania (February 24, 1990) *Saiudis* gained 73 seats in the 133-seat Supreme Council. In Estonia (March 19, 1990) the Popular Front gained over half seats in the 105-seat Supreme Council. Finally, at the end of April, the Latvian Popular Front gained 131 seats in the 201-seat Supreme Council.

Electoral victories of opposition accelerated the process of achieving independence. On March 11, 1990 the Lithuanian Supreme Council declared restoration of state's independence and the 1938 constitution. In reaction, Moscow decided to cut off oil and gas supply. The economical blockade was lifted in June 1990 when Lithuanian authorities withdrew from immediate implementation of the declaration. The Estonian Supreme Council was more careful because it declared, on 30 March, 1990, that the Soviet occupation did not cease *de iure* the existence of the pre-war Republic of Estonia. Therefore, the Estonian parliament proclaimed the onset of the restoration of the Republic of Estonia. The transitory period should come to an end with the establishment of all institutions and prerogatives of an independent state. A similar strategy was adopted by the Supreme Council of Latvia that on May 5, 1990, declared restoration of an independent state, constitution from 1922 as well as reestablishment of the pre-war name of the state.

Aspirations to independence were confirmed by referendums held in each Baltic country at the turn of February and March in 1990. In the Lithuanian referendum 90% of voters supported an independent state. In Latvia and Estonia, respectively 74% and 78% of electors voted for independence. At the same time the Baltic nations boycotted the federal referendum on the future of the Soviet Union, held on March 18, 1991.

The Soviet Union was forced to recognise state independence of the Baltic countries after the unsuccessful coup d'état in August 1991. On the 20th of August the Supreme Councils of Estonia and Latvia proclaimed full restoration of independence. This decision was accepted by the Supreme Council of the Soviet Union that on September 6, 1991, annulled the 1940 annexation of the Baltic states and announced ratification of treaties with each Baltic state defining the status of Russian army and schedule of its withdrawal. In the second half of 1991 the Baltic states outlawed the Communist Party of the Soviet Union and other organizations supporting federation with the Soviet Union. Simultaneously, the newly independent countries began to build own armies. In the years 1992–1993, in all Baltic countries presidential and parliamentary elections were held. In the first half of the 90s, Estonia and Lithuania proclaimed own constitutions and Latvia amended its own constitution from 1938. This way instigation of stable democracy in the Baltic societies was completed.

Political development of the Baltic societies may be interpreted in the categories of a victorious civil revolution. Mass civil protest movements enforced political concessions on the part of republican factions of the class of rulers. Those factions fearing impending loss of political support, sided with own citizens' fight for independence, which was testified by democratization of the republican political systems and increasing autonomy within the Soviet Union. This strategy allowed for smooth transition to independent statehood and peaceful exchange of ruling elite that under new conditions respected democratic rules of political game. Membership of those states is the Council of Europe and European Union points to the stability of built democracy.

4.1.2. Victorious Civil Revolution Leading to Growth of Power Regulation

A. Political Development of the Armenian Society

Civil revival in Armenia begun from the support and solidarity shown with Armenians inhabiting Nagorno-Karabagh, a mountainous region located in Azerbaijan.[7] At the end of 1987, the national

---

[7] This subsection is based on empirical research conducted by: Józef Darski, "Kto na Kaukazie potrzebuje Rosji. Próba panoramy politycznej" [Who Needs Russia on the

movement spread among Armenians living in Nagorno-Karabagh who claimed unification with Armenia. On February 20, 1988, the Council of Deputies of the Autonomous Region of Nagorno-Karabagh appealed to the Supreme Councils of Armenia and Azerbaijan requesting incorporation of this region to Armenia. This request was supported by Armenians from Armenia: from February 21 to 26, 1988, several thousand people demonstrated at Yerevan's Opera Square. A couple days later (February 27–28, 1988) the Armenian–Azeri conflict broke out. Several dozens of Armenians living in the village of Askeran and the town of Sumgait, near Baku, were killed. In the ensuing months the Armenian–Azeri conflict escalated. The Council of the Autonomous Region of Nagorno-Karabagh decided to leave the Azerbaijan Soviet Socialist Republic and join the Armenian Soviet Socialist Republic. This decision marks the beginning of a regular Armenian–Azeri war and ethnic purges of Armenians in Azerbaijan. Paradoxically, an earthquake of tragic consequences (December 7, 1988) calmed down political situation for several months in Armenia.

In 1989 in Armenia and Nagorno-Karabagh the national movement formed a conspirational Armenian National Army consisting of 40 thousand soldiers and in November that year founded an overt organization – the Armenian National Movement. At the end of 1989, under a growing pressure of mass civil movement, the Supreme Council, dominated by the communists, passed the bill "On Unification of the Armenian Socialist Soviet Republic and Autonomous Region of Nagorno-Karabagh".

Caucasus. An Attempt at Political Panorama], *Obóz* 33, 1998, pp. 103–141; Nora Dudwick, "Political Transformations in Postcommunist Armenia: Images and Realities", in: *Conflict, Cleavage, and Change in Central Asia and the Causasus*, ed. by Karen Dawisha, Bruce Parrott, Cambridge: Cambridge University Press, 1997, pp. 69–110; Andrzej Furier, "Niepodległość krajów zakaukaskich po rozpadzie ZSRR" [The Independence of the Caucasus Countries after the Collapse of the Soviet Union], *Obóz* 37, 2000, pp. 65–93; idem, "Od rozpadu ZSRR do niepodległej Armenii" [From Collapse of the Soviet Union to Independent Armenia], *Studia Polonijne* 22, 2001, pp. 91–107; David E. Mark, "Eurasia Letter: Russia and the New Transcaucasus", *Foreign Policy* 105, 1996, pp. 141–159; Irena Tatarzyńska, "Azja Środkowa i Zakaukazie. Zagrożenia oraz rywalizacja pomiędzy tradycyjnymi i nowymi uczestnikami wielkiej gry o wpływy" [Central Asia and the Caucasus. Threats and Competition Between Traditional and New Participants of Great Game over Influences], *Obóz* 25/26, 1993, pp. 167–178.

During elections held in June 1990 to the Supreme Council, the Communist Party won 56% of votes and the Armenian National Movement – 44%. However, as a result of a split inside the Armenian Communist Party, Vazgen Manukian, one of the ANM leaders, became Prime Minister and Levon Ter-Petrossian – Chairman of the Supreme Council. Thus, opposition seized the whole power. On August 23, 1990, the Supreme Council proclaimed "the Act of Sovereignty". At that time, the Azeri–Armenian war intensified again. Russian troops supporting Azerbaijan landed in the capital of Armenia, some other units pacified Armenian villages in Nagorno-Karabagh. These events radicalised claims of Karabagh Armenians. At the beginning of July, at the joint session of the Council of the Autonomous Region of Nagorno-Karabagh and Councils of the Districts, secession from the Soviet Union and formation of the Republic of Nagorno-Karabagh was proclaimed.

After the Moscow coup d'état, Armenian authorities decided to became independent and sever links with the Soviet Union. In a referendum held in September 1991, 95% of voters favoured state independence, which was proclaimed by the Supreme Council of Armenia on September 23, 1991. Levon Ter-Petrossian, who gained 83% of votes in the presidential elections, became first president of Armenia. However, an ongoing war (from 1992 to 1994) with Azerbaijan on Nagorno-Karabagh influenced the process of democratization in Armenia.

In the Republic of Nagorno-Karabagh there emerged a military dictatorship and social life was completely controlled by the authorities. This impacted on the political situation in Armenia. National unity, required at the time of struggle with the enemy, toned down critique and disciplined opposition. In 1994 the authorities suspended the largest opposition party (the *Dashnaktsutiun*, Armenian Revolutionary Federation) and closed down over a dozen of newspapers and journals. As a result of overt frauds and manipulations in parliamentary elections in 1995 and presidential elections in 1996, president Ter-Petrossian could firmly hold the power. But he became a hostage of Karabagh Armenians. When the president aimed to terminate a conflict with Azerbaijan in 1998, he was forced, in a series of terrorist assassinations, to resign. Dual citizenship permitted politicians from Nagorno-Karabagh to run for elections. Owing to this, presidential elections in 1998 were won by Robert Kocharian, previous leader of Nagorno-Karabagh, and since 1997 also Prime Minister of the Armenian government. Armenians from Nagorno-Karabagh were appointed to many key state posts, which was defined as the rule of the "Karabagh clan" over Armenia, and this process strengthened autocratic tendencies inside this society.

Victorious civil revolutions took place both in the Armenian society and in the Baltic societies. However, in contradistinction to Baltic societies, in Armenia, the victorious revolution ended with a civil loop. This situation could have resulted from militarisation of political development. Long-term 'hot' and later 'cold war' with Azerbaijan resulted in *the effect of regulative credit*, permitting the new Armenian political elite to increase power regulation without provoking protests of own citizens. It is profitable for the Armenian class of rulers to foster the state of international conflicts because it hampers civil protests.

B. Political Development of the Georgian Society

In Georgia, mass protest movement began in summer of 1988.[8] It culminated in spring next year when several thousand people took part in manifestations held in the capital of Georgia. However, brutal pacification of these protests radicalised this civil society. Among plethora of independent organizations, the Helsinki Union, under the

---

[8] This subsection is based on empirical research conducted by: Józef Darski, "Kto na Kaukazie potrzebuje Rosji" [Who Needs Russia on the Caucasus], op. cit.; Andrzej Furier, "Niepodległość krajów zakaukaskich po rozpadzie ZSRR" [The Independence of the Caucasus Countries after the Collapse of the Soviet Union], op. cit.; Wojciech Górecki, "Abchazja" [Abkhazia], *Prace OSW* 9, 2003, pp. 20–23; idem, "Ossetia Południowa" [South Ossetia], op. cit., pp. 23–27; David E. Mark, "Eurasia Letter: Russia and the New Transcaucasus", op. cit.; Wojciech Materski, *Gruzja* [Georgia], Warszawa: Trio, 2000; Darrell Slider, "Democratization in Georgia", in: *Conflict, Cleavage, and Change in Central Asia and the Causasus*, ed. by Karen Dawisha, Bruce Parrott, op. cit., pp. 156–201; Irena Tatarzyńska, "Azja Środkowa i Zakaukazie" [Central Asia and the Caucasus], op. cit., pp. 167–178.

leadership of Zviad Gamsakhurdia, enjoyed largest popularity and civil support. Opposition went on strikes, including hunger strikes, it organized sit-down demonstrations and blockaded highways. Under growing social pressure the republican authorities were forced to make gestures of independence. In the second half of 1989 the Supreme Council of the Georgian Soviet Socialist Republic declared sovereignty. At that same time the Supreme Council announced elections, which were held in autumn 1990 and won by the coalition "Round Table – Free Georgia", headed by Gamsakhurdia. The victorious coalition gained 155 seats in the 250-seat Supreme Council. The legislative controlled by the opposition changed the name of the state from the Georgian Soviet Socialist Republic into the Republic of Georgia and appointed Gamsakhurdia to the post of a Speaker of the Supreme Council. On March 9, 1991, the Supreme Council annulled federal treaty on the foundation of the Soviet Union, which meant separation from the Soviet Union and an onset of independent existence. On March 31, 1991, in a ballot on independence of the republic, 95% of voters voted for full independence; the turnout was 99%. On April 9, 1991, the Georgian parliament declared restoration of an independent Georgian state and appointed Gamsakhurdia President. This decision was confirmed in the first in the Soviet Union presidential elections held on May 26, 1991. Gamsakhurdia gained 86% of votes.

It is worth recognising that until mid 1991, the Georgian society developed in an analogous way to the Baltic societies. Civil movements in both societies gained mass support and managed to form own organizations. In effect, the opposition in both analysed cases, won elections and took control over republican institutions of power. Why did political development of these countries diverge? The Baltic societies succeeded in building stable democratic systems, but introduction of democracy in Georgia failed. It seems that it was a coincidence of three factors:
- internal anarchization of political life in Georgia;
- ethnic conflicts: Abkhazian-Georgian and Ossetian-Georgian wars;
- mechanism of a civil loop – concentration of power in the hands of a new political elite.

Paramilitary structures played a significant role in the political life of this country. Each political movement had own armed formations or security guards to protect themselves. Some military groups gained autonomy from their political bosses and acted on their own. One of them was *Mkhedroni* (horsemen in Georgian) headed by Jaba Ioselani, a former university professor, teatrologist, intellectual with a criminal record. *Mkhedroni* were founded at the beginning of the 90s and had from 3.000 to 5.000 members. This formation was accused of drug smuggling, robberies, and offering business "protection". When Gamsakhurdia became president, he established his own National Guard that combated with existing military groups, very often applying their own methods. Ioselani was arrested in February 1991 and sent to prison where he stayed without formal charges until the end of 1991.

The second factor consisted in ethnic conflicts on the territory of Georgia. In autumn 1990, the communist authorities of South Ossetia proclaimed the rise of the South Ossetian Socialist Soviet Republic and secession from Georgia. Georgian state did not accept this decision and in 1991 started a war. Thanks to Russian military aid, South Ossetia defended independence. Separatist tendencies emerged in Abkhazia in March 1989. On August 25, 1990, Abkhazia proclaimed sovereignty and later the authorities of that province established an independent state. Georgia refused to accept this state of affairs and went to war with an insurgent province, which lasted from August 1992 to September 1993. Russian military aid helped Abkhazians to defend their independence.

The growth of power regulation for the sake of power regulation was the third type of factors influencing development of Georgian society. This mechanism was marked by personal traits of Gamsakhurdia – namely his megalomania. For example, in summer 1991, the leader of Georgia went on strike demonstrating against the imperialistic policy of Kremlin, which apart from economical losses did not bring any profits. Nationalistic ideology summarised in a slogan "Georgia for Georgians" meant "georginisation" of public life, in practice – an appointment of Gamsakhurdia's adherents to public posts. It turned out that within a new administrative division of the state that introduced prefectures, prefects were appointed by the president. Gamsakhurdia closed mosques and took part in christianization of Islamic villages. The growth of power regulation at the expense of non-Georgian part of citizenry, on the one hand, intensified ethnic conflicts on the territory of Georgia, but, on the other, deepened national unity and support for the authorities. However, when power regulation increased at the expense of the Georgian class of citizens, the new authority was gradually losing following and citizens became more and more critical towards new power.

When on September 2, 1991, the National-Democratic Party organized a demonstration in Tbilisi, it was pacified by the police forces loyal towards Gamsakhurdia. In the wake of the pacification a wave of demonstrations against the president, who was abandoned by his supporters, ensued. In December 1991, civil protests escalated into a regular civil war. On January 2, 1992, after a month siege, the Military Council, an informal oppositional body, took the House of Parliament defended by the president and introduced the State of Emergency. Gamsakhurdia was forced to migrate. The Military Council invited Eduard Shevardnadze to stabilise the situation. Following his arrival, Shevardnadze was appointed Chairman of the State Council, a provisional parliament.

Gradually Shevardnadze consolidated his power. He won the 1992 presidential elections and the political party that supported him, the Union of Georgian Citizens, received a sizeable number of mandates in the parliamentary elections. However, the consolidation of power by the president was accompanied by election frauds, manipulations and tightened control over the mass media. This situation culminated in the ensuing waves of civil protests on November 2002, which are known as "the revolution of roses". In its aftermath Shevardnadze was forced to resign.

The victorious civil revolutions took place both in the Georgian society and in the Baltic societies. However, the outbreak of ethnic conflicts on the territory of the Georgian republic and radicalism of the anticommunist opposition led to anarchy and facilitated civil loops in the political development of the Georgian society. Such a sequence of events occurred for the first time in the years 1990–1992 and repeated in the years 1992–2002.

4.2. Progressive Secession

The political development of Western Soviet republics (Belarus, Moldova and Ukraine) and Azerbaijan in comparison with the Baltic societies distinguishes itself by smaller range of civil movement, its later institutionalization and failure to seize control over republican institutions and organs of power. In the elections to parliamentary assemblies of the Western republics in 1990, the opposition gained about 1/3 of seats. The majority of seats was taken by communists who held the whole power in the first years of independence.

4.2.1. Progressive Secession Leading to Civil Resistance (Political Development of the Ukrainian Society)

In Ukraine civil revival stimulated by Gorbachev's *perestroika* began later than in the Baltic republics – namely in the second half of 1988.[9] Earlier, independent social endeavours were limited to a handful of dissidents whose activity did not go beyond postulating equal rights to the Ukrainian language, legalisation of Greco-Catholic Church and environmental protection. First demonstration, held in autumn 1987, commemorating Ukrainian victims of the Stalinist terror, gathered about 400 protesters.

In the second half of 1988, in the milieu of Kievian writers and intelligentsia, the Initiative Group of the Popular Movement for Restora-

---

[9] This subsection is based on empirical research conducted by: Piotr Andrusieczko, Marek Figura, "Przebieg transformacji ustrojowej na Ukrainie w latach 1991–1998" [The Course of Transformation on Ukraine, 1991–1998], in: *Ścieżki transformacji* [The Paths of Transformations], ed. by Krzysztof Brzechczyn, Poznań: Zysk i S-ka, 2003, pp.117–135; Józef Darski, "Rok 1989: Jesień Ludów czy KGB?" [Autumn of the People or KGB?], *Fronda* 23/24, 2001, pp. 62–120; Andrzej Chojnowski, *Ukraina* [Ukraine], Warszawa: Trio, 1997; Jarosław Hrycak, *Historia Ukrainy, 1772–1999. Narodziny nowoczesnego narodu* [History of Ukraine, 1772–1999. The Birth of Modern Nation], transl. by Katarzyna Kotyńska, Lublin: Instytut Europy Środkowo-Wschodniej, 2000; Illya Prizel, "Ukraine between Proto-Democracy and 'Soft' Authoritarianism", in: *Democratic Change and Authoritarian Reaction in Russia, Ukraine, Belarus, and Moldova*, ed. by Karen Dawisha, Bruce Parrott, Cambridge: Cambridge University Press, 1997, pp. 330–371.

tion was established (later on called: *Rukh* which stands for Movement). At that time, patriotic masses and public meetings in support of the Movement assembled about several thousand adherents. The first congress of the Movement held from 8 to 10 September 1989, demanded more autonomy for the Ukrainian Republic in the Soviet federation.

In September 1989, in the face of growing social pressure, the first secretary of the Ukrainian Communist Party was forced to step down. In October 1989, the Supreme Council of the Ukrainian Soviet Socialist Republic granted to the Ukrainian language on the territory of the republic, the status of the state language. Also, the authorities announced free elections, which were held on March 4, 1990. In spite of civil revival and social mobilization, although limited to Western part of Ukraine, the elections to the Supreme Council of the Republic of Ukraine were won by the Communist Party. The opposition, forming the Democratic Alliance of Ukraine, won in the western part of the state, gaining 115 seats in the 450-seat parliament. At the first session of the new Council, despite protests lodged by opposition, V. Ivashko, First Secretary of the Ukrainian Communist Party, was elected Chairman of the Republican Parliament. When he was appointed Deputy of the Communist Party of the Soviet Union, Leonid Kravchuk, another Communist activist, replaced him. In July 1990, the Supreme Council proclaimed sovereignty of Ukraine; however this republic remained within the borders of the Soviet Union. Public meetings and demonstrations against new federation treaty gathered from 20 (Kiev) to 100 (Lviv) thousand people. However, in a plebiscite held in March 1991, 80% of voters supported alliance with the Soviet Union. During the August coup, oppositional deputies demanded the session of the Council be called. On August 24, 1991, 346 deputies out of 400 present, voted for the Act of Independence of Ukraine. This decision was supported by a referendum, held simultaneously with the presidential elections. In December 1991, 90% of voters supported independence. Leonid Kravchuk became first president of the sovereign Ukrainian State.

Ukrainian independence was initiated by the local class of rulers. This way, the communist elite, seceding from the Soviet Union, was able to control the process of democratization and still hold the whole power. However, civil support, in the first years of consolidation of new statehood, was contingent upon concessions made to citizens. In the first period of the independent existence, democratic system was build and elements of free market economy introduced. Therefore, from 1991 to 1994, a tendency toward democratization prevailed. However later on, concessions made by authorities, as a result of a relative weakness of civil society and social mobility, proved transitory.

Very soon, political groups coming from the former Communist Party, which gained mass support in parliamentary elections, dominated the Ukrainian political scene. In turn, anticommunist and national opposition (e.g. Chornovil in presidential elections of 1991 gained 27% of votes) was marginalised. The growth of power regulation, leading to autocratization of political system, manifested itself in political assassinations (death of Chornovil and Gongadze), concentration of political prerogatives in the hands of president, bureaucratization of economy and control of the mass media. It is estimated that 32 bills, 60 presidential decrees and 80 governmental instructions regulated economic activity. The authorities, resorting to election manipulations and frauds, stirred social unrest. In the last presidential campaign, such demeanour of authorities resulted in the outbreak of protests, known as "the Orange Revolution". In their result the second turn of elections had to be repeated.

4.2.2. Progressive Secession Leading to Growth of Power Regulation

A. Political Development of the Azerbaijan Society

The civil revival in Azerbaijan was limited to intelligentsia and groups of city dwellers.[10] The Popular Front of Azerbaijan was established in June 1989. Several months later, as a result of an agreement

---

[10] This subsection is based on empirical research conducted by: Audrey L. Altstadt, "Azerbaijan's Struggle toward Democracy", in: *Conflict, Cleavage, and Change in Central Asia and the Causasus*, ed. by Karen Dawisha, Bruce Parrott, op. cit., pp. 110–156; Tadeusz Świętochowski, *Azerbejdżan i Rosja. Kolonializm, Islam i narodowość w podzielonym kraju* [Azerbaijan and Russia. Colonialism, Islam and Nationality in Divided Country], Warszawa: ISP PAN, 1998; Irena Tatarzyńska, "Azja Środkowa i Zakaukazie" [Central Asia and the Caucasus], op. cit., pp. 167–178.

between the Popular Front and the Communist Party, the Supreme Council proclaimed sovereignty of the republic. In the elections held in 1990, the Democratic Bloc election coalition, set up by the Popular Front, won 26 out 360 seats.

This way, the whole structure of power was controlled by the aparatchiks of the Communist Party. Several days after the coup in Moscow, on August 30, 1991, the Supreme Council of the Azerbaijan Soviet Socialist Republic proclaimed independence. Next month presidential elections were held. Ayaz Mutalibov, the former first secretary of the Communist Party of Azerbaijan, was the only candidate Due to the fact that elections were held hastily, other candidates had no chance to register. Mutalibov gained 98.5% and the turnout was 86%. Admittedly, the Communist Party was dissolved, but its members were appointed to state posts. On November 1991, Mutalibov formed the National Council consisting of representatives of opposition and nomenclature. The National Council was to replace the Supreme Council and seized the whole legislative work, although the Supreme Council still existed.

In the wake of the war with Armenia, Mutalibov's popularity waned, according to charges levelled against him by the opposition, he was solely to blame for the course of war. As a result of the March demonstration organized by the Popular Front, Mutalibov was forced to resign. In June 1992, new presidential elections were held and won by Abulfez Elchibey. The new president tried to reorient internal as well external policy of Azerbeijan, seeking cooperation with Turkey and withdrawing from the Commonwealth of Independent States. However, his political fate depended on the Armenian–Azeri war. War defeats provoked putsch organized by colonel Surat Huseinov, who instigated a march on Baku, calling for Elchibey's resignations. President called Heydar Aliyev as a mediator and appointed him Chairman of the National Council. However, Huseinov refused to negotiate and insisted that President resign. Devoid of the Popular Front's political support, Elchibey stepped down. Aliyev assumed the mantle of a provisional President and Huseinov of Prime Minister. The putschits conducted a referendum legitimising the upheaval in October 1993. In autumn that year, Aliyev won the presidential elections.

The change of political elite brought about an increase in power regulation. This fact is testified by the cult of the president as well as censorship and imprisonment of political opposition. In 1995 there were five thousand political prisoners in Azerbaijan. Election frauds became inherent in election campaigns. For example, in the 1995 parliamentary elections, four out of twelve parties were disqualified and so was the case with 60% of candidates, most of whom acted on behalf of the opposition. The so-called patriarchal voting, when the head of family votes for those of kin, became a common practice. According to Western observers, elections were neither free nor fair.

The political development in Azerbaijan may be construed as a progressive secession culminating in a successful autocratization of the political system. Initial, real democratization of the society, epitomized by the change of the head of state in 1992, ended with toppling a legally chosen president. Yet, during the reign of his successor, constant growth of power regulation did not provoke any significant civil protests. The war with Armenia triggered *the effect of regulative credit* allowing, in the face of an external threat, to increase power regulation by the Azeri political elite.

B. Political Development of the Belarusian Society

Belarus developed acting impulses coming from the neighbouring republics.[11] Therefore, political changes were controlled by the ruling nomenclature. The Popular Front, main civil organization, was established in October 1988, but it was legalised three years later (June 1991). By then, local authorities of the Belarusian republic had been persecuting activists of the Front. Participants of independent demon-

---

[11] This subsection is based on empirical research conducted by: Paweł Kazanecki, "Białoruska panorama polityczna – wiosna 1993" [Belarusian Political Panorama – Spring 1991], *Obóz* 25/26, 1993, pp. 79–84; Kathleen J. Mihalisko, "Belarus: retreat to authoritarianism", in: *Democratic Change and Authoritarian Reaction in Russia, Ukraine, Belarus, and Moldova*, ed. by Karen Dawisha, Bruce Parrott, op. cit., pp. 223–282; Eugeniusz Mironowicz, "Narodziny białoruskiej suwerenności w latach 90." [The Birth of Belarusian Sovereighnty in 90s.], *Obóz* 35, 1998, pp. 87–94; Wincuk Wiaczorka, "Białoruski Front Narodowy 'Odrodzenie'" [Belarusian Popular Front "Restoration"], *Obóz* 25/26, 1993, pp. 85–98.

strations were beaten and dissipated with lachrymatory gas. Members of the Popular Front were arrested for abuse of national symbols. The police confiscated literature, press and leaflets published by independent organizations. The first constituent congress of the Popular Front was organized outside Belarus, in Vilnius, because the authorities of Minsk forbade the meeting. In spite of political repression, thousands of people joined manifestations and other forms of activity organized by the Front.

Multicandidate elections to the republican Supreme Council were held in March 1990. In Belarus, unlike in other republics, a certain number of seats (50 out of 360) was reserved for "war veterans" and other organizations. During election campaigns about one hundred thousand people participated in rallies and meetings organized by the Popular Front. In elections, the Democratic Bloc, a coalition of independent organizations set up by the Front, gained 67 out of 360 seats. It was not enough to control republican structures of power. The Belarusian Communist Party could, without any obstacles, appoint its members to most important posts. Mikalai Dzemyantsei, an apparatchik from the BCP, was elected Chairman of the Supreme Council. The first initiative of the Popular Front put on the agenda of the Supreme Council consisted in the ratification of the state sovereignty declaration. The republican authorities rejected this proposal, but following consultations with Moscow, when it turned out that the central authorities would not object, they changed their mind. On July 27, 1990, the Supreme Council declared sovereignty of the republic. However, the support of the Belarusian population for state independence remained very low. In all Soviet Union March referendum, held in 1991, 83% of voters supported remaining within the borders of the Soviet Union. The Supreme Council was able to proclaim independence of Belarus following an unsuccessful coup d'état in Moscow, on August 24, 1991. This declaration did not change, however, relations in the Belarusian power structure. The only change consisted in the dismissal of M. Dzemyantsei, Chairman of the Supreme Council. He was replaced by Stanisław Shushkevich, one of the leaders of the Popular Front. However, the opposition was unable to appoint its candidates to executive posts of power structure. In December 1991, the Popular Front collected 800 thousand signatures under petitions calling for a referendum on pre-term elections, which, according to the postulates of the opposition, were to be held in the first half of 1992. However, the Supreme Council controlled by Communists simply ignored these petitions and elections were held in a constitutional term, in 1994. It came as no surprise that the opposition, devoid of real clout, won only 25% of votes. The Communist nomenclature was the real triumpher of the parliamentary elections. The election results opened up vistas for the marginalization of the opposition. This process was precipitated a year later when Alyaksandr Lukashenka won presidential elections. Since 1995 successful autocratization of the Belarusian political system has been symbolized by the growth of Lukashenka's personal power.

C. Political Development of the Moldavian Society

In Moldova civil revival was mostly limited to the Romanian-speaking intelligentsia which in May 1989 established the Moldavian Popular Front.[12] In the elections to the Supreme Council held in February 1990, the Popular Front gained 101 out of 406 seats. Analogously to the political development of Azerbaijan, Belarus and Ukraine, civil support of the Moldavian opposition was insufficient to seize control over legislative and executive branches of power. However, the coalition with reform-oriented communist deputies provided a base for political changes in Moldova. The newly elected

---

[12] This subsection is based on empirical research conducted by: Stephen R. Bowers, Scott J. Hammond, Vasile Nedelciuc, "Moldovia: the Transformation of Post-Soviet Society", *The Journal of Social, Political and Economic Studies* 22, 1997, pp. 143–164; William Crowther, "The Politics of Democratization in Postcommunist Moldova", in: *Democratic Change and Authoritarian Reaction in Russia, Ukraine, Belarus, and Moldova*, ed. by Karen Dawisha, Bruce Parrott, op. cit., pp. 282–330; Luke March, "Socialism with Unclear Characteristics: The Moldovan Communists in Government", *Demokratizatsiya* 12, 2004, pp. 507–524; Rafał Morawiec, "Mołdawia" [Moldova], *Europa Środkowo-Wschodnia* 2, 1992, pp. 125–135; Paul D. Quinlan, "Back to the Future: An Overview of Moldova under Voronin", *Demokratizatsiya* 12, 2004, pp. 484–504; Alicja Sowińska-Krupka, "Mołdawia 1940–1989: od sowietyzacji do odrodzenia narodowego" [Moldova 1940–1989: from Sovietization to National Revival], *Studia Polityczne* 5, 1996, pp. 127–141; Jacek Wróbel, "Naddniestrze" [Transdniestria], *Prace OSW* 9, 2002, pp. 15–20.

Supreme Council declared republican sovereignty and after the Moscow coup d'état, on August 27, 1991, it proclaimed independence.

However, political development of the Moldavian society was distorted by separatist aspirations of the Russian, Ukrainian and Gagauz population. In September 1990, local communist nomenclature, aiming to protect own economic and political interests, proclaimed the Transdniestran Moldavian Soviet Socialist Republic. After the Moscow coup this usurpatory state declared full independence and renamed into the Transdniestran Moldavian Republic. Moldova, that went to war with Transdniestria (from April to July 1992), did not accept that state of affairs. Thanks to the aid of the 15th Russian Army, the Transdniestran Moldavian Republic was able to protect its sovereignty.

The threat of territorial disintegration of Moldova forced the communists and part of opposition to make a political compromise. This agreement resulted in the formation of the national consent government under the auspices of President Mircea Snegur who, manoeuvring between the followers of integration with the Commonwealth of Independent States and adherents of the union with Romania, strengthened his own position, favouring the policy of 'moldovization' of the country. However, this compromise marginalized the pan-Romanian Popular Front and blocked the process of democratization. In the succeeding parliamentary elections, the Moldavian Communists Party obtained more seats in the parliament. The communists won elections in 1998, but owing to the agreement between lesser parties, they were unable to form a government. It was possible after parliamentary elections of 2001, when the Moldavian Communist Party gained 71 seats in the 101-seat parliament. They could form the government and elect president. The monopoly of one party hampered the process of democratization. Administrative state reforms, in the wake of which 13 counties were replaced by 32 districts, pointed to the growth of power regulation. Additionally, 30% of bureaucratical personnel was changed. The new ruling elite tightened its control over radio and TV stations. Critically thinking journalists were discriminated and opposition radio programmes, press agencies, journals and newspapers were closed. The only state company, which had monopoly on press distribution, refused to circulate journals and newspapers slanted critically towards the authorities.

Consequently, the authorities broke the law in organized elections. During elections, only those unswerving towards the authorities were appointed committee members, which established a base for manipulation. At the time of campaigns, local as well as central authorities used to cut off electricity during transmissions aired by the opposition, they censored statements made by independent candidates in government controlled mass media and restrained public meetings. Western observes called the local elections held in 2003 "free but not honest".[13]

Political development of the Moldavian society can be interpreted in terms of a progressive secession. The first period of building their statehood was threatened by separatist tendencies espoused by national and ethnic minorities calling for the establishment of own political organisms or tightening links with the Soviet Union. The political compromise with the Moldovian communists was made at the expense of further democratization. The policy of 'moldavization' provided the base for territorial integrity which, in turn, marginalised the Popular Front, the most important Pan-Romanian democratic force. This paved the way for post-communist political parties, which dominated political scene and led to a slow autocratization of the whole political system of that country.

4.3. Regressive Secession
(Political Development of the Central Asian Societies)

Social life of the Central Asian societies is based on different "civilizational foundations" than that of West-European societies.[14] Class divisions, even in an enlarged version, presupposed by non-

---

[13] Paul D. Quinlan, "Back to the Future: An Overview of Moldova under Voronin", op. cit., p. 493.

[14] This subsection is based on empirical research conducted by: Erkin Abildaev, Osmon Togusakov, "System polityczny i uwarunkowania jego rozwoju" [Political System and Conditions of its Development], in: *Kirgistan. Historia – społeczeństwo – polityka* [Kyrgyzstan. History – Society – Politics], ed. by Tadeusz Bodio, Warszawa: Elipsa, 2004, pp. 340–350; Aalybek Akunov, Wojciech Bartuzi, Janat Jamankulov, "Opozycja polityczna" [The Political Opposition], ibidem, pp. 414–430; Narynbek Alymkulov, "Oblicza modernizacji politycznej państwa" [The Faces of Political Modernization of the State], ibidem, pp. 262–283; Muriel Atkin, "Thwarted democratization in Tajikistan",

Marxian historical materialism, do not prevail in these societies, as divisions are based on biological kinship: familiar, clan and tribal relations. In the first stage of the development of real socialism – an increase in power regulation – clan and tribal structures were persecuted by the communist triple-rule as they constituted the main barrier to the imposition of political domination of triple-rulership. However, in the second stage of the evolution of that system – a de-

---

in: *Conflict, Cleavage, and Change in Central Asia and the Causasus*, ed. by Karen Dawisha, Bruce Parrott, op. cit., pp. 277–312; Tadeusz Bodio, Kazak kyzy Nurgul, Wojciech Jakubowski, "Przywództwo i elity polityczne" [Leadership and Political Elites], in: *Kirgistan. Historia – społeczeństwa – polityka* [Kyrgyzstan. History – Society – Politics], ed. by Tadeusz Bodio, op. cit., pp. 392–412; Piotr Borawski, "Chanowie współczesnej Azji" [The Khans of Modern Asia], *Sprawy Polityczne* 23/24, 2003, pp. 15–37; Andrei Chebotarev, "Opozycja polityczna" [The Political Opposition], in: *Kazachstan. Historia – społeczeństwo – polityka* [Kazakhstan. History – Society – Politics], ed. by Tadeusz Bodio, Konstanty A. Wojtaszczyk, Warszawa: Elipsa, 2000, pp. 218–231; Ibadulla E. Ergashev, Wojciech Jakubowski, "Partie polityczne i organizacje społeczne Uzbekistanu" [Political Parties and Social Organisations in Uzbekistan], in: *Uzbekistan. Historia – społeczeństwa – polityka* [Uzbekistan. History – Society – Politics], ed. by Tadeusz Bodio, Warszawa: Elipsa, 2001, pp. 151–159; William Fierman, "Political Development in Uzbekistan: Democratization?", in: *Conflict, Cleavage, and Change in Central Asia and the Causasus*, ed. by Karen Dawisha, Bruce Parrott, op. cit., pp. 360–409; Eugene Huskey, "Kyrgyzstan: the Fate of Political Liberalization", ibidem, pp. 242–277; Wojciech Jakubowski, Piotr Załęski, "Organizacja systemu władzy publicznej" [The Organization of the System of Public Authority], in: *Kazachstan. Historia – społeczeństwo – polityka* [Kazakhstan. History – Society – Politics], ed. by Tadeusz Bodio, Konstanty A. Wojtaszczyk, op. cit., pp. 170–188; Daniel Łaga, "Kalendarium ważniejszych wydarzeń w historii Kazachstanu" [The Chronicle of Important Events in History of Kazakhstan], ibidem, pp. 449–469; M. Mashan, "Partie polityczne i ruchy społeczne" [Political Parties and Social Movements], ibidem, pp. 188–217; Michael Ochs, "Turkmenistan: the Quest for Stability and Control", in: *Conflict, Cleavage, and Change in Central Asia and the Causasus*, ed. by Karen Dawisha, Bruce Parrott, op. cit., pp. 312–360; Martha B. Olcott, "Democratization and the Growth of Political Participation in Kazakstan", ibidem, pp. 201–242; Lucyna Roszyk, "Transformacja uzbecka: przełom czy kontynuacja?" [An Uzbek Transformation: Turning Point or Continuation?], in: *Uzbekistan. Historia – społeczeństwa – polityka* [Uzbekistan. History – Society – Politics], ed. by Tadeusz Bodio, op. cit., pp. 171–189; idem, "Model transformacji tadżyckiej – próba rekonstrukcji" [The Model of Tajik Transformation – An Attempt at Reconstruction], in: *Tadżykistan. Historia – społeczeństwa – polityka* [Tajikistan. History – Society – Politics], ed. by Tadeusz Bodio, Warszawa: Elipsa, 2002, p. 201–231; idem, "Dylematy transformacji kirgiskiej. Między modelem a praktyką zmiany systemowej" [The Dilemmas crease in power regulation – starting from the mid 50s, tribal and clan structures begun to coexist with structures of triple-lordship. Later on, domination of local communist nomenclatures in Central Asia was directly propped up by clan and tribal ties. Usually, members of influential tribes and clans became first secretaries of republican Communist Parties, but their deputies were Russians, coming from the centre. In 1964, Dinmukhamed Kunaev, coming from the tribe of the great *zhus*, was appointed first secretary of the Communist Party of the Kazak Socialist Soviet Republic. Members of nomenclature in Kyrgyzstan usually recruited from southern clans of this republic. Uzbekistan was ruled by Sharif Rashidov, coming from the Samarkanda clan. Saparmurad Niiyazov, a member of the *Tekke* tribe, became first secretary of the Communist Party of Turkmenistan. Tajikistan was ruled by clans' representatives coming from Leninobodis and Kulob. Members of the Leninobodis clan were elected first Secretary, members of the latter – Minister of Security. Clan and tribal domination based on biological kinship, overlapping with class domination based on disposition of means of coercion, production and communication, strengthened the power of local factions of the triple-lords class. This is why despotism of local nomenclature, corruption and nepotism in societies in Central Asia was more widespread than in other republics of the Soviet Union. In a presupposed conceptual apparatus, the level of autonomy of citizens in the societies of Central Asia was lower than the level of autonomy of the metropolitan citizens, not to mention the Baltic republics.

Vitality of tribal and clan structures fundamentally weighed on the process of revitalization of autonomous civil bonds. In case of Central Asian societies, the very use of the expression "revitalization of autonomous civil bonds" is not adequate, because a Western-style

---

of Kyrgyz Transformation. Between Model and Practice of Systemic Change], in: *Kirgistan. Historia – społeczeństwa – polityka* [Kyrgyzstan. History – Society – Politics], ed. by Tadeusz Bodio, op. cit., pp. 315–333; Michael Rywkin, "Problemy narodowościowe krajów byłego ZSRR" [National Problems of the Previous Soviet Union's Countries], *Obóz* 28, 1993, pp. 83–95; Irena Tatarzyńska, "Azja Środkowa i Zakaukazie" [Central Asia and the Caucasus], op. cit., pp. 167–178; Askar Tulegulov, "Elita polityczna" [The Political Elite], in: *Kazachstan. Historia – społeczeństwo – polityka* [Kazakhstan. History – Society – Politics], ed. by Tadeusz Bodio, Konstanty A. Wojtaszczyk, op. cit., pp. 255–267.

civil society, based on autonomous, individual social relations, which take place between human beings, has never governed public life of these societies. Individuals have always represented and acted on behalf of their own family, clan or tribe. It is possible to claim, whatever it might mean in the conceptual apparatus of non-Marxian historical materialism, that during Gorbachev's *perestroika*, revitalization of tribal and clan bonds occurred. But these bonds, if coupled with triple-class rule, blocked the development of autonomous civil relations. As a result of the above, the process of revitalization of autonomous civil relations, stimulated by Gorbachev's reforms, never gained such momentum as analogous social processes in the metropolitan society and some provincial sub-societies.

Thus, liberalisation processes, coming from the centre of the empire, posed a serious threat to the rule of local communist nomenclatures. The victory of democratic forces in the Moscow coup d'état paradoxically precipitated the secession of Central Asian republics from the Soviet Union. Uzbekistan and Kyrgyzstan proclaimed independence on August 31, 1991, Tajikistan, on September 9, 1991 and Turkmenistan, on October 27, 1991. Kazakhstan gained independence last, namely after the meeting in Bialowieza, on December 16, 1991.

However, in case of the Central Asian societies, the collapse of the Soviet Empire did not lead to the collapse of the system of triple-lordship. Local factions of the triple-lord class, by proclaiming independence, defended own class interests and preserved political *status quo*.

At the level of basic relations: the class of triple-lords – citizenry, independent existence of the Central Asian societies changed nothing. Citizens of new states accepted this fact with passivity and indifference. The independent statehood did not stir enthusiasm or social revival. Suffice it to say that independent existence did not even provoke personal changes in the structure of power. New presidents of the Central Asian states previously held posts of first secretaries of their Communist Parties. So was the case with Islam Karimov – president of Uzbekistan, Nursultan Nazarbaev – president of Kazakhstan, Saparmurad Niyazov – president of Turkmenistan, Rahmon Nabiev – first president of Tajikistan. The only exception was Kyrgyzstan, where as a result of a compromise between most important tribal groups, Askar Akaev, a former scientist, became president.

At the institutional level, political divisions have not been formed yet. Authorities controled political parties and social organizations. In some countries, one-party model was overtly accepted (Tajikistan), in other, oppositional parties were banned and marginalised or – if they exist – have clearly restricted character (Kazakhstan, Kyrgyzstan). The executive branch of power dominated over the legislative and judiciary branches of power structure.

Presidential and parliamentary elections were nothing but a façade. According to Western observers, they were neither free nor fair. Referendum held in 1994 in Turkmenistan, concerning prolongation of Niyazov's presidency until 2002, might serve as a prime example. In its result, the 1997 presidential elections were cancelled. When many candidates stand for elections, potential rivals were eliminated by frauds and manipulations and had no chance to compete fairly. Organization of elections in Kazakhstan aptly illustrates this thesis. In order to prevent other candidates from launching effective election campaign, Nazarbaev unexpectedly shortened his term in October 1998 and scheduled elections for January next year. The Central Election Commission disqualified two most important rivals of the president. One of them was Kazhegeldin, former Prime Minister, and the other – Awezov, leader of the opposition party, *Azamat*. As a result of these manipulations Nazarbaev gained 81.7 % votes (turnout reached 87%).

At the level of social consciousness, the authorities wanted to legitimize its power appealing to the tradition of oriental despotism. It is claimed that a Western model of democracy is inadequate and therefore an oriental model of a democratic system is needed.

Political changes in Central Asia can be subsumed into the model of regressive secession. In spite of'being for a long time part of the Soviet Empire, civilizational distinctiveness of the Central Asian societies and vitality of tribal divisions slackened the process of revitalization of autonomous social bonds. Described situation was brought about not as a result of terror and repression of the metropolitan triple-class (although it played a role), but rather vitality of tribal structures coexisting with the structure of class domination. Since these societies are based on a very distinctive civilizational fundament, it is difficult to prognosticate their further development applying directly theses of the first model of a political society. Let us remind that according to the static assumptions of this model, if growing power regulation has passed a certain threshold, revitalization of social bonds takes place, which results in a civil revolution. In case of the Central Asian societies tribal and clan structures pose the most significant obstacle to the revitalization of autonomous social bonds. The gradual democratization of countries from this region may be stimulated by modernization, leading to individualization of social life, which will set into motion processes described in the first model of a political society in non-Marxian historical materialism. Whether this situation comes true is contingent upon processes of modernization alone. The response of non-Marxian historical materialism in this case may be twofold. Modernization processes may occur in a selective way, adjusting to interests of an autocratic political structure (casus China), or may occur in an autonomous and spontaneous way. Than, autocratic political structure would have to adjust to the interest of social classes and groups espousing modernization.

5. The Variety of Democratization in the Global Context: Summary

Developmental differentiation of the post-Soviet republics resulted from the force of two classes: rulers and citizens. The force of each class may be defined as its ability to promote own social interests in relation to each other. Such a definition of the relations between the class of citizens and rulers, allows to distinguish five developmental paths of the post-soviet societies:

(i)   victorious civil revolution leading to class peace;
(ii) victorious civil revolution leading to a civil loop;
(iii) progressive secession leading to civil resistance;
(iv) progressive secession leading to an increase in power regulation;
(v)   regressive secession leading to an increase in power regulation.

At one pole there are societies with an active and organized class of citizens who are able to make a victorious revolution. However, the outcome of these revolutions was twofold. Some revolutionary disturbances ended with the introduction of stable class peace (i) some – with a civil loop (ii). The Baltic societies (Estonia, Latvia, and Lithuania) pertain to the first group, whereas Georgia and Armenia – to the latter. At the second pole there are societies with a passive and atomised class of citizens (v). Independence initiated by local communist nomenclatures did not translate into political benefits for citizens. This is the fate of the societies of Central Asia (Kazakhstan, Kyrgyzstan, Tajikistan, Turkmenistan and Uzbekistan). Between these two opposite poles there are societies whose citizens were strong enough to force concessions on the part of authorities, but too weak to seize the whole power. In the first stage of limited democratization, citizenry gained some level of autonomy. However, in the second stage of autocratic consolidation, the mechanisms of political competition led to the growth of power regulation, which provoked (iii) or not (iv) the resistance of citizenry. The third developmental variant is represented by Ukraine, the fourth one by Azerbaijan, Belarus and Moldova.

The above can be conceived in the qualitative language of non-Marxian historical materialism. Bearing in mind a number of factors incorporated in the first model of power and its further elaboration, it seems quite a lot. First of all, it permits to present a comprehensive framework embracing political development of all post-Soviet republics. This is the greatest advantage of this conceptualization. However, problems appear as soon as we come to details. One of them is the course taken by revolutions in particular countries. Why revolutions in the Baltic societies were successful, whereas those in the Caucasus failed? This problem refers to the role of national consciousness in the process of democratization: why, in the Baltic case, national consciousness comprised a factor favouring democratization, whereas in the Caucasus case, it was one of the main obstacles to it. Another question relates to the overlap between democratic development and economical reforms: did privatisation and free-market reforms accelerate or hamper democratization? Or maybe they are neutral to the process of democratization, which displays its own dynamics, first of all, in the sphere of politics.[15] One may hope that

---

[15] Considerations on this topic in non-Marxian historical materialism were presented among others by Krzysztof Brzechczyn, "The Collapse of Real Socialism in

further concretization of the theory of power in non-Marxian historical materialism, grasping both cultural and economic dimensions of social life, shall allow for further clarification of mentioned problems.

However, thanks to the comprehensiveness of presented picture of political transformations occurring in the post-Soviet societies, it seems congruent to pose a question concerning the influence of the global context on the processes under analysis.

The global context is understood here as a coincidence of three types of factors: policy of Western European and North American states, network of international organizations (e.g. non-governmental organizations observing human rights), and international economical relations.

At the time of *perestroika*, Western countries supported territorial integrity of the Soviet Union till the very decline of this state. Just several days before the Moscow coup d'etat, President Bush went to Kiev to persuade Ukrainian leaders to moderate their demands towards Moscow. This strategy led to indifference towards democratic and independent aspirations of the Balts and their moral rights. The Baltic societies own their independence to themselves.

However, after the break-up of the Soviet Union, there emerged three kinds of political strategies adopted by the Euro-Atlantic World. It is possible to call them provisionally: *democratic support* (i), *maintenance of status quo* (ii), and *democratic encouragement* (iii). The aim of *the democratic support* strategy consists in strengthening international security and democratic consolidation of the post-Soviet countries. The Baltic states, which became members of the CE, the EU, NATO and other international organizations, are the recipients of such a policy. In the Central Asian states, ruled by the post-Soviet, yet mostly secular dictatorships, the strategy of *maintaining status quo* is adopted. This is why they impede, to a certain degree, the spread of Islamic funda-

Eastern Europe versus the Overthrow of the Spanish Colonial Empire in Latin America. An Attempt at Comparative Analsis", *Journal of Interdisciplinary Studies in History and Archaelogy*, vol. 1, no. 2, 2004, pp. 105–135, and Achim Siegel, "Entdifferenzierung, Desintegration, Re-Differenzierung. Zur Modellierung des politisch-ökonomischen Krisenzyklus in der Volksrepublik Polen", in: *Differenz und Integration. Die Zukunft moderner Gesellschaften*, ed. by Karl-Siegbert Rehberg, Opladen/Wiesbaden: Westdeutscher Verlag, 1997, pp. 363–369.

mentalism in this region. This policy was bolstered after September 11th. The strategy of *democratic encouragement* was adopted towards countries located between Russia and Central and South Europe, such as Belarus, Ukraine, Moldova, Georgia, Armenia and Azerbaijan, where. This strategy has matured slowly. At first, these countries were recognised as a grey zone pertaining, formally, or what is more important, informally, to the Russian sphere of influence. However, tightening links with the Western world strengthened civil societies in some of these countries and they gained ability to resist. The interest of Western opinion combined with an active role played by democratic states and international organizations helped to seek political compromise and routes to democratization. Ukraine and Georgia were the main beneficiaries such a policy. One may hope that democratization will spread to other countries belonging to this group.

DIA-LOGOS
Schriften zu Philosophie und Sozialwissenschaften
Studies in Philosophy and Social Sciences

Herausgegeben von
Edited by
Tadeusz Buksiński & Piotr W. Juchacz

www.peterlang.de